DISCOVERING THE GLOBAL PAST

Volume I: To 1650

DISCOVERING THE GLOBAL PAST

A LOOK AT THE EVIDENCE

SECOND EDITION

Merry E. Wiesner
University of Wisconsin—Milwaukee

William Bruce Wheeler
University of Tennessee

Franklin M. Doeringer
Lawrence University

Kenneth R. Curtis
California State University Long Beach

HOUGHTON MIFFLIN COMPANY **Boston** **New York**

Sponsoring Editor: Nancy Blaine
Editorial Associate: Gillie Jones
Senior Project Editor: Christina M. Horn
Associate Production/Design Coordinator: Christine Gervais
Senior Manufacturing Coordinator: Jane Spelman
Senior Marketing Manager: Sandra McGuire

Cover image: Ceramic bowl from Kashanor, Ravy, Persia, 13th century.
Freer Gallery of Art, Smithsonian Institution.

Printed in the U.S.A.

Library of Congress Catalog Card Number: 00133832

ISBN: 0-618-04367-5

1 2 3 4 5 6 7 8 9-DOC-05 04 03 02 01

CONTENTS

PREFACE

Almost from the founding of the United States itself, those who chose to call themselves "Americans" maintained a deep and abiding curiosity about and interest in other lands and their peoples. Indeed, although they often were characterized as provincial, narrow, and even rustic, Americans read all they could find about faraway peoples, flocked to lectures and lyceums offered by world travelers in the early nineteenth century, packed into nineteenth- and twentieth-century expositions and world's fairs to see "exotic" peoples, and even more recently became a "nation of tourists."

In order to convert this widespread curiosity into a deeper knowledge, schools began to offer classes in World History. In 1821 the first high school–level World History course was offered, at the Boston English High School, and a World History textbook (by Samuel G. Goodrich) appeared in 1828 to serve the growing teacher and student interest. Colleges and universities followed suit quickly thereafter, and in 1885 historian Mary D. Sheldon of Wellesley College first introduced the examination and analysis of primary sources into her World History (it was called "General History") course.[1]

The advent of professionally trained historians in the late nineteenth and early twentieth centuries, however, nearly spelled the end of the World History course. Essentially, these new professors charged that by trying to teach everything, the result was to teach nothing—or at least nothing in depth. By 1915 fewer than 5 percent of the high schools surveyed by the U.S. commissioner of education still taught a World History course. And after the introduction of the Western Civilization course (at Columbia University in 1919), colleges and universities too abandoned the single course in World History.[2]

And yet the curiosity that prompted the first World History courses in the early nineteenth century never abated. Indeed, with the recent emergence of the "global village," interest grew significantly. In 1982 the World History Association was founded, in part to encourage the reintroduction of World History courses and in part to assist people eager to teach such a course. As William H. McNeill, one of the founders of the modern movement to reintroduce World

1. Gilbert Allardyce, "Toward World History: American Historians and the Coming of the World History Course," in *Journal of World History*, vol. I (Spring 1990), pp. 23–76, esp. 45 and 47.
2. Ibid., pp. 30, 47.

History courses, put it, "Surely it takes only a little common sense to see that some sort of world history is the *only* way a college can do justice to students who live in a world where events in Asia, Africa, and Latin America are as likely to involve the United States in critical action as anything happening in Europe or North America."[3]

The response to the First Edition of *Discovering the Global Past* has been a gratifying one. It means that Mary D. Sheldon at Wellesley College over a century ago understood how to tap the already high level of student curiosity about faraway people. In our opinion, it also means that William H. McNeill had it right: that students understand not only the satisfaction of studying world history, but, in today's world, its *necessity.* This book honors both of these historians, as well as the countless numbers of curious and challenging students and their equally challenging teachers.

The primary goal of *Discovering the Global Past: A Look at the Evidence* is to allow students enrolled in world history courses to *do* history in the same way that we as historians do—to examine a group of original sources to answer questions about the past. The unique structure of this book clusters primary sources around a set of historical questions that students are asked to "solve." Unlike a source reader, this book prompts students to actually *analyze* a wide variety of authentic primary source material, to make inferences, and to draw conclusions in much the same way that historians do.

The evidence in this book is more varied than that in most source collections. We have included such visual evidence as coins, paintings, statues, literary illustrations, historical photographs, maps, cartoons, advertisements, and political posters. In choosing written evidence we again have tried to offer a broad sample—eulogies, wills, court records, oral testimonies, and statistical data all supplement letters, newspaper articles, speeches, memoirs, and other more traditional sources.

In order for students to learn history the way we as historians do, they must not only be confronted with the evidence but must also learn how to use that evidence to arrive at a conclusion. In other words, they must learn historical methodology. Too often methodology (or even the notion that historians *have* a methodology) is reserved for upper-level majors or graduate students; beginning students are simply presented with historical facts and interpretations without being shown how these were unearthed or formulated. Students may learn that historians hold different interpretations of the significance of an event or individual or different ideas about causation, but they are not informed of how historians come to such conclusions.

Thus, along with evidence, we have provided explicit suggestions about how one might analyze that evidence, guiding students as they reach their own conclusions. As they work through the various chapters, students will discover

3. Ibid., p. 72. Italics added.

both that the sources of historical information are wide-ranging and that the methodologies appropriate to understanding and using them are equally diverse. By doing history themselves, students will learn how intellectual historians handle philosophical treatises, economic historians quantitative data, social historians court records, and political and diplomatic historians theoretical treatises and memoirs. They will also be asked to consider the limitations of their evidence, to explore what historical questions it cannot answer as well as those it can. Instead of remaining passive observers, students become active participants.

Each chapter is divided into six parts: The Problem, Background, The Method, The Evidence, Questions to Consider, and Epilogue. Each of the parts relates to or builds upon the others, creating a uniquely integrated chapter structure that helps guide the reader through the analytical process. "The Problem" section begins with a brief discussion of the central issues of the chapter and then states the questions students will explore. A "Background" section follows, designed to help students understand the historical context of the problem. The section called "The Method" gives students suggestions for studying and analyzing the evidence. "The Evidence" section is the heart of the chapter, providing a variety of primary source material on the particular historical event or issue described in the chapter's "Problem" section. The section called "Questions to Consider" focuses students' attention on specific evidence and on linkages among different evidence material. The "Epilogue" section gives the aftermath or the historical outcome of the evidence—what happened to the people involved, the results of a debate, and so on.

Within this framework, we have tried to present a series of historical issues and events of significance to the instructor as well as of interest to the student. We have also aimed to provide a balance among political, social, diplomatic, intellectual, and cultural history. In other words, we have attempted to create a kind of historical sampler that we believe will help students learn the methods and skills used by historians. Not only will these skills—analyzing arguments, developing hypotheses, comparing evidence, testing conclusions, and reevaluating material—enable students to master historical content; they will also provide the necessary foundation for critical thinking in other college courses and after college as well.

Because the amount of material in global history is so vast, we had to pick certain topics and geographic areas to highlight, though here too we have aimed at a balance. Some chapters are narrow in focus, providing students with an opportunity to delve deeply into a single case study, while others ask students to make comparisons among individuals, events, or developments in different cultures. We have included cultural comparisons that are frequently discussed in World History courses, such as classical Rome and Han China, as well as more unusual ones, such as peasant family life in early modern central Europe and Southeast Asia.

Discovering the Global Past is designed to accommodate any format of the World History course, from the small lecture/discussion class at a liberal arts or community college to the large lecture with discussions led by teaching assistants at a sizable university. The chapters may be used for individual assignments, team projects, class discussions, papers, and exams. Each is self-contained, so that any combination may be assigned. The book is not intended to replace a standard textbook, and it was written to accompany any World History text the instructor chooses. The Instructor's Resource Manual, written by the authors of the text, offers further suggestions for class discussion, as well as a variety of ways in which students' learning may be evaluated and annotated lists of recommendations for further reading.

A note on spellings: Many of the sources presented in this book were originally written in a language other than English, and often in an alphabet other than the Western (Roman) one. Over the centuries, translators have devised various means of representing the sounds of other languages, and these conventions of translation have also changed over time. In general, we have used the most current spelling and orthographic conventions in our discussions and have left spellings as they appeared in the original translation in the sources. This means, for example, that Indian, Arabic, and Japanese words often have diacritical marks in the sources but not in our own material. For Chinese, in our own text we have used the pinyin system developed by the Chinese in the 1950s, with pinyin spellings indicated in brackets in the sources, most of which use the older Wade-Giles system.

New to the Second Edition

The Second Edition of *Discovering the Global Past* incorporates the responses to the book that we have received from our own students, as well as from student and faculty users of the book around the country. Nearly every chapter in the two volumes has received some reworking, and new chapters are included in each volume.

Volume I includes four entirely new chapters: Viking and Polynesian voyages of exploration (Chapter 6); the Black Death as it was experienced throughout Eurasia (Chapter 9); Buddhist, Muslim, and Christian pilgrimages (Chapter 13); and the interaction of agricultural villages and states in England, Japan, and the Inca world (Chapter 14). Volume II repeats the chapter on English, Japanese, and Inca agricultural villages and states and adds five additional new chapters: sugar trade and consumption in the Atlantic system (Chapter 4); constitutional responses to European expansion in Africa and the Pacific (Chapter 7); modern identity (Chapter 10); the causes and consequences of total war in World Wars I and II (Chapter 12); the Suez Crisis (Chapter 13); and the Americanization of global popular culture, exemplified through the spread of McDonald's (Chapter 15).

One of the chief goals of this revision has been to bolster the book's comparative approach to global history. By juxtaposing the seemingly divergent histories of peoples such as the Vikings and Polynesians (Volume I, Chapter 6), the authors present the student with a well-balanced set of primary sources in the exciting context of cross-cultural comparison. New comparative chapters have been added in both volumes, and popular comparative chapters from the First Edition, such as "Han and Rome: Asserting Imperial Authority (300 B.C.E.–400 C.E.)" (Volume I, Chapter 4) and "Industrializing the Nation: Germany and Japan (1860–1900)" (Volume II, Chapter 8), have been retained.

Acknowledgments

The authors thank Melvin Page for his contribution to the First Edition. We would also like to thank the many students and instructors who have helped us in our efforts. We extend our gratitude to the following professors, who read and criticized the manuscript throughout its development:

Maria S. Arbelaéz, *University of Nebraska at Omaha*

Sandy Bardsley, *Emory and Henry College*

Jurgen Buchenau, *University of North Carolina, Charlotte*

Theron E. Corse, *Fayetteville State University*

David M. Fahey, *Miami University (Ohio)*

Gayle V. Fischer, *Salem State College*

Dean T. Ferguson, *Texas A & M University, Kingsville*

Katherine L. French, *State University of New York, College at New Paltz*

Leslie Heaphy, *Kent State University, Stark Campus*

James Heitzman, *Georgia State University*

James E. Lindsay, *Colorado State University*

Nancy L. Locklin, *Maryville College*

Ronald V. Mershart, *University of Wisconsin, Superior*

Elizabeth Mary Miles, *Mt. Hood Community College*

Dane A. Morrison, *Salem State College*

Kenneth J. Orosz, *University of Maine at Farmington*

Sandra J. Peacock, *Georgia Southern University*

Josh Sanborn, *Lafayette College*

Angelika E. Sauer, *Texas Lutheran University*

Michele Scott James, *MiraCosta College*

Gordon C. Thomasson, *Broome Community College*

M. C. Weber, *Bradford College*

In addition to our colleagues across the United States, we would like to thank especially our colleagues at the University of Wisconsin—Milwaukee; the University of Tennessee, Knoxville; Lawrence University; and California State University Long Beach. Merry E. Wiesner wishes especially to thank Barbara Andaya, Judith Bennett, Philip C. Brown, Martha Carlin, Jean Fleet, Charlotte Furth, Faye Getz, Michael Gordon, Abbas Hamdani, Anne Hansen, Jean Johnson, Jeffrey Merrick, Sheilagh Ogilvie, Jean Quataert, Irene Silverblatt, Andrea Stone, Hitomi Tonomura, Jane Waldbaum, and Charlotte Weber. Bruce Wheeler would like to thank Thomas Burman, Robert Bast, Todd Diacon, J. Daniel Bing, Owen Bradley, Palmira Brummett, W. Wayne Farris, Yen-ping Hao, and Vejas Liulevicius.

Franklin M. Doeringer wishes to thank all of his colleagues in the Lawrence University Department of History for their support and interest in this project. J. Michael Hittle and Edmund M. Kern deserve particular mention for reading over portions of manuscript and offering helpful comments. He also expresses his gratitude to Jane Parish Yang and Kuo-ming Sung in the Department of East Asian Languages and Cultures for their suggestions on material pertaining to China and East Asia. Finally, he extends special thanks to Peter J. Gilbert of the Lawrence library for his unflagging help in tracking down elusive sources and obscure references. Kenneth R. Curtis would especially like to thank Christos Bartsocas, Francine Curtis, Steve Curtis, Ross Dunn, Tim Keirn, Lezlie Knox, Emilie Savage-Smith, Donald Schwartz, and his coauthors.

Finally, we would like to thank Gillie Jones, Christina Horn, and the rest of the staff at Houghton Mifflin for their support.

M.E.W.
W.B.W.
F.M.D.
K.R.C.

DISCOVERING THE GLOBAL PAST

CHAPTER ONE

THE NEED FOR WATER IN ANCIENT SOCIETIES (3100 B.C.E.–100 C.E.)

THE PROBLEM

The title of the course for which you are using this book is most likely some variation on "World Civilization." The meaning of *world* is self-evident, but why *civilization?* What distinguishes human cultures that are termed civilizations from those that are not? Though there are great differences among civilizations, all civilizations have a few features in common. The most important of these is the presence of cities; indeed, the word *civilization* comes from the Latin word *civis,* meaning "resident of a city, or citizen." Historians and archaeologists generally define a city as a place where more than five thousand people live. Remains of the earliest communities of this size have been discovered in ancient Mesopotamia, or present-day Iraq.

Why should the presence of cities be the distinguishing mark of cultural development? It is not the cities themselves but what they imply about a culture that makes them so important. Any society in which thousands of people live in proximity to one another must agree in general to certain laws or rules governing human behavior. These may be either part of an oral tradition or, as they were in ancient Mesopotamia, written down. A city must also make provision to assure its residents of a constant supply of food, which involves not only transporting food into the city from the surrounding farmland but also storing food throughout the year and preserving stockpiles for years when harvests are poor. In addition to demonstrating that people could transport and store food effectively, the presence of cities also indicates that people were producing enough surplus food to allow for a specialization of labor. If the whole work force had been devoted to farming, no one would have been available to build roads, produce storage bins, or enforce the laws on which the city depended. This specialization of labor eventually allowed some members of society the opportunity and time to build structures and produce goods that were not directly essential to daily survival. Urban residents in Mesopotamia began to erect large buildings and to decorate them with sculptures, paintings, and mosaics, to write poetry and history, and to develop religious and philosophical ideas, all of which we consider essential to a civilization. As the cities themselves grew, they needed greater and greater amounts of food, which led to further technological development.

The civilization of ancient Mesopotamia flourished in the valley of two rivers, the Tigris and the Euphrates, and other early civilizations were located in river valleys as well—the Nile in Egypt, the Indus in India, and the Yellow in China. In all of these areas, except perhaps the Indus Valley, the amount of natural rainfall is not enough to sustain the level of agricultural production required for urban populations; irrigation using river water is necessary. Rather than proving a block to further development, however, the need for irrigation in these river valleys may have been the very catalyst that prompted the growth of cities. We may never be able to know this for sure, because irrigation systems were already in place before written records appeared, and because cities and irrigation expanded together. We do know that neither could have existed without the other in Mesopotamia; cities could survive only where there was a food surplus created by irrigation, and irrigation could be implemented only where there were enough people to construct and maintain ditches and other components of the system.

Supplying cities with water was not simply a technological problem, but one with economic, legal, social, and political implications as well. We can see this significance even in words themselves: The word *rival* originally meant those who shared, and quarreled over, the water in a *rivus,* or "irrigation channel." Your task in this chapter will be to use both visual and written evidence of ancient water systems to answer the following question: How did the need for a steady supply of water affect the technological, economic, political, and legal development of ancient societies?

BACKGROUND

Though the earliest of the world's civilizations all grew up in river valleys, the technical and organizational problems they confronted were very different because the character of the rivers differed tremendously. The Tigris and Euphrates flowed very fast, carrying soil as well as water down from the highlands. This soil was extremely rich and created new farmland where the rivers emptied into the Persian Gulf. (The ancient Persian Gulf ended more than 100 miles north of its modern-day shoreline; all of that land was created as the rivers filled in the delta.) The soil also filled in the irrigation ditches, which meant that they had to be cleaned out constantly. Every year this deposit was piled on the banks until they grew so high that the cleaning could no longer be accomplished easily. At this point a new ditch was cut and the old one abandoned, a process that entailed a great deal of work and required the cooperation of everyone whose land was watered by that particular ditch.

Mesopotamian farmers used several types of irrigation. They leveled large plots of land adjacent to the rivers and main canals, building up dikes around them in what is termed basin irrigation. During the spring and other high-water times of the year, farmers knocked holes in the dikes to allow water and fresh soil in. Once the sediment had settled, they let the water flow back into the channel. Workers also built small waterways between their fields to provide water throughout the year, developing a system of perennial irrigation. In the hillier country of northern Mesopotamia, farmers built terraces with water channels running alongside them. The terraces provided narrow strips of flat land to farm, and the waterways connected to brooks and streams.

Farmers could depend on gravity to bring water to their fields during spring and flood times, but at other times water-raising machines did the work. Technicians built many different types of machines, some of which are still in use in many parts of the world today. These solved some problems, but created others; for example, farmers with machines could drain an irrigation ditch during times of low water, leaving their neighbors with nothing. How were rights to water to be decided? Solving this problem was extremely important, and the first recorded laws regarding property rights in fact involve rights to water, not rights to land. In Mesopotamia, land was useless unless it was irrigated.

Many of the irrigation techniques developed in Mesopotamia spread to Egypt or were developed independently there. Egypt, because it received even less rainfall than Mesopotamia, was totally dependent on the Nile for watering crops. Fortunately, the Nile was much easier to use than the Tigris and Euphrates because it flooded regularly, allowing easy basin irrigation. The Nile was so predictable, in fact, that the Egyptians based their 365-day calendar on its annual flooding. The Egyptians also constructed waterways and water-lifting machines for perennial irrigation. Here as well, irrigation both caused and resulted from the growth of cities. Moreover, it contributed to the power of the kings, whom the Egyptian people regarded as somehow responsible for the flood of the Nile.

The harnessing of the Yellow River in China was also closely related to the growth of centralized state power there. The Yellow is a very violent river and carries a great amount of silt—twelve times as much as the Tigris and Euphrates, and seventy times as much as the Nile. The silt, caused by deforestation and erosion in the highlands, raises the bed of the Yellow River by three feet every century, necessitating either constant dredging of irrigation canals or the continual building of higher dikes to hold back the river. The violence of the Yellow River floods—which have continued into the twentieth century—has changed the river's lower course dramatically throughout recorded history and has always led to devastation and social upheaval. Engineers in the Yellow River valley thus needed waterworks that would both protect cities and villages from flooding and at the same time irrigate fields; the earliest attempts to do both began in the seventh century B.C.E. In addition, the states that developed in the Yellow River valley received most of their taxes in the form of grain, which needed to be transported to the capital or to armies under state command. Along much of its course, the Yellow was too turbulent for transport, so canals were dug for grain barges. These three goals—flood control, irrigation, and grain transport—were not always compatible. In addition, competing armies often used waterworks as weapons, flooding the land of their rivals by building or destroying dikes. (Such tactics have also continued into the twentieth century; the dikes of the Yellow River were broken as a strategic move in 1938 during the Sino-Japanese War.)

Some of the earliest large-scale waterworks in China were the Hong Guo system of canals connecting the Yellow River with the Bian and Si Rivers, dating from the fifth or fourth century B.C.E., and the Zhengguo irrigation canal, first completed in 246 B.C.E. and still in use today. Branch canals dug from the major arteries created large irrigated areas, and farmers built water-lifting machines for the perennial irrigation of their plots. As in Mesopotamia, water rights were a contentious issue, and special officials charged with the regulation of water were appointed as early as the second century B.C.E.

Though sewers were rare in the ancient world, pipes and conduits bringing water into cities and buildings were quite common in some areas. In China, earthenware pipes fitted together in sections have been excavated from as early as the second century B.C.E., and bamboo piping appears in illustrations from slightly later. The most extensive system for bringing water into cities in the ancient world was the one built for Rome. Like the three civilizations we have already discussed, Rome also grew up on the banks of a river, the Tiber, but substantial natural rainfall in the area made extensive irrigation for agricultural purposes unnecessary. Farmers did build drainage ditches, for much of the land around Rome was marshy and was usable for agriculture only when drained. Rome's primary water problem was the lack of good drinking water; the Tiber was often brackish and unpleasant, or even unhealthy, to drink. The Chinese solved the problem of unhealthy drinking water very early by boiling theirs, but the Romans instead learned from their Near Eastern neighbors and built aqueducts, covered or uncovered channels that brought water into the cities from pristine lakes and springs. The first of Rome's aqueducts was built in 312 B.C.E., and the system was expanded continuously up to about 150 C.E. Over 300 miles of aqueducts served the city of Rome alone, with extensive networks in the outlying provinces as well. Roman engineers went to great lengths to avoid valleys but were occasionally forced to construct enormous bridges to carry the aqueduct across a gorge. Some of these bridges were over 150 feet high, and a few, such as that in Segovia, Spain, still serve to bring water to city residents. Roman construction techniques, such as the use of the arch and water-resistant cement, allowed them to build water systems undreamed of in Mesopotamia and Egypt. Legal problems were not as easily solved, however, and disputes about water rights occurred throughout Rome's long history.

THE METHOD

Historians use a wide variety of sources when exploring ancient irrigation and water-supply systems. Many of these systems were created before the development of writing, so archaeological evidence—the actual remains of ancient ditches, machines, or aqueducts—is extremely important, particularly when tracing technological development. Even when such evidence itself has completely disappeared, valuable traces remain. As you will discover in this chapter, modern landscapes often reveal the ancient uses of the land through patterns of depressions and discoloration.

The easiest way to see these patterns is through aerial photography. Analyzing aerial photographs can be difficult, for it takes a great deal of training to learn how to read ancient land-use patterns through the overlay of modern development. Occasionally the older patterns can be quite clear, however, and with only a bit of additional information, you can begin to decode them. Source 1 is an aerial photograph of the site of a pre-Roman city in Italy. Examine the picture carefully. Can you see the old grid pattern of drainage ditches, which shows up as light and dark marsh grass? The dark lines are ancient drainage ditches, the lighter areas are ancient fields, and the white parallel lines superimposed on top are part of a modern drainage system. To examine the ancient system, you will mentally have to strip away the modern system. What do you think the broader black strip at the top left is? Look at the flatness of the landscape. Would silting in be a problem?

A more sophisticated type of aerial photography involves the use of satellites, rather than airplanes. Satellites can take extremely detailed pictures of the earth's surface that reveal natural and artificially constructed features, both ancient and contemporary. The sharpest images are produced by high-resolution military satellites whose pictures are not available to the public, but low-power images produced by LANDSAT, the only U.S. commercial imaging satellite system, are adequate for most archaeological and historical purposes. Source 2 is a map of the major ancient irrigation ditches between the Tigris and Euphrates Rivers identifiable in a recent LANDSAT image. What does the extent of the system reveal about Mesopotamian technology? What does the size of this network imply about the political systems in this area—that is, would you expect the cities in Mesopotamia to be politically unified? hostile to each other? New technologies such as LANDSAT imagery not only answer elusive questions, but also guide future research. How could you use this map to plan further investigations of irrigation systems?

Aerial photography provides visual evidence of entire irrigation systems, but not of the specific tools and machines used to build them or to lift water to the fields. For these we must look to the remains of the tools themselves, or to depictions of them in tomb paintings, scrolls, mosaics, and pottery. Source 3 is the earliest depiction of irrigation ditches that has survived from ancient Egypt, carved on the head of a ceremonial mace dating from around 3100 B.C.E. The large figure in the middle is one of the early kings of Egypt, holding a hoe, flanked by two palm-fan bearers and a man holding a basket for the dirt dug up by the hoe. At the bottom are two other workmen, also with hoes, excavating or deepening the ditches. Based on what you already know about Egyptian society, would you expect the king himself to be digging ditches? Why might this mace, which signified royal authority, show the king involved in building irrigation ditches?

Some of the machines depicted in ancient paintings are still in use today, showing that many techniques for lifting water have not changed at all for thousands of years. Sources 4 to 7 show four different machines for raising water that we know were in use in ancient times: the shaduf, the saqiya, the square-pallet chain pump, and the noria. To assess their role and importance, you have to think about a number of different factors while you examine the four diagrams. Some of these factors are technical: How complicated is this machine to build? Does it have many moving parts to keep in good repair? How much water can it lift? How high can it lift it? Can it work with both flowing and stationary water? Some of the factors are economic: Does the machine require a person to operate it (thus taking a worker away from other types of labor)? Does it require a strong adult, or can it be operated by a child? Does it require the power of an animal, which must be fed and cared for? Some of the factors are both economic and political: Does the machine require more raw materials to build than one family would be likely to possess? Does it require any raw materials, such as metal, that would have to be imported? (Such questions are political because someone has to decide which families get the raw materials necessary for their fields.) Some of the factors are legal: Does the machine raise so much water that distribution would have to be regulated? At this point, you may want to make a chart summarizing your assessment of the advantages and disadvantages of each machine; such a study aid will help you make your final conclusions.

We now turn from visual to written sources. Because water was so important, mention of water systems appears very early in recorded human history. Sources 8 to 12 are written accounts of the construction or operation of water systems. Source 8 presents the sections from the Code of Hammurabi, a Babylonian legal code dating from 1750 B.C.E., that refer to irrigation. Source 9 is a description of the building of the Zhengguo [Chêng Kuo] canal in the third century B.C.E., written by the historian Sima Qian about 150 years later. In Source 10, the Roman historian Suetonius records the water-system projects undertaken by the Emperor Claudius during his reign (41–54 C.E.). Source 11 is a report of the activities of Shao Xinchen [Hsin-Ch'en], an administrator during the Han dynasty in China, dating from sometime before 33 B.C.E. Source 12 is a discussion of some of the problems associated with Rome's water system, written about 100 C.E. by Frontinus, who was commissioner of the water supply. Finally, Source 13 is a memorial dating from the first century B.C.E. by Jia Rang [Chia Jang], a specialist in flood control, answering an imperial decree that asked for opinions on river conservancy.

As you read these sources, notice first of all the technical problems that each author addresses. What particular problems in controlling, tapping, transporting, and storing water are discussed? What solutions are suggested? Then look at legal problems, most clearly presented in the selection by Frontinus and the Code of Hammurabi. How were people misusing or harming the water systems? What penalties did they incur? Who controlled the legal use of water and decided how water was to be distributed?

The written sources also include information about political and economic factors in ancient water-supply systems that is nearly impossible to gain from archaeological evidence. Careful reading can give you an insight into who paid for the construction of such systems and who stood to profit—financially or politically—from their use. What reasons other than the simple need for water led rulers to build water systems? What political and economic factors entered into decisions about how water was to be distributed?

THE EVIDENCE

Source 1 from Leo Deuel, Flights Into Yesterday: The Story of Aerial Archaeology *(New York: St. Martin's Press, 1969), p. 236. Photograph: Fotoaerea Valvassori, Ravenna.*

1. Aerial Photograph of Pre-Roman City in Italy

Source 2 from Robert MaC. Adams, Heartland of Cities; Surveys of Ancient Settlements and Land Use on the Central Floodplains of the Euphrates *(Chicago: University of Chicago Press, 1981), p. 34.*

2. Major Ancient Levees Identifiable in LANDSAT Imagery

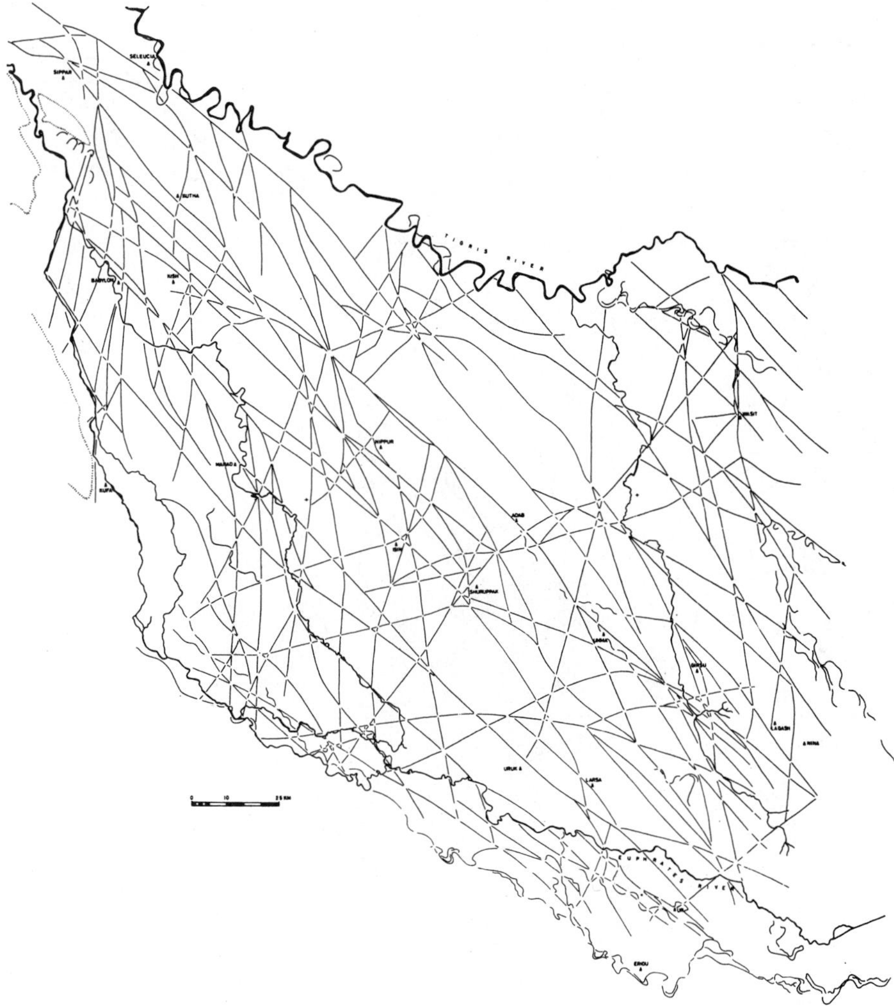

Source 3 from Walter B. Emery, Archaic Egypt *(Baltimore: Penguin, 1961), p. 43.*

3. Early Egyptian King Cutting an Irrigation Ditch, Drawn from Mace-head Carving, 3100 B.C.E.

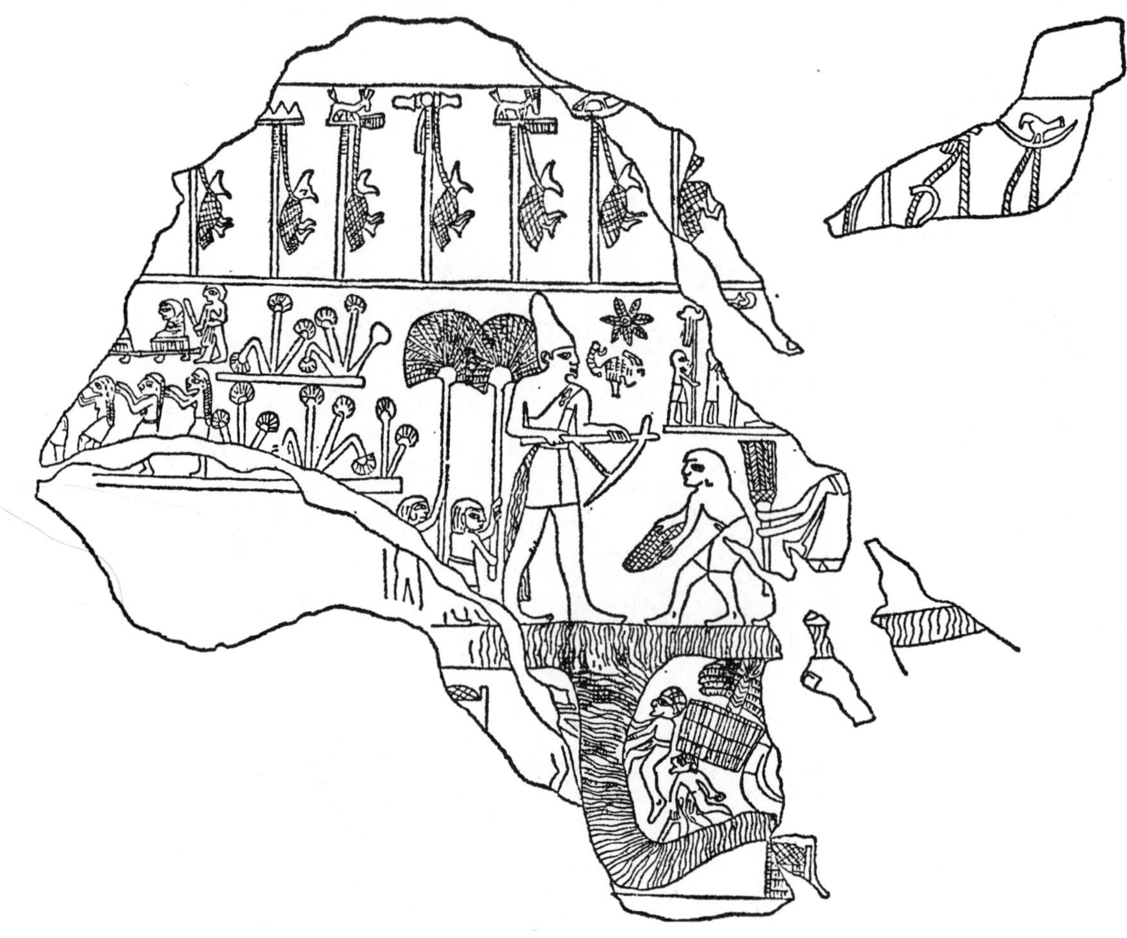

Sources 4 through 7 adapted from sketches by Merry E. Wiesner.

4. Shaduf

5. Saqiya

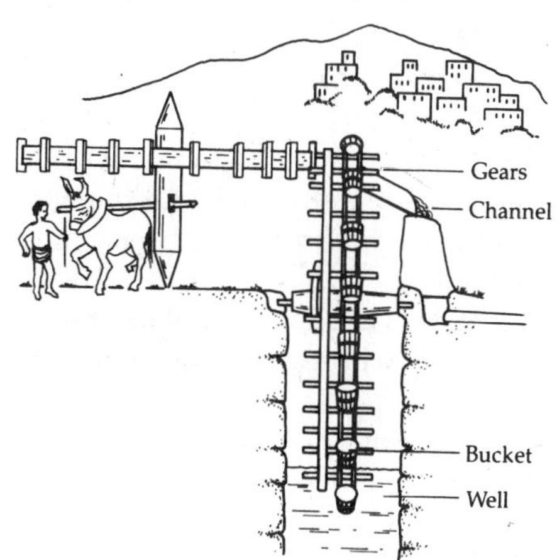

6. Square-Pallet Chain Pump

7. Noria

Source 8 from Robert F. Harper, The Code of Hammurabi *(Chicago: University of Chicago Press, 1904).*

8. Sections from the Code of Hammurabi Referring to Irrigation, 1750 B.C.E.

53. If a man neglects to maintain his dike and does not strengthen it, and a break is made in his dike and the water carries away the farmland, the man in whose dike the break has been made shall replace the grain which has been damaged.

54. If he is not able to replace the grain, they shall sell him and his goods and the farmers whose grain the water has carried away shall divide [the results of the sale].

55. If a man opens his canal for irrigation, and neglects it and the water carries away an adjacent field, he shall pay out grain on the basis of the adjacent field.

56. If a man opens up the water and the water carries away the improvements of an adjacent field, he shall pay out ten *gur* of grain per *bur* [of damaged land]. . . .

66. If a man has stolen a watering-machine from the meadow, he shall pay five shekels of silver to the owner of the watering-machine.

Source 9 from Joseph Needham, Science and Civilization in China, *Vol. 4, Pt. 3 (Cambridge: Cambridge University Press, 1974), p. 285.*

9. Sima Qian's Description of the Building of the Zhengguo Canal, ca. 100 B.C.E.

(The prince of) Han,[1] hearing that the State of Chhin[1] [Qin] was eager to adventure profitable enterprises, desired to exhaust it (with heavy activities), so that it should not start expanding to the east (and making attacks on Han). He therefore sent the hydraulic engineer Chêng Kuo [Zhengguo] (to Chhin) to persuade deceitfully (the king of) Chhin to open a canal from the Ching [Qing] River, from Chung-shan [Zhongshan] and Hu-khou [Hukou] in the west, all along the foot of the northern mountains, carrying water to fall into the river Lo in the east. The proposed canal was to be more than 300 *li*[2] long, and was to be used for irrigating agricultural land.

1. Han and Chhin were two states that bordered the Yellow River.
2. 300 *li* = 100 miles.

Before the construction work was more than half finished, however, the Chhin authorities became aware of the trick. (The king of Chhin) wanted to kill Chêng Kuo, but he [the engineer] addressed him as follows: "It is true that at the beginning I deceived you, but nevertheless this canal, when it is completed, will be of great benefit to Chhin. I have, by this ruse, prolonged the life of the State of Han for a few years, but I am accomplishing a work which will sustain the State of Chhin for ten thousand generations." The (king of) Chhin agreed with him, approved his words, and gave firm orders that the canal was to be completed. When it was finished, rich silt-bearing water was led through it to irrigate more than [667,000 acres] of alkali land. The harvests from these fields attained the level of [16 bushels] per *mou* [i.e. they became very abundant]. Thus Kuanchung (the land within the passes) became a fertile country without bad years. (It was for this reason that) Chhin became so rich and powerful, and in the end was able to conquer all the other feudal States. And ever afterwards the canal (bore the name of the engineer and) was called the Chêngkuo Canal.

Source 10 from Naphtali Lewis and Meyer Reinhold, Roman Civilization *(New York: Columbia University Press, 1955), pp. 151–152.*

10. Suetonius's Description of the Water Projects Undertaken by Emperor Claudius (r. 41–54 C.E.)

The public works which Claudius completed were great and essential rather than numerous; they were in particular the following: an aqueduct begun by Caligula; also the drainage channel of Lake Fucine and the harbor at Ostia, although in the case of the last two he knew that Augustus had refused the former to the Marsians in spite of their frequent requests, and that the latter had often been considered by the deified Julius but given up because of its difficulty. He brought to the city on stone arches the cool and abundant springs of the Claudian aqueduct . . . and at the same time the channel of the New Anio, distributing them into many beautifully ornamented fountains. He made the attempt on the Fucine Lake as much in the hope of gain as of glory, inasmuch as there were some who offered to drain it at their own cost provided the land that was drained be given them. He finished the drainage canal, which was three miles in length, partly by leveling and partly by tunneling a mountain, a work of great difficulty requiring eleven years, although he had 30,000 men at work all the time without interruption.

Source 11 from Cho-yun Hsu, Han Agriculture: The Formation of Early Chinese Agrarian Economy *(Seattle: University of Washington Press, 1980), pp. 268–269.*

11. Activities of Shao Xinchen, Han Dynasty, before 33 B.C.E.

[Shao] Hsin-ch'en [Xinchen] was promoted to be grand administrator of Nanyang. . . . Hsin-ch'en was a person of energy and plans; he took an interest in creating benefits for the people and regarded it as his urgent task to enrich them. Crossing in and out of the fields, stopping and resting even at remote villages and cantons, and having very little time for quiet living, he personally encouraged farming.

As he traveled about, he inspected the waters and springs in the commandery. He dug canals and ditches and built water gates and dikes in several tens of places in all to expand the irrigated land, which increased year by year to as much as [500,000 acres]. The people obtained benefits from this and had a surplus of stores.

Hsin-ch'en formulated regulations for the people concerning the equitable distribution of water. They were inscribed on stones and set up at the boundaries of the fields to prevent disputes over the distribution [of water].

Source 12 from B. K. Workman, editor and translator, They Saw It Happen in Classical Times *(New York: Barnes & Noble, 1964), pp. 179–181.*

12. Frontinus's Discussion of Rome's Water System ca. 100 C.E.

The New Anio[3] is drawn from the river in the district of Sinbrinum, at about the forty-second milestone along the Via Sublacensis. On either side of the river at this point are fields of rich soil which make the banks less firm, so that the water in the aqueduct is discoloured and muddy even without the damage done by storms. So a little way along from the inlet a cleansing basin was built where the water could settle and be purified between the river and the conduit. Even so, in the event of rain, the water reaches the city in a muddy state. The length of the New Anio is about 47 miles, of which over 39 are underground and more than 7 carried on structures above the ground. In the upper reaches a distance of about two miles in various sections is carried on low structures or arches.

3. An aqueduct completed under the emperor Claudius in 52 C.E.

Nearer the city, from the seventh Roman mile-stone, is half a mile on substructures and five miles on arches. These arches are very high, rising in certain places to a height of 109 feet.

. . . All the aqueducts reach the city at different levels. So some serve the higher districts and some cannot reach loftier ground. For the hills of Rome have gradually increased in height because of the rubble from frequent fires. There are five aqueducts high enough at entrance to reach all the city, but they supply water at different pressures. . . .

Anyone who wants to tap water for private consumption must send in an application and take it, duly signed by the Emperor, to the Commissioner. The latter must take immediate action on Caesar's grant, and enroll one of the Imperial freedmen to help him in the business. . . . The right to water once granted cannot be inherited or bought, and does not go with the property, though long ago a privilege was extended to the public baths that their right should last in perpetuity. . . . When grants lapse, notice is given and record made in the ledgers, which are consulted so that future applicants can be given vacant supplies. The previous custom was to cut off these lapsed supplies at once, to make some profit by a temporary sale to the landowners or even to outsiders. Our Emperor felt that property should not suddenly be left without water, and that it would be fairer to give thirty days' notice for other arrangements to be made by the interested party. . . .

Now that I have explained the situation with regard to private supply, it will be pertinent to give some examples of the ways in which men have broken these very sound arrangements and have been caught red-handed. In some reservoirs I have found larger valves in position than had been granted, and some have not even had the official stamp on them. . . .

Another of the watermen's intolerable practices to make a new outlet from the cistern when a water-grant is transferred to a new owner, leaving the old one for themselves. I would say that it was one of the Commissioner's chief duties to put a stop to this. For it affects not only the proper protection of the supply, but also the upkeep of the reservoir which would be ruined if needlessly filled with outlets.

Another financial scheme of the watermen, which they call "puncturing," must also be abolished. There are long separate stretches all over the city through which the pipes pass hidden under the pavement. I found out that these pipes were being tapped everywhere by the "puncturers," from which water was supplied by private pipe to all the business premises in the area, with the result that only a meagre amount reached the public utilities. I can estimate the volume of water stolen in this way from the amount of lead piping which was removed when these branch pipes were dug up.

Source 13 from Cho-Yun Hsu, Han Agriculture: The Formation of Early Chinese Agrarian Economy *(Seattle: University of Washington Press, 1980), pp. 266–267.*

13. Memorial from Jia Rang, 1st century B.C.E.

[Jia Rang memorialized:] ". . . Digging canals has three benefits; not digging them has three detriments. When the people are constantly exhausted by preventing floods, half of them lose their livelihood. When the water overflows the land and when the accumulated moisture evaporates, the people are made ill by the humid atmosphere. All the trees rapidly rot away, and the soil, turning alkaline, does not produce grain. When the river breaks the dikes and overflows, destruction ensues, and [the victims] become food for fish and turtles. These are the three detriments.

"If there are canals for irrigation, then the salt is washed down to the marshy ground and the spreading of the silt increases fertility. Where formerly millet and wheat were raised, even nonglutinous and glutinous rice can be produced; the productivity is increased fivefold in the high-lying land and tenfold in low-lying land. Furthermore, there is the advantage of transportation by water. These are the three benefits."

[Jia Rang next considers the possible types of irrigation projects, and proposes the building of large-scale dikes as the best policy. He describes two other alternatives to pursue if new dikes are not possible: digging new irrigation canals and repairing the old dikes. He assesses these two choices as follows.]

"At present, the number of functionaries and conscript laborers for embankments along the Yellow River in each commandery is several thousand, and the costs of cutting and buying wood and stone are several tens of millions yearly [an amount] that is sufficient to dig canals and construct water gates. Furthermore, when the people benefit from irrigation, they will urge one another to make canals, and they will not be weary even if the work is strenuous. At the same time the people's fields will be cared for and the dikes on the Yellow River will be completed. This will indeed enrich the state, make the people secure, create profit, and do away with calamities, and it will endure for several hundred years. Therefore, I consider this a medium policy. Repairing the old dikes by means of increasing the height and thickness would cost limitlessly, and we would frequently encounter calamities. This would be the worst policy."

QUESTIONS TO CONSIDER

Now that you have looked at both visual and written evidence, you will need to compile and organize the information gained from each type of source to achieve a more complete picture. Because sources for the earliest periods of human development are so scant, we need to use every shred of evidence available and use it somewhat creatively, making reasonable speculations where there is no specific evidence.

Take all the evidence about technical problems first. Keeping in mind that the ancient world had no power equipment, and no tools more elaborate than axes, hammers, saws, and drills (the Chinese and Romans also had planes and chisels), what would you gauge to be the most difficult purely technical problem involved in constructing water systems? in keeping them operating? The four diagrams of the water-raising machines are arranged in the chronological order of their development, with the shaduf as old as 2500 B.C.E. and the other three introduced hundreds of years later. Looking at your chart of the advantages and disadvantages of each machine, how do the later machines improve on the shaduf? What additional problems do these improvements create? What types of technological experimentation did the need for water encourage?

Technological advance is not always an unmitigated blessing. For example, water standing in irrigation ditches can become a fertile breeding ground for mosquitoes and other carriers of disease. Cities that depend on irrigation suffer food shortages and famine when ditches cannot be kept clear or when river levels drop. Furthermore, the diversion of so much of their water makes rivers much smaller when they finally reach their deltas, which means that the deltas become increasingly salty from sea water and eventually become unable to support the kinds of plant and animal life they originally sustained. Judging by the aerial photograph and the LANDSAT map, would you expect any of these problems in ancient Italy or Mesopotamia? In the written sources, do you find evidence of problems in the Chinese and Roman water systems that were caused by technological advance? Are any suggestions made for solving these?

Now think about what you have learned about the economic issues associated with water systems. You have no doubt noticed that tremendous numbers of people were needed to construct irrigation ditches and aqueducts. Some of the written sources, such as Suetonius and Jia Rang, give exact figures as to the number of workers. The size and complexity of the systems depicted in all the sources also imply huge work forces, given the lack of elaborate equipment. The rulers of Mesopotamia, Egypt, China, and Rome did not view the need for mass labor as an obstacle, but rather saw it as a solution to the problem of unemployment. Legend has it that the Roman emperor Vespasian, when offered a labor-saving machine, refused to use it on the grounds that it would put people out of work and lead to social unrest in Rome. You may approve of this concern for full employment, but it should also tell you something about the value of labor in ancient societies. What would you expect wages to be for construction workers? What class of people would you expect to find working on these water systems?

Large numbers of workers were needed not only in construction, but also in the maintenance of irrigation systems and the operation of water-lifting machines. What does this tell you about the value of labor? What would happen with the sudden drop in the population, such as that caused by a famine or epidemic? How would a loss of workers affect the available food supply?

The sources also reveal information about political factors associated with water systems. What does their construction indicate about the power of rulers to coerce or hire labor? How do rulers control the building and maintenance of machines and ditches? How might this affect the power and independence of local communities or of individual families? What can you surmise about the role water played in expanding centralized political power or in disputes between rival dynasties?

Finally, the sources provide evidence of legal changes necessitated by the search for, and limits of, water. Actions that had previously been unrestricted and unregulated now came under the control of public authorities, which meant that the number of enforcement agents and courts had to increase. What would this expansion of bureaucracy do to taxation levels? How did political concerns shape the regulations?

You are now ready to answer the question posed at the beginning of the chapter: How did the need for a steady supply of water affect the technological, economic, political, and legal development of ancient societies?

EPILOGUE

The irrigation and water supply systems of the ancient world required not only huge amounts of labor, but also strong central states to coerce or hire that labor and to enforce laws that kept the channels flowing. For example, each Mesopotamian city managed its own irrigation system, but the wealthy and advanced cities were attractive targets for foreign conquerers. The political history of ancient Mesopotamia was one of wave after wave of conquerers invading from the north—the Akkadians, Babylonians, Assyrians, Persians, Greeks, and finally Romans. Most of these conquerers realized the importance of irrigation and ordered the vanquished residents to maintain or expand their systems. When the Moslems conquered the area in the seventh century, they studied Mesopotamian techniques and spread these westward across northern Africa and into Spain, where centuries-old Roman irrigation systems were disintegrating.

In between these powerful conquerers, however, and after the thirteenth century, when the area was overrun by the Mongols, the irrigation ditches were often not maintained, and they silted in irreparably. The fertile farmland that had been built up in the delta became salinized from the salty waters of the Persian Gulf, making it useless for cultivation. Once the irrigation ditches were no longer functional, the cities could not survive. Centuries of irrigation combined with too little fertilization made even irrigated land less and less productive.

The benefits and problems brought by irrigation are not limited to the ancient world, however, but can be seen in many modern societies. A striking contemporary example comes from one of the parts of the world we have been studying in this chapter. Throughout the twentieth century, Egypt expanded irrigation system fed by the Nile with a series of dams, culminating in the Aswan High Dam, begun in 1960 to provide hydroelectric power and limit the free flow of water at the height of the flood season. The enormous reservoir created by the dam can also be tapped at low water times to allow for perennial irrigation. The dam does all of the things it was intended to do very well, but has also introduced some unexpected problems. The river's regular flooding had brought new fertile soil to the Nile Valley and carried away the salts that result from evaporation. Once the dam stopped the flooding, Egyptian fields began to need artificial fertilizer to remain productive, a supplement few farmers could afford. Because the soil of the Nile Valley contains much clay and so drains very slowly, the dam's steady supply of water makes many fields waterlogged and unusable. The large reservoir created by the dam sits in the middle of the Sahara Desert, losing tremendous amounts to evaporation and decreasing the total flow of water in the Nile significantly. The artificial lake also put many acres of farmland under water and forced the relocation of tens of thousands of people. The current drought in northern Africa has further lowered the level of the Nile, shrinking the amount of hydroelectric power the river can generate. Ending the flooding also allowed snails that carry bilharzia (schistosomiasis) to proliferate in the fields and irrigation ditches; bilharzia is an intestinal parasite that severely weakens its victims. Thus, like the dikes in ancient China that could be broken by flood or foreign conquest, or the levees of the Mississippi that gave way in the floods of 1993, or the irrigation of the southwestern United States that is draining underground aquifers, the Aswan High Dam has proved a mixed blessing to modern Egypt.

As you reflect on what you have discovered in this chapter, you may want to think about problems associated with the distribution of water in your own area. How does the need for water affect the political and economic structures of your city or state? What technological solutions has your area devised, and how have these worked?

CHAPTER TWO

WRITING AND POWER: DEFINING WORLD-VIEWS (1750–200 B.C.E.)

THE PROBLEM

According to Islamic tradition, when the angel Gabriel first revealed himself to Muhammad around the year 610, among the first words he spoke to Muhammad were these:

> In the name of the Lord who created all things. He has taught us the use of the pen. He taught us that which we know not.[1]

Although there is no record that Muhammad himself could either read or write, there is little doubt that the man who ultimately would be revered by Muslims as the Prophet understood the power that literacy gave to those who could read and write, a power that literate people held over those who were not literate. Thoughts could be shaped, codified, and transmitted over both distance and time. Laws (whether political, economic, or religious) could be written down and interpreted or enforced by those who could record or read them. Perhaps more important, writing gave to some the power to bind a people together by giving them a shared history, a common literature, a united world-view, and even a shared *cosmology* (a branch of philosophy that deals with the origin, process, and structure of the universe). And while the oral traditions of nonliterate peoples could be powerful, effective, and in some ways even more "democratic" (in that all who heard could thereby participate in the carrying on of laws, religion, and history), writing possessed certain advantages over an oral tradition, not the least of which being that later historians from other cultures could gain access to the history, culture, and thought of peoples of the past.

Throughout history, virtually every culture has had its own explanation of

1. Qur'an (Koran) XCVI, 1–5.

how the world was created (cosmology) and what place humans were meant to occupy in that world. In addition to commercial information and law codes, a people's explanations of creation were one of the first things they wrote down, thus demonstrating the people's own belief in the superiority of written over oral transmission. By studying these written explanations of creation, historians can come to understand a particular people's value system, its view of itself, and the relationship of the people to the world, to the universe, and to a god or gods. In addition, historians can gain an understanding of a people's own view of history. To a particular people, is history linear (resembling a straight line, from event to event), cyclical (circular, with patterns recurring), of another form, or formless (with events occurring purely at random, by chance)? In sum, by studying a people's accounts of creation, historians can learn a remarkable amount about how the people thought and even why they behaved as they did.

Your tasks in this chapter will require you to use all your analytical reading skills plus a good deal of historical imagination. In the Evidence section of this chapter you will find four written creation accounts—one from Atra-hasis of ancient Babylonia, one from the Rig Veda of ancient India, one from the Yijing (or I Ching, the Book of Changes) of ancient China, and one from the Torah (the first five books of both the Jewish and Christian Bibles) of the Israelites. First, you must read each account to learn how each of these peoples sought to explain the creation of the world. Then, using your historical imagination, show what each creation account tells us about the people who thought it critical enough to write it down—their value system, their view of history, their relationship to the universe as well as to a god or gods. In essence, then, you will be studying the cosmologies of four ancient peoples, an extremely important exercise for historians.

BACKGROUND

Forms of "written" communication are nearly as old as humanity itself. Cave paintings and etchings[2] surely were intended to transmit simple messages as well as to provide means of self-expression. Message sticks (Australia), wampum belts (Native Americans), shell designs (Nigeria), knotted cords (Tibet, Polynesia, parts of Africa), bean patterns (pre-Inca Peru), and the like—all were used to communicate uncomplicated messages.

Beginning about six thousand years ago, however, people began to develop more complex and codified (systematic, with rules) forms of written communication. Evolving first among the Sumerians of the Fertile Crescent—the land between the Tigris and Euphrates

2. Carvings or etchings on cave walls are referred to by archaeologists as petroglyphs; cave paintings are called petrograms.

Rivers—in approximately 3500 B.C.E., various types of writing on stone, clay tablets, and papyrus[3] emerged independently in Egypt, China, the Near East, Crete, Cyprus, and (by about 1000 B.C.E.) Central America. Ultimately, various cultures developed over two hundred written scripts, approximately eighty of which are still in use today.[4]

Wherever writing developed and whatever particular form it took, all types of writing can be divided into two general systems: *ideographic* and *phonetic*. Ideographic writing, known also as thought writing, evolved from using pictures to represent things or thoughts (Sumerian pictorials, Egyptian hieroglyphics, and Chinese pictographs, among others). The advantage of ideographic writing is that it is not tied to any particular spoken language and thus can be understood by people speaking a variety of tongues and dialects. The principal disadvantage of ideographic writing is that it requires the memorization of an immense number of different signs, or ideograms—four to six thousand, for example, for literate Chinese. On the other hand, in phonetic writing, each sign (or letter, in our writing) represents a particular sound, and signs are combined to make the sounds for particular words. For example, most Western Europeans employ a form of phonetic writing that uses the signs of the Roman alphabet. Regularized in the sixth century B.C.E., the Roman alphabet originally contained twenty-one signs (letters); the number was later expanded to twenty-six.[5] The chief advantages of phonetic writing are that only a few signs need to be memorized and that these signs can be grouped in an almost endless number of sound combinations to make words and to create new words.[6]

Wherever writing developed, those who mastered this skill often wielded great power and commanded enormous respect. In Egypt, scribes were exempt from physical labor, taxation, and military service. As one scribe wrote, "Put writing in your heart that you protect yourself from hard labor of any kind." Scribes were likewise respected in Mesopotamia, among the Aztecs of Central America, and later in the nations of Islam. Most societies founded schools to teach royalty, nobility, and scribes the craft of writing, but in no early culture was universal literacy considered either necessary or desirable. This was because those in power quickly realized that those who could write possessed the capacity to shape the thoughts of those who could not. The illiterate would gather

3. **papyrus:** a type of paper, developed by the Egyptians around 3100 B.C.E., that was made from the inner stems of the papyrus plant, which were pressed together with some form of adhesive; after being written on, the papyrus then was rolled into scrolls.

4. Of all the written scripts known to have existed, over twenty still are undecipherable. People who decipher ancient inscriptions or writings are known as epigraphers. For more on this exciting profession, see John Chadwick, *The Decipherment of Linear B* (Cambridge, England, 1958); Carol Andrews, *The Rosetta Stone* (London, 1981); Michael D. Coe, *Breaking the Maya Code* (New York, 1992).

5. The letters *W, J, Y, Z,* and *U* were added later.

6. An unabridged English dictionary contains approximately 500,000 words, and hundreds of new words are added to the language each decade.

(or would be forcibly gathered) to listen to the readings of edicts, proclamations, laws, or religious texts and liturgies.[7]

As noted above, along with commercial agreements and legal codes, one of the first things a people committed to writing was their own explanation of the creation of the universe, the world, and human beings. Such creation accounts often bound a people together and formed a philosophical foundation for their thoughts and actions. In this chapter, you will be analyzing the creation accounts of the Babylonians of the Fertile Crescent (written down sometime between 1750 and 1400 B.C.E.), the Indo-Aryans of ancient India (Rig Veda, written down in ca. 600 B.C.E.), the Zhou dynasty of ancient China (Yijing, parts of which can be dated roughly at 1000 B.C.E., although the section you will be reading dates from around the third century B.C.E.), and the Israelites of ancient Israel (the Torah, traditionally first read publicly by the scribe Ezra in Jerusalem in 444 B.C.E.).[8]

Historians generally agree that Mesopotamia,[9] the area between the Tigris and Euphrates Rivers (in modern-day Iraq), was the scene of the earliest civilization. It was here that a people known as Sumerians domesticated plants and animals; devised an irrigation system; constructed cities such as Ur, Uruk, and Lagash; established trade routes to lands as far away as Egypt; and developed what was probably the world's first writing system, at first pictographic but ultimately evolving into a phonetic system. Later conquerors of the Sumerians, such as the Babylonians,[10] adopted much of Sumerian culture, including its writing and its cosmology. Atra-hasis (Source 1), the Babylonian creation account, borrowed heavily from the Sumerians.

The Indo-Aryans migrated to present-day India from the northwest around 1500 B.C.E., either conquering the earlier Indus civilization or moving in after its fall. Originally a warlike and pastoral people, the Aryans quickly adapted themselves to a sedentary, food-producing life. Politically, their Vedic society was divided into a strict caste system of priests (Brahman), warriors (Kshatriya), peasants (Vaishya), and serfs (Shudra). Although the original Aryan conquerors were illiterate, the preceding Indus Valley civilization had developed a writing system that was a mixture of ideographic and phonetic forms.[11] By roughly 700 B.C.E., however, Vedic society had developed its own form of writing known as Brahmi, apparently derived from a North Semitic script.

In Vedic society, writing apparently was first used in political contexts, but soon was adopted by the Brahman to systematically collect songs, hymns, histories, and other materials that had

7. **liturgy:** a prescribed form for a public religious service; many religions have written down their liturgies in prayer books or missals.

8. See Nehemiah 8:1–8.

9. **Mesopotamia:** a Greek word meaning "land between the rivers."

10. The Babylonians were known as Amorites, a Semitic people who invaded Sumer from the west and built the city of Babylon. Their most famous ruler was Hammurabi, the author of a comprehensive law code for Babylon.

11. The Indus script is one of those that is still a mystery.

been passed orally from generation to generation. The oldest of those collections was the Rig Veda (Source 2),[12] a collection of 1,017 hymns or songs divided into ten chapters or books. Some of these songs had been present in Vedic society at least since the Indo-Aryan migration to northern India in roughly 1500 B.C.E. It is here that the society's creation accounts can be found.

In China, the Shang dynasty (ca. 1523–1027 B.C.E.) was overthrown by the Zhou (Chou), once-loyal dependents of the Shang whose military technology (including horse-drawn chariots) gave them the upper hand over their former masters. But the Zhou were wise enough to retain much of Shang culture, including its system of writing and its religious beliefs. A major part of those beliefs had to do with divination, the art of foretelling the future. Priests would take the bottom shell of a tortoise, pierce the shell with a small hole, ask a question, and then apply heat to the hole in the shell. The resulting cracks in the shell formed various patterns that the priests could then interpret in order to predict future events. By around 200 B.C.E., the Yijing (or Book of Changes) had been completed and served as an interpretive guide that substituted eight trigrams (sets of three parallel lines) and sixty-four hexagrams (six parallel lines) for the cracks in the tortoise shell. The Yijing is less a religious book than it is a volume of philosophy and ethics, and it was considered important enough to escape the great book burning of 213 B.C.E. It is in the Yijing (Source 4) that the Chinese creation account can be found.

About the time that the Indo-Aryans were moving into India and the Shang dynasty was in the process of controlling the eastern half of the Yellow River valley, in Mesopotamia and the Arabian peninsula groups of homeless nomads (referred to in Mesopotamian and Egyptian sources as "Habiru") wandered across the semiarid landscape grazing their herds. One of these groups came to be known as "Hebrews," or "Israelites" or "Jews."[13] Sometime after 1550 B.C.E., the Jews voluntarily migrated to Egypt to escape a drought, but soon were enslaved by the Egyptians. Around 1200 B.C.E., the Jews either abandoned or escaped from Egypt. The decline of both the Egyptian and Hittite empires had left a power vacuum along the eastern coast of the Mediterranean Sea, and it was here that the Israelites ultimately settled, fighting off Philistines and other peoples in order to seize and hold the land. Sometime after 925 B.C.E. (the traditional death of King Solomon), the Israelites broke into two kingdoms. The northern kingdom was destroyed by Assyrian invaders, while the southern kingdom (Judah) survived for another century and a half, until the Babylonian captivity.

Written Hebrew was one of the several offshoots of North Semitic script (another, as we have seen, was Brahmi) and was in use as early as ca. 800 B.C.E.

12. **Veda:** "wisdom, or the path to wisdom."

13. At the time, "Hebrew" referred to a social category, whereas "Israelite" was used to describe all the people of the group; "Jews" derived from the southern kingdom's surviving tribe of Judah.

The form of Hebrew writing known as Square Hebrew (for the rectangular shaping of the letters) traditionally owed its adoption to the scribe Ezra in the fifth century B.C.E. Like all Semitic scripts, Hebrew is consonantal—that is, phonetic with consonant letters or sounds (in the case of Hebrew, twenty-two), but no vowels.

Similar to the early writings of other peoples, the Torah contains the Jews' creation account, history, and laws. Traditionally, authorship is credited to Moses, although a majority of biblical scholars assert that the Torah comes from more than a single source. According to ancient tradition, Joshua had the Torah "engraved upon the stones of the altar" of the tabernacle sometime before 1100 B.C.E., a claim that most scholars dispute as much too early (the fifth century B.C.E. is more likely). Like those of other peoples, the Israelites' explanation of creation (Source 3, from the book of Genesis, which began to be stabilized around 720 B.C.E.) tells historians a great deal about the Jewish people themselves.

What does the creation account of each of the peoples excerpted in the Evidence section tell us about the people themselves? What can we discover about how they viewed the universe, themselves, the role of a god or gods, and the unfolding of history itself?

THE METHOD

When people today consult the Rig Veda, the Torah, or the Yijing, most do so either as part of their religious worship or as an inspirational guide.[14] Each of these writings, however, also is a historical document that can be examined and analyzed for what that document tells us about those who created it and those who preserved and venerated it.

As you might expect, historians approach such a document in quite different ways from members of a group for which the document is an important part of their creed or philosophy. To begin with, whenever it is possible, historians prefer to read the document in its oldest version and in its original language. In that way, mistakes made in copying or translating, as well as purposeful additions to or deletions from the original text, will not lead the historians into errors of judgment. Second, it is important to historians to know as closely as possible the date (or dates) of the document's creation. This information is valuable to historians because it enables them to study the context and understand more about the people who were living during that period, the events taking place, and the ideas in circulation. Historians call this process learning about the "climate of opinion" of a particular time period. Unfortunately, very early documents (such as the ones you will be working with in this chapter) cannot be dated very precisely because

14. Atra-hasis was lost for centuries and began to be discovered only in the mid-1800s (large parts are still missing). No contemporary people venerate it as a religious text.

they were written down only after a long period of oral transmission.

After completing these early steps, historians then are prepared to examine the document itself. When dealing with creation accounts, historians ask of each written account a series of questions: How does the account explain the creation of the universe, the world, and human beings? Is the creation divinely inspired—in other words, did a god or gods play an active role in the creation process, and for what purpose? Are human beings merely one among many objects of creation, *or* are human beings the pinnacle of the creation process? In return for creation and care, do human beings have any obligation to their creator? Finally, is the creation process in the account lineal (proceeding sequentially along a line from one event to another), cyclical (circular), of another pattern, or without pattern (formless)?

Having subjected each creation account to this series of questions, historians then are ready to ask what each document reveals about the people who created it. This will take some reading in your text about the people under scrutiny, as well as a considerable amount of historical imagination. For example, if each creation account can be seen as a life guide for those who venerate it, what does the account encourage or compel (or forbid) the true believers to do? Is the creation process *reproduced* in the lives of true believers (from birth to death)? What does that process tell you about the people who created the account?

Finally, you are ready to compare the four creation accounts and the people who committed them to memory and later to writing. Historians call this process *comparative textual analysis,* and it is one of the most basic methods of investigation used throughout all the humanities (literature, philosophy, linguistics, history, and the like). As you compare these accounts and their creators, using the questions above as initial guides, be careful *not* to fall into the habit of thinking of certain cultures or peoples as "inferior" or "superior" on the basis of how far or near a particular group's beliefs are to your own beliefs or philosophy. This is a common trap, and you must make every effort to avoid it. After all, each of the creation accounts you will be examining and analyzing was preserved by a people or peoples for thousands of years. All except Atra-hasis have become the foundation for one or more current religions or philosophies, and as such have been deemed satisfying by a group or groups for many, many generations. Historians, therefore, approach these sources with great sensitivity and respect.

Atra-hasis (Source 1), as noted above, was lost for two millennia, surviving only in some Hebrew traditions that became part of the Book of Genesis (Atra-hasis was a man who was warned of a flood by the god Enki and was urged to build a boat and escape with his family and a selection of animals). The Rig Veda (Source 2) is the oldest of the sacred texts of modern Hinduism (733 million followers in 1992). The Torah (Source 3) is considered sacred to Jews (18 million), Christians (1.8 billion), and Muslims (971 million), all of whom are referred to by Muslims as People of the Book. The Yijing (Source 4) is one of the bases of Confucianism (195 million adherents is only a guess), a westernization of the name of the great teacher K'ung Fu-tze (551–479 B.C.E.).

As you read the Evidence, be sure to take notes. One effective way of organizing your thoughts is to divide your note pages into two parts. On the left side of the page, summarize the creation account you are reading. Then, on the right side, summarize your thoughts (and questions) about the value system, the view of history, and the relationship between beings that you are able to infer from the creation account.

THE EVIDENCE

Source 1 from W. G. Lambert and A. R. Millard, Atra-hasis: The Babylonian Story of the Flood *(Oxford: Oxford University Press, 1969), pp. 57, 59, 61.*

1. Excerpts from Atra-hasis

[*The account begins with a universe that contained only the gods. The three senior gods (Anu, Enlil, and Enki) agree to divide the universe into three spheres of influence, with Anu in charge of heaven, Enlil of earth, and Enki of the water beneath the earth. The junior gods, required by Enlil to work, revolt against the senior gods. Thus the three senior gods call on Belet-ili,*[15] *the birth goddess, to create workers to serve the gods.*]

While [Belet-ili, the birth-goddess], is present,
Let the birth-goddess create offspring
And let man bear the toil of the gods.
They summoned and asked the goddess,
The midwife of the gods, wise Mami,
'You are the birth-goddess, creatress of mankind,
Create *Lullu*[16] that he may bear the yoke,
Let him bear the yoke assigned by Enlil,
Let man carry the toil of the gods.'
Nintu opened her mouth
And addressed the great gods,
'It is not possible for me to make things,
Skill lies with Enki.
Since he can cleanse everything
Let him give me the clay so that I can make it.'
Enki opened his mouth
And addressed the great gods,
'On the first, seventh, and fifteenth day of the month

15. Interestingly, Belet-ili, the birth goddess, is also referred to as Mami or Mama.

16. **Lullu:** man

I will make a purifying bath.
Let one god be slaughtered
So that all the gods may be cleansed in a dipping . . .
So that we may hear the drum for the rest of time
Let there be a spirit from the god's flesh.
Let it proclaim living (man) as its sign,
So that this be not forgotten let there be a spirit.'
In the assembly answered 'Yes'
The great Anunnaki, who administer destinies.
On the first, seventh, and fifteenth day of the month
He made a purifying bath.
We-ila, who had personality,
They slaughtered in their assembly.
From his flesh and blood
Nintu mixed clay.
For the rest [of time they heard the drum],
From the flesh of the god [there was] a spirit.
It proclaimed living (man) as its sign,
And so that this was not forgotten [there was] a spirit.
After she had mixed that clay
She summoned the Anunnaki, the great gods.
The Igigi, the great gods,
Spat upon the clay.
Mami opened her mouth
And addressed the great gods,
'You commanded me a task, I have completed it;
You have slaughtered a god together with his personality.
I have removed your heavy work,
I have imposed your toil on man.
You raised a cry for mankind,
I have loosed the yoke, I have established freedom.'
They heard this speech of hers,
They ran together and kissed her feet (saying),
'Formerly we used to call you Mami,
Now let your name be Mistress-of-All-the-Gods (Belet-kala-ili) . . .

[*As the number of humans increased, their noise bothered the gods. Therefore Enlil tried to reduce the human population through plagues and other devices. It was in this context that he summoned up the flood, from which Atra-hasis and his family escaped. It is likely that, while in captivity in Babylon, the Hebrew people heard this account.*]

Source 2 from Franklin Edgerton, trans., The Beginnings of Indian Philosophy *(Cambridge, Mass.: Harvard University Press, 1965), pp. 60–61, 67–68, 73, 74.*

2. Excerpts from Book 10 of the Rig Veda

10.72[17]

1. We will now proclaim the origins of the gods to win applause (from any) who shall behold them in a later age, as the hymns are chanted.

2. Brahmanaspati (the Lord of the Holy Word) smelted them together, as a smith. In the primal age of the gods the Existent was born from the Non-existent.

3. In the first age of the gods the Existent was born from the Non-existent. After it (the Existent) the regions were born—(after) it, from the (World-mother) in labour.

4. The world was born from the (World-mother) in labour; from the world the regions were born. From Aditi Daksa was born, from Daksa likewise Aditi (was born).[18]

5. Aditi, verily, was born, who is thy daughter, O Daksa. After her the gods were born, the blessed ones, companions of immortality.

6. When, O gods, there in the flood you stood, holding fast to one another, then from you, as from dancers, thick dust arose.

7. When, O gods, like wizard-priests, you made the worlds to swell, then you brought forth the sun that had been hidden in the sea.

8. There were eight sons of Aditi, which were born of her body. She went to the gods with seven; the (Sun-)bird she cast away.

9. With seven sons Aditi went to the primal generation (of gods). She brought back the (Sun-)bird for alternate procreation and death.

10.81

1. The seer who, in sacrificing all these worlds, took his seat as hotar-priest, our father—he, with prayer seeking wealth (i.e., sacrificing), concealing that which was first, entered into the later beings.

17. The Rig Veda is organized into ten books totaling 1,017 hymns. The number 10.72 means hymn #72 of book #10.

18. Aditi "is Mother, is Father, is Son . . . is all that is born, that will be born" (Rig Veda, 1.89). Normally, however, Aditi is taken to mean the Great Mother from whom the world was born, as well as the mother of the gods themselves. Daksa is masculine and often referred to as the "primordial cause," the original power of wisdom. Daksa's personification fluctuates throughout the Vedas.

2. What, verily, was that resting-place (support)? What manner of thing did he begin from, and how vast was it, that from which the All-maker, the all-seeing, creating the earth, unfolded the heaven by his might?

3. With eyes and face in all directions, likewise with arms and feet in all directions, he welded (as a smith) them together with his arms, with fan-bellows, creating heaven and earth, the sole god.

4. What, verily, was the wood, what the lumber, from which they carpentered out heaven and earth? You wise ones, with your wisdom inquire into that, upon what base he rested, establishing the worlds.

5. These your highest places, your lowest also, and these that are your midmost, All-maker, teach to (your) friends at the oblation, O Self-mighty One. Yourself offer sacrifice, prospering your own self (thereby).

6. O All-maker, thriving on sacrifice, do you sacrifice for yourself (i.e., create, by the cosmic "sacrifice" of creation) earth and heaven. Let other people round about stray helplessly; for us here let there be a generous patron.

7. Let us summon today for aid at the (sacrificial) contest the Lord of Holy Utterance,[19] the All-maker, who inspires the intellect. Let him take pleasure in our offerings, being helpful to all, working surely unto our support.

10.90

1. The Purusa[20] has a thousand heads, a thousand eyes, and a thousand feet. He, encompassing the world on all sides, stood out ten fingers' lengths beyond.

2. The Purusa alone is all this universe, what has been, and what is to be. He rules likewise over (the world of) immortality (viz. the gods), which he grows beyond, by (sacrificial?) food.

3. Such is the extent of his greatness; and the Purusa is still greater than this. A quarter of him is all beings, three quarters are (the world of) the immortal in heaven.

4. In his three-quarters the Purusa arose to the upper regions; a quarter of him, on the other hand, came to be here below. From this (quarter) he expanded manifoldly into the things that eat and those that do not eat (animate and inanimate beings).

19. **Lord of Holy Utterance:** the feminine version of the Lord of the Holy Word (see 10.72, verse 2), which were hymns composed by the Brahman (priests); the Brahman held contests to see who could compose the best hymns.

20. **Purusa:** man as a cosmic being, a sort of world-giant.

5. From him the Shining One (the cosmic waters) was born, from the Shining One (was born likewise) the Purusa. Being born (from the Shining One) he extended beyond the world, behind and also before.

6. When the gods, with the Purusa as oblation,[21] extended (performed) the (cosmic) sacrifice, Spring became the butter for it, Summer the firewood, Autumn the oblation.

7. They consecrated on the sacred grass this sacrifice, (namely) the Purusa, born in the beginning. With him the gods sacrificed, the Sadhyas,[22] and the Seers.

8. From this sacrifice, offered as whole-offering, the ghee-mixture[23] (the juice that flowed off) was collected; it made these animals—those of the air, of the jungle, and of the village.

9. From this sacrifice, offered as whole-offering, the stanzas of praise (the Rigveda) and the melodies (Samaveda) were produced; the meters were produced therefrom, the sacrificial formulas (Yajurveda) were produced therefrom.

10. Therefrom were produced horses, and whatever animals have (cutting-) teeth on both jaws. Cattle were produced therefrom, therefrom were born goats and sheep.

11. When they divided the Purusa (as the victim at the cosmic sacrifice), into how many parts did they separate him? What did his mouth become? What his two arms? What are declared to be his two thighs, his two feet?

12. The Brahman (priestly caste) was his mouth, his two arms became the Rajanya (warrior caste); his two thighs are the Vaisya (artisan caste), from his two feet the Sudra (serf caste) was produced.

13. The moon sprang from his thought-organ, the sun was produced from his eye; from his mouth Indra (war-god and soma-drinker) and Agni (the Fire-god), from his breath Vayu (the wind) was produced.

14. From his navel arose the atmosphere, from his head the heaven evolved; from his two feet the earth, from his ear the directions. Thus they fashioned the worlds.

15. Seven were his surrounding sticks (at the burnt-offering), thrice seven were made the pieces of kindling wood, when the gods, extending (performing) the (cosmic) sacrifice, bound the Purusa as the victim.

21. **oblation:** offering (to a deity).

22. **Sadhyas:** ancient gods or demigods.

23. **ghee:** a clarified butter, used in religious rituals.

16. With offering the gods offered the offering; these were the first (holy) institutions. Verily these powers have followed up to heaven, where are the Sadhya-gods of old.

10.129

1. Non-existent there was not, existent there was not then. There was not the atmospheric space, nor the vault beyond. What stirred, where, and in whose control? Was there water, a deep abyss?

2. Nor death nor immortality (mortals nor immortals) was there then; there was no distinction of night or day. That One breathed without breath by inner power; than it verily there was nothing else further.

3. Darkness there was, hidden by darkness, in the beginning; an undistinguished ocean was This All. What generative principle was enveloped by emptiness—by the might of (its own) fervour That One was born.

4. Desire (creative, or perhaps sacrificial, impulse) arose then in the beginning, which was the first seed of thought. The (causal) connection (bandhu) of the existent the sages found in the non-existent, searching with devotion in their hearts.

5. Straight across was stretched the (dividing-)cord of them (i.e., of the following); below (what) was there? above (what) was there? Seed-bearers (male forces) there were, strengths (female forces) there were; (female) innate power below, (male) impellent force above.[24]

6. Who truly knows? Who shall here proclaim it—whence they were produced, whence this creation? The gods (arose) on this side (later), by the creation of this (empiric world, to which the gods belong); then who knows whence it came into being?

7. This creation, whence it came into being, whether it was established, or whether not—he who is its overseer in the highest heaven, he verily knows, or perchance he knows not.

24. A suggestion that the world was created by some sort of cosmic intercourse between male powers and female powers. But, as Edgerton suggests, verses 6 and 7 strongly imply that the poet feels that he has gone too far. See *Beginnings of Indian Philosophy,* p. 73. See also Abinash Chandra Bose, *Hymns from the Vedas* (New York: Asia Publishing House, 1966), pp. 303–305.

Source 3 from The Torah: A Modern Commentary *(New York: Union of American Hebrew Congregations, 1981), pp. 18–20, 29–30, 116–117.*

3. From the First Book of Moses, called Genesis

CHAPTER 1

1] When God began to create the heaven and the earth—**2]** the earth being unformed and void, with darkness over the surface of the deep[25] and a wind[26] from God sweeping over the water—**3]** God said, "Let there be light"; and there was light. **4]** God saw that the light was good, and God separated the light from the darkness. **5]** God called the light Day, and the darkness He called Night. And there was evening and there was morning, a first day.

6] God said, "Let there be an expanse in the midst of the water, that it may separate water from water." **7]** God made the expanse, and it separated the water which was below the expanse from the water which was above the expanse. And it was so. **8]** God called the expanse Sky. And there was evening, and there was morning, a second day.

9] God said, "Let the water below the sky be gathered into one area, that the dry land may appear." And it was so. **10]** God called the dry land Earth, and the gathering of waters He called Seas. And God saw that this was good. **11]** And God said, "Let the earth sprout vegetation: seed-bearing plants, fruit trees of every kind on earth that bear fruit with the seed in it." And it was so. **12]** The earth brought forth vegetation: seed-bearing plants of every kind, and trees of every kind bearing fruit with the seed in it. And God saw that this was good. **13]** And there was evening and there was morning, a third day.

14] God said, "Let there be lights in the expanse of the sky to separate day from night; they shall serve as signs for the set times—the days and the years; **15]** and they shall serve as lights in the expanse of the sky to shine upon the earth." And it was so. **16]** God made the two great lights, the greater light to dominate the day and the lesser light to dominate the night, and the stars. **17]** And God set them in the expanse of the sky to shine upon the earth, **18]** to dominate the day and the night, and to separate light from darkness. And God saw that this was good. **19]** And there was evening and there was morning, a fourth day.

20] God said, "Let the waters bring forth swarms of living creatures, and birds that fly above the earth across the expanse of the sky." **21]** God created the great sea monsters, and all the living creatures of every kind that creep, which

25. Some Hebraic scholars point out that this phrase ("surface of the deep") echoes a "Mesopotamian creation story where it is told that heaven and earth were formed from the carcass of the sea dragon, Tiamat." *The Torah: A Modern Commentary,* p. 18.

26. **wind:** also translated as "spirit."

the waters brought forth in swarms; and all the winged birds of every kind. And
God saw that this was good. **22]** God blessed them, saying, "Be fertile and
increase, fill the waters in the seas, and let the birds increase on the earth."
23] And there was evening and there was morning, a fifth day.

24] God said, "Let the earth bring forth every kind of living creature: cattle,
creeping things, and wild beasts of every kind." And it was so. **25]** God made
wild beasts of every kind and cattle of every kind, and all kinds of creeping
things of the earth. And God saw that this was good. **26]** And God said, "Let us
make man in our image, after our likeness. They shall rule the fish of the sea, the
birds of the sky, the cattle, the whole earth, and all the creeping things that creep
on earth." **27]** And God created man in His image, in the image of God He created him; male and female He created them. **28]** God blessed them and God said
to them, "Be fertile and increase, fill the earth and master it; and rule the fish of
the sea, the birds of the sky, and all the living things that creep on earth."

29] God said, "See, I give you every seed-bearing plant that is upon all the
earth, and every tree that has seed-bearing fruit; they shall be yours for food.
30] And to all the animals on land, to all the birds of the sky, and to everything
that creeps on earth, in which there is the breath of life, [I give] all the green plants
for food." And it was so.[27] **31]** And God saw all that He had made, and found it
very good. And there was evening and there was morning, the sixth day.

CHAPTER 2

1] The heaven and the earth were finished, and all their array. **2]** On the seventh
day God finished the work which He had been doing, and He ceased on the seventh day from all the work which He had done. **3]** And God blessed the seventh
day and declared it holy, because on it God ceased from all the work of creation
which He had done.

4] Such is the story of heaven and earth when they were created.

When the LORD God made earth and heaven—**5]** when no shrub of the field
was yet on earth and no grasses of the field had yet sprouted, because the LORD
God had not sent rain upon the earth and there was no man to till the soil, **6]** but
a flow would well up from the ground and water the whole surface of the
earth—**7]** the LORD God formed man from the dust of the earth. He blew into
his nostrils the breath of life, and man became a living being.

8] The LORD God planted a garden in Eden, in the east, and placed there the
man whom He had formed. **9]** And from the ground the LORD God caused to
grow every tree that was pleasing to the sight and good for food, with the tree
of life in the middle of the garden, and the tree of knowledge of good and
bad. . . .

27. Many biblical scholars assert that humans and other animals were herbivores (exclusively vegetarian) until after the Flood, when they became omnivores (eating all kinds of food, including the flesh of other animals). See Genesis 9:3 and Isaiah 11:7.

15] The LORD God took the man and placed him in the garden of Eden, to till it and tend it. **16]** And the LORD God commanded the man, saying, "Of every tree of the garden you are free to eat; **17]** but as for the tree of knowledge of good and bad, you must not eat of it; for as soon as you eat of it, you shall die."[28]

18] The LORD God said, "It is not good for man to be alone; I will make a fitting helper for him." **19]** And the LORD God formed out of the earth all the wild beasts and all the birds of the sky, and brought them to the man to see what he would call them; and whatever the man called each living creature, that would be its name. **20]** And the man gave names to all the cattle and to the birds of the sky and to all the wild beasts; but for Adam no fitting helper was found. **21]** So the LORD God cast a deep sleep upon the man; and, while he slept, He took one of his ribs and closed up the flesh at that spot. **22]** And the LORD God fashioned the rib that He had taken from the man into a woman; and He brought her to the man. **23]** Then the man said, "This one at last / Is bone of my bones / And flesh of my flesh. / This one shall be called Woman, / For from man was she taken." **24]** Hence a man leaves his father and mother and clings to his wife, so that they become one flesh.

[*Disobeying God's command, Adam and Eve ate the forbidden fruit, were cursed by God, and were banished from the Garden. Their first two children were Cain and Abel. Out of jealousy, Cain murdered Abel and was even further banished. Adam and Eve had many more children. After several generations, humans had become corrupt, and God determined to punish them by flooding the land. He warned righteous Noah, who gathered his family and all species in an ark, which survived the flood. Many generations later, people attempted to build a tower to reach heaven, but were confounded by God, who caused them to begin speaking different languages. Many generations later, God appeared to Abram, offering to make a covenant (contract) with him.*]

CHAPTER 17

1] When Abram was ninety-nine years old, the LORD appeared to Abram and said to him, "I am El Shaddai.[29] Walk in My ways and be blameless. **2]** I will establish My covenant between Me and you, and I will make you exceedingly numerous."

3] Abram threw himself on his face, as God spoke to him further, **4]** "As for Me, this is My covenant with you: You shall be the father of a multitude of nations. **5]** And you shall no longer be called Abram, but your name shall be Abraham, for I make you the father of a multitude of nations. **6]** I will make you exceedingly fertile, and make nations of you; and kings shall come forth from

28. Given the fact that Adam did not die immediately upon eating the forbidden fruit, perhaps a better translation might be "you shall lose your immortality."

29. **El Shaddai:** God Almighty.

you. **7]** I will maintain My covenant between Me and you, and your offspring to come, as an everlasting covenant throughout the ages, to be God to you and to your offspring to come. **8]** I give the land you sojourn in to you and your offspring to come, all the land of Canaan, as an everlasting possession. I will be their God."

9] God further said to Abraham, "As for you, you and your offspring to come throughout the ages shall keep My covenant. **10]** Such shall be the covenant between Me and you and your offspring to follow which you shall keep: every male among you shall be circumcised. **11]** You shall circumcise the flesh of your foreskin, and that shall be the sign of the covenant between Me and you. **12]** And throughout the generations, every male among you shall be circumcised at the age of eight days. As for the homeborn slave and the one bought from an outsider who is not of your offspring, **13]** they must be circumcised, homeborn and purchased alike. Thus shall My covenant be marked in your flesh as an everlasting pact. **14]** And if any male who is uncircumcised fails to circumcise the flesh of his foreskin, that person shall be cut off from his kin; he has broken My covenant."

15] And God said to Abraham, "As for your wife Sarai, you shall not call her Sarai, but her name shall be Sarah. **16]** I will bless her; indeed, I will give you a son by her. I will bless her so that she shall give rise to nations; rulers of peoples shall issue from her." **17]** Abraham threw himself on his face and laughed, as he said to himself, "Can a child be born to a man a hundred years old, or can Sarah bear a child at ninety?" **18]** And Abraham said to God, "Oh that Ishmael might live by Your favor!" **19]** God said, "Nevertheless, Sarah your wife shall bear you a son, and you shall name him Isaac; and I will maintain My covenant with him as an everlasting covenant for his offspring to come. **20]** As for Ishmael, I have heeded you. I hereby bless him. I will make him fertile and exceedingly numerous. He shall be the father of twelve chieftains, and I will make of him a great nation. **21]** But My covenant I will maintain with Isaac, whom Sarah shall bear to you at this season next year." **22]** And when He was done speaking with him, God was gone from Abraham.

23] Then Abraham took his son Ishmael, and all his homeborn slaves and all those he had bought, every male in Abraham's household, and he circumcised the flesh of their foreskins on that very day, as God had spoken to him. **24]** Abraham was ninety-nine years old when he circumcised the flesh of his foreskin, **25]** and his son Ishmael was thirteen years old when he was circumcised in the flesh of his foreskin. **26]** Thus Abraham and his son Ishmael were circumcised on that very day; **27]** and all his household, his homeborn slaves and those that had been bought from outsiders, were circumcised with him. . . .

Source 4 from Cary F. Baynes, trans., The I Ching [Yijing], or Book of Changes, *3d ed. (Princeton: Princeton University Press, 1967), pp. 280, 283–287, 293–296, 328–335.*

4. From Yijing, Commentary on the Appended Judgments

Heaven is high, the earth is low; thus the Creative and the Receptive are determined. In correspondence with this difference between low and high, inferior and superior places are established.

Movement and rest have their definite laws;[30] according to these, firm and yielding lines are differentiated.

Events follow definite trends, each according to its nature. Things are distinguished from one another in definite classes. In this way good fortune and misfortune come about. In the heavens phenomena take form; on earth shapes take form. In this way change and transformation become manifest.

Therefore the eight trigrams succeed one another by turns, as the firm and the yielding displace each other.[31]

Things are aroused by thunder and lightning; they are fertilized by wind and rain. Sun and moon follow their courses and it is now hot, now cold.

The way of the Creative brings about the male.

The way of the Receptive brings about the female.

The Creative knows the great beginnings.

The Receptive completes the finished things.

The Creative knows through the easy.

The Receptive can do things through the simple.

What is easy, is easy to know; what is simple, is easy to follow. He who is easy to know attains fealty. He who is easy to follow attains works. He who possesses attachment can endure for long; he who possesses works can become great. To endure is the disposition of the sage; greatness is the field of action of the sage.

By means of the easy and the simple we grasp the laws of the whole world. When the laws of the whole world are grasped, therein lies perfection. . . .

The Book of Changes contains the measure of heaven and earth; therefore it enables us to comprehend the tao[32] of heaven and earth and its order.

Looking upward, we contemplate with its help the signs in the heavens; looking down, we examine the lines of the earth. Thus we come to know the circumstances of the dark and the light. Going back to the beginnings of things

30. The *Book of Changes* is concerned primarily with understanding and predicting what appears to be constant and random change. ("Everything flows on and on like this river, without pause, day and night."—K'ung Fu-tze)

31. **displace each other:** an example of cyclical change.

32. **tao:** the way.

and pursuing them to the end, we come to know the lessons of birth and of death. The union of seed and power produces all things; the escape of the soul brings about change. Through this we come to know the conditions of outgoing and returning spirits.

Since in this way man comes to resemble heaven and earth, he is not in conflict with them. His wisdom embraces all things, and his tao brings order into the whole world; therefore he does not err. He is active everywhere but does not let himself be carried away. He rejoices in heaven and has knowledge of fate, therefore he is free of care. He is content with his circumstances and genuine in his kindness, therefore he can practice love.

In it are included the forms and the scope of everything in the heavens and on earth, so that nothing escapes it. In it all things everywhere are completed, so that none is missing. Therefore by means of it we can penetrate the tao of day and night, and so understand it. Therefore the spirit is bound to no one place, nor the Book of Changes to any one form. . . .

When in early antiquity Pao Hsi [Baoxi][33] ruled the world, he looked upward and contemplated the images in the heavens; he looked downward and contemplated the patterns on earth. He contemplated the markings of birds and beasts and the adaptations to the regions. He proceeded directly from himself and indirectly from objects. Thus he invented the eight trigrams in order to enter into connection with the virtues of the light of the gods and to regulate the conditions of all beings.

He made knotted cords and used them for nets and baskets in hunting and fishing. He probably took this from the hexagram of THE CLINGING.

When Pao Hsi's clan was gone, there sprang up the clan of the Divine Husbandman.[34] He split a piece of wood for a plowshare and bent a piece of wood for the plow handle, and taught the whole world the advantage of laying open the earth with a plow. He probably took this from the hexagram of INCREASE.

When the sun stood at midday, he held a market. He caused the people of the earth to come together and collected the wares of the earth. They exchanged these with one another, then returned home, and each thing found its place. Probably he took this from the hexagram of BITING THROUGH.

When the clan of the Divine Husbandman was gone, there sprang up the clans of the Yellow Emperor, of Yao, and of Shun. They brought continuity into their alterations, so that the people did not grow weary. They were divine in the transformations they wrought, so that the people were content. When one change had run its course, they altered. (Through alteration they achieved continuity.) Through continuity they achieved duration. Therefore: "They were blessed by heaven. Good fortune. Nothing that does not further."

The Yellow Emperor, Yao, and Shun allowed the upper and lower garments

33. More commonly known as Fuxi (ca. 2953–2838 B.C.E.), who is credited with constructing the eight trigrams based on cracks in a tortoise shell, from which was developed the system of Yijing.

34. **Shennong:** the teacher of agriculture to humans.

to hang down, and the world was in order. They probably took this from the hexagrams of THE CREATIVE and THE RECEPTIVE.

They scooped out tree trunks for boats and they hardened wood in the fire to make oars. The advantage of boats and oars lay in providing means of communication. (They reached distant parts, in order to benefit the whole world.) They probably took this from the hexagram of DISPERSION.

They tamed the ox and yoked the horse. Thus heavy loads could be transported and distant regions reached, for the benefit of the world. They probably took this from the hexagram of FOLLOWING.

They introduced double gates and night watchmen with clappers, in order to deal with robbers. They probably took this from the hexagram of ENTHUSIASM.

They split wood and made a pestle of it. They made a hollow in the ground for a mortar. The use of the mortar and pestle was of benefit to all mankind. They probably took this from the hexagram of PREPONDERANCE OF THE SMALL.

They strung a piece of wood for a bow and hardened pieces of wood in the fire for arrows. The use of bow and arrow is to keep the world in fear. They probably took this from the hexagram of OPPOSITION.

In primitive times people dwelt in caves and lived in forests. The holy men of a later time made the change to buildings. At the top was a ridgepole, and sloping down from it there was a roof, to keep off wind and rain. They probably took this from the hexagram of THE POWER OF THE GREAT.

In primitive times the dead were buried by covering them thickly with brushwood and placing them in the open country, without burial mound or grove of trees. The period of mourning had no definite duration. The holy men of a later time introduced inner and outer coffins instead. They probably took this from the hexagram of PREPONDERANCE OF THE GREAT.

In primitive times people knotted cords in order to govern. The holy men of a later age introduced written documents instead, as a means of governing the various officials and supervising the people. They probably took this from the hexagram of BREAKTHROUGH.

QUESTIONS TO CONSIDER

One of the first truths that historians come to appreciate is that people from different cultures not only think differently about various subjects (such as life, death, and cosmology) but also use different thought patterns when attempting to solve a problem. Thus we must determine not only what people of the past think, but also how they think.[35] Accounts or interpretations of

35. The same can be said about the study of writing itself. For example, fewer than half of the systems of writing that exist (or are known to have existed) begin at the top left of a page and move from left to right, then drop down one line and repeat the process. Some peoples' systems require writing right to left, some vertically (either top to bottom or bottom to top), and some circularly, and a few (like the Aztec script of Central America) have no particular form at all.

creation are excellent sources from which to deduce not only how a particular culture thinks about creation, but how it thinks in general.

Sumero-Babylonian traditions had more than one account of the creation and of the early history of human beings, of which Atra-hasis probably is the oldest. Written in cuneiform script using a stylus on soft clay that later was baked to harden it, the Atra-hasis creation epic is still fragmentary, and parts of the broken tablets are still being discovered in excavations.

Why did the gods decide to create human beings? What, therefore, is the purpose of humans? How were the first humans constructed by Belet-ili? What materials were used? Why was it necessary to kill the junior god We-ila? What was We-ila's "contribution" to humans? In your opinion, what does this tell about the Babylonians' concept of human beings? Of their gods?

The first thing that we discover about Vedic culture is that it has not one creation account but several. In Rig Veda 10.72, the creation of the universe is compared to the birth of a human child. Who is Aditi, and what function does she perform? But how was Aditi created (see verses 2–5)? Note that these verses have a cyclical pattern: Aditi is born and gives birth and in turn is born. This cyclical thought pattern would become a key component of Hindu philosophy (Westerners are most familiar with it in the Hindu doctrines of *karma* and reincarnation—see R.V. 10.81, verse 1).

R.V. 10.81 is interesting for two reasons. First, this creation account, unlike that in 10.72, is quasi-monotheistic (monotheism is belief in one god), in this case called the All-maker. But might that All-maker in fact be Aditi herself (both are feminine)? More interesting are the questions asked in verses 2 and 4. If originally there was nothing (10.72 called it the "Non-existent"), then where did the materials to make the world come from? Does the hymn's composer answer those questions?

In R.V. 10.90, the universe itself (Purusa) is masculine and encompasses everything, including the gods. Note, however, the cyclical thinking again in verse 5, and in verse 6, in which Purusa (the universe) is himself sacrificed by the gods to create all other things. What is the implication about how humans are to honor this creation process? How does this creation account support and justify the Vedic caste system?

In R.V. 10.129, the author begins by emphasizing the nothingness that preceded creation. And then, mysteriously, That One was born. But what role (if any) did That One play in creation? What about the male forces and female forces? Where did those forces come from? What feelings does the author convey in verses 6 and 7?

The narrative of creation in the Torah is a familiar one to Jews, Christians, and Muslims, and is quite different from the accounts in the Rig Veda. Almost immediately, however, we see that we are confronted not with *one* creation account in the Torah, but with *two*. Notice that Genesis 1:1 through 2:4 contains one account and, immediately following, Genesis 2:5–24 is *another* account, in some ways markedly different. In your view, what are the principal differences between the two creation accounts in Genesis? Can you explain why there are two accounts? Why do you think that both accounts were included and have remained stable fixtures in Genesis for over 2,700 years?

In the Torah, it is extremely clear that the Israelites (and the later Christians and Muslims) were strict monotheists. Moreover, the one god of the Torah exhibits human traits—intent, desire, love, satisfaction, anger, and other emotions—and is given a voice that speaks to many people. And even more important, God has made some specific promises to and demands on the humans He created, most especially the ancient Israelites (the "Chosen People," as explicitly stated in Genesis 17:2). What were those demands? What was the covenant?

In contrast to the Torah, the Yijing not only lacks an account of a divinely inspired or god-caused creation, but also seems almost unconcerned about these questions at all. Gods do appear (Heaven, the high god, is most prominent), but more as abstract models for humans to emulate than as powers to worship or obey. Instead, the Yijing is a search for order, for patterns that can be discovered in the heavens and then later on earth—the patterns of birth and of life and of death.

How can the Creative and the Receptive be seen in the universe? Can any patterns be discerned and applied to the world? In this way, "man comes to resemble heavens and earth, he is not in conflict with them." One can see day and night (and day again) in the heavens. To what could you compare that cycle on earth?

How is Pao Hsi (Baoxi) treated in the Yijing? Obviously, he was not a god, but he was nicknamed "the inventor" by millions in later years. What did Pao Hsi "invent"? The remainder of the excerpt traces a line of creative leaders or sages. What were their contributions? How did they "discover" these things? What was the final (the highest) gift of the holy men? Finally, how did those who venerated the Yijing think about creation?

EPILOGUE

The development of writing held out many advantages for a culture. Important commercial agreements (water rights, real estate titles, merchant contracts, bills of sale) could be recorded and handed down with considerably more precision, often giving the ownership of property and goods more security and status. Laws and proclamations also could be codified, read in public, and enforced with more regularity. Finally, works of religion, philosophy, and literature could bind a people together, give them a sense of their past and of mission, and shape and mold their collective thought.

For these reasons, a people's written accounts of creation were never merely interpretations of the origins of the universe, the world, and human beings. The Torah revealed the Jews' (and later Christians' and Muslims') belief in a purposeful deity who created humans for a specific purpose and made a covenantal agreement with Abraham and his descendants that required worship and obedience to God's laws in return for God's blessing and protection. Not only did the Rig Veda strengthen Indian thinking about the cyclical laws that governed birth, life, and death, but it also legitimized the Aryan caste system of priests, warriors, peasants, and serfs. The Yijing called the Chinese to meditation about the interrelationships of all things—past, present, and future. Indeed, these creation accounts as well as all others (and there are literally dozens) contain much more than a simple relating of origins.

Just as writing offered cultures that possessed it certain advantages, so also the ability to read and write elevated certain individuals, elite groups, and classes *within* a culture. To begin with, it was these people who had the power to make and enforce laws, to mold and sanction beliefs, and to exercise authority over the illiterate. As soon as a particular group had established a political or religious canon,[36] its next step often was to punish those who violated or opposed the established orthodoxy.

There is little doubt that literate elites tried to limit the spread of writing. But ultimately such restraint was almost impossible. The invention of the printing press in the mid-fifteenth century in Mainz (Germany) made it possible for writing to reach an almost limitless audience.[37] As a result, literacy in Western Europe increased dramatically. Once political and religious canons could be read by many, however, disputes erupted, often over the "proper" interpretation of these canons. Yet once Pandora's box had been opened, it was nearly impossible to close it again.

Ultimately, widespread literacy strengthened the cultures in which it occurred and gave them great advantages over those in which literacy was more limited or confined. In the long run, near-universal literacy tended to support political stability and continuity, in part because of earlier political revolts and changes that, ironically, literacy often had instigated, and in part because literate cultures could develop and disseminate technology and economic systems that more often led toward economic abundance. It may be no accident that in the world's most prosperous economies (Germany, Japan, the United States, the Scandinavian nations, the United Kingdom, France, and the like), illiteracy is negligible and political stability is prevalent, whereas in the world's poorest nations (such as Chad, Niger, Afghanistan, and Bangladesh), illiteracy is rampant and political systems are extremely unstable.[38]

It would take centuries before the relationship between widespread literacy, economic abundance, and political stability would be fully understood. And yet as early as the prophet Muhammad, people appreciated the fact that writing meant power, and that the pen (or carving tool or stylus or quill or brush or whatever writing instrument) could be mightier than the sword.

36. **canon:** code of law.

37. In fact, printing, movable type, and paper all had been invented in China over five hundred years earlier.

38. Estimates from 1995 show Niger with an astounding 86 percent illiteracy, Afghanistan with 68.5 percent, Bangladesh with 62 percent, and Chad with 52 percent (*The World Almanac and Book of Facts*, 1999).

CHAPTER THREE

REPRESENTING THE HUMAN FORM

(1400 B.C.E.–1500 C.E.)

THE PROBLEM

In the last chapter, you explored the role that writing and written texts played in shaping the world-views of several early civilizations. As important as they are, however, written texts are only one of the types of sources available for learning about early cultures.

In many of the world's cultures, the transmission of information continued to be entirely oral, and in those that developed writing, the number of people who could read and write was very small, so that written texts were not a part of most people's lives. However, almost all of the world's cultures produced decorated items or adorned the walls of some buildings. These objects and decorations are what we would now call "art," and they can provide important evidence about both literate and nonliterate cultures.

Artistic evidence has been used to answer a wide range of historical questions about early cultures. Some of these are technical: What level of engineering skill in a culture would enable it to construct certain types of buildings? What technological processes did a culture use in the production of pottery, metalwork, or other items? Some are economic: What proportion of a culture's wealth went into the production of what types of artistic products? Who paid for and benefited from artistic production? Some questions are aesthetic: How skillful were certain artists? How would one describe an individual artist's or a civilization's style, particularly in comparison to those of others? Some are cultural: Why were certain subjects depicted, and depicted the way they were? What did a civilization view as important enough to include in its permanent visual record?

The questions that we might term aesthetic or cultural are perhaps the most tricky for historians or art historians, particularly if they involve comparisons between civilizations.

Assessing the skill of an artist requires not only appreciating the technical aspects of production, but also understanding ideas about the purpose of artistic products as well as the cultural context in which the artist worked. We may be able to say immediately that we "like" or "don't like" an artistic product, but we certainly need information on the culture in which it was created to assess its meaning and use it as historical evidence. It is often difficult to gain much understanding of a culture from a few pieces of artistic evidence, particularly when we view them, not where they were intended to be displayed, but on a gallery wall or in a museum case. Thus, using artistic evidence is in some ways a circular process: We learn about a culture from the available written and artistic sources, then use that background to analyze a single piece of art, which may in turn make us change or refine our ideas about the written record or other artistic creations, and eventually may lead to new conclusions about the culture as a whole.

Analysis of individual pieces of artistic evidence is thus an important tool for historians. It is often difficult to view pieces in their original setting—they may have been removed, or we may not be able to travel to distant lands—so our only access to such evidence is via museums or in books of reproductions. In this chapter we use such reproductions of sculpture and painting to investigate five different cultures: Egypt in the New Kingdom (1400–1200 B.C.E.), Archaic and Classical Greece (600–350 B.C.E.), Buddhist India (200 B.C.E.–600 C.E.), classic Maya (600–900 C.E.), and western Africa during the ascendancy of Ile-Ife and Benin (1100–1500 C.E.). In all five of these cultures, one of the most common subjects for artistic presentation was the human form. Our questions for this chapter, questions that are aesthetic and cultural, focus on this one subject: How do these cultures depict the human form? What do these depictions tell us about the values of these cultures?

BACKGROUND

Though most historians and art historians regard some knowledge of a culture as important for an understanding of its artistic products, there are those who discount such a prerequisite. Some people, though usually not art historians, assert that aesthetic judgments are not culturally or historically based, but rather derive from universal standards, so that "good" art, or at least a masterpiece, is recognizable to all. Others contend that knowing about a culture shapes one's impressions too strongly, making it impossible to view an artistic product objectively. To them what is most important is seeing with a fresh eye, and they stress that to use visual evidence correctly, we must both sharpen our powers of observation and also *unlearn* previous ideas about art.

You may agree with either or both of these arguments and wish to test them with this chapter. To do this, turn immediately to the Evidence and look carefully at each sculpture or painting. Record your general impressions, and also write down your initial responses to the central questions for the chapter. (This will enable you later to assess how much even a slight understanding of a culture may alter your viewing.) Do any of these impressions or answers come from what you already know about any one of these cultures, or do they come solely from looking at the art?

As we turn now to background information, we begin with characteristics common to all of the sources. For each of the three cultures, the sculptures and paintings are arranged roughly in chronological order, though they span different amounts of time. All the pieces served some sort of religious or political function and come from tombs, religious buildings such as temples, or royal residences. In all of these cultures except Classical Greece, rulers were regarded as links between human society and the gods, so that the distinction between the religious and political realms is somewhat artificial; even in Greece, religion was viewed as having a political function, binding the residents of one area together. All the pieces were created in cultures that believed in *anthropomorphic* gods; in other words, at least some of their gods were conceptualized in human form so that human form and divine power were linked. In all five cultures, making an image of a god or a godlike hero or leader and honoring that image were seen as meritorious, and thus the creative process was linked to spiritual and religious values.

In ancient Egypt, art was an integral aspect of religion, with much of the art that has survived made not for human eyes but for the inside of tombs, part of the Egyptian cult of the dead. The Egyptians had an extremely strong belief in the afterlife, an afterlife that was very much like life in this world and that required both physical objects and funeral rituals to attain. In the Archaic Period and the Old Kingdom (about 3100–2200 B.C.E.), only the pharaoh was regarded as capable of achieving a full afterlife. Nobles built their tombs as close to his as possible, pledging in carved inscriptions to continue their allegiance to the pharaoh after death; if he engaged their services, they, too, might achieve eternal life. In the Middle and New Kingdoms (ca. 2050–1085 B.C.E.), eternal life was viewed as a hope for all, as long as the body was preserved through mummification and the spirit was led to Osiris, the god of the dead, through the proper mortuary ceremonies. Funerary objects and statues or paintings of the deceased all helped lead him or her to Osiris by depicting the deceased in rituals that assured eternal life. Throughout all periods of ancient Egyptian history, the statue of a deceased person in a tomb or temple was regarded as a home for his or her *ka,* the spirit or immortal alter ego, which entered the sculpture during a funeral ritual. The *ka* within the sculpture made the deceased a participant in festivities held in the temple even after death. Though we might view this preoccupation with death and the afterlife as morbid and reflecting a rejection of life, it does not seem to have been so for the ancient Egyptians whose portraits and tomb paintings have been preserved; they enjoyed their life here on earth so much that they simply wanted to continue it after death.

Because most statues were regarded as substitutes for a particular deceased person, and paintings were to show the deceased involved in activities or rituals, it was extremely important that depictions be recognized as the correct individual. Egyptian artists achieved this objective not by individualistic portraiture of a physical likeness, but by painting or inscribing the name on the statue or painting. The portrait itself could then be used to depict stereotyped qualities: Plumpness represented wealth and well-being; signs of age, maturity and wisdom; a trim build, confidence and vitality. Egyptian art also sought to link the impermanent individual clearly to the permanent office or occupation, so it was important to include unmistakable symbols of office—a scribe was always portrayed with a scroll, and the pharaoh with the crown of Upper and Lower Egypt and a crooked staff. The emphasis on permanence emerges in many aspects of Egyptian art, most noticeably perhaps in the continuity over thousands of years in the basic style of portraying the human body. By the Middle Kingdom there was some attempt to individualize facial features, but the bodies remained stock types and the faces continued to be idealized.

Egyptian artists attempted to portray scenes or figures not as they appeared to the eye, but as they actually were, what we might call a depiction of their essence. Thus individual figures are not foreshortened or drawn from one particular vantage point, for one's vantage point might easily change; instead they are shown in a way that presents many sides or angles at once. The most famous example of this is the Egyptian way of depicting the human body, which you can see most clearly in Sources 2 and 4. The Egyptian way of setting elements in a scene is also one that does not reproduce a visual image, but reflects the content of what is being represented. Thus, artists use what is sometimes termed an *aspective* rather than a *perspective* approach, basing the size of the figures not on their placement in the scene, but on their importance in the social hierarchy.

Many of the earliest Greek depictions of the human form were also from tombs or temples, the male *kouros* and female *kore* figures. These were not portraits or ceremonial substitutes for the deceased the way Egyptian tomb sculptures were, but rather were erected in memory of an individual or by a living person to fulfill a vow to the gods. These large stone sculptures began to be made in Greece beginning in the mid-seventh century B.C.E., and many art historians have linked them stylistically with much earlier Egyptian statuary. In contrast to the permanence of Egyptian depictions, however, the portrayal of the human body in Greece changed rapidly over the next two hundred years, with sculptors basing their work more and more on actual human anatomy. This concern with the way that the body actually looked can also be observed in Greek painting. Unfortunately, most large-scale Greek paintings have been lost, but Greek pottery was frequently decorated with painted figures and scenes that allow us to see human forms in a setting.

Along with the kore and kouros figures, Greek statuary from the Archaic period (about 630–480 B.C.E) also portrayed gods and mythological heroes, who are sometimes part divine and sometimes fully human. Because the gods bore no physical sign of their divinity, it is often difficult to tell exactly who is being depicted unless the subject is accompanied by a standard symbol such as the sea god Poseidon's trident or the hero Herakles' lion skin. Gods and heroes continued to be the most common subject matter for Greek sculpture in the Classical period (about 480–330 B.C.E.), with actual historical events shown only rarely, although mythological events appear frequently, especially in reliefs.

Greek pottery often shows mythological scenes, but it also depicts everyday life—women weaving, men banqueting, people going in and out of doors. Some of its subjects are pornographic, showing men with prostitutes or gods and satyrs chasing nymphs. Because of such subject matter, pottery has traditionally been viewed as having no religious or ceremonial significance. This view has recently changed somewhat, as scholars have recognized that, for example, the banqueting scenes not only depict the setting in which the pottery was actually used, but also envision a certain type of afterlife for those using it. The doors may not be simply entrances of houses, but also the gateway between this life and the next. The mythological scenes are not simply decorative, but are meant to reinforce cultural norms.

The Greek view of the human body was determined by philosophy as well as religion, particularly after the time of Plato (427–347 B.C.E.). Plato saw the human body as in some ways a microcosm of the universe (an idea that influenced Western thought until the time of the Renaissance), a universe that was itself a living creature. Both the body and the universe are material and perishable, but the soul is immortal, as is the perfect form of the universe and all that exists within it. For Plato, these perfect forms, which are sometimes called "ideal types," were not simply mental constructs but had an existence somewhere and were actually more "real" than the transitory, material world around us. (The notion of ideal types, or idealism, has also been a long-lasting one in Western thought. It operates, for instance, in many people's understanding of such concepts as justice. Their concept of a just society comes not so much from observing societies that actually exist in the world as from abstract principles regarding what might be termed "ideal justice.") As a proponent of idealism, Plato scorned the attempts of the artists and sculptors who were his contemporaries to depict the human body based on visual observation. Plato thought the chief purpose of art was to represent eternal forms as understood by the soul, not to imitate fleeting external appearances. He praised Egyptian art for its elevated portrayals, and he regarded mathematical forms as the most beautiful because their beauty was absolute and not based on—or biased by—either intellectual or physical points of view.

In many ways, sculptors in India working within both Buddhist and Hindu traditions fit Plato's ideal better than did his Athenian contemporaries. In Indian religion and philosophy, the purpose of sculpture is not to depict the physical body but to give concrete shape to an invisible spirit within the body. Indian artists sought to give visible form to the living principles within the body, conceptualized as breath (*prana*) and sap (*rasa*). *Prana* pushes against the walls of the body, making the skin appear taut and keeping the body erect, so that the muscles are less important. Indian sculpture does not aim to record the appearance or structure of the body, but instead to express the awareness of life within the body, of the breath that sustains and moves the body. Sculptors achieve this, not by looking at other bodies as models, but by feeling the breath and pulse of life within their own bodies and by meditating or contemplating. There is a link between the body and the natural world, which also has breath and sap. When a sculpture was completed, it was consecrated by a priest, given the breath of life. Then it was placed in a position within a temple where it could be seen, worshiped, and perhaps eventually copied, for the replication of images was considered auspicious.

Buddhist teachings did not reject earlier Indian ideas about art or the body, but built on them. The religious teachings generally termed Buddhism were first taught in India by Siddhartha Gautama, a nobleman living in the sixth century B.C.E. who came to be known as the Buddha, or the Awakened One. Buddhist teachings are extremely complex, although at their heart is an emphasis on morality, meditation, and achieving wisdom. Part of the wisdom one strives to achieve is the understanding that there is nothing permanent, including the individual soul, and that the ideal state of being (*nirvana*) is a life that transcends individual desires. On achieving nirvana, an individual would become awakened to a transcendental eternal realm of being, that is, a buddha.

Over the centuries, many divisions developed within Buddhism, one of the most significant being a split beginning in the first century B.C.E. over how strictly one needed to follow the Buddhist path in order to achieve nirvana. Mahayana Buddhism taught that many people, not simply a small spiritual elite of monks, could become fully buddha, an idea that gave this branch of Buddhism a wide popular base. As it spread, Mahayana Buddhism absorbed a number of local deities, transforming them to fit with Buddhist ideas by turning them into guardians of the Buddha, or *bodhisattvas.* A bodhisattva is a being who has almost achieved nirvana but decides instead to turn away from this final, blissful, transcendental state to help others on their way to becoming buddha. Although bodhisattvas had human bodies, they were no longer subject to the physical limitations of human life and were often worshiped in their own right. Their merits could be shared by their worshipers, and their intervention, combined with devotion, could allow the worshiper to achieve nirvana. The Buddha himself had been a bodhisattva in his earlier lives, and stories of his actions and exploits during these previous lives became an important part of Buddhist literature.

Though there was no explicit prohibition on portraying the Buddha as Buddha, there are no images of him until several centuries after his death; he was symbolized by an empty throne or a hemispheric mound containing a relic, termed a *stupa*. With the spread of Mahayana Buddhism, people became more devoted to Buddha's person and not simply his teachings, so they wanted physical likenesses. Images of the Buddha showed up first on coins and temple railings and, by the first century C.E., as free-standing sculpture. Sculptors adopted existing ideas about portraying the body to the portrayal of the Buddha's body, striving to produce a sacred image that both transcended and represented perfect human beauty. The links between the body and the natural world were stressed in the shapes of the Buddha's body parts, and a system of proportions was developed based on the height of the head or the breadth of the finger. These calculations for the correct proportions of the Buddha were based not on actual human anatomy, but on the magical properties of certain numbers, and they became the standard for images of the Buddha for centuries.

Representations of the human form among the Mayas share a number of features with those of ancient Egypt. As in Egypt, most large-scale art was produced to record the deeds and actions of rulers; Maya buildings are almost like billboards, with huge reliefs depicting religious and political messages. It was thus important that the individuals depicted be recognized, which Maya artists accomplished sometimes by showing them with specific distinctive physical features, but more often by identifying them by name in the writing that almost always accompanies pictures of people. The Mayas also built pyramids, which served both as temples and as graves for kings, who were viewed as interceding between the gods and people both in this life and after death; concerns about the afterlife show up in much Maya art, just as they do in Egypt.

In contrast to the Egyptians, however, the Mayas were not unified under a single ruler, but lived in cities ruled by separate royal lineages. Scholars used to think that the Mayas were a peaceful people concerned primarily with astronomical and religious issues; this view was altered dramatically after 1960, when scholars began to learn to read Maya writing, which told of great battles and extolled rulers who were victorious over other kings. Writing and art also portray gruesome bloodletting rituals involving kings and their families as well as captives; blood was a potent substance for the Mayas, and the blood of their rulers was particularly powerful. (All hereditary aristocracies conceptualize what distinguishes rulers from everyone else in terms of blood, of course; even the weak monarchs of today have "royal blood.") Like Egyptian hieroglyphics, Maya writing is a combination of signs that stand for certain whole words and phonetic symbols; it was painted with a brush on pottery and in books made from the bark of fig trees, and inscribed on stone, wood, jade, and shell objects. The earliest writing dates from the first century B.C.E.; because Maya artists included the dates on the events they depicted (and because scholars have learned how to interpret these dates), we are able to trace some aspects of their history very specifically. Artists and scribes belonged to certain families and sometimes included their own names as well as those of their subjects on their work, so that, unlike the case with many ancient peoples, we can know the identity of certain artists. Writing and artistic production were viewed as in some ways beyond human capacity, and a number of gods were associated with writing; these god-scribes are sometimes portrayed as animals—as rabbit-scribes, as in Source 17, or, more commonly, as monkey-scribes.

The sculptures and paintings reproduced here all date from the period 600–900 C.E., which scholars label the late classic period. (Like that of ancient Greece, Maya cultural history is generally divided into preclassic, classic, and postclassic periods.) During that period, the Mayas living in hundreds of large and small cities, ruled by lineages that both intermarried and engaged in warfare with one another, built large buildings, and recorded their own histories. These reproductions come from three of those cities, Palenque, Bonampak, and Yaxchilan, all located in the southwestern part of the area inhabited by Maya people, now in southern Mexico.

Given the warm and damp climate of central America, most painted Maya artwork has disappeared; most of what survives is thus carved or formed out of more permanent materials such as stone, stucco, or jade. (Many books were also destroyed by Spanish Christian authorities in the sixteenth and seventeenth centuries because these authorities considered Maya writing, which often concerned religious and mythological subjects, to be demonic; only four preconquest Maya books survive today.) Much of this is in the form of reliefs carved on vertically set slabs of stone (called *stelae*) or panels, and some of it is very difficult to see because it has weathered over the centuries, so that art historians and archaeologists make drawings of the pictures and writing in order to study them more closely. Source 16 is, in fact, a copy based on the original painting, as the painting itself is very faint and difficult to see. Many of these reliefs are also extremely complex, with writing, people, gods, and natural objects entwined and interwoven over the entire surface; all of these have symbolic meanings, and deciphering them is thus very complicated. The objects shown here are therefore somewhat unusual in that they are relatively simple and the carvings are still sharp enough to be seen without the aid of a drawing.

In other ways, the pieces reproduced here are quite typical of Maya art. In contrast to the Greeks, who showed the human form primarily through the depictions of gods and heroes, the Mayas showed actual people and actual historical events, although rulers were often dressed as gods. Source 14 is a stucco portrait head of King Pacal of Palenque (ruled 615–683) from his burial tomb; Source 15 shows a king of Yaxchilan, Shield Jaguar, and his wife, Lady Xoc, in a bloodletting ritual that took place on October 28, 709; Source 16 is one of the wall murals from Bonampak, which portray various events in the life of the ruler Chaan-muan from the 790s. In all of these, and in the portrayal of a mythological scene in Source 17, bodies are shown in realistic proportions, with clothing and accessories depicted in great detail. In the reliefs and the painting, people are shown primarily in a side view, with the heads always shown from the side. This allows the artist to highlight one of the most distinctive aspects of the ideal human form for classic-period Mayas: the flat, elongated forehead, achieved by molding infants' skulls in this shape while they were still pliable. Nobles and deities are also generally portrayed with large, curved noses, another sign of status (this is sometimes enhanced, as it is in Source 14, with a decorative nosepiece, probably made of latex rubber). Captives and conquered peoples, by contrast, are often shown with blunt noses and domed foreheads.

Like that from ancient Egypt, much of the art from Nigeria in the eleventh through the sixteenth centuries that has survived comes primarily from royal courts, where professional artists—smiths, sculptors, jewelers, and so on—produced items for royal families and other powerful individuals. Not surprisingly, much of this art depicts kings and queens, either alone or surrounded by their supporters, servants, and assistants. There were a number of small kingdoms in this area during this period, linked both politically and artistically. According to tradition, in the thirteenth century the people of Benin (called the Edo people) asked the ruler or *oni* of the Yoruba kingdom of Ile-Ife to send them a king. This *oni,* Oranyan, sent one of his sons, who became the first king or *oba* of Benin. The first *oni* of Ile-Ife is regarded as the son of the Yoruba god of creation, Olorun, and Ile-Ife continued to be viewed as the spiritual and mythical center of the world by the rulers of Benin; subsequent rulers in Benin continued to receive their symbols of office from the *oni* of Ile-Ife. Those rulers also admired the art of Ile-Ife, for tradition holds that a later *oba* of Benin requested that the *oni* of Ile-Ife send him a bronzesmith to teach the smiths in his kingdom.

Given these connections, it is not surprising that the earliest art from Benin looks much like that of Ile-Ife, but within a relatively short period of time, artists from Benin had developed a completely different style. The portraits from Ile-Ife, especially those in terra cotta, depict men and women with extremely individualized features; careful attention is given to the contours and musculature of the face. Many of them are wearing elaborate headdresses that indicate their high status, or have holes on the face, indicating that originally crowns or other royal regalia were attached. Some have holes around the mouth and chin for the attachment of a beaded veil, common for Yoruba kings. (The striping pattern on some faces is thought to represent a veil.) The terra-cotta heads come from full figures, whereas those made from metal were crafted simply as heads and may have been used to show off royal garments and symbols of office. The exact identity of most of these portraits is unknown, although Source 19 is regarded by many scholars as representing the *oni* Obalufon. Though the portraits are individualized, they are also somewhat idealized: Like Egyptian portraits, they show only people with calm and peaceful expressions, which was viewed as reflecting inner dignity and self-control;

like Greek sculpture, they show only women and men in the prime of life.

In contrast to the portraits from Ile-Ife, which generally show single individuals without much decoration, those from Benin often show multiple figures and, like Maya reliefs, are loaded with symbolic and ceremonial objects. Though they continued to have contacts with artists in Ile-Ife, artists in Benin appear to have become less interested in capturing the individuality of their subjects than in providing information about court life and events; individuals are identified by clothing and symbols representing their office, not by distinctive facial features. The *oba,* his relatives, and other chiefs are generally shown with symbols of power, such as fish, leopards, or elephant trunks, and wearing huge necklaces and headdresses of red coral beads. These beads were restricted to the royal family and high court officials, as they were believed to have been stolen from Olokun, the god of the seas and waters and the source of all worldly riches; when the king was wearing beaded garments, he was regarded as having powers similar to those of a god.

Many of the artistic items that have survived from Benin in this period are ceremonial plaques showing the *oba* and other individuals, an artistic form that may have been modeled on pictures in books brought to Africa by Portuguese missionaries and merchants. In contrast to the depiction of the human form in Egyptian and Maya art, in Benin figures are shown frontally, usually standing, although the *oba* himself is occasionally seated. The plaques are symmetrical, with the *oba* or symbols that represented him in the middle; this fit with Edo ideas of the perfect hierarchical society, in which everything revolved around the *oba,* the axis of the world. As in Egyptian art, the figures are not only positioned but also proportioned according to their status; the *oba* is the largest, with various other figures of different sizes around him. All of the figures are usually placed against a flat background carved with "river-leaves," the leaves of the water-god Olokun, whose domain was thought to surround that of the earthly *oba.* The figures themselves do not stand on anything, but float on this background. The heads are often slightly enlarged in relation to the body, for the Yoruba people of Ile-Ife and the Edo people of Benin regarded the head as the site of a person's nature (*iwa*) and life force (*ase*); as in India, the purpose of representations of the body was to make these living principles within the body visible.

THE METHOD

The single most important method for using visual sources was stated at the beginning of the Background section—**look at them**. This may seem self-evident, and we may feel that our "looking" skills are well honed because of the visual culture of advertising and television in which we live. Too often, however, we view visual material as merely illustrations of a text (this is often how graphics are integrated into textbooks) and don't really look at the images themselves. To answer the first question in this chapter, turn to the Evidence (which you may already have done if you decided to do the pretest suggested in the Background section). Look carefully at Sources 1 through 4, all of which present pharaohs, queens, or members of the royal family of Egypt. What do you notice most about these figures; in other words, what details stand out? What words would you use to describe the individuals as they are portrayed? How do their expression and stance sway your description? How would you compare the portrayal of humans with that of animals—for example, the birds in Source 2? How would you compare the portrayal of Queen Nefertari in Source 4 with that of the goddess Isis in the same tomb painting? How would you compare the depiction of the pharaoh Tut-ankh-amon in Source 1 with that of the pharaoh Ramesses II in Source 3? How is clothing depicted in these examples of Egyptian art?

Now look at the artistic evidence from Greece, Sources 5 through 9. What main differences do you see in the depiction of the human form in the kore and kouros figures from the early sixth century B.C.E., Sources 5 and 6? How would you compare these to the statue of the Egyptian pharaoh in Source 3? Would you make any distinction in your comparisons between the body and the head? Judging by the vase painting in Source 7 and the sculpture in Source 8, what changes do you see in the representation of the human form over the next century? What differences do you see between the depiction of female and male forms in Source 7? Now look at Source 9, which is about one hundred years more recent than Source 8 and is one of the first depictions of the nude female form in Greek art. (Until this period, the only women depicted nude were prostitutes; even Aphrodite, the goddess of love and beauty, was shown clothed.) What words would you use to describe Aphrodite as she is shown here? Looking at Sources 8 and 9, what differences do you see in the way male and female bodies are depicted?

Now look at the examples from India, Sources 10 through 13. What details stand out in these portrayals? How would you describe the body of the female deity (*yakshi*) in Source 10? How would you compare this with the female bodies portrayed in Egyptian and Greek art? Sources 11 and 12 show the Buddha. How does his body differ from the bodies in the other sources? How would you describe his expression and demeanor? How would you compare the treatment of clothing in these two sculptures with the treatment of clothing in Egyptian and Greek sculpture? Source 13 is a bodhisattva, usually identified as Vajrapani because he is holding a thunderbolt. (Bodhisattvas can often be identified only by items they wear or carry, for no names are inscribed on these sculptures. Both Egyptian tomb sculptures and Greek statues were mostly inscribed, but in Greece the inscriptions often have been destroyed or are missing, so that we identify them as well by their dress or other details.) How would you describe the bodhisattva's body? his stance? his clothing? How would you compare these with those of the Buddha? with those of a Greek male body such as the one in Source 8?

Now look at the Maya examples, Sources 14 through 17. How would you describe the portrayal of the ruler's body in Sources 15 and 16? How would you compare that to the portrayal of the captives' bodies in Source 16? How would you compare the portrayal of male and female bodies, both those of Shield Jaguar and Lady Xoc in Source 15 and those of the goddesses who serve God L in Source 17? What do you notice about the clothing and headdresses of the kings and nobles? How do these compare with the clothing of the gods and goddesses? Source 16 shows King Chaan-muan's judgment of prisoners after their defeat in a great battle (shown on other wall paintings in this room). How does the artist use the placement of figures and their body positions to enhance the effect of the action and communicate the status of the people portrayed? How would you compare this with the other paintings of humans in action (that of the pharaoh in Source 2 and that of Theseus and the Amazons in Source 7)? How would you describe God L and his attendants in the scene of the underworld in Source 17?

Now look at the examples from Ile-Ife and Benin, Sources 18 through 21. How would you describe and compare the expressions of the individuals in Sources 18 and 19? How does the artist who made Source 20 communicate the status of the individual portrayed? How does the artist who made Source 21 communicate the status of the various individuals portrayed? What do you notice about the dress and headdresses of the individuals in Source 21? Sources 18 and 19 come from one culture, the Ile-Ife, and Sources 20 and 21 from another culture, Benin, that was nearby but developed slightly later. How would you compare the portrayal of the human form in the two cultures? Most of the individuals portrayed represent rulers, just as do most of the individuals in the Egyptian and Maya examples. How would you compare the portrayal of rulers in these three cultures?

From looking at the Sources and considering questions like those suggested above, you can formulate your answer to the first question for this chapter: How do these five cultures depict the human form? Answering the second question—what do these depictions tell us about the values of these cultures?—involves extrapolating from the sources and combining your observations with your previous knowledge of the cultures. Here you (or any historian) must be more speculative, for we generally can't know exactly how individuals living at the time a statue or painting was made looked at it, or how their view of the artist's intent differed from ours. We must also be especially careful, when using visual sources, to choose ones that are representative or typical rather than unusual. (On this issue, you will have to either trust our choice of evidence or do some further research in books of reproductions or museums in your area.)

These reservations apply, of course, just as much to historical arguments based on written sources as to those based on visual evidence, and in both cases the best method of historical interpretation is the same: Stick as closely as possible to arguments that are based on the sources themselves. In this case, then, your exploration of the values of these cultures needs to be based primarily on the careful observations you have already made.

Think about your observations of

the depiction of the body in Egypt. Whose bodies are shown? What does their stance or expression indicate were admirable qualities in such individuals? What do the similarities between the depictions of Isis and Nefertari indicate about Egyptian ideas about the relationship between the human (or at least the royal) and the divine?

Next, think about the Greek art. Why might the depiction of the body become more anatomically accurate earlier than that of the head? Why might the Greeks have broken with the Egyptian pattern and portrayed men nude, even in scenes (such as the battle scene in Source 7) in which men were not normally naked? What might account for the differences in the portrayal of male and female nudes you noted in Sources 8 and 9? Though we generally think of nakedness as revealing, are there certain facts that nakedness obscures?

Now turn to the Indian art. What does Source 10 indicate about cultural attitudes toward the female body? How does this portrayal of a goddess differ from those of Egyptian or Greek female deities (Isis in Source 4 and Aphrodite in Source 9)? What does the Buddha's expression indicate about the qualities admired in a leader? How does this differ from the qualities suggested in the depictions of the Egyptian pharaohs and Greek heroes? What do the differences you have noted between the Buddha and the bodhisattva indicate about attitudes toward each of these revered individuals?

Now turn to the Maya art. What does the portrayal of Lady Xoc engaged in a bloodletting ritual along with her husband indicate about the status of noblewomen in Maya culture? What might the similarities in the portrayals of the gods and goddesses in Source 17 and the humans in the other sources indicate about Maya ideas of the relationship between the human and the divine? What might the judgment scene in Source 16 indicate about the handling of prisoners and about Maya attitudes toward nakedness? How would you compare this with Greek attitudes toward nakedness?

Next, think about the western African art. What might the two heads from Ile-Ife (and others like them) indicate about the relative status of men and women in the upper classes? How does this compare with the impression you have gained from the art of the other cultures in this chapter? In modern cultures, veiling is often perceived as negative, a restriction of the individual. Thus, why might rulers, of all people, wear veils that covered part of their faces? What might this indicate about west African ideas of rulership, as compared with those of the ancient Egyptians or classic-era Mayas?

THE EVIDENCE

Source 1: Griffith Institute/Ashmolean Institute, Oxford.

1. Tut-ankh-amon and his wife Ankhesenam, from Tut-ankh-amon's Tomb, ca. 1350 B.C.E.

Source 2: Courtesy of the Trustees of the British Museum.

2. Nebamum Hunting Birds, with his Wife and Servant, from his Tomb at Thebes, ca. 1400 B.C.E.

Source 3: Hirmer Fotoarchiv.

3. Statues of King Ramesses II and his Wife, Queen Nefertari, at Luxor, ca. 1250 B.C.E.

The statue of Nefertari is much smaller than that of Ramesses; her head is just below his knee.

4. Wall Painting from Nefertari's Tomb near Thebes, ca. 1250 B.C.E.

The goddess Isis is holding an ankh—the symbol of life—to Nefertari's nostrils.

Source 5: Archaeological Receipts Fund/National Archaeological Museum, Athens.

5. Anavyssos Kouros, Attica near Athens, ca. 525 B.C.E.

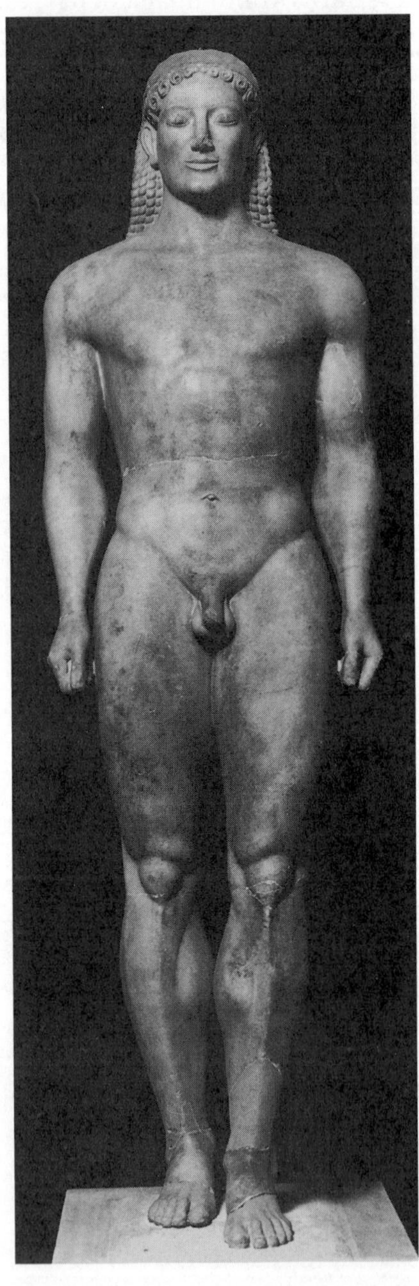

Source 6: Archaeological Receipts Fund/Acropolis Museum, Athens.

6. Peplos Kore, Athens, ca. 530 B.C.E.

Source 7: Courtesy of the Trustees of the British Museum.

7. Theseus and the Amazons, from an Attic Red-figured Krater,[1] ca. 440 B.C.E.

1. **Krater:** a wide, two-handled bowl common in ancient Greece.

Source 8: Alinari/Art Resource, NY.

8. Polykleitos, *Doryphoros* or *"The Canon,"* ca. 440 B.C.E. (Roman copy)

Source 9: Biblioteca Apostolica Vaticana.

9. Praxiteles, *Aphrodite of Knidos,* ca. 340 B.C.E. (Roman copy)

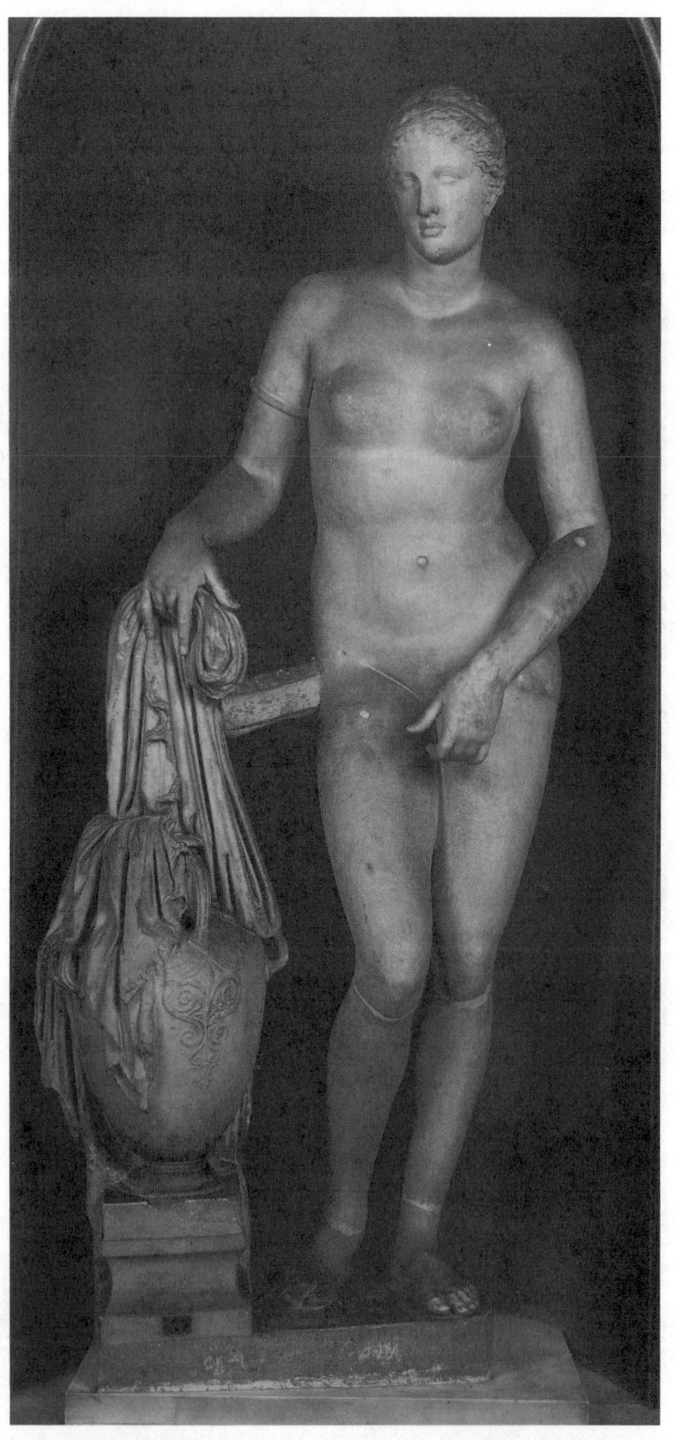

Source 10: Archaeological Survey of India.

10. Yakshi, from a Pillar at the Great Stupa of Bharhut, ca. 100 B.C.E.

Source 11: John C. Huntington.

11. Standing Buddha, from Gandhara, ca. 200 C.E.

Source 12: Robert Fisher.

12. Preaching Buddha, from Sarnath, ca. 475 C.E.

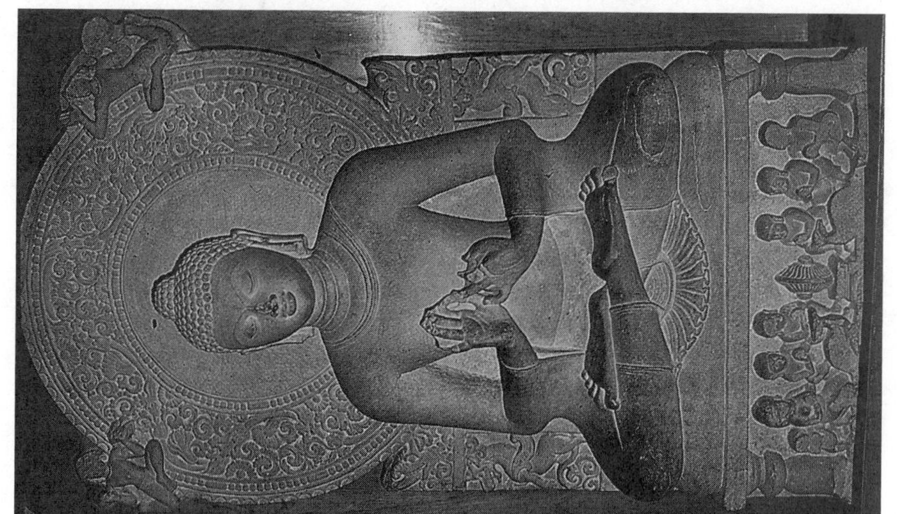

Source 13: Metropolitan Museum of Art. L.1993.51.5. Lent by the Kronos Collections.

13. Bodhisattva Vajrapani, Nepal, 6th or 7th century C.E.

Source 14: Museo Nacional de Antropologia México/Art Resource, NY.

14. Head of Pacal the Great, from His Tomb at Palenque, 684 C.E.

15. Door Lintel Showing King Shield Jaguar and Lady Xoc in a Bloodletting Ritual, 709 C.E.

Source 16: From copies made by Antonio Tejeda Fonseca, in Mary Ellen Miller, The Murals of Bonampak *(Princeton, Princeton University Press, 1986). Photograph © Tozzer Library of Harvard College Library, Harvard University.*

16. Mural at Bonampak Showing King Chaan-muan Judging Defeated Enemies, 792 C.E.

Source 17: The Art Museum, Princeton University. Museum purchase, gift of the Hans A. Widenmann (Class of 1918) and Dorothy Widenmann Foundation. © 2001 Trustees of Princeton University. Roll-out photo © Justin Kerr.

17. Vase Painting Showing God L, Several Goddesses, and Rabbit-Scribe, ca. 600–900 C.E.

Source 18: British Museum/Werner Forman/Art Resource, NY.

18. Terra-cotta Head of a King, Ife, ca. 1000–1200 C.E.

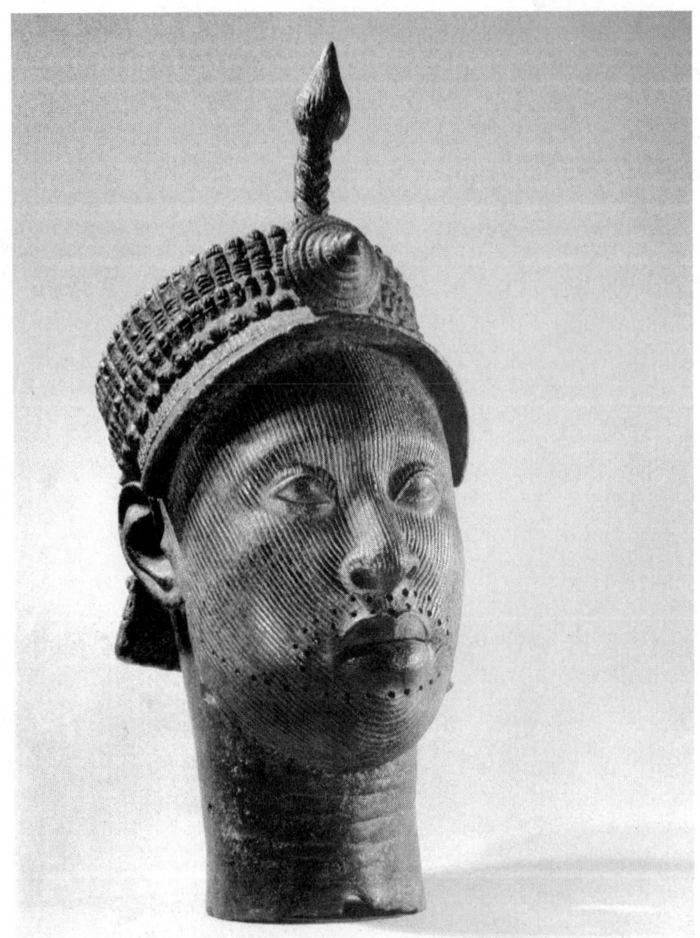

Source 19: Reproduced by courtesy of the Trustees of the British Museum.

19. Copper Obalufon Mask, Ife, 1000–1200 C.E.

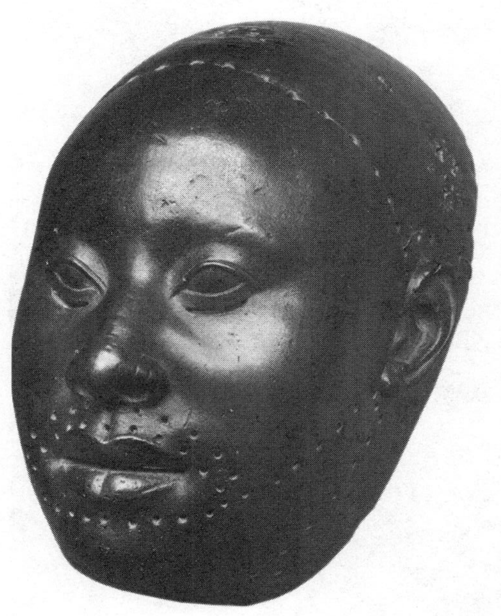

Source 20: Reproduced by courtesy of the Trustees of the British Museum.

20. Brass Head of Queen Mother, Benin, ca. 1500

Source 21: The British Museum/Art Resource, NY.

21. Brass Plaque Depicting the Oba Esigie, Benin, ca. 1500

QUESTIONS TO CONSIDER

As you examine the evidence for this chapter, you may be discovering that your viewing is shaped to a greater or lesser extent both by what you already know about one or more of the cultures and by your previous experience with sculpture and paintings of the human form. Some of the sources may thus seem very familiar, whereas others may appear strange and exotic. This has caused some people who work with visual evidence to deny that we can ever view things with the "fresh eye" that other scholars deem indispensable. Does your experience in working with the evidence in this chapter lead you to support either side of this dispute? If you did the pretest, did your observations and impressions change after reading the Background section?

Though all of the evidence in this chapter depicts the human form, some of the portrayed individuals were regarded as fully human, some as fully divine, and many as both human and divine or as moving between a human and a divine state. Do these differences affect the way these individuals are depicted? What does this tell you about the five cultures?

When making any sort of cultural comparison, it is often easiest to think in terms of similarities and differences. What similarities have you found in the depictions of the human body among the five cultures? Are there any words that you could use accurately to describe the bodies in all or most of the sources? Do any of these words suggest cultural values that may be similar? Do any two of the cultures handle representations of the human body in a similar fashion? What might this tell you about other ways in which these two cultures are similar? What do you see as the most important differences among the sculpture and painting from the five cultures? Are any of these the result of technological differences (such as differences in the material out of which the sculpture is made), or do they indicate cultural differences?

You are now ready to answer the central questions for this chapter: How do these five cultures depict the human form? What do these depictions tell us about the values of these cultures?

EPILOGUE

In all of the cultures we have investigated here, a certain way of depicting the human form came to be accepted as the norm and was then copied extensively. This copying took place both within a single culture, as artists learned the expected forms and styles, and between cultures, as artists traveled to new places or adopted the styles of works made elsewhere.

In Egypt, this copying was largely internal, as forms developed in the Old Kingdom were repeated for thousands of years. There were occasional deviations from this, such as that under the pharaoh Akhenaton (ruled ca. 1372–1354 B.C.E.), who abandoned traditional

Egyptian religion in favor of the worship of one god, the sun god Aton. Akhenaton supported an artistic style that was much more naturalistic, and paintings of him show him with narrow shoulders and a pot belly. As soon as he died, however, his new religious system was abandoned, and both art and religion returned to their traditional form. This artistic form was even adopted centuries after the fall of pharaonic Egypt by the Macedonian dynasty of the Ptolemies, who were established as rulers through the conquests of Alexander the Great. The most famous of the Ptolemies, Cleopatra (69–30 B.C.E.), the sister and wife to Ptolemy XII, had herself portrayed looking very similar to Nefertari in Source 4, using this archaic form to stress her link with the ancient pharaohs.

The way in which the human body was portrayed in fourth-century B.C.E. Greece (Sources 8 and 9) was even more influential than that of Egypt. These depictions came to be regarded by later Greeks and Romans as the ultimate standard of perfection, and these pieces were copied and recopied hundreds of times. (This is very fortunate, for the Greek originals have in many cases been lost, and what remains are Roman copies; Sources 8 and 9 are actually Roman copies of the originals.) The Roman historian Pliny (ca. 23–79 C.E.), in fact, noted that Polykleitos' sculpture of the athlete (Source 8) was "called the Canon by artists, who drew from it the rudiments of art as from a code," and judged Praxiteles' Aphrodite (Source 9) the finest statue "not only by Praxiteles but in the whole world."[2] When Romans took or copied Greek images, they generally took them out of their religious setting as temple statuary and placed them in gardens, homes, or public squares. The statues thus lost their religious functions as objects of veneration and became secular objects prized primarily for their aesthetic appeal.

Greek style from this period, which has come to be called classical in the West, has been consciously emulated during many periods since, including the Italian Renaissance, the French Revolution, and the early decades of the United States. You need only to visit your state capitol or other local government buildings to assess the ways in which classical Greek standards still influence our portrayal of heroes and leaders.

Like Greek art, Buddhist art in India is generally regarded as having gone through a formative period and then achieved a level of perfection regarded as classical. Source 11 comes from the formative period, from an area of western India called Gandhara (now a part of Afghanistan) in which artists may have been influenced by Greek statues or sculptors. Sources 12 and 13 come from northern India or Nepal in the Gupta period (ca. 300–600 C.E.), a time during which the Gandharan merged with styles from other parts of India. The Gupta period was one of Indian cultural expansion into central and southeastern Asia, and Gupta styles were copied over a very broad area. Just as in Egypt, there were periods of deviation followed by

2. Pliny, *Historia naturalis,* xxxiv, 55, and xxxvi, 20. Quoted in Gisela M. A. Richter, *A Handbook of Greek Art* (New York: Da Capo Press, 1987), pp. 120, 141.

a return to the classical style for the Buddha and bodhisattvas. In areas of southeast Asia, such as Cambodia, where the ruler was viewed as a god-king, the statues often looked slightly like the ruling king, although they still were not portraits in the modern sense. Unlike Greek statuary, Buddhist images did not lose their religious function, for they were copied because of their sanctity, not solely because of their artistic merit. Images modeled on those of Gupta India are still produced today for use in worship, particularly in areas where Buddhism is strong, such as Sri Lanka and parts of southeast Asia.

As we have seen, Maya art also had a classical period, the time from roughly 200 to 900 C.E., during which most of the dynastic records were kept and the most elaborate images were carved and painted. The Mayas themselves drew on the artistic traditions of the Olmecs, who had preceded them as a major civilization in Mexico, and passed on many of their artistic and architectural achievements to various groups that later dominated central America, including the Toltecs and the Aztecs. Maya art after the classical period, such as that at Chichén Itzá in the Yucatan, blended classical Maya elements, such as reliefs of warriors with clothing and ornaments similar to those in the sources in this chapter; elements from other groups in Mexico, such as round temples and depictions of the atlatl (a type of spear-thrower); and new elements, such as long colonnades of pillars.

In western Africa, we have already noted one example of external influence, the ways in which the art (and perhaps artists) from Ile-Ife shaped that of Benin; art from Ife also influenced art in other centers of Yoruba culture, as well as in more distant parts of Africa to which Ile-Ife was connected by trading networks. West Africa provides examples of long-standing traditions and the influence of earlier styles within a single culture as well, for ideas about the ways in which the portrayal of the human form expresses the inner character and life force continue to be important for artists throughout Nigeria today. In fact, of all the items reproduced here, the only one that remains in its original setting and maintains much of its original significance is the bronze Obalufon mask (Source 19), which is still in a shrine in the palace of the *oni* reigning at Ife in central Nigeria. Thus, like Greek statuary and Gupta images of the Buddha, images of the human form from western Africa are shaping portrayals of the body by contemporary artists.

Because of the international nature of today's artistic culture, artists are not restricted to their own tradition in terms of their portrayal of the human form. They may intentionally copy or pattern what they do on centuries-old images from many cultures, or they may unintentionally bring aspects of items or images they have seen into their work. As you may have discovered in this chapter, seeing (and creating) with completely fresh eyes may be very difficult, even in an artistic culture, like that in the contemporary West, that prizes the new more than the traditional.

CHAPTER FOUR

HAN AND ROME:

ASSERTING IMPERIAL AUTHORITY

(300 B.C.E.–400 C.E.)

THE PROBLEM

Shi Huangdi, the Chinese monarch who in 221 B.C.E. created the first truly imperial realm in East Asia, awed his advisers by the scale of his success. "Now your Majesty has raised a righteous army to punish the oppressors and bring peace and order to all under heaven, so that everywhere within the seas has become our provinces and districts," they told him, observing that this was a feat "which has never once existed from remote antiquity onwards."[1] In their eyes, he had conquered not a kingdom but a world. And because no one to their knowledge had ever done so before, they had trouble envisioning a state that was able to govern on such a vast scope. Half a world away, the leaders of Rome faced a nearly identical problem. Having wrested North Africa, present-day Spain, and southern France away from Carthage in 201 B.C.E. and then conquering Greece and Anatolia (contemporary Turkey) by 133 B.C.E., the city-state of Rome found itself in control of nearly all of the Mediterranean world.

Emerging almost simultaneously at opposite extremes of Eurasia, these two great empires welded their respective spheres together with such success that they initiated new stages of political development. No longer mere regional powers, they had become world states whose rule extended over many different peoples and cultures. As such, they had to be redefined and justified in new and broader terms. Although their immense size made this endeavor somewhat unique, the Roman and Han empires were by no means the first to

1. These remarks appear in a biography of Shi Huangdi in the *Records of the Historian (Shiji)* by the historian Sima Qian. The version quoted here comes from Raymond Dawson's translation, *Historical Records* (New York: Oxford University Press, 1994), p. 84.

face such a task. Throughout history rulers have tried to secure the loyalty and obedience of their people by portraying their authority and the state through which they exercised it in the best possible light.

Such efforts to legitimize political power offer important insights into the way people in different times and cultures have viewed the state and political authority. Current states, for example, generally present themselves as embodiments of a single ethnic group or "nation," whose members share a common language and culture. According to modern beliefs, such national groups form a "people" with a "natural right" to self-rule. So governments today claim to derive their authority from their people and to reflect popular opinion in their policies. The idea of popular sovereignty seems reasonable today because it accords with current assumptions about human nature and politics. But people of other times and places with different assumptions might well consider the concept absurd.

To presume, then, that the people of the Han and Roman empires understood political authority much as modern people do courts problems. Conquerors of many peoples and cultures, these empires exemplified a very different kind of multinational state that had to be justified in terms of universality rather than exclusivity. Efforts to portray these empires as nation-states or even as ancestral forms of modern nations involve all sorts of anachronistic assumptions that project present ideas into the past. To overcome this danger, we need to discover how the builders of the Han and Roman states conceived of political authority within the constraints of their own political traditions. And that is the task facing you in this chapter. In the Evidence section, you will find two sets of primary materials dealing with imperial rule, one Roman and one Chinese. Investigate both to determine the answers to these questions: How did each of these peoples redefine political authority to suit a new level of world mastery? What do their views of imperial authority tell us about the ways in which they understood the state and its power?

BACKGROUND

Neither the Han nor the Roman empire emerged through a sudden, unexpected revolution. On the contrary, both evolved as final, logical outcomes of long processes of regional integration. Some general remarks about the origins of these empires, therefore, will provide a context for better understanding their transformation from regional to world powers. Tracing their rise will also provide insight into the political traditions to which they were heir. For though both innovated freely, they primarily shaped new identities by reinterpreting older, indigenous ideas and institutions. As a result, it would be difficult to understand how the builders of these empires conceived of them without reference to the historical circumstances out of which each evolved.

The Han state clearly owed a heavy debt to the past. For one thing, much of its institutional structure derived directly from the short-lived Qin dynasty, officially inaugurated by Shi Huangdi in 221 B.C.E.[2] Despite that conqueror's boast that his dynasty would rule the new empire for ten thousand years, his early death little more than a decade later created a power vacuum that brought its swift collapse. For a few years, civil war raged as rival provincial leaders restored local kingdoms and vied with one another for regional mastery. But finally one warlord, Liu Bang, overcame all other contenders and reimposed imperial unity. The Han dynasty, which he proclaimed in 202 B.C.E., proved a far more lasting regime than the one it replaced, surviving in its basic form for nearly four centuries before it was swept away by rebellion and mutiny in a series of upheavals that began in 184 C.E.

Despite the change of rulers, much of the basic structure of the Qin regime persisted under the Han, whose early rulers slowly modified its institutions to meet changing conditions. Throughout history, therefore, Qin and Han have often been linked together and deemed, as they will be here, but two phases of a single stage of imperial development. The fact that ancient records carefully distinguish between them, however, points up an important difference between the Chinese political tradition and the European: In China, states were named in terms of dynasties, or ruling families, rather than in terms of territories, peoples, or institutional structures. Viewed from this perspective, Rome would appear to be not one but a series of different empires, named after successive ruling houses like the Julian and Flavian lines.

Though novel in scope, neither the Qin nor the Han ascension marked an abrupt departure from earlier political patterns. Indeed, much of their imperial system evolved out of the efforts of territorially more limited kingdoms, some ethnically Chinese and some not, to create centralized monarchies during the preceding third and fourth centuries B.C.E. Qin was itself initially just one of a half-dozen or so of these kingdoms, which fought so incessantly with one another during these centuries that later ages termed the era the Warring States Period. Because it succeeded in centralizing faster than its rivals, Qin proved better able to mobilize its resources and so conquered them. But many of these rivals, too, including Qin's chief contender for imperial mastery, a great southern kingdom called Chu, followed their own programs of centralization. Out of their collective experiments evolved many important, new institutions like autocratic kingship, centralized provincial administration, civil bureaucracy, mass military organization, and standardized legal codes, all of which the

2. Chinese terms appear in the modern *pinyin* system of romanization, with the often more familiar Wade-Giles spelling sometimes given in parentheses. The name Qin sounds approximately like the English word "chin," and the first emperor's title is pronounced something like *shur hwang dee.*

later Qin and Han empires adapted to their own purposes.

The Warring States era also supplied a diverse body of new ideas about the nature and purpose of the state. As in earlier times, Confucianism remained a significant intellectual force. A practical political doctrine developed from the ideas taught by Confucius (in *pinyin* Kung Fu Zi, ca. 551–479 B.C.E.), early Confucianism advocated government based on ethical principles rather than on mere expediency or a ruler's whims. Confucius himself directed his followers to seek such principles in an old ruling house called the Zhou, claiming that its kings exemplified the highest ethical ideal, a rare quality called *ren,* translated variously as humanity, goodness, and benevolence. Later followers like the idealistic Mencius (Mengzi, ca. 371–288 B.C.E.) and the third-century B.C.E. rationalist Xunzi (Hsün Tzu) offered updated Confucian interpretations to suit the altered conditions of the Warring States Period. All, however, insisted that inherent human goodness made coercion unnecessary and argued that governments should rely on moral persuasion rather than force to win support. Only "sages," people endowed with extraordinary ethical virtue and intellectual ability, could in their view establish such regimes, and thus they claimed that rulers should turn government over to a well-trained, upright elite.

Other schools of thought, however, advocated different modes of sagely rule. Proponents of a political brand of Daoism (Taoism), a doctrine associated with a sixth-century B.C.E. figure named Laozi (Lao Tzu), proposed a doctrine of paternalistic, *laissez-faire* rule. In their view, secretive sage rulers trusted in the great Way (*Dao*) that orders the natural world to keep their people content and harmonious. And a group known as the Legalists propounded a theory of outright autocracy. Likening most people to unruly animals, they claimed that the only means to achieve any social order was to allow those few individuals who overcame their base emotions to serve as enlightened despots. Using a strict system of rewards and punishments, these elevated autocrats were then to train their fellow humans to behave in orderly ways, much as dogs are trained.

Despite wide disagreement on how to achieve order and stability, all these schools of thought bequeathed a common legacy to later empires. First, all anticipated an end to the era of multiple kingdoms. Although they sharply differed as to how unification of their cultural world would be achieved, none doubted its likelihood—or desirability. They thus spoke of a state including all *Tianxia,* or "Underheaven," that is, a state stretching across the entire earth. Their idea of a world-wide state, however, was colored by assumptions of cultural difference.

For they expected this realm to develop around a core area located in the Central Plains of north China, the homeland of ethnic Chinese, then known as the *Xia.* Much earlier, at the start of the first millennium B.C.E., when united under the loose rule of the Zhou dynasty, this region had dominated regional politics. The collapse of Zhou power in the eighth century B.C.E. brought political fragmentation and the loss of regional mastery. But the people of this area continued to enjoy high cultural status in the centuries that followed, winning their petty principalities recognition as the *zhung guo* or "central states." When arguing for regional integration, Warring States thinkers reinterpreted the meaning of this term, understanding it to mean a single Central State that could serve as the core of a greater world polity.

Advocates of integration also fostered the belief that a world-state would be founded by the same kind of *sheng ren* or "sage" that was said to have founded the Zhou dynasty. Thus they encouraged a second assumption: that Underheaven would be united by a special kind of person. Unique to this tradition, the sage had no counterpart in Western thought. The figure may have evolved out of the semidivine forebears of ancient north Chinese clans, to whom old foundation myths ascribe all sorts of wondrous powers. But by Warring States times, sages seem to have been seen as purely human geniuses who personally created all of human culture, including its social and political order. Already, a number of thinkers were advancing historical schemes in which a line of sages seemingly guided humankind out of barbarism and onto the path of civilization. These schemes encouraged the idea that all great changes, including the founding of new states, depended on the leadership of such an event-making figure.

Warring States thinkers introduced a third assumption about any future world-state. Caught up in a wave of recent cosmological speculation, many argued that a strict correspondence existed between natural and human order. In their opinion, all political shifts occurred in concert with larger changes in the natural world. Confucian writers developed a special version of this idea, claiming that a conscious power whom they called *Tian* or "Heaven" willed this correspondence. Borrowing from old apologists who had justified the Zhou monarchy's power on the basis of Heavenly authority, Mencius claimed that Heaven gave true sages a special Heavenly Mandate or charge to found new regimes. He thus helped to revive an old Zhou belief that its kings were "Sons of Heaven," destined to serve as its agent among all humankind. From such concepts emerged a unique theory that universal states would rise and fall in dynastic cycles responsive to Heavenly bidding.

Rome, too, inherited a rich legacy from its Mediterranean forerunners. But it developed out of a very different milieu, one in which city-states rather than regional kingdoms dominated the political scene. The political tradition connected with such city-states celebrated the uniqueness and autonomy of small communities in which a select citizenry enjoyed special privileges. Even in imperial times, the Romans continued to identify with their own distinct origin as a small Latin "republic." Based on the idea of a *res publica,* or "public thing," held in common by a body of people, the ancient republic was a form of government in which authority was thought to reside in a group of citizens rather than in one family or one individual. Only those whom the citizens chose to represent them could thus legitimately rule the community. In early Rome, as in most Mediterranean city-states, only a small portion of the community actually possessed citizenship and could select rulers. Nonetheless, even this limited form of popular participation in government created a strong sense of communal identity that was lacking in East Asia. Compared to the highly standardized Qin–Han imperial system, in which provincial administrations tolerated no local deviation nor any form of communal power, the Roman Empire appeared more like a federation of semiautonomous cities and provinces than like a fully integrated domain.

In its earliest stages, of course, the Roman Empire arose out of just such a league. Beginning as a small Latin city-state on the Tiber River in central Italy in the eighth century B.C.E., it gradually expanded through the conquest of neighboring cities until by 272 B.C.E. it controlled the whole of the Italian peninsula. Thereafter, the decline of Greek power to the east and the rise of a rival Carthaginian hegemony in the west drew Rome into a wider involvement in the Mediterranean world. Within less than a century and a half more, the Roman republic extended its rule over most of the Mediterranean basin. This imperial success, however, placed an enormous burden on Rome's republican institutions, creating a period of political crisis during the mid–first century in which factional strife and civil war threatened to destroy the state.

This process intensified when the chief republican institution, a patrician council known as the Senate, accorded Julius Caesar dictatorial powers so that he could carry out a program of comprehensive reform. Although out of deference to republican tradition Caesar rejected the outright title *rex* ("king"), he became a monarch in all but name in 44 B.C.E. when the Senate voted him a lifetime dictatorship. His assassination that year briefly halted the transition toward monarchical rule, but it resumed little more than a decade later when Caesar's grandnephew Octavian convinced the Senate to name him dictator, too. By a further act of the Senate in 27 B.C.E., Octavian became *imperator* or "emperor," and under the new title Augustus completed the transition from republic to monarchy. From then until the empire's disintegration in the early fifth century, Caesarian-style emperors ruled over the Roman state.

Although an outgrowth of the Roman political situation, this monarchy increasingly reflected the influence of the Hellenistic[3] states of the eastern Mediterranean that Rome eventually absorbed. Most of these were monarchies still ruled by descendants of the followers of Alexander the Great, the Greek conqueror who in the fourth century B.C.E. briefly created the predecessor of a Mediterranean world-state by annexing the Persian Empire to his own much expanded kingdom of Macedonia. Fascinated by Near

3. **Hellenistic:** refers to the people of the eastern Mediterranean who after the time of Alexander the Great became Greek in their ways and outlook, though not necessarily Greek in ancestry; it derives from the word *Hellene,* the name the ancient Greeks gave themselves.

Eastern forms of kingship, Alexander had himself declared a god like the Egyptian pharaohs and ruled in the autocratic manner of the Persian warrior kings. Although Alexander's empire broke apart after his death, successors in Egypt and Asia Minor kept alive the tradition of posing as god kings, bequeathing it in turn to their Roman conquerors in the first century B.C.E.

In other areas, too, Hellenistic culture and thought influenced Roman political life. Two Athenian philosophers of the fourth century B.C.E., Zeno and Epicurus, proved particularly influential on later Roman thought. Epicurus, a strict materialist, denied that there was any purpose or meaning to the world other than what humans made of it. He thus counseled followers to seek a quiet life of simple human pleasures. Zeno argued an almost opposite position, contending that a divine spirit worked mysteriously through all things to manifest cosmic harmony. Humans, he felt, provided a special medium through which this spirit operated. He accordingly urged people to recognize human fellowship and to dedicate themselves to a life of service to others and, through it, to the purpose of the divine will. In speaking of a broader human fellowship united by a common purpose, Zeno gave the Mediterranean area a concept of world community that could replace the localism of the city-state. His doctrine, known as Stoic philosophy, thus promoted a more cosmopolitan outlook on the eve of Rome's great expansion.

These Hellenistic ideas helped prepare the way for Rome's creation of an empire by providing terms with which to envision a universal state. Hellenistic writers, especially the Stoics, popularized the idea that the Mediterranean basin formed a single cultural domain, called the "ecumene,"[4] because its inhabitants, whatever their language and ethnicity, shared a common legacy of Greek ways and Greek thought. Out of this developed the later concept of a single Western civilization made up of diverse peoples united by a common classical tradition. Hellenistic thinkers, however, wanted political as well as cultural integration. They thus encouraged hopes that a divine, or at least a divinely inspired, figure would emerge to unite the whole Mediterranean world and help humankind realize its oneness in a new kind of universal state. Rome's eventual conquest of most of this area naturally seemed a fulfillment of their prophetic desires. And Roman emperors easily came to equate their *imperium* or "rule" with an assumed divine mission to order the entire globe, or *orbis terrarum* (literally "world sphere") as they called it.

4. **ecumene:** from the Greek word *oikoumene* ("the inhabited world"); the term, like the Chinese "underheaven," signifies a worldwide or universal sphere.

THE METHOD

The problem at issue here—how the builders of the Han and Roman empires understood their imperial authority—certainly involves aspects of political and institutional history. Yet, it pertains more to what people thought than to what they did. The study of what people of the past thought falls largely in the realm of intellectual history, a branch of history that seeks to trace the development of ideas and their impact on society. For all that they may appear to lack the concreteness of political events and institutions, ideas too can be recovered, providing we tap the right kind of evidence.

Written materials, of course, yield the most information on complex political ideas, for they typically reveal them in the fullest detail. Government documents like degrees, announcements, and commemorative statements give evidence of the official perspective, whereas individual histories, critiques, memoirs, and letters reveal something of the private viewpoints of the time. But written materials by no means exhaust all possibilities. As any visitor to a modern capital city quickly discovers, buildings, monuments, and artworks also express public ideals in powerful ways. Unlike written documents, which make sense only to literate elites, materials of this sort "speak" to a broader segment of the population through the language of visual symbols. In earlier times, when education and literacy were restricted, they probably played a greater role than written texts in conveying basic notions of the state and political authority to the populace. For that reason, we include visual materials as well as written documents in the Evidence section of this chapter.

Evidence presented here on the early Chinese empire includes both sorts of artifact. Source 1 is a selection from a famous biography of Qin Shi Huangdi contained in an early Chinese history of the world called the *Shiji,* or *Records of the Historian.* Compiled in the late second century B.C.E. by the Han scholar Sima Qian, it incorporates a number of older documents along with the texts of certain stone inscriptions made at the first emperor's own order in 219 and 218 B.C.E. The photographs that serve as Sources 2 and 3 illustrate this emperor's tomb. Source 4 includes parts of essays written by Dong Zhongshu (Tung Chung-shu), a Confucian adviser to Han emperor Wudi (Wu-ti, r. 141–87 B.C.E.), and Source 5 is the text of a decree issued by Han emperor Wendi (Wen-ti) in 178 B.C.E. Sources 4 and 5 both reflect later views of the Qin-Han monarchy.

The Roman material, too, is visual as well as textual. Source 6, an excerpt from the *Res Gestae Divi Augusti,* or *The Achievements of the Divine Augustus,* sets forth the feats for which Rome's first emperor, Caesar Augustus (r. 27 B.C.E.–14 B.C.E.), wished to be remembered in his own words. Source 7, an excerpt from a work called *Roman History,* presents a different view of the accomplishments of Augustus by the third-century historian Cassius Dio. Source 8, a Roman coin, and Sources 9 and 10, a Roman monument called Trajan's Column, present visual images of the monarchy that were intended to influence the less literate. Additional official statements by later Roman emperors comprise Sources 11 and 12; both of these are inscriptions carved on the walls of public temples in the eastern part of the Roman Empire.

As Sources 1 and 5 demonstrate, political ideas tend to be discussed most intensely when governments first emerge or when they undergo crisis. More apt to feel threatened and vulnerable at these times, leaders often take much greater pains than normal to explain their actions so as to consolidate their power. They issue special proclamations asserting their legitimacy and experiment with new guises through which to portray themselves and their power. Rivals, too, speak out more freely at such moments, whether to challenge authority or to voice alternative views. Material from such critical moments, therefore, provides an especially rich source of political ideas, and you will find a number of such items included here. But even the less intense level of political "talk" that continues in ordinary times may reflect important aspects of a political tradition. Governments, for example, often take advantage of routine statements to reaffirm basic ideals and conventional claims, as do private interests. The very repetitiousness of such messages may, in fact, prove more revealing of commonplace assumptions than more carefully authored statements.

In assessing the following materials, try to distance yourself from modern political assumptions and look for the unfamiliar. One way to do so is to pay special attention to the unusual terms and images that appear with any frequency. In written sources, "keywords," or special terms that appear again and again and seem critical to an understanding of the text, provide a useful starting point for analysis. Because their uniqueness makes modern translation difficult, many will appear in their original language, like the Latin *imperium* or the Chinese *huangdi.* But even when translated, most of these should catch your eye because of their oddity, if not their frequency. Where in modern political discourse, for example, would you find people talking about "sages" or "ovations"? Write these words down and note any passages that offer hints to their meaning. You may have to work back and forth among several of these passages, using clues from one to illuminate others. But if you do so carefully for both sets of evidence, you should end up with a basic vocabulary list of important political terms for each of the two traditions. In a similar way, look for significant factors in the visual materials to add to your list, and ask yourself if they correlate in any way to the keywords.

An approach of this sort, which requires you first to identify the basic words and images of the evidence, will force you to respect the integrity of the evidence and enable you to confront it on its own terms. But doing so will not automatically give you an answer to the central question of this chapter—how did the builders of the Han and Roman empires conceive of and justify their political authority? To get to that point, you will need to ask yourself what each set of key elements collectively indicates about the nature of imperial rule. Keeping a few fundamental considerations in mind at this point should help you piece the evidence together into a larger picture. First, ask yourself what in each case the state seems to embody. Is it a land, an ideal, a people, or something else? A second, closely related question to consider involves the purpose of imperial rule. Modern states, which usually claim to represent a nation, often cite securing the liberty and well-being of their people as their primary purpose. But throughout history other kinds of states have asserted different ends. Some, for example, have claimed to be embodiments of religious movements or churches with divine purposes to fulfill. Others have posed as bearers of cultural traditions, which they presume to defend or promote. Frequently they link this purpose to some higher order or power that thus bestows an ultimate sanction on their power. Logically, a third question to consider, then, is who or what authorizes imperial rule.

Once you have reached some general conclusions about the way in which Han and Roman rulers each understood their imperial authority, compare the differences and similarities between them. Juxtaposing one against the other should highlight what is unique to each. You will no doubt remark with what distinct "voices" early Chinese and Roman sources speak; patterns of rhetoric and style differ as much as, if not more than, basic political beliefs. Think what these differences imply about the gulfs between cultures and the difficulty of interpreting one in terms of the other. Yet, at the same time, note how similar some Roman and Chinese ideas of authority seem relative to the modern notion of popular sovereignty. How do you think people today would react to these ideas? Time, in this case centuries, creates gaps between people that are not easily bridged.

THE EVIDENCE

Source 1 from Raymond Dawson, Historical Records *(New York: Oxford University Press, 1994), pp. 63–70.*

1. From Sima Qian, *The Annals of Qin,* ca. second century B.C.E.

Now Qin for the first time had unified all under Heaven and instructions were given to the Chief Minister and the Imperial Secretary saying: "On another occasion the King of Hann offered us his territory and handed over his seal, requesting to become a frontier vassal, but having done so he turned his back on the agreement and formed a north–south alliance with Zhao and Wei to rebel against Qin, so we raised troops to punish them and took their king prisoner. I consider this to be a good thing since it practically brought an end to the fighting. . . . With my own insignificant person I have raised troops to punish violence and chaos and, with the support of the sacred power of the ancestral temples, the six kings have all admitted their crimes, and order is magnificently restored in all under Heaven. Now if the title is not changed there will be no means of praising these achievements and transmitting them to later generations. You are to discuss the imperial title."

Chief Minister Wang Wan, Imperial Secretary Feng Jie, Superintendent of Trials Li Si, and others all said: "In days of old the territory of the Five Emperors was 1,000 *li* square, and beyond this was the territory of the feudal princes and of the barbarians. Some of the feudal princes came to court and some did not, for the Son of Heaven was unable to exercise control. Now Your Majesty has raised a righteous army to punish the oppressors and bring peace and order to all under Heaven, so that everywhere within the seas has become our provinces and districts and the laws and ordinances have as a result become unified. This is something which has never once existed from remote antiquity onwards, and which the Five Emperors did not attain. Your servants have carefully discussed this with the scholars of broad learning and, as in antiquity there was the Heavenly August, the Earthly August, and the Supreme August, and the Supreme August was the most highly honoured, so your servants, risking death, submit a venerable title, and propose that the King should become 'the Supreme August.' His commands should be 'edicts,' his orders should be 'decrees,' and the Son of Heaven should refer to himself as 'the mysterious one.' " The King said: "Omit the word 'supreme' and write 'august' and pick out the title of 'emperor' used from remote antiquity, so that the title will be 'August Emperor.' The rest shall be as you suggest." And an edict was issued saying that it should be done. King Zhuangxiang was to be posthumously honoured as "the Supreme August on High."

The Chief Minister Wang Wan and others said: "The states are newly defeated and the territories of Yan, Qi, and Chu are distant, so if we do not establish kings for them there will be no means of bringing order to them. We beg to set up your sons in authority, but it is up to the Supreme One alone to favour us with his agreement." The First Emperor handed down their suggestion to the ministers, and they all thought this would be expedient. But the Superintendent of Trials Li Si advised: "Only after an extremely large number of sons and younger brothers and people of the same surname had been enfeoffed by King Wen and King Wu did they win the adherence of the distant, and then they attacked and smote each other and behaved like enemies. And when the feudal states wrought vengeance on each other more and more, the Zhou Son of Heaven was incapable of preventing them. Now all within the seas has been unified thanks to Your Majesty's divine power, and everywhere has been turned into provinces and districts. And if your sons and the successful officials are richly rewarded from the public revenues, that will be quite sufficient to secure easy control. If there is no dissension throughout the Empire, then this is the technique for securing tranquillity. To establish feudal states would not be expedient." The First Emperor said: "It is because of the existence of marquises and kings that all under Heaven has shared in suffering from unceasing hostilities. When, thanks to the ancestral temples, all under Heaven has for the first time been brought to order, if states are reintroduced, this will mean the establishment of armies, and it would surely be difficult to seek peace in those places. The advice of the Superintendent of Trials is right."

So the Empire was divided into thirty-six provinces, and a governor and army commander and an inspector were established for each. The people were renamed "the black-headed people," and there were great celebrations. The weapons from all under Heaven were gathered in and collected together at Xianyang and were melted down to make bells and stands and twelve statues of men made of metal, each 1,000 piculs in weight, to be set up in the courts and palaces. All weights and measures were placed under a unified system, and the axle length of carriages was standardized. For writings they standardized the characters.

In the twenty-eighth year the First Emperor travelled eastwards through his provinces and districts and ascended Mount Zouyi. He set up a stone tablet, and after discussion with the various Confucian scholars of Lu an inscription was carved on the stone extolling the virtue of Qin. They also discussed the matter of the *feng* and *shan* sacrifices[5] and the sacrifices to mountains and rivers. So next he ascended Mount Tai, set up a stone tablet, and made the *feng* sacrifice. As he descended and there was a violent onset of wind and rain, he rested under a tree, which was consequently enfeoffed as fifth-rank grandee. He made the *shan* sacrifice at Liangfu. The stone tablet that he had set up was inscribed with the following words:

When the August Emperor came to the throne, he created regulations and made the laws intelligent, and his subjects cherished his instructions.

In the twenty-sixth year of his rule, he for the first time unified all under Heaven, and there were none who did not submit.

In person he made tours of the black-headed people in distant places, climbed this Mount Tai, and gazed all around at the eastern limits.

His servants who were in attendance concentrated on following his footsteps, looked upon his deeds as the foundation and source of their own conduct, and reverently celebrated his achievements and virtue.

5. ***feng* and *shan* sacrifices:** sacrifices to Heaven appropriate only to a supreme ruler.

As the Way of good government circulates, all creation obtains its proper place, and everything has its laws and patterns.

His great righteousness shines forth with its blessings, to be handed down to later generations, and they are to receive it with compliance and not make changes in it.

The August Emperor is personally sage, and has brought peace to all under Heaven, and has been tireless in government.

Rising early and retiring late, he has instituted long-lasting benefits, and has brought especial glory to instructions and precepts.

His maxims and rules spread all around, and far and near everything has been properly organized, and everyone receives the benefits of his sagely ambitions.

Noble and base have been divided off and made clear, and men and women conform in accordance with propriety, and carefully fulfil their duties.

Private and public are made manifest and distinguished, and nothing is not pure and clean, for the benefit of our heirs and successors.

His influence will last to all eternity, and the decrees he bequeaths will be revered, and his grave admonitions will be inherited for ever.

In the twenty-ninth year the First Emperor made a tour in the east. When he reached Bolangsha in Yangwu, he was startled by bandits. They looked for them but did not find them, so he ordered a grand search throughout the Empire for ten days. He ascended Zhifu and had an inscription made on stone with the following words:

In the twenty-ninth year, the time being in the middle of spring, when the sunny season had just started,

The August Emperor made a tour in the east, and during his travels he ascended Zhifu, and his gaze shone upon the sea.

The servants who were in attendance observed him in admiration, recalled his blessings and glory, and reflected upon and sang the praises of what he initiated.

In creating the government, the great sage established the laws and regulations, and made manifest the guiding principles.

Abroad he taught the feudal lords, gloriously bestowing the blessings of culture, and spreading enlightenment by means of the principles of righteousness.

The Six States remained aloof, insatiable in greed and violence, and the atrocities and killings did not cease.

The August Emperor felt pity for the multitude, and then sent forth chastising armies, and displayed with determination his military power.

He made his punishments just and his conduct sincere, and his awesome glory spread around, and no one did not submit.

He wiped out the strong and violent, rescued the black-headed people, and restored order to the four quarters.

Everywhere he bestowed enlightened laws, and made warp and woof for all under Heaven, to provide a model for all eternity.

He has become great indeed, and within the whole universe we accept and obey his sage-like intent.

All his servants sing the praises of his achievements, and request to inscribe them on stone, so that they may be displayed and handed down as a constant rule.

He then proceeded to the east of Bohai, passed through Huang and Chui, did a complete tour of Mount Cheng, ascended Zhifu, and set up a stone tablet there extolling the virtue of Qin and then left.

He then went south and ascended Langye and, since he greatly enjoyed it, he stayed for three months. Then he moved 30,000 households of the black-headed people to the foot of Langye terrace, giving them tax and labour exemption for twelve years. When he built Langye terrace, he set up a stone inscription extolling the virtue of Qin, to make clear that he had achieved his ambition. It said:

In his twenty-eighth year, the August Emperor makes a beginning.

Laws and standards are corrected and adjusted, as a means of recording the myriad things.

Thus he clarifies human affairs, and brings concord to father and son.

With sagacity, wisdom, humaneness, and righteousness, he has made manifest all principles.

In the east he has pacified the eastern lands, and thus he has inspected officers and men.

When this task had been magnificently accomplished, he then turned towards the sea.

Through the achievements of the August Emperor, the basic tasks are diligently worked on.

Farming is put first and non-essentials are abolished, and it is the black-headed people who are made wealthy.

All people under Heaven, have heart and mind in unison.

Implements are given a uniform measure, and the characters used in writing are standardized.

Wherever the sun and moon shine, wherever boats and carts carry goods.

Everyone completes his destiny, and nobody does not get what he wants.

He makes things move in accord with the seasons, such is the August Emperor.

Source 2: Cultural Relics Publishing House.

2. Grave Mound of Qin Shi Huangdi at Mt. Li

Source 3: Julian Calder/Tony Stone.

3. Flanking Pit of Excavated Tomb of Qin Shi Huangdi

Source 4 from William Theodore de Bary et al., eds., Sources of Chinese Tradition *(New York: Columbia University Press, 1960), pp. 178–179.*

4. From Dong Zhongshu (Tung Chung-shu), Essays on Kingship

HOW THE WAY OF THE KING JOINS THE TRINITY

Those who in ancient times invented writing drew three lines and connected them through the middle, calling the character "king" [王]. The three lines are Heaven, earth, and man, and that which passes through the middle joins the principles of all three. Occupying the center of Heaven, earth, and man, passing through and joining all three—if he is not a king, who can do this?

Thus the king is but the executor of Heaven. He regulates its seasons and brings them to completion. He patterns his actions on its commands and causes the people to follow them. When he would begin some enterprise, he observes its numerical laws. He follows its ways in creating his laws, observes its will, and brings all to rest in humanity. The highest humanity rests with Heaven, for Heaven is humaneness itself. It shelters and sustains all creatures. It transforms them and brings them to birth.

The ruler holds the position of life and death over men; together with Heaven he holds the power of change and transformation. There is no creature that does not respond to the changes of Heaven. The changes of Heaven and earth are like the four seasons. When the wind of their love blows, then the air will be mild and the world teem with life, but when the winds of their disfavor come forth, the air will be cold and all things die. When they are joyous the skies are warm and all things grow and flourish, but from their wrath comes the chill wind and all is frozen and shut up.

THE THREEFOLD OBLIGATIONS OF THE RULER

The ruler is the basis of the state. In administering the state, nothing is more effective for educating the people than reverence for the basis. If the basis is revered then the ruler may transform the people as though by supernatural power, but if the basis is not revered then the ruler will have nothing by which to lead his people. Then though he employ harsh penalties and severe punishments the people will not follow him. This is to drive the state to ruin, and there is no greater disaster. What do we mean by the basis? Heaven, earth, and man are the basis of all creatures. Heaven gives them birth, earth nourishes them, and man brings them to completion. Heaven provides them at birth with a sense of filial and brotherly love, earth nourishes them with clothing and food, and man completes them with rites and music. The three act together as hands and feet join to complete the body and none can be dispensed with. . . .

Source 5 from Dun J. Li, The Essence of Chinese Civilization *(New York: Van Nostrand, 1967), pp. 116–117.*

5. Han Wendi (Wen-ti), *On the Eclipse of the Sun*

I have heard that Heaven installs rulers to govern the people it creates and that it will warn a ruler with natural disasters if he has lost virtue or if his rule has become unjust.

On the eleventh month of this year there was an eclipse of the sun. No natural disaster can be more serious than this: Heaven has reproached me!

I have inherited the duty of protecting the temples of our imperial ancestors. A simple and insignificant person though I was, I was called to become the king of all people and scholars. I am solely responsible for all occurrences on earth, be they good or evil. In administering the vast empire, I am assisted by some of my closest minister-advisers.

I have lost my virtue indeed as my inability to take care of my people has aroused the wrath of the sun, the moon, and the stars. Let it be known that immediately after this decree is issued, all of you should think seriously about my shortcomings and inform me on happenings that I have not been able to hear and see myself. Report your findings to me directly! Moreover, you are urged to recommend to me the virtuous, the upright, the honest, and the outspoken so that I can benefit from their counsel and advice. Be it also decreed that all of you are to be diligent at your tasks and that you are to reduce taxes and corvée [enforced labor] duties among my subjects.

Source 6 from Res Gestae Divi Augusti *in Naphtali Lewis and Meyer Reinhold, eds.,* Roman Civilization: Selected Readings, *vol. 1 (New York: Columbia University Press, 1955), pp. 562–572.*

6. From Caesar Augustus, *The Achievements of the Divine Augustus*

Below is a copy of the accomplishments of the deified Augustus by which he brought the whole world under the empire of the Roman people, and of the moneys expended by him on the state and the Roman people, as inscribed on two bronze pillars set up in Rome.

1. At the age of nineteen, on my own initiative and at my own expense, I raised an army by means of which I liberated the Republic, which was oppressed by the tyranny of a faction. For which reason the senate, with honorific decrees, made me a member of its order in the consulship of Gaius Pansa and Aulus Hirtius [43 B.C.E.], giving me at the same time consular rank in voting, and granted me the *imperium.* It ordered me as propraetor, together with the consuls, to see to it that the state suffered no harm. Moreover, in the same year, when both consuls had fallen in the war, the people elected me consul and a triumvir for the settlement of the commonwealth.

2. Those who assassinated my father I drove into exile, avenging their crime by due process of law; and afterwards when they waged war against the state, I conquered them twice on the battlefield [the two battles of Phillippi (42 B.C.E.)].

3. I waged many wars throughout the whole world by land and by sea, both civil and foreign, and when victorious I spared all citizens who sought pardon. Foreign peoples who could safely be pardoned I preferred to spare rather than to extirpate. About 500,000 Roman citizens were under military oath to me. Of these, when their terms of service were ended, I settled in colonies or sent back to their own municipalities a little more than 300,000, and to all of these I allotted lands or granted money as rewards for military service. I captured 600 ships, exclusive of those which were of smaller class than triremes.

4. Twice I celebrated ovations, three times curule triumphs, and I was acclaimed *imperator* twenty-one times. When the senate decreed additional triumphs to me, I declined them on four occasions. I deposited in the Capitol laurel wreaths adorning my *fasces* [an emblem of Roman authority] after fulfilling the vows which I had made in each war. For successes achieved on land and on sea by me or through my legates under my auspices the senate decreed fifty-five times that thanksgiving be offered to the immortal gods. Moreover, the number of days on which, by decree of the senate, such thanksgiving was offered, was 890. In my triumphs there were led before my chariot nine kings or children of kings. At the time I wrote this, I had been consul thirteen times, and I was in the thirty-seventh year of my tribunician power [14 C.E.]. . . .

6. In the consulship of Marcus Vinicius and Quintus Lucretius, and again in that of Publius Lentulus and Gnaeus Lentulus, and a third time in that of Paullus Fabius Maximus and Quintus Tubero [in 19, 18, and 11 B.C.E.], though the Roman senate and people unitedly agreed that I should be elected sole guardian of the laws and morals with supreme authority, I refused to accept any office offered me which was contrary to the traditions of our ancestors. The measures which the senate desired at that time to be taken by me I carried out by virtue of the tribunician power. In this power I five times voluntarily requested and was given a colleague by the senate. . . .

10. My name was inserted, by decree of the senate, in the hymn of the Salian priests. And it was enacted by law that I should be sacrosanct in perpetuity and that I should posseses the tribunician power as long as I live. I declined to become *pontifex maximus* in place of a colleague while he was still alive, when the people offered me that priesthood, which my father had held. A few years later, in the consulship of Publius Sulpicius and Gaius Valgius, I accepted this priesthood, when death removed the man who [had] taken possession of it at a time of civil disturbance; and from all Italy a multitude flocked to my election such as had never previously been recorded at Rome. . . .

20. I repaired the Capitol and the theater of Pompey with enormous expenditures on both works, without having my name inscribed on them. I repaired the conduits of the aqueducts which were falling into ruin in many places because of age, and I doubled the capacity of the aqueduct called Marcia by admitting a new spring into its conduit. I completed the Julian Forum and the

basilica which was between the temple of Castor and the temple of Saturn, works begun and far advanced by my father, and when the same basilica was destroyed by fire, I enlarged its site and began rebuilding the structure, which is to be inscribed with the names of my sons; and in case it should not be completed while I am still alive, I left instructions that the work be completed by my heirs. In my sixth consulship [28 B.C.E.] I repaired eighty-two temples of the gods in the city, in accordance with a resolution of the senate, neglecting none which at that time required repair. In my seventh consulship [27 B.C.E.] I reconstructed the Flaminian Way from the city as far as Ariminum, and also all the bridges except the Mulvian and the Mínucian. . . .

26. I extended the frontiers of all the provinces of the Roman people on whose boundaries were peoples not subject to our empire. I restored peace to the Gallic and Spanish provinces and likewise to Germany, that is to the entire region bounded by the Ocean from Gades to the mouth of the Elbe river. I caused peace to be restored in the Alps, from the region nearest to the Adriatic Sea as far as the Tuscan Sea, without undeservedly making war against any people. My fleet sailed the Ocean from the mouth of the Rhine eastward as far as the territory of the Cimbrians, to which no Roman previously had penetrated either by land or by sea. The Cimbrians, the Charydes, the Semnones, and other German peoples of the same region through their envoys sought my friendship and that of the Roman people. At my command and under my auspices two armies were led almost at the same time into Ethiopia and into Arabia which is called Felix; and very large forces of the enemy belonging to both peoples were killed in battle, and many towns were captured. In Ethiopia a penetration was made as far as the town of Napata, which is next to Meroe; in Arabia the army advanced into the territory of the Sabaeans to the town of Mariba.

27. I added Egypt to the empire of the Roman people. Although I might have made Greater Armenia into a province when its king Artaxes was assassinated, I preferred, following the precedent of our ancestors, to hand over this kingdom, acting through Tiberius Nero, who was then my stepson, to Tigranes, son of King Artavasdes and grandson of King Tigranes. And afterwards, when this same people revolted and rebelled, after I subdued it through my son Gaius, I handed it over to the rule of King Ariobarzanes, son of Artabazus, king of the Medes, and after his death to his son Artavasdes. When the latter was killed, I dispatched to that kingdom Tigranes, a scion of the royal family of Armenia. I recovered all the provinces extending beyond the Adriatic Sea eastward, and also Cyrenae, which were for the most part already in the possession of kings, as I had previously recovered Sicily and Sardinia, which had been seized in the slave war. . . .

34. In my sixth and seventh consulships, after I had put an end to the civil wars, having attained supreme power by universal consent, I transferred the state from my own power to the control of the Roman senate and the people.

For this service of mine I received the title of Augustus by decree of the senate, and the doorposts of my house were publicly decked with laurels, the civic crown was affixed over my doorway, and a golden shield was set up in the Julian senate house, which, as the inscription on this shield testifies, the Roman senate and people gave me in recognition of my valor, clemency, justice, and devotion. After that time I excelled all in authority, but I possessed no more power than the others who were my colleagues in each magistracy.

35. When I held my thirteenth consulship, the senate, the equestrian order, and the entire Roman people gave me the title of "father of the country" and decreed that this title should be inscribed in the vestibule of my house, in the Julian senate house, and in the Augustan Forum on the pedestal of the chariot which was set up in my honor by decree of the senate. At the time I wrote this document I was in my seventy-sixth year. . . .

Source 7 from Cassius Dio, Roman History *in Naphtali Lewis and Meyer Reinhold, eds.,* Roman Civilization: Selected Readings, *vol. 1 (New York: Columbia University Press, 1955), pp. 557–559.*

7. From Cassius Dio, *Roman History*

POWERS AND TITLES OF THE EMPEROR

In this way the power of both people and senate passed entirely into the hands of Augustus, and from this time there was, strictly speaking, a monarchy; for monarchy would be the truest name for it, even if two or three men later held the power jointly. Now, the Romans so detested the title "monarch" that they called their emperors neither dictators nor kings nor anything of this sort. Yet, since the final authority for the government devolves upon them, they needs must be kings. The offices established by the laws, it is true, are maintained even now, except that of censor; but the entire direction and administration is absolutely in accordance with the wishes of the one in power at the time. And yet, in order to preserve the appearance of having this authority not through their power but by virtue of the laws, the emperors have taken to themselves all the offices (including the titles) which under the Republic possessed great power with the consent of the people—with the exception of the dictatorship. Thus, they very often become consuls, and they are always styled proconsuls whenever they are outside the *pomerium.* The title *imperator* is held by them for life, not only by those who have won victories in battle but also by all the rest, to indicate their absolute power, instead of the title "king" or "dictator." These latter titles they have never assumed since they fell out of use in the constitution, but the actuality of those offices is secured to them by the appellation *im-*

perator. By virtue of the titles named, they secure the right to make levies, collect funds, declare war, make peace, and rule foreigners and citizens alike everywhere and always—even to the extent of being able to put to death both *equites* and senators inside the *pomerium*—and all the other powers once granted to the consuls and other officials possessing independent authority; and by virtue of holding the censorship they investigate our lives and morals as well as take the census, enrolling some in the equestrian and senatorial orders and removing others from these orders according to their will. By virtue of being consecrated in all the priesthoods and, in addition, from their right to bestow most of them upon others, as well as from the fact that, even if two or three persons rule jointly, one of them is *pontifex maximus,* they hold in their own hands supreme authority over all matters both profane and sacred. The tribunician power, as it is called, which once the most influential men used to hold, gives them the right to nullify the effects of the measures taken by any other official, in case they do not approve, and makes their persons inviolable; and if they appear to be wronged in even the slightest degree, not merely by deed but even by word, they may destroy the guilty party as one accursed, without a trial. The emperors, it should be explained, do not think it lawful to be tribunes, inasmuch as they all belong to the patrician class, but they assume the power of the tribunes in its entirety, as it was at its height; and the number of the years of their rule is counted from the assumption of this power, the theory being that they receive it annually along with those who actually hold the office of tribune. These, then, are the institutions they have taken over from the Republic, each essentially in its traditional form and with the same title, so as to give the impression of possessing no power that has not been granted them. . . .

Thus by virtue of these Republican titles they have clothed themselves with all the powers of the government, so that they actually possess all the prerogatives of kings without the usual title. For the appellation "Caesar" or "Augustus" confers upon them no actual power but merely shows in the one case that they are the successors of their family line, and in the other the splendor of their rank. The name "Father" perhaps gives them a certain authority over us all—the authority which fathers once had over their children; yet it did not signify this at first, but betokened honor and served as an admonition both to them to love their subjects as they would their children, and to their subjects to revere them as they would their fathers. . . .

Source 8: Courtesy of the Trustees of the British Museum.

8. Roman Coin of the Reign of Emperor Nero (r. 54–68)

Source 9: Alinari/Art Resource, NY.

9. Trajan's Column, Rome

10. Detail from Trajan's Column

Source 10 from Bildarchiv Foto Marburg/Art Resource, NY.

Source 11 from V. Ehrenberg and A. H. M. Jones, trans., Documents Illustrating the Reigns of Augustus and Tiberius, *1976, p. 72.*

11. Roman Temple Inscription in Myra, Lycia (Asia Minor)

Divine Augustus Caesar, son of a god, imperator of land and sea, the benefactor and saviour of the whole world, the people of the Myrians.

Marcus Agrippa, the benefactor and saviour of the province, the people of the Myrians.

Source 12 from E. M. Smallwood, trans., Documents Illustrating the Principates of Gaius, Claudius and Nero, *1967, p. 64.*

12. Edict and Speech of Nero to the Greeks

Imperator Caesar proclaims:

Since I wish to reward most noble Greece for its good will and piety towards me, I order that as many as possible from this province attend at Corinth on November 29th.

When crowds had gathered in convention, he delivered the following address:

Men of Greece, I bestow upon you an unexpected gift—though anything may be anticipated from my generosity—a gift of such a size that you were incapable of asking for it. All you Greeks who inhabit Achaea and what until now was the Peloponnese, receive freedom and immunity from taxation, something you have not all had even in your most prosperous times, for you have been slaves either to foreigners or to each other. I wish that I might have bestowed this gift when Greece was at her peak, so that more might enjoy my beneficence. For this reason I hold the times to blame for having reduced the size of my beneficence. But, as it is, I bestow the beneficence upon you not out of pity but out of good will and I reward your gods, whose constant care for me on land and sea I have enjoyed, because they have made it possible for me to bestow such great benefactions. For other principes have conferred freedom on cities, but only Nero has done so even on a province.

[In response, the following decree of Acraephia was issued, proclaiming Nero a god.]

The high-priest of the Augusti for life and of Nero Claudius Caesar Augustus, Epaminondas, son of Epaminondas, proclaimed (submitted by him for prior consideration to the council and people):

Since the lord of the entire world, Nero, pontifex maximus, in his 13th year of tribunician power, father of his country, New Sun that has shone on the Greeks, has decided to bestow beneficence upon Greece and has rewarded and shown piety towards our gods, who have stood by him everywhere for his care and safety; since he, Nero, Zeus the Liberator, the one and only greatest imperator of our times, friend of the Greeks, has bestowed the eternal indigenous, native freedom that had formerly been taken from the Greeks, he has shown his favour, he has brought back the autonomy and freedom of the past and to this great and unexpected gift has added immunity from taxation, quite complete, which none of the previous Augusti gave us. For all these reasons it has been decided by the magistrates and councillors and people to worship him at the existing altar dedicated to Zeus the Saviour, and to inscribe upon it "To Zeus the Liberator, Nero, forever" and to erect statues of Nero Zeus the Liberator and the goddess Augusta Messallina in the temple of Ptoian Apollo to share it with our ancestral gods, so that, when these things have been done, our city may be seen to have poured out every honour and piety upon the house of the lord Augustus Nero; it has also been decided to inscribe the decree on a column set beside Zeus the Saviour in the market-place and on the temple of Ptoian Apollo.

QUESTIONS TO CONSIDER

As you read and studied the individual pieces of evidence looking for clues about the ways the builders of the Han and Roman empires conceived of and justified imperial authority, you probably noted some shifts of emphasis. Later rulers and their advisers often embellished the ideas of the founding emperors. The founder of the Chinese empire, Qin Shi Huangdi, based much of his claim to an exalted imperial position on his success in conquering "all lands within the four seas." But subsequent rulers, who were not themselves conquerors, needed to develop other justifications for their power. Do you detect a similar shift in the Roman materials?

The stone inscriptions in Source 1 probably best reflect Qin Shi Huangdi's own view of his authority. Though they hail his military victories and worldwide conquest, note the claim that he inaugurated a new age by unifying the Six States and standardizing all laws and norms "wherever the sun and moon shine." Note, too, the references to his sageliness, a quality reflected in the title *Huangdi* (*Huang-ti*), which he adopted. Both words compounded into this title, though often translated "August Emperor" as here, came from terms applied to ancient sages whom tradition portrayed as the creators of human civilization. What does "sage" seem to imply in the emperor's biography? Why do you think the first emperor identified himself with this figure?

In addition to setting up stone markers and other monuments to celebrate his accomplishments while alive, Shi Huangdi constructed a huge tomb out on a plain some fifty kilometers away from his capital city to preserve his fame in death. This practice, which Han emperors continued on a more modest scale, gave him another way to shape his public image. Revisit Source 2, the photograph of his burial mound at Mt. Li. Originally an earthen pyramid 47 meters tall, this mound stood within a 2-square-kilometer enclosure that contained a virtual underground palace. As the detail of one of the excavations shows (Source 3), the area all around was honeycombed with pits filled with thousands of pottery figures. The overwhelming majority of these figures are soldiers like those shown here. What image of authority does this monument and its legions of clay figures imply? How does it compare with the images of conqueror, unifier, and sage presented in the biography?

Qin Shi Huangdi tried to link his rule with higher powers. These included his own deified ancestors and an impersonal cycle of cosmological forces believed to shape human events. But later Han emperors, who patronized Confucianism, elaborated this tendency further. In Source 4, Dong Zhongshu (Tung Chung-shu), a court Confucian adviser, explains how a ruler serves the higher moral power of Heaven, the deity with whom Confucians linked cosmic order. What does his statement that "the king is but the executor of Heaven" imply about the nature of imperial authority? What purpose does it ascribe to the state? And what does it mean to say "the ruler is the basis of the state"? Source 5, a decree issued by the Han Emperor Wendi, expresses the full development of the idea that Han emperors had a special mandate from Heaven to rule. But note that an emperor could lose this charge. Confucians argued that since Heaven gave ethical rulers mandates to rule, it could likewise withdraw authority from the unworthy. What according to Wendi's decree seems to bring Heaven's displeasure—and how does he expect Heaven to show it? Confucians used the doctrine of heavenly warnings to press for a professional bureaucracy schooled in their values as a check on arbitrary rule. Can you gather from this decree how the doctrine empowered imperial officials as well as emperors?

Source 6, *The Achievements of the Divine Augustus,* or *Res Gestae Divi Augustus,* issued by Augustus Caesar, provides a comparable Roman counterpart to Qin Shi Huangdi's stone inscriptions. It, too, came to be inscribed on stone, as copies were carved on the walls of temples throughout the Roman Empire. More autobiographical and personal than Shi Huangdi's inscriptions, it nonetheless served much the same purpose: to explain Augustus's new titles and power. Notice, however, that despite the name of the work, Augustus himself makes no claim to divinity here. Nor does he presume to be a new kind of ruler by right of any transcendent power, divine or natural. Although he points out how he has enlarged the Roman Empire, he does not claim to be a world conqueror, much less the creator of a new state. Saying only that he "liberated the Republic, which was oppressed by the tyranny of a faction," he presents himself as a restorer, not an innovator, and carefully professes not to transgress "the traditions of our ancestors."

Yet, as Augustus notes, not only did the Roman people elect him consul, the highest executive office in the Republic, the Senate voted him the extraordinary title of *imperator,* or emperor. Again and again he attributes his authority to these two sources. Their importance in the state was symbolized by the universal inscription S.P.Q.R., signifying *Senatus Populusque Romanus* ("The Senate and the Roman People"), on Roman standards and monuments. As the "sole guardian of the laws and morals with supreme authority" elected by the Roman Senate and people, what kind of imperial ruler did Augustus presume to be? In keeping with his elected offices, Augustus often preferred to use another title bestowed upon him by the Senate—*princeps,* meaning "first" among his fellow citizens. What kind of legitimization do these claims imply? In what sense did it qualify him to assume the title "father of the country," which he asserts so prominently at the end of this laudatory piece.

In his *Roman History,* the third-century historian Cassius Dio questions Augustus's pose as mere restorer of the Republic. In Source 7, an excerpt from this work, Cassius Dio argues that Augustus and subsequent Roman emperors actually wrested all power from the Senate and people and instituted an autocratic system of monarchy in which the *imperator* became an absolute ruler. Behind the façade of their republican titles, he charges, Augustus and his successors assumed "all the prerogatives of kings without the usual title." They absorbed not only all civil authority in this way, he says, but other authority, too. For they took the title *pontifex maximus,* or high priest of the official Roman pantheon of gods, along with their profane offices and honors. Indeed, one of the few surviving statues of Augustus portrays him in this priestly role. What support do you suppose he and his successors expected to add to their status through this title?

Later emperors continued to present themselves as high priest as well as civic father, chief executive, and, of course, heir to Augustus. Look at Source 8, a *sesterius* or bronze coin minted during the time of Emperor Nero (r. 54–68). Long accustomed to commemorating leading citizens on state coinage, the Romans found it natural to mint money bearing imperial portraits under the empire. These portraits and the legends accompanying them, of course, provided emperors with an excellent way to propagandize their public images. Notice all the names and titles appearing on the face of the coin reproduced here. Beginning at the lower left, the coin gives the emperor's personal name, Nero Claudius, then affirms his relationship to Caesar Augustus through his adopted father, Germanicus. Then around the rim follow abbreviated versions of his four most prized titles: PM for *Pontifex*

Maximus, TRP for *Tribunicia Potestate* or tribuneship (an office supposedly representing the lower or plebeian class of the empire), IMP for *Imperator*, and PP for *Pater Patriae* or "father of the country." How do these titles compare with those assumed by Augustus?

Besides asserting civil and religious authority, a number of later emperors chose to portray themselves as military commanders and conquerors. Emperor Trajan (r. 98–117), who began his political career as a general, especially popularized this role. He not only commissioned statues of himself in full armor and minted coins bearing his image as a warrior, but raised a great column in Rome to depict his generalship. Source 9 shows this column. Although built primarily to hold aloft a huge statue of Trajan in military dress, the column also publicizes his most famous campaign, a war fought against the Dacians on the Balkan peninsula. Battle scenes like the one shown in Source 10 spiraled up its entire length, recalling a tradition of battlefield leadership going back to Alexander the Great and the Persian monarchs whom he imitated. Like similar monuments and victory arches raised in Rome by other emperors, Trajan's Column openly celebrates military conquest. What kind of imperial authority do these images evoke?

The image of a world conqueror closely parallels another theme that eventually affected the way Roman emperors characterized themselves and their authority: the tradition of world savior. In the eastern lands of the empire, rulers had often claimed not only to represent gods but to *be* gods in their own right. Rome's newly conquered subjects in this quarter, therefore, readily accorded the emperors divine status. Source 11, a commemorative inscription from the time of Caesar Augustus carved on a temple in Myra, a city on the Mediterranean coast in present-day Turkey, shows this trend well underway. Note how it characterizes the first emperor as "divine Augustus Caesar" and calls him "son of a god," implying that his adoptive father, Julius Caesar, was divine, too. And observe how it lauds him as "benefactor and savior of the whole world," far more than just a restorer of Roman liberties.

By the time of Nero, the cult of imperial divinity encouraged even more exaggerated claims, like those in Source 12, an inscription from Acraephia. Issued by a priest in the service of the Augusti, or imperial cult, on the occasion of Nero's decision to grant many Greek cities special tax immunity, it equates Nero, "lord of the entire world," with the greatest of Greek gods, Zeus—here characterized as Liberator and Savior. By the end of the fourth century, Emperor Diocletian, who ruled from the eastern half of the realm, regularly equated himself with Zeus or his Roman equivalent, Jupiter. Contrast this form of divine monarchy with Augustus's own more modest view of sovereignty. How does it change the nature and justification of imperial authority?

As you compare this vision of a divinely led empire with the Han idea of a Heavenly ordained ruler, ask yourself why religious beliefs of this sort became so entwined with political institutions in both imperial traditions. How would people today react if their leaders claimed to have special divine or religious powers? Modern assumptions about the separation of state and religion make it difficult for us to understand why political supremacy might be equated with sacred power. But clearly this equation occurred in both ancient Rome and China. What other common features do you find in these two traditions that contrast with modern practice or belief? Think for a moment about the gender implied in all of these images of imperial rule. How different would it be if the Han rulers had claimed to be "children" of Heaven or the Roman emperors proclaimed themselves "parents" of the country. What does the masculine nature of the expressions imply about ancient Roman and Chinese notions of power?

EPILOGUE

Although extremely powerful for a few centuries, neither Han nor Rome proved immune to eventual decay. Internal conflicts and divisions strained their administrative structures to the breaking point, and as central authority ebbed, their empires fragmented in the face of rebellions and invasions. To their subjects, this collapse entailed far more than the end of political regimes. It meant the break-up of world order and the start of extended eras of change, turmoil, and insecurity at both ends of the Eurasian continent. Among other results, such change brought an end to regional unity and world-states.

The Han collapsed first, following a generation of court intrigues and coups in the second half of the second century that allowed imperial power to drift away from reigning emperors into the hands of palace eunuchs who lacked any claim to virtue or legitimacy. Uncertain of the bureaucracy's loyalty, they hesitated in the face of a wave of popular insurrections that exploded in the Yellow River plain in 184 following a devastating plague. United by millenarian bands known as Yellow Turbans, pledged to found a revolutionary "Heavenly State of Great Peace," the rebels nearly toppled the Han. For lack of central forces, provincial governors and local elites had to organize their own resistance against the rebels. After quelling the rebellions, therefore, they refused to disband their forces and relinquish local control. Nervously building up their power, they became de facto warlords and began to vie with each other for wider influence. Eventually one of their number, a general named Cao Cao, set himself up in the capital as protector of the impotent throne and used his armies to prolong nominal Han rule for a few decades more. But when his son deposed the last Han emperor in order to ascend the throne himself in 220, many provincial magnates refused to recognize his authority and partitioned the empire into warring fragments. Despite a brief reunification of the imperial territories at the end of the third century, further civil strife soon broke out again, and all hope of imperial restoration crumbled as waves of invaders swept across the frontiers to engulf north China.

Imperial Rome lasted longer, but eventually it, too, fragmented. Although for reasons different from those in China, rivalry around the throne weakened the monarchy. Left with inadequate resources, provincial leaders failed to deal with mounting domestic problems and frontier dangers. Emperor Diocletian (r. 284–305) and his immediate successors tried to overhaul the administrative structure of the empire and enhance imperial prestige. Constantine (r. 306–337), who shifted the capital away from Rome to his namesake city, Constantinople, enjoyed brief success. But the benefits of these belated reforms did not last long, and by the end of the fourth century, the decline had begun anew. Eventually the relentless pressure of German tribes along the Rhine and Danube frontier brought about the empire's final collapse. Following the Gothic invasion and sack of Rome in 410, outsiders overran and divided up the empire's western half. With the loss of Rome and most of the Latin-speaking lands, the eastern half, ruled from Constantinople, began to evolve into a very different kind of Greek empire known as Byzantium.

Despite their fall, both empires left enduring legacies of institutions and ideas, including ideals of universal empire and imperial authority. After a lapse of nearly three and a half centuries, East Asians succeeded in resurrecting a great imperial state under the Sui and Tang dynasties of the sixth through the ninth centuries. Though altered in subsequent centuries, this imperial state essentially survived intact until 1911, when the last *huangdi,* or sage lord, abdicated in the face of the revolution that instituted a westernized Chinese republic. And to this day, the Chinese still call themselves in their own language *Han ran*—the "people of Han." In the West, the imperial ideal proved more elusive, and though Europeans tried on occasion to revive the Roman Empire, none of their endeavors fully succeeded. Justinian's effort in the sixth century to rebuild it from a Byzantine base failed, as did Charlemagne's ninth-century attempt to restore it from his Frankish kingdom. Yet the mystique of the Caesars persisted into modern times, leading the Germans and Russians to appropriate the name for their rulers in *Kaiser* and *Czar.* Napoleon, who rode to power in France on the first tide of modern nationalism, showed how powerful that aura remained at the start of the nineteenth century when he gladly abandoned republican scruples to grasp the old title *imperator* for himself. And both Mussolini and Hitler evoked it again in the twentieth century in the symbols of their authoritarian power. As many have observed, the papacy preserves a more benign version of the Roman monarchy into the present.

The lasting power of these imperial ideals suggests that they embodied some of the most deeply rooted assumptions and beliefs from within their respective cultural spheres. A final point worth considering, therefore, is the degree to which they may continue to influence contemporary political life. Some, for example, claim to see vestiges of assumed sagehood in the "great Helmsman" Mao Zedong (Mao Tse-tung), who, after all, proclaimed the advent of a new socialist age with global significance from a balcony overlooking Tiananmen Square in Beijing—a square whose very name, derived from the adjacent entrance to an old imperial palace, means the Gate of Heavenly Peace! And how many modern republics still revere a military figure who became "father of his country" by virtue of restoring the lost liberty of a people through some presumed divine grace?

CHAPTER FIVE

INTERNATIONAL RELIGIOUS COMMUNITIES (300 B.C.E.–800 C.E.)

THE PROBLEM

In the last chapter, we examined the growth of large empires in the ancient world, noting the technical and bureaucratic structures that enabled them to grow and flourish. In this chapter, we explore another way in which large territories were brought or held together: through allegiance to a set of religious ideas or a religious figure. Of the thousands of religions practiced in the world today, three claim large numbers of adherents throughout the world: Buddhism, Christianity, and Islam. Each of these began as a small group of followers around a single leader and then was transformed, slowly or quickly, into an international religious community. In the case of Buddhism and Christianity, this occurred several centuries after the lives of the initial leaders, Siddhartha Gautama, called the Buddha (ca. 563–483 B.C.E.), and Jesus of Nazareth (ca. 5 B.C.E.–29 C.E.). In the case of Islam, this growth began during the lifetime of the initial leader, Muhammad (ca. 570–632 C.E.), and continued for many centuries after his death.

For each of these religions, the transformation from small sect to international community was accomplished by individuals who also had what we would term secular political power; in other words, they were political as well as religious leaders. In the case of Buddhism, the person generally regarded as dramatically expanding Buddhism both within and beyond the Indian subcontinent was the Mauryan emperor Ashoka (ruled ca. 273–232 B.C.E.). In the case of Christianity, the Roman emperor Constantine (ruled 306–337 C.E.), the first emperor to become a Christian, is usually seen as the key figure. In the case of Islam, Muhammad himself and the first four caliphs who succeeded him, termed the "patriarchal caliphs"—

Abu Bakr (ruled 632–634), Umar (ruled 634–644), Uthman (ruled 644–656), and Ali (ruled 656–661)—spread Islam across Arabia and into Persia and North Africa, setting the pattern for later, more extensive expansion into Europe, Africa, and Asia.

In each of these cases, the individuals involved, or those close to them, have left us a record of these transformations and what they were attempting to accomplish. Your task in this chapter will be to use a variety of sources to answer these questions: How did political leaders within Buddhism, Christianity, and Islam encourage the growth of their chosen religious community? What differences and similarities do you see in their actions and in what they viewed as most important in the lives of these communities?

BACKGROUND

Studying the history of any religious movement can pose special problems for historians. We may have more trouble achieving unbiased assessments of the history of religion than of other historical topics because of our intellectual, spiritual, or emotional commitments to certain religious ideas. This does not mean, however, that we should avoid religious topics—to do so would make it impossible for us to understand the past—but instead that we should be aware of our own prejudices and approach all religions with respect. Our job as historians is to understand people's religious ideas within their historical context and to see how religious faith has manifested itself in historically observable phenomena; it is not to judge whether certain religious ideas are right or wrong, true or false.

Difficulties in being objective when studying the history of religion can stem not only from our own personal religious commitments, but also from the nature of the sources available. Very few religious sources were written simply to describe what happened; more often, they were written to express central doctrines or to win converts. Even those sources that do describe historical events, such as the actions of the political leaders we are examining in this chapter, were often written for the added purpose of spreading the faith. Many of these were composed long after the events occurred, and so later developments colored the ways in which they were recorded. In some cases, these written records were based on extensive oral traditions, but they are now our only source for the events they describe, and we have no way to check their accuracy. They may relate events that were viewed at the time as clearly miraculous—visions in the sky, voices from heaven—but also as having actually happened. Luckily, we as historians do not need to take a stand on the historicity of such events. What is important for us is that people believed that they had happened and acted accordingly.

In talking about any religious group, we often make distinctions between history, tradition, and myth, but the lines between these are never sharp and are frequently contested. It is important to recognize, however, that tradition and myth are not the same; when historians use the phrase "according to tradition, . . . " they are not saying that an event is completely mythological but simply commenting on the limits of their sources. In many religions, deep divisions developed quite early not only about the religious meaning of certain events, but also about when certain things happened and whether they happened at all. Thus, not only can our sources be obscure, they can also be contradictory. Often there is no way to resolve the contradiction, and we simply have to say "according to this tradition . . . whereas according to that tradition. . . ." These divisions within religions were often more bitterly contested than differences between religions, and indeed, discords within religions continue to shape the contemporary world in profound and sometimes violent ways.

Keeping in mind these cautionary thoughts about the evaluation of all religious sources, we can now focus more specifically on the context for the sources we include here. Because we are examining the actions of certain leaders in regard to their religious communities, the evidence focuses on that aspect of their reigns. Your textbook can provide you with more general information about Ashoka and the Mauryan Empire, Constantine's reign in the Roman Empire, and the lives of Muhammad and the patriarchal caliphs.

The Mauryan emperor Ashoka was the grandson of the founder of the Mauryan Empire, Chandragupta, who had defeated one of the generals of Alexander the Great in 304 B.C.E. and expanded his holdings to include most of the Indian subcontinent. Ashoka grew up at the royal court at Pataliputra in the Ganges River valley, where many religious traditions mingled—Brahmanism, Jainism, Buddhism—and where ideas about the role of the ruler were openly debated and discussed. The most extensive consideration of these was a treatise on government traditionally attributed to one of Chandragupta's ministers, the Brahmanical teacher Kautilya, titled *Arthashastra,* in which power and benevolence were described as the two main objectives of kingship.

At some point in his life, Ashoka accepted Buddhism, although traditions vary about exactly who converted him. They also vary about the timing of some events within Buddhism that probably occurred during or shortly before or after Ashoka's reign, such as formal splits because of disagreements about various interpretations of the Buddha's teaching. Certain aspects of the practice and prevalence of Buddhism at that time are very clear, however: We know, for example, that people often went on pilgrimages to the holy places associated with the Buddha's life, built mounds called *stupas* to house Buddhist relics, and supported communities of monks and nuns called the *sangha;* Buddhism was well established in central India, and had begun to spread north to Kashmir and south to the Deccan plateau; and a canon of sacred texts, attributed to the Buddha, had begun to appear.

Like Ashoka, the Roman emperor Constantine underwent a religious conversion some time after he became an adult, though there are discrepancies in the sources and differences of opinion among historians about exactly when this was and how complete an acceptance and understanding of Christianity Constantine evidenced. Constantine was the son of Emperor Constantius, but his claim to the throne was challenged by a number of rivals. Though his troops elected him emperor in 306, the emperorship itself was divided at the time in a complex way, and Constantine did not become sole sovereign until 324, after he had defeated all other claimants. Much of Constantine's early reign was thus spent in warfare, and he became extremely concerned with establishing structures and institutions that would make the Roman Empire more united.

Christianity appeared to Constantine to be just such a unifying force. Christianity had originally been largely ignored by high-level Roman authorities, who regarded it as a sect within Judaism and therefore of little consequence. There were sporadic persecutions in the first century C.E., but there was no concerted campaign to annihilate Christianity. These persecutions may have actually helped Christianity spread, as the heroism of martyrs often impressed those who watched their public executions and who later became Christians themselves. As more non-Jews converted, Roman authorities became more concerned, particularly because Christians refused to participate in the sacrifices and ceremonies honoring the traditional Roman gods. These ceremonies were patriotic as well as religious to the Romans, for they were carried out for the good of the state and often specifically held to assure military victory. Persecution was thus stepped up in the second and third centuries, and it became particularly vicious during the reigns of those emperors who were most concerned about the health of the empire. By this point it was too late to stop the spread of Christianity, which had a growing following among people of all classes throughout the Roman Empire and a strong bureaucratic structure based on regional officials termed bishops. There is great disagreement among historians about how much of the Roman population had become Christian by the time of Constantine, but it was certainly a sizable minority.

The history of Islam is very different from that of Buddhism and Christianity in that it was both a religious and a political community from the beginning; Muhammad was in some ways his own Constantine. Like both Ashoka and Constantine, Muhammad experienced a religious conversion when he was an adult, but, unlike them, he was a merchant rather than a ruler. He lived in Mecca, an important trading and religious center on the Arabian peninsula, which was divided into different tribal groups and lacked the leadership of a single ruler. Muhammad's conversion involved visions of angelic beings who ordered him to preach a message of a single God and to become God's Prophet, which he began to do in his hometown of Mecca. While he slowly gathered followers there, he also provoked a great deal of resistance and in 622 migrated with his followers to Medina—this event, termed the *hijra,* marks the beginning of the Muslim calendar. At Medina, Muhammad was much more successful, and by his death in 632 he had unified most of the Arabian peninsula into a religious/political community (termed the *umma*) of *Muslims,* a word meaning "those who comply with or submit to God's will." (The first umma was formed by the Charter of Medina in 622 and included the local Jewish community, which established a precedent for the later protection of Jews under Islam.)

Muhammad's revelations were written down by his followers during his lifetime and shortly thereafter were organized into an authoritative text, the Qur'an, regarded by Muslims as the direct words of God (Allah) to his prophet Muhammed and therefore especially revered. (These revelations were in Arabic. If Muslims use translations into other languages, they do so alongside the original Arabic.) At the same time, other sayings and accounts of Muhammad, which gave advice on matters that went beyond the Qur'an, were collected into books termed *hadith;* Muslim tradition (*sunna*) consists of both the Qur'an and the hadith. Unfortunately for the Muslim community, neither the Qur'an nor the hadith gave clear guidance about how successors to Muhammad were to be chosen, but a group of Muhammad's closest followers elected Abu Bakr, who was a close friend of the Prophet's and a member of a small tribe affiliated with the Prophet's tribe, as caliph, meaning "successor." This election set a precedent for the ratification of the subsequent patriarchal caliphs, though it was unsuccessfully opposed militarily by other Arab tribes. A more serious challenge developed later among supporters of the fourth caliph, Ali. Ali claimed the caliphate because of his blood ties with Muhammad—he was the Prophet's cousin and son-in-law—and because Muhammad had designated him as *imam,* or "leader." He was assassinated in 661, five years after becoming caliph, and his supporters began to assert that he should rightly have been the first caliph and that all subsequent caliphs were usurpers. These supporters of Ali—termed *shi'at Ali* or *Shi'ites*—saw Ali and subsequent imams as the divinely inspired leaders of the community, whereas the larger body of Muslims who accepted the first elections—termed *Sunnis*—regarded the caliphs as political leaders. Since Islam did not have an organized church and priesthood, the caliphs had an additional function of safeguarding and enforcing the religious law (*sharia*) with the advice of scholars (*ulama*), particularly the jurists, judges, and scholastics who were knowledgeable about the Qur'an and hadith.

THE METHOD

In reading the two central questions for this chapter, you no doubt noted that the first is largely informational and the second is comparative. This order is not accidental, for historians must first uncover information about past societies before they can begin to make comparisons. Indeed, many historians choose to devote their entire lives to the intensive study of a single culture and time period and are not especially interested in comparative questions. World history courses, including probably the one you are enrolled in, tend to provoke comparative questions, however, and some historians would argue that to a certain degree *all* history is comparative. By this they mean that we approach all other cultures from the vantage point of our own, and thus we can understand them only by comparing them to what is familiar and known. They stress that these comparisons may be implicit, but they are inescapable. Other historians, though, dispute this point and argue that the best history writing seeks to be highly objective and, as much as possible, to constrain the historian's own cultural background from intruding.

Whatever they think about *implicit* comparisons, historians who make *explicit* comparisons in their work recognize that these must be derived and expressed very carefully. Not only must historians think about the ways in which the events, individuals, or developments that are the subjects of their study are comparable, but they must also think about the ways in which the sources available to them are comparable. Very often the types of records left by one culture are quite different from those left by another, even regarding matters as central as political leadership. Thus, as you begin to make comparisons between the actions and ideas of the leaders who are the focus of this chapter, you will need to think about how your ideas—and the connections and comparisons you are making—are shaped by the types of sources you are using.

Most of the sources for this chapter are written; they consist primarily of pronouncements of the political leaders themselves or the writings of historians or other commentators who were members of the leader's community. In no case does our evidence come from someone who was hostile to the individuals or their actions. (This is another aspect of the evidence you need to keep in mind.) Your primary method will be careful reading, and we advise you first to work on gathering information and then to go back and make your comparisons. You may find it useful to list all the actions and ideas of the leaders described in the sources, so as to summarize their roles in your own words before you begin to make comparisons.

Sources 1 through 3 all relate to King Ashoka. Source 1 is a selection of some of the so-called rock and pillar edicts, which are the best record we have of Ashoka's reign. These are inscriptions that King Ashoka ordered carved in stone on large rocks in prominent places or on tall pillars that he had erected for this purpose. The edicts are found in a number of different locations throughout Ashoka's large empire, particularly along the borders. They were written in Prakrit, the language spoken at Ashoka's time, and are the oldest surviving written documents of historical importance in India. Read these edicts carefully. What convinced Ashoka that he should change the way he was ruling and acting? What does he now see as the main aim of his reign? What actions has he done to promote this aim? How does he relate to the community of Buddhist monks and nuns (the sangha, sometimes spelled Samgha)? How does he say he treats those who follow religions other than Buddhism, and how does he advise his subjects to treat people with different religious ideas?

Source 2 is a photograph of one of the Ashokan pillars, topped with a single lion. (Other pillars are topped with three lions, an emblem that is now on the state seal of India and Indian coins, or lions and the Buddhist wheel of law, an emblem reproduced on India's flag.) Each of these pillars—more than thirty have been discovered—was transported hundreds of miles from the same quarry and polished very smooth before it was inscribed. Why might Ashoka have regarded this effort as important? Why would pillars such as these be an effective way to relay the information you have just read? How would the pillars complement the visits by officials and by Ashoka himself?

The other major type of source we have for Ashoka's reign is legends, oral traditions about him that did not die out when the Mauryan Empire collapsed but spread throughout India and beyond its borders. Some of these were written down in the Pali language as part of the chronicles from the island of Sri Lanka, where Buddhist tradition holds that Ashoka's son Mahendra and daughter Samghamitra spread Buddhism. Others were written down in Sanskrit in northern India and gradually collected into a single text called the *Asokavadana.* Source 3 is from this text, relating an incident from Ashoka's life after he converted to Buddhism. When we use legends and oral traditions in historical investigations, the most important question to ask ourselves is not whether the events really happened, but why followers of an individual tell and retell them—in other words, how these oral traditions worked to support the followers' ideas. Why would the Buddhist followers of Ashoka tell this story? How does it fit with Ashoka's statements about his own ideas and reign as inscribed in the rock and pillar edicts?

Sources 4 through 6 concern the Roman emperor Constantine. Like the evidence about Ashoka, many of the records that survive from Constantine's reign are official edicts and proclamations, though these were written on papyrus and parchment rather than being inscribed on pillars. Source 4 comprises a series of edicts issued by Constantine regarding Christianity, beginning with the original edict of toleration from 311 signed by three of the then four rulers of the Roman Empire: Lactantius, Licinius, and Constantine. The remaining edicts were issued by Constantine alone and are reprinted here in chronological order. They cover a range of actions that Constantine took either directly on behalf of the Christian church or because he was inspired by Christian ideas. Some indicate his opinion toward those following other systems of belief. Reading them will allow you to begin developing your ideas about Constantine's role.

The most important record we have of Constantine's life is a biography written shortly after his death by the historian and Christian bishop Eusebius of Caesarea (ca. 263–339?), a close adviser to Constantine. As Constantine's friend and an official in the Church, Eusebius expressed a particular point of view in his biography, but many of the events he discusses, such as Constantine's proclamations and military battles, are recorded in other sources as well. Other events are not verifiable, but, as with the legends surrounding King Ashoka, the stories about Constantine came to be considered true by later Christians. Source 5 is a series of selections from Eusebius's *Life of Constantine.* As you read these excerpts, note the actions Constantine takes in regard to the Christian church and the statements he makes about it. What convinces Constantine that he should become a Christian? How does he relate to the bishops, the Church's key officials? What does he see as most important for the Church? How do the events related here fit with the imperial edicts you read in Source 4? How might Eusebius's position as an official in the Church shape the way he reports history?

Like Ashoka, Constantine erected large monuments to his rule, most notably the Arch of Constantine in Rome. In Source 5, you discover smaller ways in which he portrayed his religious sentiments and celebrated his reign, through coins and portraits. Source 6 shows two of these coins, one portraying Constantine with a halo and another, two soldiers with the *labarum,* the special standard that was made for the army after Constantine's vision. Why might Constantine have thought it important to issue coins with symbols such as these? Why would coins be an effective means of communicating ideas?

When we turn to the transformation of Islam from small sect to international religious community, we can no longer look at the actions of just one individual, but we must explore those of a series of rulers. Here we have four basic types of sources: the Qur'an, the hadith, histories and biographies written after the fact, and legal or other commentaries on the actions of rulers and ideas about rulership. As you read Sources 7 through 10, you need to think about how the purpose for which each was written might have shaped the discourse.

Source 7 is several verses from the Qur'an regarding the duties of believers to authorities, the rewards for believers, the treatment for those who did not accept the Prophet's words, and the attitudes Muslims were to have toward Jews and Christians. Source 8 is a selection of sayings ascribed to the Prophet from three different collections of hadith, again addressing the duties of believers toward their leaders and leaders toward the community. Because the hadith record sayings and traditions that were handed down orally for several generations, they are generally prefaced by a listing of the names of those who related them back to the early years of Islam. According to both the Qur'an and the hadith, what are the most important duties of the leaders toward the community? of the community toward leaders? What developments are to be most guarded against? How are those who are not Muslims to be treated?

Source 9 is a selection from the earliest biographer of Muhammad whose work has survived, Ibn Ishaq, who was born in Medina in 707 and died in Baghdad in 773. (The Muslim calendar uses the hijra, Muhammad's migration from Mecca to Medina in 622, as its starting date, written as A.H.; in that dating system, Ibn Ishaq's dates are A.H. 85–151.) As with Eusebius's biography of Constantine, many of the incidents recorded have been confirmed by archaeological findings and other sources, so that it is regarded as generally reliable, though, like Eusebius, the author writes from the point of view of a committed follower and admirer. As you read Source 9, note the kinds of actions by which Muhammad spread his message. How were those who opposed him to be handled? What were the most important aspects of the Muslim community? Source 10 is from the *Book of Land-tax* by Abu Yusuf (died A.H. 182/798 C.E.), a legal scholar who wrote a lengthy book of advice for his sovereign, the caliph Harun al-Rashid. Though this evidence comes from a later period, Abu Yusuf relates a number of incidents about the earliest caliphs as part of his instructions to the present one. What actions and advice of the patriarchal caliphs Abu Bakr and Umar does he describe and praise here? What do they advise their successors?

Unlike Christianity and Buddhism, Islam avoided portraying humans or animals in its sacred art; thus the Qur'an and the hadith are never illustrated with figures, though they are often decorated with lavish designs. This convention did not extend to histories, however, and Source 11 is an illustration from one of the most famous Muslim histories, the *Jami' al-tawarikh* (World History) of Rashid al-Din, an adviser to the Muslim ruler Uljaytu (ruled 1304–1316 C.E.). This work was produced, of course, long after the early development of Islam, but its text and illustrations depict what later Muslims saw as important from their early history. Source 11 is a picture of Muhammad (the figure on the far right), addressing Ali and other Muslim leaders before the battle of Badr in the year A.H. 2, which was the first victory of Muhammad's followers against the Meccans. What aspects of Muhammad's leadership does this painting highlight?

You should now have a list of actions and ideas for each of the three individuals—and their religious communities—that are the focus of this chapter, and you have probably begun to see ways in which to compare them. As you develop your comparisons further, you may wish to turn to the Questions to Consider section for additional suggestions.

THE EVIDENCE

Source 1 from The Edicts of Aśoka, *ed. and trans. N. A. Nikam and Richard McKeon (Chicago: University of Chicago Press, 1959), pp. 27–29, 30, 34, 51–52, 58, 66, 67–68.*

1. Selections from Ashoka (Aśoka), Rock and Pillar Edicts

The Kaliṅga country[1] was conquered by King Priyadarśī, Beloved of the Gods,[2] in the eighth year of his reign. One hundred and fifty thousand persons were carried away captive, one hundred thousand were slain, and many times that number died.

Immediately after the Kaliṅgas had been conquered, King Priyadarśī became intensely devoted to the study of Dharma,[3] to the love of Dharma, and to the inculcation of Dharma.

The Beloved of the Gods, conqueror of the Kaliṅgas, is moved to remorse now. For he has felt profound sorrow and regret because the conquest of a people previously unconquered involves slaughter, death, and deportation.

But there is a more important reason for the King's remorse. The Brāhmaṇas and Śramaṇas [the priestly and ascetic orders] as well as the followers of other religions and the householders—who all practiced obedience to superiors, parents, and teachers, and proper courtesy and firm devotion to friends, acquaintances, companions, relatives, slaves, and servants—all suffer from the injury, slaughter, and deportation inflicted on their loved ones. Even those who escaped calamity themselves are deeply afflicted by the misfortunes suffered by those friends, acquaintances, companions, and relatives for whom they feel an undiminished affection. Thus all men share in the misfortune, and this weighs on King Priyadarśī's mind.

[Moreover, there is no country except that of the Yōnas (that is, the Greeks) where Brahmin and Buddhist ascetics do not exist] and there is no place where men are not attached to one faith or another.

Therefore, even if the number of people who were killed or who died or who were carried away in the Kaliṅga war had been only one one-hundredth or one one-thousandth of what it actually was, this would still have weighed on the King's mind.

King Priyadarśī now thinks that even a person who wrongs him must be forgiven for wrongs that can be forgiven.

1. **Kaliṅga:** the modern state of Orissa on the east coast of India.
2. **King Priyadarśī:** Ashoka's name for himself, meaning "Beloved of the Gods."
3. **Dharma:** a complex term with many shades of meaning, involving piety, morality, ethics, order, duty, mutual understanding, justice, and peace.

King Priyadarśī seeks to induce even the forest peoples who have come under his dominion [that is, primitive peoples in the remote sections of the conquered territory] to adopt this way of life and this ideal. He reminds them, however, that he exercises the power to punish, despite his repentance, in order to induce them to desist from their crimes and escape execution.

For King Priyadarśī desires security, self-control, impartiality, and cheerfulness for all living creatures.

King Priyadarśī considers moral conquest [that is, conquest by Dharma, *Dharma-vijaya*] the most important conquest. He has achieved this moral conquest repeatedly both here and among the peoples living beyond the borders of his kingdom. . . .

Wherever conquest is achieved by Dharma, it produces satisfaction. Satisfaction is firmly established by conquest by Dharma [since it generates no opposition of conquered and conqueror]. Even satisfaction, however, is of little importance. King Priyadarśī attaches value ultimately only to consequences of action in the other world.

This edict on Dharma has been inscribed so that my sons and great-grandsons who may come after me should not think new conquests worth achieving. If they do conquer, let them take pleasure in moderation and mild punishments. Let them consider moral conquest the only true conquest.

This is good, here and hereafter. Let their pleasure be pleasure in morality [*Dharma-rati*]. For this alone is good, here and hereafter. . . .

My highest officials, who have authority over large numbers of people, will expound and spread the precepts of Dharma. I have instructed the provincial governors, too, who are in charge of many hundred thousand people, concerning how to guide people devoted to Dharma.

King Priyadarśī says:

Having come to this conclusion, therefore, I have erected pillars proclaiming Dharma. I have appointed officers charged with the spread of Dharma, called *Dharma-mahāmātras.* I have issued proclamations on Dharma. . . .

King Priyadarśī says:

My officers charged with the spread of Dharma are occupied with various kinds of services beneficial to ascetics and householders, and they are empowered to concern themselves with all sects. I have ordered some of them to look after the affairs of the Saṁgha [the Buddhist religious orders], some to take care of the Brahmin and Ajīvika ascetics, some to work among the Nirgranthas [the Jaina monks], and some among the various other religious sects.

King Priyadarśī honors men of all faiths, members of religious orders and laymen alike, with gifts and various marks of esteem. Yet he does not value either gifts or honors as much as growth in the qualities essential to religion in men of all faiths.

This growth may take many forms, but its root is in guarding one's speech to avoid extolling one's own faith and disparaging the faith of others improperly or, when the occasion is appropriate, immoderately.

The faiths of others all deserve to be honored for one reason or another. By honoring them, one exalts one's own faith and at the same time performs a service to the faith of others. By acting otherwise, one injures one's own faith and also does disservice to that of others. For if a man extols his own faith and disparages another because of devotion to his own and because he wants to glorify it, he seriously injures his own faith.

Therefore concord alone is commendable, for through concord men may learn and respect the conception of Dharma accepted by others.

King Priyadarśī desires men of all faiths to know each other's doctrines and to acquire sound doctrines. Those who are attached to their particular faiths should be told that King Priyadarśī does not value gifts or honors as much as growth in the qualities essential to religion in men of all faiths. . . .

Aśoka [Ashoka], Beloved of the Gods, issues the following proclamation:

For more than two and a half years, I have been a lay disciple [*upāsaka*] of the Buddha. More than a year ago, I visited the Saṁgha [the Buddhist religious orders], and since then I have been energetic in my efforts. . . .

The Saṁgha of the monks and the Saṁgha of the nuns have each been united to continue united as long as my sons and great-grandsons rule and as long as the sun and moon shine.

The monk or nun who disrupts the Saṁgha shall be required to put on white robes [instead of the customary yellow][4] and to live in non-residence (*anabasasi*). It is my desire that the Saṁgha be united and endure forever.

Everywhere in my dominions local, provincial, and state officials shall make a tour of their districts every five years to proclaim the following precepts of Dharma as well as to transact other business:

Obedience to mother and father; liberality to friends, acquaintances, relatives, priests, and ascetics; abstention from killing living creatures; and moderation in spending money and acquiring possessions are all meritorious.

4. **to put on white robes:** to leave the order of monks or nuns.

Source 2: Borromeo/Art Resource, NY.

2. Ashokan Pillar with a Single-Lion Capital at Vaishali, India

Source 3: from John S. Strong, The Legend of King Aśoka: A Study and Translation of the Aśokāvadāna *(Princeton: Princeton University Press, 1983), pp. 234–236.*

3. From the *Asokavadana*

Not long after King Aśoka had come to have faith in the Teaching of the Buddha, he started honoring Buddhist monks, throwing himself at their feet wherever he saw them, in a crowd, or in a deserted place.

Now Aśoka had a minister named Yaśas, and although he had the utmost faith in the Blessed One,[5] he said, one day, to the king: "Your majesty, you ought not to prostrate yourself before wandering mendicants of every caste, and the Buddhist monks do come from all four castes."

To this Aśoka did not immediately respond. Sometime later, however, he told all his ministers that he needed to have the heads of various sorts of creatures, and he asked one of them to bring him the head of such and such an animal, and another to bring him the head of another animal, and so on. Finally, he ordered Yaśas to bring him the head of a human being.

Now when the ministers had gathered all these heads, Aśoka ordered them to go to the market place and sell them. Soon, all of the heads had been sold, except Yaśas's human head that no one would buy. Aśoka then told Yaśas to give his head away, but, even though it was gratis, still no one would take it.

Ashamed at his lack of success, Yaśas came back to Aśoka and said:

O king, the heads of cows, asses, sheep, deer, and birds—
all were sold to people for a price;
but no one would take this worthless human head,
even free of charge.

"Why is that?" Aśoka asked his minister, "why wouldn't anyone accept this human head?"

"Because it disgusted them," Yaśas replied.

"Oh?" said the king, "is it just this head that is disgusting or the heads of all human beings?"

"The heads of all humans," answered Yaśas.

"What?" said Aśoka, "is my head disgusting as well?"

Out of fear, Yaśas did not want to tell him the real fact of the matter, but the king ordered him to speak the truth, and finally he answered: "Yes."

After forcing this admission out of his minister, Aśoka then revealed to him his purpose in doing so: "You, sir, are obsessed with matters of form and superiority, and because of this attachment you seek to dissuade me from bowing down at the feet of the monks."

5. **the Blessed One:** the Buddha.

But if I acquire some merit
by bowing down a head so disgusting
that no one on earth would take it,
even free of charge,
what harm is there in that?
You, sir, look at the caste (jāti)
and not at the inherent qualities of the monks.
Haughty, deluded, and obsessed with caste,
you harm yourself and others.
When you invite someone,
or when it is time for a wedding,
then you should investigate the matter of caste,
but not at the time of Dharma.
For Dharma is a question of qualities,
and qualities do not reflect caste.
If a man of prominent family
happens to resort to vice,
the world censures him.
How then should one not honor virtue
when displayed by a man of low birth?
It is on account of men's minds
that their bodies are reviled or honored;
the minds of the Buddhist monks are pure,
therefore I honor them.

Source 4 from (a) Henry Bettenson, ed., Documents of the Christian Church *(Oxford: Oxford University Press, 1963), p. 15; (b–f) Theodosian Code, trans. and rpt. Maude Aline Huttman,* The Establishment of Christianity and the Proscription of Paganism, *Columbia University Studies in History, Economics and Public Law, no. 60 (New York: AMS Press, 1967), pp. 152, 154, 161–162, 163, 164.*

4. Constantinian Edicts

A. *EDICT OF TOLERATION,* 311

Among our other regulations to promote the lasting good of the community we have hitherto endeavoured to restore a universal conformity to the ancient institutions and public order of the Romans; and in particular it has been our aim to bring back to a right disposition the Christians who had abandoned the religion of their fathers. . . . 3. After the publication of our edict ordering the Christians to conform to the ancient institutions, many of them were brought to order through fear, while many were exposed to danger. 4. Nevertheless, since many still persist in their opinions, and since we have observed that they now neither show due reverence to the gods nor worship their own God, we therefore, with our wonted clemency in extending pardon to all, are pleased to grant indulgence to these men, allowing Christians the right to exist again and to set up their places of worship; provided always that they do not offend against public order. 5. We will in a further instruction explain to the magistrates how they should conduct themselves in this matter. In return for this indulgence of ours it will be the duty of Christians to pray to God for our recovery, for the public weal and for their own; that the state may be preserved from danger on every side, and that they themselves may dwell safely in their homes.

B. OCT. 31, 313 (?)

The Emperor Constantine Augustus. We have learned that the clergy of the Catholic Church are so harrassed by a faction of heretics as to be burdened with nominations to office and common public business, contrary to the exemptions granted to them. Wherefore, it is ordered that if your gravity[6] should find anyone thus annoyed, another man is to be substituted for him, and from henceforth, men of the religion above mentioned are to be protected from wrongs of this kind.

C. MARCH 21, 315 (316?)

The same [Constantine] Augustus to Eumelius.[7] If any one, on account of the crimes in which he is detected, should be condemned to the arena or the mines, by no means let him be branded in the face, although both on his hands and legs the penalty of his condemnation may be marked in a single brand; while the face which is formed in the likeness of heavenly beauty shall not be dishonored.

D. MAY 15, 319

The same [Constantine] Augustus to the People.

We prohibit all soothsayers, priests of prophecy, and those who are wont to administer such rites, from entering a private house, or, under the guise of friendship, from crossing another's threshold. And if they despise this law penalties shall be meted out to them. You, who think this applies to yourselves, go to the public altars and shrines, and celebrate your customary ceremonies, for we do not forbid the full services of ancient tradition from being conducted in the day time.

6. It is unclear to whom this edict was addressed.

7. **Eumelius:** the Vicar of Africa.

E. DEC. 17, 320 (321?)

The Emperor Constantine to Maximus.[8]

If a part of our palace, or any other public building, be struck by lightning, let the customs of the old religion be observed and the haruspices[9] be consulted for the meaning of the omen, and let their words be very carefully brought together and reported to us. Permission for the practice of the custom should also be granted to others, provided that no household sacrifices are made, for these are specifically forbidden.

F. JULY 3, 321

The same [Constantine] Augustus to the People.

Every man, when dying, shall have the right to bequeath as much of his property as he desires to the holy and venerable Catholic Church. And such wills are not to be broken.

Source 5 from Eusebius, Life of Constantine the Great, *trans. Ernest Cushing Richardson, Library of Nicene and Post-Nicene Fathers, second series, vol. 1. (Grand Rapids, Mich.: Eerdmans, 1979), pp. 489, 490–491, 494, 513–514, 523, 525–526, 534, 544, 545, 546.*

5. Selections from Eusebius, *Life of Constantine*

Thus then the God of all, the Supreme Governor of the whole universe, by his own will appointed Constantine, the descendant of so renowned a parent, to be prince and sovereign: so that, while others have been raised to this distinction by the election of their fellow-men, he is the only one to whose elevation no mortal may boast of having contributed. . . .

Being convinced, however, that he [Constantine] needed some more powerful aid than his military forces could afford him, on account of the wicked and magical enchantments which were so diligently practiced by the tyrant,[10] he sought Divine assistance, deeming the possession of arms and a numerous soldiery of secondary importance, but believing the co-operating power of Deity invincible and not to be shaken. He considered, therefore, on what God he might rely for protection and assistance. . . .

8. **Maximus:** the Prefect of the City of Rome.
9. **haruspices:** a traditional Roman religious authority who interpreted the meaning of lightning and other natural events.
10. **the tyrant:** referring to two of Constantine's rivals for authority in the empire, Severus and Galerius.

Accordingly he called on him with earnest prayer and supplications that he would reveal to him who he was, and stretch forth his right hand to help him in his present difficulties. And while he was thus praying with fervent entreaty, a most marvelous sign appeared to him from heaven, the account of which it might have been hard to believe had it been related by any other person. But since the victorious emperor himself long afterwards declared it to the writer of this history,[11] when he was honored with his acquaintance and society, and confirmed his statement by an oath, who could hesitate to accredit the relation, especially since the testimony of after-time has established its truth? He said that about noon, when the day was already beginning to decline, he saw with his own eyes the trophy of a cross of light in the heavens, above the sun, and bearing the inscription, CONQUER BY THIS. At this sight he himself was struck with amazement, and his whole army also, which followed him on this expedition, and witnessed the miracle.

He said, moreover, that he doubted within himself what the import of this apparition could be. And while he continued to ponder and reason on its meaning, night suddenly came on; then in his sleep the Christ of God appeared to him with the same sign which he had seen in the heavens, and commanded him to make a likeness of that sign which he had seen in the heavens, and to use it as a safeguard in all engagements with his enemies.

At dawn of day he arose, and communicated the marvel to his friends: and then, calling together the workers in gold and precious stones, he sat in the midst of them, and described to them the figure of the sign he had seen, bidding them represent it in gold and precious stones. And this representation I myself have had an opportunity of seeing.

Now it was made in the following manner. A long spear, overlaid with gold, formed the figure of the cross by means of a transverse bar laid over it. On the top of the whole was fixed a wreath of gold and precious stones; and within this, the symbol of the Saviour's name, two letters indicating the name of Christ by means of its initial characters, the letter P being intersected by X in its centre: and these letters the emperor was in the habit of wearing on his helmet at a later period. . . .[12]

Thus the pious emperor, glorying in the confession of the victorious cross, proclaimed the Son of God to the Romans with great boldness of testimony. And the inhabitants of the city, one and all, senate and people, reviving, as it were, from the pressure of a bitter and tyrannical domination, seemed to enjoy purer rays of light, and to be born again into a fresh and new life. All the nations, too, as far as the limit of the western ocean, being set free from the calamities which had heretofore beset them, and gladdened by joyous festivals, ceased not to praise him as the victorious, the pious, the common benefactor: all, in-

11. that is, Eusebius.

12. This sign—a cross and the first two letters in Christ's name on the top of a long pole—was called the *labarum*.

deed, with one voice and one mouth, declared that Constantine had appeared by the grace of God as a general blessing to mankind. . . .

The emperor also personally inviting the society of God's ministers, distinguished them with the highest possible respect and honor, showing them favor in deed and word as persons consecrated to the service of his God. Accordingly, they were admitted to his table, though mean in their attire and outward appearance; yet not so in his estimation, since he thought he saw not the man as seen by the vulgar eye, but the God in him. He made them also his companions in travel, believing that He whose servants they were would thus help him. Besides this, he gave from his own private resources costly benefactions to the churches of God, both enlarging and heightening the sacred edifices, and embellishing the august sanctuaries of the church with abundant offerings.

He likewise distributed money largely to those who were in need, and besides these showing himself philanthropist and benefactor even to the heathen, who had no claim on him; and even for the beggars in the forum, miserable and shiftless, he provided, not with money only, or necessary food, but also decent clothing. . . . In short, as the sun, when he rises upon the earth, liberally imparts his rays of light to all, so did Constantine, proceeding at early dawn from the imperial palace, and rising as it were with the heavenly luminary, impart the rays of his own beneficence to all who came into his presence. It was scarcely possible to be near him without receiving some benefit, nor did it ever happen that any who had expected to obtain his assistance were disappointed in their hope. . . .

[*In an edict to the provinces,
Constantine stated:*]

"My own desire is, for the common good of the world and the advantage of all mankind, that thy people should enjoy a life of peace and undisturbed concord. Let those, therefore, who still delight in error, be made welcome to the same degree of peace and tranquillity which they have who believe. For it may be that this restoration of equal privileges to all will prevail to lead them into the straight path. Let no one molest another, but let every one do as his soul desires. Only let men of sound judgment be assured of this, that those only can live a life of holiness and purity, whom thou callest to a reliance on thy holy laws. With regard to those who will hold themselves aloof from us, let them have, if they please, their temples of lies: *we* have the glorious edifice of thy truth, which thou hast given us as our native home. We pray, however, that they too may receive the same blessing, and thus experience that heartfelt joy which unity of sentiment inspires. . . ."

[In 325, Constantine called the Council of Nicaea and addressed the bishops assembled there as follows.]

"[I]n my judgment, intestine strife within the Church of God is far more evil and dangerous than any kind of war or conflict; and these our differences appear to me more grievous than any outward trouble. . . .

"Delay not, then, dear friends: delay not, ye ministers of God, and faithful servants of him who is our common Lord and Saviour: begin from this moment to discard the causes of that disunion which has existed among you, and remove the perplexities of controversy by embracing the principles of peace. For by such conduct you will at the same time be acting in a manner most pleasing to the supreme God, and you will confer an exceeding favor on me who am your fellow-servant. . . ."

All these things the emperor diligently performed to the praise of the saving power of Christ, and thus made it his constant aim to glorify his Saviour God. On the other hand he used every means to rebuke the superstitious errors of the heathen. Hence the entrances of their temples in the several cities were left exposed to the weather, being stripped of their doors at his command; the tiling of others was removed, and their roofs destroyed. . . .

How deeply his soul was impressed by the power of divine faith may be understood from the circumstance that he directed his likeness to be stamped on the golden coin of the empire with the eyes uplifted as in the posture of prayer to God: and this money became current throughout the Roman world. His portrait also at full length was placed over the entrance gates of the palaces in some cities, the eyes upraised to heaven, and the hands outspread as if in prayer. . . .

With regard to those who were as yet ignorant of divine truth, he provided by a second statute that they should appear on each Lord's day on an open plain near the city, and there, at a given signal, offer to God with one accord a prayer which they had previously learnt. He admonished them that their confidence should not rest in their spears, or armor, or bodily strength, but that they should acknowledge the supreme God as the giver of every good, and of victory itself. . . . The emperor himself prescribed the prayer to be used by all his troops. . . .

Hence it was not without reason that once, on the occasion of his entertaining a company of bishops, he let fall the expression, "that he himself too was a bishop," addressing them in my hearing in the following words: "You are bishops whose jurisdiction is within the Church: I also am a bishop, ordained by God to overlook whatever is external to the Church." And truly his measures corresponded with his words; for he watched over his subjects with an episcopal [as a bishop] care, and exhorted them as far as in him lay to follow a godly life.

Source 6: Top photograph from the Ashmolean Museum, Oxford. Bottom photograph is Courtesy of the Trustees of the British Museum.

6. Two Constantinian Coins

Source 7 from A. J. Arberry, The Koran Interpreted *(Oxford: Oxford University Press, 1964).*

7. Selections from the Qur'an

O you who believe! Obey God and obey the Prophet and those of you who hold authority. (Sura 4:59)

God has promised those of you who believe and do wholesome deeds that He will surely make you successors in the land, as he made successors of those before you, and He will surely establish for them as their service (*dīn*) what He approves for them, and exchange for them, after their fear, security: "They shall serve Me, not associating with Me anything." (Sura 24:55)

There is no compulsion in matters of faith. Distinct now is the way of guidance from error. He who turns away from the forces of evil and believes in God, will surely hold fast to a handle that is strong and unbreakable, for God hears all and knows everything. (Sura 2:256)

Say (O Muslims): We believe in God and that which is revealed unto us and that which was revealed unto Abraham and Ishmael and Isaac and Jacob, and the tribes, and that which Moses and Jesus received, and that which the Prophets received from their Lord. We make no distinction between any of them, and unto Him we have surrendered. (Sura 2:136)

Source 8 from (a) Al-Muttaqi, Kanz-al-'Ummāl, *in Bernard Lewis, ed. and trans.,* Islam from the Prophet Muhammad to the Capture of Constantinople, *vol. 1 (New York: Oxford University Press, 1987), p. 150; (b) Al-Khaṭīb al-Tibrīzī,* Niches of Lamps, *in John Alden Williams, ed.,* Themes of Islamic Civilization *(Berkeley: University of California Press, 1971), pp. 65–67; (c) An-Nawawī,* The Forty Traditions, *in Arthur Jeffrey, ed.,* A Reader on Islam: Passages from Standard Arabic Writings Illustrative of the Beliefs and Practices of Muslims *(Gravenhage: Mouton and Company, 1962), p. 154.*

8. Selections from the Hadith

a. I charge the Caliph after me to fear God, and I commend the community of the Muslims to him, to respect the great among them and have pity on the small, to honor the learned among them, not to strike them and humiliate them, not to oppress them and drive them to unbelief, not to close his doors to them and allow the strong to devour the weak.

b. Bukhārī and Muslim, from Abū Hurayra: The Messenger of God, may God's blessing and peace be on him, said "Whoever obeys me obeys God, and whoever disobeys me disobeys God. Whoever obeys the Commander obeys me, and he who disobeys him disobeys me."

Muslim, from Umm al-Ḥuṣayn: The Messenger, may God bless him and give him peace, said "Even if a mutilated slave is made your commander, and he leads you in accord with the Book of God, hear him and obey."

Bukhārī, from Anas: The Messenger of God, the blessing of God and peace be upon him, said "Hear and obey, though an Abyssinian slave with a head like a raisin be placed over you."

Bukhārī and Muslim, from 'Umar's son: The Messenger of God—God's benediction and peace upon him—said "Hearing and obeying are incumbent on a Muslim man, so long as he is not ordered to disobey God. When he is ordered to do that, there is no hearing it and no obeying." 'Alī reported a similar tradition.

Bukhārī and Muslim, from 'Umar's son: The Messenger said—may God give him peace and blessing—"Is not each of you a shepherd, who must answer for his flock? The Imām of the people is a shepherd, and is answerable for his flock. A man is the shepherd of the people in his house, and he is answerable for his flock. A woman is shepherdess of her husband's house and children, and is answerable for them, and a slave is the shepherd of his master's wealth and is answerable for that. Thus each of you is a shepherd, and each of you is responsible for his flock."

Muslim, from 'Arfaja: I heard the Messenger of God, peace and God's blessing be upon him, say "If anyone comes to you when you are united under one man, and tries to split you or divide your Umma, then kill him."

Bayhaqī, from 'Umar's son: The Prophet, God bless him and give him peace, said "The Government (*al-Sultān*) is the shadow of God on the earth; all of His servants who are oppressed shall turn to it. When it is just, it shall be rewarded, and the flock must be grateful. When it is tyrannical, the burden is upon it, and the flock must be patient."

c. From Abu Najih al-Irbad ibn Sariya, with whom may God be pleased, who said: The Messenger of God, may God's blessing and peace be upon him, preached a sermon whereby our hearts were made afraid and our eyes dropped tears, so we said: "O Messenger of God, it is as though this were a farewell sermon, so give us a testamentary exhortation." He said: "My testamentary exhortation to you is that you have a pious fear of God, magnified and exalted be He; that you hearken and obey, even though it should be a slave who is appointed over you. He among you who lives long enough will see great disagreement, so take care to observe my custom and the custom of the Rightly Guided Caliphs [that is, the first four: Abu Bakr, Umar, Uthman, and Ali], holding on to them with your molar teeth. Beware of matters newly introduced, for every innovation is an error." So Abu Dawud relates it, as does al-Tirmidhi, who says, "An excellent, sound Prophetic tradition."

Source 9 from Ibn Ishaq, The Life of Muhammad, Apostle of Allah, *ed. and trans. Michael Edwards (London: The Folio Society, 1964), pp. 35, 36–37, 41, 54, 65, 74, 104, 150, 156–157, 165.*

9. Selections from Ibn Ishaq, *The Life of Muhammad, Apostle of Allah*

When Muhammad was forty years old Allah sent him as a prophet of mercy to the people of the visible and of the invisible worlds, and to all mankind. . . .

Every year the apostle of Allah spent a month praying at Hira and fed the poor who came to him; and when he returned to Mecca he walked round the Kaba[13] seven or more times, as it pleased Allah, before entering his own house. In the month of Ramadan,[14] in the year when Allah designed to bestow grace upon him, the apostle of Allah went to [Mount] Hira as usual, and his family accompanied him. In the night the angel Gabriel came with the command of Allah. The apostle of Allah later said, "He came while I was asleep, with a cloth of brocade whereon there was writing, and he said, 'Read.' I replied, 'I cannot read it.' Then he pressed the cloth on me till I thought I was dying; he released his hold and said, 'Read.' I replied, 'I cannot read it.' And he pressed me again with it, till I thought I was dying. Then he loosed his hold of me and said, 'Read.' I replied, 'I cannot read it.' Once more he pressed me and said, 'Read.' Then I asked, 'What shall I read?' And I said this because I feared he would press me again. Then he said, 'Read in the name of the Lord thy creator; who created man from a drop of blood. Read, thy Lord is the most bountiful, who taught by means of the pen, taught man what he knew not.' Accordingly I read these words, and he finished his task and departed from me. I awoke from my sleep, and felt as if words had been graven on my heart.

"Afterwards I went out, and when I was on the centre of the mountain, I heard a voice from heaven, saying, 'O Muhammad! Thou art the prophet of Allah, and I am Gabriel.' I raised my head to look at the sky, and lo! I beheld Gabriel in the shape of a man with extended wings, standing in the firmament, with his feet touching the ground. And he said again, 'O Muhammad! Thou art the apostle of Allah, and I am Gabriel.' I continued to gaze at him, neither advancing nor retreating. Then I turned my face away from him to other parts of the sky, but in whatever direction I looked I saw him in the same form. I remained thus, neither advancing nor retreating, and Khadija [Muhammad's first

13. **Kaba:** a house containing a black stone venerated by Arabs before Muhammad, which was retained as the most holy place in Islam.

14. **Ramadan:** ninth month of the Muslim lunar year, which came to be viewed as holy because the first of Muhammad's revelations occurred during this month.

wife] sent messengers to search for me. They went as far as the highest part of Mecca and again returned to her, while I remained standing on the same spot, until the angel departed from me and I returned to my family. . . ."

Soon several men and women had made their profession of Islam and it was much discussed in Mecca. Then Allah commanded his apostle to make public the revelation and to invite the people to accept it; hitherto, for the three years since his first revelation, it had been kept secret by the apostle. Allah said to him, "Publish that which thou hast been commanded, and turn away from the idolaters."

When the apostle began to spread Islam among his people as Allah had commanded him, they did not gainsay him until he began to abuse their idols; but when he had done this, they accused him of seeking power, denied his revelation, and united to injure him. The companions of the apostle of Allah went into the valleys to pray, unknown to the people; and once, whilst Sad and several companions of the apostle were at prayer, they were discovered by idolaters who heaped insults upon them, condemned their deeds, and provoked them to fight. Then Sad struck an idolater with the jawbone of a camel, and wounded him; and this was the first blood shed in Islam.

The apostle of Allah never failed to attempt the conversion of any man of note or position who came to Mecca. . . .

When Allah gave His apostle permission to wage war, the promise to fight immediately became a condition of allegiance to Islam. This had not been so at the first meeting on the hillside, when homage was paid "in the manner of women"; Allah had not then given His apostle permission to fight. He had given permission neither to wage war nor to shed blood, but only to call men to Allah, to endure insults patiently, and to pardon the ignorant. Some of the followers of the apostle had therefore been forced to flee from persecution into the countryside, some to Abyssinia, others to Medina and elsewhere.

[*Muhammad and his followers left Mecca for Medina.*]

The apostle of Allah remained in Medina until the following year when his mosque and his dwellings were built. He worked on them with his own hands to encourage his followers. Islam in Medina soon became so complete that only a handful of houses remained whose tenants had not made profession of Islam.

[*After a defeat of Meccan forces, Muhammad said:*]

"'. . . Whenever you win plunder, a fifth shall belong to Allah and His apostle, and his kindred, and orphans, and the poor, and the traveller.

"'. . . When you meet an army in battle, stand firm and remember Allah, that you may prosper; and do not quarrel, lest My cause should suffer. Be not like those who make parade of their deeds in pursuit of the approbation of men, but act purely for the sake of Allah and for His reward in giving your religion victory; work only for this, and covet nothing else. . . . Prepare against the infidels what force you are able, that you may strike terror into your enemy and that of Allah. And whatever you shall expend for the religion of Allah, it shall be repaid unto you, and you shall not be without reward. But if they incline to peace, do you also incline to peace; and trust in Allah, for He heareth and knoweth all things. . . ."

The apostle sent out expeditions to the surrounding territory to invite the people to Allah, but not to kill. . . . The apostle of Allah specially exhorted the rich to furnish money and beasts of burden and they did so, hoping for the eternal reward; Uthman was the most liberal of them, and the apostle said, "Allah! Be pleased with Uthman; for I am pleased with him!"

When the apostle of Allah had conquered Mecca and completed the campaign of Tabuk, and when al-Taif[15] had surrendered and made profession of Islam, deputations of Arabs arrived from all directions. This, the ninth year after the Hijra, was called the Year of Deputations. The Arabs had delayed professing Islam until they saw how the affair between the apostle and the Quraysh[16] would end, because the Quraysh were the leaders of men, the people of the Kaba and of the sacred territory, and they were acknowledged as the descendants of Ishmael, son of Abraham. Not one chief of the Arabs denied this. But when Mecca was conquered and the Quraysh submitted to Islam, the Arabs knew that they themselves were not strong enough to wage war or to show enmity to the apostle of Allah. So they entered into the religion of Allah in droves, arriving from all directions.

Source 10 from Abū Yūsuf, Kitāb al-Kharāj, *in John Alden Williams, ed.,* Themes of Islamic Civilization *(Berkeley: University of California Press, 1971), pp. 68–69, 72.*

10. From Abu Yusuf (d. A.H. 182/798 C.E.), *Book of Land-tax*

"I have heard," says Abū Yūsuf, "from Ismā'īl ibn Abī Khālid, on the authority of Zubayd ibn al-Ḥārith, that when death was drawing near to Abū Bakr, he sent for 'Umar to make him the Caliph, his successor, and people said 'Will you appoint as Caliph over us this hard, harsh man to be hard and harsh to us? What will you say to your Lord when you meet Him having appointed 'Umar over us?' He said 'Would you frighten me with my Lord? I shall tell Him "God, I have appointed over them the best of Thy people!" ' Then he sent for 'Umar

15. **Tabuk** and **al-Taif:** cities in the northern part of Arabia.
16. **Quraysh:** Muhammad's tribe, the leading tribe in Mecca.

and said 'I shall give you a piece of advice such that if you follow it, nothing will be dearer to you than your death when it comes, and if you do not follow it, nothing will be more hateful to you than the death you shall not escape. You have obligations to God at night that He will not accept from you by day, and obligations by day that He will not accept at night, and a work of supererogation is not accepted until after the performance of the obligatory works. The scales on Judgement Day will not weigh lighter for anyone than for those who sought light things, and they will not weigh heavier for anyone than for the man who sought justice in the world. . . . I have only appointed you my successor thinking of those whom I leave behind me. For I was a Companion of the Prophet, and saw one who preferred us to himself, and our people to his own family, so that we should give to them from the abundance of what is given to us. You have been my companion, and you have seen that I have only followed the path of him who was before me, and the first thing I counsel you against, 'Umar, is your self, for every self has selfish desires, and if one gives in to one of them, it demands another. Beware also of those persons among the Companions of the Messenger of God who have filled their bellies and raised their eyes. Every man of them loves himself, and all of them will be in perplexity if one of them stumbles. Take care that that one is not you. They will never cease to fear you so long as you fear God, or cease to go straight with you so long as your way is straight. That is my counsel to you, and now I wish you farewell.' "

When 'Umar was dying, he left this advice: "I advise my successor to fear God, and to respect the rights and the merits of the first emigrants to Medina; and as to the Anṣār, who lived in Medina, and in the Faith, to accept their good deeds and to be indulgent to the bad among them. As to the people of the garrison towns, they are the help of Islam, the fury of the enemy, and the bringers of wealth, so he should take only their superfluity, and by their agreement. I advise him as to the beduins that they are the source of the Arabs, and the raw stuff of Islam, and he should take only a little of their possessions, to return to the poorest among them. As to the protected peoples, let him fulfill his agreement with them and fight their enemies and not burden them beyond their endurance. . . . "

Source 11 from The Nasser D. Khalili Collection of Islamic Art. MSS 727, folio 66a.

11. Muhammad Addresses Ali and Other Leaders Before the Battle of Badr, from Rashid al-Din, *Jami'al-tawarikh*

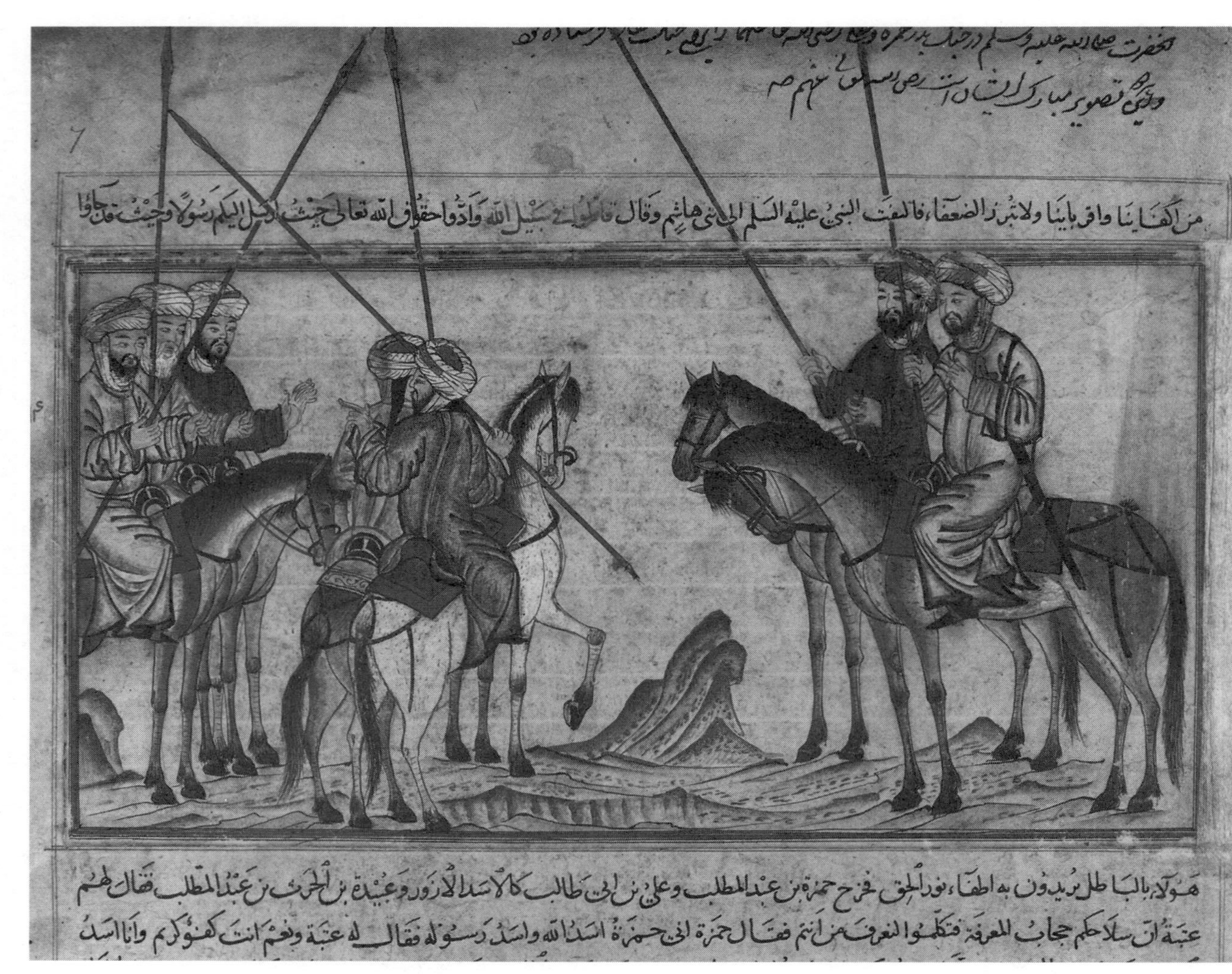

QUESTIONS TO CONSIDER

Before you begin to make specific comparisons between the leaders and their methods of advancing their religious commitments, you should probably step back a minute and think about the different types of sources you have used. In some cases, there are quite comparable sources for two cases, but not for the third. For example, it is clear that both Ashoka and Constantine ordered the edicts included in the evidence to be inscribed or issued; we have nothing directly comparable for Muhammad. Our ability to compare the edicts of Ashoka and Constantine stops with the texts themselves, however, for though we have quite a bit of evidence about how Constantine and his successors enforced his edicts and proclamations, we have no way of knowing what impact Ashoka's edicts had on his actual reign. The language in which Ashoka's edicts were written ceased to be spoken shortly after his reign, so subsequent generations could not read them; in fact, the script in which they were written was deciphered for the first time only in 1837. Unlike the stories of Constantine told by Eusebius and others, the legends that grew up about Ashoka, including the one you read here, did so without reference to his actual edicts; people claimed the inscriptions referred to events in the legends, but they had no way of actually reading them the way Roman Christians could the laws and proclamations of Constantine.

For another example of similarity, the biographies of Eusebius and Ibn Ishaq are more like each other than the *Asokavadana.* All of these contain material that may be in the realm of legend, but we can check both Eusebius and Ibn Ishaq against other sources, something that is not possible for the *Asokavadana.* Eusebius in particular also notes his source when he is telling something his readers may have difficulty believing; in the section on Constantine's vision of the cross, for example, he stresses that Constantine himself told him about this, using "he said" rather than relating the story directly the way most of the biography is written. This same noting of sources appears even more prominently in the hadith (Source 8), where it serves to stress the authenticity of the words of Muhammad. Most of the hadith were actually written in the two centuries after Muhammad's life, when Islam had already split into Sunni and Shi'ite factions, and they are interpreted so as to argue one point of view or another. As you can see, for example, Source 8c gives a Sunni view of Muhammad's last words.

Keeping the limitations of our sources in mind, then, you can begin to compare the actions and ideas of the individuals and groups. Ashoka, Constantine, and Muhammad all had clear conversion experiences. How would you compare these and the actions that resulted directly from them? How do these experiences shape their attitudes toward military conquest as a means of expanding a religious community? What humanitarian aims develop after the conversions, and how do they seek to achieve these?

All of these leaders had to deal with dissenters—both people who followed other religious traditions and those within their own religion who disagreed with them. How did the leaders enforce their own views? What did they advise regarding the toleration of those who disagreed? How important was unity within their religious community to these leaders? Ashoka and Constantine each had to foster a relationship with a body of clergy that already existed, the Buddhist sangha and the Christian bishops. How would you characterize their relationship with these clerics? Where did ultimate authority lie in terms of making religious policy? (For some of these questions, the sources may give contradictory information, and you may wish to turn to your textbook for further information, or else simply note the contradiction.)

The sources for each of the three groups make explicit reference to the conflict between social status and religious status or authority. How do the leaders treat individuals of modest social status but high religious or moral status? What advice do they give to their followers in this regard? The relationship between church and state is much discussed in the contemporary American political scene. What do these sources reveal about this relationship in these three religious traditions? In the minds of these leaders, should the religious community and the political community be unified, related, or separate?

Though all of these sources describe the actions of real individuals, they also convey what each tradition regarded as qualities of the ideal ruler. How would you compare the ideal ruler in these three traditions? What qualities would ideal religious communities exhibit under the leadership of such individuals? From your initial lists and comparisons, you are now ready to answer the central questions in this chapter: How did political leaders within Buddhism, Christianity, and Islam encourage the growth of their chosen religious community? What differences and similarities do you see in their actions and in what they viewed as most important in the lives of these communities?

EPILOGUE

The three religions we have explored in this chapter are three of the four largest religions found in the world today: Buddhism has around 309 million adherents, Christianity 1.8 billion, and Islam 950 million.[17] (The fourth major world religion is Hinduism with 720 million adherents, though it is more concentrated in certain geographic areas than the other three.) All three of these continue to be missionary religions; that is, they seek new converts just as they did in the days of Ashoka, Constantine, and Muhammad. Some of the issues we have explored in this chapter continue to be matters of concern or over the cen-

17. These numbers represent 1992 statistics and come from David Chrystal, ed., *The Cambridge Factfinder* (Cambridge: Cambridge University Press, 1993). There are, of course, many ways to count allegiance to religion, and the numbers change every day, so these are estimates.

turies have become even more complicated.

For example, each of these religions has splintered further since the periods we focused on in this chapter. Shortly after Ashoka's reign, Buddhism split into two main groups, Mahayana and Theravada (sometimes called Hinayana), and then continued to divide into a number of different sects. Christianity gradually divided into two main churches, Roman Catholicism and Eastern Orthodoxy, and the Roman Catholic Church was further split by the Protestant Reformation in the sixteenth century. New Christian denominations are created every year as groups choose to emphasize certain aspects of Christian teaching. The rift between Shi'ites and Sunnis was only the first of many within Islam, for Shi'ites themselves divided into two major groups, and other sects developed as well. Thus the unity sought by the leaders we have investigated has not been achieved, although there are movements within each of these three religions today to heal internal schisms or at least to downplay them in a desire for tolerance and understanding.

As these three religions have expanded, they have continued to confront the issue of the relationship between church and state, between the religious and political community. In some cases, the relationship is extremely intimate, in that all three are official state religions in some countries of the world. This role may have a widely differing impact, however. In some of the countries of the Middle East, for example, Islam structures almost all aspects of life, whereas in some European countries that are officially Christian, few people attend church and the church has little impact on national policies. Even in those countries where the power of the state church is extremely strong, there are still disputes about overlapping or conflicting authority and the proper role of religious leaders: Should they be spiritual guides or heads of state?

On the other hand, many adherents of these religions live in countries where their religion is not the one sanctioned by the state, or where there is no official state religion, such as the United States. They, and their religious leaders, thus have to address the issues we have explored in this chapter in a different way. What should the relationship between the religious and political communities be in a country of religious pluralism? How should a person's allegiance to a country be weighed against allegiance to a religion? What are the limits of acceptable diversity within a religious community, and who has the power of exclusion? How do you handle someone who violates what is viewed as God's law in a religious tradition but has broken no state laws? Should there be a line between church and state, between the sacred and profane? Should political leaders follow the path of Ashoka, Constantine, and Muhammad and seek to expand their own religion, or should such crusades be left to those who do not hold public office?

None of these were issues when religion was closely tied to membership in a particular tribe or residence in a particular village, but as religions became international, as they came to be practiced by people over large geographic areas, the questions became pressing and problematic. Conflicts within and between religious communities are some of the most bitter, deadly, and long-lasting in the world today, and the words of Ashoka, carved in stone over two thousand years ago, still bear repeating: "The faiths of others all deserve to be honored for one reason or another. By honoring them, one exalts one's own faith and at the same time performs a service to the faith of others. By acting otherwise, one injures one's own faith and also does disservice to that of others."

CHAPTER SIX

VIKINGS AND POLYNESIANS:

EXPLORING NEW WORLDS

(300–1100)

THE PROBLEM

William Fitzhugh, the curator of a new exhibit on Vikings at the Smithsonian Institution, has recently warned that the historical record has badly distorted our view of early Scandinavians. "Only in the past 20 years or so," he points out, "have archeological and other studies begun to provide information that fleshes out and in some cases contradicts or even replaces the historical record. . . . This contrasts sharply with the early accounts, which were all from Europe, were inevitably based on victims' reports, and were extremely one-sided."[1]

The portrayal of Vikings represents a common historical problem: how people who left few or no writings of their own appear in the historical record. The study of history has traditionally been based on evidence gleaned from written sources. But this approach has forced us to view the past almost exclusively from the vantage point of literate people, the ones who kept written records—often a small minority. The narrowness of their perspective, troubling enough with regard to their own societies, becomes highly problematic when they discuss neighbors who were nonliterate or who failed to keep historical records. For they often lacked a complete or dispassionate picture of those whose "history" they presumed to tell.

This chapter addresses the problem of how to deal with these voiceless people of history by looking at two outstanding examples that have begun to attract considerable attention of late, the Vikings and the Polynesians. Both were long relegated to the role of archetypal "barbarians," either

1. William Fitzhugh's remarks appeared in an interview on a *Nova* program on the Vikings, for which a partial transcript has been made available on *Nova*'s web site, **http://www.pbs.org/wgbh/nova/vikings/who.html.**

as brutal despoilers in the case of the Vikings or as noble savages in the case of the Polynesians. Recently, however, some scholars have begun to argue that both of these seafaring peoples developed advanced maritime technologies that allowed them to carry out significant voyages of discovery, trade, and colonization long before the modern age of Western European exploration began and thus merit greater acknowledgment for their accomplishments.

Most of these findings come from nontraditional methods of historical study. Many depend upon the use of techniques that allow us to interpret the past through "material culture" or physical remains. With these methods, historians not only recover artifacts from the past but deduce from them information about how their makers lived and thought. New ways of studying oral traditions handed down by nonliterate people have also supplied historians with yet another set of tools. Together with recent scientific techniques, these approaches allow us to explore the world of formerly "voiceless" peoples as never before. In this chapter, you will have a chance to compare evidence relating to the Vikings and Polynesians that derives from some of these new approaches as well as from more traditional sources.

Your task in looking over this material is to decide how seriously these new findings need to be taken. That question is not a simple one to resolve, for it involves dealing with a number of other questions as well. First and foremost, of course, is there sufficient evidence to indicate that these peoples did carry out major voyages of discovery and colonization? Second, if they did, what was significant about these achievements from a historical point of view? That is to say, what impact or effect did they have on other peoples, past or present? This last issue raises a still broader question to think about, although the answer is not to be found in the evidence: What value is there in studying people whose experience and feats have long been lost or forgotten?

THE BACKGROUND

Reconsideration of the Vikings' reputation dates from the early 1960s, when the Norwegian Helge Ingstad and his archaeologist wife, Anne Stine Ingstad, discovered the remains of a Scandinavian settlement in North America at L'Anse aux Meadows on the Newfoundland coast of Canada. Although scholars had long known of Icelandic sagas or tales that spoke of Viking visits to a place called *Vinland,* or Wine Land, west of Greenland, they had dismissed them as fanciful. But evidence found at L'Anse aux Meadows revealed that some Vikings did make it to America around the year 1000, nearly five centuries before Columbus's celebrated voyage of 1492. In the years since 1960, further work has shown that the Viking discovery of America was only one part of a vast maritime expansion of Scandinavian people during the years from 750 to 1050, an era that has come to be called the Viking Age. To appreciate the scale of this expansion, which reached from the Casian Sea to the shores of Labrador, look at the map on page 146.

Before their great expansion began, the Vikings dwelt in southern Scandinavia, where their forebears had settled in late Roman times. An offshoot of Germanic peoples, they were already differentiating into Danes, Norwegians, and Swedes, but they still shared a common language, called Norse, and continued to worship old Germanic gods like Odin, Thor, and Frey. Because of the harsh winters and short growing seasons in their homeland, they could not rely entirely on cereal crops for food and engaged in herding, hunting, and trapping to survive. Given the territorial demands of this lifestyle, they usually lived dispersed on individual farms or in small hamlets. Political unification was difficult under these circumstances, and regional lords called *Jarls* ruled through local landed elites. Beneath these freemen, who could hold estates, command others, and speak out in a council known as a *thing,* was an enslaved class of *thralls* burdened with menial work.

Living around the North Sea, Scandinavians early came to rely on ships for communication and trade. Archaeological finds from Denmark reveal that people there devised the forerunner of the famous "longboat" well before the Viking Age. Fourth-century ships unearthed in a Danish bog at Nydam Mose already show most of its characteristics: the tall, matching, upcurved bow and stern, the "clinker-built" or overlapping oak side planks, and the open hull fitted with dozens of long oars. Only the addition of a mast and woolen sail, innovations that came in the seventh or eighth century, were required to complete the evolution of this unique craft. Shallow in draft to negotiate the fiords and coastal streams of Scandinavia yet flexibly built to withstand the forces of ocean storms, the Viking longboat was the basis of a maritime tradition that was unequaled in Europe until the Portuguese and Spanish developed an alternative one in the fifteenth century.

Such ships enabled Viking expansion, but they did not cause it. Christian churchmen, beginning with Alcuin, attributed it to God's doing, deeming Viking raids punishment for religious laxity. But an eleventh-century Saxon cleric claimed that it resulted from overpopulation and poverty in the Viking homeland. His view accords with accounts in a thirteenth-century Icelandic source called the *Landnámábok* or *Book of Settlement.* It portrays early Norse émigrés to the Atlantic islands as landless sons, social outcasts, and political refugees—all forced by adversity to leave their homes in search of opportunities elsewhere, much like later European immigrants to the New World.[2]

Whatever its causes, Viking emigration flowed in many directions. Danes spread south across modern Holland and France, then on to England or down through Spain into the Mediterranean. Swedes swept east across the Baltic Sea into Slavic lands to the

2. Adam of Bremen, *History of the Archbishops of Hamburg-Bremen,* trans. Francs J. Tscan (New York: Columbia University Press, 1959), p. 211.

Viking Expansion

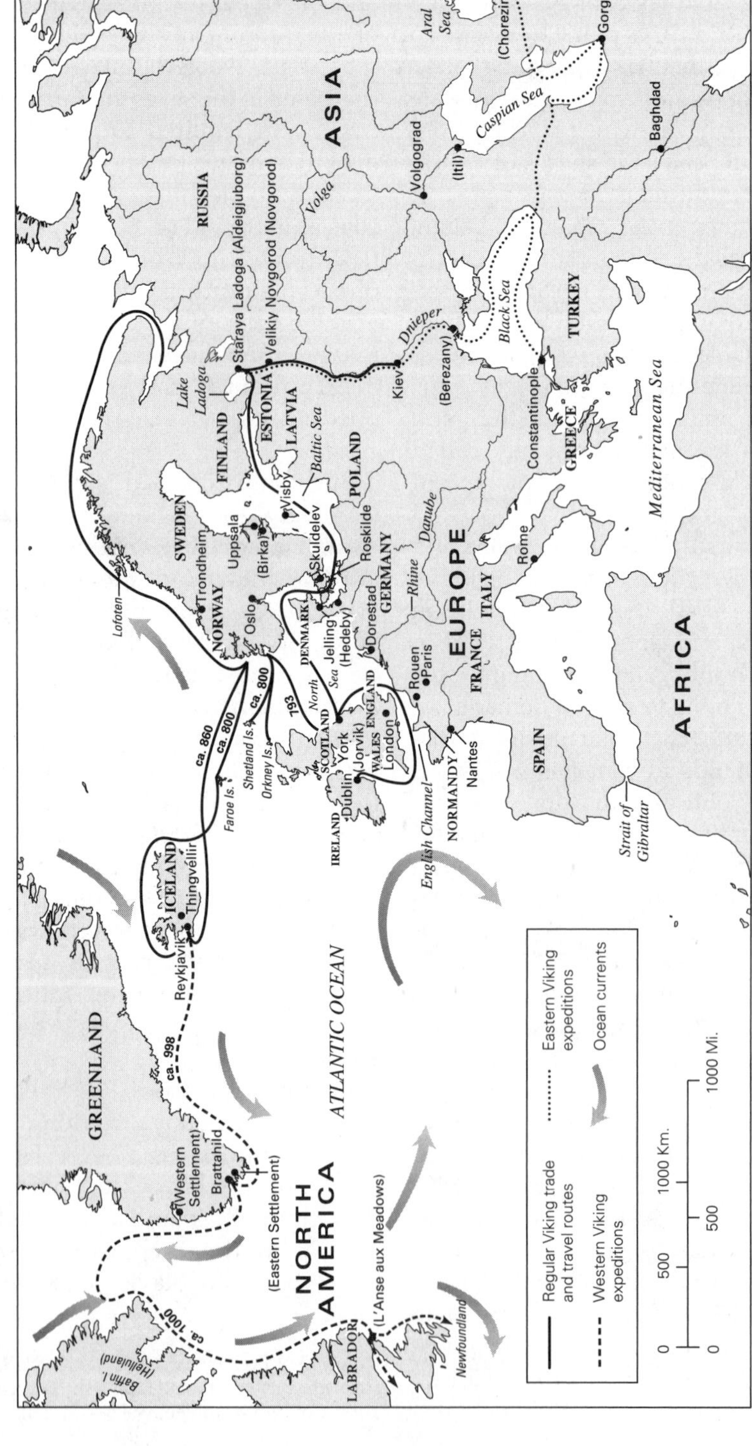

Source: Adapted from National Geographic, *vol. 197, no. 5 (May 2000): 12–13. Map by Laszlo Kubinyi/NGS Image Collection.*

fringes of the Byzantine and Islamic worlds. And Norwegians ventured west, hopping from one island to another across the North Atlantic. Settled neighbors seldom grasped the full scope of this exodus. Western Europeans were as unfamiliar with Viking voyages across the Atlantic or down the Volga River in Russia as Eastern peoples were of their western migrations Slavs called them the *Rus* (a Baltic term later appropriated by Russians), while Byzantine Greeks, who prized their fighting ability and recruited them as mercenaries, called them Varangians. Such names meant nothing to Western Europeans, who dubbed them the Normanni or Normans, meaning men of the north. When meeting former members of the Varangian Guard who were accompanying a Byzantine embassy, Frankish rulers were amazed to learn that they were akin to the Normans.

Most of these migrations began as small enterprises organized by a local chieftain to explore opportunities abroad. If successful, the chieftain would return to recruit additional chieftains and their war bands to accompany him on larger expeditions to establish beachheads from which they could march inland to pillage the countryside and collect *danegeld,* or tribute. If unopposed, they would proceed to seize land and impose their rule over the indigenous people, creating colonies that would attract further immigration from Scandinavia. By the late ninth century, Viking colonies spread across most of northern Europe and the North Atlantic. Swedes not only established important trade sites like Staraja Ladoga and Novgorod in Russia but founded the first known state there at Kiev. Meanwhile, Danes overran much of Britain after carving out enclaves throughout the coastal Netherlands and France, and Norwegians seized the Faroe, Orkney, and Shetland Islands before planting the first European settlements in Iceland and Greenland. Some of these lands, like the duchy of Normandy in France, they held as nominal fiefs under local rulers, but more often they ruled them independently, as they did in the British Isles, where they established separate kingdoms centered in York, Dublin, and the Isle of Man.

Contact between these enclaves and the Viking homeland nourished trade. Centers like Birka in Sweden and Heddeby in Denmark became rich and important cities as commerce flowed into them from regional markets as far off as Dublin and York in the west and Staraja Ladoga and Kiev in the east. For a while, a vast network of Viking-controlled trade linked the North Atlantic and Middle East into a single great market with Europe. Danish and Norwegian rulers made occasional efforts to unify this far-flung Viking world. Knut the Great of Denmark almost succeeded in the early eleventh century, bringing the Danes, Norwegians, English, Atlantic outliers, and some Swedes together in a brief-lived northern empire that lasted until his death in 1035. But his reign marked both the apogee of the Viking world and the start of its collapse. Over the ensuing two centuries, it broke apart as assimilation into local populations and conversion to Christianity deprived it of a common Scandinavian language and identity.

Pacific Migrations

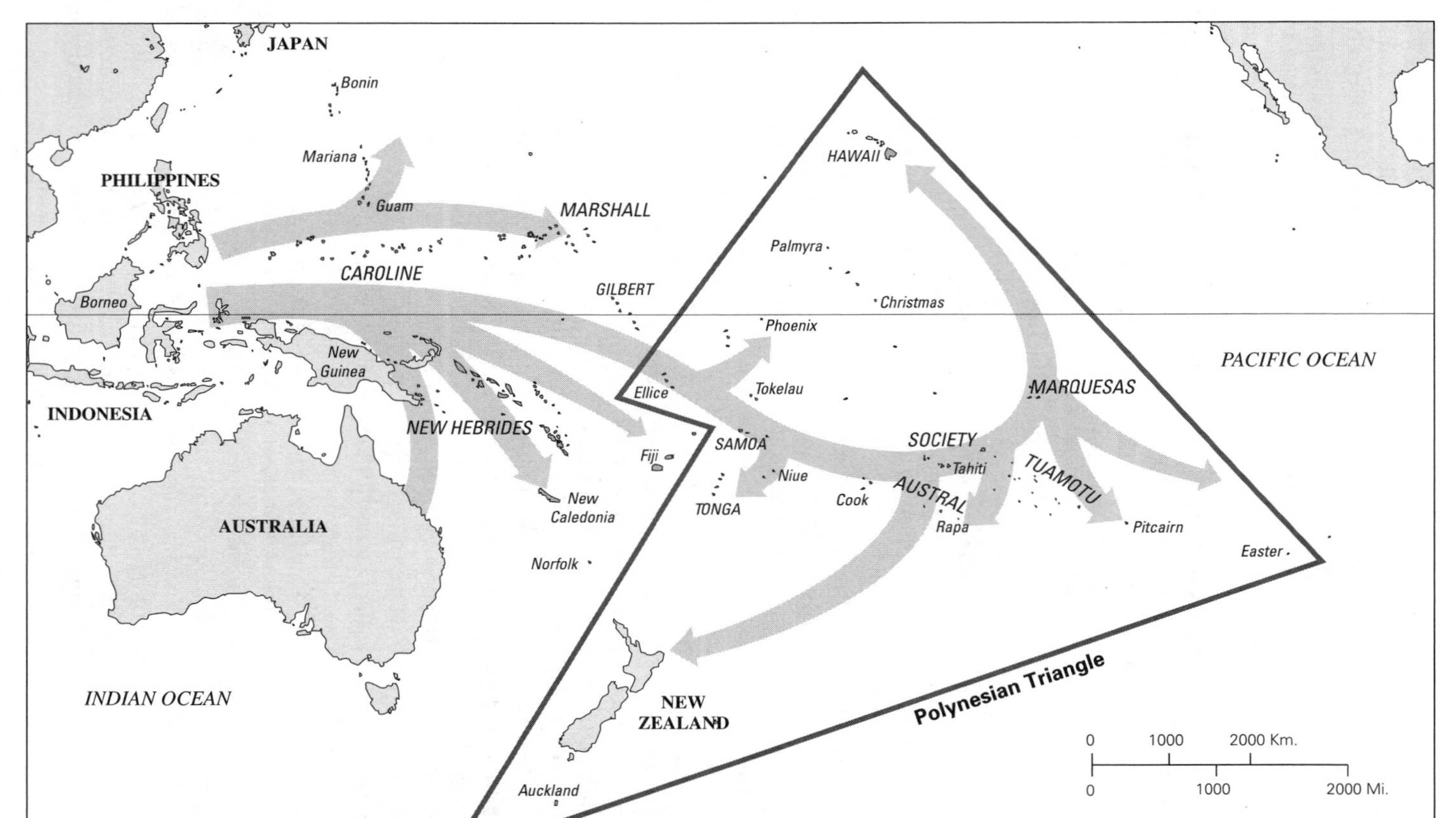

Source: Tommy Holmes, The Hawaiian Canoe *(Honolulu: Editions Limited, 1981), p. 4.*

A similar expansion and fragmentation occurred among the Polynesian peoples of the Pacific, although they are much less well understood. Long ignored by scholars, Polynesia began to attract attention in 1947 when adventurers captained by a modern "Viking," the Norwegian Thor Heyerdahl, sailed a balsa raft from Peru to Raroia Atoll in the Tuaomotu Islands to prove that South American Indians could have peopled the region. Though Heyerdahl's subsequent effort to elaborate his theory of South American colonization in a popular book called *Kon-tiki,* published in 1952, generated many scholarly rebuttals, his dramatic voyage had much the same effect on Polynesian studies as the Ingstads' discovery of the L'Anse aux Meadows site had on Viking studies, sparking a new era of research based upon innovative approaches. Until then, little was known of the Polynesian past, for the Polynesians (with but one exception) neither possessed writing themselves nor encountered literate people who could record their history until Europeans reached the Pacific in the sixteenth century. By then, most Polynesians had lost the ability to conduct distant voyages and, following long isolation on widely scattered islands, had only vague memories left of their origins.

Recent discoveries, however, suggest that their ancestors spread four thousand miles across the central Pacific to colonize the vast complex of islands known as Polynesia. As you can see from the map on page 148, most of Polynesia falls within a great triangle with its points at Hawaii in the north, New Zealand in the southwest, and Easter Island in the east, although a scattering of outlying islands stretches westward between Melanesia and Micronesia. Despite being dispersed over an area twice the size of the United States, Polynesians remain a relatively homogeneous population, speaking closely related languages of the Austronesian family that derive from a single ancestral form spoken back around 1500 B.C.E. Archaeological findings, though sparse for Polynesia as a whole, shed some light on that formative era. They show that from 1500 to 500 B.C.E., a Lapita culture with a distinctive pottery tradition flourished along an island chain running from New Guinea through Fiji to Tonga and Samoa. Not yet true farmers, the Lapita people were horticulturists who set plants out in temporary clearings created by slash and burn methods. But they already grew taro, yams, and breadfruit, the staples of later Polynesian life, and kept the region's only domesticated animals: pigs, chickens, and dogs. They must have already been good sailors, too, for they spread over closely spaced islands as far as Tonga and Samoa. Unlike the low atolls and rocky islands of the western Pacific, these islands are high and volcanic, with features more akin to those further east in the central Pacific. Here, where clay and stone materials were sparse and plant and animal life restricted, Lapita colonists had to adapt to a more typically Polynesian environment, fashioning baskets in place of clay pots, making implements out of shells and pumice rather than hard rock, and turning from the land to the sea for food. Tonga and Samoa thus seem most likely to be the places where

Polynesians first emerged as a distinct people.

Before they could voyage into the central and eastern Pacific, where distances between islands were much greater, however, they had to perfect better craft than the outrigger canoes that ostensibly brought their Lapita ancestors to Tonga and Samoa from islands further west. The outrigger canoe, probably devised in Southeast Asia long before the Lapita people emerged, was a simple vessel made by hollowing out a single log and lashing a separate float to one side to improve its balance. Limited in size and low in the water, it was suitable only for offshore fishing and short trips between near islands on a calm sea, not voyages of a month or more over thousands of miles of stormy seas with large groups of people who had to be fed. For such voyages, early Polynesians developed a different craft, a twin-hulled vessel similar to a modern catamaran. Although called canoes, these were true ships and could be as much as ninety to a hundred feet in length. Their twin hulls were built up of separate planks, tied edge to edge in carvel fashion (as opposed to the clinker or overlapped construction of Viking ships). Beams lashed across the hulls bound them into a single assembly and supported wide decks and even raised platforms that could hold considerable cargo or passengers. Although such vessels could be rowed by oarsmen, they were equipped with masts and triangular sails to take advantage of the wind whenever possible. Using ships of this sort, Polynesians leapfrogged from island to island across four thousand miles of open ocean, probably using the position of stars on the horizon and an intimate knowledge of winds, currents, and bird flights to chart their way.

As Polynesians dispersed over the Pacific, differences evolved that distinguished one island people from another. Those who dwelled on resource-poor atolls and islands, which could not sustain large populations, lived in small-scale, usually egalitarian communities. But on bigger islands and archipelagoes like Tonga, Samoa, and the Society, Hawaiian, and Easter Islands, as on New Zealand, populous societies with a high degree of stratification developed. By the time Europeans reached the area, hereditary chieftains ruled many of these areas. Often distinguishing themselves as a caste apart, they used their elevated status to exercise life-and-death power over kinsmen. Aided by centralized governments, many were capable of organizing a sufficient number of workers to build large burial mounds and monumental stone structures, terrace hillsides for taro beds, and construct fleets of oceangoing canoes. But because of the great distances between island groups, the local chiefdom remained the usual polity throughout Polynesia. Trade, too, was largely local, although archaeological findings indicate that long-distance exchanges did take place, if only through successive stages of barter between adjacent archipelagos. Isolation also affected religious practice. Worship varied from one archipelago to another despite a common polytheism. Cults of the sea god Tangaroa prevailed in the west, while eastern Polynesians worshiped a more eclectic pantheon featuring the war god Tu along with Rongo and Tane, gods of horticulture and procreation. Most eastern Polynesians nonetheless retained legends of a sacred homeland in the west called Hawaiki, of which the names Hawaii and Savai'i, an island in the Samoan chain, are variants. Perhaps Savai'i, which contains the ruins of an impressive ceremonial site built on a great stone mound, had a special cult role that inspired such legends. Similar *marae* or temple complexes became even more elaborate in eastern Polynesia, where they were raised on stepped pyramids or stone terraces adorned with effigies of spirits such as the *Moai* of Easter Island.

That island, the easternmost that Polynesians settled, became a focus of controversy when Thor Heyerdahl led an archaeological expedition there in 1955 to seek traces of Native American movements into the Pacific. Only 2,500 miles off the coast of Chile, to which it now belongs, Easter Island lies within plausible sailing distance of Latin America, but no proof of Native American colonization has been found there. Less certain is whether Easter Islanders had contact with mainland America in pre-Columbian times. Striking resemblances between the stonework and art found on the island and that in the Andes as well as the existence on Easter Island of the only known system of writing in Polynesia, the ideographic *rongorongo* script, hint at possible connections with literate Amerindian peoples. Unfortunately, like the Viking communities in Greenland, this Polynesian outpost underwent a sharp demographic and cultural decline in late traditional times. After Peruvian slavers decimated its population in 1862, no elders survived who could read the island's unique script or keep alive memories of its past.

THE METHOD

In the Evidence section that follows, you will encounter material used by scholars to reconstruct the lost worlds of the Vikings and Polynesians. You may notice a considerable difference in the nature of the sources presented for each people. In part this is because physical remains survive far better in the northern bogs and tundra of the Vikings' homelands than they do in tropical islands, and so we have far richer materials through which to study the Vikings than we have for the Polynesians. Also, the Vikings have attracted much more present-day study than the Polynesians, often from European descendants who are culturally akin to them. We are thus usually able to "read" Viking materials better and to get more out of them. Keep these factors in mind as you look over the evidence and consider how this situation affects our picture of the two peoples' respective activities.

As you might expect, the evidence is presented in two parts, one focused on the Vikings and the other on the Polynesians. Each opens with documents that reflect early efforts by outsiders to portray the people in question, followed by sources drawn from recent scholarship that try to illuminate them through their own artifacts and traditions. Compare the information presented through each. An important issue to be addressed here is the degree to which more recent material "fleshes out and in some cases contradicts or even replaces the historical record," as Fitzhugh put it. So consider how newer evidence adds to or changes our picture of the Vikings and Polynesians.

The section on the Vikings begins with a chronicle by a Saxon or German cleric known only as Adam of Bremen. In the 1060s he set out to record the history of the Catholic archbishops of Hamburg-Bremen but added digressions on the Scandinavians, whom they were then seeking to convert to Christianity. Though favorable to Scandinavians overall, he held a low opinion of the Viking adventurers who raided into Saxony. Source 2, an illustration from a manuscript on the life of St. Aubin dating from the same century, gives a similar view, portraying Vikings as they may have looked to clerics whose churches and monasteries they looted along the French coast.

Source 3 presents a very different image. Erected near a warrior's grave, this ninth-century stone from Gotland, Sweden, depicts a crew's journey to Valhalla, the legendary resting place of heroes. It shows the warrior god Odin riding his eight-legged horse Sleipnir, while one of his *valkyries*, or battle maidens, welcomes the crew to his realm. The ship is remarkably similar to the remnants of actual Viking vessels uncovered by archaeologists, like the one shown in Source 4, a photograph of the Oseberg *drakkar* or long ship discovered in a grave mound in Norway. The next items suggest where Vikings went in such ships and what they did. Source 5 consists of runic inscriptions on stones raised over the graves of Scandinavian notables to memorialize their feats at home and abroad. Source 6, a hoard or treasure trove of the sort often buried throughout Viking lands for religious or security reasons, yields more clues to Scandinavian activities abroad. Coins found in such hoards bear dates and mint marks that tell when and where they were obtained, and distinctive items of jewelry can be identified with their lands of origin.

That Scandinavians made it even farther afield can be deduced from the next items. Source 7, an excerpt from the *Greenlanders' Saga*, a prose tale produced during the thirteenth-century flowering of Icelandic literature, portrays Norwegian efforts to explore and settle the Atlantic isles. Though fictional, its version of Greenland's colonization and the exploration of Vinland parallels other Icelandic accounts and may preserve lore left by early settlers who knew firsthand about such affairs.[3] As Source 8, an archaeological plan of the L'Anse aux Meadows site, shows, the foundations of the long, narrow houses found there exactly conform in outline to the distinctive sod farmhouses that Scandinavians built in timber-poor Iceland. Along with a typical Viking bronze pin and stone lamp found at the site, these

3. L'Anse aux Meadows was only a temporary camp, and the exact location of Vinland remains unclear. The issue of its location has been complicated by a so-called Vinland map that emerged in the 1960s, only to be soon discredited.

foundations establish a Viking presence in North America.

Source 9, which begins the Polynesian section, comes from the *Polynesian Researches* of William Ellis, an early American missionary in the Pacific. Published in 1833, it was one of the first efforts by a sympathetic Westerner to describe Polynesians in detail. Still, Ellis missed no opportunity to point out their uncivilized ways and what he termed their "licentiousness and moral degradation." The open sexuality and tolerance for premarital and homosexual activity that drew his contempt fascinated other early Western visitors to Polynesia. William Hodges's 1776 painting *Tahiti Revisited,* a detail of which appears as Source 10, reveals this reaction, portraying Polynesians as "noble savages" at home with nature and with their bodies. An official artist on explorer James Cook's expedition to the Pacific in the 1770s, Hodges helped to foster this view in paintings on his return to London. By the nineteenth century, it had become a cliché in European art and literature, often used as a foil to Victorian stuffiness and prudery.

Efforts to dispel such stereotypes began only in the twentieth century as a few Western scholars became interested in the history of the Pacific peoples and tried to overcome the lack of early written records by looking for other kinds of evidence on the Polynesian past. One of the earliest approaches was to study maritime technology throughout the Pacific for clues about the way people moved into the region and settled where they did. But, because wood and fiber rot quickly in the tropics, no actual examples of the ancient vessels made of these materials survived for them to find. Petroglyphs or stone pictures such as those from Hawaii shown in Source 11 give a rough approximation of what ancient Polynesian double-hulled canoes may have looked like. Using such hints along with details gleaned from boat builders still active elsewhere in the Pacific, modern researchers have attempted reconstructions like the *Hokule'a,* depicted in Source 12. On voyages like the one charted on the map, they have also shown that such craft could sail closely enough into the wind to contend with the westerly trade winds and accurately find their way from one archipelago to another relying on traditional methods of navigation.

Memories of such voyages and links to other islands survived among Polynesians in popular traditions long after many had lost the ability to continue long-range travel, as Source 13 attests. Excerpted from an early-nineteenth-century work called *Hawaiian Antiquities,* this material represents an attempt by its author, a traditional Hawaiian poet and storyteller named David Malo, to preserve oral accounts in writing before they were lost. Having learned to read and write Hawaiian at a missionary school, Malo was clearly influenced by Western ideas of historical narrative. Source 14, stories collected directly from elders on the islands of Rennel and Bellona by Western ethnographers in the 1950s, more directly reproduces the way oral traditions deal with historical events. Both, however, indicate that Polynesians did retain some memory of their own origins and the connections between distant island groups.

To trace these origins in more detail, modern historians have turned to linguists for help. By studying similarities and dissimilarities in related languages, they have worked out the chart shown here as Source 15 to indicate the likely steps by which Polynesians colonized different island groups. It is based on the assumption that as colonists who struck out to settle new islands lost regular contact with their former homelands, their speech evolved differently, eventually forming a new dialect or even a new language. The pattern of linguistic evolution may thus roughly chart the stages and paths of Polynesian movement across the Pacific. Historians have also sought the aid of ethnobotanists, who study how different cultures identify and use plants. Source 16 presents some of their findings on the origin and distribution of plants introduced into Polynesia by humans. Not surprisingly, the places from which most of these plants must have been obtained hint at a basic movement eastward out of Asia into Polynesia through the western Pacific. But the presence of several South American plants spread widely throughout Polynesia also hints at contacts with the New World and movement back westward.

Similarities between Polynesian and Andean art and architecture provide another suggestion of contact. Source 17 illustrates how, in the eyes of some, the *Moai* ancestral figures of Easter Island mark an intermediate step in the development of Polynesian *tiki* or sacred effigies out of Latin American models like the stella from Tiahuanaco, Peru. Advocates of this view also argue that the close-laid stone terraces on which these Easter Island figures were erected, as well as similar terraces in Hawaii and the stepped pyramids of ancient Tahiti, derive from Andean prototypes. But without direct archaeological proof of contact between Polynesians and Native Americans, such claims remain conjectural.

THE EVIDENCE

Source 1 from Adam of Bremen, History of the Archbishoprics of Hamburg-Bremen, *trans. Francis J. Tschan (New York: Columbia University Press, 1959), pp. 75–76, 190–191.*

1. From Adam of Bremen, *History of the Archbishoprics of Hamburg-Bremen,* 11th century

BOOK TWO, XXXI.

At that time a fleet [994] of pirates whom our people call Ascomanni landed in Saxony and devastated all the coastland of Frisia and Hadeln.[4] And as they went up the mouth of the Elbe River, they fell upon the province. Then the chief men of the Saxons met, and although their forces were small, engaged the Barbarians, who had left their ships at Stade, which is a convenient port and stronghold on the Elbe. Mighty and memorable, but exceedingly unhappy, was the battle in which, though it was manfully contested on both sides, our men finally proved too few. The victorious Swedes and Danes completely destroyed the whole Saxon troop. Captured there were the margrave Siegfried, Count Dietrich and other distinguished men whom the barbarians dragged to the ships with their hands tied behind their backs, and their feet shackled with chains. After that the barbarians ravaged the whole province with impunity. But since one of the captives, the margrave Siegfried, stealthily slipped away by night with the aid of a certain fisherman and escaped, the pirates forthwith fell into a rage and, mocking all the nobles whom they had in chains, severed their hands and feet and cut off their noses. Thus maimed and half dead, they cast them upon the land. . . .

BOOK FOUR, VI.

There is very much gold in Zealand,[5] accumulated by the plundering of pirates. These pirates, called Vikings by the people of Zealand, by our people, Ascommani, pay tribute to the Danish king for leave to plunder the barbarians who live about this sea in great numbers. Hence it also happens that the license granted them with respect to enemies is frequently misused against their own people. So it is true they have no faith in one another, and as soon as one of them

4. **Ascomanni:** literally "shipmen," but conveying the sense of pirates or sea raiders. Frisia and Hadeln roughly corresponded with the modern Netherlands and the North Sea coastal portion of Germany. Saxony, the northwestern part of modern Germany, was then a province in the Carolingian empire.

5. **Zealand:** a Danish island in the North Sea between the Jutland Peninsula and modern Sweden.

catches another, he mercilessly sells him into slavery, either to one of his fellows or to a barbarian. In many other respects, indeed, both in their laws and their customs, do the Danes run contrary to what is fair and good. None of these points appears to me to be worth discussing, unless it be that they immediately sell women who have been violated and that men who have been caught betraying his royal majesty or in some other crime would rather be beheaded than flogged. No kind of punishment exists among them other than the ax and servitude, and then it is glorious for a man who is convicted to take his punishment joyfully. Tears and plaints and other forms of compunction, by us regarded as wholesome, are by the Danes so much abominated that one may weep neither over his sins nor over his beloved dead. . . .

Source 2: Bibliothèque nationale de France. Manuscript 01 NAL 1390 Fol 7.

2. Illuminated French Manuscript on Life of St. Aubin, St. Aubin Abbey, ca. 1100

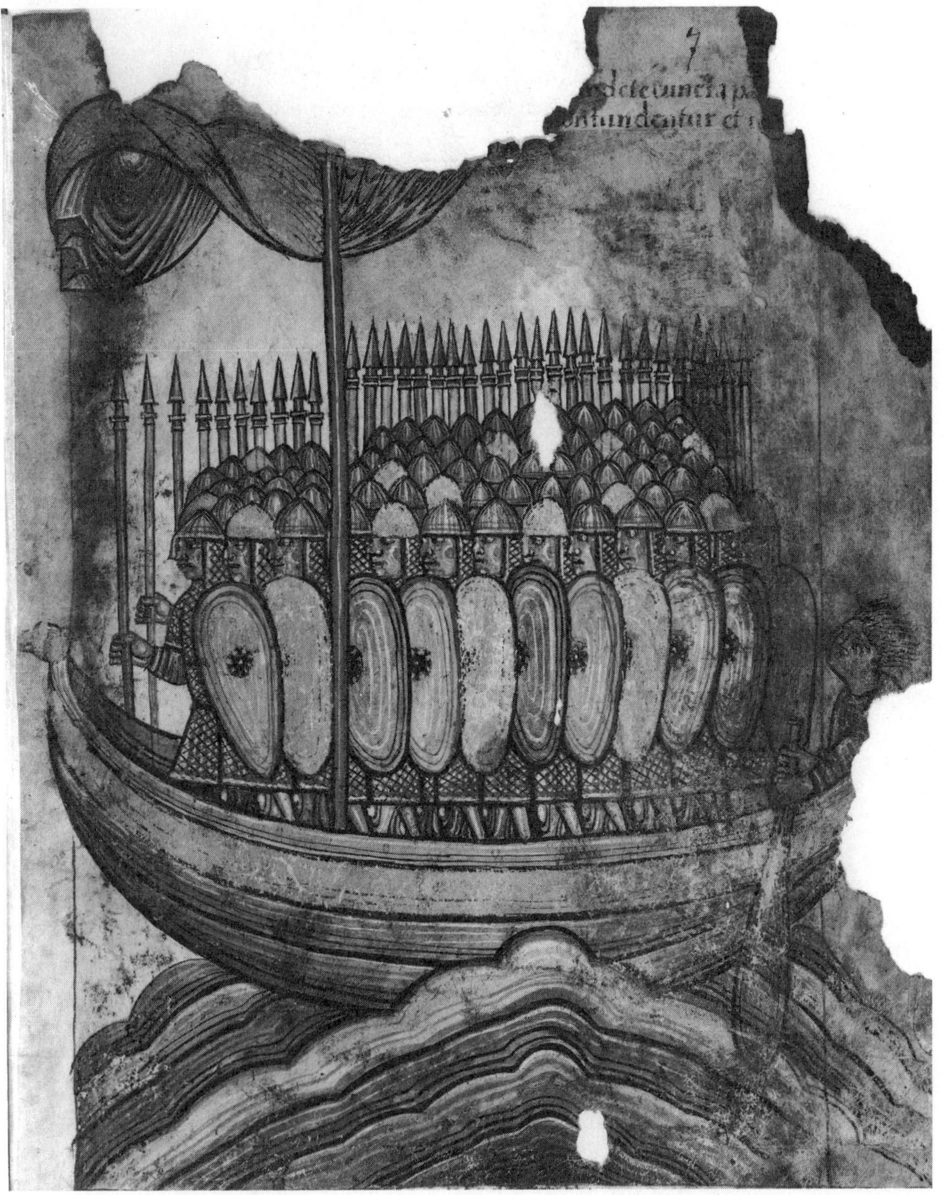

Source 3: Antikvarisktopografiska arkivet/National Heritage Board, Stockholm.

3. Memorial Stone, Gotland, Sweden, 8th to 9th century

Source 4: University Museum of Cultural Heritage/University of Oslo.

4. Oseberg Viking Ship, Norway, 9th to 10th century

Source 5 from R. I. Paige, Runes *(Berkeley and Los Angeles: University of California Press, 1987), pp. 46–51.*

5. Runic Memorial Inscriptions, Germany, Norway, and Sweden

1. Haddeby Stone, Schleswig, Germany: "[This stone was raised by Thórófr, Svein's retainer for his comrade Eiríkr] who met his death when *drengiar* . . . besieged Haddeby. He was master of a ship, and a very good *drengr.*"[6]

2. Uppland Stone, Uppland, Sweden: "Áli had this stone put up in his own honour. He took Knútr's *danegeld* in England. May God help his soul!"[7]

3. Veda Stone, Uppland, Sweden: "[Irenmuder set up this stone.] He bought this estate and made his money in the east, in Gardar."[8]

4. Fjuckby Stone, Uppland, Sweden: "[Liótr set up this stone in memory of his son, Áki.] He was master of a freighter, docking in the harbors of Greece. He died at home."

5. Gripsholm Stone, Södermanland, Sweden: "Tola set up this stone in memory of her son Haraldr, Ingvarr's brother. Like men they went far to seek gold, and in the east they fed the eagle. Died south, in Serkland."[9]

6. Dynna Pillar, Opland, Norway: "Gunnvor, Thrýdrik's daughter, made a bridge in memory of her daughter, Ástrídr. She was the most skilful girl in Hadeland."

6. ***drengr:*** a young warrior; *drengiar* is its plural form.
7. ***danegeld:*** "Danish gold," the money Danish invaders exacted from the Anglo-Saxons in England.
8. **Gardar:** the name Scandinavians used for eastern Russia.
9. **Serkland:** Norse for "Saracen land," the usual European term for Muslim territories.

Source 6 from Vikings: The North Atlantic Saga, *ed. William W. Fitzhugh and Elizabeth I. Ward (Washington and London: Smithsonian Institution Press, 2000) p. 120. Photo: University Museum of Cultural Heritage, Oslo, Norway.*

6. Buried Viking Hoard, Hon, Norway

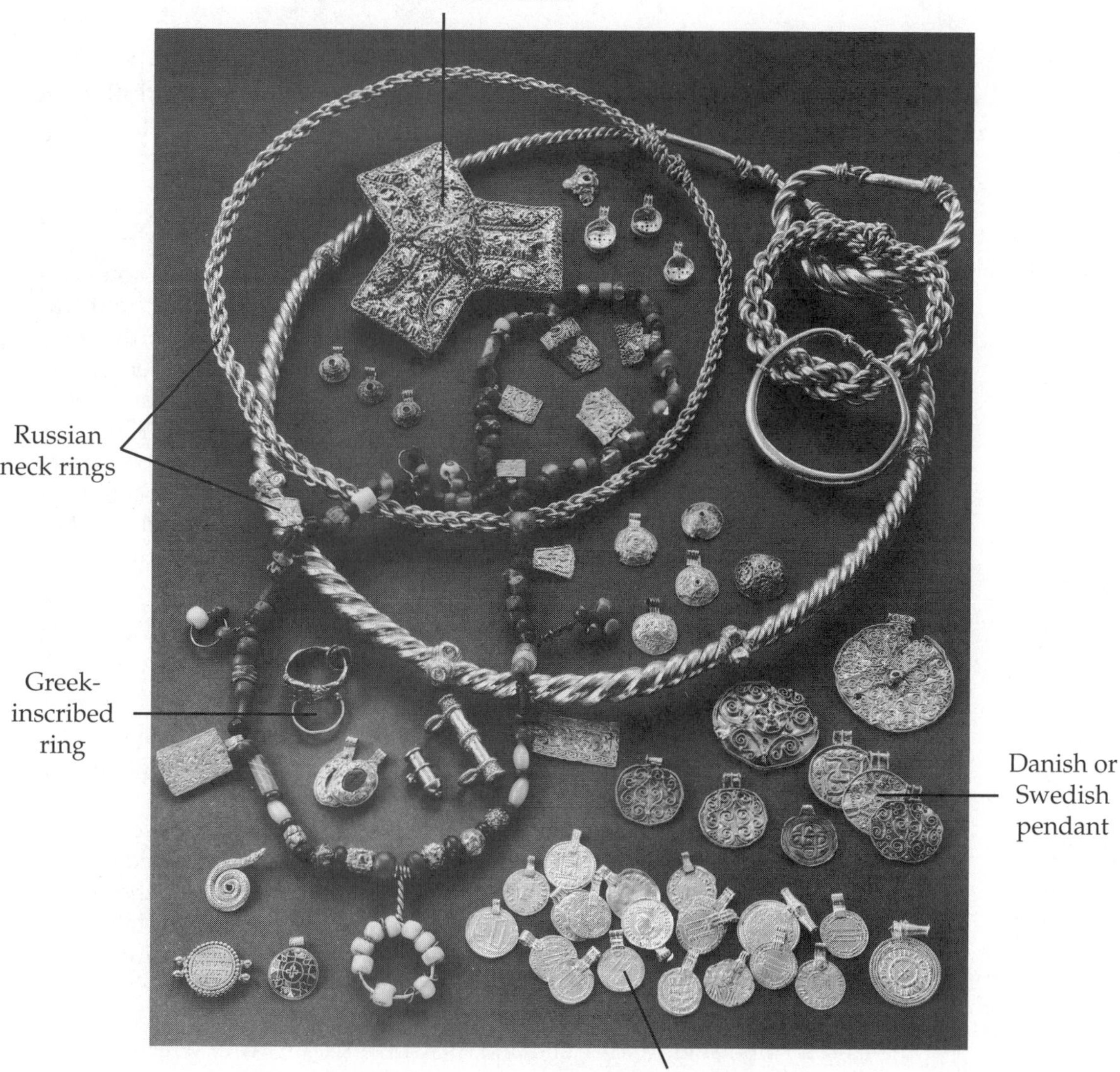

Source 7 from Gwyn Jones, The Norse Atlantic Saga *(London: Oxford University Press, 1964), pp. 142–152.*

7. From *Greenlanders' Saga,* 13th century

I

Learned men tell us that this same summer Eirik the Red went off to colonize Greenland, thirty-five [some versions say twenty-five] ships set sail from Breidafjord and Borgarfjord, but only fourteen of them succeeded in getting there. Some were forced back and some perished. . . .

II

[Bjarni Herjolfsson, an Icelander, away in Norway when his father accompanied the settlers to Greenland, decided to follow him in his own ship, but was blown off course.] . . . Then their following wind died down, and north winds and fogs overtook them, so that they had no idea which way they were going. This continued over many days, but eventually they saw the sun and could then get their bearings [or determine the quarters of the heavens]. They now hoisted sail, and sailed that day before sighting land, and debated among themselves what land this could be. To his way of thinking, said Bjarni, it could not be Greenland . . . [for] the land was not mountainous and was covered with forest, with low hills there, so they left the land to port of them and let their sheet turn towards the land.

III

[After more landfalls, none of which he was willing to explore, Bjarni reached Greenland itself.] . . . There was now much talk about voyages of discovery. Leif, son of Eirik the Red of Brattahlid, went to see Bjarni Herjolfsson, bought his ship from him, and found her a crew, so that they were thirty-five all told. . . .

. . . They now prepared their ship and sailed out to sea once they were ready, and they lighted on that land first which Bjarni his people had lighted on last. They sailed to land there, anchor and put off a boat, then went ashore, and could see no grass there. The background was all great glaciers, and right up to the glaciers from the sea as it were a single slab of rock. The land impressed them as barren and useless. "At least," said Leif, "it has not happened to us as to Bjarni over this land, that we failed to get ourselves ashore. I shall now give the land a name, and call it Helluland, Flatstone Land." After which they returned to the ship.

After that they sailed out to sea and lighted on another land. This time too they sailed to land, cast anchor, then put off a boat and went ashore. The country was flat and covered with forest, with extensive white sands wherever they went, and shelving gently to the sea. "This land," said Leif, "shall be given a name in accordance with its nature, and be called Markland, Wood Land." After which they got back down to the ship as fast as they could.

From there they now sailed out to sea with a north-east wind and were at sea two days before catching sight of land. They sailed to land, reaching an island which lay north of it. . . . After which they returned to their ship and sailed into the sound which lay between the island and the cape projecting north from the land itself. . . . Later they decided to winter there and built a big house.

There was no lack of salmon there in river or lake, and salmon bigger than they had ever seen before. The nature of the land was so choice, it seemed to them that none of the cattle would require fodder for the winter. No frost came during the winter, and the grass was hardly withered. Day and night were of a more equal length there than in Greenland or Iceland. On the shortest of winter the sun was visible in the middle of the afternoon well as at breakfast time.

One evening it turned out that a man of their company was missing. This was Tyrkir the German. Leif was greatly put out by this, for Tyrkir had lived a long while with him and his father, and had shown great affection for Leif as a child. He gave his shipmates the rough edge of his tongue, then turned out to go and look for him, taking a dozen men with him. But when they had got only a short way from the hall there was Tyrkir coming to meet them. . . .

"Why are you so late, foster-father," Leif asked him, "and parted this way from your companions."

By way of a start Tyrkir held forth a long while in German, rolling his eyes all ways, and pulling faces. They had no notion what he was talking about. Then after a while he spoke in Norse. "I went no great way further than you, yet I have a real novelty to report. I have found vines and grapes."

. . . They slept overnight, then in the morning Leif made this announcement to his crew. "We now have two jobs to get on with, and on alternate days must gather grapes or cut vines and fell timber, so as to provide a cargo of such things for my ship. . . ."

. . . Leif gave the land a name in accordance with the good things they found in it, calling it Vinland, Wineland; after which they sailed out to sea and had a good wind till they sighted Greenland and the mountains under the glaciers.

IV

There was now much discussion of Leif's expedition to Vinland. His brother Thorvald considered that the land had been explored in too restricted a fashion. So Leif said to Thorvald, "If you want to, go you to Vinland, brother, in my ship. . . ."

. . . Next summer Thorvald set off eastwards with the merchantship and further north along the land . . . and into the mouth of the next fjord they came to, and to a headland jutting out there which was entirely covered with forest.

They brought the ship to where they could moor her, thrust out a gangway to the shore, and Thorvald walked ashore with his full ship's company. "This is a lovely place," he said, "and here I should like to make my home." Then they made for the ship, and saw three mounds on the sands up inside the headland. They walked up to them and could see three skin-boats there, and three men under each. So they divided forces and laid hands on them all, except for one who got away in his canoe. The other eight they killed, and afterwards walked back to the headland, where they had a good look round and could see various mounds on up the fjord which they judged to be human habitations. Then after this so great a drowsiness overtook them that they could not keep awake, and all fell asleep. Then a cry carried to them, so that they were all roused up, and the words of the cry were these: "Rouse ye, Thorvald, and all your company, if you would stay alive. Back to your ship with all your men, and leave this land as fast as you can!" With that there came from inside the fjord a countless fleet of skin-boats and attacked them. . . . The Srælings kept shooting at them for a while, but then fled away, each one as fast as he could [leaving the party intact, save for Thorvald, who was mortally wounded].

. . . Then they stayed there that winter and gathered grapes and vines for the ship. The following spring they prepared to leave for Greenland, and brought their ship into Eiriksfjord, and the news they had to tell Leif was great news, indeed.

Source 8 site plan from Anne S. Ingstad, The Discovery of a Norse Settlement in America *(Oslo: Norwegian University Press, 1977); reconstructed Stöng Farmhouse from James Graham-Cambell,* The Viking World *(New Haven and New York: Ticknor & Fields, 1980), p. 81.*

8. Site Plan, L'Anse aux Meadows, Newfoundland, Canada and House, Stöng, Iceland

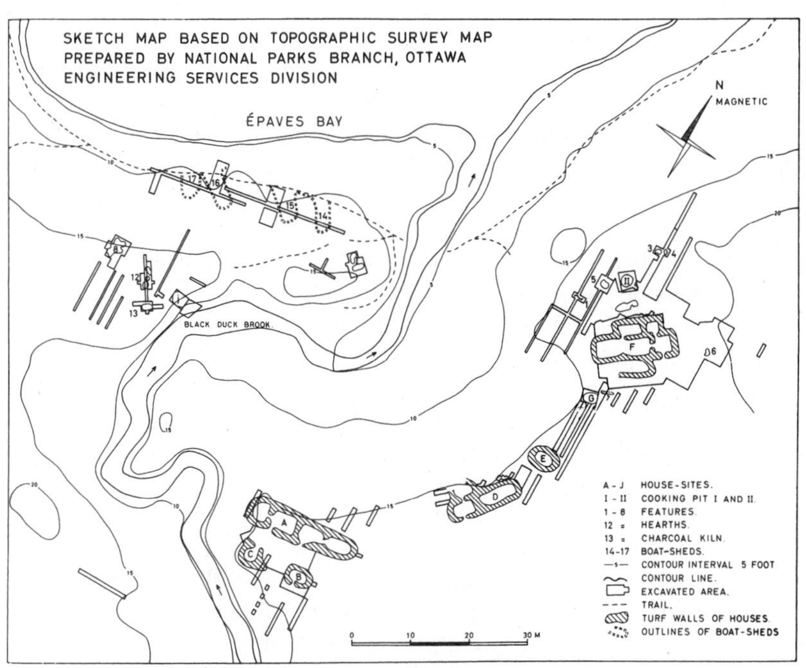

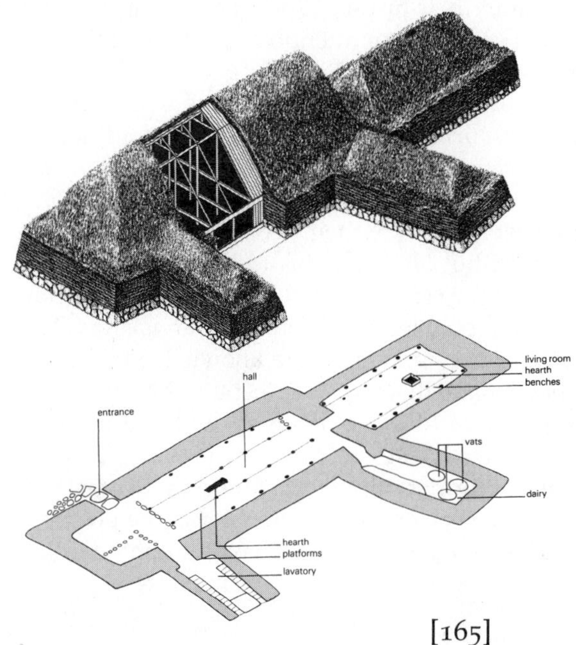

Source 9 from William Ellis, Polynesian Researches, *vol. I (New York: J. & J. Harper, 1833), pp. 72, 86–87, 95, 97, 106.*

9. from William Ellis, *Polynesian Researches,* 19th century

. . . The greater part of Polynesia appears to be inhabited by those who present in their physical character many points of resemblance to the Malay and South Americans, but yet differ materially from either, and seem to form an intermediate race.

Next to their hospitality, their cheerfulness and good nature strike a stranger. They are seldom melancholy or reserved, always willing to enter into conversation, and ready to be pleased, and to attempt to please their associates. They are generally careful not to give offense to each other: but though, since the introduction of Christianity, families dwell together, and find an increasing interest in social intercourse, yet they do not realize that high satisfaction experienced by members of families more advanced in civilization. . . .

Their humour and jests were, however, but rarely what might be termed innocent sallies of wit; they were in general low and immoral to a disgusting degree. . . . Awfully Dark, indeed, was their moral character, and notwithstanding the apparent mildness of their disposition, and the cheerful vivacity of their conversation, no portion of the human race was ever perhaps sunk lower in brutal licentiousness and moral degradation than this isolated people.

To a missionary, the business of whose life is with the people among whom he is stationed, everything relating to their history is, at least, interesting; and the origin of the islanders has often engaged our attention, and formed the subject of our inquiries. The early history of a people destitute of all records, and remote from nations in whose annals contemporaneous events would be preserved, is necessarily involved in obscurity. The greater part of the traditions of this people are adapted to perplex rather than facilitate the investigation.

The origin of the inhabitants of the Pacific is involved in great mystery, and the evidences are certainly strongest in favor of their derivation from Malayan tribes inhabiting the Asiatic islands; but allowing this to be their source, the means by which they have arrived at the remote and isolated stations they now occupy are inexplicable. If they were peopled from the Malayan islands, they must have possessed better vehicles and more accurate knowledge of navigation than they now exhibit, to have made their way against the constant trade-winds prevailing within the tropics, and blowing regularly, with but transient and uncertain interruptions, from east to west. . . .

. . . The monuments or vestiges of former population found in these islands are all exceedingly rude, and therefore warrant the inference that the people to whom they belong were rude and uncivilized, and must have emigrated from a nation but little removed from a state of barbarism—a nation less civilized than those must have been who could have constructed vessels, and traversed this ocean six or seven thousand miles against the prevailing winds, which must have been the fact, if we conclude they were peopled only by the Malays.

On the other hand, it is easy to imagine how they could have proceeded from the east. The winds would favour their passage, and the incipient stages of civilization in which they were found would resemble the condition of the aborigines of America far more than that of the Asiatics. . . .

10. Detail from William Hodges, *Tahiti Revisited,* 1776

Source 11 from Tommy Holmes, The Hawaiian Canoe *(Honolulu: Editions Limited, 1981), pp. 154–155. Both photos: Ray Mains.*

11. Petroglyphs of Hawaiian Canoes

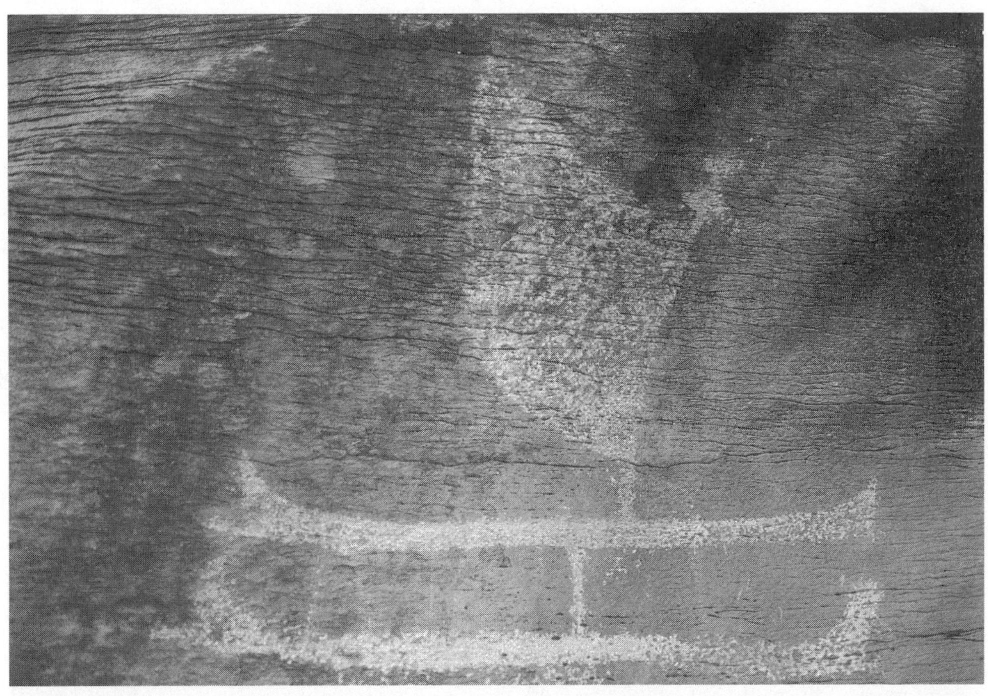

Source 12 photo from Tommy Holmes, The Hawaiian Canoe *(Honolulu: Editions Limited, 1993, p. 7. Photo: Ed George/NGS Collection, 1976/10514-5; map reprinted by permission from Ben F. Finney, "Voyaging Canoes and the Settlement of Polynesia,"* SCIENCE *(1977), 196: 1277–1285. Copyright 2001 American Association for the Advancement of Science.*

12. Reconstructed Double-Hulled Hawaiian Canoe *Hokule'a* and Route of Its Voyages

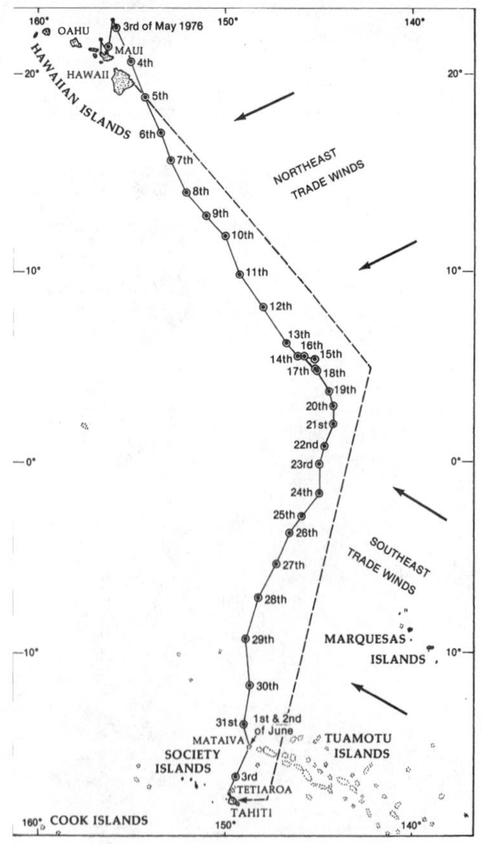

Source 13 from David Malo, Hawaiian Antiquities *(Moolelo Hawaii), trans. Nathaniel Emerson (Honolulu, Bishop Museum, 1951), pp. 4–7.*

13. From David Malo, *Hawaiian Antiquities,* early 19th century

CHAPTER 4

4. It is thought that this people came from lands near Tahiti and from Tahiti itself, because the ancient Hawaiians at an early date mentioned the name of Tahiti in their *mele,* prayers, and legends.[10]

7. Perhaps because of their affection for Tahiti and Hawaii they applied the name Kahiki-nui to a district of Maui, and named this group . . . Hawaii. . . .[11]

8. The following is one way by which knowledge regarding Tahiti actually did reach these shores: we are informed (by historical tradition) that two men named Paao and Makua-kaumana, with a company of others, voyaged hither, observing the stars as a compass; and that Paao remained in Kohala, while Makua-kaumana returned to Tahiti.

10. Paao continued to live in Kohala until the kings of Hawaii became degraded and corrupted (*hewa*); then he sailed away to Tahiti to fetch a king from thence. Pili (Kaaiea) was that king and he became one of Hawaii's line of kings (*papa alii*).

13. There is also a tradition of a man named Moikeha, who came to this country from Tahiti in the reign of Kala, king of Hawaii.

15. When Kila [Moikeha's son] was grown up he in turn sailed on an expedition to Tahiti, taking his departure, it is said, from the western point of Kahoolawe, for which reason that cape to this day called Ke-ala-I-kahiki (the route to Tahiti).

16. Kila arrived in safety at Tahiti and on his return to these shores brought back with him Laa-mai-Kahiki [his son, whose name meant Tahiti-born Laa]. On the arrival of Laa was introduced the use of the *kaekeeke* drum. An impetus was given at the same time to the use of sinnet in canoe lashing (*aha hoa waa*),

10. **mele:** a traditional song or chant. Malo cites several traditional *mele* and prayers (*hainaki*) that make reference to Kahiki, generally assumed to be the Hawaiian pronunciation of Tahiti. One, a prayer to the god Lono, claims "The stem of Lono links our dynasties with Kahiki," (p. 146).

11. Many eastern Polynesian peoples had legends and songs recalling an ancient homeland called Hawaii or Hawaiki, a term that may have referred to western Polynesian as a whole or perhaps just a similar-sounding island like Savai'i in Samoa.

together with improvements in the plaited ornamental knots or lashings, called *lana-lana*. . . .

17. The Hawaiian are thought to be of one race with the people of Tahiti and the islands adjacent to it. The reason for this belief is that the people closely resemble each other in their physical features, language, genealogies, traditions (and legends) as well as in (the names of) their deities. It is thought that very likely they came to Hawaii in small detachments.

19. It seems probable that this was the case from the fact that in Tahiti they have large canoes called *pahi;* and it seems likely that its possession enabled them to make their long voyages to Hawaii. The ancients are said to have been skilled also in observing the stars, which served them as a mariner's compass directing their course.

Source 14 from Samuel H. Elbert and Torben Monberg, From the Two Canoes. Oral Traditions of Rennell and Bellona *(Honolulu and Copenhagen: University of Hawaii Press, 1965), pp. 82, 174–176, 188, 257, and 301.*

14. Excerpts from the Oral Traditions of Rennell and Bellona

Text 124 Story of the Voyage of the Ancients, told by Basiana, April 13, 1958

1. The coming of the voyage of the ancients, that reached Rennell and Bellona here. They made no settlement, but first just traveled about on Bellona here and on Rennell and looked about. Afterwards they made their settlements, and made their two temples brought from 'Ubea.[12] The name of the great temple that Tongo brought was Teuse and Manga-ma'ubea. They dug up the earth and made the settlement of the gods there, and erected the house there. The house was very sacred.—

12. **Ubea:** the name the Polynesians of Bellona and Rennel used for their homeland.
Bellona and **Rennell:** "outliers" or western extensions of Polynesia in the Solomon Islands about 200 miles south of Guadalcanal. 'Ubea was probably Uvea Island, located about midway between Samoa and Fiji, over 1,200 miles to the east.

Text 153 The Story of the Seven Originals, told by Tupe'uhi, March 19, 1958

1. The seven originals were brought here from 'Ubea and had different gods, and Kaitu'u had two. The Taupongi clan, Ekeitehua; and the Sau clan, theirs was Baabenga. 2. The Tanga clan's were Guatupu'a and Tepoutu'igangi.... Sikigimoemoe was the god of the Nikatemono clan. 3. The Puka clan and the Togo clan had their gods, but their names are not known....[13]

Text 66 From the story of Kaitu'u and Taupongi, told by Taupongi, December 12, 1958

1. Taupongi and Tanga and Ngoha and Nikatemono and Puka and Sau and To'a and Suki and Pua made the search for land. These are the things which they brought from 'Ubeangango (West-'Ubea): two black stones and the temple named Mangama'ubea and the life-of-the-land [staff]. 2. [They] came and arrived at the eastern 'Ubea, where a person was strolling.... 3. And Tanga and Pua said as follows: "What is your name?" And [he] said: "I am Kaitu'u...." 6. ... And they took [him] to Tongo, his classificatory uncle, and they cast off away from eastern 'Ubea and came this way.

Text 67 Kaitu'u, told by Tetamogi, January 6, 1958

[*Kaitu'u, whom the original migrants met on eastern 'Ubea, joined the group with his own kinsmen because he dreamed that two gods wanted him to carry them to a new location.*]

10. After his dream [Kaitu'u] awoke at daylight and made preparations and boarded the double canoe of Tahasi and To'a and Suke, the two chiefs and owners of the canoe. Kaitu'u's wife is not known. 11. The mother was taken aboard, her name being Nautaga. Togo made preparations. These people were uncle and nephew, Togo and Kaitu'u. 12. Togo boarded the canoe with his two gods, two stones named Tepoutapu (the-sacred-post), a male god, and Guatupu'a and Gau'eteaki (two names), a goddess. 13. [They all] boarded the canoe and got settled there; Kaitu'u and his mother and his two gods, and Togo and his two gods sat in the lesser hull. 14. And Tahasi and To'a and Suki sat in the main

13. The original Polynesian migrants who set out from western 'Ubea represented seven clans, but only two chiefs, Kaitu'u and Taupongi, made it safely to Rennell and Bellona with their followers intact.

hull. 15. Casting off from 'Ubea, coming this way, going and landing at many islands. 16. Coming this way, landing at a land, not knowing the name of the land, To'a and Suki were killed by the people of this land. 17. Casting off the canoe, coming this way, landing at another land. So Tahasi was also killed. The two people who had been chiefs and owners of the canoe were no more. 18. Kaitu'u and Togo were left, and [they] got into the main canoe and left the other hull.

Text 66 From the story of Kaitu'u and Taupongi, told by Taupongi, December 12, 1958

9. And Tongo and Kaitu'u boarded the main hull [of the double] canoe, and came and reached Henuatai (Marine-land). And the sea was rough, and the black stone sank [into the sea], and the people of the canoe came ashore at Henuatai, where [they] hammered and broke a stalactite and replaced the black stone with it, and slept in the neighborhood.

14. . . . And all the people then took the canoes through the reef out to the sea and said: "Tengenga is my woman." 15. . . . There were one hundred [people]; all were out to sea. Only the double canoe was left on the shore, and only Tongo and Kaitu'u stayed upon it. . . .

18. When Tongo and Kaitu'u came out, the whole fleet of canoes had sunk. Only the one belonging to Taupongi was left. And Tongo took on board a man and his wife of another clan.

19. And in this way Tongo went on picking up all the clans. And the woman of the Tanga clan said: "Every clan now survives, each through one couple [*baaghabu*], but my clan will die out." 20. And Tongo picked up the Tanga clan in the double canoe, and [they] were now seven. And then the two canoes came this way, the double canoe in front and behind the one belonging to Taupongi. When [they] met rough seas, the double canoe fell astern, and so the one belonging to Taupongi was ahead.

22. [They] came and reached Ahanga at the lake and came to the north side of Rennell. Came on and came out from the point at Kangiata, and Bellona here appeared. 28. . . . And the two canoes came ashore, [people] went up and walked about in Ahanga and danced their sauhongi.

Text 5 Story of Ekeitehua, told by Taupongi, January 2, 1959

4. The canoe belonging to Kaitu'u, the double canoe, came from 'Ubea, but the canoe belonging to Taupongi came here first. It was a small canoe, its name was *hua*. And the canoe came and arrived here at Bellona, and installed its district

god here and named [him] Ekeitehua. [They] called his district god that name because he arrived before the double canoe.[14]

Text 67 Kaitu'u, told by Tetamogi, January 6, 1958

[*Conflict subsequently broke out with an indigenous people called the* hiti *already living on the island when they killed Togo in a dispute over the spoils of a hunt.*]

49. Then Kaitu'u stayed with the *hiti* and then thought he would revenge his uncle Togo, so Kaitu'u stood and fought the *hiti,* and Kaitu'u killed the *hiti,* and in revenge for Togo, killed and ate [the *hiti*].

14. Kaitu'u made the voyage in a great double canoe, whereas Taupongi had only a lesser small canoe or outrigger. But because the latter arrived first, his descendants called their clan god Ekeitehua: "rest-on-the-small-canoe."

Source 15 based on charts in Patrick V. Kirch, The Evolution of the Polynesian Chiefdoms *(Cambridge and London: Cambridge University Press, 1984), pp. 43, 27.*

15. Development Sequence of Polynesian Languages

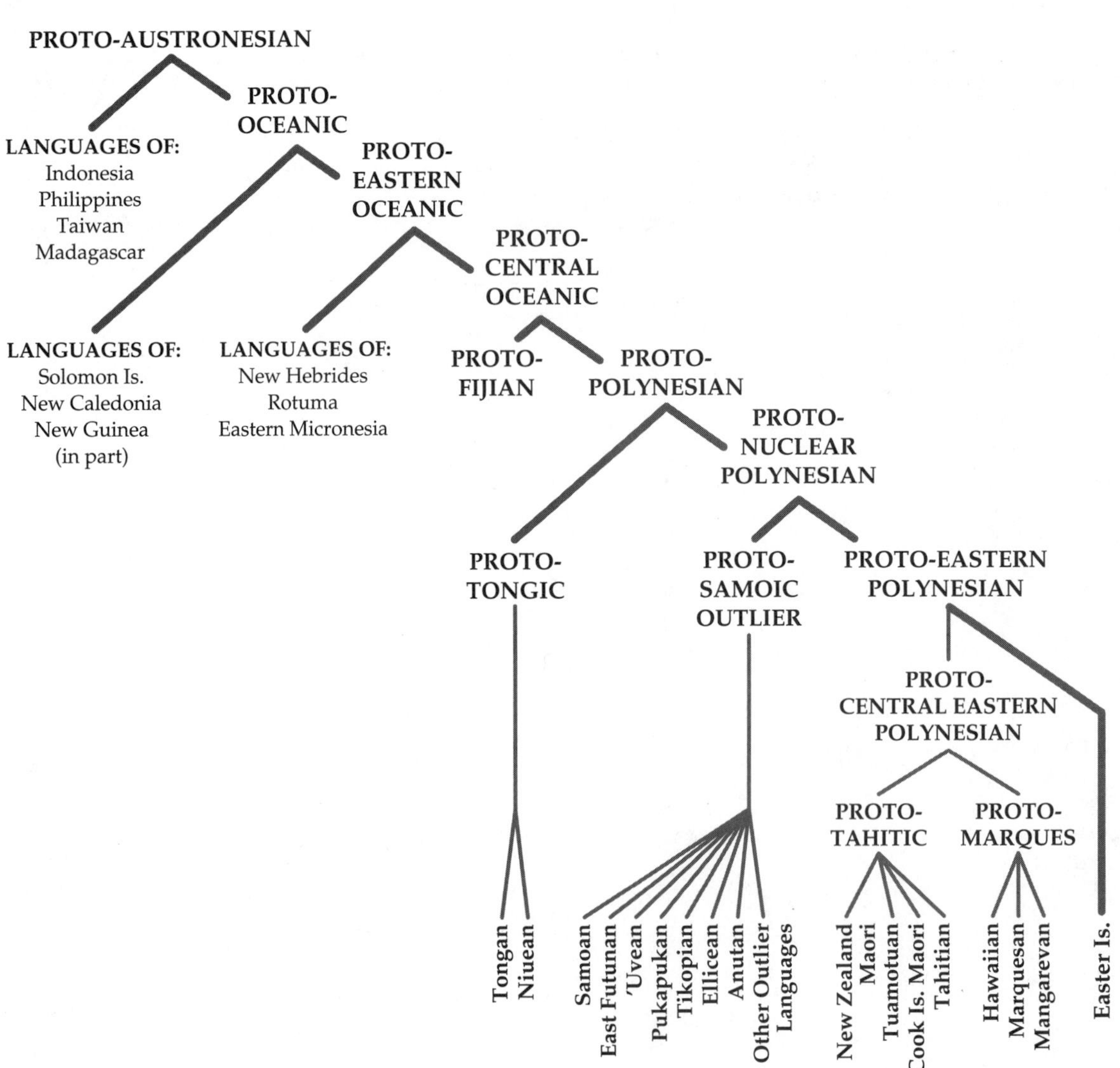

Source 16 charts created from data in W. Arthur Whistler, "Polynesian Plant Introduction," from Islands, Plants, and Polynesians. An Introduction to Polynesian Ethnobotony, *ed. Paul Allen Cox and Sandra Anne Banack (Portland, Ore.: Dioscorides Press, 1991), pp. 41–66.*

16. Plant Species Introduced into Polynesia Before European Contact

(a) Origin of 72 known plant species introduced into Polynesia

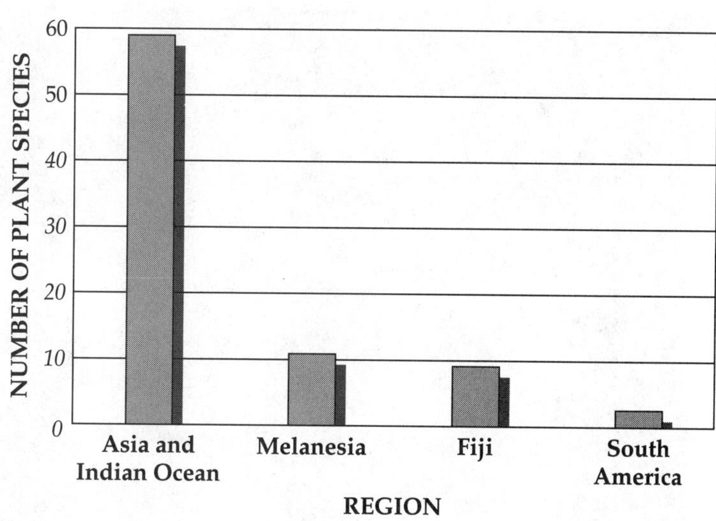

(b) Distribution in Polynesia of three plant species of South American origin

	Islands					
Species	*Tonga*	*Samoa*	*Cook*	*Society*	*Marquesas*	*Hawaii*
Ipomea batatas Sweet potato	P	P	P	P	P	P
Lagenaria siceraria bottle gourd	—	—	P	P	P	P
Solanum repandum fruit-bearing shrub	P	P	P	P	P	Modern?

Note: **P** indicates the presence of a plant. *Solanum repandum* is found in Hawaii, but it was probably a modern plant introduction.

Source 17: Photo (a): Superstock #53/534/A/R59B; Photo (b): Tony Morrison/South American Pictures, #BBA0211D; Photo (c): Jo Anne Van Tilburg, Easter Island *(London: British Museum Press, 1994), p. 119. Drawing by Cristian Arevalo Pakarati; Photo (d): Vanadis Expedition/ British Museum.*

17. Monolithic Statues

(a) Ahu Akivi Platform, Easter Island

(b) Tiahuanaco Stella

(c) Easter Island Moai

(d) Marquesan Tiki

QUESTIONS TO CONSIDER

Begin your review of the evidence on the Vikings by asking how early historical documents like Sources 1 and 2 portrayed them. One way to approach this task with regard to Source 1 is to list the descriptive terms that Adam of Bremen uses to describe the Vikings. Taken together, what image do these terms evoke? Adam, like many chroniclers, employs stories and anecdotes to dramatize his account and provide representative examples of behavior. Do these present a consistent picture of Vikings? In particular, how does the story of Margrave Siegfried reflect on the Vikings' image as warriors? Compare this view with the one that emerges in the discussion of Danish morals and character. Does Adam accord any positive traits to the Danes or the Swedes? Now turn to Source 2 and ask yourself what specific aspect of Viking life this picture illustrates, and in what perspective. Does it challenge or reinforce the image provided by Adam's account? Does either suggest a heroic people or a people with significant historical accomplishments?

By contrast, look at how Source 3, the memorial stone, presents the subject of a party of Viking warriors. In what context are they shown here, and how does this affect the perspective? Do these seem to be treacherous, greedy, or disloyal men? Compare the ship depicted here with the one illustrated in Source 2. Which shows details of such things as hull outline, rigging, and sails, which would affect the seaworthiness of a craft? By implication, which shows a craft that might be capable of an extended journey? Now compare the ship on the memorial stone with the one found at Oseberg. How well do they agree in details? Does the Oseberg vessel seem like a crude and clumsy craft? Replicas of such ships, which were up to ninety feet in length and sixteen feet in breadth, have been made and sailed across the Atlantic since the 1890s, leaving little doubt about their seaworthiness. How do such ships compare with those of later European explorers?

In going over the inscriptions in Source 5, note where Vikings went and how far they traveled. Note, too, what they did. Were they just pirates? What other activities did they pursue? Most inscriptions record the feats of men, but women did not go unrecognized, as you can see from the sixth inscription. How does this inscription in particular contrast with Adam's claim that Danes lacked compunction over the dead? Relying on what you have learned from these inscriptions, how do you think the Viking owner of the Hon hoard obtained the items displayed in Source 6? Note the places where these objects were made. How do you think they were obtained? Items from Western Europe may have come from pillaging, but Vikings did not raid the Muslim city of Bagdhad or the Bzyantine capital, Constantinople.

Source 7, the *Greenlander's Saga*, reveals still other Viking activities. Why did men like Erik the Red sail to Greenland? Assuming crews of the size Leif recruited for his ship, how many people accompanied his father to Greenland? How does this venture compare with later European attempts to start colonies in North America? The voyages to Vinland later made by Leif and his brother Thorvald may have been for more than exploration, to judge from the cargoes they elected to bring back. Why might timber and grapes be of value to colonists in Greenland and Iceland? As you might guess from looking at the Icelandic farmhouse shown in Source 8, these are cold, northern lands with sparse forest cover that demanded extreme adaptation if settlers were to survive. The Vikings had to learn how to use the sparse materials at hand in these new places, and then developed a distinctive kind of sod building. Compare the outline of the house foundations (marked A–J) on the archaeological site plan of L'Anse aux Meadows with that of the reconstructed Icelandic farmhouse shown at the bottom of the page. Do you see the resemblance? Conditions further south on the North America coast were more favorable. Does the saga suggest why Vikings did not settle there?

As you turn to the material on the Polynesians, note how differently their "barbarism" is portrayed in Source 9, Ellis's account. What are the words Ellis uses to characterize them and what do the qualities these words evoke suggest—savage warriors, dignified chieftains, or degraded children? Compare the image you get of them here with the one conveyed in Hodges's painting, Source 10. By focusing on nude women bathing in a lush tropical setting, Hodges provided a very selective view of Polynesian life. Does it contrast sharply with Ellis's view or other views of South Sea islanders that you have encountered? What does such a view imply about these people? Would you expect such people to plan and carry out arduous projects or have expert knowledge about navigation? Consider in this context Ellis's doubt that Polynesian ancestors came from Asia.

Like Ellis, many early Western observers felt that "a nation but little removed from a state of barbarism" could not "have constructed vessels, and traversed this ocean six or seven thousand miles against prevailing winds." But Source 11, the Hawaiian petroglyphs, indicates otherwise. Compare the canoes scratched on these rocks—particularly the outline of their hulls and sails—with Source 12, the photo of a replica of a traditional oceangoing canoe. Successful voyages over thousands of miles by replicas such as *Hokule'a* show that such vessels could cross vast stretches of open ocean. And as the map of *Hokule'a*'s voyages proves, their triangular rig would allow them to sail close enough into the wind to avoid being blown off course to the west.

As Sources 13 and 14 verify, memories of such voyages were kept alive in oral traditions. Note the number of trips between Tahiti and Hawaii listed in Source 14. Were any two-way? Why were such voyages undertaken, and what consequences did they have? Clearly settlement was one motive, but on what scale did it take place? How did such migrants find their way on such voyages? Stories from Rennell and Bellona in Source 15 give more detail on Polynesian colonization. What led the Seven Originals to leave 'Ubea? How many people set out, and how many arrived? What prized possessions did they bring with them? Like the Vikings in Vinland, these newcomers encountered prior occupants. Were their relations more amicable? What do you make of their treatment of the *hiti*? Rennell and Bellona lie far west of Uvea, the likely 'Ubea from which the Seven Originals came, suggesting two-way traffic across the Pacific.

The linguistic evidence presented in Source 15, however, shows that the main direction of Polynesian movement was from west to east. New branches in the line of language development probably occurred as groups broke away from older populations to settle a new home. What locations would then mark key stages in the migration of peoples into Polynesia? Find these on the map and note the course of migration that they indicate. Notice that this route runs counter to the direction of the trade winds. What does this fact imply about navigation into the Pacific from Asia—or South America. Source 16 provides data on the diffusion of South American plants into the Pacific. What does this suggest about human movements into the area? The interpretation of Source 17, the stone figures, is more problematic, because all representations of the human form look somewhat alike. But note that all are free-standing figures carved in similar crouching positions with arms clasped around their midriffs and large, staring eyes. Note, too, the similar headdress on both the Easter Island *Moai* and the South American stella. If we could prove that the Polynesians reached America from the west, would that feat give them new significance in history?

EPILOGUE

Both the Vikings and the Polynesians suffered from declines that cost them their seagoing prowess. Without the means of continuing long-range voyages, their scattered settlements lost touch with one another and sank into isolation and obscurity. Eventually most Viking states outside of Scandinavia foundered, as migrant communities died out or were assimilated into indigenous populations. Vinland was abandoned early, and by the fourteenth century the Greenland colonies had vanished, too. Settlements elsewhere fared little better, being incorporated into new states created and governed by other peoples. Only the duchy of Normandy in France, whose Duke William went on to conquer England in 1066, and Iceland endured to preserve some of their legacy. But in these lands, as in Scandinavia proper, conversion to Christianity and adoption of Western European ways brought a break with tradition and a loss of old identity. We know less about the course of events in Polynesia. However, when Europeans arrived in the Pacific, most eastern Polynesian peoples had lost their ability to build and sail the double canoes of the past. Trade and communication between major island groups had ceased, and little remained to indicate that Polynesians had once crossed the ocean on voyages of discovery and colonization.

Only recently have we begun to see how great a break occurred and how worthwhile it may be to rediscover the lost worlds of people like the Vikings and the Polynesians. The picture that is emerging from modern studies of these two peoples, though certainly more detailed for the Vikings than for the Polynesians, shows in both cases not savages, but sophisticated peoples with a surprising degree of material and cultural development. Their transoceanic exploration, trade, and colonization certainly narrowed the great ocean barriers of the Atlantic and Pacific. And long before Columbus launched Western Europe's celebrated age of discovery with his expedition of 1492, they may have closed the final gap between the Old World and the New.

CHAPTER SEVEN

TWO FACES OF "HOLY WAR":[1]

CHRISTIANS AND MUSLIMS

(1095–1270s)

THE PROBLEM

According to the Book of Matthew in the Christian New Testament, after his resurrection from the dead, Jesus appeared before his eleven remaining disciples in Galilee, where he commanded them, "Go ye, therefore, and teach all nations, baptizing them in the name of the Father, and of the Son, and of the Holy Ghost, [t]eaching them to observe all things whatsoever I have commanded you."[2] Similarly, in the Qur'an (Koran), the book containing the revelations to Islam's founder, Muhammad ibn Abdullah, the Prophet commanded his followers to "Invite [all] to the way of your Lord . . . For your Lord knows best who has strayed from His Path, and who receives guidance."[3] Thus Christianity and Islam, both of which saw themselves as the keepers of God's ultimate revelation of Himself to humanity, from their respective beginnings had built within their doctrines the commandment to proselytize and spread to include all peoples.

At their beginnings, neither Christianity nor Islam preached the expansion of the faiths by use of the sword. Muhammad counseled his followers to make converts "with wisdom and beautiful preaching; and argue with them in ways that are best and most gracious,"[4] while earlier the apostle Paul, himself a convert to Christianity, wrote to his fellow Christians in Rome to "follow after the things that make for peace, and things therewith one may

1. The term *holy war* is of European origin, first coined by Friedrich Schwally in his book *Der Heilege Kreig im alten Israel [Holy War in Ancient Israel]* (Leipzig, 1901).

2. King James Version (KJV) 28:19–20. See also Acts 1:8.

3. Qur'an, Sūra 16:125.

4. Ibid.

edify another," so that "through your mercy they also may obtain mercy."[5]

Yet ultimately both Christians and Muslims were willing to spread their respective faiths by force. As Christians swelled in numbers, they increasingly embraced violence both to punish unbelievers and heretics and to expand the faith. For justification, they often reached back into the Old Testament, in which Israelites had been told to "utterly destroy them [unbelievers], as the Lord thy God hath commanded thee."[6] For their part, after the *hijra*[7] of Muhammad and his followers to Medina, the Prophet began to report revelations of *jihads al-sayf* (jihads of the sword). Originally the term *jihad* was shorthand for *jihad fi sabil Allah* (struggle in the path of God) and had no relation to warfare at all. Most often the term referred to an *internal* struggle of a Muslim against temptations, or a particular internal struggle against Muslim heretics or impious leaders. But, as noted above, within a few years of the *hijra*, Muhammad was saying such things as "Whoever fights in the path of God, whether he be killed or be victorious, on him We shall bestow a great reward," and "those who strive and fight has He distinguished above those who sit [at home] by a great reward."[8]

5. Romans 14:19, 11:31, KJV.

6. Deuteronomy 20:17, KJV.

7. **hijra:** the flight or emigration of Muhammad from Mecca to Medina, in 622 C.E.

8. Qur'an, Sūra 4:74, 95. Muhammad's revelations in the Qur'an are in order of length, with the longest sūra first. For one interpretation of the *chronology* of the revelations, see Reuven Firestone, *Jihad: The Origins of Holy War in Islam* (New York: Oxford University Press, 1999), pp. 67–91, 115–125.

For centuries the proponents of these two religions maintained comparatively good relations with one another. In lands conquered by Muslims, Christians and Jews (known to Muslims as "People of the Book") were able to practice their respective faiths so long as they paid tribute and taxes to Muslim political authorities. Christians and Jews also were able to make pilgrimages to Jerusalem. And in Italy and Spain, Muslims lived in close proximity to Christians for hundreds of years without major altercations. Yet while their respective intellectual elites shared knowledge with one another, the two kept a careful—and enforced—distance. The papacy labeled Christians who dealt with Muslims as traitors and warned that such treason meant loss of all their property. For their part, most Muslims thought Western Christians were primitive and had little to teach them (Usamah ibn-Munqidh called Christians "animals").

Sometime after 1071 C.E., however, that brittle peace was broken. Seljuk Turks, new converts to Islam who interpreted the term *jihad* in its most warlike way, seized control of Jerusalem from the more tolerant Abbasid Muslims. On November 27, 1095, in a field of Clermont, France, Pope Urban II called on Western Christians to undertake a *peregrinatio* (pilgrimage) to capture Jerusalem from the Muslims.[9] By the time the first Christian army arrived in Palestine in 1098, written accounts by one side about the other had

9. Those Christians who went on these expeditions referred to themselves as "pilgrims." The term *crusade* (from the French word *croix*, "cross" in English) was not used for some time.

been circulated and read (or listened to). Appearing when they did during the period Europeans refer to as the Crusades, there is little doubt that these accounts created perceptions and stereotypes in the minds of Christians who had never met Muslims, and vice versa. Moreover, it is clear that these accounts helped to formulate ideas in each camp of how the other should be treated.

Your tasks in this chapter are twofold. First, by examining the accounts written by Christians and by Muslims, determine the impressions that each side created of the other. Second, reach some conclusions about how those perceptions and stereotypes (whether accurate or inaccurate) might have influenced the ways in which Christians and Muslims chose to deal with one another.

Before you begin, we must issue a note of caution. From the evidence provided by Christians, you will *not* be able to determine what Muslims were *really* like, but only what Christians perceived (or wanted their readers to perceive) Muslims were like. This is equally true of the Muslim accounts. Indeed, it is quite possible that some of the writers had never even met the people about whom they were writing. Even so, what you *do* learn will prove extremely important, for perceptions, impressions, and stereotypes are often just as powerful as facts in prompting individuals to action. To paraphrase historian Claude Van Tyne, what people *think* is true may be more important to them than what is *really* true.

BACKGROUND

The 500s and early 600s was a period of great change in the Arab world. Increased trade had brought a new level of prosperity, but that prosperity in turn had produced tribal and class divisions. Old values of tribal unity and sharing wealth were giving way to new values of individual and family accumulation. At the same time, Arabs began to feel a strong sense of religious inferiority. Neighboring Jews and Christians (with whom Arab merchants traded) boasted that their respective faiths were superior to other religions because they were built on divine revelations, something Arabs had not received. Hence one could say that the Arabian peninsula was in economic, social, political, and intellectual crisis.

The appearance of Muhammad ibn Abdullah (ca. 570–632) ultimately solved each of these crises. Orphaned at an early age and raised by an uncle, Muhammad became a merchant, traveling in mercantile caravans as far as Palestine, where he surely became familiar with both Judaism and Christianity. Marriage to a wealthy widow freed him from the need to work long hours to make a living, and the extremely pious merchant spent a good deal of time in meditation and prayer.

Around the year 610, Muhammad began to experience what he said were divine revelations from God (*Allah* in Arabic) and God's messengers (he claimed that his first vision was of the angel Gabriel). Gathering around him a small group of followers, he began to preach what he insisted was not a new religious faith but a reform of Arabs' traditional faith. Initially, Muhammad's message was a simple one: There was but one God (Allah), the same God, he said, who was worshiped by Jews and Christians; humans must prepare themselves for a last judgment; it was the duty of each believer to care for the poor and oppressed and to work to create a just society based on God's will and divine revelations. One can see how Muhammad and his teachings filled several needs in Arabic society. He advocated Arab unity over class and tribal divisions, care for the poor in a region of growing prosperity but unequal distribution of wealth, and Islam's parity with other religions because of the revelations Muhammad experienced.[10]

By the time of Muhammad's death in 632, most people living in the Arabian peninsula had become Muslims. Muhammad's successor Abu Bakr (called a *caliph,* or "successor to the Prophet") ordered that all of Muhammad's revelations be collected and printed in one book, the Qur'an (Koran), which was published in 651. Muslims accepted the teachings of both Jews and Christians (the most significant exception being the Christian assertion of Jesus' deity) and claimed that Muhammad was the last and ultimate prophet in a long line that included Abraham, Moses, and Jesus.

The death of Abu Bakr in 634 brought Umar to the caliphate. Under Umar, Arabs launched a series of wars to expand their power to North Africa, the Middle East, India, China, and Europe. In addition to the religious imperative, there also were economic reasons for these wars of expansion, especially the extension of trade routes under Arab control and the reaping of tribute paid by vanquished peoples. Jews and Christians living in conquered lands were allowed to practice their faiths, but economically and politically they were definitely second-class citizens. Christians were allowed to make pilgrimages to Jerusalem, a holy city that they now shared with Jews and Muslims.[11]

Beneath the surface, however, Islam was never as unified as Muslims claimed. In 656 the third caliph, Uthman, was murdered, and a division soon arose among Muslims as to who would succeed him. The two resulting groups, the Sunnis and the Shi'ites, also differed over whether caliphs, like the Prophet, were divinely inspired.[12] In time, the split became permanent, and even today it is the source of much internal strife within Islam. Thus, by the time Christians from Western Europe began their own "holy war" in 1097 (later called by Europeans the

10. *Islam,* in Arabic, means "submission (to God)," and a *Muslim* is "one who submits."

11. Muslims believed that Muhammad ascended to heaven from the Dome of the Rock, located in Jerusalem on the very site of the Temple where Jesus taught, which was destroyed by Roman armies in the first century. In 691, Caliph Abd al-Malik built a pavilion on the rock. Both Christians and Muslims believed that the rock possessed curative powers, and pilgrims chipped off fragments to take them home.

12. The name *Sunni* was derived from the Arabic word *Sunna,* a collection of the Prophet's sayings and instructions for conduct in certain situations. *Shi'ite* is Arabic for "supporter" or "partisan."

First Crusade), the Muslim world was badly fragmented and vulnerable to outside intrusions.

At the same time that the Muslim world was becoming increasingly divided, Western Europe was showing signs of increased energy. After centuries of comparatively modest population increases, suddenly population grew more rapidly, creating a surplus agricultural population and a resulting desire for more land. For example, it has been estimated that between about 950 and 1347 (the year the Black Death first appeared in Europe), the population of Europe increased threefold—in some areas, like Saxony, it increased tenfold. At the same time, trade with the eastern Mediterranean grew significantly, which fed the desires, especially in the commercial cities of Italy, for more trade connections with the Middle East. Finally, the social order produced a class of knightly warriors who were anxious to extend their power through combat.

Politically, however, Europe was even more fragmented than the Muslim world. Kings, for the most part weak, were unable to enforce peace within their domains. In an effort to keep the lords of Europe away from each other's throats as well as to enhance the power of the papacy, popes in the eleventh century attempted to promote the Peace of God movement among Christians. European nobles, the movement proclaimed, would not engage in warfare against one another.

The Peace of God movement shows that the power of the popes was increasing and that religious enthusiasm was on the rise in Europe. Itinerant preachers whipped up crowds into fevers of religious excitement in which visions and miracles of healing were reported. In about the year 1000, an old Christian myth was revived and spread throughout much of Europe. Before the second coming of Christ and the resulting end of the world, the story went, an emperor from the West would be crowned in Jerusalem and would battle the Antichrist in that holy city. The circulation of this myth was especially rampant during the widespread famine of 1033.

Hence a number of factors were pushing Christian Europe toward its own version of a "holy war." Population growth spurred a hunger for land, and, in turn, a drive for new lands to be brought under Europeans' control gained momentum. The knightly warriors could maintain the Peace of God among Christians while at the same time uniting to battle "pagans" elsewhere. Crusades could also increase the power of the papacy and would direct the religious enthusiasm toward a productive end. Therefore, when Pope Urban II in 1095 issued his call for a crusade, many Christians took up the cry "God wills it!" "You should be especially aroused," Urban challenged his listeners at Clermont, "by the knowledge that . . . the holy places are shamelessly misused and sacrilegiously defiled with their filth." The first armies set off in August 1097[13]; they captured Jerusalem on July 15, 1099.

13. A ragtag army of peasants led by the itinerant holy man Peter the Hermit began its march earlier, slaughtered Jews, on its way across Europe, and was wiped out before reaching Palestine. It has been estimated that one-fourth of all "crusaders" (more often they referred to themselves as pilgrims) died on their way to the Holy Land.

Earlier Muslim incursions into North Africa, the eastern Mediterranean, Sicily, Italy, Spain, and southern France did not mean that they had learned a great deal about Christian Europe, or that European Christians had learned a great deal about them. Instead, what is striking is the apparent utter lack of curiosity that each side displayed toward the other. Beginning about the time of the First Crusade, however, the number of written accounts by both Christians and Muslims increased dramatically. Your tasks are to determine what the perceptions presented were *and* how they helped to shape opinion on how the other side was to be treated.

THE METHOD

The Evidence section of this chapter contains three Muslim accounts of European crusaders and two European Christian accounts of Muslims. Usamah ibn-Munqidh (1095–1188) was born in Syria and educated by private tutors; he was a merchant and government administrator, and knew Europeans quite well. Source 1 is his account of the "curious" crusaders. For his part, Ibn al-Athir (1160–1233) was one of three brothers, all of whom became noted Arabic scholars. He traveled extensively to collect material for his historical writing, and in Source 2, he glories in the 1187 retaking of Jerusalem. Imad ad-Din (1125–1201) was a scholar who was best known as a secretary to the sultan Saladin. Source 3 is an excerpt from his *History of the Fall of Jerusalem.*

As to the Christian sources, *History of the Jerusalem Journey* (Source 4) is by Peter Tudebode, a priest who accompanied the warriors on the First Crusade. One or possibly two of his brothers were killed in battle during the siege of Antioch. Some controversy continues to surround Peter Tudebode's account because many scholars believe that some of it was plagiarized from earlier writers. Since you are concerned with the perceptions that readers or listeners might have gleaned from the account, whether Tudebode actually saw some of what he chronicled or not is less important than those perceptions.

The final account, *A History of Deeds Done Beyond the Sea* by William of Tyre (Source 5), is almost certainly the most widely read account by a Christian of the Crusades. William was born around 1130 in or near Jerusalem to European parents. He was extremely well educated both in Palestine and in Europe and had command of six languages, including Arabic and Persian. He was ordained a Roman Catholic priest, returned to what Christians referred to as the Holy Land, and was made Archbishop of Tyre, a position he held from 1175 to approximately 1185. By the time Saladin conquered Jerusalem in 1187, William had disappeared from view and probably had died.

At first glance, all of these sources present some potential problems. To begin with, we cannot be certain that any of the authors were eyewitnesses to the events they describe. For example, some events that William of Tyre wrote about took place before he was born. To be sure, as secretary to Saladin, Imad ad-Din was in an excellent position to witness the events that he recounted. But that is not proof that he actually *did* see them, and we cannot be sure how much he embellished what he saw or heard.

And yet, in this chapter, these are not the obstacles that they might be elsewhere. This is because, as noted above, we are seeking the *perceptions* that each side had of the other and the images and stereotypes that were deliberately created for a myriad of purposes (one pilgrim on the First Crusade, the Fulcher of Charters, described people "so tall that they can mount elephants as easily as horses").[14] Each author is attempting to create an impression in the minds of readers. To that end, he may accurately report events, or he may liberally exaggerate, interpret, or simply invent. That these writers were helping to create or perpetuate what ultimately would become very unhealthy stereotypes that in some cases continue to exist today does not appear to have bothered them in the least. Indeed, for some of these men, such stereotypes were good things that people should believe when facing their enemies.

As you finish each selection, think of some adjectives that readers of the account might have used to describe "the enemy." Keep a running list of these adjectives as you proceed through the evidence. Be willing also to read between the lines. Sometimes a particular author, in genuinely trying to describe or explain a specific incident, may have nevertheless created a perception in the minds of his readers, intentionally or unintentionally. Be alert for such instances.

Keep the central questions of the chapter in mind: In the written accounts by Muslims and Christians, what impressions did each side create of the other? How might those perceptions or stereotypes have influenced the way each side chose to deal with and treat each other, both during and after the period Europeans refer to as the Crusades?

14. See Fulcher of Charters, *A History of the Expedition to Jerusalem, 1095–1127,* trans. Frances Rita Ryan (Knoxville: University of Tennessee Press, 1969), p. 287.

THE EVIDENCE

MUSLIMS ON CHRISTIANS

Source 1 from Usamah ibn-Munqidh, An Arab-Syrian Gentleman and Warrior in the Period of the Crusades, *trans. Philip K. Hitti (New York: Columbia University Press, 1929; reprint, Princeton: Princeton University Press, 1987), pp. 161–169.*

1. Usamah ibn-Munqidh Describes the Franks

Their lack of sense.—Mysterious are the works of the Creator, the author of all things! When one comes to recount cases regarding the Franks,[15] he cannot but glorify Allah (exalted is he!) and sanctify him, for he sees them as animals possessing the virtues of courage and fighting, but nothing else; just as animals have only the virtues of strength and carrying loads. I shall now give some instances of their doings and their curious mentality.

In the army of King Fulk, son of Fulk, was a Frankish reverend knight who had just arrived from their land in order to make the holy pilgrimage and then return home. He was of my intimate fellowship and kept such constant company with me that he began to call me "my brother." Between us were mutual bonds of amity and friendship. When he resolved to return by sea to his homeland, he said to me:

> My brother, I am leaving for my country and I want thee to send with me thy son (my son, who was then fourteen years old, was at that time in my company) to our country, where he can see the knights and learn wisdom and chivalry. When he returns, he will be like a wise man.

Thus there fell upon my ears words which would never come out of the head of a sensible man; for even if my son were to be taken captive, his captivity could not bring him a worse misfortune than carrying him into the lands of the Franks. However, I said to the man:

> By thy life, this has exactly been my idea. But the only thing that prevented me from carrying it out was the fact that his grandmother, my mother, is so fond of him and did not this time let him come out with me until she exacted an oath from me to the effect that I would return him to her.

Thereupon he asked, "Is thy mother still alive?" "Yes," I replied. "Well," said he, "disobey her not." . . .

15. Most Muslims called all the crusaders "Franks" even though they knew full well that they were not all French.

Their curious medication.—A case illustrating their curious medicine is the following:

The lord of al-Munayṭirah wrote to my uncle asking him to dispatch a physician to treat certain sick persons among his people. My uncle sent him a Christian physician named Thābit. Thābit was absent but ten days when he returned. So we said to him, "How quickly hast thou healed thy patients!" He said:

> They brought before me a knight in whose leg an abscess had grown; and a woman afflicted with imbecility. To the knight I applied a small poultice until the abscess opened and became well; and the woman I put on diet and made her humor wet. Then a Frankish physician came to them and said, "This man knows nothing about treating them." He then said to the knight, "Which wouldst thou prefer, living with one leg or dying with two?" The latter replied, "Living with one leg." The physician said, "Bring me a strong knight and a sharp ax." A knight came with the ax. And I was standing by. Then the physician laid the leg of the patient on a block of wood and bade the knight strike his leg with the ax and chop it off at one blow. Accordingly he struck it—while I was looking on—one blow, but the leg was not severed. He dealt another blow, upon which the marrow of the leg flowed out and the patient died on the spot. He then examined the woman and said, "This is a woman in whose head there is a devil which has possessed her. Shave off her hair." Accordingly they shaved it off and the woman began once more to eat their ordinary diet—garlic and mustard. Her imbecility took a turn for the worse. The physician then said, "The devil has penetrated through her head." He therefore took a razor, made a deep cruciform incision on it, peeled off the skin at the middle of the incision until the bone of the skull was exposed and rubbed it with salt. The woman also expired instantly. Thereupon I asked them whether my services were needed any longer, and when they replied in the negative I returned home, having learned of their medicine what I knew not before. . . .

Another wants to show to a Moslem God as a child.—I saw one of the Franks come to al-Amīr Mu'īn-al-Dīn (may Allah's mercy rest upon his soul!) when he was in the Dome of the Rock and say to him, "Dost thou want to see God as a child?" Mu'īn-al-Dīn said, "Yes." The Frank walked ahead of us until he showed us the picture of Mary with Christ (may peace be upon him!) as an infant in her lap. He then said, "This is God as a child." But Allah is exalted far above what the infidels say about him!

Franks lack jealousy in sex affairs.—The Franks are void of all zeal and jealousy. One of them may be walking along with his wife. He meets another man who takes the wife by the hand and steps aside to converse with her while the husband is standing on one side waiting for his wife to conclude the conversation. If she lingers too long for him, he leaves her alone with the conversant and goes away.

Here is an illustration which I myself witnessed:

When I used to visit Nāblus, I always took lodging with a man named Mu'izz, whose home was a lodging house for the Moslems. The house had windows which opened to the road, and there stood opposite to it on the other side of the road a house belonging to a Frank who sold wine for the merchants. He would take some wine in a bottle and go around announcing it by shouting, "So and so, the merchant, has just opened a cask full of this wine. He who wants to buy some of it will find it in such and such a place." The Frank's pay for the announcement made would be the wine in that bottle. One day this Frank went home and found a man with his wife in the same bed. He asked him, "What could have made thee enter into my wife's room?" The man replied, "I was tired, so I went in to rest." "But how," asked he, "didst thou get into my bed?" The other replied, "I found a bed that was spread, so I slept in it." "But," said he, "my wife was sleeping together with thee!" The other replied, "Well, the bed is hers. How could I therefore have prevented her from using her own bed?" "By the truth of my religion," said the husband, "if thou shouldst do it again, thou and I would have a quarrel." Such was for the Frank the entire expression of his disapproval and the limit of his jealousy. . . .

Ordeal by water.—I once went in the company of al-Amīr Mu'īn-al-Dīn (may Allah's mercy rest upon his soul!) to Jerusalem. We stopped at Nāblus. There a blind man, a Moslem, who was still young and was well dressed, presented himself before al-Amīr carrying fruits for him and asked permission to be admitted into his service in Damascus. The amīr consented. I inquired about this man and was informed that his mother had been married to a Frank whom she had killed. Her son used to practice ruses against the Frankish pilgrims and cooperate with his mother in assassinating them. They finally brought charges against him and tried his case according to the Frankish way of procedure.

They installed a huge cask and filled it with water. Across it they set a board of wood. They then bound the arms of the man charged with the act, tied a rope around his shoulders and dropped him into the cask, their idea being that in case he was innocent, he would sink in the water and they would then lift him up with the rope so that he might not die in the water; and in case he was guilty, he would not sink in the water. This man did his best to sink when they dropped him into the water, but he could not do it. So he had to submit to their sentence against him—may Allah's curse be upon them! They pierced his eyeballs with red-hot awls. . . .

Source 2 from Francesco Gabrieli, Arab Historians of the Crusades *(Berkeley: University of California Press, 1969), pp. 141–142, 144.*

2. Ibn al-Athir, The Capture of Jerusalem, 1187

When the Franks saw how violently the Muslims were attacking, how continuous and effective was the fire from the ballistas and how busily the sappers were breaching the walls, meeting no resistance, they grew desperate, and their leaders assembled to take counsel. They decided to ask for safe-conduct out of the city and to hand Jerusalem over to Saladin.[16] They sent a deputation of their lords and nobles to ask for terms, but when they spoke of it to Saladin he refused to grant their request. "We shall deal with you," he said, "just as you dealt with the population of Jerusalem when you took it in 492/1099, with murder and enslavement and other such savageries!" The messengers returned empty-handed. Then Baliān ibn Barzān asked for safe-conduct for himself so that he might appear before Saladin to discuss developments. Consent was given, and he presented himself and once again began asking for a general amnesty in return for surrender. The Sultan still refused his requests and entreaties to show mercy. Finally, despairing of this approach, Baliān said: "Know, O Sultan, that there are very many of us in this city, God alone knows how many. At the moment we are fighting half-heartedly in the hope of saving our lives, hoping to be spared by you as you have spared others; this is because of our horror of death and our love of life. But if we see that death is inevitable, then by God we shall kill our children and our wives, burn our possessions, so as not to leave you with a *dinar* or a *drachma* or a single man or woman to enslave. When this is done, we shall pull down the Sanctuary of the Rock and the Masjid al-Aqsa and the other sacred places, slaughtering the Muslim prisoners we hold—5,000 of them—and killing every horse and animal we possess. Then we shall come out to fight you like men fighting for their lives, when each man, before he falls dead, kills his equals; we shall die with honour, or win a noble victory!" Then Saladin took counsel with his advisers, all of whom were in favour of his granting the assurances requested by the Franks, without forcing them to take extreme measures whose outcome could not be foreseen. "Let us consider them as being already our prisoners," they said, "and allow them to ransom themselves on terms agreed between us." The Sultan agreed to give the Franks assurances of safety on the understanding that each man, rich and poor alike, should pay ten *dinar*, children of both sexes two *dinar* and women five *dinar*. All who paid this sum within forty days should go free, and those who had not paid at the end of the time should be enslaved. Baliān ibn Barzān offered 30,000 *dinar* as ransom for the poor, which was accepted, and the city surrendered on Friday 27 rajab/2 October 1187, a memorable day on which the Muslim flags were hoisted over the walls of Jerusalem. . . .

The Grand Patriarch of the Franks left the city with the treasures from the Dome of the Rock, the Masjid al-Aqsa, the Church of the Resurrection and others, God alone knows the amount of the treasure; he also took an equal quantity of money. Saladin made no difficulties, and when he was advised to sequestrate

16. **Saladin:** Muslim sultan Salah ad-Din, whose real name was Yusuf ibn-Ayyub. *Salah-ad-Din* means "Rectifier of the Faith," a name Yusuf took up when he began his jihad against Christians.

the whole lot for Islām, replied that he would not go back on his word. He took only the ten *dinar* from him, and let him go, heavily escorted, to Tyre.

At the top of the cupola of the Dome of the Rock there was a great gilded cross. When the Muslims entered the city on the Friday, some of them climbed to the top of the cupola to take down the cross. When they reached the top a great cry went up from the city and from outside the walls, the Muslims crying the *Allāh akbar* in their joy, the Franks groaning in consternation and grief. So loud and piercing was the cry that the earth shook. . . .

Source 3 from Francesco Gabrieli, Arab Historians of the Crusades *(Berkeley: University of California Press, 1969), pp. 136–137, 148–149, 163, 170–171, 204, 207.*

3. From Imad ad-Din, *History of the Fall of Jerusalem*

At the same time as the King was taken the "True Cross"[17] was also captured, and the idolaters who were trying to defend it were routed. It was this cross, brought into position and raised on high, to which all Christians prostrated themselves and bowed their heads. Indeed, they maintain that it is made of the wood of the cross on which, they say, he whom they adore was hung, and so they venerate it and prostrate themselves before it. They had housed it in a casing of gold, adorned with pearls and gems, and kept it ready for the festival of the Passion, for the observance of their yearly ceremony. When the priests exposed it to view and the heads (of the bearers) bore it along all would run and cast themselves down around it, and no one was allowed to lag behind or hang back without forfeiting his liberty. Its capture was for them more important than the loss of the King and was the gravest blow that they sustained in that battle. The cross was a prize without equal, for it was the supreme object of their faith. To venerate it was their prescribed duty, for it was their God, before whom they would bow their foreheads to the ground, and to which their mouths sang hymns. They fainted at its appearance, they raised their eyes to contemplate it, they were consumed with passion when it was exhibited and boasted of nothing else when they had seen it. They went into ecstasies at its reappearance, they offered up their lives for it and sought comfort from it, so much so that they had copies made of it which they worshipped, before which they prostrated themselves in their houses and on which they called when they gave evidence. So when the Great Cross was taken great was the calamity that befell them, and the strength drained from their loins. Great was the number of the

17. The religious excitement in Europe led to the "discovery" of numerous relics both before and during the Crusades. Some of these relics were portions of the "True Cross" of Christ's crucifixion (see above), the Holy Lance (that pierced Jesus's side), and the Crown of Thorns. Thus, the loss of what was believed to have been the cross to Saladin was a devastating blow to the crusaders.

defeated, exalted the feelings of the victorious army. It seemed as if, once they knew of the capture of the Cross, none of them would survive that day of ill-omen. They perished in death or imprisonment, and were overcome by force and violence.

Here[18] are pictures of the Apostles conversing, Popes with their histories, monks in their cells, priests in their councils, the Magi with their ropes,[19] priests and their imaginings; here the effigies of the Madonna and the Lord, of the Temple and the Birthplace, of the Table and the fishes, and what is described and sculpted of the Disciples and the Master, of the cradle and the Infant speaking. Here are the effigies of the ox and the ass, of Paradise and Hell, the clappers and the divine laws. Here, they say, the Messiah was crucified, the sacrificial victim slain, divinity made incarnate, humanity deified. Here the dual nature was united, the cross was raised, light was extinguished and darkness covered the land. Here the nature was united with the person, the existent mingled with the non-existent, the adored Being was baptized and the Virgin gave birth to her Son.

They continued to attach errors like this to the object of their cult, wandering with false beliefs far from the true forms of faith, and said: "We shall die in defence of our Lord's sepulchre, and we shall die in fear of its slipping from our hands; we shall fight and struggle for it: how could we not fight, not contend and join battle, how could we leave this for them to take, and permit them to take from us what we took from them?" They made far-reaching and elaborate preparations, stretching out endlessly to infinity. They mounted deadly weapons on the walls, and veiled the face of light with the sombre curtain of walls. They sent out their demons, their wolves ran hither and thither, their impetuous tyrants raged; their swords were unsheathed, the fabric of their downfall displayed, their blazing firebrands lit. . . .

When Jerusalem was purified of the filth of the hellish Franks and had stripped off her vile garments to put on the robe of honour, the Christians, after paying their tax, refused to leave, and asked to be allowed to stay on in safety, and gave prodigious service and worked for us with all their might, carrying out every task with discipline and cheerfulness. They paid "the tax for protection permitted to them, humbly." They stood ready to accept whatever might be inflicted on them, and their affliction grew as they stood waiting for it. Thus they became in effect tribute-payers, reliant upon (Muslim) protection; they were used and employed in menial tasks and in their position they accepted these tasks as if they were gifts.

The Franks had cut pieces from the Rock,[20] some of which they had carried to Constantinople and Sicily and sold, they said, for their weight in gold, making

18. **Here:** refers to the Church of the Holy Sepulchre, a church that Christians believed enclosed the sites of Jesus' crucifixion and the tomb from which they claim, he was resurrected.

19. **Magi . . . ropes:** refers to the Qur'an XX, 69, which describes Egyptian Magi casting down ropes before Moses and making them appear to be serpents.

20. See note 11.

it a source of income. When the Rock reappeared to sight the marks of these cuts were seen and men were incensed to see how it had been mutilated. Now it is on view with the wounds it suffered, preserving its honour for ever, safe for Islam, within its protection and its fence. This was all done after the Sultan left and after an ordered pattern of life had been established. . . .

There arrived by ship three hundred lovely Frankish women, full of youth and beauty, assembled from beyond the sea and offering themselves for sin. They were expatriates come to help expatriates, ready to cheer the fallen and sustained in turn to give support and assistance, and they glowed with ardour for carnal intercourse. They were all licentious harlots, proud and scornful, who took and gave, foul-fleshed and sinful, singers and coquettes, appearing proudly in public, ardent and inflamed, tinted and painted, desirable and appetizing, exquisite and graceful, who ripped open and patched up, lacerated and mended, erred and ogled, urged and seduced, consoled and solicited, seductive and languid, desired and desiring, amused and amusing, versatile and cunning, like tipsy adolescents, making love and selling themselves for gold, bold and ardent, loving and passionate, pink-faced and unblushing, black-eyed and bullying, callipygian[21] and graceful, with nasal voices and fleshy thighs, blue-eyed and grey-eyed, broken-down little fools. . . .

Among the Franks there were indeed women who rode into battle with cuirasses [armor breastplates] and helmets, dressed in men's clothes; who rode out into the thick of the fray and acted like brave men although they were but tender women, maintaining that all this was an act of piety, thinking to gain heavenly rewards by it, and making it their way of life. Praise be to him who led them into such error and out of the paths of wisdom! On the day of battle more than one woman rode out with them like a knight and showed (masculine) endurance in spite of the weakness (of her sex); clothed only in a coat of mail they were not recognized as women until they had been stripped of their arms. Some of them were discovered and sold as slaves; and everywhere was full of old women. These were sometimes a support and sometimes a source of weakness. They exhorted and incited men to summon their pride, saying that the Cross imposed on them the obligation to resist to the bitter end, and that the combatants would win eternal life only by sacrificing their lives, and that their God's sepulchre was in enemy hands. Observe how men and women led them into error; the latter in their religious zeal tired of feminine delicacy, and to save themselves from the terror of dismay (on the day of Judgment) became the close companions of perplexity, and having succumbed to the lust for vengeance, became hardened, and stupid and foolish because of the harm they had suffered. . . .

21. **callipygian:** having shapely buttocks.

EUROPEANS ON MUSLIMS

Source 4 from Peter Tudebode, Historia de Hierosolymitano Itinere (History of the Jerusalem Journey), *trans. John Hugh Hill and Laurita L. Hill (Philadelphia: American Philosophical Society, 1974), pp. 54–55, 58–59, 115.*

4. From Peter Tudebode, *History of the Jerusalem Journey*

The Turkish attack was so overwhelming that our men took to their heels over the nearest mountain or the most convenient path; and those who were swift of foot survived, but the laggards met death for the name of Christ. More than one thousand knights or footmen martyred on that day rose joyfully to heaven and, bearing the stole of customary white-robed martyrdom, glorified and praised our triune God in whom they happily triumphed; and they said in unison: "Our God! Why did you not protect our blood which was shed today for your name?"

Following a different road, Bohemond with a few knights gave his horse free rein and sped to the assembled group of beset crusaders. Burning with anger over the death of our men, we invoked the name of Jesus Christ and, being assured of the crusade to the Holy Sepulchre, moved as a united front against our foes and joined in battle with one heart and mind. The Turks, enemies of God and us, stood around stunned and paralyzed with fear because they thought that they could overwhelm and slaughter us as they had done the troops of Raymond and Bohemond.

But Omnipotent God permitted no such thing. Knights of the true God, protected on all sides by the sign of the Cross, rushed pell-mell and courageously struck the Turks. In the ensuing rout the besieged scurried to safety by way of the narrow bridge to Antioch. The survivors, who could not push their way through the jam of people and horses, were snuffed out in everlasting death, and their miserable souls returned to the devil and his legions. We knocked them in the head and drove them into the river with our deadly lances so that the waters of the swift Orontes seemed to flow crimson with Turkish blood. If by chance one of them crawled up the bridge posts or struggled to swim to land, he was wounded. All along the river banks we stood pushing and drowning the pagans in the pull of the rapid stream.

The din of battle coupled with the screams of Christians and Turks rang out to the elements, and the rain of missiles and arrows darkened the sky and obscured the daylight. Strident voices within and without Antioch added to the noise. Christian women of Antioch came to loopholes on the battlements, and in their accustomed way secretly applauded as they watched the miserable plight of the Turks. Armenians, Syrians, and Greeks, willingly or unwillingly, by daily orders of the tyrannical Turkish leaders, sped arrows against us. Twelve Turkish emirs in line of duty met death in soul and body as well as fifteen hundred of their most experienced and brave soldiers who were also the core of Antioch's defense.

The survivors in Antioch did not have the *esprit de corps* to shout and gibber by day and night as had been their custom. Only night broke off the skirmishing of crusaders and their opponents and so ended the fighting, the hurling of javelins, the thrusting of spears, and the shooting of arrows. So by the strength of God and the Holy Sepulchre the Turks no longer possessed their former spirit, either in words or deeds. As a result of this day, we refitted ourselves very well in horses and other necessities. . . .

On another day the Turks led to the top of an Antiochian wall a noble knight, Rainald Porchet, whom they had imprisoned in a foul dungeon. They then told him that he should inquire from the Christian pilgrims how much they would pay for his ransom before he lost his head. From the heights of the wall Rainald addressed the leaders: "My lords, it matters not if I die, and I pray you, my brothers, that you pay no ransom for me. But be certain in the faith of Christ and the Holy Sepulchre that God is with you and shall be forever. You have slain all the leaders and the bravest men of Antioch; namely, twelve emirs and fifteen thousand noblemen, and no one remains to give battle with you or to defend the city."

The Turks asked what Rainald had said. The interpreter replied: "Nothing good concerning you was said."

The emir, Yaghi Siyan, immediately ordered him to descend from the wall and spoke to him through an interpreter: "Rainald, do you wish to enjoy life honorably with us?"

Rainald replied: "How can I live honorably with you without sinning?"

The emir answered: "Deny your God, whom you worship and believe, and accept Mohammed and our other gods. If you do so we shall give to you all that you desire such as gold, horses, mules, and many other worldly goods which you wish, as well as wives and inheritances; and we shall enrich you with great lands."

Rainald replied to the emir: "Give me time for consideration"; and the emir gladly agreed. Rainald with clasped hands knelt in prayer to the east; humbly he asked God that He come to his aid and transport with dignity his soul to the bosom of Abraham.

When the emir saw Rainald in prayer, he called his interpreter and said to him: "What was Rainald's answer?"

The interpreter then said: "He completely denies your god. He also refuses your worldly goods and your gods."

After hearing this report, the emir was extremely irritated and ordered the immediate beheading of Rainald, and so the Turks with great pleasure chopped off his head. Swiftly the angels, joyfully singing the Psalms of David, bore his soul and lifted it before the sight of God for Whose love he had undergone martyrdom.

Then the emir, in a towering rage because he could not make Rainald turn apostate, at once ordered all the pilgrims in Antioch to be brought before him with their hands bound behind their backs. When they had come before him, he ordered them stripped stark naked, and as they stood in the nude he commanded that they be bound with ropes in a circle. He then had chaff, firewood, and hay piled around them, and finally as enemies of God he ordered them put to the torch.

The Christians, those knights of Christ, shrieked and screamed so that their voices resounded in heaven to God for whose love their flesh and bones were cremated; and so they all entered martyrdom on this day wearing in heaven their white stoles before the Lord, for Whom they had so loyally suffered in the reign of our Lord Jesus Christ, to Whom is the honor and glory now and throughout eternity. Amen. . . .

When our lords saw these atrocities, they were greatly angered and held a council in which the bishops and priests recommended that the crusaders hold a procession around the city. So the bishops and priests, barefooted, clad in sacred vestments, and bearing crosses in their hands, came from the church of the Blessed Mary, which is on Mount Zion, to the church of Saint Stephen, the Protomartyr, singing and praying that the Lord Jesus Christ deliver his holy city and the Holy Sepulchre from the pagan people and place it in Christian hands for His holy service. The clerks, so clad, along with the armed knights and their retainers, marched side by side.

The sight of this caused the Saracens to parade likewise on the walls of Jerusalem, bearing insignia of Mohammed on a standard and pennon. The Christians came to the church of Saint Stephen and there took their stations as is customary in our processions. In the meantime the Saracens stood on the walls, screamed, blared out with horns, and performed all kinds of acts of mockery. To add insult to injury they made from wood a cross similar to the one on which, pouring forth His blood, the most merciful Christ redeemed the world. Afterward they inflicted great sorrow upon the Christians when, in the sight of all, they beat upon the cross with sticks and shattered it against the walls, shouting loudly, "*Frango agip salip*," which means "Franks, is this a good cross?"

Source 5 from William of Tyre, A History of Deeds Done Beyond the Sea, *2 vols., trans. Emily Atwater Babcock and A. C. Krey (New York: Columbia University Press, 1943), vol. 1, pp. 60, 68–69, 306–307; vol. 2, p. 323.*

5. From William of Tyre, *A History of Deeds Done Beyond the Sea*

In the time of the Roman Emperor Heraclius, according to ancient histories and Oriental tradition, the pernicious doctrines of Muhammad had gained a firm foothold in the Orient. This first-born son of Satan falsely declared that he was a prophet sent from God and thereby led astray the lands of the East, especially Arabia. The poisonous seed which he sowed so permeated the provinces that his successors employed sword and violence, instead of preaching and exhortation, to compel the people, however reluctant, to embrace the erroneous tenets of the prophet. . . .

There was a certain infidel living in the city, a treacherous and wicked man, who persecuted our people with insatiable hatred. This man was determined to devise some scheme that would bring about their destruction. One day, he stealthily threw the carcass of a dog into the temple court, a place which the custodians—and indeed the whole city as well—were most careful to keep scrupulously clean. Worshippers who came to the temple to pray the next morning found the mouldering body of the unclean animal. Almost frantic, they at once roused the whole city with their cries. The populace quickly ran to the temple, and all agreed that without question the Christians were responsible for the act. Need more be said? Death was decreed for all Christians, since it was judged that by death alone could they atone for such an act of sacrilege. The faithful, in full assurance of their innocence, prepared to suffer death for Christ's sake. As the executioners, with swords unsheathed, were about to carry out their orders, however, a young man, filled with the spirit, came forward and offered himself as the sacrifice. "It would be most disastrous, O brethren," he said, "that the entire church should die in this way. Far better were it that one man should give his life for the people, that the whole Christian race may not perish. Promise me that annually you will reverently honor my memory and that the respect and honor due to my family shall be maintained forever. On these terms, at the command of God, I will deliver you from this massacre." The Christians heard his words with great joy and readily granted what he asked. They promised that, on the day of palm branches, in perpetual memory of him, those of his lineage should bear into the city, in solemn procession, the olive which signifies our Lord Jesus Christ.

The young man then gave himself up to the chief men of Jerusalem and declared that he was the criminal. In this way he established the innocence of the other Christians, for, when the judges heard his story, they absolved the rest and put him to the sword. Thus he laid down his life for the brethren and, with pious resignation, met death, that most blessed sleep, confident that he had acquired grace in the sight of the Lord. . . .

There was a certain noble of the Turkish race named Balas living in that part of the country, who had formerly been the lord of Seruj. At that time, he had been allied by treaty with the count, and before the Latins arrived in such numbers the two had been on very friendly terms. This man perceived that Baldwin's affection toward him had become less. Led either by his own feelings of resentment, or possibly by the request of the citizens, he went to the count and begged as a favor that he would come personally to receive the one fortress which still remained in his [Balas's] possession. He declared that Baldwin's favor would be all-sufficient for him and would be esteemed as a valuable heritage. He said also that he intended to bring his wife and children, with all he possessed, to Edessa and pretended to stand in great fear of his fellow countrymen, because he had become so friendly with the Christians. To carry out this wish, the count was persuaded to set a day to visit the place. At the time appointed, he set out with two hundred knights and marched to the fortress, whither Balas had preceded him. The latter, however, had secretly strengthened the defenses of the castle by introducing a hundred valiant knights, splendidly armed. This force was concealed inside in such a way that not a man was visible.

When Baldwin arrived before the castle, Balas begged that he would take only a few of his staff with him into the fortress. He gave as an excuse for this request the risk of danger to his property if the entire force were introduced. His persuasive words almost induced the count to accede to his wishes in every respect. Fortunately, however, some of the wise noblemen in attendance on Baldwin had a certain foreboding of treachery. Almost by force they held the count back against his protest and prevented his entering the castle. They rightly distrusted the evil designs of the rascal and judged it safer that the trial be first made by others. The count acquiesced in this prudent counsel. He ordered twelve of his bravest men, well armed, to enter the place. Meanwhile, he himself with the rest of his band remained quietly outside near by until he should see with his own eyes the result of the experiment. No sooner had the gallant band entered than they fell victims to the perfidious treachery of the wicked Balas. For the hundred Turks mentioned above at once emerged from their hiding places, armed to the teeth. They seized the betrayed knights and, in spite of their efforts to resist, threw them into chains. This result distressed the count greatly. Anxious about the fate of his loyal men whom he had lost by so dastardly a trick, he drew nearer to the castle and earnestly admonished Balas to remember the oath of fidelity which he had taken. On the strength of this fealty, he urged him to return the prisoners so treacherously seized and to receive instead a large sum of money as ransom. Balas absolutely refused to consider this proposition, however, unless Seruj were returned to him. The count perceived that he could do nothing more, for the castle was situated on a steep precipice and was impregnable both because of its strength and because of the skill with which it was built. . . .

The reason for the title caliph is as follows: Muhammad, their prophet, or rather their destroyer, who was the first to draw the peoples of the East to this kind of superstition, had as his immediate successor one of his disciples named Abu-Bakr. The latter was succeeded in the kingdom by Omar, son of Khattab, who was likewise followed by Uthman, and he by Ali, son of Abu-Talib. All these prophets were called caliphs, as were also all who followed them later, because they succeeded their famous master and were his heirs. But the fifth in the succession from Muhammad, namely Ali, was more warlike than his predecessors and had far greater experience in military matters than his contemporaries. He was, moreover, a cousin of Muhammad himself. He considered it unfitting that he should be called the successor of his cousin and not rather a great prophet himself, much greater, in fact, than Muhammad. The fact that in his own estimation and that of many others he was greater did not satisfy him; he desired that this be generally acknowledged. Accordingly, he reviled Muhammad and spread among the people a story to the effect that the Angel Gabriel, the propounder of the law, had actually been sent to him from on high but by mistake had conferred the supreme honor on Muhammad. For this fault, he said, the angel had been severely blamed by the Lord. Although these claims seemed false to many from whose traditions they differed greatly, yet others believed them, and so a schism developed among that people which has lasted even to the present. Some maintain that Muhammad is the greater and, in fact, the greatest of all prophets, and these are called in their own tongue, Sunnites; others declare that Ali alone is the prophet of God, and they are called Shiites.

QUESTIONS TO CONSIDER

Begin with the three Muslim accounts of Christians. Usamah's account (Source 1) is extremely valuable not only because he was well acquainted with Christians but also because he offers his readers numerous examples to support his main view of his European Christian foes. Examine and analyze each of Usamah's illustrations. What point is he trying to make by relating the story of the Frank who wanted to take Usamah's son back to Europe to make him a "wise man"? How does this story shed light on Usamah's perception of the Franks? Similarly, Usamah describes in some detail two medical "case studies," comparing the European remedies to the Muslim treatment. What does he intend his readers to think after reading about those two patients? Would readers get the same impressions from his account of the Christians' "ordeal by water"? What are those impressions likely to have been? In his "God as a child" story, Usamah is remarkably restrained (see later accounts by Muslims and Christians of each other's faith). What point is communicated?

Because the subject reappears in Imad ad-Din's account, the subject of male-female relations deserves to be examined a bit more closely. In the "lack of jealousy" story, Usamah offers a very curious tale of a Frank who returns home to find his wife in bed with another man. What impression of European Christians do you think Usamah intends to give? What would his readers' reactions have been?

Ibn al-Athir's account (Source 2) is primarily concerned with Saladin's conquest of Jerusalem in 1187, and his portraits of European crusaders seem extremely vague. From reading the two accounts (the first of Franks suing for surrender terms and the second of Franks leaving the city), what impressions would readers get of the European crusaders? What adjectives best describe their behavior?

It matters little that Imad ad-Din's view (Source 3) of Christianity contains a number of errors and misperceptions—each side was remarkably ignorant of the other's faith. What is important is the perception of Christian beliefs that he attempts to convey. What impressions would Imad's readers have gathered from his story of the devotion of the European crusaders to the "True Cross"? How is the Church of the Holy Sepulchre depicted by Imad? How does he describe the treatment of Muslim holy sites by Christians? What stereotypes of European crusaders would that likely have put in the minds of Imad's readers? Finally, Imad portrays two groups of Frankish women. What do the descriptions tell readers about European women—and men?

Finally, reexamine each of the Muslim accounts. Do you notice any threads that are common to all three sources?

Like their Muslim counterparts, Western writers also recounted the immediate transportation of fallen warriors' souls to heaven (see, for example, the immensely popular *Song of Roland*, written by an anonymous author around 1100 about the Battle of Roncesvalles in 778).[22] Roman Catholic priest Peter Tudebode also wrote of Christian souls transported immediately to heaven (the martyrdom of Rainald Porchet) and the "everlasting death" of the Turks. According to Peter Tudebode, how does the Turkish emir react to the faithfulness of Rainald? What perceptions was Peter Tudebode trying to communicate to his readers in that account? in his account of Muslims' mockery of crosses?

William of Tyre was the Christian chronicler most familiar with Palestine and its Muslim population. Yet the first paragraph makes it clear that, to William, Muhammad is the"first-born son of Satan," a false prophet whose successors were converted to Islam by force. Interestingly, the "dog carcass" story and the "Balas trap" story both sketch the same stereotype of Muslims. What is that stereotype?

Now repeat for the Christian writers the process that you followed for the Muslim writers; that is, look for any common themes or stereotypes that all the accounts share.

As you examined and analyzed the Muslim and the European accounts, you doubtless noticed that some of the perceptions held by Muslims and European Christians about each other were remarkably similar. What similarities did you identify? How do you account for them?

Finally, without being too explicit, all of the accounts advocate ways in which the other side should be treated. How do the perceptions (and misperceptions) lead directly to those conclusions? What attitudes and behaviors do you think might have been recommended? To answer these questions, you will have to exercise some historical imagination. Put yourself in the position of an intelligent but uninformed person who is reading these accounts soon after they were written. How do the implicit stereotypes affect your view of how the targeted group should be treated? Explain.

22. *The Song of Roland* is based on a battle in which the rear guard of Charlemagne's army was overwhelmed and slaughtered by Basques. Writing during the First Crusade, however, the author substituted Muslims for Basques in the epic.

EPILOGUE

The perceptions that Muslims and European Christians had of one another made it almost inevitable that the wars later known in the West as the Crusades would be carried on with extreme ferocity. As some of the evidence above suggests, civilians and combatants often were slaughtered indiscriminately, as Christians were exhorted to "slay for God's love," and both Muslim and Christian warriors were promised immediate admission to heaven if they died while fighting in a holy war (jihad).[23] Although no accurate estimates of losses are available (some historians insist the Crusades cost the West between 4 and 5 *million* people out of a total population of around 50 million, a figure most historians believe is too high), it can be said that fewer than one-half of the pilgrims who set out on a crusade ever returned. Muslim losses, although not that high, were also frightful.

Gradually the crusading spirit declined in the West, partly because of the meager results they achieved and partly because Europe had turned to other concerns. The Black Death struck Europe in 1347, killing over five times the number felled in the Crusades. England lost between a quarter and a half of its total population to the plague, and the number of deaths were just as appalling in other parts of Europe and Asia (the plague had struck China in 1331, and a more serious outbreak occurred in 1353). In addition, the Hundred Years War (1337–1453) kept Europe in an almost perpetual state of upheaval, diverting its attention from any future crusades. In the Muslim world, political disunity and the Mongol threat turned Muslim attention away from Europeans. Too, the so-called crusader states (four European-ruled principalities on the eastern shores of the Mediterranean) all had succumbed again to Muslim control.

One would expect that the long period of contact between the Muslim and Christian worlds would have produced a great deal of cross-fertilization of culture, ideas, goods, and knowledge. Indeed, this was the case, although more of these kinds of exchanges took place in Spain and Italy than in the Middle East. From the Arabs, the West acquired a great deal of knowledge of medicine, astronomy, chemistry, physics, and mathematics. Paper, invented in China, was adopted by the Arabs and transmitted to Europe.[24] Arabs had preserved a great deal of Greek philosophy (much of which had been lost in the West), and it was by way of the Arabs that Europe "rediscovered" Aristotle. Arabic courtly

23. St. Bernard wrote that "a Christian glories in the death of a pagan because Christ is glorified; the liberality of the King [God] is revealed in the death of the Christian, because he is led out to his reward." Quoted in Norman Daniel, *Islam and the West: The Making of an Image*, rev. ed. (Oxford: Oneworld Publishing, 1993), p. 136.

24. In medicine, the Arab *al-Qanun* (The Canon) became *the* medical textbook in the West. In physics the Arabs gave the West the pendulum; in astronomy a more accurate method of predicting an eclipse; in mathematics the field of algebra (practically an Arab creation), the zero, and the decimal point. Before Europeans borrowed paper from the Arabs, they wrote on papyrus or parchment.

literature (adab) was translated and became the bases of some European literature (including Shakespeare's *Taming of the Shrew*). Trade between the two worlds was intensified.

Not surprisingly, Muslims borrowed almost nothing from the West. The Islamic world simply didn't think it had much to learn from the West. Muslims did adopt some European clothing and liked some European food, but these were minor compared to what Muslims exported to Europeans.

Yet, although the spirit of holy warfare declined in both the Muslim and Christian worlds, the perceptions and misperceptions that each side created of the other remained strong for centuries, and one can find their unhealthy residues even today in the struggles between the West and Iran and (later) Iraq, in the Arab-Israeli conflicts, and in the reemergence of Islamic fundamentalism. Behind the struggles over oil and geopolitics lie images, perceptions, and stereotypes that are centuries old and durable even today.

Writing at the time of the Crusades, Friar Felix Fabari wrote of Muslims, "The easterners are men of a different kind to us, they have other passions, other ways of thinking, other ideas . . . they are influenced by other stars. . . ." Even as Westerners have come to learn a great deal more about Islamic religion, society, politics, and the arts, the notions of Fabari and others remain.

CHAPTER EIGHT

ROMANCES AND BEHAVIOR IN ARISTOCRATIC JAPAN AND ITALY (1000–1350)

THE PROBLEM

Until the twentieth century, "history" for the most part meant the story of rulers and armies, the rise and fall of kings and empires. Thus events in the private lives of men and women are rarely mentioned in the chronicles that form the basis of much of our knowledge of premodern societies (unless they affected political developments). People's emotions and desires were viewed as even less appropriate subjects for historical record.

This does not mean, however, that earlier cultures discounted the role of emotions or were not interested in how emotions shaped human action. They simply did not explore feelings in histories or biographies, but in fiction. Writers created characters whose desires led them to great heights and depths, and readers avidly followed their emotional adventures. Sometimes writers borrowed characters from oral traditions or myths, telling familiar stories in new ways or making up fresh situations. At other times they invented characters whose stories then became part of oral tradition as those who could read told or read the stories to those who could not. In time these fictional romances became an important part of the literary heritage of many cultures.

Romances may be fiction, but, like all types of writing, they grow out of a specific cultural and historical background; every culture has a limited repertoire of assumptions and concepts that shape even fictional characters. Authors create characters as individuals with certain physical and emotional qualities, and then place them in settings and make them act in ways that will be believable to the reader. If romances thus reflect their own culture, they also help to shape it, as readers often learn what is expected of a woman or man faced with a certain dilemma by reading how these fictional characters responded. Romances do not teach directly like sermons or collected sayings of wise elders, but they usually give a clear idea of what is desirable and undesirable behavior. For later readers, like us, they also can provide details about aspects of life in the past that official histories never mention, such as styles of clothing or ideals of appearance.

Romances or other types of fiction therefore offer insights into earlier cultures that cannot be gained from official or academic histories alone. Your task in this chapter is a two-part one. First, you will use two romances from sharply divergent cultures—Murasaki Shikibu's *The Tale of Genji* from tenth-century Japan and Giovanni Boccaccio's *The Elegy of Lady Fiammetta* from fourteenth-century Italy—to explore aspects of private life and the relations between men and women. How do romances both portray and shape conventional standards of male and female behavior? Second, you need to think about these sources as well as more contemporary fiction to answer the question: What special problems arise in using fiction as a historical source?

BACKGROUND

The two romances in this chapter come from cultures that are widely separated chronologically and geographically, and yet they share certain characteristics. Both Murasaki's Japan and Boccaccio's Italy were aristocratic cultures in which a person's social level and family of birth largely determined his or her opportunities in life, but in which there was at least some social mobility. Both were urban cultures, for Murasaki the capital city of Heian Kyo (later Kyoto) and for Boccaccio the northern Italian city of Florence, both large cities by premodern standards, with populations of about 100,000. Both cities were the centers of a cultural flowering at the time these works were written, enjoying literature and art supported by the city's wealthiest and most powerful families (in Florence this cultural revival is termed the Renaissance).

There were also similarities between the two cultures in some aspects of language and learning. In both places, a learned language was normally used for history, philosophy, and other types of serious literature—Chinese in the case of Japan and Latin in the case of Italy—but an increasing number of works were being produced in the vernacular—Japanese and Italian. Women were excluded from most institutionalized learning in both cultures, so they were less likely to know the learned language; vernacular literature thus differed from learned literature in that it was aimed at an audience of both men and women. One's learning was to be worn lightly in both places, with men and to some degree upper-class women expected to be familiar with the established literary tradition and quote easily from it, but not to be pedantic.

In both cultures families had a great deal to say about whom their sons and daughters married, for marriage among the upper classes was regarded as an opportunity to increase family wealth and prestige. Affection between spouses, though nice, was hardly an adequate basis for marriage. In both Heian Kyo and Florence, upper-class women spent most of their lives indoors, somewhat secluded from public life, and did not hold official positions of power; they could inherit and own property but generally had to have a man look after their legal affairs, as they did not appear in court on their own behalf. In both cultures men were regarded as superior to women, an attitude that derived from religious beliefs. In Heian Japan, Buddhism taught that a woman could not be reborn into a higher category without first being born as a man; in Renaissance Florence, Christianity taught that women were responsible for bringing sin into the world. Both cultures accepted a sexual double standard, with extramarital affairs regarded as completely normal for men and openly discussed.

In other ways Heian Japan and Renaissance Italy differed dramatically. In Japan, Buddhism mixed easily with other religions and traditional ideas, so that people's individual belief systems were a blend with many sources, what we usually term *syncretism*. Astrology, omens, and notions about lucky and unlucky days and directions often influenced their actions. Buddhism taught that all worldly things are transitory and people should strive to control their passions, to the point of eliminating desire; after death, a person's soul migrated into another body, which could be higher or lower in status depending on his or her actions in the present life. The most proper attitude was one of *aware*, a gentle melancholy toward the world's passing things. Because of the quickness with which they fade, flowers captured the essence of these ideas, and both men and women used flowers and perfume to express their thoughts.

Though most men had only one wife, among the aristocracy polygamy was quite common. A man's first wife, chosen carefully by the two families to enhance their economic and political power, was generally the most important. Great attention was paid to a family's status at court, for the Heian aristocracy was divided into many ranks, with the highest receiving great privileges in terms of tax exemptions and household staffs provided by the government. Distinctions in rank were maintained by imperial edicts and law codes that stipulated, for example, where families of each rank could live, what kind of carriages they could travel in, and what they could wear. The marriage procedure included certain rituals that bestowed a religious blessing and assured that the community recognized the two persons as a couple; secondary wives were also often joined to their husband with a similar ritual, giving them the same legal status as the first wife. If a man was especially wealthy or important, he might also have official concubines who joined his household in a ceremony only slightly less elaborate than those for his wives. All of these women might live in the same household, although aristocratic houses were large and spread-out, with each wife and concubine inhabiting (and rarely leaving) her own quarters. Men also pursued frequent short- or long-term love affairs with women who did not live in their households, and as long as these women were not married, they were not stigmatized for such affairs and could later make perfectly honorable marriages. Wives, concubines, and even siblings or half-siblings often lived in the same house for years without seeing one another. Women were usually secluded behind screens or shades from all men except their closest family members, so that only their sleeves or shadows could be seen, although these shades were made of thin materials and voices in the next room could be heard easily. The shades were rolled up only on the hottest days, with houses thus quite dark and gloomy.

Because of this physical separation of men and women, contact between them often began with letter writing. People fell in love through writing, placing great importance not only on the content of letters, but on the words chosen, the way these were drawn, and the color combinations of inks and papers. Men tended to write in Chinese characters, whereas women wrote in *kana,* a phonetic script of Japanese as it was spoken. Their letters and literary works often contained Chinese poetry, however, for familiarity with classical Chinese poetry was essential for well-bred aristocrats of both sexes. Artistic sensitivity to painting and music was also expected, as was at least some skill in painting or playing a musical instrument.

In Renaissance Florence, Christianity was the religion of most of the population, although educated individuals were certainly familiar with the myths and stories about the classical Greek and Roman gods and goddesses. One of the distinctive features of Renaissance culture was an emphasis on classical studies and a conscious return to classical ideas and forms, a movement termed *humanism.* In the same way that Japanese aristocrats quoted Chinese poems, well-educated Italians referred to classical mythology to enrich and broaden their letters and other writings. People did not believe in this mythology in a religious sense, however, for unlike Buddhism, which accommodated other beliefs and encouraged syncretism, Christianity required its followers to repudiate other religions. Like Buddhism, Christianity encouraged believers to concentrate on the life to come, although this was not a life within another body as in Buddhism, but a life after death in either heaven or hell. Christianity did not regard passion or strong emotions as evil in themselves but felt these should be channeled into religious purposes. In fact, love and longing for God were often expressed in Christian literature in highly emotional terms that would have seemed very strange to people living in Heian Japan.

Men in Renaissance Florence could have only one wife at a time, though because of high death rates many people married more than once during their lives, and many households contained combinations of full siblings, half-siblings, and step-siblings. By this time Christianity rejected concubinage, so that although wealthy men often had mistresses, this relationship had no legal standing. A man might set his mistress up in an independent household and support her financially, but he would not move her into the household with his wife. Upper-class women were not out in public working the way lower-class women were, or conducting business the way upper-class men were, but they were not as secluded as the women in Heian Japan. Wealthy families often ate festive meals together in full view of all their neighbors, and women attended religious ceremonies and public celebrations regularly. Thus there were more chances for men and women to see each other, and though letter-writing was important, it was not as essential for making romantic contacts as it was in Japan.

When we turn from the social and literary background of these two works to the authors themselves, the differences are more striking than the similarities. Murasaki Shikibu (978–ca. 1030) was the daughter of an ambitious government official and gained an education in classical Chinese literature and history by sitting in on the lessons her father provided for her brother. At about age twenty she married a much older man who died soon afterward, leaving Murasaki with a daughter. For a while she lived in seclusion and probably began work on *The Tale of Genji* during this time. In about 1005 her father secured a position for her as a lady-in-waiting to the empress, and Murasaki was welcomed into the imperial court. During this time she worked on a diary as well as on *Genji* and was joined in her literary pursuits by a number of other women. The most famous of these was Sei Shonagon, the author of *The Pillow Book,* a collection of stories and descriptions of upper-class Heian life; Murasaki's daughter also became a well-known author.

The Tale of Genji is extremely long and complex, over twice as long as *War and Peace* and containing over 430 characters. Virtually every facet of it has provoked intense argument since it was written. We do not know exactly what order Murasaki wrote it in, because to some degree each chapter stands alone and often circulated independently. *Genji* appeared long before the invention of the printing press, so those who wished to have the book for themselves had to copy it or pay someone to do so. It quickly became a classic, and one modern commentator has estimated that there have been more than ten thousand books about *Genji* since the original was written. Its reputation and complexity led later Japanese critics to doubt whether it could really have been written by a woman, although Murasaki's authorship is not questioned at all today. (This often happened with great literary works written by women throughout the world, and Japan is unusual in that almost all its literary classics were written by women. This was the result of the fact that men regarded Chinese as the apropriate language for their writings, a feeling so strong that when men did write in Japanese, they pretended that their works were written by women. The opposite pattern is found throughout most of the rest of the world: women used male pen names to make it more likely that their works would be taken seriously.)

Giovanni Boccaccio (1313–1375) was the illegitimate son of a northern Italian merchant and an unknown mother. His father provided him with a good education, hoping that he would become a lawyer. Instead, Boccaccio became a writer, first gaining a reputation at the court of Naples in southern Italy, and then in Florence, where he became friends with the most famous poet and humanist of his time, Petrarch (1304–1374). Under Petrarch's influence, Boccaccio became a scholar of Greek and continued to write both Latin and Italian works. He never married, though he did father five children.

Shortly after his move to Florence, sometime between 1343 and 1345, Boccaccio wrote *The Elegy of Lady Fiammetta,* which apparently became quite popular because over seventy manuscript copies survive from around Europe. He also wrote satires, poetry, biographies, mythological treatises, geographical dictionaries, and commentaries on the works of other writers.

Several years after writing *Fiammetta,* Boccaccio wrote his greatest work, the *Decameron,* a collection of one hundred stories about men and women of all social classes who exhibit both good and bad human qualities—anger, despair, deceit, tenderness, jealousy. The *Decameron* is usually regarded as the first significant prose work in Italian, and it served as the model for many later works in Italian and other vernacular European languages. In contrast to the situation in Japan, writing in the vernacular in Europe did not become the province of female authors, for men wrote the major works in both Latin and the newly developing literary languages of Italian, French, English, and German. Both Petrarch and Boccaccio doubted the importance of their Italian works late in life, preferring their more serious Latin volumes, but it was the Italian ones that were to have the greatest influence. Female authors in Europe did write works modeled on Petrarch's sonnets and Boccaccio's *Decameron,* but no female-authored title in Europe would attain the status of *The Tale of Genji.*

THE METHOD

All types of sources from the past must be used very carefully, for even those that appear simply to relate historical facts, such as events during the reign of a monarch, or the births and deaths of family members, were written for a specific purpose and with a specific audience in mind. This is even more the case when we use fiction, for what the authors are attempting to tell is not a true story but a story that will interest readers and that supports a certain theme or thesis. Unless letters or other documents from authors tell us directly what points they are attempting to make, we must also be tentative in concluding the intent of the author in a literary piece; it might have been quite different from what we infer, particularly for works as old as *The Tale of Genji* or *The Elegy of Lady Fiammetta.*

Literary conventions also shape fictional works. All authors, even the most innovative, work within certain literary forms. For instance, they decide whether their work will be poetry or prose, whether it will be first-person narrative or third-person, whether they as an author will speak in the narrative or not. They choose which language to write in and adjust their vocabulary to suit the audience. They decide whether to base their characters on real individuals and whether to use actual historical events as the setting for the plot. Because they are also influenced by their own reading, they often model their work on earlier works, incorporating familiar themes and motifs. Other authors intentionally break with tradition, adding unexpected plot twists and unconventional characters, but their stories are effective precisely because both they as authors and we as readers realize that they are doing this. Thus even stories that violate the customary plot lines or characterizations expect readers to be familiar with certain conventions. (You can see this most easily in satire. A dialogue, for example, between the Lone Ranger and Tonto in which the Lone Ranger begins with "How! Me Lone Ranger, him Tonto" is recognizable as satire only if you know that these are normally Tonto's lines.)

Because of the literary nature of your sources in this chapter, and because you will be reading only excerpts from these works, it might be helpful for you to know the plot of each work before you begin. *The Tale of Genji* is the story of Genji, the son of the emperor and his favorite concubine, a woman whom the emperor loves so much that all the rest of the court is jealous. This jealousy and ill-will are so strong that they lead to the death of Genji's mother while he is still a small child. Though Genji grows up at court, becoming a handsome and talented young man, he is officially relegated to the status of a commoner and can never hope to become emperor himself. (His name, in fact, is actually that of the nonroyal clan to which he is assigned, the Genji.) He is married off to a princess slightly older than himself, Princess Aoi, a member of the most powerful clan, the Fujiwaras. He becomes good friends with her brother, To-no-Chujo, and they both have many love affairs. In one of these, To-no-Chujo has a daughter by a woman with whom he has lost contact; Genji later finds the woman and has a brief affair with her, during which she dies while lying next to Genji because of the jealous spirit of another of Genji's lovers. Guilt drives Genji to find her daughter, Tamakazura, and he presents her at court as if she were his own daughter. Genji himself secretly fathers a son by the woman who has taken his mother's place as the emperor's favorite concubine and has a number of other children. Later he falls in love with Tamakazura, but she rejects him; he then reveals her true parentage to both her and her father, and she assumes a position at court. Genji also takes in the abandoned daughter of another prince, Lady Murasaki, whom he weds after his first wife dies; Murasaki is often thought of as the romantic heroine of the story, as she becomes Genji's favorite. (The author of *The Tale of Genji* also gets her name from this character. We do not know what her real name was, as women in Heian Japan were usually simply referred to by their father's or brother's titles. "Shikibu" is in fact a title once held by the author's father, and the nickname "Murasaki" may have been given to her by a witty courtier who had read part of *Genji*.) Genji builds a large house for his many women and their children, and the plot becomes more complex as their various stories are told. Genji dies shortly after Murasaki does, and the final third of the book relates stories about his younger brother and other characters.

The plot of *The Elegy of Lady Fiammetta* is much less complicated because the work is much shorter. The unnamed female narrator, like Genji well brought up and physically attractive, marries and is quite content in her life until she falls in love with a stranger. The two see each other as often as they can, and her lover gives them each a nickname, Panfilo ("loves all") and Fiammetta ("little flame"), so that they can talk about their feelings in the presence of others. On the pretext of going to visit his dying father, Panfilo leaves, promising to return on a specific date. He does not return, and Fiammetta learns that he has fallen in love with, and married, another woman. The rest of the book recounts Fiammetta's emotions and actions as she compares her situation with that of other abandoned women.

Murasaki Shikibu did not set her story in the distant past, but in the near past in a milieu familiar to her readers. Although she was not explicit in providing historical details, she does refer to past emperors and events, and most commentators believe her story to have been set sometime between 900 and 925, or about a century before she wrote *Genji*. Though Genji and the other characters in the book are not actual historical people, they correspond loosely to real figures, and when the emperor ruling during her lifetime heard *Genji* being read aloud, he commented: "She [Murasaki Shikibu] must have read the *Chronicles of Japan* . . . she seems very learned." The clan of Lady Aoi and her brother To-no-Chujo, the Fujiwaras, had no rivals by Murasaki's time, and some commentators have seen in the book a critique of the power that they held (though Murasaki herself was a member of a lesser branch of the Fujiwaras).

The "historical" Fiammetta has also been a concern of scholars and readers since Boccaccio's day, particularly because she is a character not only in this work but in many of his other poems and prose works as well. In some of Boccaccio's poems and prefaces, he describes her as his inspiration, leading literary scholars to speculate about just who she was. Maria d'Aquino, an illegitimate daughter of Robert of Naples, was proposed as a possibility, with the love affair reconstructed from Boccaccio's literary works. Unfortunately there is no historical evidence of Maria d'Aquino's existence, and even the literary record yields conflicting evidence about the details of their love affair, particularly if *The Elegy of Lady Fiammetta* is read as a description of reality. Recent scholars have given up the search for the historical Fiammetta and instead examine what roles she plays in Boccaccio's fiction and speculate about why he chose to use her as a device in so many of his works. Dante and Petrarch, two other central figures in the Italian Renaissance, also wrote many works in which they claimed to be inspired by female characters—Beatrice in the case of Dante and Laura in the case of Petrarch—so that such speculations involve not only Boccaccio but Italian Renaissance literature in general.

Now that you know something of the background and plot of these two works, you can begin reading the excerpts carefully. Our focus in this chapter is the fictitious portrayal of male and female behavior, and the social opinions of the authors that emerge from this portrayal. As you read, you may wish to make a few notes: How are the characters themselves described, physically and emotionally? What actions by the characters are presented in a positive light? Which are presented negatively? What actions are narrated in a matter-of-fact manner, with little comment from the authors? What basic ideas about what is important in life emerge from the authors' portrayals of their characters' actions? Who do the authors surmise should be or will be reading their works? Why do they think people should read them? Assuming the audiences are as expected, what messages about acceptable male and female behavior might they receive? Are the messages clear, or are there alternative ways to interpret what happens to the characters?

As you read, keep in mind our second question as well: What special problems arise in using fiction as a historical source? As you do this, it will be helpful to think about more recent fictional portrayals of relations between men and women in books, films, and songs, such as *Gone with the Wind, Titanic,* or hundreds of romance novels and country music songs. Fictional characters are often interesting because they are extraordinary, or at least have extraordinary experiences. Are they thus models for normal behavior, or are they countermodels whose experiences are meant to contrast with the normal? If they are countermodels, does this limit the ways in which we can use these texts as reflections of reality? Might we be safer in using fiction solely as a source for historical details—such as styles of dress or tastes in architecture—rather than as a source for ideas about acceptable human behavior?

THE EVIDENCE

Source 1 from Murasaki Shikibu, The Tale of Genji, *trans. Edward Seidensticker (New York: Alfred Knopf, 1976), pp. 20–22, 32–35, 40–46, 436–439.*

1. From Murasaki Shikibu, *The Tale of Genji*

[*Genji has married Lady Aoi and has had a number of love affairs; because of his good looks and many talents, he comes to be called "shining."*]

"The shining Genji": it was almost too grand a name. Yet he did not escape criticism for numerous little adventures. It seemed indeed that his indiscretions might give him a name for frivolity, and he did what he could to hide them. But his most secret affairs (such is the malicious work of the gossips) became common talk. If, on the other hand, he were to go through life concerned only for his name and avoid all these interesting and amusing little affairs, then he would be laughed to shame. . . .

It had been raining all day. There were fewer courtiers than usual in the royal presence. Back in his own palace quarters, also unusually quiet, Genji pulled a lamp near and sought to while away the time with his books. He had Tō no Chūjō with him. Numerous pieces of colored paper, obviously letters, lay on a shelf. Tō no Chūjō made no attempt to hide his curiosity.

"Well," said Genji, "there are some I might let you see. But there are some I think it better not to."

"You miss the point. The ones I want to see are precisely the ones you want to hide. The ordinary ones—I'm not much of a hand at the game, you know, but even I am up to the ordinary give and take. But the ones from ladies who think you are not doing right by them, who sit alone through an evening and wait for you to come—those are the ones I want to see."

It was not likely that really delicate letters would be left scattered on a shelf, and it may be assumed that the papers treated so carelessly were the less important ones.

"You do have a variety of them," said Tō no Chūjō, reading the correspondence through piece by piece. This will be from her, and this will be from *her,* he would say. Sometimes he guessed correctly and sometimes he was far afield, to Genji's great amusement. Genji was brief with his replies and let out no secrets.

"It is I who should be asking to see *your* collection. No doubt it is huge. When I have seen it I shall be happy to throw my files open to you."

"I fear there is nothing that would interest you." Tō no Chūjō was in a contemplative mood. "It is with women as it is with everything else: the flawless ones are very few indeed. This is a sad fact which I have learned over the years. All manner of women seem presentable enough at first. Little notes, replies to this and that, they all suggest sensibility and cultivation. But when you begin sorting out the really superior ones you find that there are not many who have to be on your list. Each has her little tricks and she makes the most of them, getting in her slights at rivals, so broad sometimes that you almost have to blush. Hidden away by loving parents who build brilliant futures for them, they let word get out of this little talent and that little accomplishment and you are all in a stir. They are young and pretty and amiable and carefree, and in their boredom they begin to pick up a little from their elders, and in the natural course of things they begin to concentrate on one particular hobby and make something of it. A woman tells you all about it and hides the weak points and brings out the strong ones as if they were everything, and you can't very well call her a liar. So you begin keeping company, and it is always the same. The fact is not up to the advance notices."

Tō no Chūjō sighed, a sigh clearly based on experience. Some of what he had said, though not all, accorded with Genji's own experience. "And have you come upon any," said Genji, smiling, "who would seem to have nothing at all to recommend them?"

"Who would be fool enough to notice such a woman? And in any case, I should imagine that women with no merits are as rare as women with no faults. If a woman is of good family and well taken care of, then the things she is less than proud of are hidden and she gets by well enough. When you come to the middle ranks, each woman has her own little inclinations and there are thousands of ways to separate one from another. And when you come to the lowest—well, who really pays much attention?"

They talked on, of the varieties of women. . . .

At this point two young courtiers, a guards officer and a functionary in the ministry of rites, appeared on the scene, to attend the emperor in his retreat. Both were devotees of the way of love and both were good talkers. . . .

"Let me tell you a story about a foolish woman I once knew," said Tō no Chūjō. "I was seeing her in secret, and I did not think that the affair was likely to last very long. But she was very beautiful, and as time passed I came to think that I must go on seeing her, if only infrequently. I sensed that she had come to depend on me. I expected signs of jealousy. There were none. She did not seem to feel the resentment a man expects from a woman he visits so seldom. She waited quietly, morning and night. My affection grew, and I let it be known that she did indeed have a man she could depend on. There was something very appealing about her (she was an orphan), letting me know that I was all she had.

"She seemed content. Untroubled, I stayed away for rather a long time. Then—I heard of it only later—my wife found a roundabout way to be objectionable. I did not know that I had become a cause of pain. I had not forgotten, but I let a long time pass without writing. The woman was desperately lonely and worried for the child she had borne. One day she sent me a letter attached to a wild carnation." His voice trembled.

"And what did it say?" Genji urged him on.

"Nothing very remarkable. I do remember her poem, though:

" 'The fence of the mountain rustic may fall to the ground.
Rest gently, O dew, upon the wild carnation.'

"I went to see her again. The talk was open and easy, as always, but she seemed pensive as she looked out at the dewy garden from the neglected house. She seemed to be weeping, joining her laments to the songs of the autumn insects. It could have been a scene from an old romance. I whispered a verse:

" 'No bloom in this wild array would I wish to slight.
But dearest of all to me is the wild carnation.'

"Her carnation had been the child. I made it clear that my own was the lady herself, the wild carnation no dust falls upon.

"She answered:

"'Dew wets the sleeve that brushes the wild carnation.
The tempest rages. Now comes autumn too.'

"She spoke quietly all the same, and she did not seem really angry. She did shed a tear from time to time, but she seemed ashamed of herself, and anxious to avoid difficult moments. I went away feeling much relieved. It was clear that she did not want to show any sign of anger at my neglect. And so once more I stayed away for rather a long time.

"And when I looked in on her again she had disappeared.

"If she is still living, it must be in very unhappy circumstances. She need not have suffered so if she had asserted herself a little more in the days when we were together. She need not have put up with my absences, and I would have seen to her needs over the years. The child was a very pretty little girl. I was fond of her, and I have not been able to find any trace of her. . . .

The guards officer took up again. "In women as in men, there is no one worse than the one who tries to display her scanty knowledge in full. It is among the least endearing of accomplishments for a woman to have delved into the Three Histories and the Five Classics; and who, on the other hand, can go through life without absorbing something of public affairs and private? A reasonably alert woman does not need to be a scholar to see and hear a great many things. The very worst are the ones who scribble off Chinese characters at such a rate that they fill a good half of letters where they are most out of place, letters to other women. 'What a bore,' you say. 'If only she had mastered a few of the feminine things.' She cannot of course intend it to be so, but the words read aloud seem muscular and unyielding, and in the end hopelessly mannered. I fear that even our highest of the high are too often guilty of the fault."

[*Genji goes to visit his wife at her house at Sanjo but cannot spend the night there because he has broken a directional taboo on his journey. He decides to spend the night at the household of the governor of Kii, who has just had a new garden with ponds and brooks built near his house.*]

Having heard that his host's stepmother, who would be in residence, was a high-spirited lady, he listened for signs of her presence. There were signs of someone's presence immediately to the west. He heard a swishing of silk and young voices that were not at all displeasing. Young ladies seemed to be giggling self-consciously and trying to contain themselves. The shutters were raised, it seemed, but upon a word from the governor they were lowered. There was a faint light over the sliding doors. Genji went for a look, but could find no opening large enough to see through. Listening for a time, he concluded that the women had gathered in the main room, next to his. . . .

Genji found a cool place out near the veranda and lay down. His men were quiet. Several young boys were present, all very sprucely dressed, sons of the host and of his father, the governor of Iyo. There was one particularly attractive lad of perhaps twelve or thirteen. Asking who were the sons of whom, Genji learned that the boy was the younger brother of the host's stepmother, son of a guards officer no longer living. His father had had great hopes for the boy and had died while he was still very young. He had come to this house upon his sister's marriage to the governor of Iyo. He seemed to have some aptitude for the classics, said the host, and was of a quiet, pleasant disposition; but he was young and without backing, and his prospects at court were not good.

"A pity. The sister, then, is your stepmother?"

"Yes."

"A very young stepmother. My father had thought of inviting her to court. He was asking just the other day what might have happened to her. Life," he added with a solemnity rather beyond his years, "is uncertain."

"It happened almost by accident. Yes, you are right: it is a very uncertain world, and it always has been, particularly for women. They are like bits of driftwood." . . .

The wine was having its effect, and his men were falling asleep on the veranda.

Genji lay wide awake, not pleased at the prospect of sleeping alone. He sensed that there was someone in the room to the north. It would be the lady of whom they had spoken. Holding his breath, he went to the door and listened.

"Where are you?" The pleasantly husky voice was that of the boy who had caught his eye.

"Over here." It would be the sister. The two voices, very sleepy, resembled each other. "And where is our guest? I had thought he might be somewhere near, but he seems to have gone away."

"He's in the east room." The boy's voice was low. "I saw him. He is every bit as handsome as everyone says."

"If it were daylight I might have a look at him myself." The sister yawned, and seemed to draw the bedclothes over her face.

Genji was a little annoyed. She might have questioned her brother more energetically.

"I'll sleep out toward the veranda. But we should have more light." The boy turned up the lamp. The lady apparently lay at a diagonal remove from Genji. "And where is Chūjō?[1] I don't like being left alone."

"She went to have a bath. She said she'd be right back." He spoke from out near the veranda.

All was quiet again. Genji slipped the latch open and tried the doors. They had not been bolted. A curtain had been set up just inside, and in the dim light he could make out Chinese chests and other furniture scattered in some disor-

1. **Chūjō:** one of her ladies-in-waiting.

der. He made his way through to her side. She lay by herself, a slight little figure. Though vaguely annoyed at being disturbed, she evidently took him for the woman Chūjō until he pulled back the covers.

"I heard you summoning a captain," he said, "and I thought my prayers over the months had been answered."[2]

She gave a little gasp. It was muffled by the bedclothes and no one else heard.

"You are perfectly correct if you think me unable to control myself. But I wish you to know that I have been thinking of you for a very long time. And the fact that I have finally found my opportunity and am taking advantage of it should show that my feelings are by no means shallow."

His manner was so gently persuasive that devils and demons could not have gainsaid him. The lady would have liked to announce to the world that a strange man had invaded her boudoir.

"I think you have mistaken me for someone else," she said, outraged, though the remark was under her breath.

The little figure, pathetically fragile and as if on the point of expiring from the shock, seemed to him very beautiful.

"I am driven by thoughts so powerful that a mistake is completely out of the question. It is cruel of you to pretend otherwise. I promise you that I will do nothing unseemly. I must ask you to listen to a little of what is on my mind."

She was so small that he lifted her easily. As he passed through the doors to his own room, he came upon the Chūjō who had been summoned earlier. He called out in surprise. Surprised in turn, Chūjō peered into the darkness. The perfume that came from his robes like a cloud of smoke told her who he was. She stood in confusion, unable to speak. Had he been a more ordinary intruder she might have ripped her mistress away by main force. But she would not have wished to raise an alarm all through the house.

She followed after, but Genji was quite unmoved by her pleas.

"Come for her in the morning," he said, sliding the doors closed.

The lady was bathed in perspiration and quite beside herself at the thought of what Chūjō, and the others too, would be thinking. Genji had to feel sorry for her. Yet the sweet words poured forth, the whole gamut of pretty devices for making a woman surrender. . . .

. . . She was weeping. He had his hands full but would not for the world have missed the experience.

"Why must you so dislike me?" he asked with a sigh, unable to stop the weeping. "Don't you know that the unexpected encounters are the ones we were fated for? Really, my dear, you do seem to know altogether too little of the world."

"If I had met you before I came to this,"[3] she replied, and he had to admit the truth of it, "then I might have consoled myself with the thought—it might have

2. Chujo means "captain," the rank that Genji holds.

3. That is, before she was married.

been no more than self-deception, of course—that you would someday come to think fondly of me. But this is hopeless, worse than I can tell you. Well, it has happened. Say no to those who ask if you have seen me."

One may imagine that he found many kind promises with which to comfort her.

The first cock was crowing and Genji's men were awake.

"Did you sleep well? I certainly did."

"Let's get the carriage ready."

Some of the women were heard asking whether people who were avoiding taboos were expected to leave again in the middle of the night.

Genji was very unhappy. He feared he could not find an excuse for another meeting. He did not see how he could visit her, and he did not see how they could write. Chūjō came out, also very unhappy. He let the lady go and then took her back again.

"How shall I write to you? Your feelings and my own—they are not shallow, and we may expect deep memories. Has anything ever been so strange?" He was in tears, which made him yet handsomer. The cocks were now crowing insistently. He was feeling somewhat harried as he composed his farewell verse:

"Why must they startle with their dawn alarums
When hours are yet required to thaw the ice?"

The lady was ashamed of herself that she had caught the eye of a man so far above her. His kind words had little effect. She was thinking of her husband, whom for the most part she considered a clown and a dolt. She trembled to think that a dream might have told him of the night's happenings.

This was the verse with which she replied:

"Day has broken without an end to my tears.
To my cries of sorrow are added the calls of the cocks." . . .

[*Genji attempts to use the woman's young brother as a go-between, sending messages to her through him.*]

He treated the boy like a son, making him a constant companion, giving him clothes from his own wardrobe, taking him to court. He continued to write to the lady. She feared that with so inexperienced a messenger the secret might leak out and add suspicions of promiscuity to her other worries. These were very grand messages, but something more in keeping with her station seemed called for. Her answers were stiff and formal when she answered at all. She could not forget his extraordinary good looks and elegance, so dimly seen that night. But she belonged to another, and nothing was to be gained by trying to interest him. His longing was undiminished. He could not forget how touchingly fragile and confused she had seemed. . . .

[Much later in the novel, To-no-Chujo's daughter Tamakazura, Genji's second wife Murasaki, and one of Genji's concubines, the Akashi lady, spend their time at Genji's house at Rokujo in cultural pursuits.]

The rains of early summer continued without a break, even gloomier than in most years. The ladies at Rokujo amused themselves with illustrated romances. The Akashi lady, a talented painter, sent pictures to her daughter.

Tamakazura was the most avid reader of all. She quite lost herself in pictures and stories and would spend whole days with them. Several of her young women were well informed in literary matters. She came upon all sorts of interesting and shocking incidents (she could not be sure whether they were true or not), but she found little that resembled her own unfortunate career. There was *The Tale of Sumiyoshi,* popular in its day, of course, and still well thought of. She compared the plight of the heroine, within a hairbreadth of being taken by the chief accountant, with her own escape from the Higo person.[4]

Genji could not help noticing the clutter of pictures and manuscripts. "What a nuisance this all is," he said one day. "Women seem to have been born to be cheerfully deceived. They know perfectly well that in all these old stories there is scarcely a shred of truth, and yet they are captured and made sport of by the whole range of trivialities and go on scribbling them down, quite unaware that in these warm rains their hair is all dank and knotted."

He smiled. "What would we do if there were not these old romances to relieve our boredom? But amid all the fabrication I must admit that I do find real emotions and plausible chains of events. We can be quite aware of the frivolity and the idleness and still be moved. We have to feel a little sorry for a charming princess in the depths of gloom. Sometimes a series of absurd and grotesque incidents which we know to be quite improbable holds our interest, and afterwards we must blush that it was so. Yet even then we can see what it was that held us. Sometimes I stand and listen to the stories they read to my daughter, and I think to myself that there certainly are good talkers in the world. I think that these yarns must come from people much practiced in lying. But perhaps that is not the whole of the story?"

She pushed away her inkstone. "I can see that that would be the view of someone much given to lying himself. For my part, I am convinced of their truthfulness."

He laughed. "I have been rude and unfair to your romances, haven't I. They have set down and preserved happenings from the age of the gods to our own. *The Chronicles of Japan* and the rest are a mere fragment of the whole truth. It is your romances that fill in the details.

4. **Higo:** an obnoxious rural suitor of Tamakazura.

"We are not told of things that happened to specific people exactly as they happened; but the beginning is when there are good things and bad things, things that happen in this life which one never tires of seeing and hearing about, things which one cannot bear not to tell of and must pass on for all generations. If the storyteller wishes to speak well, then he chooses the good things; and if he wishes to hold the reader's attention he chooses bad things, extraordinarily bad things. Good things and bad things alike, they are things of this world and no other.

"Writers in other countries approach the matter differently. Old stories in our own are different from new. There are differences in the degree of seriousness. But to dismiss them as lies is itself to depart from the truth. Even in the writ which the Buddha drew from his noble heart are parables, devices for pointing obliquely at the truth. To the ignorant they may seem to operate at cross purposes. The Greater Vehicle is full of them, but the general burden is always the same. The difference between enlightenment and confusion is of about the same order as the difference between the good and the bad in a romance. If one takes the generous view, then nothing is empty and useless."

He now seemed bent on establishing the uses of fiction.

"But tell me: is there in any of your old stories a proper, upright fool like myself?" He came closer. "I doubt that even among the most unworldly of your heroines there is one who manages to be as distant and unnoticing as you are. Suppose the two of us set down our story and give the world a really interesting one."

"I think it very likely that the world will take notice of our curious story even if we do not go to the trouble." She hid her face in her sleeves.

"Our curious story? Yes, incomparably curious, I should think." Smiling and playful, he pressed nearer.

"Beside myself, I search through all the books,
And come upon no daughter so unfilial.

"You are breaking one of the commandments."

He stroked her hair as he spoke, but she refused to look up. Presently, however, she managed a reply:

"So too it is with me. I too have searched,
And found no cases quite so unparental."

Somewhat chastened, he pursued the matter no further. Yet one worried. What was to become of her?

Murasaki too had become addicted to romances. Her excuse was that Genji's little daughter insisted on being read to.

"Just see what a fine one this is," she said, showing Genji an illustration for *The Tale of Kumano.* The young girl in tranquil and confident slumber made her think of her own younger self. "How precocious even very little children seem to have been. I suppose I might have set myself up as a specimen of the slow, plodding variety. I would have won that competition easily."

Genji might have been the hero of some rather more eccentric stories.

"You must not read love stories to her. I doubt that clandestine affairs would arouse her unduly, but we would not want her to think them commonplace."

What would Tamakazura have made of the difference between his remarks to her and these remarks to Murasaki?

"I would not of course offer the wanton ones as a model," replied Murasaki, "but I would have doubts too about the other sort. Lady Atemiya in *The Tale of the Hollow Tree,* for instance. She is always very brisk and efficient and in control of things, and she never makes mistakes; but there is something unwomanly about her cool manner and clipped speech."

"I should imagine that it is in real life as in fiction. We are all human and we all have our ways. It is not easy to be unerringly right. Proper, well-educated parents go to great trouble over a daughter's education and tell themselves that they have done well if something quiet and demure emerges. It seems a pity when defects come to light one after another and people start asking what her good parents can possibly have been up to. Yet the rewards are very great when a girl's manner and behavior seem just right for her station. Even then empty praise is not satisfying. One knows that the girl is not perfect and looks at her more critically than before. I would not wish my own daughter to be praised by people who have no standards."

He was genuinely concerned that she acquit herself well in the tests that lay before her.

Source 2 from Giovanni Boccaccio, The Elegy of Lady Fiammetta, *ed. and trans. Mariangela Causa-Steindler and Thomas Mauch (Chicago and London: University of Chicago Press, 1990), pp. 1, 3–4, 7–8, 25–26, 113–115, 116, 119, 124–125, 127, 156, 157, 159.*

2. From Giovanni Boccaccio, *The Elegy of Lady Fiammetta*

Here begins the book called The Elegy of Lady Fiammetta, *sent by her to women in love.*

PROLOGUE

Unhappy people customarily take greater pleasure in lamenting their lot when they see or hear that someone else feels compassion for them. Therefore, since I am more eager to complain than any other woman, to make certain that the cause of my grief will not grow weaker through habit but stronger, I wish to recount my story to you, noble ladies, and if possible to awaken pity in you, in whose hearts love perhaps dwells more happily than in mine. And I do not care if my speech does not reach the ears of men; in fact if I could, I would entirely keep it away from them, for the harshness of one of them is still so alive in me that I imagine the others to be like him, and I would expect jeering laughter from them rather than compassionate tears. I pray that you alone, in whom I recognize my own open-mindedness and inclination for misfortunes, may be my readers; and as you read, you will find neither Greek myths embellished with many lies, nor Trojan battles befouled with much blood, but stories of love stirred by innumerable desires; in them, there will appear before your eyes the wretched tears, the impetuous sighs, the doleful voices, and the stormy thoughts that have troubled me with constant torment and have taken away from me appetite, sleep, joyful memories, and treasured beauty all at once. . . .

At that season when the newly clad earth displays her beauty more than at any other time of the year, I came into the world born of noble parents and welcomed by a benign and generous Fortune. Cursed be the day I was born, more detestable to me than any other! How much luckier it would have been if I had not been born or if I had been led from that wretched birth to my tomb, or if I had not lived longer than the teeth sown by Cadmus and if Lachesis had cut her threads as soon as she had spun them.[5] Innumerable woes, now the sad reason for my writing, would have found a conclusion at a tender age. But what is the use of lamenting this now? I am here all the same, and it has pleased and still pleases God that I should be here.

As has been said, I was welcomed into the world's most sublime pleasures, and I grew up in them; from infancy to delightful childhood I was raised by a revered teacher from whom I learned all the manners suitable to a young noblewoman. And as my body grew with the passing of time, my charms, which were the specific cause of my troubles, multiplied. Alas, what pride I took in them, although I was still young, and how I improved on them with care and artful means upon hearing them praised by many people!

But once I had passed from childhood to a more mature age, trained by nature stirring within me, I learned of the desires lovely young women can arouse in young men, and I became aware that my beauty in particular, an unwelcome gift to anyone who wishes to live virtuously, set afire young men my own age as well as other noblemen. By various means which I then hardly understood, they tried countless times to kindle in me the same fire which was burning in them, and which in the future would not only warm me but would consume me more than any other woman. I was also insistently urged by many of them to enter into marriage; but when among those many, one suitable to my station in

5. **Cadmus:** a Greek hero who, after his companions were killed by a dragon, took the dragon's teeth and sowed them; the teeth turned into soldiers who immediately killed one another. **Lachesis:** one of the three Fates, goddesses who measure out and cut the threads of each person's life, thus controlling destiny.

every respect obtained me, the pestering throng of suitors lost nearly all hope and stopped pursuing me with their behavior. Therefore, duly satisfied with such a husband, I lived in bliss until the raging passion later took hold of my young mind with a fire I had never felt before. Alas, there was never anything which might please me or any other woman that was not quickly granted to my satisfaction. I was my young husband's sole good and only joy, and I loved him just as he loved me. Oh, how much happier than any other woman I could call myself, had such love lasted in me forever!

While I was living contentedly, and as I was being continually entertained, Fortune, who is quick to overturn human affairs, became envious of the very gifts she had bestowed and wished to retract her favors, but not knowing where to place her venom, with subtle guile she made misfortune find its way through my very own eyes. . . .

[*She describes going out for holiday celebrations and how her beauty impressed both men and women.*]

While I went on in this way, seldom looking at others but much admired by many and believing that my beauty captivated other people, it happened that someone else's beauty unfortunately captured me. And as I was already close to that fateful moment which was to be the cause of certain death or of a life more wretched than any other, I was moved by an unknown spirit, and with my eyes raised in due solemnity, I gazed piercingly through the crowd of surrounding youths, and apart from everyone else, alone and leaning against a marble column, exactly opposite me, I saw a young man; moved by an inevitable fate, I did something I had never done before with anyone else: I began to take mental stock of him and his manner. I must say that according to my judgment, which was still free from the influence of love, he was very handsome and very pleasing in his gestures, and he was dressed most nobly; his soft curly beard still barely shadowed his cheeks as a clear sign of his youth, and he stared at me, no less adoring than cautious, across the crowd of men. To be sure, I had the strength to refrain from looking at him for long, but neither the estimation of the other things just mentioned, nor any other incident could dissuade me from thinking about him, even if I made an effort. Since his image was already imprinted upon my mind, I observed it within myself with a certain quiet delight as if I were adducing new reasons to confirm the judgment I had made of him.

But during these intermittent looks, since I was not protecting myself from love's snares, at one point I stared into his eyes much more intently than usual, and in them I seemed to read words that said, "O woman, our blessedness lies in you alone!" I would certainly lie if I said that these words displeased me; on the contrary, they pleased me so much that they drew from my breast a soft sigh, accompanied by these words: "And mine in you." But I became conscious of myself and deprived him of them. To what avail? What had not been said, the heart understood by itself, and it kept within itself that which might have allowed me to remain free, if it had been said.

So from that moment on I granted more power of judgment to my foolish eyes and indulged them with more of what they had come to desire; and certainly if the gods, who draw all things to their predetermined end, had not deprived me of understanding, I could have remained my own woman, but I put off to the very end all consideration and followed my appetite, and I immediately became susceptible to being caught; for not unlike fire which leaps from one spot to another, a most subtle ray of light left the young man's eyes and hit my own, and it did not rest there satisfied, but by some mysterious route it suddenly reached my heart and penetrated it. Terrified at this sudden visitation, my heart drew all its vital powers to itself, leaving me all pale and chilled. But I did not remain this way for long before the opposite happened; and not only did I feel my heart grow warm again, but as my energies returned to their proper places, they brought with them such a heat that it drove away my pallor and made me very red and as hot as fire; and as I looked at the one from whom this came, I sighed. From that moment on, I could not have any other thought than to please him. . . .

[*She is able to see her beloved regularly, and they talk about their feelings in the presence of others by using the names Panfilo and Fiammetta for each other.*]

His desire and my own made each day drag on one after the other, tense with expectation, and each of us bore this with bitterness because one would show it to the other by speaking cryptically, and the other would appear extremely disdainful, just as you ladies do, who may be looking for the strength to do what you would like to do most and which you know women who are loved usually do. Thus, somewhat mistrustful of me in this matter, and more lucky than wise in what happened to him and with more impudence than talent, he found a convenient time and place and obtained from me that which I wanted just as much as he did, although I feigned the contrary. Surely, if this were the reason for my loving him, I would confess to feeling a sorrow unlike any other every time this came back into my mind; but (and may God be my witness in this) this incident was and is the least important reason for the love I carry for him; however, I don't deny that I cherished it then, as I do now.

And what woman would be so unwise as not to want something she adores close by rather than far away? And the greater the love, would she not wish it all the closer? I say then, that after such an event, which in the past I had imagined but had never experienced, and under these circumstances, fate and our wits helped us to solace ourselves at length and with immense pleasure not once but many times, although it seems to me now that the time then flew by faster than any wind. But while we were living those happy moments, as Love, whom I can offer as my only witness, can truly tell, he was never allowed to come to me without fear, since he came to me only in secret. Oh how he adored my chamber and how cheerfully it always welcomed him! I have seen him revere it more than any temple. Oh how many tender kisses and amorous embraces, and how many nights were spent talking more than if it were daytime, and how many pleasures, dear to each lover, we had there during those joyful hours! . . .

[*Panfilo then leaves, promising to return on a certain date. He does not; instead he marries someone else. Fiammetta sinks into despair and confides in the old woman who had been her childhood nurse.*]

"Even in the most sizzling corner of hell, with its most terrible tortures for those who are damned, there is no punishment like mine. Tityus[6] is cited as an example of excruciating pain by ancient authors who say that vultures continually peck at his ever-renewing liver, and I certainly do not consider this a meagre punishment, but it is nothing in comparison with mine, because while the vultures peck at his liver, a thousand fears, stronger than any bird's beak, continually tear my heart apart. Similarly, they say that Tantalus[7] is dying of hunger and thirst while surrounded by waters and fruit, but placed in the middle of worldly pleasures, affectionately hungry for my lover and unable to have him, I certainly suffer as much as he does, or more, since the proximity of the waves and the nearby fruit give him some hope that sometime he will be able to satisfy himself fully, but I now completely despair of anything in which I had hoped to find my consolation, and since I love more than ever the one who by his own free will is kept in someone else's power, I have been deprived of all hope. . . .

. . . Death would therefore not be grievous to me, but a relief from grief. So let my dear husband come and take revenge for himself and at the same time free me from suffering; let his knife slit open my miserable bosom and let him take out my aching soul, my love, and my sorrow all at the same time with much blood; may he tear apart my heart, the holder of these things, as the principal deceiver and as the one who shelters his enemies, just as the perpetrated inequity deserves."

When my old nurse saw that I had ceased speaking and was deep in tears, she began talking softly to me:

"My dear girl, what are you saying? Your words are useless and your intentions terrible. I am very old and have seen many things in this world, and I have certainly been familiar with the love affairs of many ladies, and even though I

6. **Tityus:** a handsome giant who attempted to seduce Zeus's wife Hera; she punished him by condemning him to Hades, where vultures feed on his liver.

7. **Tantalus:** a son of Zeus punished for a crime against the gods by being placed in a pool of water that receded every time he bent to drink, and near a fruit tree with branches that sprung away every time he reached to pick fruit.

am not to be counted among you, I have nevertheless been well acquainted with the poisonous love which weighs just as heavily on humble people as on more powerful ones, and more so at times, since the poor have fewer ways open to satisfy their desire than do those people who with their riches find them in their leisure; besides, I have never felt (or heard it said) that which you speak of as being so painful to you and nearly impossible, is as hard as you indicate. And even if such grief were extremely great, you should not let it consume you, as you are doing, to the point that you seek death, which you are asking for more out of anger than reason. . . . He is also not the first to do such a thing, nor are you the first to whom this has happened. Jason abandoned Hypsipyle in Lemnos to return to Medea in Thessaly; Paris left Oenone in the forest of Ida and went back to Helen in Troy; and Theseus left Ariadne in Crete to join Phaedra in Athens;[8] but neither Hypsipyle nor Oenone nor Ariadne killed themselves, rather, by putting aside their futile thoughts, they forgot their false lovers. . . .

Not once but many times my wise nurse spoke to me in this fashion, believing that she could chase my sufferings away and restrict my worries to those about dying, but few or none of her words touched my preoccupied mind fruitfully; most of them were lost to the four winds; each day my disease invaded my aching soul more and more, and so I lay on my sumptuous bed with my face down and hidden by my arms, turning over in my mind a variety of grand things. . . .

[*Fiammetta decides to commit suicide.*]

. . . I started out towards the stairs leading to the highest part of my lodgings; and having already broken out of my bedchamber and crying loudly, I looked wildly around all of the house and said in a weak, broken voice:

"O home that was so hostile to me when I was happy, stand eternal and let my lover know of my fall if he returns; and you, my dear husband, comfort yourself and look right away for a wiser Fiammetta. Dear sisters, relatives, any other women companions and friends, faithful maidservants, live on in the good graces of the gods."

With these words I was angrily pushing myself along a disgraceful course, but my old nurse, like someone aroused from sleep by a frenzy, left her spinning, amazed at seeing this, suddenly lifted her very heavy limbs and began screaming and following me as fast as she could. With a voice I found hard to believe, she said:

"My girl, where are you running? What madness is driving you? Is this the result of my words in which you said you had taken comfort? Where are you going? Wait for me!"

Then, even more loudly she screamed:

8. **Hypsipyle:** the daughter of the king of Lemnos, who bore Jason two sons before he left her for Medea. **Oenone:** a young Trojan shepherdess whom Paris married and deserted; she refused to heal him when he received his fatal wounds but later felt remorse and threw herself on his funeral pyre. **Ariadne:** the daughter of the king of Crete, who fell in love with Theseus and helped him escape from the Labryinth; he later abandoned her on the island of Naxos.

"Maids, come and stop this insane woman and calm her madness."

Her shouting served no purpose, and her laborious running even less: I seemed to have grown wings, and I was running towards my death faster than any wind. But unexpected circumstances, contrary to good as well as to evil intentions, saved my life, because while my very long garments could have been a hindrance to my purpose for their length, they did not impede my running, but somehow, as I was hurrying, they tangled themselves around a sharp piece of wood and halted my impetuous flight, and no matter how hard I pulled, not a piece of them came free. Because of this my heavy nurse reached me as I was trying to untangle them; red in the face and screaming, I remember saying to her:

"You wretched old woman, if you care for your life, go away. You think you are helping me, but you are harming me; let me die now while I am disposed toward it with the greatest will, because he who stops from dying the one who wishes to die does not do anything else but kill him; you are killing me, in the belief that you are saving me from death, and like an enemy you try to prolong my suffering."

My tongue was shouting, my heart was ablaze with ire, and my frantic hands, intending to untangle, were entangling myself, and no sooner did I think of the alternative of disrobing than my screeching nurse reached me and hindered me as much as she could; but once I became free, all of her strength would have been inadequate, if at her screams the young maids had not rushed in from everywhere and held me fast.

[*Her nurse tells her that it is cowardly and dishonorable to commit suicide, and she becomes calmer.*]

There is no anger that burns so fiercely that it does not become very cold with the passing of time. I saw myself for several days in the state I am depicting and clearly recognized the truth in my wise nurse's words, and I bitterly regretted my past folly. But even though my madness consumed itself in time and vanished, my love did not change at all because of it; on the contrary, I was left with the melancholy I used to feel at other such incidents, and I could hardly bear the idea that I had been abandoned for another woman.

[*Throughout the rest of the book, Fiammetta continues to compare her situation with that of abandoned women from antiquity and mythology, and argues that her pain is even greater. In the final chapter, Fiammetta speaks directly to her book.*]

O dear little book of mine, snatched from the near burial of your lady, here it is that your end has come more quickly than that of our misfortunes, as is my wish; therefore, just as you have been written by my own hand and in many places damaged by my tears, present yourself to women in love; if, as I strongly hope, pity guides you, and if the rules of Love have not changed since we became miserable, those women will gladly receive you. . . .

If by chance you should fall into the hands of a woman who manages the affairs of the heart so well as to laugh at our sorrows and reprove us for being insane, bear the mocking with humility; it is the least of our troubles; remind her that Fortune is fickle and can very quickly make you and me joyous, and her like us, in which case we would return her laughter, mockery for mockery.

And if you find another who cannot keep her eyes dry as she reads but is sad and full of compassion for our misfortunes and multiplies your blotches with her tears, gather them within you along with my own, and consider them holy. . . .

Live then. No one can deprive you of this, and remain an eternal example to happy and unhappy people of your lady's anguish.

QUESTIONS TO CONSIDER

The first scene from *The Tale of Genji* included in the evidence is a discussion between Genji, his friend and brother-in-law To-no-Chujo, and several courtiers about women. Reread the first paragraph; what is it that Genji feels he would be "laughed to shame" about? What does To-no-Chujo's attitude about Genji's many letters from women reveal about expectations for men's behavior? (Remember that Genji is the husband of his sister.) What does his discussion about women in theory, and the story he then tells about one of his affairs, reveal about expectations for female behavior? for male? What role does social class play in these expectations? (When To-no-Chujo speaks of "rank," he is talking about levels of social status *within* the aristocracy. Common people almost never appear in *The Tale of Genji* or other literature from Heian Japan.) What role does poetry play in the interchanges between women and men? What do the comments of the guards officer reveal about attitudes toward learned women? Why do you think Murasaki Shikibu included this, considering that she was highly learned herself?

The next scene occurs later in the same chapter; Genji spends the night at the household of the governor of Kii after spending the day with his wife. How do Genji's actions fit with the expectations for male behavior that you have already discovered? How do the lady's fit with those for female behavior? Why do you think Murasaki does not disclose her name? What is the reaction of her lady-in-waiting, Chujo, to the events? What does the episode say about marriage among the aristocracy in Heian Japan?

The final scene in Source 1 occurs much later in the book, when Genji comes upon Tamakazura and other women reading romance novels. Who does he expect will read romances? What purpose do they serve, in his opinion? How does this compare with the type of storytelling he and his friends engage in, as we have just seen? How does his attitude toward the purpose of novels differ when he is talking to Tamakazura, To-no-Chujo's daughter to whom he was attracted, and to Murasaki about their own daughter? What does he see as the relation between novels and real life? Based on these statements, how might he answer our second question, about using novels as historical sources?

Turn now to the selections from *The Elegy of Lady Fiammetta.* To whom does Fiammetta address her book, both at the beginning and at the end? What does her discussion of her appearance and upbringing reveal about expectations for women in Renaissance Italy? How does she describe her marriage and her husband? her first glimpse of her beloved? her first feelings of true love? What does the choice of names her beloved uses reveal (or foreshadow) about subsequent events in the story? What role do classical mythological figures play in Fiammetta's account? What is her nurse's response to her tragedy? What does the nurse have to say about the role of social class in love affairs?

By now, you have probably noticed some similarities—and some distinct differences—between the two works themselves and the attitudes toward male and female behavior and the relations between men and women they convey. How would you compare the attraction of Fiammetta toward her beloved and of Genji toward the unnamed lady, his host's stepmother? How is love itself described in the two works? What is the connection between sexual relations and shame or honor in the two? How is it different for men versus women? How would you compare the reactions of Chujo, the unnamed lady's lady-in-waiting, and Fiammetta's nurse? What role does fate, or Fortune, play in the two works? How do the ideals for male and female beauty differ in the two?

In both of these selections, an author of one sex is describing the feelings and opinions of members of the other—Murasaki creates the conversations of men about women in the first excerpt, and Boccaccio's entire elegy is spoken through the voice of Fiammetta. How might this have shaped the way they told their stories? Other than in Heian Japan, most of the literature that has been preserved from all periods before the twentieth century was written by men. Because of this, we often must rely on male-authored texts to learn about women's attitudes or lives. How would you use *Genji,* which is actually written by a woman, differently from *Fiammetta,* which is only written in a female voice, to draw conclusions about women's ideas or expectations for female behavior? Does the sex of the author shape your willingness to view fictional portrayals as authentic and representing reality?

To address the second question, imagine that you are a historian working hundreds of years from now, with popular romance novels and country music lyrics as your only source for early twenty-first-century culture. What impressions would you get of male and female behavior? of the relations between men and women? In what ways would these impressions be misleading? Do these same issues emerge when we consider the limitations of *Genji* and *Fiammetta* as historical sources?

Now that you have read the selections, you can develop answers to the two central questions for this chapter. How do romances both portray and shape conventional standards of male and female behavior? What special problems arise in using fiction as a historical source?

EPILOGUE

By two centuries after *The Tale of Genji* was written, scholars in Japan were trying to produce a complete, authoritative version from the many manuscript and partial copies that existed, and the work was considered required reading for anyone who wanted to be considered learned. Thus *Genji* became a classic, in the same way that Homer's *Iliad* and Virgil's *Aeneid* did in Europe. Like these works, *Genji* was revered not only as great literature, but as a historical source, a description of the way things had actually been in Genji's time. Like many classics, it was also viewed as a commentary on the way things were *supposed* to be, and thus it was used by scholars as a way to criticize what they perceived as a cultural decline in their own day. Even people who had not read it became familiar with many scenes and characters because these were discussed in other literary works or depicted in art, in the same way that people who have not read the *Iliad* know about the Trojan War it chronicles. In fact, some scholars would say that *Genji* served one of the functions of the Bible in the West—not, of course, as a source of religious teaching and inspiration, but as a common point of cultural reference with people alluding to it all the time and assuming everyone was familiar with the stories it contained.

The Elegy of Lady Fiammetta did not achieve this status as a classic, although Boccaccio's *Decameron* did, its stories becoming the basis for artistic and literary works and Boccaccio attaining status as an author whose name was familiar even to people who had not read his works. *Fiammetta* thus does not create a literary tradition, but it fits into one that is common in Western literature, the tradition of the abandoned woman. As you have read, Fiammetta and her nurse compare her situation to that of many women from classical history and mythology who have likewise been loved and left behind. Male authors only rarely write in a female voice in the West, but when they do, it is often to tell a story of feeling abandoned, either by a lover or by God, as romantic and religious feelings are often linked in Western literature in a way they are not in Japan.

The popularity of romances did not end in Murasaki's or Boccaccio's time, of course, but continues to our own, which is why it was probably quite easy for you to think of contemporary examples when addressing the second question. Like *Genji* and *Fiammetta,* contemporary romances both portray and shape standards of male and female behavior. Though it may be somewhat embarrassing for you to admit it, can you identify ways in which your own ideas of conventional behavior have been shaped by reading or viewing fictional romances? What would you see as contemporary romantic conventions—in other words, how do you expect people in these stories and songs to act? What would you most like to tell that future historian that we spoke about earlier to ignore in these fictional portrayals? What do you think Murasaki and Boccaccio might have most wished we had ignored in our reading of their work?

CHAPTER NINE

FACING THE BLACK DEATH

(1300–1400)

THE PROBLEM

Ring around the rosies
A pocket full of posies
Ashes, ashes, all fall down.

For centuries, English and American children at play have chanted this seemingly nonsensical rhyme. For all their innocence, however, these children have been transmitters of historical memory. The "rosies" to which this song refers are "buboes," the ugly protuberances at the neck, armpits, or groin that are the horrible sign of bubonic plague. The "pocket full of posies" refers to the clump of flowers that medieval Europeans might clutch in their hands and hold before their noses in a futile attempt to keep the plague at bay. And when today's children collapse to the ground as they chant "all fall down," they unknowingly recreate piles of burning corpses.

This simple children's song records the terror of the Black Death, the epidemic of bubonic plague that struck Europe in the middle of the fourteenth century and killed somewhere between a quarter and a third of its people. Those who exhibited the telltale buboes usually had less than three days to live. Those who contracted the pneumatic form of the illness, spread by respiration from person to person, would be perfectly healthy one day and dead the next. "Ring around the rosies" shows how ancient memories of dramatic events can be retained in the popular imagination.

When the plague epidemic hit Europe in 1347–1348, people faced the crisis with little useful knowledge about how the plague was spread or how it could be treated. One thing they did know: The disease had come from the east. While most historical attention has been focused on the Black Death in Europe, historians have followed through on that single bit of knowledge and now understand that the fourteenth-century outbreak of the plague was a *pandemic,* that is, a widespread epidemic that struck most of Eurasia and North Africa almost simultaneously. The tragedy of the Black Death was not limited to a single corner of the world, and it has therefore become a major topic among world historians.

Where did the plague come from? Why did it arise so suddenly and spread so rapidly? What could be done about it? Societies across Eurasia and North Africa were faced with these questions in the fourteenth century. Your task in this chapter will be to examine a number of contemporary accounts of the Black Death drawn from both Christian and Islamic sources. How did these authors answer the questions posed above? What were some of the medical, religious, political, and economic reactions to the Black Death? Do you see any similarities between Christian and Muslim reactions? Or are there some fundamental differences in how people from the two religious traditions dealt with the plague?

BACKGROUND

The answers to some of these questions are not absolutely clear even today, but we certainly know a great deal more about bubonic plague than did the Asian, European, and African victims of the fourteenth-century pestilence. Much of our scientific knowledge about bubonic plague comes from studies conducted in the late nineteenth and early twentieth centuries. In the 1890s a devastating new outbreak of plague afflicted Asia; millions died in India and China. Stirred to action, bacteriologists identified the bacterium that causes bubonic plague and the cycle of infection that produces epidemics of the disease. Fleas drink the blood of infected rats, after which the bacteria multiply in the flea's gut. When the flea bites another rat, the bacteria are regurgitated into the open wound. Usually this cycle of infection is limited to fleas and their rodent hosts. Under special circumstances, however, the fleas jump from their rodent hosts and bite people instead.

Thus the spread of the bubonic plague in the 1890s, as in earlier epidemics, resulted from increasing human contact with infected fleas and rats. This knowledge, however, still does not explain why it is that in certain times and places bubonic plague spreads with such speed and ferocity. Plague-infested rodent populations have lived in close proximity to humans from time immemorial. In such areas plague is *endemic,* that is, always present. But its effects among humans are usually minimized and localized by the small size of the affected population, their lack of contact with the wider world, and popular knowledge of the local environment, which often permits the development of folk strategies that lessen human contact with infected rodents.

Plague becomes *epidemic,* spreading to previously unaffected areas, when these balances are upset. A sudden growth in the rat population, environmental changes that drive rats carrying infected fleas into closer contact with humans, economic or cultural changes that challenge the folk wisdom that had kept the plague at bay—all have been implicated in the spread of plague epidemics. Finally, in order for a pandemic to occur—for the plague bacillus to infect huge numbers of humans very suddenly across vast distances—even more substantial changes must have taken place in the interactions between humans and the environment and among different societies.

Such was indeed the case in the fourteenth century. One factor may have been environmental changes in Inner Asia. A period of drought may have forced infected rat populations into closer contact with human societies in search of food and water. But human actors were certainly involved as well, as we see in William McNeill's imaginative reconstruction.[1] In his view, it was the great Mongol warriors who unwittingly created the conditions for the Black Death. It was the Mongols' conquests and the vast expansion of trade that accompanied their empire building that facilitated the spread of plague from a localized outbreak in China in 1331, through the Central Asian steppes in the 1330s, to the ports of the Black Sea and the Mediterranean in the 1340s, and finally to the most densely populated areas of Europe, Western Asia, and North Africa in 1347–1348.

The Mongol era saw an unprecedented unification of Eurasia, not only militarily and politically, but commercially and even environmentally as well. This was the thirteenth- and fourteenth-century world in which famous travelers such as the Italian Marco Polo (1254–1324) and the North African Ibn Battuta (1304–1368) crossed from one end of Eurasia to the other with unprecedented ease. Little did the merchants and other intercontinental travelers realize that in their saddlebags and on their carts and ships, plague-infested fleas had stowed away, ready to spread the disease to rodents and humans at the other end of their journey. By 1339 the plague was found in Samarkand, a famous Central Asian stopping point on the Silk Road. By 1345 it had reached the Volga River and the Caucasus Mountains. By 1347 it had reached the ports of the Black Sea, Constantinople, and Alexandria, and within a year it had spread to Mecca, Damascus, Tunis, Venice, and Paris. Far-away London was hit in 1349. In all of these areas the plague led to a devastating loss of population: By some estimates, the population of Egypt did not return to its pre-1347 level until the nineteenth century. The effects of the Black Death in Europe were so fundamental that the pandemic is often cited as one of the main causes of the decline of feudalism and the rise of the new ideas and institutions that would usher in the modern age.

Very little of this was known to the victims of the Black Death. Yet they could not have been expected to accept this scourge without attempts to find an explanation and a remedy. What caused the plague, and what could be done about it? There was, of course, no

1. William H. McNeill, *Plagues and Peoples* (New York: Anchor, 1977).

single answer to these questions. A great deal depended on religious beliefs: The responses of Latin Christians, Orthodox Christians, Muslims, Jews, Zoroastrians, Buddhists, and followers of other faiths were at least partially determined by the specific traditions of their religions.

In Western Europe, the Black Death struck at societies that had experienced several centuries of economic growth, population increase, and relative political stability. The "high middle ages" were a period of spiritual optimism, as demonstrated by the magnificent cathedrals erected in the twelfth through early fourteenth centuries. With the growth of cities came an expansion of long-distance trade; Europeans came into greater contact with the rest of the Eurasian world. They had no way of knowing that increased contact with the wider world would bring the danger of a plague epidemic.

The *Dar-al-Islam* ("Abode of Islam") was at the epicenter of political and military events in Eurasia, and was both more stimulated and more destabilized than Western Europe by Asian-centered events such as the rise of the Mongols and the coming of the Turks. When the Mongols overran Baghdad in 1258, they not only brought the Abbasid caliphate to an end but also severed a link of authority between the Prophet and the caliphs ("successors") that has never to this day been reestablished. Muslims in Western Asia had therefore experienced cataclysmic political change less than a century before the arrival of the Black Death. By the early fourteenth century, Muslims often felt a sense of faded glory, of the best times having already passed, whether one looked at the fairly recent fall of the Abbasid caliphate or at the glorious time when the Prophet Muhammad ruled the *umma* (community) with a perfect mixture of spiritual and political authority. Though the demographic effects of the Black Death were quite similar in Europe and the Middle East, these differences of experience and outlook conditioned the responses of various societies to this crisis.

Generalizations are just that; we should not let them obscure the very real differences that occur within given societies and between particular individuals. Even within a single tradition, people reacted to the trauma of the Black Death quite differently, and popular responses were frequently quite different from the policies adopted by secular and religious authorities. In Western Europe, for example, groups known as *flagellants*, convinced that the plague was sent by God as a punishment for their sins, beat themselves bloody as a form of penance. Others sought solace and deliverance through quiet contemplation. In Islamic lands, some regarded the Black Death as a blessing, guaranteeing a place in heaven to those who suffered it in dignity as an unfathomable expression of God's will. But in these same societies there were also those who resorted to magic, trying to find some secret combination of words or numbers that would protect them. It is variations on these themes that you will explore in the readings that follow.

THE METHOD

As you consider the texts and images that follow, keep three side-by-side lists:

- On the first list, note every idea that you encounter that has to do with the ***cause*** of the pestilence. You may want to differentiate *ultimate* causes (e.g., divine intervention) from *immediate* causes (e.g., environmental factors and human activities).
- On the second list, write down every idea you find that has to do with the ***consequences*** of the plague for the societies and individuals concerned. You may want to differentiate the demographic, social and political, economic, religious, and psychological consequences of the Black Death as reported in the sources.
- On the third list, keep track of all the actions that are described or recommended for ***curing*** or in some other way ***coping*** with the Black Death. As you add items to this list, you may want to consider the question of how effective these measures might have been.

When you encounter the same idea in more than one document, make a note of how many times it occurs and whether it is found only in Christian documents, only in Muslim ones, or in both. When these lists are completed, you should have the material you need to make comparisons between the documents and to generalize about the main questions at issue: How did people interpret the causes of the plague, what were its effects, and how did people respond to this calamity?

The paragraphs below provide some historical context to help you make sense of each of the readings. You will want to refer back to this section as you consider the evidence.

The first document is taken from a book that many consider to be the greatest work of history written by a Muslim of this period, Ibn Khaldun's *Introduction to History* (Source 1). Ibn Khaldun, a well-known Arab philosopher, historian, and statesman, was centrally concerned with describing and analyzing various types of civilization; he anticipated the work of later world historians by placing a great emphasis on environmental conditions in explaining how different civilizations arise and develop.

The next three documents, by contrast, give us a much more immediate and intimate portrait of the plague as it affected three very different cities: Florence, Damascus, and Constantinople. Giovanni Boccaccio was a literary scholar as well as one of the great writers of his day. His *Decameron* (Source 2) is renowned for its glorious tales of late medieval Florentine life, for bringing us much closer to the real world of kitchens, bedrooms, shop fronts, and back alleys than any previous work in European literature. The *Decameron* is a work of fiction, but these opening pages, where Florentine reactions to the plague are described, have the ring of truth.

The passage from Ibn Battuta is similar to Boccaccio in its close description of civic reactions to the plague. The greatest of medieval Arab geographers,

Ibn Battuta was one of the most widely traveled men of his age, and his *Travels in Asia and Africa* (Source 3) is an important source of information about the world of Islam in the fourteenth century. In this passage he describes a procession in the city of Damascus. Though he does not dwell on the fact, we know that Ibn Battuta was deeply affected by the Black Death: His own mother was carried away by the plague. Family tragedy also infuses the reading from Ioannes Cantacuzenos (Source 4), better known as the Byzantine Emperor John VI. Adronikos, the young man whose death is mentioned in this passage, was John VI's own son. In 1355, eight years after this tragic event, John VI abdicated his throne and retired to a monastery. This passage is taken from the history of the Byzantine Empire he wrote while in retirement. While the other documents in this chapter come from either the Latin Christian or the Islamic tradition, this one represents an Orthodox Christian viewpoint.

Among the major elements of the account of Jean de Venette, a Carmelite friar (Source 5), are the great importance that Christians placed on dying a "good death" and the challenges that the huge mortality of 1348 posed to their doing so. Sudden death and the possibility of burial in unconsecrated ground were particularly horrible for people who believed that an eternity in hell awaited any soul that was not adequately prepared. Jean de Venette also comments, like Boccaccio, on the effects of the epidemic on standards of social conduct and morality. It is also important to note that this account indicates that some believed that the Black Death was caused by the evil actions of particular groups of people. The attacks on Germany's Jewish population that he describes are a chilling anticipation of the genocide that would take place six hundred years later; 1349 was neither the first nor the last time that one response to harsh times has been to find a scapegoat.

The next source is a visual one, a reproduction of a painting that is included because it gets at both human and cosmological dimensions of the Black Death as it was experienced in Europe (Source 6). In interpreting this painting, it might be helpful to think in terms of several sets of contrasts. First, compare the left and right sides of the lower part of the painting, with the corpse in the foreground as a bridge between the two. Second, compare the lower and upper portions of the painting. St. Sebastian, who is seen near the top of the painting in a position of prayer, was one of several saints who became identified as offering help to plague victims. Sebastian was a soldier in the Roman army who was put to death for his adherence to Christianity. St. Sebastian was always represented with arrows piercing his flesh, a torture equivalent to being pierced by the hidden arrows of the plague. (Muslims also made a connection between being shot with arrows and being infected by bubonic plague: There were those who thought that the disease entered the human body by being shot with invisible arrows by evil *jinn,* or spirits.) The prayer to St. Sebastian (Source 7) exemplifies the concept of the "intercession of the saints." If God himself seemed too distant to be appealed to directly, you could pray to a saint to intercede on your behalf.

The following four documents all relate to the Black Death in the Islamic world. The quotation from theologian and legal scholar Muhammad ibn Isma'il (Source 8), while very brief, is of the greatest importance. There is a strong tendency in Islam to judge current behavior and practice in relation not only to a sacred text but also to historical precedent. In addition to the Qur'an, the accounts of the life and times of Muhammad as given in the *hadith*, the stories of the Prophet's life collected and codified in later generations, give believers the guidance they need for correct behavior, individual as well as social and political, in almost every situation. While the Qur'an itself has little to say about the plague, the three statements from the hadith proposed by Ibn Isma'il helped establish an understanding of the plague that was shared by most Muslim theologians. They are therefore powerfully authoritative. Those in the Islamic world who thought differently had to justify their positions in relation to this orthodoxy. In contract, Ibn al-Khatib's perspective (Source 9) is a medical one, and his conclusions do not necessarily conform to the orthodoxy. His perspective is that of a physician, interested in concrete causes and cures, rather than that of a lawyer or theologian interested in the interpretation of texts for their own sake.

In addition to the medical perspective, there were other Islamic responses to the Black Death. Mysticism and magic have long had a role in the Islamic world, and the catastrophe of the Black Death seems to have reinforced these trends. Muslims do not have saints to pray to, but in the Sufi brotherhoods they do have spiritual leaders whose blessings can continue even after death. Visiting the graves of departed holy men, while not sanctioned by some Islamic thinkers, became a much more common practice in this period. While Sufi mystics usually accept the basic theological premises of the Islamic legal traditions, they try to go beyond them by finding a direct connection with the Divine. Often this involves achieving a meditative state through constant repetition of one or more of the many names they attribute to God. It is possible that the surge of interest in Islamic mysticism in the late medieval period may be at least partly attributable to the spiritual quest of Muslims seeking solace from the harsh world of the plague.

The images reproduced in Source 10 point to another response to the plague: the use of cryptograms—combinations of numbers, letters, or words—to stave off the epidemic. Often these strategies relied on the use of specific Qur'anic verses or names for God. The use of devices such as amulets was not, of course, limited to the Islamic world. However, because Muslims are not allowed to find relief and help from the types of portraits and statues that were familiar to medieval Christians, they were more likely to use the type of figurative devices shown in this source. The idea that salvation could come from writing a holy verse on a slip of paper, dissolving the ink in water, and then drinking it may have been opposed by orthodox thinkers like Ibn al-Isma'il, but it gave people a sense that there was something they could do other than simply accept their deaths as a martyrdom. The use of numbers to interpret the world, like the similar use of the stars by astrologers, could give people a sense of an underlying order of things when they were faced with the apparent randomness with which the plague chose its victims.[2] For Muslims, meditation on mathematical symbols or sacred words, like the Christian contemplation of statues or other sacred images, could help believers focus on the divine.[3]

Ibn al-Wardi was an eyewitness to the spread of the plague in Aleppo (Syria), who died of the disease in 1349. The selection from his account of the plague (Source 11) seems less consistent than the accounts of some other authors, and in fact some of his arguments may even seem contradictory: If the plague for Muslims is really "a martyrdom and a reward," why would one seek to escape it? In spite of, or perhaps even because of, such inconsistencies, Ibn al-Wardi has a great deal to say about popular beliefs related to our core questions: Where did the plague come from, what were its consequences, and what could people do about it?

The following three selections give us varying European accounts of the causes of and remedies for the plague. The Fifteenth-Century Treatise on the Pestilence, reproduced as Source 12, gives the conventional Christian interpretation of that time. Thus, just as Ibn al-Khatib had to struggle with Islamic religious orthodoxy in his assertion of medical causes and cures for the plague, so the Paris Medical Faculty (Source 13) had to justify their effort to go beyond this type of strictly religious explanation. The Paris doctors distinguished their mode of inquiry from that of religious authorities by grounding their analysis in the works of the classical tradition of medicine, with reference to such figures as Hippocrates and Galen. (Though they do not acknowledge it in this passage, these doctors were deeply indebted to the Iranian Muslim physician Ibn Sina, whose very influential medical text synthesizing classical and Islamic medical knowledge had been trans-

2. Historian Michael Dols writes, "Obviously, the cryptograms show a great variety, being composed of words, letters, numbers, symbols, or any combination of these. . . . Their symbolism is often not readily apparent. In some instances, there is a perfect square in which the sum is always the same whether the numbers are added horizontally, vertically or diagonally, or when any group of four contiguous numbers are added together. . . . The instructions state that when the quadrants were completed by the inclusion of the numbers outside the diagram the square would avert the plague. . . . These magic quadrants may have been used in numerous ways, but it is certain that they were often inscribed on metal amulets." (From Michael Dols, *The Black Death in the Middle East* [Princeton: Princeton University Press, 1977], pp. 138–139)

3. Michael Dols elaborates, "Ibn Haydur relates that his teacher informed him that one night in the year 764/1362–63 he had gone to bed and thought about the epidemic of plague that was rampant in this year. He slept badly because of the distress caused by the epidemic. In his sleep, he saw a man take a small book from his own library and bring it to him. The man laid his hand on the last line on the right side of the page of the book and said: 'These names will intercede for you during the epidemic, and read them in this manner—'Oh Living One, Oh Patient One, Oh Loving One, Oh Wise One.' . . . When it was morning he told his friends about the dream. Among them was [one] who, when he heard the recitation of the names of God in this manner, said that these names were engraved on rings. . . . The stone engraved in this way would guard a person against the burning fever that accompanied plague, if he drank water in which the ring had been submerged." (Dols, *The Black Death*, pp. 133–135)

lated into Latin in the twelfth century.) While the references to astrology and the "four humors" may not seem very scientific to us, this document represents the most sophisticated medical thinking of its day. The selection entitled "A Wholesome Medicine Against the Plague" (Source 14) reminds us that while reaction to the plague in Europe could take such violent forms as self-flagellation and attacks on Jews, there were many other Christians who were more moderate and balanced in their response.

These readings on the Black Death have taken us across many intellectual and cultural frontiers. The final reading, in which the great Humanist philosopher Petrarch (Source 15) describes the death of his friends, brings us back down to the most basic, human level. As we read Petrarch's letter, can we really imagine what it would have been like to be living in such circumstances?

THE EVIDENCE

Source 1 from Michael Dols, The Black Death in the Middle East *(Princeton: Princeton University Press), 1977, p. 270; Ibn Khaldun,* The Muqaddimah; *trans. Franz Rosenthal (Princeton: Princeton University Press, 1967), pp. 136–137.*

1. From Ibn Khaldun, *The Muqaddimah: An Introduction to History*

Civilization in the East and West was visited by a destructive plague which devastated nations and caused populations to vanish. It swallowed up many of the good things of civilization and wiped them out. It overtook the dynasties at the time of their senility, when they had reached the limit of their duration. . . .

In the later (years) of dynasties, famines and pestilences become numerous. . . .

. . . There is much unrest and bloodshed, and plagues occur. The principal reason for the latter is the corruption of the air (climate) through (too) large a civilization (population). It results from the putrefaction and the many evil moistures with which (the air) has contact (in a dense civilization). Now, air nourishes the animal spirit and is constantly with it. When it is corrupted, corruption affects the temper of (the spirit). If the corruption is strong, the lung is afflicted with disease. This results in epidemics, which affect the lung in particular. (Even) if the corruption is not strong or great, putrefaction grows and multiplies under (its influence), resulting in many fevers that affect the tempers, and the bodies become sick and perish. The reason for the growth of putrefaction and evil moistures is invariably a dense and abundant civilization such as exists in the later (years) of a dynasty. . . . This is obvious. Therefore, it has been clarified by science in the proper place that it is necessary to have empty spaces and waste regions interspersed between civilized areas. This makes circulation of the air possible. . . .

God determines whatever He wishes.

Source 2 from Giovanni Boccaccio, The Decameron, *trans. Mark Musa and Peter Bondanella (New York: W. W. Norton, 1982), pp. 6–12.*

2. From Giovanni Boccaccio, *The Decameron*

Let me say, then, that thirteen hundred and forty-eight years[4] had already passed after the fruitful Incarnation of the Son of God when into the distinguished city of Florence, more noble than any other Italian city, there came a deadly pestilence. Either because of the influence of heavenly bodies or because of God's just wrath as a punishment to mortals for our wicked deeds, the pestilence, originating some years earlier in the East, killed an infinite number of people as it spread relentlessly from one place to another until finally it had stretched its miserable length all over the West. And against this pestilence no human wisdom or foresight was of any avail; quantities of filth were removed from the city by officials charged with the task; the entry of any sick person into the city was prohibited; and many directives were issued concerning the maintenance of good health. Nor were the humble supplications rendered not once but many times by the pious to God, through public processions or by other means, in any way efficacious; for almost at the beginning of springtime of the year in question the plague began to show its sorrowful effects in an extraordinary manner. . . . Neither a doctor's advice nor the strength of medicine could do anything to cure this illness; on the contrary, either the nature of the illness was such that it afforded no cure, or else the doctors were so ignorant that they did not recognize its cause and, as a result, could not prescribe the proper remedy (in fact, the number of doctors, other than the well-trained, was increased by a large number of men and women who had never had any medical training); at any rate, few of the sick were ever cured, and almost all died after the third day of the appearance of the previously described symptoms (some sooner, others later), and most of them died without fever or any other side effects.

This pestilence was so powerful that it was transmitted to the healthy by contact with the sick, the way a fire close to dry or oily things will set them aflame.

4. In Boccaccio's day, Florentines began the first of each year not with the first of January, as is done today, but rather with the traditional date of the Annunciation (March 25).

And the evil of the plague went even further: not only did talking to or being around the sick bring infection and a common death, but also touching the clothes of the sick or anything touched or used by them seemed to communicate this very disease to the person involved. . . . The plague described here was of such virulence in spreading from one person to another that not only did it pass from one man to the next, but, what's more, it was often transmitted from the garments of a sick or dead man to animals that not only became contaminated by the disease but also died within a brief period of time. My own eyes, as I said earlier, were witness to such a thing one day: when the rags of a poor man who died of this disease were thrown into the public street, two pigs came upon them, and, as they are wont to do, first with their snouts and then with their teeth they took the rags and shook them around; and within a short time, after a number of convulsions, both pigs fell dead upon the ill-fated rags, as if they had been poisoned. From these and many similar or worse occurrences there came about such fear and such fantastic notions among those who remained alive that almost all of them took a very cruel attitude in the matter; that is, they completely avoided the sick and their possessions, and in so doing, each one believed that he was protecting his own good health.

There were some people who thought that living moderately and avoiding any excess might help a great deal in resisting this disease, and so they gathered in small groups and lived entirely apart from everyone else. They shut themselves up in those houses where there were no sick people and where one could live well by eating the most delicate of foods and drinking the finest of wines (doing so always in moderation), allowing no one to speak about or listen to anything said about the sick and the dead outside; these people lived, entertaining themselves with music and other pleasures that they could arrange. Others thought the opposite: they believed that drinking excessively, enjoying life, going about singing and celebrating, satisfying in every way the appetites as best one could, laughing, and making light of everything that happened was the best medicine for such a disease; so they practiced to the fullest what they believed by going from one tavern to another all day and night, drinking to excess; and they would often make merry in private homes, doing everything that pleased or amused them the most. This they were able to do easily, for everyone felt he was doomed to die and, as a result, abandoned his property, so that most of the houses had become common property, and any stranger who came upon them used them as if he were their rightful owner. In addition to this bestial behavior, they always managed to avoid the sick as best they could. And in this great affliction and misery of our city the revered authority of the laws, both divine and human, had fallen and almost completely disappeared, for, like other men, the ministers and executors of the laws were either dead or sick or so short of help that it was impossible for them to fulfill their duties; as a result, everybody was free to do as he pleased.

Many others adopted a middle course between the two attitudes just described: neither did they restrict their food or drink so much as the first group nor did they fall into such dissoluteness and drunkenness as the second; rather, they satisfied their appetites to a moderate degree. They did not shut themselves up, but went around carrying in their hands flowers, or sweet-smelling herbs, or various kinds of spices; and they would often put these things to their noses, believing that such smells were a wonderful means of purifying the brain, for all the air seemed infected with the stench of dead bodies, sickness, and medicines.

Others were of a crueler opinion (though it was, perhaps, a safer one): they maintained that there was no better medicine against the plague than to flee from it; convinced of this reasoning and caring only about themselves, men and women in great numbers abandoned their city, their houses, their farms, their relatives, and their possessions and sought other places, going at least as far away as the Florentine countryside—as if the wrath of God could not pursue them with this pestilence wherever they went but would only strike those it found within the walls of the city! Or perhaps they thought that Florence's last hour had come and that no one in the city would remain alive.

And not all those who adopted these diverse opinions died, nor did they all escape with their lives; on the contrary, many of those who thought this way were falling sick everywhere, and since they had given, when they were healthy, the bad example of avoiding the sick, they in turn were abandoned and left to languish away without any care. The fact was that one citizen avoided another, that almost no one cared for his neighbor, and that relatives rarely or hardly ever visited each other—they stayed far apart. This disaster had struck such fear into the hearts of men and women that brother abandoned brother, uncle abandoned nephew, sister left brother, and very often wife abandoned husband, and—even worse, almost unbelievable—fathers and mothers neglected to tend and care for their children as if they were not their own.

Thus, for the countless multitude of men and women who fell sick, there remained no support except the charity of their friends (and these were few) or the greed of servants, who worked for inflated salaries without regard to the service they performed and who, in spite of this, were few and far between; and those few were men or women of little wit (most of them not trained for such service) who did little else but hand different things to the sick when requested to do so or watch over them while they died, and in this service, they very often lost their own lives and their profits. . . . Between the lack of competent attendants that the sick were unable to obtain and the violence of the pestilence itself, so many, many people died in the city both day and night that it was incredible just to hear this described, not to mention seeing it! Therefore, out of sheer necessity, there arose among those who remained alive customs which were contrary to the established practices of the time.

It was the custom, as it is again today, for the women relatives and neighbors to gather together in the house of a dead person and there to mourn with the women who had been dearest to him; on the other hand, in front of the deceased's home, his male relatives would gather together with his male neighbors and other citizens, and the clergy also came, many of them or sometimes just a few, depending upon the social class of the dead man. Then, upon the shoulders of his equals, he was carried to the church chosen by him before death with the funeral pomp of candles and chants. With the fury of the pestilence increasing, this custom, for the most part, died out and other practices took its place. And so not only did people die without having a number of women around them, but there were many who passed away without having even a single witness present, and very few were granted the piteous laments and bitter tears of their relatives; on the contrary, most relatives were somewhere else, laughing, joking, and amusing themselves; even the women learned this practice too well, having put aside, for the most part, their womanly compassion for their own safety. . . .

The plight of the lower class and, perhaps, a large part of the middle class was even more pathetic: most of them stayed in their homes or neighborhoods either because of their poverty or because of their hopes for remaining safe, and every day they fell sick by the thousands; and not having servants or attendants of any kind, they almost always died. Many ended their lives in the public streets, during the day or at night, while many others who died in their homes were discovered dead by their neighbors only by the smell of their decomposing bodies. The city was full of corpses. The dead were usually given the same treatment by their neighbors, who were moved more by the fear that the decomposing corpses would contaminate them than by any charity they might have felt toward the deceased: either by themselves or with the assistance of porters (when they were available), they would drag the corpse out of the home and place it in front of the doorstep, where, usually in the morning, quantities of dead bodies could be seen by any passerby; then they were laid out on biers, or for lack of biers, on a plank. . . . Moreover, the dead were honored with no tears or candles or funeral mourners; in fact, things had reached such a point that the people who died were cared for as we care for goats today. Thus it became quite obvious that the very thing which in normal times wise men had not been able to resign themselves to, even though then it struck seldom and less harshly, became as a result of this colossal misfortune a matter of indifference to even the most simpleminded people.

So many corpses would arrive in front of a church every day and at every hour that the amount of holy ground for burials was certainly insufficient for the ancient custom of giving each body its individual place; when all the graves were full, huge trenches were dug in all of the cemeteries of the churches and into them the new arrivals were dumped by the hundreds; and they were packed in there with dirt, one on top of another, like a ship's cargo, until the trench was filled. . . .

Oh, how many great palaces, beautiful homes, and noble dwellings, once filled with families, gentlemen, and ladies, were now emptied, down to the last servant! How many notable families, vast domains, and famous fortunes remained without legitimate heir! How many valiant men, beautiful women, and charming young boys, who might have been pronounced very healthy by Galen, Hippocrates, and Aesculapius (not to mention lesser physicians), ate breakfast in the morning with their relatives, companions, and friends and then in the evening dined with their ancestors in the other world!

Source 3 from Ibn Battuta: Travels in Asia and Africa, 1325–1354, *trans. and selected by H. A. R. Gibbs (New York: August M. Kelley, 1969), pp. 305, 68–69.*

3. From *Ibn Battuta, Travels in Asia and Africa, 1325–1354*

Early in June we heard at Aleppo that the plague had broken out at Gaza, and that the number of deaths there reached over a thousand a day. On travelling to Hims I found that the plague had broken out there: about three hundred persons died of it on the day that I arrived. So I went on to Damascus, and arrived there on a Thursday. . . .

One of the celebrated sanctuaries at Damascus is the Mosque of the Footprints (al-Aqdám), which lies two miles south of the city, alongside the main highway which leads to the Hijáz, Jerusalem, and Egypt. It is a large mosque, very blessed, richly endowed, and very highly venerated by the Damascenes. . . . I saw a remarkable instance of the veneration in which the Damascenes hold this mosque during the great pestilence, on my return journey through Damascus in the latter part of July 1348. The viceroy Arghún Sháh ordered a crier to proclaim through Damascus that all the people should fast for three days and that no one should cook anything eatable in the market during the daytime. For most of the people there eat no food but what has been prepared in the market. So the people fasted for three successive days, the last of which was a Thursday, then they assembled in the Great Mosque, amírs, sharífs, qádís, theologians, and all the other classes of the people, until the place was filled to overflowing, and there they spent the Thursday night in prayers and litanies. After the dawn prayer next morning they all went out together on foot, holding Korans in their hands, and the amírs barefooted. The procession was joined by the entire population of the town, men and women, small and large; the Jews came with their Book of the Law and the Christians with their Gospel, all of them with their women and children. The whole concourse, weeping and supplicating and seeking the favour of God through His Books and His Prophets, made their way to the Mosque of the Footprints, and there they remained in supplication and invocation until near midday. They then returned to the city and held the Friday service, and God lightened their affliction; for the number of deaths in a single day at Damascus did not attain two thousand, while in Cairo and Old Cairo it reached the figure of twenty-four thousand a day.

Source 4 from Christos S. Bartsocas, "Two Fourteenth Century Descriptions of the 'Black Death,'" Journal of the History of Medicine, *October 1966, pp. 395–397.*

4. From Ioannes Cautacuzenos (John VI of Byzantium), *Historarum*

Upon arrival in Byzantium she [the empress] found Andronikos, the youngest born, dead from the invading plague, which starting first from the Hyperborean Scythians, attacked almost all the sea coasts of the world and killed most of their people. For it swept not only through Pontus, Thrace and Macedonia, but even Greece, Italy and all the islands, Egypt, Libya, Judaea and Syria, and spread throughout almost the entire world.

So incurable was the evil, that neither any regularity of life, nor any bodily strength could resist it. Strong and weak bodies were all similarly carried away, and those best cared for died in the same manner as the poor. No other [major] disease of any kind presented itself that year. If someone had a previous illness he always succumbed to this disease and no physician's art was sufficient; neither did the disease take the same course in all persons but the others, unable to resist, died the same day, a few even within the hour. Those who could resist for two or three days had a very violent fever at first, the disease in such cases attacking the head; they suffered from speechlessness and insensibility to all happenings and then appeared as if sunken into a deep sleep. . . .

Great abscesses were formed on the legs or the arms, from which, when cut, a large quantity of foul-smelling pus flowed and the disease was differentiated as that which discharged much annoying matter. Even many who were seized by all the symptoms unexpectedly recovered. There was no help from anywhere; if someone brought to another a remedy useful to himself, this became poison to the other patient. Some, by treating others, became infected with the disease. It caused great destruction and many homes were deserted by their inhabitants. Domestic animals died together with their masters. Most terrible was the discouragement. Whenever people felt sick there was no hope left for recovery, but by turning to despair, adding to their prostration and severely aggravating their sickness, they died at once. No words could express the nature of the disease. All that can be pointed out is that it had nothing in common with the everyday evils to which the nature of man is subject, but was something else sent by God to restore chastity. Many of the sick turned to better things in their minds, by being chastened, not only those who died, but also those who overcame the disease. They abstained from all vice during that time and they lived virtuously; many divided their property among the poor, even before they were attacked by the disease. If he ever felt himself seized, no one was so ruthless as not to show repentance of his faults and to appear before the judgment seat of God with the best chance of salvation, not believing that the soul was incurable or unhealed. Many died in Byzantium then, and the king's son, Andronikos, was attacked and died the third day.

Source 5 from Rosemary Horrox, The Black Death *(Manchester: Manchester University Press, 1994), pp. 55–57.*

5. From the Chronicle of Jean de Venette

In 1348 the people of France, and of virtually the whole world, were assailed by something more than war. For just as famine had befallen them, as described in the beginning of this account, and then war, as described in the course of the account, so now pestilences broke out in various parts of the world. In the August of that year a very large and bright star was seen in the west over Paris, after vespers, when the sun was still shining but beginning to set. It was not as high in the heavens as the rest of the stars; on the contrary, it seemed rather near. And as the sun set and night approached the star seemed to stay in one place, as I and many of my brethren observed. Once night had fallen, as we watched and greatly marvelled, the great star sent out many separate beams of light, and after shooting out rays eastwards over Paris it vanished totally: there one minute, gone the next. Whether it was a comet or something else—perhaps something condensed from some sort of exhalations which then returned to vapour—I leave to the judgment of astronomers. But it seems possible that it presaged the incredible pestilence which soon followed in Paris and throughout the whole of France, as I shall describe.

As a result of that pestilence a great many men and women died that year and the next in Paris and throughout the kingdom of France, as they also did in other parts of the world. . . .

. . . During the epidemic the Lord, of his goodness, deigned to confer such grace on those dying that, however suddenly they died, almost all of them faced death as joyfully as if they had been well prepared for it. Nor did anyone die without making confession and receiving the last sacrament. So that more of those dying would make a good end, Pope Clement mercifully gave the confessors in numerous cities and villages the power to absolve the sins of the dying, so that as a result they died the more happily, leaving much of their land and goods to churches or religious orders since their right heirs had predeceased them.

Men ascribed the pestilence to infected air or water, because there was no famine or lack of food at that time but, on the contrary, a great abundance. One result of this interpretation was that the infection, and the sudden death which it brought, were blamed on the Jews, who were said to have poisoned wells and rivers and corrupted the air. Accordingly the whole world brutally rose against them, and in Germany and in other countries which had Jewish communities many thousands were indiscriminately butchered, slaughtered and burnt alive by the Christians.[5] The insane constancy shown by them and their wives was amazing. When Jews were being burnt mothers would throw their own children into the flames rather than risk them being baptised, and would then hurl themselves into the fire after them, to burn with their husbands and children.

It was claimed that many wicked Christians were discovered poisoning wells in a similar fashion. But in truth, such poisonings, even if they really happened, could not have been solely responsible for so great a plague or killed so many people. There must have been some other cause such as, for instance, the will of God, or corrupt humours and the badness of air and earth; although perhaps such poisonings, where they did occur, were a contributory factor. The mortality continued in France for most of 1348 and 1349 and then stopped, leaving many villages and many town houses virtually empty, stripped of their inhabitants. Then many houses fell quickly into ruin, including numerous houses in Paris, although the damage there was less than in many places.

When the epidemic was over the men and women still alive married each other. Everywhere women conceived more readily than usual. None proved barren, on the contrary, there were pregnant women wherever you looked. Several gave birth to twins, and some to living triplets. But what is particularly surprising is that when the children born after the plague started cutting their teeth they commonly turned out to have only 20 or 22, instead of the 32 usual before the plague. I am unsure what this means, unless it is, as some men say, a sign that the death of infinite numbers of people, and their replacement by those who survived, has somehow renewed the world and initiated a new age. But if so, the world, alas, has not been made any better by its renewal. For after the plague men became more miserly and grasping, although many owned more than they had before. They were also more greedy and quarrelsome, involving themselves in brawls, disputes and lawsuits. Nor did the dreadful plague inflicted by God bring about peace between kings and lords. On the contrary, the enemies of the king of France and of the Church were stronger and more evil than before and stirred up wars by land and sea. Evil spread like wildfire.

What was also amazing was that, in spite of there being plenty of everything, it was all twice as expensive: household equipment and foodstuffs, as well as merchandise, hired labour, farm workers and servants. The only exception was property and houses, of which there is a glut to this day. Also from that time charity began to grow cold, and wrongdoing flourished, along with sinfulness and ignorance—for few men could be found in houses, towns or castles who were able or willing to instruct boys in the rudiments of Latin.

5. The Jews had been expelled from France by Philip the Fair in 1322.

Source 6: Walters Art Gallery, Baltimore.

6. Lieferinxe, *St. Sebastian Interceding for the Plague-Stricken*

Source 7 from Rosemary Horrox, The Black Death *(Manchester: Manchester University Press, 1994), pp. 125–126.*

7. A Prayer to St. Sebastian

O St Sebastian, guard and defend me, morning and evening, every minute of every hour, while I am still of sound mind; and, Martyr, diminish the strength of that vile illness called an epidemic which is threatening me. Protect and keep me and all my friends from this plague. We put our trust in God and St Mary, and in you, O holy Martyr. . . . Be with us always, and by your merits keep us safe and sound and protected from plague. Commend us to the Trinity and to the Virgin Mary, so that when we die we may have our reward: to behold God in the company of martyrs.

Source 8 from William H. McNeill, Plagues and Peoples *(New York: Anchor, 1977), p. 198.*

8. Citations from the Hadith

When you learn that epidemic disease exists in a county, do not go there; but if it breaks out in the county where you are, do not leave.

He who dies of epidemic disease is a martyr.

It is a punishment that God inflicts on whom he wills, but He has granted a modicum of clemency with respect to Believers.

Source 9 from Manfred Ullman, Islamic Medicine *(Edinburgh: Edinburgh University Press, 1978), pp. 94–95.*

9. An Arab Doctor's Medical Perspective on the Black Death

If one asks, 'How can you admit the assertion, there is infection, when the revealed word (*ash-shar'*) denies this?' we answer: that infection exists, is confirmed by experience, research, insight and observation and through constantly recurring accounts. These are the elements of proof. For him who has treated or recognized this case, it cannot remain concealed that mostly the man who has had contact with a patient infected with this disease must die, and that, on the other hand, the man who has had no contact remains healthy. So it is with the appearance of the illness in a house or quarter because of a garment or a vessel;

even an earring can destroy him who puts it in his ear, and all the inhabitants of the house. The illness can first appear in a town in a single house; then, from there, it can break out among individual contacts, then among their neighbours, relatives, and especially their visitors, until the breach becomes even greater. The illness can appear in coastal towns that enjoyed good health until there lands in them a man with plague, come from across the sea, from another coast where the plague already exists, as reports tell. The date of the appearance of the illness in the town tallies with the date of debarcation of this man. Many remained healthy who kept themselves strictly cut off from the outside world, like the pious Ibn-Abī-Madyan in Salé. He belonged to those who believed in contagion. He had stored up provisions for a long period and bricked up his door behind him and his large family. The town succumbed but during that period, he was not deprived of a single soul. One had repeatedly heard that places which lie remote from highways and traffic remained untouched. But there is nothing more wonderful at this time than the prison camp of the Muslims—may God free them!—in the Arsenal of Seville: there were thousands but the plague did not touch them although it practically destroyed the town itself. The report is also correct that the itinerant nomads living in tents in North Africa and elsewhere remained healthy because there the air is not shut in and the corruption proceeding from it could only gain a slight hold. . . .

But it belongs to principles which one may not ignore that a proof taken from tradition (Hadīth), if observation and inspection are contrary, must be interpreted allegorically. In this matter it is essential that it should be interpreted in accordance with the views of those who hold the theory of contagion. There are numerous compassionate passages in revealed scripture, for example, the utterance of the Prophet: 'an owner of sick animals should not drive these to the owner of healthy animals.'

Source 10 from Michael Dols, The Black Death in the Middle East *(Princeton: Princeton University Press, 1977), pp. 139, 135.*

10. Cryptograms

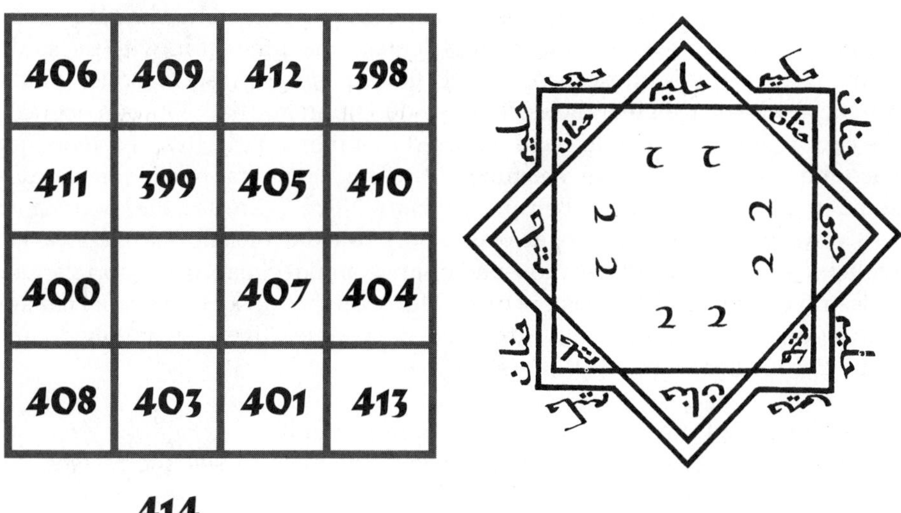

406	409	412	398
411	399	405	410
400		407	404
408	403	401	413

Source 11 from "Ibn al-Wardi's Risalah al naba' 'an al-Waba,' *A Translation of a Major Source for the History of the Black Death in the Middle East," in* Near Eastern Numismatics, Iconography, Epigraphy and History: Studies in Honor of George C. Miles, *ed. Dickran K. Kouymjian (Beirut: American University, 1974), pp. 447–450, 452–455.*

11. From Ibn al-Wardi, "An Essay on the Report of the Pestilence"

God is my security in every adversity. My sufficiency is in God alone. Is not God sufficient protection for His servant? Oh God, pray for our master, Muhammad, and give him peace. Save us for his sake from the attacks of the plague and give us shelter.

The plague frightened and killed. It began in the land of darkness. Oh, what a visitor! It has been current for fifteen years. China was not preserved from it nor could the strongest fortress hinder it. The plague afflicted the Indians in India. It weighed upon the Sind. It seized with its hand and ensnared even the lands of the Uzbeks. . . . The plague increased and spread further. It attacked the Persians, . . . and gnawed away at the Crimea. . . . The plague destroyed mankind in Cairo. . . . It stilled all movement in Alexandria. . . .

Oh Alexandria, this plague is like a lion which extends its arm to you.
Have patience with the fate of the plague, which leaves of seventy men only seven.

Then, the plague turned to Upper Egypt. It, also, sent forth its storm to Barqah. The plague attacked Gaza, and it shook 'Asqalān severely. The plague oppressed Acre. The scourge came to Jerusalem and paid the *zakāt* [with the souls of men]. It overtook those people who fled to the al-'Aqsā Mosque, which stands beside the Dome of the Rock. If the door of mercy had not been opened, the end of the world would have occurred in a moment. It, then, hastened its pace and attacked the entire maritime plain. The plague trapped Sidon and descended unexpectedly upon Beirut, cunningly. Next, it directed the shooting of its arrows to Damascus. There the plague sat like a king on a throne and swayed with power, killing daily one thousand or more and decimating the population. It destroyed mankind with its pustules. May God the Most High spare Damascus to pursue its own path and extinguish the plague's fires so that they do not come close to her fragrant orchards.

Oh God, restore Damascus and protect her from insult.
Its morale has been so lowered that people in the city sell themselves for grain. . . .

Oh God, it is acting by Your command. Lift this from us. It happens where You wish; keep the plague from us. Who will defend us against this horror other than You the Almighty? . . .

How many places has the plague entered. It swore not to leave the houses without its inhabitants. It searched them out with a lamp. The pestilence caused the people of Aleppo the same disturbance. . . .

Oh, if you could see the nobles of Aleppo studying their inscrutable books of medicine. They multiply its remedies by eating dried and sour foods. The buboes which disturb men's healthy lives are smeared with Armenian clay. Each man treated his humours and made life more comfortable. They perfumed their homes with ambergris and camphor, cyperus and sandal. They wore ruby rings and put onions, vinegar, and sardines together with the daily meal. They ate less broth and fruit but ate the citron and similar things.

If you see many biers and their carriers and hear in every quarter of Aleppo the announcements of death and cries, you run from them and refuse to stay with them. In Aleppo the profits of the undertakers have greatly increased. Oh God, do not profit them. Those who sweat from carrying the coffins enjoy this plague-time. Oh God, do not let them sweat and enjoy this. . . .

We ask God's forgiveness for our souls' bad inclination; the plague is surely part of His punishment. We take refuge from His wrath in His pleasure and from His chastisement in His restoring.

They said: the air's corruption kills. I said: the love of corruption kills.
How many sins and how many offenses does the crier call our attention to. . . .

This plague is for the Muslims a martyrdom and a reward, and for the disbelievers a punishment and a rebuke. When the Muslim endures misfortune, then patience is his worship. It has been established by our Prophet, God bless him and give him peace, that the plague-stricken are martyrs. This noble tradition is true and assures martyrdom. And this secret should be pleasing to the true believer. If someone says it causes infection and destruction, say: God creates and recreates. If the liar, disputes the matter of infection and tries to find an explanation, I say that the Prophet, on him be peace, said: who infected the first? If we acknowledge the plague's devastation of the people, it is the will of the Chosen Doer. So it happened again and again.

I take refuge in God from the yoke of the plague. Its high explosion has burst into all countries and was an examiner of astonishing things. Its sudden attacks perplex the people. The plague chases the screaming without pity and does not accept a treasure for ransom. Its engine is far-reaching. The plague enters into the house and swears it will not leave except with all of its inhabitants. "I have an order from the *qāḍī* to arrest all those in the house." Among the benefits of this order is the removal of one's hopes and the improvement of his earthly works. It awakens men from their indifference for the provisioning of their final journey.

One man begs another to take care of his children, and one says goodbye to his neighbors.
A third perfects his works, and another prepares his shroud.
A fifth is reconciled with his enemies, and another treats his friends with kindness.
One is very generous; another makes friends with those who have betrayed him.
Another man puts aside his property; one frees his servants.
One man changes his character while another mends his ways.
For this plague has captured all people and is about to send its ultimate destruction.
There is no protection today from it other than His mercy, praise to be God.

Nothing prevented us from running away from the plague except our devotion to the noble tradition. Come then, seek the aid of God Almighty for raising the plague, for He is the best helper. Oh God, we call You better than anyone did before. We call You to raise from us the pestilence and plague. We do not take refuge in its removal other than with You. We do not depend on our good health against the plague but on You. We seek Your protection, Oh Lord of creation, from the blows of this stick. We ask for Your mercy which is wider than our sins even as they are the number of the sands and pebbles. We plead with You, by the most honored of the advocates, Muhammad, the Prophet of mercy, that You take away from us this distress. Protect us from the evil and the torture and preserve us. For You are our sole support; what a perfect trustee!

Source 12 from Rosemary Horrox, The Black Death *(Manchester: Manchester University Press, 1994), pp. 193–194.*

12. A Fifteenth-Century Treatise on the Pestilence

It should be known to all Christians that pestilence, and every other manifestation of God's vengeance, arises because of sin. . . . Pestilence arises from a multitude of sins, but most especially from swearing worthless, deceitful and meaningless oaths.

If I am asked what is the cause of pestilence, what is its physical cause and by what means can someone save himself from it, I answer to the first question that sin is the cause, as set forth above. To the second question I say that it arises from the sea, as the evangelist says: 'There shall be signs in the sun and in the moon and in the stars; and upon the earth distress of nations, by reason of the confusion of the roaring of the sea and of the waves'.[6] For the devil, by the power committed to him, when the seas rise up high, is voiding his poison, sending it forth to be added to the poison in the air, and that air spreads gradually from place to place and enters men through the ears, eyes, nose, mouth, pores and the other orifices. Then if the man has a strong constitution, nature can expel the poison through ulcers, and if the ulcers putrify, are strangled and fully run their course the patient will be saved, as can be clearly seen. But if the poison should be stronger than his nature, so that his constitution cannot prevail against it, then the poison instantly lays siege to the heart, and the patient dies within a short time, without the relief which comes from the formation of ulcers.

To the third question I say that during the pestilence everyone over seven should be made to vomit daily from an empty stomach, and twice a week, or more often if necessary, he should lie well wrapped up in a warm bed and drink warm ale with ginger so that he sweats copiously, and he should never touch the sheets after that until they have been cleansed of the sweat, for if the person sweating had been in contact with the pestilence a healthy man could catch the plague from the sheets unless they have been well washed. And as soon as he feels an itch or prickling in his flesh he must use a goblet or cupping horn to let blood and draw down the blood from the heart, and this should be done two or three times at intervals of one or two days at most. And if he should feel himself oppressed deep within the body, then he should let blood in the nearest veins,

6. Luke 21.25. This occurs in a list of the signs which will precede Christ's second coming and the end of the world.

either in the arms or in the main veins of the feet. Likewise something which is extremely poisonous in itself may be of service in excluding the plague. And if a healthy adult does as I have described, they can save themselves whenever a great pestilence occurs.

Source 13 from Rosemary Horrox, The Black Death *(Manchester: Manchester: Manchester University Press, 1994), pp. 158–163.*

13. From Report of the Paris Medical Faculty, October 1348

Seeing things which cannot be explained, even by the most gifted intellects, initially stirs the human mind to amazement; but after marvelling, the prudent soul next yields to its desire for understanding and, anxious for its own perfection, strives with all its might to discover the causes of the amazing events. For there is within the human mind an innate desire to seize on goodness and truth. As the Philosopher makes plain, all things seek for the good and want to understand.[7] To attain this end we have listened to the opinions of many modern experts on astrology and medicine about the causes of the epidemic which has prevailed since 1345. However, because their conclusions still leave room for considerable uncertainty, we, the masters of the faculty of medicine at Paris, inspired by the command of the most illustrious prince, our most serene lord, Philip, King of France, and by our desire to achieve something of public benefit, have decided to compile, with God's help, a brief compendium of the distant and immediate causes of the present universal epidemic (as far as these can be understood by the human intellect) and of wholesome remedies; drawing on the opinions of the most brilliant ancient philosophers and modern experts, astronomers as well as doctors of medicine. And if we cannot explain everything as we would wish, for a sure explanation and perfect understanding of these matters is not always to be had (as Pliny says in book II, chapter 39: 'some accidental causes of storms are still uncertain, or cannot be explained'), it is open to any diligent reader to make good the deficiency.

We shall divide the work into two parts, in the first of which we shall investigate the causes of this pestilence and whence they come, for without knowledge of the causes no one can prescribe cures. In the second part we shall include methods of prevention and cure. There will be three chapters in the first part, for this epidemic arises from a double cause. One cause is distant and from above, and pertains to the heavens; the other is near and from below and pertains to the earth, and is dependent, causally and effectively, on the first cause.

7. "The Philosopher" is Aristotle.

Therefore the first chapter will deal with the first cause, the second with the second cause, and the third with the prognostications and signs associated with both of them. There will be two treatises in the second part. The first will deal with medical means of prevention and cure and will be divided into four chapters: the first on the disposition of the air and its rectification; the second on exercise and baths; the third on food and drink; the fourth on sleeping and waking, emptiness and fullness of the stomach and on the emotions. The second treatise will have three chapters: the first on universal remedies; the second on specific remedies appropriate to different patients; the third on antidotes.

CHAPTER 1 OF THE FIRST PART: CONCERNING THE UNIVERSAL AND DISTANT CAUSE

We say that the distant and first cause of this pestilence was and is the configuration of the heavens. In 1345, at one hour after noon on 20 March, there was a major conjunction of three planets in Aquarius. This conjunction, along with other earlier conjunctions and eclipses, by causing a deadly corruption of the air around us, signifies mortality and famine—and also other things about which we will not speak here because they are not relevant. Aristotle testifies that this is the case in his book *Concerning the causes of the properties of the elements,* in which he says that mortality of races and the depopulation of kingdoms occur at the conjunction of Saturn and Jupiter, for great events then arise, their nature depending on the trigon in which the conjunction occurs. And this is found in ancient philosophers, and Albertus Magnus in his book, *Concerning the causes of the properties of the elements* (treatise 2, chapter 1) says that the conjunction of Mars and Jupiter causes a great pestilence in the air, especially when they come together in a hot, wet sign, as was the case in 1345. For Jupiter, being wet and hot, draws up evil vapours from the earth and Mars, because it is immoderately hot and dry, then ignites the vapours, and as a result there were lightnings, sparks, noxious vapours and fires throughout the air.

These effects were intensified because Mars—a malevolent planet, breeding anger and wars—was in the sign of Leo from 6 October 1347 until the end of May this year, along with the head of the dragon, and because all these things are hot they attracted many vapours; which is why the winter was not as cold as it should have been. And Mars was also retrograde and therefore attracted many vapours from the earth and the sea which, when mixed with the air, corrupted its substance. Mars was also looking upon Jupiter with a hostile aspect, that is to say quartile, and that caused an evil disposition or quality in the air, harmful and hateful to our nature. This state of affairs generated strong winds (for according to Albertus in the first book of his *Meteora,* Jupiter has the property of raising powerful winds, particularly from the south) which gave rise to excess heat and moisture on the earth; although in fact it was the dampness which was most marked in our part of the world. And this is enough about the distant or universal cause for the moment.

CHAPTER 2 OF THE FIRST PART: CONCERNING THE PARTICULAR AND NEAR CAUSE

Although major pestilential illnesses can be caused by the corruption of water or food, as happens at times of famine and infertility, yet we still regard illnesses proceeding from the corruption of the air as much more dangerous. This is because bad air is more noxious than food or drink in that it can penetrate quickly to the heart and lungs to do its damage. We believe that the present epidemic or plague has arisen from air corrupt in its substance, and not changed in its attributes. By which we wish it be understood that air, being pure and clear by nature, can only become putrid or corrupt by being mixed with something else, that is to say, with evil vapours. What happened was that the many vapours which had been corrupted at the time of the conjunction were drawn up from the earth and water, and were then mixed with the air and spread abroad by frequent gusts of wind in the wild southerly gales, and because of these alien vapours which they carried the winds corrupted the air in its substance, and are still doing so. And this corrupted air, when breathed in, necessarily penetrates to the heart and corrupts the substance of the spirit there and rots the surrounding moisture, and the heat thus caused destroys the life force, and this is the immediate cause of the present epidemic.

And moreover these winds, which have become so common here, have carried among us (and may perhaps continue to do so in future) bad, rotten and poisonous vapours from elsewhere: from swamps, lakes and chasms, for instance, and also (which is even more dangerous) from unburied or unburnt corpses—which might well have been a cause of the epidemic. Another possible cause of corruption, which needs to be borne in mind, is the escape of the rottenness trapped in the centre of the earth as a result of earthquakes—something which has indeed recently occurred. But the conjunctions could have been the universal and distant cause of all these harmful things, by which air and water have been corrupted.

CHAPTER 3: CONCERNING PROGNOSTICATION AND SIGNS

Unseasonable weather is a particular cause of illness. For the ancients, notably Hippocrates, are agreed that if the four seasons run awry, and do not keep their proper course, then plagues and mortal passions are engendered that year. Experience tells us that for some time the seasons have not succeeded each other in the proper way. Last winter was not as cold as it should have been, with a great deal of rain; the spring windy and latterly wet. Summer was late, not as hot as it should have been, and extremely wet—the weather very changeable from day to day, and hour to hour; the air often troubled, and then still again, looking as if it was going to rain but then not doing so. Autumn too was very rainy and misty. It is because the whole year here—or most of it—was warm and wet that the air is pestilential. For it is a sign of pestilence for the air to be warm and wet at unseasonable times.

Wherefore we may fear a future pestilence here, which is particularly from the root beneath, because it is subject to the evil impress of the heavens, especially

since that conjunction was in a western sign. Therefore if next winter is very rainy and less cold than it ought to be, we should expect an epidemic round about late winter and spring—and if it occurs it will be long and dangerous, for usually unseasonable weather is of only brief duration, but when it lasts over many seasons, as has obviously been the case here, it stands to reason that its effects will be longer-lasting and more dangerous, unless ensuing seasons change their nature in the opposite way. Thus if the winter in the north turns out to be cold and dry, the plagues might be arrested.

We have not said that the future pestilence will be exceptionally dangerous, for we do not wish to give the impression that it will be as dangerous here as in southern or eastern regions. For the conjunctions and the other causes discussed above had a more immediate impact on those regions than on ours. However, in the judgement of astrologers (who follow Ptolemy on this) plagues are likely, although not inevitable, because so many exhalations and inflammations have been observed, such as a comet and shooting stars. Also the sky has looked yellow and the air reddish because of the burnt vapours. There has also been much lightning and flashes and frequent thunder, and winds of such violence and strength that they have carried dust storms from the south. These things, and in particular the powerful earthquakes, have done universal harm and left a trail of corruption. There have been masses of dead fish, animals and other things along the sea shore, and in many places trees covered in dust, and some people claim to have seen a multitude of frogs and reptiles generated from the corrupt matter; and all these things seem to have come from the great corruption of the air and earth. All these things have been noted before as signs of plague by numerous wise men who are still remembered with respect and who experienced them themselves.

No wonder, therefore, that we fear that we are in for an epidemic. But it should be noted that in saying this we do not intend to exclude the possibility of illnesses arising from the character of the present year—for as the aphorism of Hippocrates has it: a year of many fogs and damps is a year of many illnesses. On the other hand, the susceptibility of the body of the patient is the most immediate cause in the breeding of illnesses, and therefore no cause is likely to have an effect unless the patient is susceptible to its effects. We must therefore emphasise that although, because everyone has to breathe, everyone will be at risk from the corrupted air, not everyone will be made ill by it but only those, who will no doubt be numerous, who have a susceptibility to it; and very few indeed of those who do succumb will escape.

The bodies most likely to take the stamp of this pestilence are those which are hot and moist, for they are the most susceptible to putrefaction. The following are also more at risk: bodies bunged up with evil humours, because the unconsumed waste matter is not being expelled as it should; those following a bad life style, with too much exercise, sex and bathing; the thin and weak, and persistent worriers; babies, women and young people; and corpulent people with a ruddy complexion. However those with dry bodies, purged of waste matter, who adopt a sensible and suitable regimen, will succumb to the pestilence more slowly.

We must not overlook the fact that any pestilence proceeds from the divine will, and our advice can therefore only be to return humbly to God. But this does not mean forsaking doctors. For the Most High created earthly medicine, and although God alone cures the sick, he does so through the medicine which in his generosity he provided. Blessed be the glorious and high God, who does not refuse his help, but has clearly set out a way of being cured for those who fear him. And this is enough of the third chapter, and of the whole first part.

Source 14 from Rosemary Horrox, The Black Death *(Manchester: Manchester University Press, 1994), p. 149.*

14. A Wholesome Medicine Against All Infirmities

The advice of the reverend father Dom Theophilus of Milan, of the order of St Benedict, against the plague; also a most wholesome medicine against all infirmities. Note it well.

Whenever anyone is struck down by the plague they should immediately provide themselves with a medicine like this. Let him first gather as much as he can of bitter loathing towards the sins committed by him, and the same quantity of true contrition of heart, and mix the two into an ointment with the water of tears. Then let him make a vomit of frank and honest confession, by which he shall be purged of the pestilential poison of sin, and the boil of his vices shall be totally liquified and melt away. Then the spirit, formerly weighed down by the plague of sin, will be left all light and full of blessed joy. Afterwards let him take the most delightful and precious medicine: the body of our lord and saviour Jesus Christ. And finally let him have himself anointed on the seat of his bodily senses with holy oil. And in a little while he will pass from transient life to the incorruptible country of eternal life, safe from plague and all other infirmities.

Compared with this all other remedies of doctors are futile and profit little against the plague, which God keeps for the chastisement of sin and which is without remedy save through him and his power.

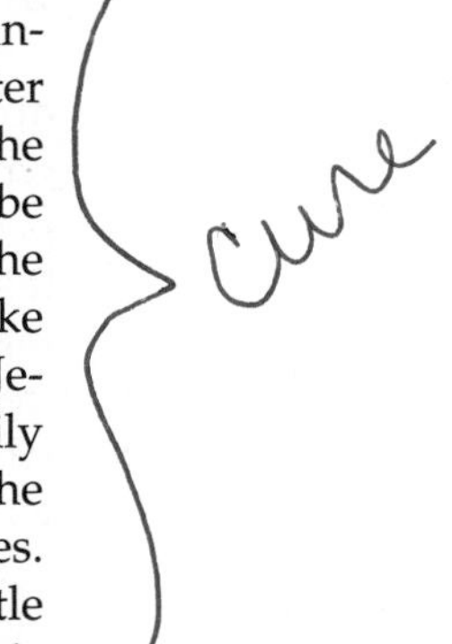

Source 15 from Rosemary Horrox, The Black Death *(Manchester: Manchester University Press, 1994), pp. 248–249.*

15. From Petrarch, "Letters on Familiar Matters"

a. What are we to do now, brother? Now that we have lost almost everything and found no rest. When can we expect it? Where shall we look for it? Time, as they say, has slipped through our fingers. Our former hopes are buried with our friends. The year 1348 left us lonely and bereft, for it took from us wealth which could not be restored by the Indian, Caspian or Carpathian Sea. Last losses are beyond recovery, and death's wound beyond cure. There is just one comfort: that we shall follow those who went before. I do not know how long we shall have to wait, but I know that it cannot be very long—although however short the time it will feel too long. . . .

b. There remained to me at least something salvaged from the wreck of last year: a most brilliant man, and (you must take my word for it) one great in action and counsel, Paganino da Milano, who after numerous proofs of his virtue became very dear to me, and seemed worthy of your friendship as well as mine. He was on the way to becoming another Socrates, displaying almost the same loyalty and good fellowship, and that friendship which lies in sharing good and bad fortune and in baring the hidden places of the heart in a trusting exchange of secrets.

How much he loved you, how much he longed to see you—you whom he could see only with the eyes of imagination. How much he worried about your safety during this shipwreck of the world. I was amazed that a man unknown to him could be so much loved. He never saw me graver than usual without becoming anxious himself and asking, 'Is something wrong? How is our friend?' But when he heard that you were in good health he would cast aside his fears with wonderful alacrity.

And this man (I speak it with many tears, and would speak it with more but my eyes are drained by previous misfortunes and I should save some tears for whatever may befall in the future), this man, I say, was suddenly seized by the pestilence which is now ravaging the world. This was at dusk, after dinner with his friends, and the evening hours that remained he spent talking with us, reminiscing about our friendship and shared concerns. He passed the night in extreme pain, which he endured with an undaunted spirit, and then died suddenly the next morning. None of the now-familiar horrors were abated, and within three days all his children and household followed him.

Go, mortals, sweat, pant, toil, range the lands and seas to pile up riches you cannot keep; glory that will not last. The life we lead is a sleep; whatever we do, dreams. Only death breaks the sleep and wakes us from dreaming. I wish I could have woken before this.

QUESTIONS TO CONSIDER

Now that you have looked at the evidence and made a list of the causes and consequences of the Black Death and the reactions to it, we can draw out some more detail and make some more systematic comparisons.

What, ultimately, caused the Black Death? Astrological causation is mentioned by the doctors of Paris, and several other authors refer to the alignment of the heavens or the actions of heavenly bodies. But was this really the ultimate cause? For most Christians and Muslims, the ultimate cause almost certainly had to be God. The documents you have examined make this clear, but a question still remains: *Why* would God bring such a pestilence to humanity? Taking the documents from Christian writers first, what seems to have been the most common answer to that question? The "Fifteenth-Century Treatise of the Plague" is characteristic in this regard, and also gives us an idea of the larger historical framework within which medieval Christians might understand the cause of the Black Death.

If we then compare the Islamic documents, a contrast becomes apparent: Meditations on God's intentions seem to be much less prominent in these sources. As Ibn Khaldun says, "God determines whatever He wishes." In general, Muslims are more reluctant than Christians to make authoritative pronouncements about God's intentions. The most rigid position articulated in these texts, Ibn Isma'il al Bukhari's relation of the *hadith,* implies that the plague is sent directly by God to the victim, as a punishment to the infidel and as a martyrdom (and therefore a blessing) to the Believer. No other explanation is necessary: God's will is unknowable. Nevertheless, you may be able to identify at least one passage from a Muslim writer who, like his Christian counterparts, ascribes a specific motivation for God's activities.

We find a greater range of possibilities when we turn from the ultimate causes in heaven to the immediate causes on earth. The first reading, from Ibn Khaldun, introduces us to the general area of environmental and demographic causation. While Ibn Khaldun locates the Black Death in a great scheme of the rise and fall of civilizations, other authors look more closely at particular environmental factors. As you look through the list of possible causes that you have identified in the documents, select those that have to do with environmental conditions or the size and distribution of population. From what you know of the "real" causes of the plague, how astute were these observations?

Many of our texts also refer to the means by which the plague is *transmitted* from one place to another and from one person to another. Again, issues of environment and demography are involved. How would you characterize the various theories of transmission, and which do you find to have been closest to the mark? Again, some variation between Christian and Islamic sources may be noted. The "orthodox" Islamic position, represented here by Muhammad ibn Isma' il, relies on an interpretation of the *hadith* that claims that since the disease is sent directly by God, there can be no belief in transmission through infection or contagion. How do the other Islamic authors react to this position?

Apart from theories of causation and transmission that refer to divine, heavenly, or environmental causes, there are also some texts that refer to the conscious activities of evil human beings who spread the disease on purpose. How were they said to have done so, and why? What groups were most likely to be singled out for such accusations, and what fate did they suffer as a consequence?

If we move from the question of causation to the question of the consequences of the Black Death, the most likely thing to notice first are the reports of mortality. How many people are said to have died? What percentage of the population is said to have been affected? How accurate do you think these reports might be?

Apart from the sheer number of people who died, many of the texts comment on the social, political, and economic effects of the Black Death. How did people's responses to the calamity affect social relationships within communities, between neighbors, between different social groups, and within families? According to the various authors, did the plague bring people closer together or push them apart? Were previously established forms of authority strengthened or weakened? How might some people benefit economically from the devastation of the plague? Does it seem that the changes in these societies brought about by the plague were temporary or permanent? Do the social, political, and economic effects of the plague seem to have been more concern to Christian or to Islamic commentators?

Many of these questions are posed in our sources in terms of public and private morality. As you compare entries in your list of consequences of the Black Death, also be aware of the contrast between those authors who saw standards of morality declining in the wake of the plague, and those who reported that at least some people were becoming more virtuous. What were some of the most striking examples of the breakdown of social conventions and the decline in morality? Under what circumstances might some people actually improve their behavior, and how might that positive response be shown?

What of the psychological effects of the plague? Several of the documents give us a close and immediate sense of the despair felt by survivors of the plague who had seen their friends and family carried away: Ioannes Cantacuzenos and Petrarch come to mind. Apart from those human emotions with which we can no doubt relate, however, there is another set of psychological concerns with which we may not immediately empathize. For medieval Christians in particular, it was of the greatest importance to die a "good death." This meant that one was properly prepared to leave this world for the next. One needed to be spiritually prepared, having received confession and the last rites of the Church. It was best if one had an opportunity to take leave of friends and family. After death, an elaborate wake and funeral ceremony would help the soul of the departed into heaven, as would the continued prayers of those left behind. Burial in consecrated ground was absolutely essential. From your reading of the documents in which such questions are raised, what might have been the psychological and emotional effects of the Black Death on medieval Christians? How might the reactions of Muslims have differed if they interpreted the *hadith* to mean that for Believers the plague was a martyrdom that guaranteed them a place in Heaven?

The ultimate logic of despair is to do nothing. If the plague really was sent by God and the doctors could do nothing about it, then why do anything other than simply wait to die? Perhaps you can find evidence of such attitudes in some of the documents, but clearly most people were on the lookout for things they could do to protect themselves and their communities. The Christian painting and Islamic cryptograms demonstrate how people might use visual images both to externalize their fears and to invoke divine aid as a protection from the plague.

In fact, many of the responses intended to remedy the situation were religious in nature. What seem to have been the most common religious activities that groups and individuals could pursue to protect themselves from the plague, or at least alleviate their suffering? Which ones seem to have been most approved of by religious leaders, or organized by them on behalf of the community? Were there other remedies that, while religious in inspiration, might have been disapproved of by the Catholic Church or by the most orthodox Islamic thinkers?

Other remedies that people might take involved changes in their living situations: People might change either where they lived, with whom they lived, or both. What different types of examples of this pattern did you find in the documents? How much of a change did they represent from previous social practices? Did the commentators seem to approve or disapprove of these strategies? Were they effective?

There were also attempts at medical solutions to the problem, involving both diagnosis and remedy. The prescriptions could involve changes of diet, alteration of lifestyle, and the use of specific medications and cures, as well as "civic" solutions involving urban authorities. Which sources do you think are the most "medical" in their approach? Did you find any diagnoses or remedies that you thought were more sensible than others?

Now that you have drawn some comparisons and reached some conclusions, you may want to step back and consider more generally the people who lived through the Black Death as depicted in these documents. It is difficult for us, perhaps, to suspend our judgment when looking at the thoughts and beliefs of people who lived long ago in very different cultural, religious, and technological circumstances. But if we make the effort, we will be better able to engage the people of the past on their own terms. What, then, have you learned about the inner worlds of medieval Christians and Muslims through your work in this chapter?

EPILOGUE

The world afflicted by the Black Death more than seven centuries ago may seem quite remote from our own. Advances in medical science now shield us from such devastation. Or do they? Is the lesson to be drawn from an examination of epidemic disease in world history really all that comforting? Two of the essential preconditions for the plague pandemic of the fourteenth century, increasing population density and a growth in intercontinental trade, should sound familiar to us today. In fact, Ibn Khaldun saw it as a general rule of history that civilizations create the conditions of their own collapse. The growth of population in general, and of cities in particular, and the growth of trade and overall prosperity seem to Ibn Khaldun to lead almost inevitably to a catastrophic decline marked by famine and pestilence.

We do not need to be as fatalistic as Ibn Khaldun to recognize that the connection between plagues and peoples is not merely a matter of history. Yet the tremendous strides of medical science have tended to blind us to this fact. Over the past century, sustained efforts to bring cleaner food, water, and living conditions to growing populations made significant headway, at least in the world's more prosperous regions. At the same time, medical science grew ever more sophisticated at identifying and attacking epidemic diseases—witness the development of the polio vaccine, the eradication of smallpox, the creation of more and more powerful antibiotics, and a huge reduction in the rates of tuberculosis and syphilis. It seemed that the age-old problem of epidemic disease was well on its way to solution.

This complacency was shattered by the AIDS outbreak of the 1980s. Differences of opinion are still to be found concerning the origin of AIDS. Since it is often the case that viruses develop in wild or domesticated animals and then somehow make the leap to human beings, it is possible that one or more of the HIV-related viruses endemic amongst certain species of monkeys in Africa made such a transition, perhaps when a hunter was infected by the blood of his kill. In the past, such a virus would probably have had only a local impact. In today's world, however, that infected hunter is likely to travel to a city, spreading the virus outside its original confined environment. That city is likely to be connected to an international airport. A disease that might once have been confined to a small group or region now stands a much better chance of becoming a global epidemic. Whatever the origin of HIV-AIDS, there is no doubt that the conditions of modernity have contributed to the spread of the disease.

HIV-AIDS is only the most notorious of the new diseases that have appeared in the past two decades. We could add Ebola virus, Lyme disease, Legionnaire's disease, Lassa fever, and many others to the list. At the same time, there has been a resurgence of old scourges that we once thought were on their way out, and the rise of more deadly forms of diseases such as malaria and encephalitis. As Arno Karlen points out, we are constantly and unwittingly creating the conditions that make this possible:

> We provide new ecological niches for microbes by tilling fields and domesticating animals, and by bringing into existence gardens and second-growth forests, villages and cities, homes and factories. We give them new homes in discarded truck tires and water tanks, air conditioners and hospital equipment. We transport them by automobile, ship and airplane. We alter their opportunities and affect their evolution

> when we change our abodes, our sex behavior, our diets, our clothing. The faster we change ourselves and our surroundings, the faster new infections reach us. In the past century we have changed the biosphere as much as any glacial change or meteor impact ever has. So we and microbes are dancing faster than ever in order to survive each other. As we do so, the burdens on our environment and our immune defenses increase.[8]

Far from having conquered epidemic disease, we seem to have speeded up the process in a way that threatens to get out of hand. As in the period reviewed in this chapter, population growth and expanded intercontinental trade bring both opportunity and danger.

Karlen advises us to be concerned, but not to despair. Our immune systems are very powerful and highly adaptable. Perhaps even more important, history shows that the human race has been through this before and has always survived. Then as now our responses are conditioned by our cultural presuppositions. As we think back on the tragic story of the Black Death, perhaps our attitude should be one of understanding and appreciation for the way our forebears dealt with problems that we still face today.

8. Arlo Karlen, "The New Epidemic," in *The Black Death*, ed. Dan Nardo (San Diego: Greenhaven, 1999), p. 126.

CHAPTER TEN

TRANS-ASIAN CONTACTS:

THE BASIS OF A WORLD SYSTEM

(900–1450)

THE PROBLEM

In recent years interest has been growing in a global approach to history—that is, a focus on the connections between states and regions rather than on their isolated development. This methodology reflects current awareness that a new level of world integration began to emerge in the early modern era, roughly speaking, during the years from 1500 to 1750. In that period, increasing contacts—initially economic and demographic but eventually political and even cultural—began drawing once separate peoples and cultures together in previously unimagined ways. Not only did African, Asian, and European peoples heighten their contacts with one another in this era, but they also became involved with whole "new worlds" in the Americas and Oceania. As connections multiplied, what people in one part of the globe did began to affect all others as never before. Ultimately people everywhere found themselves living in a so-called global village, a single, worldwide community. This kind of community is often called a "world system."

Actually, a world system need not span the globe. As used in this phrase, the word *world* means only a separate or self-contained region. The parts of such a region, though closely connected and interdependent enough to make up a unified system, simply have to remain isolated from those of other regions to form a "world" of their own. In earlier stages of history, in fact, several such systems may have existed simultaneously in different parts of the globe. A world system, then, does not necessarily entail everyone everywhere.

The modern world system, of course, did cover the whole earth. Developed initially through the efforts of Western Europeans to link other regions to their homeland in maritime networks of commerce and colonization, it centered on the North Atlantic Ocean. But in its heyday, the system spread far beyond its Atlantic hub to include the entire globe. Given the important role Western Europeans played in creating this global network, generations of historians looked to the rise of Europe as the key dynamic in modern history. But recent scholarship has begun to suggest that in drawing the world together Europeans may, in fact, have depended on the existence of a still older system in whose development they played only a modest role.

Although not as extensive as the modern world system, which became fully global in scope, this earlier one brought the peoples and cultures of the Old World into contact with one another. Based on long-distance trans-Asian connections that flourished from the tenth through the fifteenth century, it centered around Central Asia and the Indian Ocean rather than Europe and the North Atlantic. Europeans, who were then in the midst of their medieval period, remained largely marginal to it. Yet, as Columbus's voyages in search of the "Indies" attest, the lure of its enormous wealth played an important part in stimulating the later European expansion that proved so instrumental in the formation of the truly global modern system. Better understanding of this earlier system, then, may lead us not only to push back the time frame of global integration but also to rethink the origins of the modern world and especially the role non-European peoples may have played in its inception.

The Atlantic or modern world system, although initially arising out of a network of relatively free trade, ultimately evolved into an imperialistic order based upon unequal relationships in which certain peoples dominated others politically and culturally. Was this equally true of the earlier world system centered around Asia? Or did it have an entirely different character? In trying to determine the nature of this system, keep the following questions in mind: What kinds of enterprises drew people together? Who were the chief participants, and where did they come from? And finally, where and how did they interact? On the basis of your answers to these questions, you should be able to derive at least a general picture of this older system. How would you characterize it?

BACKGROUND

Long-distance contact across Asia stretches far back through history. Ultimately most travel and communication shifted toward the sea and maritime routes across the Indian Ocean. But in early days, dating back to the first millennium of the common era, contact occurred through overland routes that wound across the arid interior of Central Asia. One overland route in particular stood out. Often called the Silk Road because of the large amount of silk that flowed westward across it from China, it provided the main link between eastern and western Eurasia throughout antiquity and most of the period known in Europe as the Middle Ages.

For millennia, great mule and camel trains, known as caravans, plodded slowly across this inland route, stimulating the rise of rich commercial cities along its course. But because the pack animals could carry only limited loads, early trade was restricted to small lots of lightweight goods. For this reason, merchants in the trade preferred to deal in expensive luxury goods like silks, carpets, porcelain, and metalware that had a high ratio of value to weight. To pay the high cost of such goods and of outfitting caravans, merchants generally banded together into companies so that they could pool funds and bargain collectively. Usually these companies hired professional caravaneers to oversee the pack trains. And since in antiquity Persian and other Iranian-speaking peoples made up the majority of the population along the trade route, they provided most of its professional carriers. Persian, in fact, served as the original trade language, some of whose words—like the word *caravan* (from old Persian *kārwān*)—continue in use even today.

The eastern terminus of the Silk Road lay in the markets of China's inland cities. From China, it threaded northwestward through the Tarim Basin and around the sandy wastes of the Taklamakan Desert to the high passes of the snow-covered Pamir Mountains or the more northerly Tienshan range. From there it descended into the Caspian region, where it forked into two legs. One ran west through the Caucasus Mountains to termini along the Black Sea; the other turned south to Persia, branching again, westward toward the Mediterranean and eastward to India. Because of the rugged and arid nature of most of the terrain this route traversed, adjoining areas lacked large populations, and long stretches of desolate land separated settled sites. These conditions fostered a tradition of political separatism in which small city-states and autonomous kingdoms prevailed, and people remained local in their allegiances. But the constant flow of travelers through the area kept inhabitants up-to-date on happenings elsewhere. They thus became purveyors of new fashions and ideas as well as goods, and they passed major religions like Buddhism and Islam from one civilization to another.

The spread of Islam across the inland route, which followed the Arab conquest of Persia in the mid-600s, drew the peoples of Inner Asia closer together, offsetting in part their diversity. In the next few centuries, Islamicized cities along the inland route prospered as never before, benefiting from the growing volume of trade occasioned by development at both extremes of Asia. In the east, the Tang dynasty (618–907), based in Changan in north China, created a vast empire stretching from the Pacific to the Pamirs that stimulated economic growth throughout East Asia (see the map on page 274). Similar growth also occurred in western Asia under the Abbasid dynasty (750–1258), based in Baghdad, which built an equally immense Muslim state extending from the eastern Mediterranean to the Iranian plateau. The demand for new goods generated in these two giants dramatically increased the commerce and traffic flowing between them.

Profits derived from this trade made the cities along the caravan route among the wealthiest and most sophisticated in the world. People from adjoining areas thus flocked to them, including waves of Turkic-speaking migrants, who were drifting westward off the steppes or grasslands of East Asia. Conversion to Islam helped these Turkic migrants to blend into existing Iranian communities, but they remained a distinct population that began to outnumber the original inhabitants and to alter local traditions. Turkic rulers, known as *khans*, even began to succeed in building large regional states called *khanates*. But it was still another incoming group, the Mongols, who first unified the area under a single government.

The Mongols first penetrated the area when Chingis Khan reached the fringes of the trade route after defeating the Xixia state southwest of the Mongolian steppes and invading its western neighbor, Karakhitai, in the early 1200s. In the decades that followed, Mongol khans conquered westward to Baghdad, destroying the last Abbasid caliph there in 1258. By then, however, the Mongol empire had split into four parts. The lands along the old Silk Road formed the core of one of these, known as the Khanate of Jagadai. Richest of the four, Jagadai's resources encouraged its rulers to break with the supreme khanate further to the east and so outlive its collapse in the mid-1300s. Jagadai became the base of a new Central Asia empire under the Turko-Mongolian Khan Timur that lasted until his death in 1405. Under Mongol control, trade and travel expanded to new levels. Military traffic, of course, increased tremendously since the Mongols dispatched great armies back and forth across Central Asia. But diplomatic contacts increased, too, as neighboring peoples sought to negotiate with and placate the khans. Mongol rulers also welcomed foreign merchants into their lands, hoping to sell them *ortaqs*, or trade monopolies, and to recruit them as administrators. Marco Polo, for example, was recruited in just this way along with many other "colored eyes," as the Western émigrés were known.

By the Mongol era, however, much trans-Asian traffic had already begun shifting southward onto the Indian Ocean. Although the causes remain unclear, this trend was probably the result of explosive economic growth that began in eastern and western Asia during the Tang and Abbasid periods. In both regions the development of commercial economies, based upon affluent, urban markets with rising populations, spawned a rising demand for bulky commodities and foodstuffs. The volume of these new goods probably exceeded what overland caravans could handle. Because ships could carry greater cargoes of goods at lower cost, they posed a logical alternative—once navigational improvements made sailing across the open ocean relatively safe. Eventually, as maritime travel proved its reliability, more and more of the luxury trade, too, shifted south to the sea, drawing other forms of traffic along with it. Thus began a long, slow decline in the

Thirteenth-Century Asia

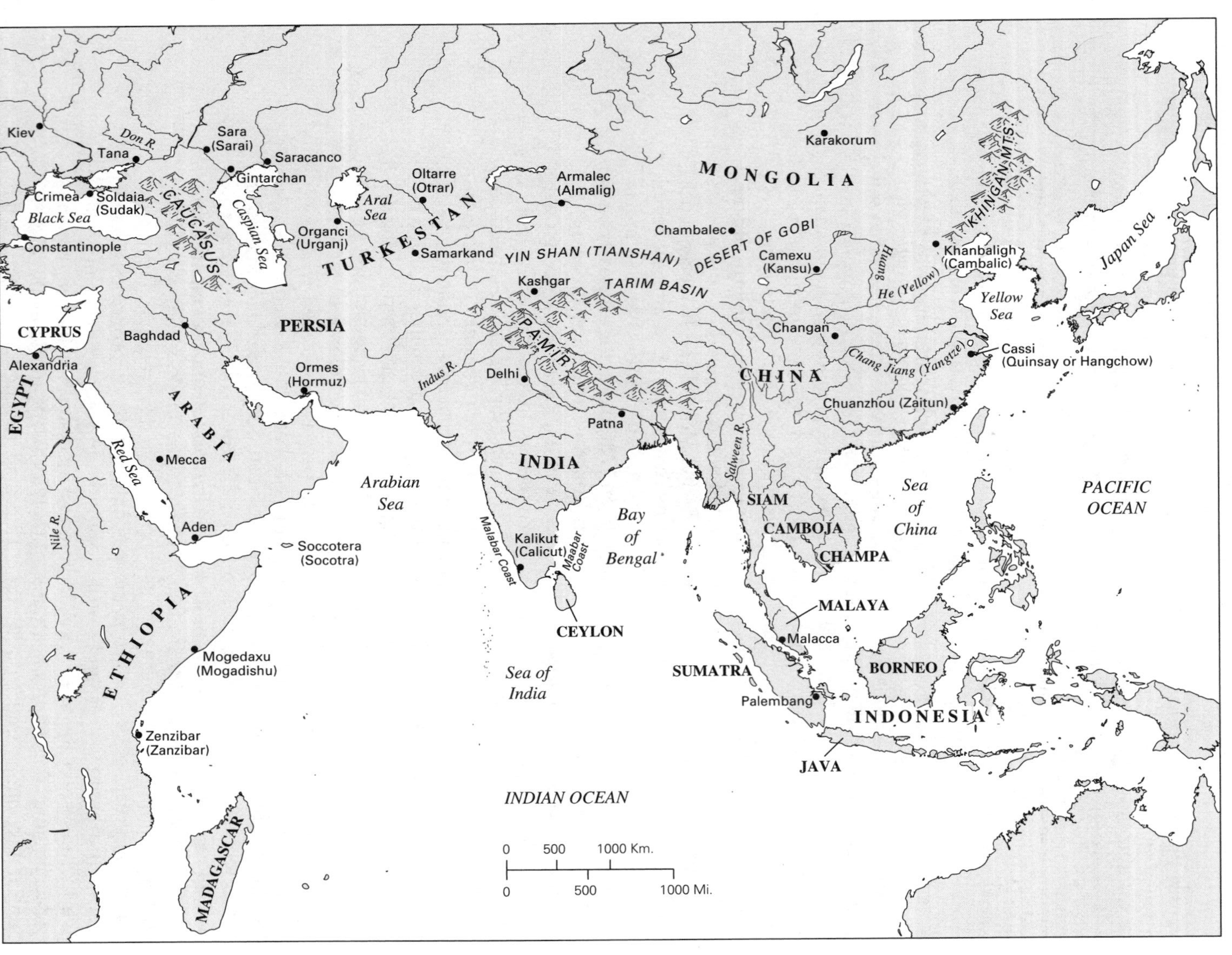

wealth and importance of Central Asia and its great cities.

Although travel by sea ultimately became easier than by land, seafaring also posed its problems. For one thing, travel across the Indian Ocean depended on the right winds. Powerful air fronts known as monsoons control the weather across the Indian Ocean and in the adjacent equatorial regions of Africa and the South Pacific. These fronts result from permanent high-pressure areas created at the equator by the evaporation of tropical waters. The warm, humid masses of air they produce flow northward all year, but during part of the year the build-up of temporary high-pressure zones over the mountains of Africa, western Asia, and northern India creates a counterflow of air that pushes them back south. This annual ebb and flow of air gives the Indian Ocean a two-season climate: A dry spell lasting from October to April annually alternates with an onslaught of heavy rains from April to October. The reversal of prevailing breezes that accompanies this seasonal shift creates two distinct sailing seasons.

For half of the year from April through September, the southwest monsoon winds blow toward India and up along the Indochina coast, making travel from west to east or south to north relatively easy. But then, when the northeast monsoon sweeps down off the land beginning in October, the winds veer sharply about and blow toward the southwest for the next six months. During this period, travel east or north becomes difficult, but ships sailing on a southern or western heading have favorable winds. Because older sailing vessels took more than six months to cross the area, this seasonal shift of winds forced them to lay over for several months in ports they could reach conveniently during periods of favorable breezes. Ships from Arabia and Persia reached these points along the western coast of India, whereas those coming down from Indonesia and East Asia found safe harbor along the tip of the Malay peninsula or on the nearby island of Java. These havens became great emporia in their own right, for they became centers of intermediate trade as well as places for re-outfitting during the lay-over season.

The need to break voyages at these sites produced a natural division of maritime traffic in Asia into three zones: one in the South Pacific, one in the western Indian Ocean, and one lying in between, in the eastern Indian Ocean. Two outlying areas—the Mediterranean and coastal northeastern Asia—fed additional traffic into the system from opposite ends of the Old World. The lack of direct sea links between the Mediterranean and the Indian Ocean, however, forced overland transshipment of all goods and people between them, creating a sharp break between the central zones and this western extension. Originally dominated by Byzantine Greeks, in the eleventh and twelfth centuries, trade at this end came under the control of Italians from Venice and Genoa. No such break marked the eastern extension. Traffic there flowed directly into the ports of southeastern China whose merchant communities dominated most of the trade throughout the whole eastern region.

Iranian-speaking peoples, who conducted much of the overland trade, initially pioneered long-distance sea travel as well. Operating from home ports along the Persian Gulf, they developed many of the early sailing routes across the Indian Ocean. But Arabs living along the Gulf and the Red Sea soon joined them, venturing even farther to Indonesia and south China, where they not only traded in season but planted resident communities. Chinese sources, in fact, indicate that by the ninth century as many as 100,000 Arabs dwelt in Canton, the chief southern port of the Tang empire. Further expansion of trade, particularly in the tenth and eleventh centuries, apparently created more traffic than these pioneers could handle. Besides, as Turkic migrations and the Mongol conquest disrupted key markets in the Muslim world, waning profits at home made it hard for Persians and Arabs to retain commercial mastery throughout the entire trade area. Indigenous people, of course, had always participated in trade with them, conducting the secondary wholesale and commodity markets that supplied them with goods. As Muslim dominance faltered, locals merely expanded into the long-distance trade.

In time, Indians, Indonesians, and Chinese thus entered the long-distance trade too, giving Asian maritime traffic a very cosmopolitan character. Because most of the newcomers limited their operations to one of the natural subregions of the system, cultural differences reinforced natural divisions. Despite much sharing of technologies and commercial practices, groups in each zone developed their own ways of operating. Even shipbuilding varied markedly from one locale to another, and as the three principal sailing vessels of the area—Arabian *dhows,* Malay *praus,* and Chinese *junks*—demonstrate, each tradition was unique.

A tradition of political as well as cultural diversity persisted across this vast maritime region, and no single state ever united it. Impressive empires did occasionally emerge on its margins, such as the Abbasid caliphate in western Asia, the sultanate of Delhi in India, and various Chinese states established both before and after the Mongol conquest. But none of them ever came close to dominating the maritime area as the Mongols did the inland trade region. Far from hindering the movement of goods and people throughout the area, lack of political unity may have promoted it.

As the huge Ming Chinese fleets that circumnavigated the entire area in the early fifteenth century prove, some of the larger Asian empires certainly had the potential to control the sea lanes. From 1407 to 1433 Ming fleets, numbering in the hundreds of ships, made a total of seven voyages into the Indian Ocean in an extraordinary display of might. But neither the Ming empire nor any other Asian power sought to emulate the Mongol example on land by actually trying to conquer and control the entire maritime area. A few like the Mamluk sultanate of Egypt, which emerged in the thirteenth century, did attempt to police portions of the region. And occasionally a local potentate would impose taxes on local traffic and trade. True maritime trade empires based on the conquest of ports and control of sea lanes, however, came only later when the Portuguese arrived and introduced new monopolistic tactics to the area in the sixteenth century. Until then, small city-states and local kingdoms prevailed throughout the region, fostering a tradition of open ports and free trade.

Such political fragmentation promoted large-scale piracy. But it also encouraged a flexible system of trade in which many small merchants exchanged a wide variety of goods throughout many markets. In this preindustrial age, regional specialization had not yet become pronounced. Goods could often be obtained from many sources, and when they became scarce in one place, they were usually available elsewhere. So, too, if certain ports became inaccessible, others equally good could generally be found. This flexibility cushioned the trade from local disruptions, but it made business decisions much harder to make. Merchants and ship masters had to anticipate volatile market and port conditions months in advance, a task further complicated by the long lay-overs. They had to make shrewd guesses not only about what to take where on their outbound run, but also about how to find suitable goods for their return voyage. These conditions stimulated a great deal of experimentation. For that reason, people, goods, and ideas circulated widely throughout the system, making it an important channel for cross-cultural contact and trade.

THE METHOD

To evaluate the nature of these trans-Asian contacts, we would ideally like to have detailed statistics about trade and travel throughout the area. Unfortunately the kinds of documents that would provide such information—like caravansary registries, port records, ship manifests, or merchant contracts—have not yet come to light. Given the climate in much of the area over which these contacts occurred, they probably never will, since most such materials would long ago have rotted away even if they had been put aside in some safe place. In their absence, we can never build any detailed, statistical models of the system nor reconstruct all of its elements with precision. So we have to content ourselves with far more impressionistic—and imprecise—evidence.

Such evidence includes mainly the letters, diaries, and travel accounts of people who journeyed through the system, brief references in histories and surveys, and a few artifacts and illustrations. Even materials of this sort are rare for the period from the ninth through the twelfth centuries. So most of the sources here date from the thirteenth century or later.

Source 1 comes from the *Book of Description of Countries,* written by a fourteenth-century Italian businessman, Francis Balducci Pegolotti, who worked for a major Florentine firm, the house of Bardi. Intended as a practical survey of commerce of the day, it tells what a western merchant entering the overland trade with Asia from the Black Sea would find. A somewhat earlier travel account from the mid-thirteenth century appears as Source 2; written by a European monk named William of Rubruck, it records his journey on a diplomatic mission to the Mongols for a French king across terrain described by Pegolotti. Source 3 shows the kind of ox-cart both mention as the usual vehicle for overland travel. Balancing these Western accounts are entries from a travel diary kept by a thirteenth-century Chinese, Li Zhichang, who journeyed over the eastern half of the area from China to Chingis Khan's camp in Samarkand (Source 4).

The rest of the materials focus on the maritime parts of the system. Source 5 is a letter sent back to Europe in 1292 by a Franciscan monk from Italy, John of Monte Corvino, who passed through India on his way to the Mongol court as a papal envoy. John's letter gives a thorough overview of trade and traffic in the western part of the Indian Ocean at this time. The kind of ship he mentions is illustrated in Source 6: the Arab dhow. East Africa, of course, formed part of this sphere, and Source 7, taken from the *Travels of Marco Polo,* details what the famous Venetian traveler discovered there on his return to Europe at the end of the thirteenth century. Source 8, from a work by the fourteenth-century Muslim traveler Ibn Battuta, provides a glimpse of the eastern half of the maritime region. Shipping there depended on the Chinese junk, depicted in Source 9. And the final piece of evidence, Source 10, from the official Chinese history of the Ming dynasty, the *Ming Shi,* shows Zheng He's use of such new seapower on his spectacular voyages across the entire region from 1402–1433.

The relative abundance of travelers' accounts from different parts of the area during the thirteenth century suggests that the scope and frequency of contacts was increasing dramatically at this time. Most writers took pains to supply useful advice to those countrymen back home whom they seemed to assume would follow in their footsteps. Like tourists today, they devoted attention to practical aspects of travel and to local attractions likely to interest future visitors. They also carefully recorded whatever specific information about their immediate business might prove helpful to successors. Those with mercantile interests, for instance, listed new foods, fabrics, and other goods of potential trade value, whereas diplomatic emissaries noted local politics and alliances. Such accounts give us a rough picture of the broader system.

The wonder of discovery that fills so many of these accounts, however, warns us that cross-cultural contacts were still at an early stage. Descriptions of novelties and far-fetched tales compete with practical observations. And expressions of bewilderment, disbelief, and even disgust often punctuate the narratives. These features point out that the writers on whom we rely for information on the system were often outside observers who, out of ignorance, may have misunderstood what they saw. Strong religious and cultural beliefs, moreover, often colored their reactions—and may on occasion have affected their observations as well.

So we must treat this material critically to factor out the false and improbable. Historians often deal with this problem by checking one source against another. Details that appear in several accounts are more likely to be reliable than those found only once. When such cross-checking is impossible, historians look for clues that a given writer may have had deeper knowledge of a certain place by virtue of long residence there or other special circumstances. Distinguishing between different kinds of information also helps. What a visiting trader reports about goods and their availability in a port, for instance, can probably be accepted more readily than his remarks about local religious customs or diplomatic initiatives.

With this advice in mind, look over the material that follows for information on the nature of the system. As you will soon discover, commercial relations played a substantial role, so you need to pay special attention to trade within the region. Try to determine not only what was traded but who traded it where and with whom. Begin by trying to work out the physical networks of commerce. What were the principal trade routes and what areas did they connect? Where did goods enter the system and to whom did they eventually pass? Who conducted the trade to such points and how did goods get exchanged at intermediary emporia or lay-overs? What does the overall pattern of trade suggest about the extent and nature of relations between different areas and peoples? How far did goods circulate? Were certain areas economically more developed—more "advanced"—than others, or were all roughly equal?

Look for other kinds of activities occurring within the system, too. Political and religious concerns motivated many of the contacts noted in these sources. What or who inspired them? Empires and religious spheres seem to have been expanding into new territories during this period. Where did they meet? And what did their confrontations indicate about the larger political and religious dynamics of Eurasia? Do you see indications of material or technological borrowing? What attracted notice, and by whom? Do you find hints that some regions seemed technologically more advanced than others and thus served as a source of innovation to others? Finally, do you see signs of cultural exchange, whether of concrete items like foodstuffs and artistic creations or of abstract ideas and beliefs?

Once you have listed different kinds of contacts, consider how they fit together as a whole. Think about the relative frequency and importance of certain activities over others. Did any dominate? Think, too, about the people involved in these activities. Were some more important than others? If so, why? Did the importance of certain people contribute to a predominance of their country or region over others either economically, politically, or culturally? What do your findings indicate about this early stage of global integration? Was it characterized by hierarchical or relatively equal relations between peoples and areas? What does this reveal about the early stages of global integration? Finally, note how all such questions require you to think in terms of a much larger entity than a single cultural area. The idea of such a system forces us to think about how the focus of historical study affects what we see.

THE EVIDENCE

Source 1 from Henry Yule, Cathay and the Way Thither, *vol. 3 (London: The Hakluyt Society, 1914), pp. 143–155.*

1. From Francis Balducci Pegolotti, *Book of Description of Countries,* ca. 1320s

CHAPTER I.
INFORMATION REGARDING THE JOURNEY TO CATHAY, FOR SUCH AS WILL GO BY TANA AND COME BACK WITH GOODS.

In the first place, from Tana [Taman] to Gintarchan may be twenty-five days with an ox-waggon, and from ten to twelve days with a horse-waggon. On the road you will find plenty of *Moccols,* that is to say, of *gens d'armes.* And from Gintarchan to Sara [Sarai] may be a day by river, and from Sara to Saracanco, also by river, eight days. You can do this either by land or by water; but by water you will be at less charge for your merchandize.

From Saracanco to Organci [Urghanj] may be twenty days' journey in camel-waggon. It will be well for anyone travelling with merchandize to go to Organci, for in that city there is a ready sale for goods. From Organci to Oltrarre [Ortrar] is thirty-five to forty days in camel-waggons. But if when you leave Saracanco you go direct to Oltrarre, it is a journey of fifty days only, and if you have no merchandize it will be better to go this way than to go by Organci.

From Oltrarre to Armalec [Almalig] is forty-five days' journey with pack-asses, and every day you find Moccols. And from Armalec to Camexu [Kansu?] is seventy days with asses, and from Camexu until you come to a river called_______is forty-five days on horseback; and then you can go down the river to Cassai [Quinsay, i.e. Hangchow], and there you can dispose of the *sommi* of silver that you have with you, for that is a most active place of business. After getting to Cassai you carry on with the money which you get for the *sommi* of silver which you sell there; and this money is made of paper, and is called *balishi.* And four pieces of this money are worth one *sommo* of silver in the province of Cathay. And from Cassai to Gamalec [Cambalec], which is the capital city of the country of Cathay, is thirty days' journey.[1]

CHAPTER II.
THINGS NEEDFUL FOR MERCHANTS WHO DESIRE TO MAKE THE JOURNEY TO CATHAY ABOVE DESCRIBED.

In the first place, you must let your beard grow long and not shave. And at Tana you should furnish yourself with a dragoman [interpreter]. And you must not try to save money in the matter of dragomen by taking a bad one instead of a good one. For the additional wages of the good one will not cost you so much as you will save by having him. And besides the dragoman it will be well to take at least two good men servants, who are acquainted with the Cumanian tongue [language of the Kipchak Turks]. And if the merchant likes to take a woman with him from Tana, he can do so; if he does not like to take one there is no obligation, only if he does take one he will be kept much more comfortably than if he does not take one. Howbeit, if he do take one, it will be well that she be acquainted with the Cumanian tongue as well as the men.

And from Tana travelling to Gintarchan you should take with you twenty-five days' provisions, that is to say, flour and salt fish, for as to meat you will find enough of it at all the places along the road. And so also at all the chief stations noted in going from one country to another in the route, according to the number of days set down above, you should furnish yourself with flour and salt fish; other things you will find in sufficiency, and especially meat.

The road you travel from Tana to Cathay is perfectly safe, whether by day or by night, according to what the merchants say who have used it. Only if the merchant, in going or coming, should die upon the road, everything belonging to him will become the perquisite of the lord of the country in which he dies, and the officers of the lord will take possession of all. And in like manner if he die in Cathay. But if his brother be with him, or an intimate friend and comrade calling himself his brother, then to such an one they will surrender the property of the deceased, and so it will be rescued.

And there is another danger: this is when the lord of the country dies, and before the new lord who is to have the lordship is proclaimed; during such intervals there have sometimes been irregularities practised on the Franks, and other foreigners. (They call *Franks* all the Christians of these parts from Romania westward.) And neither will the roads be safe to travel until the other lord be proclaimed who is to reign in room of him who is deceased.

Cathay is a province which contained a multitude of cities and towns. Among others there is one in particular, that is to say the capital city, to which is great

1. Cathay is an old name for China. Though but a single "province" in the vast Mongol empire, by the time of Kubilai Khan, China was the site of the "City of the Khan," Khanbaligh, the Mongol capital, which later became the modern Chinese city of Beijing. Quinsay, now the modern city of Hangchow, was an older, native Chinese capital.

resort of merchants, and in which there is a vast amount of trade; and this city is called Cambalec. And the said city hath a circuit of one hundred miles, and is all full of people and houses and of dwellers in the said city.

You may calculate that a merchant with a dragoman, and with two men servants, and with goods to the value of twenty-five thousand golden florins, should spend on his way to Cathay from sixty to eighty *sommi* of silver, and not more if he manage well; and for all the road back again from Cathay to Tana, including the expenses of living and the pay of servants, and all other charges, the cost will be about five *sommi* per head of pack animals, or something less. And you may reckon the *sommo* to be worth five golden florins. You may reckon also that each ox-waggon will require one ox, and will carry ten cantars Genoese weight; and the camel-waggon will require three camels, and will carry thirty cantars Genoese weight; and the horse-waggon will require one horse, and will commonly carry six and half cantars of silk, at 250 Genoese pounds to the cantar. And a bale of silk may be reckoned at between 110 and 115 Genoese pounds.

You may reckon also that from Tana to Sara the road is less safe than on any other part of the journey; and yet even when this part of the road is at its worst, if you are some sixty men in the company you will go as safely as if you were in your own house.

Anyone from Genoa or from Venice, wishing to go to the places abovenamed, and to make the journey to Cathay, should carry linens with him, and if he visit Organci he will dispose of these well. In Organci he should purchase *sommi* of silver, and with these he should proceed without making any further investment, unless it be some bales of the very finest stuffs which go in small bulk, and cost no more for carriage than coarser stuffs would do.

Merchants who travel this road can ride on horseback or on asses, or mounted in any way that they list to be mounted.

Whatever silver the merchants may carry with them as far as Cathay the lord of Cathay will take from them and put into his treasury. And to merchants who thus bring silver they give that paper money of theirs in exchange. This is of yellow paper, stamped with the seal of the lord aforesaid. And this money is called *balishi;* and with this money you can readily buy silk and all other merchandize that you have a desire to buy. And all the people of the country are bound to receive it. And yet you shall not pay a higher price for your goods because your money is of paper. And of the said paper money there are three kinds, one being worth more than another, according to the value which has been established for each by that lord.

And you may reckon that you can buy for one *sommo* of silver nineteen or twenty pounds of Cathay silk, when reduced to Genoese weight, and that the *sommo* should weigh eight and a half ounces of Genoa, and should be of the alloy of eleven ounces and seventeen deniers to the pound.

You may reckon also that in Cathay you should get three or three and a half pieces of damasked silk for a *sommo;* and from three and a half to five pieces of *nacchetti* of silk and gold, likewise for a *sommo* of silver.

Source 2 from Christopher Dawson, The Mongol Mission *(London: Sheed & Ward, 1955), reprinted as* Mission to Asia *(New York: Harper Torchbooks, 1966), pp. 91–92, 114–115.*

2. From *The Journey of William of Rubruck,* 1253

Be it known therefore to your holy Majesty that in the year of Our Lord one thousand two hundred and fifty-three on the seventh of May we entered the Sea of Pontus [Black Sea] which is commonly called the Greater Sea. It is one thousand four hundred miles in length, as I learned from merchants, and is divided into two parts, for about the middle of it there are two points of land, one in the north and the other in the south.

. . . In the middle of the south side, as it were at the apex, there is a city called Soldaia [Sudak], which looks towards Sinopolis, and all the merchants coming from Turkey and wishing to go to northern lands make their way thither, and similarly those coming from Russia and northern territories who wish to cross to Turkey. The latter bring squirrel and ermine and other valuable furs, while the former carry materials of cotton or bombax, silk stuffs and sweet-smelling spices. To the east of this province is a city called Matrica [Taman]; here the river Tanais [Don] empties itself into the Sea of Pontus through an opening twelve miles wide.

Before this river reaches the Sea of Pontus it forms a kind of sea [Sea of Azov] towards the north, which is seven hundred miles in breadth and length and nowhere reaches a depth of more than six paces; consequently large vessels do not enter it, but merchants from Constantinople going to the aforesaid city of Matrica send their barks as far as the river Tanais in order to buy dried fish, namely sturgeon and barbot and other fish in enormous quantities.

And so we reached Soldaia on May 21st. Certain merchants from Constantinople had arrived before us and had announced that envoys were coming thither from the Holy Land who wished to visit Sartach. Now I had preached publicly on Palm Sunday in St. Sophia's that I was not an envoy either of you or anybody else, but that I was going among these unbelievers in accordance with our Rule. Then when we landed the said merchants warned me to mind my words, for they had given out that I was an envoy, and if I were to deny that I was such, then I would not be allowed to proceed.

Thereupon I spoke in the following manner to the prefects of the city or rather to their deputies, for the prefects had gone to Baatu in the winter bearing their tribute and had not yet returned. "We heard it told of your lord Sartach in the Holy Land that he was a Christian and the Christians rejoiced exceedingly over this fact, especially the most Christian lord, the King of the French, who is on a pilgrimage there and is fighting against the Saracens in order to wrest the Holy Places from their hands: for this reason I desire to go to Sartach and bring to him a letter of my lord the King, in which he admonishes him concerning the good estate of the whole of Christendom." They received us with joy and lodged us in the episcopal church. The Bishop of that church had been to Sartach and he told me many good things about him which I, for my part, was not to discover later.

They then gave us the choice as to whether we would like carts with oxen, or pack horses, to carry our belongings. The merchants from Constantinople advised us to accept the carts and even to buy covered carts for ourselves like the ones the Ruthenians use for carrying their furs, and into these to put such of our things as I did not wish to unpack every day; for if I took the horses, I should have to unload them at every stopping place and pack them on to other horses; moreover I would be able to ride at a more gentle pace with the oxen. I followed their advice, but it was bad advice for I was on the road for two months before I reached Sartach: a journey I could have completed in one month if I had gone with horses.

On the advice of the merchants I had brought with me from Constantinople fruit, muscatel wine and choice biscuits to present to the chief men of the city so that I might be granted permission to travel about, since they look with no favourable eye upon anyone coming to them empty-handed. On failing to find the prefects of the city there, I placed all these things in a cart, as I was told that Sartach would be delighted with them, if only I could get them as far as him.

So we set off on our journey about June 1st with our own four covered carts and with two others I had received from them in which was carried bedding for sleeping on at night. They gave us five horses to ride on, for we were five in number, myself, my companion Friar Bartholomew of Cremona, Gosset the bearer of this letter, Abdullah the interpreter, and a boy, Nicholas, whom I had bought at Constantinople out of the alms you gave me. They also gave us two men who drove the carts and looked after the oxen and horses.

And so we travelled with great hardship from place to place, until, a few days before the feast of St. Mary Magdalene [July 22nd, 1253], we reached the great river Tanais which separates Asia from Europe, as the river of Egypt separates Asia from Africa.

So we walked for three days without coming across a soul, and just when we as well as the oxen were tired out and we did not know where we could find the Tartars, suddenly two horses came running up to us; we caught them with great joy and our guide and the interpreter mounted them, so that they could look and see in what direction we could find some people. When at last on the fourth day we came across some men we rejoiced like shipwrecked mariners on reaching port.

Source 3: Courtesy of the Trustees of the British Museum.

3. Tang Chinese Ox-Cart

Source 4 from Arthur Waley, The Travels of an Alchemist *(London: Routledge and Sons, 1923), pp. 79, 82–83, 85–86, 92–93, 113.*

4. From Li Zhichang, *The Travels of Chang Chun,* 1221

On the 27th day of the eighth month (September 15th) we reached the foot of the Yin Shan [Tianshan Mountains]. Here some Uighurs came out to meet us, and presently we reached a small town. The ruler of the place brought us grape-wine, choice fruits, large cakes, huge onions, and strips of Persian linen, a foot for each person.

Looking south towards the Yin Shan we saw three sharp peaks standing out against the sky. The Master made a poem about them and presented it to the student Li Po-hsiang (this student is a phrenologist). After passing through two other towns we reached Chambalig. The ruler is an Uighur and an old friend of Chinkai. He brought with him all his family and a number of Hui-ho priests, who came a long way out to meet us. Upon our arrival we were entertained upon a terrace and the Uighur ruler's wife gave us grape-wine, and also put in front of us water-melons that weighed as much as a measure each, and sweet melons as large as (porcelain) pillows. Their scent and taste is quite different from what we are used to in China; but the garden-vegetables are the same as ours. A priest came and waited upon the Master. By means of an interpreter he asked this priest what scriptures he read. He replied that since he had received the tonsure and submitted to the rules of the order, he had worshipped the Buddha and followed no other teaching; which was natural enough, for the dominions of the T'ang dynasty extended to this place. But west of this one finds no Buddhist priests, the Hui-ho people only worshipping the western quarter.

One more stage brought us to the town of Almalig, which we reached on the 27th day of the ninth month. We were met by the Moslem ruler of the place and the Mongol darugachi (governor) with their retinues. They gave us lodging in a fruit-garden to the west. The natives call fruit *a-li-ma,* and it is from the abundance of its fruits that the town derives its name. It is here that they make the stuff called "tu-lu-ma" which gave rise to the popular story about a material made from "sheep's wool planted in the ground." We now procured seven pieces of it to make into winter clothes. In appearance and texture it is like Chinese willow-down—very fine, soft and clean. Out of it they make thread, ropes, cloth and wadding.

The farmers irrigate their fields with canals; but the only method employed by the people of these parts for drawing water is to dip a pitcher and carry it on the head. Our Chinese buckets delighted them.

On the eighteenth day of the eleventh month (December 3rd, 1221) after crossing a great river, we reached the northern outskirts of the mighty city of Samarkand. The Civil Governor his Highness I-la, together with the Mongol and local authorities, came to meet us outside the town. They brought wine and set up a great number of tents. Here we brought our wagons to a stop.

After a time we entered the city by the north-east gate. The town is built along canals. As no rain falls during the summer and autumn, two rivers have been diverted so as to run along every street, thus giving a supply of water to all the inhabitants. Before the defeat of the Khwārizm Shah there was a fixed population here of more than 100,000 households; but now there is only about a quarter this number, of whom a very large proportion are native Hui-ho. But these people are quite unable to manage their fields and orchards for themselves, and are obliged to call in Chinese, Kitai and Tanguts. The administration of the town is also conducted by people of very various nationality. Chinese craftsmen are found everywhere. The Master's words were translated into Mongo by A-hai. The Emperor was delighted with his doctrine and on the nineteenth, when there was a bright night, sent for him again. On this occasion too he was much pleased by what he heard, and sent for the Master to his tent once more on the twenty-third (October 29th). He was here treated with the same regard as before and the Emperor listened to him with evident satisfaction. He ordered that the Master's words should be recorded, and especially that they should be written down in Chinese characters, that they might be preserved from oblivion. To those present he said: "You have heard the holy Immortal discourse three times upon the art of nurturing the vital spirit. His words have sunk deeply into my heart. I rely upon you not to repeat what you have heard." During the remainder of the Imperial Progress to the east, the Master constantly discoursed to the Emperor concerning the mysteries of Tao.

Source 5 from Henry Yule, Cathay and the Way Thither, *vol. 3 (London: The Hakluyt Society, 1914), pp. 58–67.*

5. John of Monte Corvino, Letter from India, ca. 1292

To you Friar Bartholomew of Santo Concordio, your brother in all things, Menentillus of Spoleto, wisheth health and wisdom in Christ!

And because I wot of the great curiosity that you have in regard to all science, and that, much as you do know, you would fain know everything and especially things that are new to you; and in truth that you are one whose desire is to have knowledge and information of all kinds; therefore transcribe I for you certain matters just as they have been written from India by a certain Minorite Friar (the travelling companion of Brother Nicolas of Pistoia, who died in Upper India), when on his way to the court of the Lord of all India. The bringer of the letter I have seen and spoken with, and it was in his arms that the said Brother Nicholas did die. The letter was to the effect following:

"*Concerning the state of things as to the country itself in Upper India.* The condition of the country of India aforesaid is this. The land is well enough peopled; and there be great cities therein, but the houses are wretched, being built of sandy mud, and usually thatched with leaves of trees. Hills there are few; rivers in some places are many, in others few. Springs there are few or none; wells in plenty; and the reason is this, that water is generally to be found at the depth of two or three paces, or even less. This well water is indeed not very good to drink, for it is somewhat soft and loosens the bowels; so they generally have tanks or excavations like ponds, in which they collect the rain water, and this they drink. They keep few beasts. Horses there are none, except it be in possession of the king and great barons. Flies there be few, and fleas none at all. And they have trees which produce fruit continually, so that on them you find fruit in every stage up to perfect ripeness at one time. In like manner they sow and reap at almost all seasons, and this because it is always warm and never cold. Aromatic spices are to be had good cheap, some more so and some less so, according to what spices they be. They have trees that produce sugar, and others that produce honey, and others that produce a liquor that has a smack of wine. And this the natives of those countries use for drink. And those three things are to be had at very small cost. And the pepper plant is here also. It is slender and knotty like a vine; and indeed 'tis altogether very like a vine, excepting that it is more slender, and bears transplanting.

"Ginger is a reed-like plant, and, like a cane-root, it can be dug and transplanted. But their canes here are more like trees, being sometimes a cubit in girth and more, with slender prickly branches round about, and small leaves.

"The Brazil tree is a slender lofty and thorny tree, all red as it were, with leaves like fern. The Indian nuts are as big as melons, and in colour green like gourds. Their leaves and branches are like those of the date tree.

"The cinnamon tree is of a medium bulk, not very high, and in trunk, bark, and foliage, is like the laurel; indeed, altogether it resembleth the laurel greatly in appearance. Great store of it is carried forth of the island which is hard by Maabar.

"The state of things as regards the inhabitants of India is as follows:—The men of this region are idolaters, without moral law, or letters, or books. They have indeed an alphabet which they use to keep their accounts, and to write prayers or charms for their idols; albeit they have no paper, but write upon leaves of trees like unto palm leaves. They have no conscience of sin whatever. They have idol-houses in which they worship at almost all hours of the day; for they never join together in worship at any fixed hour, but each goes to worship when it pleases himself. And so they worship their idols in any part of these temples, either by day or by night. They frequently set forth their fasts and feasts, but they have no fixed recurring day to keep, either weekly or monthly. Their marriages take place only at one time of the year; and when the husband dies the wife cannot marry again. The sin of the flesh they count not to be sin, nor are they ashamed to say so.

"In the regions by the sea are many Saracens, and they have great influence but there are few of them in the interior. There are a very few Christians, and Jews, and they are of little weight. The people persecute much the Christians, and all who bear the Christian name.

"But India is a region of great extent, and it hath many realms and many languages. And the men thereof are civil and friendly enough, but of few words, and remind me somewhat of our peasants. They are not, strictly speaking, black, but of an olive colour, and exceedingly well formed both women and men. They go barefoot and naked, except that they wear a cloth round the loins, and boys and girls up to eight years of age wear nothing whatever, but go naked as they came from their mother's womb. They shave not the beard; many times a day they wash; bread and wine they have none. Of the fruits that we make use of they have few or none; but for their daily food they use rice and a little milk; and they eat grossly like pigs, to wit, with the whole hand or fist, and without a spoon.

"The state of things in regard to the Sea of India is this. The sea aboundeth greatly with fish; and in some parts of it they fish for pearls and precious stones. The havens are few and bad; and you must know that the sea here is the Middle Sea or Ocean. Traversing it towards the south there is no continent found but islands alone, but in that sea the islands are many, more than 12,000 in number. And many of these are inhabited, and many are not.

"You can sail (upon that sea) between these islands and Ormes and (from Ormes) to those parts which are called [Minibar] is a distance of 2,000 miles in a direction between south and south-east; then 300 miles between east and south-east from Minibar to Maabar, which (latter however) you enter steering to the north; and from Menabar [Maabar?] you sail another 300 miles between north-east and north to Siu Simmoncota. The rest I have not seen, and therefore I say nothing of it.

"The shores of the said sea in some places run out in shoals for 100 miles or more, so that ships are in danger of grounding. And they cannot make the voyage but once a year, for from the beginning of April till the end of October the winds are westerly, so that no one can sail towards the west; and again 'tis just the contrary from the month of October till March. From the middle of May till the end of October the wind blows so hard that ships which by that time have not reached the ports whither they are bound, run a desperate risk, and if they escape it is great luck. And thus in the past year there perished more than sixty ships; and this year seven ships in places in our own immediate neighbourhood, whilst of what has happened elsewhere we have no intelligence. Their ships in these parts are mighty frail and uncouth, with no iron in them, and no caulking. They are sewn like clothes with twine. And so if the twine breaks anywhere there is a breach indeed! Once every year therefore there is a mending of this, more or less, if they propose to go to sea. And they have a frail and flimsy rudder like the top of a table, of a cubit in width, in the middle of the stern; and when they have to tack, it is done with a vast deal of trouble; and if it is blowing in any way hard, they cannot tack at all. They have but one sail and one mast, and the sails are either of matting or of some miserable cloth. The ropes are of husk.

"Moreover their mariners are few and far from good. Hence they run a multitude of risks, insomuch that they are wont to say, when any ship achieves her voyage safely and soundly, that 'tis by God's guidance, and man's skill hath little availed.

"This letter was written in Maabar, a city of the province of Sitia in Upper India, on the 22nd day of December in the year of our Lord MCCX (CII or CIII)."

Source 6: Bibliothèque nationale de France.

6. Illustration of Arab Dhow, 13th century

Source 7 from Travels of Marco Polo, *trans. Manuel Komroff (New York: Liveright Publishing Corp., 1953), pp. 312–315.*

7. From *Travels of Marco Polo,* ca. 1290s

OF THE GREAT ISLAND OF MADAGASCAR

Leaving the island of Soccotera [Socotra], and steering a course between south and south-west for a thousand miles, you arrive at the great island of Madagascar, which is one of the largest and most fertile in the world. In circuit it is three thousand miles.

The inhabitants are Saracens, or followers of the law of Mahomet [Muhammad]. They have four sheikhs, which in our language may be expressed by "elders," who divide the government amongst them. The people subsist by trade and manufacture, and sell a vast number of elephants' teeth, as those animals abound in the country, as they do also in that of Zenzibar, from whence the exportation is equally great.

The island is visited by many ships from various parts of the world, bringing assortments of goods consisting of brocades and silks of various patterns, which are sold to the merchants of the island, or bartered for goods in return. They make large profits.

Ships do not visit other numerous islands lying further south; this and the island of Zenzibar alone being frequented. This is because of the sea current that runs with such force towards the south that it renders their return impossible. The vessels that sail from the coast of Malabar for this island, perform the voyage in twenty or twenty-five days, but in their returning voyage are obliged to struggle for three months; so strong is the current of water, which constantly runs to the southward.

OF THE ISLAND OF ZENZIBAR

Beyond the island of Madagascar lies that of Zenzibar, which is reported to be in circuit two thousand miles. The inhabitants worship idols, have their own peculiar language, and do not pay tribute to any foreign power. They are large in stature, but their height is not proportioned to the bulk of their bodies. Were it otherwise, they would appear gigantic.

They are, however, strongly made, and one of them is capable of carrying what would be a load for four of our people. At the same time, he would require as much food as five. They are black, and go naked, covering only the private parts of the body with a cloth. Their hair is so crisp, that even when dipped in water it can with difficulty be drawn out. They have large mouths, their noses turn up towards the forehead, their ears are long, and their eyes so large and frightful, that they have the aspect of demons. The women are equally ill-favoured, having wide mouths, thick noses, and large eyes. Their hands, and also their heads, are large and out of proportion.

Many trading ships visit the place, which barter the goods they bring for elephants' teeth and ambergris [perfume ingredient found in whale intestines], of which much is found on the coasts of the island, in consequence of the sea abounding with whales.

Source 8 from Travels of Ibn Battuta, *ed. and trans. Samuel Lee (New York: Burt Franklin, n.d.), pp. 169–170, 172–173.*

8. From *Travels of Ibn Battuta,* ca. 1353

The first town we entered in the country of Malabar was that of Abi Sardar which is small, and is situated on a large estuary of the sea. We next came to the city of Kākanwar, which is large, and also upon an estuary of the sea. It abounds in the sugar-cane. The Sultan is an infidel. He sent his son as a pledge to our vessel, and we landed accordingly, and were honourably received. He also sent presents to the ship, as marks of respect to the Emperor of India. It is a custom with them, that every vessel which passes by one of their ports shall enter it, and give a present to its Sultan; in this case they let it pass, but otherwise they make war upon it with their vessels, they then board it out of contempt, and impose a double fine upon the cargo, just in proportion to the advantage they usually gain from merchants entering their country.

We next arrived at the city of Manjarūn, which is situated upon a large estuary of the sea, called the *"estuary of the wolf,"* and which is the greatest estuary in the country of Malabar. In this place are some of the greatest merchants of Persia and Yemen. Ginger and black pepper are here in great abundance. The king of this place is the greatest of the kings of Malabar, and in it are about four thousand Mohammedan merchants. The king made us land, and sent us a present.

We next came to the town of Hīlī, which is large and situated upon an estuary of the sea. As far as this place come the ships of China, but they do not go beyond it; nor do they enter any harbour, except that of this place, of Kālikūt, and of Kawlam.

The city of Hīlī is much revered both by the Mohammedans and infidels, on account of a mosque, the source of light and of blessings, which is found in it. To this seafaring persons make and pay their vows, whence its treasury is derived, which is placed under the control of the principal Moslem. The mosque maintains a preacher, and has within it several students, as well as readers of the Korān, and persons who teach writing.

We next came to Kālikūt, one of the great ports of the district of Malabar, and in which merchants from all parts are found. The king of this place is an infidel, who shaves his chin just as the Haidarī Fakeers of Room do. When we approached this place, the people came out to meet us, and with a large concourse brought us into the port. The greatest part of the Mohammedan merchants of this place are so wealthy, that one of them can purchase the whole freightage of such vessels as put in here; and fit out others like them. Here we waited three months for the season to set sail for China: for there is only one season in the year in which the sea of China is navigable. Nor then is the voyage undertaken, except in vessels of the three descriptions following: the greatest is called a junk, the middling sized a zaw, the least a kakam. The sails of these vessels are made of cane-reeds, woven together like a mat; which, when they put into port, they leave standing in the wind. In some of these vessels there will be employed a thousand men, six hundred of these sailors, and four hundred soldiers. Each of the larger ships is followed by three others, a middle-sized, a third, and a fourth sized. These vessels are no where made except in the city of El Zaitūn [Chuanzhou] in China, or in Sīn Kīlān, which is Sin El Sin. They row in these ships with large oars, which may be compared to great masts, over some of which five and twenty men will be stationed, who work standing. The commander of each vessel is a great Emir. In the large ships too they sow garden herbs and ginger, which they cultivate in cisterns (made for that purpose), and placed on the sides of them. In these also are houses constructed of wood, in which the higher officers reside with their wives; but these they do not hire out to the merchants. Every vessel, therefore, is like an independent city. Of such ships as these, Chinese individuals will sometimes have large numbers: and, generally, the Chinese are the richest people in the world.

Source 9 from John E. Vollmer et al., Silk Roads, China Ships *(Toronto: Royal Ontario Museum), p. 100. Illustration: Jim Loates/Visutronx.*

9. Artist's Rendition of a Chinese Junk, ca. 12th or 13th century

Source 10 from Ming Shi, *trans. Dun J. Li, in* The Civilization of China *(New York: Scribner's, 1975), pp. 279–281.*

10. From Zhang Ting-yu et al., *Zheng He's Voyages,* 1402–1483

Cheng Ho [Zheng He], a native of Yunnan, was popularly known as San-pao the Grand Eunuch. At one time he served as a staff member in the feudatory of King Ch'eng; later he was promoted to the position of grand eunuch in recognition of his contribution to King Ch'eng's successful revolt against Emperor Ming Hui-ti [r. 1399–1402]. After his accession to the throne, Emperor Yung-lo, the former King Ch'eng, suspected that his defeated predecessor Hui-ti might have escaped from Nanking and be residing somewhere in the South Seas and wanted very much to know his whereabouts. Besides, he wished to glorify Chinese arms in the remote regions and show off the wealth and power of the Central Kingdom. It was this combination of motives that promoted him to launch Cheng Ho's voyages.

In the sixth month of the third year of Yung-lo [1405] Cheng Ho and his deputy Wang Ching-hung, as ordered by the emperor, proceeded with their journey to the Western Ocean. Well furnished with treasure and accompanied by more than 27,800 officers and men, they sailed in sixty-two giant ships, each of which measured forty-four *chang* [ca. 517 feet] in length and eighteen *chang* [ca. 212 feet] in width. The ships left the Liuchia River [near modern Shanghai] for the sea and then sailed southward to Fukien wherefrom they proceeded with sails full-blown to Champa. From Champa the Chinese envoys visited one country after another. They read the imperial decree that demanded the submission of the kingdoms they visited and rewarded generously those rulers who agreed to submit. As for those who chose not to obey, force was used to assure their compliance.

In the ninth month of the fifth year of Yung-lo [1407] Cheng Ho returned to the capital and presented to the emperor tribute-bearing envoys from the kingdoms he had visited. The emperor was greatly pleased and granted titles and financial rewards to all of those who had been presented to him. Cheng Ho also brought back many prisoners of war, including the captured king of Palembang.

Palembang was formally known as Sanfuch'i whose ruler, a Chinese named Ch'en Tsu-yi, had been active as a pirate in the South Seas before he was captured by Cheng Ho. When Cheng Ho demanded his surrender, he said he would, but in secret he was planning to launch an attack upon Cheng Ho's ships. Once the perfidy was recognized, Cheng Ho attacked and won a decisive victory. Ch'en Tsu-yi was captured alive and later brought to Peking. He was executed shortly afterward.

In the ninth month of the sixth year of Yung-lo [1408] Cheng Ho sailed again for Ceylon. Upon his arrival, the king of Ceylon, a man named Alagakkonara, invited him to visit his city with fine promises. Once inside the city, Cheng Ho was presented with a demand for gold and silk; moreover, Alagakkonara had already ordered an attack on the Chinese ships. Taking advantage of the fact that practically all the Ceylonese troops had been out of the city for this attack, Cheng Ho personally led two thousand soldiers to attack the city itself. The surprise worked, and Alagakkonara and his family, together with many high-ranking officials, were captured alive. The Ceylonese troops hurried back to rescue their king, only to be routed by the Chinese. In the sixth month of the ninth year of Yung-lo [1411] the captured Ceylonese, including their king, were presented to the Chinese emperor for a determination of their fate. The emperor decided to forgive them and ordered them to be returned to Ceylon. By then all of Indochina had been pacified and brought under Chinese jurisdiction. Frightened by Chinese might, more and more kingdoms sent envoys to China to pay their tribute.

Cheng Ho served three emperors with distinction and conducted seven voyages altogether. Among the more than thirty kingdoms he had visited were the following: Champa, Java, Camboja, Palembang, Siam, Calicut, Malacca, Borneo, Sumatra, Aru, Cochin, Quilon, Chola, Cail, Jurfattan, Koyampadi, Ceylon, Lambri, Pahang, Kelantan, Hormus, Brawa, Maldives, Sunda, Mogedoxu, Malinde, Sana, Zufar, Juba, Bengal, Mecca, Lide, and Battak.[2] The amount of treasure he brought to China from these kingdoms was of course enormous, but the expense to China herself was even more staggering. Beginning in the Hsüan-teh period [1426–35] these kingdoms, occasionally, still sent tribute missions to China, but they could not be compared with the tribute missions of the Yung-lo period [1403–24] that were not only more sumptuous but also more frequent. By then Cheng Ho had become too old to undertake any strenuous task. Long after his death, however, his achievement was still so highly regarded that Chinese generals and admirals, whenever serving abroad, kept mentioning it as a way to impress foreigners. Even laymen spoke of the Seven Voyages of the Grand Eunuch as a most outstanding event of the Ming dynasty.

2. Champa is part of modern Vietnam. Java, Palembang, Borneo, Sumatra, Aru, Lambri, Sunda, Lide, and Battak form part of modern Indonesia. Camboja is modern Cambodia; Siam is modern Thailand. Calicut, Cochin, Quilon, Chola, Cail, Jurfattan, Koyampadi, Maldives, and Bengal are located on the coast of modern India. Malacca, Pahang, and Kelantan are located in the Malay Peninsula. Hormus is located at the head of the Persian Gulf; Sana, Zufar, and Mecca are located on the Arabian Peninsula. Brawa, Mogedoxu, Malinde, and Juba are located on the eastern coast of Africa.

QUESTIONS TO CONSIDER

Filled with so many details, many of which seem obscure, this material can be overwhelming. But remember that you are trying to discern the overall structure and nature of interregional contacts, not every detail. To that end, first familiarize yourself with the historical map that appears on page 273. Then, as you look at each source, ask how it speaks to the basic questions posed at the start of this chapter: How extensive was this trans-Asian system? And does it constitute a significant step in world integration?

Source 1 gives a broad view of the overland silk route in the early fourteenth century. Its author, Francis Balducci Pegolotti, did not travel the Silk Road himself but, drawing on information from other European travelers, hoped to encourage his firm to enter the Asian trade, which other Italian merchants had found very lucrative. Notice how he views the enterprise from the perspective of a Mediterranean trader. From where did Pegolotti assume an Italian merchant party would begin? By what general route and using what conveyance would they travel? To whom might they turn for aid on the way besides the "moccols," or Mongols? What sort of capitalization and currency would such a party require? What trade goods does Pegolotti recommend securing? Finally, what can you infer from his account about the ease and extent of overland trade?

Source 2 gives another European view of travel across Inner Asia. Its author, William of Rubruck, though a Fleming from one of Europe's most commercially advanced areas, was not interested in trade. He was a Christian monk whom Louis IX of France secretly sent to Asia in 1253 to negotiate an alliance with the Mongols. Louis was directing a crusade against the Muslim Mamluks of Egypt and hoped to secure aid from the Mongols, who were already assailing the Caspian frontiers of the Muslim world. William's immediate goal was to sound out a local Mongol ruler called Sartak or Sartach, who governed the Crimean area for Batu, head of the western khanate of Kypchak. But ultimately he crossed the whole of Asia to meet Mongka Khan at his Mongolian capital, Karakorum. On his arrival he found he was not the only European emissary there. The pope, too, had sent people to seek an alliance with Mongka Khan against Muslims. How would you characterize this kind of interregional contact? But look from whom William sought advice on his way. Like the merchants who helped him, he used the Pontus or Black Sea as his gateway to Asia. Mongol fighting with the Abbasid caliphate had already shifted the western end of trade northward from Persia and the eastern Mediterranean to this locale, allowing Greek, Armenian, and Italian traders in the area to take advantage of the situation. In this context, note William's comments about goods flowing into the area from Russia and Turkey.

Constantinople was the chief Western emporium for the Asian trade, but William outfitted his party for overland travel at Soldaia, a city on the southern shore of the Crimean Peninsula. His first goal, Matrica or Taman on the northeastern coast of the Black Sea at the mouth of the Tanais (Don) River, was the true embarkation point to the East. An Italian colony outside the city of Azak (modern Azov), it served as a key transshipment point at the western end of the Silk Road during the Mongol era. Check what Pegolotti, who called it Tana, says about Taman. How long, judging from William's date entries, did it take to reach this point from Constantinople? Beyond lay open steppe or grassland, running past Batu's headquarters on the Etilia (Volga) River all the way to Mongolia. William offers a clear picture of his traveling party: six ox-carts for goods, five riding horses, two companions, a slave boy, and Abdullah (his dragoman, or Turkic interpreter and guide), plus two caravaneers. Compare this party with Pegolotti's ideal merchant group. What does the size of such parties suggest about security along the way? Both sources indicate that ox- or camel-carts provided the usual conveyance for goods across Inner Asia. Look at Source 3, which illustrates such a vehicle. How much cargo do you think six such carts could hold? What kinds of goods would most likely be shipped this way over long distances?

Conditions at the eastern end of Inner Asia can be glimpsed in Source 4, a travel diary kept by a Chinese named Li Zhichang. Li accompanied a famous religious master on a trip in 1221 to meet Chingis Khan, the founder of the Mongol Empire, who had summoned him to an audience to find out more about the Chinese doctrine of Taoism. When their party arrived in Mongolia, however, they discovered that the khan had already left Karakorum to begin his Inner Asian conquests. So, equipped with carts, a cavalry escort, and the Mongol guide Chinkai, they set out along a northern leg of the old Silk Road for Transoxiana above modern Afghanistan, where they caught up with Chingis Khan near the city of Samarkand.

Li's party, of course, traveled on a religious mission. Unlike William of Rubruck, who a generation later tried without success to interest Mongka Khan in his beliefs, Li's master not only wins a hearing but inspires his host to record his teachings. Look for other indications of the religious contacts in the sources that follow. Pay particular attention to references to Islam. The Mongols showed little interest in this religion, but as you can see here, it prevailed all along the Silk Road from the Black Sea to China. By the thirteenth century, in fact, most residents across this region were Turkic-speaking Muslims like the Uighurs who hosted Li's party en route.

Li points out, however, that other peoples were moving among them. Who were they, and what did they contribute to the area? The large scale movements of people in the Mongol era apparently accelerated the sharing of products and technology across Eurasia. In this context, think about Li's keen interest in what to him were the exotic foods and products of the far west. Notice his remarks about grape wine, "Persian" linen, and cotton, a fiber still so rare in China that he termed it "sheep's wool planted in the ground." Li's attention to new plants and foodstuffs has parallels in other sources. What does it imply about contemporary contacts? His comment about the local Turkic farmers' delight in Chinese buckets also suggests something about the way technology, too, may have been spreading. Do you find similar evidence elsewhere?

Li's destination, Samarkand, was once the greatest mercantile center and crossroads in all Inner Asia. But note what Li says about its condition at the time of his visit. Dislocations late in the thirteenth century led to further decline in the overland trade, shifting commerce and travel southward to sea routes across the Indian Ocean. Source 5 suggests how this shift affected the western side of this maritime sphere. Because a rebellion by the Mongol ruler of Jagadai closed travel across Inner Asia, John had to make his way east by the sea route. It took him years to reach his destination, Cambalec or Khanbaligh, the new "city of the Khan," built by Kubilai Khan during the 1260s to replace Karakorum. In another letter sent back to Europe from Khanbaligh in 1305, John recommends the land route to China over the sea lanes. It takes only five or six months to cross, he says, and is "safer and more secure." By contrast, he finds the sea passage "long and perilous since it involves two sea voyages, the first of which is about the distance of Acre [in Palestine] from the province of Provence, but the second is like the distance between Acre and England, and it may happen that the journey is scarcely completed in two years."[3]

Source 5, John's earlier letter, tells what he found during the first stage of his trip from the Middle East to India. It gives a general survey of Upper India—the area along the western shore of India from the Indus down to the rich commercial cities of the Malabar coast. Southward lay Lower India, then considered a different realm. As John indicates, travelers reached these lands by sailing across the "Sea of India" from Ormes (Hormuz) on the Persian Gulf. Pay special attention to what he says about the sailing seasons that prevailed along this leg and the risks incurred by those who ignored them. What other hazards besides off-season gales does he mention as a danger to mariners in this area? Despite such risks, many ships must have been sailing this route, judging from John's claim of no less than sixty perishing during the year of his stay. Most were probably small Arab dhows like the one shown as Source 6. Notice which of these caught John's eye. As he remarks, such ships sailed to western India for cargoes of aromatics, fruits, spices, and pears. How much of such cargo do you think these dhows could safely carry?

These exotic goods attracted traders to the Malabar coast not only from Hormuz and western Asia, but from China and Africa, too. Relations between this area and the East African coast, which lay due west, were so

3. These remarks appear in a "Second Letter of John of Monte Corvino" translated in Raymond Dawson, *Mission to Asia* (New York: Harper Torchbooks, 1965), p. 226.

common that the region around the Horn of Africa near modern Ethiopia was called Middle India. Fed by goods from several large empires in the interior as well as Aden on the Red Sea, coastal East Africa formed an important adjunct to the India trade. In Source 7 Marco Polo cites its commercial significance, and particularly that of Madagascar and Zanzibar (Zenzibar, in the selection), on his return to Europe along the water route in 1293 or 1294. Notice what goods the area supplied—and absorbed. Where do you suppose the "silks" bartered here were obtained? Marco Polo's comments on Zanzibar's black inhabitants shows that the world of the Indian Ocean included people of many types. His depictions, of course, betray obvious racial bias. Do such feelings infect any of the other sources? How often do the source writers take care to distinguish racial traits? Do these seem as important to them as ethnic or religious differences?

Religion certainly caught the eye of some. Note which religions figure in these accounts. By the thirteenth century, Islam had spread throughout the entire trade area, and Muslim communities could be found in almost every port from Mogadishu on the African coast to Zaitun in China. John of Corvino observes the "many Saracens," or Arabs, who lived along the Malabar coast in India. They were probably traders and their descendants who settled there permanently to work as brokers for the seasonal influx of Arab and Persian merchants. Though he declares that they had "great influence," he remains strangely silent about why. He nowhere explains, for example, that "the Lord of all India" was a Turkic Muslim whose sultanate of Delhi ruled the northern part of the subcontinent under the nominal authority of the Abbasid caliphate.

By contrast, the fourteenth-century Arab traveler from North Africa, Ibn Battuta, left a detailed picture of Islam's impact across the Indian Ocean. As he notes in Source 8, an account written near the end of his career, Muslims lived all along its coasts. Notice not only what he says about resident Muslims—their homelands, numbers, and occupations—but what he records about their efforts to spread their beliefs. For all that he extols the wealth of Muslim merchants from Yemen and Persia, Ibn Battuta deems the Chinese "the richest people in the world." During the thirteenth and fourteenth centuries, they served as principal carriers in the eastern half of the trade between India and the Pacific. In a passage not given here, Ibn Battuta praises Zaitun or Chuanzhou, China's chief emporium on the eastern end of the trade, as "one of the finest in the world" where as many as one hundred great ships docked at once.[4] Note his reaction to Chinese shipping, which represented the most advanced maritime technology of the time.

Chinese seamen already used the compass and other modern navigational devices on the long and difficult run to India. And the Arabs, who introduced their innovations westward,

4. Quoted in *Travels of Ibn Battuta,* ed. and trans. Samuel Lee (New York: Burt Franklin, n.d.), p. 213.

regarded the Chinese ocean-going junks as the largest and safest ships of the time. Compare Ibn Battuta's description with the illustration in Source 9. Consider how much more such ships carried than the small dhows common in the western half of the trade realm or the carts and pack animals on overland routes. According to Marco Polo, who also praised Chinese ships, the largest had crews of three hundred men and carried "from five to six thousand baskets, or mat bags of pepper."[5] What does this suggest about the relative volume and wealth of trade within different parts of the system?

The huge ocean-going ships of China afforded its rulers unrivaled sea power. Kubilai Khan, the greatest of all the Mongol emperors, quickly grasped its potential, sending fleets of captured junks to invade both Japan and Indonesia at the end of the thirteenth century. Though the invasions failed, his armadas demonstrated the value of large, state-maintained navies. During the subsequent Ming dynasty, which restored native rule in China, the Yongle emperor thus revived an imperial fleet. Originally built for an invasion of Vietnam, this armada later projected Ming power far abroad when its commander, Zheng He, convinced the emperor to let him sail the convoy to the Indian Ocean on the seven voyages of 1402–1433 mentioned earlier.

The last document here, Source 10, gives the highlights of these voyages into the "Western" or Indian Ocean. Notice what it says about the motive behind the expeditions. Given this purpose, why do you suppose Zheng He made the Indian Ocean his destination? In thinking about this question, consider what ports he visited and what they collectively represented at the time of his voyages. In addition to the extent of their circuits, note the scale of these fleets. How do they compare with the later efforts of European states to send ships to the Indies? Think what outfitting fleets of this magnitude for voyages of several years must have entailed. Here again is some indication of China's economic stature at the time as well as its potential maritime power.

5. These remarks appear in *The Travels of Marco Polo*, ed. Manuel Komroff (New York: Liveright Publishing Corp., 1953), p. 261.

EPILOGUE

For reasons that remain unclear, this early world system, flourishing in the thirteenth century, began to change toward the end of the fourteenth. Various conjectures have been made about the possible causes, but much more study needs to be done before any conclusions can be drawn. Clearly the break-up and collapse of the Mongol imperium in the mid-fourteenth century were important contributing factors. A vast state, the Mongol Empire at its height foreshadowed the later Western empires of the modern world system in both its transcontinental size and its pluralism. It not only unified Inner Asia politically, making overland travel and trade across the whole breadth of the continent relatively safe, but stimulated new levels of interaction among the peoples all around its periphery. One unfortunate result of this heightened contact, however, was a diffusion of diseases. Mongol invaders appear to have spread bubonic plague to China and the Crimea, from which places it spread to the rest of Asia and Europe during the mid-fourteenth century. Decimating whole cities, particularly in Europe, where it was known as the Black Death, this devastating disease not only weakened Mongol power but speeded the decline of Central Asia and its ancient trade centers.

Changes in China, too, contributed to the fragmentation of the trans-Asian system. Perhaps the wealthiest of that system's regions and its largest source of trade, China may well have been its single most crucial component. Because of internal economic changes and Ming policies, however, Chinese trade and contact with the rest of the system declined dramatically in the second half of the fifteenth century. The Ming decision to abandon its fleets may have been decisive in this regard. The lure of unprotected shipping and rich ports along the China coast attracted huge bands of international pirates. Rather than build another navy to police its offshore waters, the Ming regime decided to close its ports, fortify the coastline, and withdraw into semi-isolation to discourage pirate attacks. Along with shifts in domestic markets, this closure policy drastically cut back Chinese foreign commerce, capital, and shipping, depriving the Indies trade of key components without which it probably could not continue as before.

Despite these changes, interregional trans-Asian trade and relations did not end abruptly in the fifteenth century. India still remained an important heart of widespread commerce. But the intensity as well as the frequency of economic, political, and cultural contacts across Asia evaporated. As traditional connections weakened or shifted to new alignments, the network of trade and travel centered around Central Asia and the Indian Ocean slowly dissolved. When Vasco da Gama's two Portuguese ships appeared in the Indian Ocean in 1498 after rounding Africa from the west, the process was already well underway. By then, of course, Christopher Columbus's misguided attempt to reach the Indies by sailing westward from Spain in 1492 had put Europeans in contact with the Americas. In the age of European colonialism that followed, a new world system straddling the North Atlantic soon emerged, gradually displacing the older trans-Asian one. Its once thriving cities were relegated to peripheral status in emergent empires centered in Atlantic ports like Lisbon, Amsterdam, and London. Yet in the early stages of building their own modern empires, Portugal, Holland, and Britain all coveted control of the Indies, attesting to the value of this once great hub even in its decline.

CHAPTER ELEVEN

REGIONAL METROPOLISES:

CONSTANTINOPLE AND TENOCHTITLÁN

(1160–1521)

THE PROBLEM

As noted in an earlier chapter, the words for civilization in most Western European languages derive from the Latin term for a city, *civitas*. The implied connection between high cultural attainment and "civic" or urban life reflects a measure of truth. First emerging in the third millennium B.C.E., in what has sometimes been termed the urban revolution, cities provided dynamic, new foci for human development. Within the next few millennia, they appeared not only across the entire breadth of Eurasia but in Africa and America as well. Originally small, largely self-contained city-states, urban communities began to change with the widening of political, religious, and economic networks during the centuries that immediately preceded the start of the common era. As imperial capitals, religious seats, or trade emporia, a few centers here and there began to evolve into cities on a scale much larger and far more complex in nature. Over the next thousand years, some of these, like imperial Rome in the West and Changan in East Asia, grew into a new kind of city that served as the hub of a huge, far-flung region. To contemporaries they were not just the biggest urban areas in their respective spheres but regional "metropolises," world-class cities that outranked all peers. Typically seats of political and religious power as well as cultural and economic magnets, they attracted polyglot populations from all over a vast hinterland. Long before the advent of modern mass society, therefore, great international cities began to emerge as transregional, cosmopolitan centers.

Although imposing in their own ways, these premodern metropolises were quite different from the big cities of the twentieth century. Built before the Industrial Revolution and the emergence of modern utilities and mass transit, they had to solve basic urban problems of housing, supply, sanitation, and transportation with far fewer technological means. For that very reason, of course, economics and technology played a smaller role in shaping them. Both the modern industrial city, whose concentric rings of commercial, manufacturing, and residential zones centered around a "downtown" complex of railroad depots and office buildings, and the contemporary "edge city" with its malls, airports, and theme parks strung out along arterial highways typically evolved in haphazard response to the changing technologies and material needs of mass, democratic societies. Older cities, though certainly affected by physical considerations, tended to be shaped more by ideals than by material concerns. And the patterns and rhythms of life within them conveyed a very different urban experience from that of the modern West. To comprehend the nature of any premodern metropolis, therefore, we need to free ourselves from current conceptions of what constitutes a city.

Unfortunately, neither historians nor others who study cities have agreed on a simple, generic definition, and efforts to list a comprehensive set of urban characteristics have generally met with much criticism. For in addition to such commonly accepted features as the presence of a large population, a ruling elite or class, diversified manufacturing, and long-distance trade, regionally unique traits like the possession of writing or metallurgy complicate the issue. Lewis Mumford in his classic study *The City in History* thus cautions: "No single definition will apply to all its manifestations and no single description will cover all its transformations."[1] In truth, a certain amount of consensus does exist. All scholars, for example, agree that urban life entails a high concentration of people living together in some sort of interdependent community. And most regard a population of about five thousand as the minimum necessary for a true city. Furthermore, experts generally concur that cities are primarily nonagricultural communities with formal institutions that provide diverse services to surrounding areas as well as to their own inhabitants. But beyond these few essentials, cities have varied widely in size, role, and character, making it difficult to generalize about their historical identity. For that reason, an understanding of any urban type has to be sought first and foremost through an analysis of actual examples.

This chapter accordingly asks you to consider two of the world's greatest cities in late traditional times, roughly speaking, from about the twelfth through the fifteenth centuries. The two presented here, Constantinople and Tenochtitlán, do not represent especially unique examples for this era, which coincides with the end of the Middle Ages in Europe. Other contemporary metropolises such as Baghdad or the Chinese city of Hangzhou would serve equally well as case studies. The choice of Constantinople and Tenochtitlán, however, highlights the global nature of the phenomena, con-

1. Lewis Mumford, *The City in History: Its Origins, Its Transformations, Its Prospects* (New York: Harcourt Brace Jovanovich, 1961), p. 3.

trasting as it does two cities, one in the Mediterranean and the other in Mesoamerica, that were quite literally worlds apart. Moreover, because Western Europeans visited and recorded their impressions of both sites during this era, this choice invites implicit comparisons with their homelands where truly great urban centers had yet to develop.

Your task in this chapter is to determine what the characteristics of these two great cities were. Go over the materials presented in the Evidence section for each of the cities, looking for information on the dominant physical features. Then think about what these features represent in terms of urban life or activities. The prominence of railroad stations, factories, office buildings, and department stores at the heart of most modern cities, for example, provides clear indications of their industrial and commercial nature. What physical elements stood out in Constantinople and Tenochtitlán, and how do these elements provide clues to these cities' identity and nature? Once you have arrived at some idea of what each city was like, compare them to see if they shared enough common features to represent a generic type. By considering what characterized them, you should not only discover what these metropolises were like in their heyday but gain some insight into the nature of big, pre-modern cities in general.

BACKGROUND

Although differing in many respects, Constantinople and Tenochtitlán both achieved regional preeminence primarily as imperial capitals. First and foremost seats of government, they represented conscious attempts by rulers to legitimize political authority. For this reason, both were built in imitation of older and more renowned centers of power whose grandeur and might their founders hoped to regain. Yet neither remained merely a political seat. Each in its own way became a major religious site and a hub of interregional trade as well as the dominant center of high culture in its sphere. Nonetheless, their fortunes remained closely tied to those of the empires that they represented, and when these fell, both cities quickly lost their original grandeur.

Of the two, Constantinople was by far the older, but its rise to fame as a Roman capital came late in its history. The city dates back to 658 B.C.E., when Greek colonists from Megara first settled it. Named Byzantium in honor of their leader Byzas, it remained no more than a provincial port throughout most of antiquity. Its only noteworthy feature was its location: It stood at the tip of a promontory jutting out into the narrow strait, known as the Bosphorus, that separates Europe from Asia. This strait connects the Black Sea to the north with the Sea of Marmara to the south and through it—and the even narrower channel of the Hellespont—to the Aegean entrance of the Mediterranean. By imperial times, Roman expansion into

Greece and Asia Minor made this waterway the most important artery in the rich, eastern half of the empire. With the decline of Rome and its western provinces in the fourth century C.E., this eastern portion of the empire gained ever greater importance as a reservoir of wealth and manpower. And Byzantium, perched upon an easily defended headland dominating the most crucial waterway in the East, assumed new strategic value. It was apparently this strategic consideration that led Emperor Constantine to select the city as a replacement for Rome in 324 when he sought a better base from which to revive the empire.

Though Rome itself had ceased to be the actual imperial residence for some time before this change, it continued to hold great symbolic importance. In selecting Byzantium, therefore, Constantine apparently made much of its similarity with the older capital, particularly the fact that it, like Rome, stood among hills. To enhance the similarity, he refurbished the city in typical Roman style. But Constantinople, or "Constantine's city," as the site came to be called after its formal consecration in 330, was a seaport rather than an inland center. Built on a triangular peninsula, it faced water on two sides: the Sea of Marmara on the south and a deep inlet off the Bosphorus on the north. This inlet, called the Golden Horn because of its crescent-like shape, provided the city with a well-protected deep-water harbor that made it one of the best ports in the Mediterranean world. Taking full advantage of the maritime character of the site, its original Megaran founders had concentrated most of their public buildings in Greek fashion atop a tall hill, named the Acropolis, that overlooked the water at the very tip of the peninsula. The sea and seafarers thus dominated the city.

Byzantium differed from Rome in another respect as well. Imperial Rome rose to fame without walls, adding them only in 268 when the growing threat of barbarian invasion from across the Alps led Emperor Aurelius to see to the city's defenses. But the unsettled conditions of his time led Constantine to wall off Byzantium's landward side immediately, giving the city a well defined western boundary. Later, Emperor Theodosius built an even more massive rampart farther to the west, considerably enlarging the city, and subsequent rulers raised sea walls along both the Golden Horn and the Marmaran shore. These defenses, which gave Constantinople a reputation for impregnability, attracted attention throughout the West and made the city a frequently copied prototype for the walled cities of medieval times.

Despite its extensive fortification, however, Constantinople ultimately covered four times the area of Rome. The heart of the city remained near the tip of the peninsula, where Constantine refurbished existing buildings and added what came to be called simply the Great Palace. As the first Christian emperor and one who actively patronized his faith, Constantine also built a number of churches throughout the city. Later emperors continued his interest in public construction. Emperor Theodosius not only built new land walls to the west of those erected under Constantine to enlarge the city but also added many internal monuments and improvements. Even more lavish, however, was Emperor Justinian, who launched an extensive building program to renovate the city as part of his effort to revitalize the Roman state. Along with many secular works, he ordered the construction of St. Sophia, a colossal church designed to be the greatest and most impressive building in all Christendom. During Justinian's reign from 527 to 565, in fact, the city probably reached the peak of its development with a population somewhere around 500,000 to 600,000—far in excess of that of contemporary Rome, which had shrunk rapidly in size as well as in stature.

By the time of Justinian, the city assumed the basic layout that it was to retain for the better part of the next millennium. Public life centered around a complex of buildings that stood just southwest of the Acropolis, the original heart of the city, near the tip of the peninsula. These included not only the Great Palace and the church of St. Sophia, the chief seats, respectively, of imperial political and religious life, but a great stadium-like race course called the Hippodrome and the Baths of Zeuxippus, both of which offered important public entertainments. Between them passed the Mese, or "Midway," the city's principal street. This grand avenue ran westward from the foot of St. Sophia to the Forum of Theodosius, where it forked into branches that continued out to the two most important entry points in the landward walls—the Golden Gate and the Gate of Charisos—which opened to the main imperial highways linking the city to the rest of the empire. Along its approximately two-mile course stood additional forums, colonnaded squares in which markets and other public affairs could be conducted with some shelter from the weather. The largest and most imposing of these, the Forum of Theodosius, also served as the terminus of the raised aqueduct, built by order of Emperor Valens, that kept the many fountains and cisterns of the city filled with an adequate supply of fresh water. Most private homes and shops lined the secondary streets that branched off the Mese to thread their way up and down the six hills across which the city spread.

The decline of imperial might and wealth following Justinian's reign curtailed further building, and subsequent rulers added little to the city other than an occasional small church or monument. Moreover, by the eighth century, dwindling imperial fortunes together with a series of earthquakes and plagues appear to have severely reduced the population to perhaps a third or less of its peak figure. Thus it was a much smaller city that survived to become the regional metropolis of the Western world during Europe's Middle Ages. It was also a more complex city, combining its original Roman heritage with strong Greek and Christian influences. In its layout and most prominent secular buildings, of course, Constantinople continued to reflect the urban ideals of ancient Rome. But because of the Hellenistic culture of its populace, who spoke mainly Greek, the city's distinctly eastern character soon overpowered its Latin legacy. This feature was especially marked in religious affairs, for the city served as the seat of the Orthodox Christian faith whose churches conformed to the Greek or Eastern rites rather than those of Rome. Moreover, as an important trade as well as political and religious center throughout the Middle Ages, the city continued to attract people from all over the Mediterranean and Asia Minor. Its many foreign quarters, filled with Italians, Jews, Armenians, and Slavs, gave it a cosmopolitan flavor that was enriched by a constant influx of still more exotic traders and diplomats coming from as far away as Britain and Persia.

Relative to Constantinople, Tenochtitlán was a young city. Founded by a people known as the Aztecs in the fourteenth century, the city quickly grew from a small local center into the largest city in the Americas as they expanded their control over Mesoamerica. The Aztecs, a Nahuatl-speaking group who called themselves the Mexica or Tenocha, came late into this area from an original homeland located somewhere in the arid lands farther to the northwest. According to their legends, they had dwelt there in a city called Azatlán, the "Place of the Herons," built on a paradisiacal island located in the midst of a desert lake. At the beginning of the twelfth century, however, they and seven neighboring tribes left their homeland at the order of their chief god, Huitzilopochtli, on a long migration southward. By the century's end they reached the shores of a new lake, Lake Texcoco, high up in the Valley of Mexico, where for nearly a century, they served indigenous tribes as mercenaries. In 1325, however, the Aztecs retreated into the marshes of Lake Texcoco to found a new city of their own at a site where, in fulfillment of a prophecy attributed to their god Huitzilopochtli, they found an eagle perched on a cactus growing out of a stone.

The city they erected in the marshes took its name, Tenochtitlán—the "Place of the Prickly Pear Cactus"—from this prophecy. And the image of an eagle on a cactus not only provided a glyph or written emblem for the city but, combined with a sheaf of spears, served as the imperial symbol of the Aztecs. Like the founders of Constantinople, the Aztec builders of Tenochtitlán developed their city in imitation of an older ideal. But two different models influenced its design. One was the legendary paradise, Azatlán, in imitation of which they founded their new city on an island off the southwestern shore of Lake Texcoco. But in actual layout, Tenochtitlán followed another more historic model, an impressive ruin lying less than fifty miles away in the northeastern part of the Valley of Mexico.

All that remained of a great city dating back to the middle of the first millennium of the common era, this deserted ruin exercised a tremendous influence over all the peoples of Mesoamerica. The Aztecs, who knew nothing of its builders' identity, called it simply Teotihuacán, or the "City of the Gods," on the assumption that only divine beings could have built so grand a place. Despite extensive archaeological work in recent decades, we know little more about its builders than the Aztecs did. This first great metropolis of the Americas, however, clearly attests to a long prior tradition of urban development in the area. At its height around the year 500 C.E.,

Teotihuacán may have been home to as many as 200,000 people, making it one of the world's largest cities at the time. Even more impressive than its immense pyramids, its great residential quarters and workshops, or its vast market compound is its careful layout around an expansive avenue of monumental buildings leading to the city's titanic Pyramid of the Sun. In spite of the grandeur of their city, Teotihuacán's inhabitants began to drift away sometime after 750 for reasons still unknown to us, eventually leaving it an empty ruin. Even in abandonment, the old site continued to serve as an urban model for subsequent Central American people. None, however, succeeded as well as the Aztecs in recapturing its grandeur.

In order to duplicate the monumental scale of Teotihuacán, the Aztecs had to expand their original island site through extensive landfills and hydraulic projects, allowing them to enlarge its shoreline and connect it with an adjacent island that held a separate community named Tlaltelolco. As part of this endeavor, they also found a solution to the damaging alkalinity of the landlocked Lake Texcoco: They built a huge dike across the southwest corner to isolate streams bringing in fresh water from the brackish main body of the lake lying east and north of the city. Within this fresh water zone, they reclaimed many acres of marshland around the city's edge for agricultural use by building up *chinampas,* floating fields of heaped-up mud and vegetation anchored in place with stakes and willow trees. In addition, they built great causeways to the north, south, and west to link the island complex to the mainland. These connected the city to trade routes that fanned out across the Valley of Mexico, making it the hub of a mammoth network of commerce that spread across the whole of Central America.

Because the northern community of Tlaltelolco developed independently until conquered and annexed by the expanding Aztecs in the 1470s, the island complex retained two distinct populations, each focused upon its own *teocalli,* or ceremonial center. That of Tenochtitlán proper occupied the geographic center, but the more northerly *teocalli* of Tlaltelolco outshone it in magnificence. Both featured enormous enclosures containing temples and priestly quarters around which clustered ancillary markets, administrative courts, and palaces. Beyond these great centers spread a maze of streets and canals along which stood many smaller markets, workshops, and residential sections. Made primarily of stucco-covered adobe, most of the buildings in these latter sections were low, one- or two-storied structures that adjoined open courtyards. Those in Tenochtitlán were organized into four wards dispersed around the central temple enclosure.

By its zenith at the end of the fifteenth century, this prodigious urban complex probably held 200,000 to 300,000 people, a population greater than that of any contemporary European city, including Constantinople. But this figure fails to include the population of the half dozen or so satellite communities that developed on the shore of the lake, particularly where the causeways began. The larger metropolitan area of Tenochtitlán, therefore, may well have contained a population twice or more in size, making it one of the world's greatest urban areas at the time. Many of these people were not Aztecs but older inhabitants of the region whose city-states had been subjected to Aztec rule. They and other ethnic groups who migrated into the metropolitan area from more distant vassal states or came as traveling merchants infused it with a very diverse population. A constant flow into the city of tribute missions and organized merchant groups from as far away as the deserts of the north and Yucatan to the south added even more to its cosmopolitanism. Many of these immigrant groups and visitors tended to settle in separate neighborhoods and markets where they perpetuated their own customs and languages, adding great cultural variety to the city's life.

THE METHOD

The physical remains of old cities, whether ancient or more recent, provide the best information about their main features. Ideally, then, we should turn to archaeology, the science that studies the material culture of the past, for evidence about the nature of these early metropolises. But because modern Mexico City and Istanbul overlie old Tenochtitlán and Constantinople, archaeologists have not been able to do the extensive work required to uncover them. Although occasionally new construction, particularly in Mexico City, has allowed them to excavate a few important sites, for the most part they have not been able to do much fieldwork. So historical archaeology, or the investigation of material sites built in historical times, provides only limited evidence for us to use in understanding these particular cities.

As a result, the bulk of our information must come from documents. You will find two sets in the Evidence section that follows, one for Constantinople and one for Tenochtitlán. Sources 1 and 2 present eyewitness accounts of Constantinople left behind by two medieval European travelers, Benjamin of Tudela, a Spanish rabbi who visited the city in the course of a long trip across the Mediterranean in the years 1160–1173, and Robert of Clari, a French soldier who took part in the sack of the city in 1203 by Western Europeans bound on the Fourth Crusade. You can identify many of the sites they describe in Source 3, a medieval illustrated map of Constantinople. Source 4 provides an illustration of the most celebrated of these, the great church of St. Sophia. Two Byzantine accounts complete this picture of medieval Constantinople: Source 5, an account from the *Historia* of the chronicler George Acropolites, describes an imperial procession through the city in celebration of its recovery from invaders in 1261 by Emperor Michael VIII; and Source 6, an imperial Chrysobull (or decree) of 1082, sheds light on economic matters in the city.

Similar materials reflect life in Tenochtitlán at its height. Source 7 comes from a letter written by the Spanish conqueror of the city, Hernan Cortés, to King Charles V of Spain, and Source 8 presents the recollections of one of his lieutenants, Bernal Días del Castillo, as recorded in his history *The Discovery and Conquest of Mexico.* A parallel visual record appears in Source 9, a Spanish map of the city made at the time of its conquest in the sixteenth century. Source 10 shows a line drawing of the excavated site of the Great Temple area, and Source 11, an Aztec drawing from the so-called Florentine Codex, depicts the Great Temple that formed the city's central feature. This Codex, an illustrated manuscript now in Madrid, preserves Aztec accounts of traditional life as transcribed into both Nahuatl and Spanish by Bernardino de Sahagún soon after the conquest. Source 12 consists of excerpts from several such accounts of city sights from this invaluable testament.

Interpreting the sources for Tenochtitlán presents special problems. Unlike the Byzantines, the Aztecs had no writing system of their own, and so the oldest written descriptions of their capital date from the time of its downfall and come from the hands of the Europeans who destroyed it. Despite their obvious appreciation of many aspects of Tenochtitlán, such observers hardly viewed the city with dispassionate eyes, and their remarks need to be considered cautiously. The inhabitants of Constantinople, of course, did write, and they left us considerable records of their own. But here, too, we must be wary of problems. Many of the surviving accounts come from outsiders who either passed through the city themselves or obtained their information second-hand from other visitors. And outsiders necessarily view places from an unusual perspective.

Before historians can use such testimony, then, they have to determine its degree of credibility. Obvious cultural and religious biases leading to overexaggerations and false observations are often easy to spot. Those who openly glorify their own cultural or religious superiority, for example, may well play down the impressiveness of what they have seen elsewhere. Other factors, however, may cause more subtle distortions. Invaders often inflate the size and splendor of conquered sites to enhance their reputation at home or to awe rivals. Be aware, too, that outsiders generally have interests and purposes quite different from those of the inhabitants, and they may frequent only certain quarters to the exclusion of others. For example, a religious pilgrim might remain unaware of the activities of a market or craft quarter, whereas a merchant hurrying to sell his wares could be completely oblivious to major religious sites. So as you analyze the materials that follow, try to discern not only who wrote each account but for whom and why. The answers to these questions should tell you which source may be more believable for a particular aspect of city life. By then crosschecking and integrating pieces from different accounts, you should be able to obtain a reasonably clear and accurate picture of what these cities were like.

Begin this attempt by trying to determine what physical features stood out most in each of these cities. Did certain districts or complexes catch the eye of visitors more than others? What constituted the most imposing public monuments and civic symbols? Were there special places for work, residence, and entertainment? How did people move about within the city, and where did the principal lines of access take them? Once you have a list of these features, locate each of them on the maps included and give some thought to the general pattern that emerges. Ask yourself how the parts interrelated and what elements seemed most to shape the overall layout of the city. Do any clear centers of city life seem to stand out from others? Can you tell what sorts of activities dominated city life?

Once you have gained a general sense of the layout and chief structures of each city, ask yourself what such features indicate about the course of events in Constantinople and Tenochtitlán. Try to determine from the physical elements those chief concerns or activities around which public life revolved. Did certain of them predominate? Were there, for example, defensive works? What would such features indicate about urban life and the relationship between the cities and their surrounding countryside? What, if anything, seemed to provide the locus for communal life? Were there large open spaces or public buildings where crowds could gather? What would they have done there? What provisions existed for mass movement and supply of resources like food? Similarly, try to determine what most defined civic identity through a consideration of the nature of public spaces and monuments. Did certain complexes command more notice than others? What did they house or commemorate? Who would have participated in or benefited from them?

On the basis of this analysis, ask yourself what such elements suggest about the function and nature of these early metropolises. Both were obviously imperial capitals, but were they merely political centers? To what extent did they also function as important focal points for economic, religious, or cultural life? It might help to compare them with more recent cities. Think for a moment how cities are laid out today and what features dominate contemporary urban landscapes. Note how airports, freeways, corporate headquarters, malls, and theme parks reflect the pattern and rhythm of the contemporary urban life with its emphasis on commercial activities and preoccupation with *mass* mobility, consumerism, and entertainment. What do the features of Constantinople and Tenochtitlán reveal about the nature of earlier urban life? Whose interests did they most seem to serve? How might you define or characterize such cities?

THE EVIDENCE

Source 1 from Manuel Komroff, ed., Contemporaries of Marco Polo *(New York: Liveright, 1928), pp. 264–267.*

1. From Benjamin of Tudela, *Travels of Rabbi Benjamin of Tudela,* 1160–1173

The circumference of the city of Constantinople is eighteen miles; one-half of the city being bounded by the continent, the other by the sea, two arms of which meet here; the one a branch or outlet of the Russian, the other of the Spanish sea. Great stir and bustle prevails at Constantinople in consequence of the conflux of many merchants, who resort thither, both by land and by sea, from all parts of the world for purposes of trade, including merchants from Babylon and from Mesopotamia, from Media and Persia, from Egypt and Palestine, as well as from Russia, Hungary, Patzinakia, Budia, Lombardy and Spain. In this respect the city is equalled only by Baghdad, the metropolis of the Mahometans [Muhammadans].

At Constantinople is the place of worship called St. Sophia, and the metropolitan seat of the Pope of the Greeks, who are at variance with the Pope of Rome. It contains as many altars as there are days of the year, and possesses innumerable riches, which are augmented every year by the contributions of the two islands and of the adjacent towns and villages. All the other places of worship in the whole world do not equal St. Sophia in riches. It is ornamented with pillars of gold and silver, and with innumerable lamps of the same precious materials.

The Hippodrome is a public place near the wall of the palace, set aside for the king's sports. Every year the birthday of Jesus the Nazarene is celebrated there with public rejoicings. On these occasions you may see there representations of all the nations who inhabit the different parts of the world, with surprising feats of jugglery. Lions, bears, leopards, and wild asses, as well as birds, which have been trained to fight each other, are also exhibited. All this sport, the equal of which is nowhere to be met with, is carried on in the presence of the king and the queen.

King Manuel has built a large palace for his residence on the sea-shore, near the palace built by his predecessors; and to this edifice is given the name of Blachernes [Blachernae]. The pillars and walls are covered with pure gold, and all the wars of the ancients, as well as his own wars, are represented in pictures. The throne in this palace is of gold, and ornamented with precious stones; a golden crown hangs over it, suspended on a chain of the same material, the length of which exactly admits the emperor to sit under it. This crown is ornamented with precious stones of inestimable value. Such is the lustre of these diamonds, that, even without any other light, they illumine the room in which they are kept. Other objects of curiosity are met with here which it would be impossible to describe adequately.

The tribute, which is brought to Constantinople every year from all parts of Greece, consisting of silks, and purple cloths, and gold, fills many towers. These riches and buildings are equalled nowhere in the world. They say that the tribute of the city alone amounts every day to twenty thousand florins, arising from rents of hostelries and bazaars, and from the duties paid by merchants who arrive by sea and by land. The Greeks who inhabit the country are extremely rich, and possess great wealth in gold and precious stones. They dress in garments of silk, ornamented with gold and other valuable materials. They ride upon horses, and in their appearance they are like princes. The country is rich, producing all sorts of delicacies, as well as abundance of bread, meat, and wine. They are well skilled in the Greek sciences, and live comfortably, "every man under his vine and his fig tree." The Greeks hire soldiers of all nations, whom they call barbarians, for the purpose of carrying on their wars with the sultan of the Thogarmim, who are called Turks. They have no martial spirit themselves, and, like women, are unfit for warlike enterprises. . . .

No Jews dwell in the city with them; they are obliged to reside beyond the one arm of the sea, where they are shut in by the channel of Sophia on one side, and they can reach the city by water only, when they want to visit it for purposes of trade. The number of Jews at Constantinople amounts to two thousand Rabbanites and five hundred Caraites, who live on one spot, but divided by a wall. The principals of the Rabbanites, who are learned in the law, are the rabbi Abtalion, Obadiah, Aaron Khuspo, Joseph Sargeno and Eliakim the elder. Many of them are manufacturers of silk cloth, many others are merchants, some being extremely rich; but no Jew is allowed to ride upon a horse, except Solomon Hamitsri, who is the king's physician, and by whose influence the Jews enjoy many advantages even in their state of oppression, which is very severely felt by them; and the hatred against them is increased by the practise of the tanners, who pour out their filthy water in the streets and even before the very doors of the Jews, who, being thus defiled, become objects of contempt to the Greeks.

Their yoke is severely felt by the Jews, both good and bad; for they are exposed to be beaten in the streets, and must submit to all sorts of bad treatment. Still the Jews are rich, good, benevolent, and religious men, who bear the misfortunes of their exile with humility. The quarter inhabited by the Jews is called Pera.

Source 2 from Robert of Clari, The Conquest of Constantinople, *trans. Edgar Holmes McNeal (New York: W. W. Norton, 1969), pp. 101, 102–103, 105, 107, 108–110, 111–112.*

2. From Robert of Clari, *Conquest of Constantinople,* 1203

Not since the world was made, was there ever seen or won so great a treasure or so noble or so rich, not in the time of Alexander nor in the time of Charlemagne nor before nor after. Nor do I think, myself, that in the forty richest cities of the world there had been so much wealth as was found in Constantinople. For the Greeks say that two thirds of the wealth of this world is in Constantinople and the other third scattered throughout the world. . . .

When the city was captured and the pilgrims were quartered, as I have told you, and the palaces were taken over, then they found in the palaces riches more than a great deal. And the palace of Boukoleon was very rich and was made in such a way as I shall tell you. Within this palace, which was held by the marquis, there were fully five hundred halls, all connected with one another and all made with gold mosaic. And in it there were fully thirty chapels, great and small, and there was one of them which was called the Holy Chapel, which was so rich and noble that there was not a hinge nor a band nor any other part such as is usually made of iron that was not all of silver, and there was no column that was not of jasper or porphyry or some other rich precious stone. . . .

[And there was another palace in the city, called the palace of Blachernae.] And there were fully twenty chapels there and at least two hundred chambers, or three hundred, all connected with one another and all made of gold mosaic. And this palace was so rich and so noble that no one could describe it to you or recount its great nobility and richness. In this palace of Blachernae there was found a very great treasure, for one found there the rich crowns which had belonged to former emperors and the rich ornaments of gold and the rich cloth of silk and gold and the rich imperial robes and the rich precious stones and so many other riches that no one could number the great treasure of gold and silver that was found in the palaces and in many other places in the city. . . .

Then the pilgrims regarded the great size of the city, and the palaces and fine abbeys and churches and the great wonders which were in the city, and they marveled at it greatly. And they marveled greatly at the church of Saint Sophia and at the riches which were in it.

Now I will tell you about the church of Saint Sophia, how it was made. Saint Sophia in Greek means Sainte Trinité ["Holy Trinity"] in French [*sic*].[2] The church of Saint Sophia was entirely round, and within the church there were domes, round all about, which were borne by great and very rich columns, and

2. Robert of Clari apparently knew no Greek and so misunderstood the meaning of the church's name. *Saint Sophia* means "Holy Wisdom," not "Holy Trinity."

there was no column which was not of jasper or porphyry or some other precious stone, nor was there one of these columns that did not work cures. . . .

Elsewhere in the city there is another gate which is called the Golden Gate. On this gate there were two elephants made of copper which were so large that it was a fair marvel. This gate was never opened except when an emperor was returning from battle after conquering territory. And when an emperor returned from battle after conquering territory, then the clergy of the city would come out in procession to meet him, and the gate would be opened, and they would bring out a chariot of gold, which was made like a cart with four wheels, such as we call a *curre.*

Now in another part of the city there was another marvel. There was an open place near the palace of Boukoleon which was called the Games of the Emperor. This place was a good bowshot and a half long and nearly a bowshot wide. Around this place there were fully thirty rows of seats or forty, on which the Greeks used to mount to watch the games, and above these rows there was a loge, very dainty and very noble, where the emperor and the empress sat when the games were held, and the other high men and ladies. And if there were two sides playing at the same time, the emperor and the empress would wager with each other that one side would play better than the other, and so would all the others who watched the games.

. . . Now about the rest of the Greeks, high and low, rich and poor, about the size of the city, about the palaces and the other marvels that are there, we shall leave off telling you. For no man on earth, however long he might have lived in the city, could number them or recount them to you. And if anyone should recount to you the hundredth part of the richness and the beauty and the nobility that was found in the abbeys and in the churches and in the palaces and in the city, it would seem like a lie and you would not believe it.

Source 3 from the British Library.

3. Illustrated Map of Constantinople, 13th century

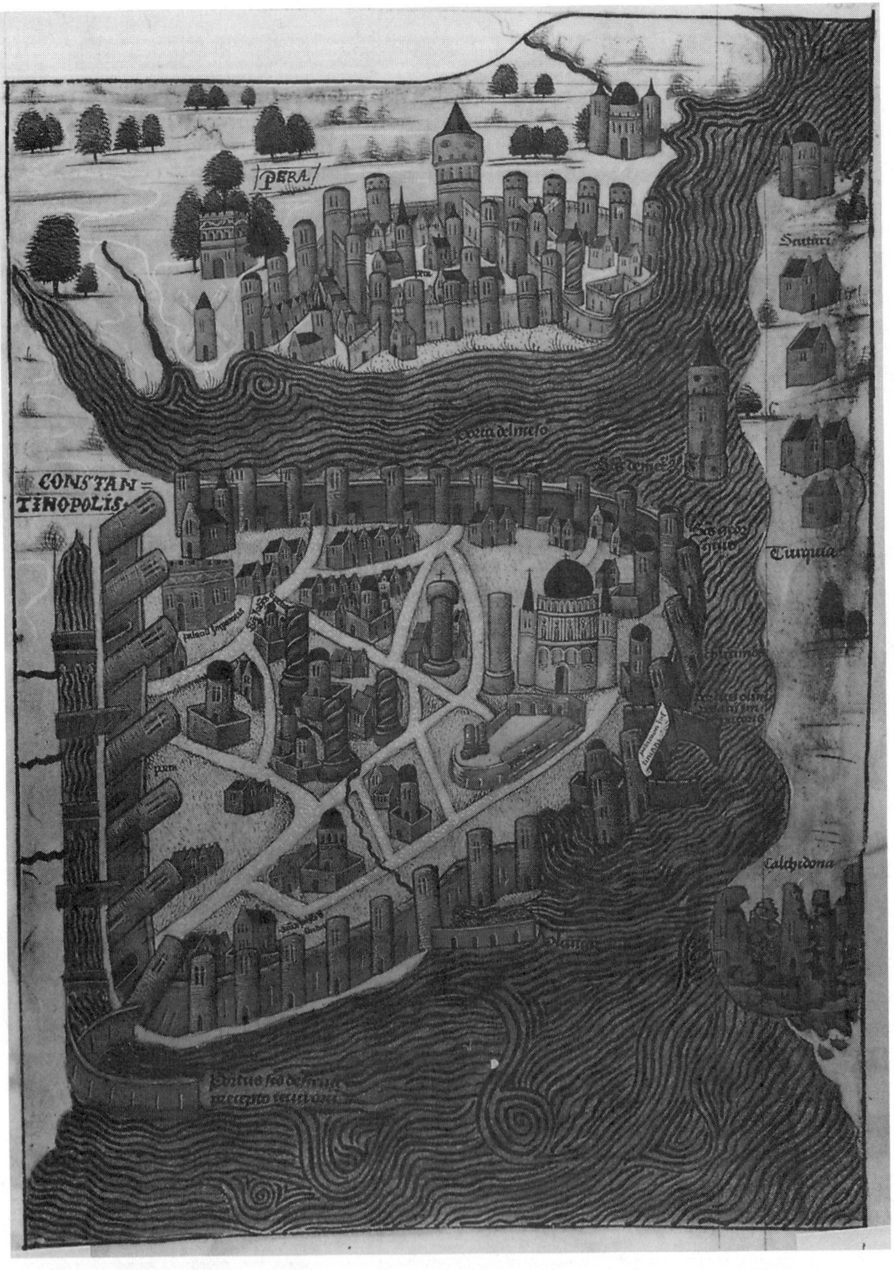

Source 4 : Bildarchiv Foto Marburg/Art Resource, NY.

4. Interior, Saint Sophia

Source 5 from George Acropolites, Historia, *ed. A. Heisenberg, in Deno John Geanakoplos,* Byzantium *(Chicago: University of Chicago Press, 1984), pp. 374–375.*

5. George Acropolites, "The Byzantine Recovery of Constantinople: Thanksgiving and Celebration," 1261

The emperor [Michael VIII Palaeologus] reached Constantinople on the fourteenth day of August, but he did not wish to enter the city the same day, so he pitched his tents in the monastery of Cosmidion. . . . And after spending the night there and arising, he made his entrance as follows: since the Patriarch Arsenios was not present . . . it was at once necessary that one of the prelates pronounce the prayers. George, metropolitan of Cyzicus . . . whom they call Kleidas, fulfilled this task. Getting up on one of the towers of the Golden Gate and having with him also the icon of the *Theotokos,* the image named after the monastery of the *Hodegetria,* he recited prayers for all to hear. Then the emperor, putting aside his mantle, fell to his knees on the ground, and with him all those behind fell to their knees. And after the first prayer was over, the deacon motioned them to rise, and all standing chanted *Kyrie eleison* [Lord have mercy] one hundred times.

When this was over, another prayer was recited by the prelate. And then the same thing happened as after the first. And this was done until the completion of all the prayers. When the religious part of the ceremony had been performed, the emperor entered the Golden Gate in a way which honored God more than the emperor, for he marched on foot with the icon of the Mother of God preceding him. And he went up to the monastery of Studius, and after leaving there the icon of the most immaculate Mother of God, he mounted his horse and went to the Church of the Wisdom of God [St. Sophia]. There he worshiped Our Lord Christ and rendered proper thanks to him. Then he arrived at the Great Palace and the Byzantine population was filled with great and immense joy and exultation. For there was no one who could not dance or exult with joy, being scarcely able to believe this event because of its unexpectedness and the enormous outpouring of jubilation. Since it was necessary that the patriarch also be in Constantinople, . . . after a few days the emperor entered the holy building, the temple of Great Wisdom, in order that he might hand over the *cathedra* [the patriarch's throne] to the prelate. And finally there assembled with the emperor all the notables of the archons and the entire multitude. Then the emperor, taking the arm of the patriarch, said, "Take your throne now, O lord, and enjoy it, that of which you were so long deprived."

Source 6 from G. Tafel and G. Thomas, eds., Urkunden zur Älteren Handelsund Staatsgeschichte der Republik Venedig, *in Deno John Geanakoplos,* Byzantium *(Chicago: University of Chicago Press, 1984), pp. 286–287.*

6. Chrysobull Detailing Extraordinary Privileges for the Venetians, 1082

No one is ignorant of those things which have been done by the faithful Venetians, how after they had gathered together different types of ships, they came to Epidamnus (which we call Dyrrachium) and how they provided for our assistance numerous seaborne fighting men, how their fleet conquered by force the wicked expedition [of the Normans], and how they lost some of their own men. We also know how even now they continue to be our allies, and about those things which have been done by their rowers [*thalattokopi*], men who work on the sea. Even if we should not mention this, everyone knows it perfectly well.

Wherefore, in recompense for their services of this kind, Our Majesty decrees through this present chrysobull, that the Venetians annually receive a gift of twenty pounds [of gold], so that they might distribute this among their own churches in whatever manner they see fit. . . . In addition, those workshops situated in the quarter of Perama [on the Golden Horn across from Pera], together with their upper chambers, which have an entrance and exit throughout, which extend from the Ebraica [gate] up to the Vigla [gate], both inhabited or uninhabited, and in which Venetians and Greeks stay—[all of] these we grant to them as factories, as well as three docks [*scalae*] which end in this aforementioned area. We also grant to St. Akyndinos the property, that is, a mill, lying alongside this church, which belongs to the house of Peter and which has an income of twenty bezants [Byzantine gold coins]. Similarly, we give the church of the Holy Apostle Andrew in Dyrrachium, together with all the imperial payments except the one which is set aside there to be given to the [harbor] barges.

It is also granted to the Venetians that they may conduct business in every type of merchandise in all parts of the empire, that is around great Laodicea, Antioch, Mamistra, Adana, Tarsus, Attalia, Strobilos, Chios, Ephesus, Phocea, Dyrrachium, Valona, Corfu, Bonditza, Methone, Coron, Nauplia, Corinth, Thebes, Athens, Negropont, Demetrias, Thessalonika, Chrysopolis, Perithorion, Abydos, Redestos, Adrianople, Apros, Heraclea, Selymbria, and the megalopolis itself [Constantinople], and indeed in all other places which are under the authority of our pious clemency, without their paying anything at all for any favor of commerce or for any other condition on behalf of their business—[payments] which are made to the fisc [*demosion*] such as the *xylokalamos, limenatikos, poriatikos, kaniskios, hexafolleos, archontikios* [i.e. charges for mooring ships, disembarking, and unloading cargo, and taxes on imports, exports, purchases, and sales], and exemption from all other taxes which have to be paid to engage in commerce. For in all places of business Our Majesty has given them the permission that they be free of such exactions. And the Venetians are removed [from the authority of] the *eparchos parathalassitos* [sic] himself, the *heleoparochos*, the *genikos*, the *chartularii*, the *hypologoi*, and of all officials of this sort. Let no one who carries out imperial or other duties presume to be contemptuous of the provisions which have been specified here. For permission has been granted to the Venetians to deal in whatever types of goods and merchandise anyone may mention, and they have the ability to make any purchase and remain free from all exactions [*dationes*].

Source 7 from Hernan Cortés: Letters from Mexico, *ed. and trans. A. R. Pagden (New York: Grossman, 1971), pp. 83–84, 102–106, 107–108, 109.*

7. Letter of Hernan Cortés to Charles V, King of Spain

This great city of Temixtitan [Tenochtitlán] is built on the salt lake, and no matter by what road you travel there are two leagues from the main body of the city to the mainland. There are four artificial causeways leading to it, and each is as wide as two cavalry lances. The city itself is as big as Seville or Córdoba. The main streets are very wide and very straight; some of these are on the land, but the rest and all the smaller ones are half on land, half canals where they paddle their canoes. All the streets have openings in places so that the water may pass from one canal to another. Over all these openings, and some of them are very wide, there are bridges made of long and wide beams joined together very firmly and so well made that on some of them ten horsemen may ride abreast. . . .

This city has many squares where trading is done and markets are held continuously. There is also one square twice as big as that of Salamanca, with arcades all around, where more than sixty thousand people come each day to buy and sell, and where every kind of merchandise produced in these lands is found; provisions as well as ornaments of gold and silver, lead, brass, copper, tin, stones, shells, bones, and feathers. . . .

Finally, besides those things which I have already mentioned, they sell in the market everything else to be found in this land, but they are so many and so varied that because of their great number and because I cannot remember many of them nor do I know what they are called I shall not mention them. Each kind of merchandise is sold in its own street without any mixture whatever; they are very particular in this. Everything is sold by number and size, and until now I have seen nothing sold by weight. There is in this great square a very large building like a courthouse, where ten or twelve persons sit as judges. They preside over all that happens in the markets, and sentence criminals. There are in this square other persons who walk among the people to see what they are selling and the measures they are using; and they have been seen to break some that were false. . . .

There are, in all districts of this great city, many temples or houses for their idols. . . .

Amongst these temples there is one, the principal one, whose great size and magnificence no human tongue could describe, for it is so large that within the precincts, which are surrounded by a very high wall, a town of some five hundred inhabitants could easily be built. All round inside this wall there are very elegant quarters with very large rooms and corridors where their priests live. There are as many as forty towers, all of which are so high that in the case of the largest there are fifty steps leading up to the main part of it; and the most important of these towers is higher than that of the cathedral of Seville. . . .

There are three rooms within this great temple for the principal idols, which are of remarkable size and stature and decorated with many designs and sculptures, both in stone and in wood. Within these rooms are other chapels, and the doors to them are very small. Inside there is no light whatsoever; there only some of the priests may enter, for inside are the sculptured figures of the idols, although, as I have said, there are also many outside.

There are in the city many large and beautiful houses, and the reason for this is that all the chiefs of the land, who are Mutezuma's [Montezuma's] vassals, have houses in the city and live there for part of the year; and in addition there are many rich citizens who likewise have very good houses. All these houses have very large and very good rooms and also very pleasant gardens of various sorts of flowers both on the upper and lower floors.

Along one of the causeways to this great city run two aqueducts made of mortar. Each one is two paces wide and some six feet deep, and along one of them a stream of very good fresh water, as wide as a man's body, flows into the heart of the city and from this they all drink. The other, which is empty, is used when they wish to clean the first channel. Where the aqueducts cross the bridges, the water passes along some channels which are as wide as an ox; and so they serve the whole city.

Canoes paddle through all the streets selling the water; they take it from the aqueduct by placing the canoes beneath the bridges where those channels are, and on top there are men who fill the canoes and are paid for their work. At all the gateways to the city and at the places where these canoes are unloaded, which is where the greater part of the provisions enter the city, there are guards in huts who receive a *certum quid* of all that enters. I have not yet discovered whether this goes to the chief or to the city, but I think to the chief, because in other markets in other parts I have seen this tax paid to the ruler of the place. Every day, in all the markets and public places there are many workmen and craftsmen of every sort, waiting to be employed by the day. The people of this city are dressed with more elegance and are more courtly in their bearing than those of the other cities and provinces, and because Mutezuma and all those chieftains, his vassals, are always coming to the city, the people have more manners and politeness in all matters. Yet so as not to tire Your Highness with the description of the things of this city (although I would not complete it so briefly), I will say only that these people live almost like those in Spain, and in as much harmony and order as there, and considering that they are barbarous and so far from the knowledge of God and cut off from all civilized nations, it is truly remarkable to see what they have achieved in all things.

Source 8 from Bernal Díaz del Castillo, The Discovery and Conquest of Mexico, *trans. A. P. Maudsley (New York: Farras, Straus and Cudahy, 1956), pp. 191–192, 215–219.*

8. From Bernal Díaz del Castillo, *The Discovery and Conquest of Mexico*

Our Captain and all of those who had horses went to Tlaltelolco on horseback, and nearly all of us soldiers were fully equipped, and many Caciques whom Montezuma had sent for that purpose went in our company. When we arrived at the great market place, called Tlaltelolco, we were astounded at the number of people and the quantity of merchandise that it contained, and at the good order and control that was maintained, for we had never seen such a thing before. . . . In this way one could see every sort of merchandise that is to be found in the whole of New Spain. . . .

When we arrived near the Great Cue and before we had ascended a single step of it, the Great Montezuma sent down from above, where he was making his sacrifices, six priests and two chieftains to accompany our Captain.[3] On ascending the steps, which are one hundred and fourteen in number, they attempted to take him by the arms so as to help him to ascend (thinking that he would get tired) as they were accustomed to assist their lord Montezuma, but Cortés would not allow them to come near him. When we got to the top of the great Cue, on a small plaza which has been made on the top where there was a space like a platform with some large stones placed on it, on which they put the poor Indians for sacrifice, there was a bulky image like a dragon and other evil figures and much blood shed that very day.

So we stood looking about us, for that huge and cursed temple stood so high that from it one could see over everything very well, and we saw the three causeways which led into Mexico, that is the causeway of Iztapalapa by which

3. Diaz uses the term *Cue* to refer to the tall, flat-topped pyramid on which the Aztecs built their temples. Note his care in recounting its impressive height, some 114 steps above the surrounding plaza.

we had entered four days before, and that of Tacuba, and that of Tepeaquilla, and we saw the fresh water that comes from Chapultepec which supplies the city, and we saw the bridges on the three causeways which were built at certain distances apart through which the water of the lake flowed in and out from one side to the other, and we beheld on that great lake a great multitude of canoes, some coming with supplies of food and others returning loaded with cargoes of merchandise; and we saw that from every house of that great city and of all the other cities that were built in the water it was impossible to pass from house to house, except by drawbridges which were made of wood or in canoes; and we saw in those cities Cues and oratories like towers and fortresses and all gleaming white, and it was a wonderful thing to behold; then the houses with flat roofs, and on the causeways other small towers and oratories which were like fortresses.

After having examined and considered all that we had seen we turned to look at the great market place and the crowds of people that were in it, some buying and others selling, so that the murmur and hum of their voices and words that they used could be heard more than a league off. Some of the soldiers among us who had been in many parts of the world, in Constantinople, and all over Italy, and in Rome, said that so large a market place and so full of people, and so well regulated and arranged, they had never beheld before.

Then our Cortés said to Montezuma: "Your Highness is indeed a very great prince and worthy of even greater things. We are rejoiced to see your cities, and as we are here in your temple, what I now beg as a favour is that you will show us your gods and Teules." Montezuma replied that he must first speak with his high priests, and when he had spoken to them he said that we might enter into a small tower and apartment, a sort of hall, where there were two altars, with very richly carved boardings on the top of the roof. On each altar were two figures, like giants with very tall bodies and very fat, and the first which stood on the right hand they said was the figure of Huichilobos their god of War. . . . Then we saw on the other side of the left hand there stood the other great image the same height as Huichilobos, and it had a face like a bear and eyes that shone, made of their mirrors which they call *Tezcat,* and the body plastered with precious stones like that of Huichilobos, for they say that the two are brothers; and this Tezcatepuca was the god of Hell and had charge of the souls of the Mexicans, and his body was girt with figures like little devils with snakes' tails. The walls were so clotted with blood and the soil so bathed with it that in the slaughter houses of Spain there is not such another stench.

Source 9: Newberry Library.

9. Spanish Illustrated Map of Tenochtitlán, Printed in Nuremberg, 1524

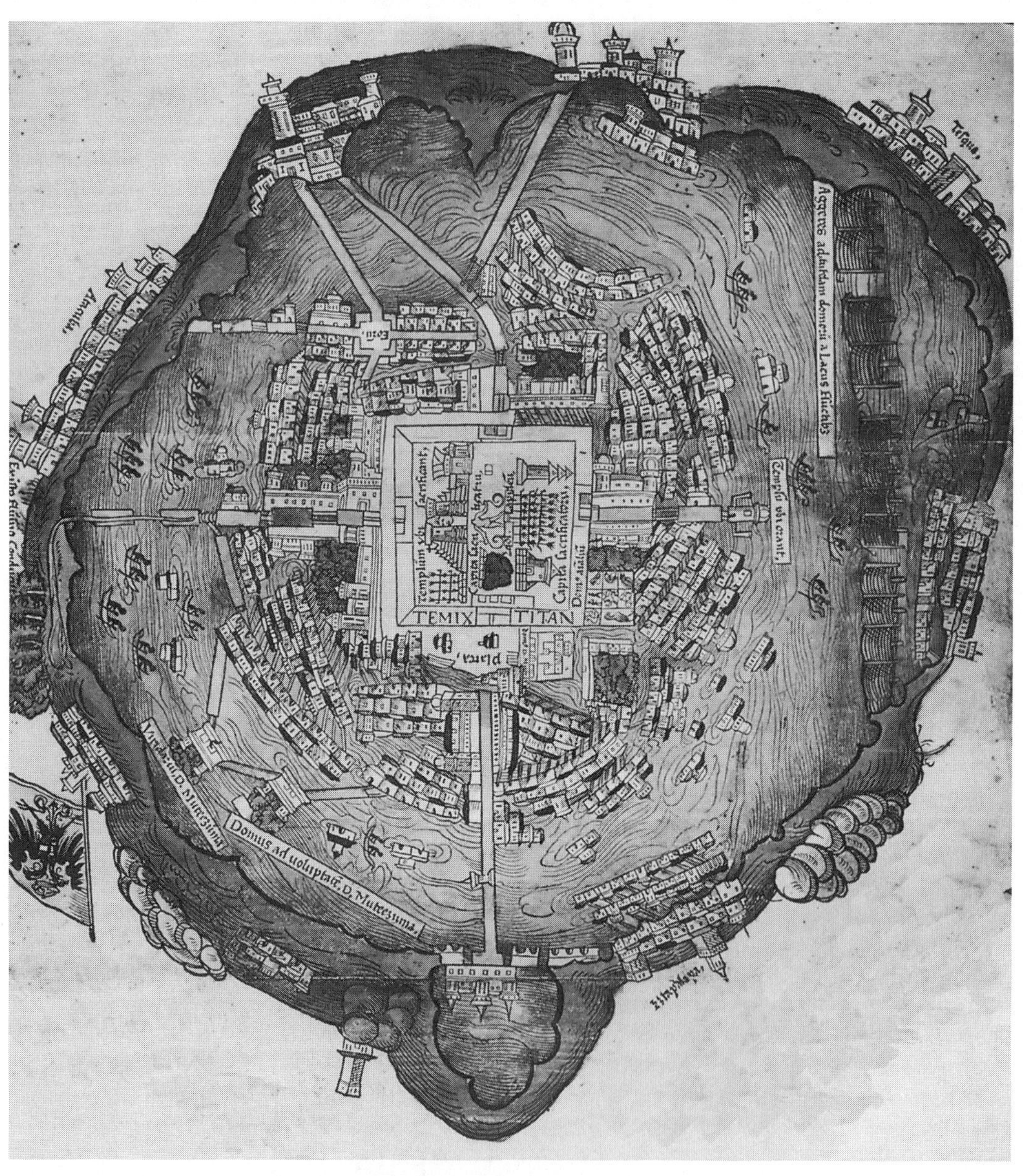

Source 10: Museo del Templo Mayor. Photographer: Saturnino Vallejo y German Zuniga.

10. The Excavated Site of the Great Temple Enclosure

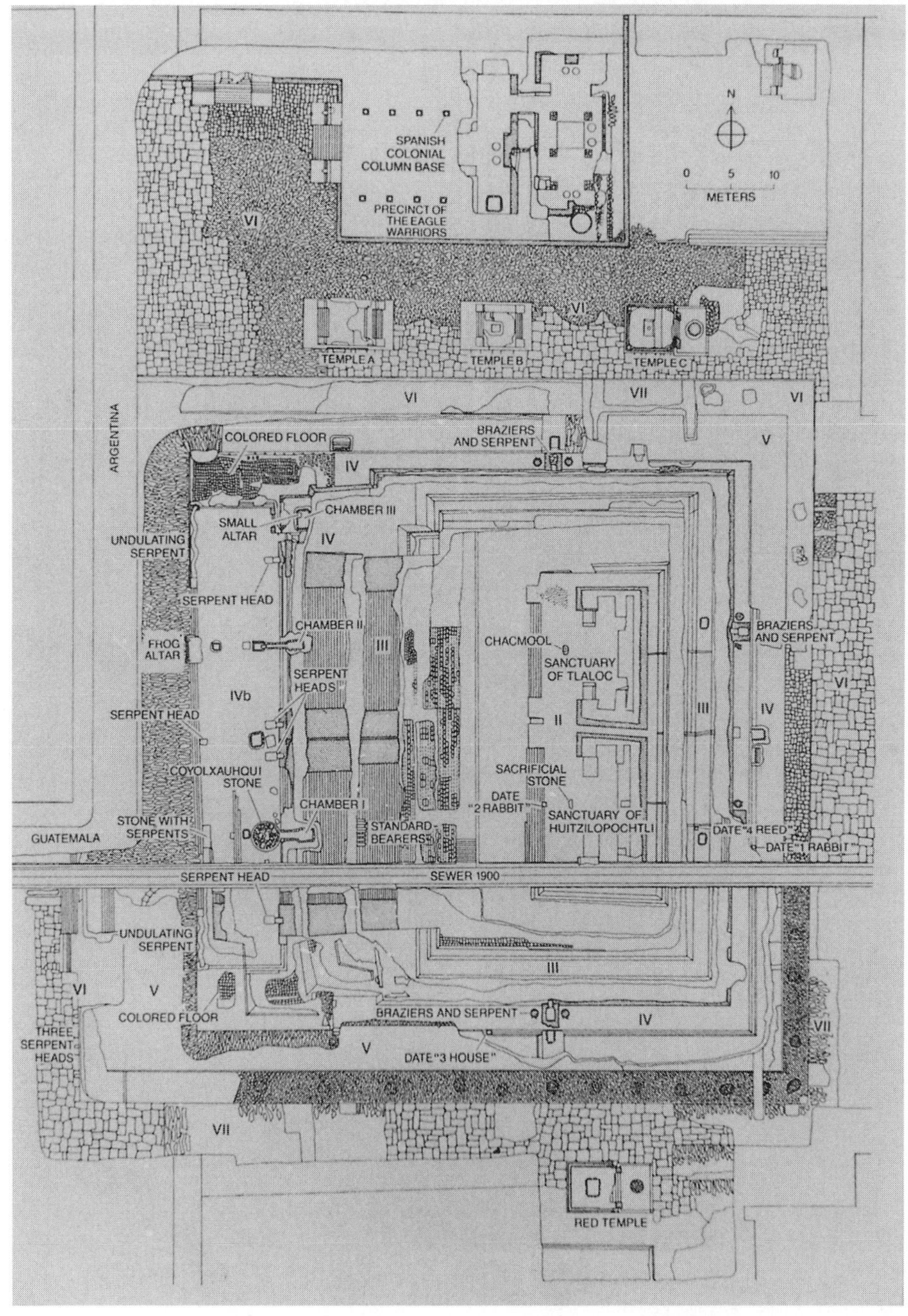

Source 11 from Bernardino de Sahagún, Historia de las Cosas de Nueva España, *trans. Arthur J. O. Anderson and Charles E. Dibble (Santa Fe, N.M.: The School of American Research and the University of Utah, 1954). Photograph: Courtesy, Patrimonio Nacional, Biblioteca Real.*

11. The Great Temple Enclosure at Tenochtitlán, from the Florentine Codex

Source 12 from Bernardino de Sahagún, Historia de las Cosas de Nueva España, *trans. Arthur J. O. Anderson and Charles E. Dibble (Santa Fe, N.M.: The School of American Research and the University of Utah, 1954), Part XII, pp. 269, 270–271, Part IX, pp. 29, 58.*

12. From Bernardino de Sahagún, The Florentine Codex

TEOCALLI

It means house of the god. In idolatrous times it was named *teocalli.* It is high, just an artificial mountain with levels, with steps. Some have one hundred steps, etc. And on its summit there stood two small houses, or just one; there the image of the demon, the devil, was guarded. This *teocalli* has levels, a landing, a stairway, a junction; it has a house, a house standing; it has a parapet, a column; it has columns.

It has a portal, corners, an entrance, a covering to the entrance, a stone column, a column, a door bar, a façade, a frontispiece, a wooden enclosure. It is roofed with thin slabs, with planks; it is uncovered; it is protected, with a parapet, with conduits. It is high, very high, very good, surpassingly good. It is a place to show, a place to exhibit.

TECPANCALLI

It means the house of the ruler, or the government house, where the ruler is, where he lives, or where the rulers or the townsmen, the householders, assemble. It is a good place, a fine place, a palace; a place of honor, a place of dignity. There is honor, a state of honor.

It is a fearful place, a place of fear, of glory. There is glory, there are glories, things are made glorious. There is bragging, there is boasting; there are haughtiness, presumption, pride, arrogance. There is self-praise, there is a state of gaudiness. There is much gaudiness, there is much arrogance—a state of arrogance. It is a place where one is intoxicated, flattered, perverted. There is a condition of knowledge; there is knowledge. It is a center of knowledge, of wisdom.

The ruler, when he beheld and knew that the common folk and vassals were very fretful, then commanded that the ball game be played, in order to animate the people and divert them. He commanded the majordomos to take out the rubber ball, and the girdles, and the leather hip guards, and the leather gloves with which the ruler's ball players were dressed and arrayed. And things were arranged on the ball court; there was sprinkling, there was sanding, there was sweeping.

On the two sides, on either hand, it was limited by walls, very well made, in that the walls and floor were smoothed. And there, in the very center of the ball court, was a line, drawn upon the ground. And on the walls were two stone, ball court rings. He who played caused [the ball] to enter there; he caused it to go in. Then he won all the costly goods, and he won everything from all who watched there in the ball court. His equipment was the rubber ball, the leather gloves, girdles, and leather hip guards.

QUESTIONS TO CONSIDER

As you go over the sources in search of clues that will help you determine the nature of these early metropolises, look for features that reappear in more than one account. Benjamin of Tudela and Robert Clari, the authors of Sources 1 and 2, had different reasons for visiting Constantinople, and their personal interests may have affected what they saw and remembered of the city. Yet both call attention to three of the city's dominant structures: St. Sophia, the Boukoleon palace, and the Hippodrome. Symbolic of the city's mixed Christian, Roman, and Greek heritage, these buildings all stood near the base of the original Acropolis. They formed the Capitolium, a central complex where the great thoroughfare known as the Mese, the city's main artery, began its course out to the landward walls. Together with public baths and the nearby Forum of Constantine, they defined the heart of the city as well as the administrative center of the imperial government. All three provided dramatic arenas for public spectacles. But note how, according to both sources, all three, including the stadium, housed religious as well as imperial functions. What explains the close connection between sports, religion, and politics in the life of this city? Would this same combination be likely in a twentieth-century city?

You can easily locate these and other major sites in Source 3, an illustrated medieval map of Constantinople. The map clearly shows one of the city's most often remarked features—its great encircling walls. What do such fortifications suggest about the city's relationship to the surrounding countryside and its regional position? Built by a series of early emperors, these walls were primarily intended to protect the administrative machinery of the empire. Most of the major government buildings, in fact, clustered together near the Capitolium. If you look at the apex of the triangular peninsula that juts out into the water on the map, you can see this area. Can you identify any of the buildings depicted?

The domed structure is the church of St. Sophia, or "Holy Wisdom." Why does it appear so large? St. Sophia was the biggest building then known in the Christian world, and, as Source 4 shows, it did enclose a vast space under its dome. But its size here is probably symbolic of its eminent role as the seat of the patriarch or head of the Greek Orthodox Church and the sacred light it was said to radiate throughout the Byzantine Empire. Like the entire complex of which it formed the hub, the church served an important civic function, too. It provided a staging area for great public processions that proceeded down the Mese to the Golden Gate, symbolically the most important entry into the city. Something of their appearance can be glimpsed in Source 5, which describes the return of Emperor Michael VIII Palaeologus into the city following its recovery from the Crusaders. Note how St. Sophia plays a prominent role in the celebrations. Of course, as the drawing of the city shows, and Robert of Clari's account confirms, many smaller churches, abbeys, and imperial monuments dotted the rest of the cityscape. What do they tell about this metropolis?

Perhaps less obvious in the general accounts of Constantinople is its role as a major seaport and center of economic activity. The medieval map clearly reveals the city's maritime character showing many *porta,* or sea gates, giving direct access to the waterfront. Think for a moment how the encircling sea would have eased problems of sanitation, transportation, and supply in a premodern city of this size. Constantinople's proximity to important sea routes also promoted a great deal of trade and industry. Both Rabbi Benjamin and Robert of Clari hint at this aspect of the city's life. Notice how both dwell on the fabulous material wealth of the city, the one finding it comparable only to Baghdad, the center of the Muslim world, and the other rating it as without peer. Much of this wealth derived from what the rabbi called "the conflux of many merchants" who came "from all parts of the world," giving the city a very cosmopolitan and mercantile character. Whom does he specifically mention as inhabitants or visitors? By the eleventh century, Italians dominated most of the commerce in the eastern Mediterranean and Black Seas. What role did they play in the life of Constantinople?

Source 6, a Chrysobull, or imperial edict, authorizing Venetian trade rights, not only indicates the extent of their privileges but affords a brief glimpse into the complex economic life of the city. Note its mention of specialized workshops, factories, mills, docks, and barges as well as its list of various taxes levied on different port activities and commercial transactions. Clearly commerce and manufacturing flourished in Constantinople during Europe's Middle Ages. Observe, too, the high concentration of Venetians in a section of the city along the fashionable port side of the Golden Horn called Perama—just opposite the separate walled community of Pera, which, according to Rabbi Benjamin, served as the Jewish quarter and a center of silk manufacturing. Apparently the splendid harbor of the Golden Horn had drawn most of the economic activity and commercial wealth of the city to its shores by this time. The map hints at this trend in its depiction of many multistoried houses in these quarters, presumably the residences of rich merchants. The allure of this essentially mercantile quarter seems to have attracted members of the political elite, too. Can you find the Blanchernae Palace overlooking the water of the Golden Horn near the end of the land wall? What might this indicate about the impact of the sea and commerce on the character of the city?

Water influenced the layout of Tenochtitlán even more than that of Constantinople, for it was an island city, surrounded on all sides by water. Its watery setting, of course, was an inland lake, as the city stood on a high plateau far from the sea. The Spanish conquistadors Hernan Cortés and Bernal Díaz made much of this setting, as you can see from Sources 7 and 8. Note that both remark on the lake's contribution to the city's defense as well as to its transportation system. Because of Lake Texcoco—and the strength of Aztec forces—the city needed no walls. Instead of ramparts, therefore, the most impressive external features of the city were the great causeways that linked it with the lakeshore. As Cortés writes, two of these doubled as aqueducts, bringing an ample supply of fresh water into the city from landward sources. These causeways appear clearly in Source 9, an early Spanish map of the city. Notice their great extent as well as the many outlying communities that clustered around their junction with the shore. This drawing also shows the great wickerwork dike built east of the city to hold back brackish water and the many channels weaving in and out of the *chinampas* (floating fields) on its perimeter. What impression do you gain from these documents about the likely role waterways played in the city's life? Would they have facilitated trade over a vast region? Or would they merely have made a widely dispersed urban area possible in the premodern period?

Of the various causeways, the most impressive seems to have been the one that entered from the south, along which Cortés and his party first entered the city. As he relates, this causeway, which began in the satellite city of Ixtapalapa and spanned Lake Xochimilco before continuing across Lake Texcoco proper, led directly to the enclosure of the Great Temple that formed the center of Tenochtitlán. Within the walls of this temple, built high on a pyramid of stone, stood sanctuaries dedicated to the Aztecs' patron god Huitzilpochtli and the rain god Tlaloc. All around it, Cortés says, spread towers and courts inhabited by priests. A large plaza, which served as the main market, occupied the area in front of this enclosure, and various imperial and noble residences flanked it on either side. Like the Capitolium of Constantinople, this entire complex, known as the Great Teocalli, provided the main focus of public life. The drawing of the excavated site shown in Source 10 gives some idea of its original layout. It was named after the large temple, or *teocalli,* that loomed over it, but, as you can see, it contained many other components. How do these compare with those of the Capitolium in Constantinople?

The nature of the activities that occurred around the Great Temple complex can be inferred from Díaz's detailed description of the similar, though somewhat larger, *teocalli* of Tlatelolco, the neighboring city that became virtually one with the Aztec capital after its conquest. Note Díaz's open astonishment at the number of people and the amount of goods in the arcaded marketplace associated with this compound, as well as his keen interest in the wealth seen there. Like Constantinople, Tenochtitlán served as a regional economic center whose merchants, according to Díaz, traded in "every sort of merchandise that is to be found in the whole of New Spain," that is, all of Mesoamerica. His description of the marketplace at Tlateloco matches Cortés's portrayal of a great square in the city "twice as big as that of Salamanca" where "more than sixty thousand people come each day to buy and sell." They both note the orderliness of the trading as well as the wide variety of produce on display. To what do they attribute this order?

Díaz shows equal astonishment over the vast court of the temple itself and the Great Cue (pyramid) that stood in its center. From the summit, the highest point in the city, he could look out beyond the immediate precincts of the capital to survey the entire metropolitan area spread out across the shores of the surrounding lakes. His comparisons of Tenochtitlán's size with that of Europe's great cities of the time, including Constantinople, merit special notice. One of Cortés's letters to Charles V echoes Díaz's praise of Tenochtitlán, claiming that even "in Spain there is nothing to compare" with the main palace adjacent to the Tenochtitlán *teocalli* in which the Aztec ruler Montezuma lived. But both accounts evince disgust over the ceremonies conducted in its temple enclosures, for Europeans found the human sacrifice practiced by the Aztecs as part of their religion upsetting. What does Díaz reveal about his feelings on this issue? Clearly he regards Europeans as culturally superior in this respect, though they, too, engaged in mass killing under other circumstances and did not refrain from eventually slaughtering large numbers of Aztecs.

Source 11, an Aztec drawing of the Great Temple enclosure at Tenochtitlán, illustrates the kind of sacrificial ceremonies that so repulsed the Spaniards. At the top center appears the Great Temple itself with sacrificial blood streaming down the steps from its two sanctuaries. Like many other Mesoamerican peoples, the Aztecs considered blood to be a source of vitality that supported the cycle of life. They thus sacrificed people in order to replenish the vitality of the gods, who they believed returned it to humanity in full measure through the fecundity of life. Although only a few victims were killed in ordinary rituals, as many as eighty thousand prisoners were sacrificed here on the altar stones in victory celebrations following the conquest of rival states. On these latter occasions, the Aztecs invited vassal chieftains and allied rulers to witness the gory spectacle, suggesting that such rites had important political as well as religious functions. What might these have been? How may such activities have shaped the way in which neighboring peoples understood the nature or significance of the city?

As you can see from a comparison with the excavated site, the drawing of the Great Temple provides a faithful picture of this ceremonial heart of the city where its people sought daily renewal through sacrifice. Note, in this context, Díaz's account of the emperor personally assisting the priests in such rites as part of a state religion. In Tenochtitlán, like Constantinople, palace and temple stood together, creating an almost inseparable focus for public life. As Source 12 indicates, both the *teocalli,* or "house of god," and the *tecpancalli,* or "house of the ruler," were designed to awe people with the power and grandeur of their residents. The description of the ball games played in the courts adjacent to the Great Temple complex shows a similar purpose in the imperial patronage of sports. Compare the alliance of religious and athletic events here with those of the Hippodrome at Constantinople. To what extent did public life in both cities focus on a display of ruling powers, whether human or divine? What does this fusion of sacred and secular suggest about their nature as cities?

EPILOGUE

Because of their grandeur and wealth in late traditional times, both Constantinople and Tenochtitlán attracted the attention of covetous outsiders who eventually brought them to grief. The Spanish conquest and sack of Tenochtitlán in 1521 are, of course, generally well known. For all of his earlier admiration of the city, after seizing control of it, Cortés set about its complete destruction. He had already torn down the great dike during his attack on the city, destroying its immediate agricultural environs; and after occupying it, he ordered all the principal buildings razed, the waterways filled in with the rubble, and most of its former inhabitants relocated, claiming the need to purge it of its barbaric religious cults. A Nahuatl lament for the dying city preserves some of the anguish this destruction wrought: "Let me not be angry that the grandeur of Mexico is to be destroyed./ The smoking stars gather together against it; the one who cares for flowers is about to be destroyed."[4] Using the labor of allied tribes whom he brought to the area, Cortés built a new, Spanish-style colonial settlement renamed Mexico City upon the ruins of the old Aztec capital. Ironically, the builders of the new city erected the Metropolitan Cathedral over part of the old *teocalli* enclosure on a site adjacent to their colonial headquarters (where the present National Palace stands), thus perpetuating in a new form the close conjunction of temple and palace.

Constantinople's plight was neither as dramatic nor as complete, but Constantine's city, too, suffered from invasion. The first of these came in 1203 when "Latin" participants of the Fourth Crusade, diverted from their original purpose by the lure of Constantinople's wealth and what they deemed its heretical Greek church, sacked and occupied the city. Remarking that "they revealed their race to be lovers of gold," a Byzantine chronicler complained that "these Westerners spared neither the living nor the dead" when they looted the city and showed "complete indifference and impiety" in stripping St. Sophia and other

4. This lament is translated by Daniel G. Brinton in his *Ancient Nahuatl Poetry* (New York: AMS Press, Inc., 1969), p. 123; this version is a reprint of an older edition printed in Philadelphia in 1890.

churches of all valuables.[5] Though dominated by Venetians, who coveted Constantinople's economic superiority, most of these so-called Latin conquerors were Franks, who, after thoroughly looting its moveable wealth, attempted to control the city for the next few decades. But a great fire that broke out during their occupation had devastated nearly half the city; and under their subsequent colonial rule, Constantinople not only failed to rebuild but slid into a rapid economic decline.

Thus, though restored to Greek control under Michael VIII Palaeologus in 1261, the city never regained its former wealth or stature. Its trade and territories passed gradually into the hands of others, and by the early fifteenth century it was reduced to a shadow of its original glory, with wide empty spaces within its walls given over to orchards and fields of grain or filled with crumbling ruins. As a result of their declining fortunes, the Byzantines could not stem the tide of Turkish-speaking Muslim people moving in from the east. In 1453 one of these, known as the Ottoman Turks, seized the city and ended Byzantine rule for good. Unlike the earlier Latin conquerors, however, they successfully rebuilt the city under the name Istanbul to serve as the capital of an expansionary, new Islamic empire that straddled the Bosphorus and spread westward into Europe as well as southeastward into Palestine and Africa. Symbolically, they transformed St. Sophia into a mosque and built a new imperial residence, known as the Topkapi Sarayi, nearby on the old Acropolis, reaffirming afresh the traditional importance of temple and palace in the city's identity.

The role that Western Europeans played in the decline of both of these metropolises merits some thought. Many of the sources imply that religious beliefs underlay their violent behavior. And their almost obsessive interest in gold and other material wealth is also well documented. As various of the above accounts demonstrate, Venetians, Franks, and later Spaniards, too, found these cities far richer than anything they knew. Their often naive amazement over the wealth and size of such metropolises points out the relative "underdevelopment" of urban centers in their homelands during this era. Because of this relative backwardness, Westerners later tended to equate the emergence of great urban centers with modern economic development. An appreciation of the scope of premodern metropolises like Constantinople, Tenochtitlán, Baghdad, Hangzhow, and Osaka, however, calls this view into question. Their impressive scale, in fact, suggests that efforts to understand world history using Western European patterns of development as a standard may be misleading.

5. These remarks by Nicetas Chomates appear in an excerpt from his *Historia* translated in Deno John Geanakoplos, *Byzantium* (Chicago: University of Chicago Press, 1984), p. 371.

CHAPTER TWELVE

MEDICINE AND REPRODUCTION IN THE WEST AND THE EAST (1000–1600)

THE PROBLEM

Along with ideas about how the world began, every human culture has developed theories regarding what we now term *reproduction,* that is, the process by which humans and other animals give rise to offspring. These have varied widely throughout history, and human reproduction in particular has often been linked to religious beliefs and ritualistic practices. In some belief systems, gods reproduce themselves in ways that are similar to human reproduction or make positive statements about reproduction, thus giving reproduction divine sanction. In others, reproduction is regarded as evil or negative, established by malevolent deities or demons as a way to dissuade humans from their true spiritual goals. In still others, reproduction is linked to cosmic forces that are conceptualized not as gods but as basic qualities such as order and disorder or harmony and chaos.

Reproduction was not only a religious issue, however, but also from very early times a matter of medical concern. Though all aspects of health and disease were viewed as influenced by divine will and action, human intervention was generally regarded as acceptable. (There were some who opposed this view, however, as there continue to be today in groups such as the Christian Scientists.) This intervention might take the form of prayers and intercessions, but it also included treatments that were not primarily religious. Some of the earliest records from ancient Egypt, for example, indicate that doctors identified and treated such diseases as diabetes, bronchitis, hemorrhoids, and skin cancer. In ancient Greece, philosophers such as Aristotle (384–322 B.C.E.) and physicians such as Hippocrates (ca. 460–ca. 370 B.C.E.) were interested not simply in clinical practice, but also in developing medical theories about the way in which the body—and the mind—operates. In China, notions of illness being caused by one's ancestors or by demons were supplemented as early as the fourth century B.C.E. by diagnoses based on observing patients, listening to their breathing, feeling their pulse, and discussing their pains and other symptoms.

For many of these ancient practitioners and theorists, reproduction was an essential part of medical knowledge and practice; Aristotle, for example, wrote an entire treatise on it, *The Generation of Animals.* His ideas, and those of other ancient Greek-speaking authorities, became the basis for theories of reproduction and treatment of reproductive difficulties—as well as most other ailments—for nearly two thousand years in the Near East, North Africa, and Europe. In China, the *Huangdi Neijing* (translated as "The Yellow Emperor's Manual of Corporal Medicine" or "The Yellow Emperor's Inner Canon"), a collection of medical treatises compiled perhaps as early as the second century B.C.E., includes discussions of sexual development and reproduction. This, too, became the basis for both theories of reproduction and treatment of reproductive problems over a huge area, including not only China but also Korea, Japan, and Southeast Asia, for thousands of years. In both the West and the East, later authors built on ancient works, creating bodies of medical literature that were translated into many languages and spread over vast areas, even coming to influence each other to some degree in terms of procedures and prescriptions. (These two schools were supplemented by additional theories and treatments that developed first in India.) Western and Eastern medicine are often set against each other, but in terms of ideas regarding reproduction and treatments of reproductive problems, there were also many similarities. Your task in this chapter is to compare and contrast works from these two traditions: What were their basic ideas regarding reproduction? How were these translated into practical advice for patients and medical practitioners? In what issues do you see similarities, and where do you find differences?

BACKGROUND

The Western medical tradition came primarily from the ancient Greeks, most notably Hippocrates and Galen (ca. 130–ca. 200 C.E.). Galen is credited with over five hundred works, mostly on medical topics, based on earlier medical knowledge and his own observation and experimentation. His interests were so wide-ranging and his findings became so influential that his work was considered authoritative for centuries—until the seventeenth century or later in Europe and until the nineteenth to a large degree in the Arabic world. Like the writings of Aristotle on other scientific subjects, the word of Galen was considered nearly as authoritative as the Hebrew and Christian scriptures and the Muslim Qur'an.

Galen's ideas and writings were copied and taught within the Roman Empire (he lived for much of his life in Rome, though he continued to write in Greek) and, after the collapse of the western Roman Empire, within the eastern Roman or Byzantine Empire, particularly at Alexandria, Athens, and Edessa. During the fifth and sixth centuries, the Byzantine emperors ordered many medical schools to close, and the physicians and scientists moved further eastward, first to Jundishapur in Persia. Here they came into contact with Indian and Persian medical teachings and combined these with Greek teachings into a single system. Once the Muslims conquered this area, many physicians moved to Baghdad, the capital of this part of the Islamic world, where they were welcomed at the caliph's court. Most of these physicians retained their allegiance to Christianity or Judaism, but they also learned Arabic and began to translate medical texts into Arabic. Under the leadership of Rhazes (Arabic al-Razi, 860–932), the main hospital in Baghdad became a center of clinical observation and the treatment of disease.

While Rhazes was celebrated for his accurate observations, the most influential Islamic medical writer was Avicenna (Arabic Ibn Sina, 980–1037), who was also a philosopher and interpreter of Aristotle. Avicenna was dubbed "Prince of Physicians" throughout both Europe and the Islamic world, and his major work, the *Canon of Medicine,* brought together medical traditions from a number of different cultures. Written originally in Arabic, this work was later translated into Latin and other languages; it became the most important book for all students of medicine within Islam and, in its Latin version, for medical students in Europe until the seventeenth century. In the *Canon,* Avicenna discusses the general principles of health and disease, the diseases of particular organs and those that affect the whole body, such as fever, and simple and compound drugs; ideas about reproduction and the treatment of reproductive ailments are found throughout the work.

At the time that physicians in the Islamic world were translating Greek works and developing their own theories of health and disease, medical treatment in Europe was largely in the hands of local healers. With the collapse of the Roman Empire in the West, the ability to read Greek declined and schools that taught medicine disappeared, and so learned medicine lagged far behind that in Islam; before the eleventh century, only two or three of Galen's works were available in Latin, whereas over one hundred were available in Arabic. This began to change in the tenth and eleventh centuries, when a few cities in Europe gradually developed first informal and then formal centers of medical training. The most prominent of these was at Salerno in southern Italy, where male and female medical practitioners received training first through apprenticeship and then in an organized medical school. Individuals associated with Salerno, such as the convert from Islam and later Benedictine monk Constantine the African (f. 1065–1085), began to translate medical works out of Arabic. These translations included writings by Galen and Hippocrates that had originally been written in Greek and those by Rhazes, Avicenna, and other Islamic physicians that were originally written in Arabic. Constantine often did not translate whole works, but combined the ideas of many authors—and his own—on particular subjects; reproduction is a key issue in his treatise *On Coitus* and his treatise *On Human Nature.* Gradually copies of all of Constantine's works spread throughout Europe and, combined with those of other translators and commentators, formed the program of study at the medical faculties that were beginning to be organized as part of the newly developing universities in such cities as Paris and Bologna.

The Galenic/Islamic tradition was one in which medical ideas were very closely linked to philosophy and to ideas about the natural world in general. Prime among these was the notion of the four bodily *humors,* four fluids—blood, phlegm, black bile, and yellow bile—contained in the body that influenced bodily health. Each individual was thought to have a characteristic temperament or *complexion,* determined by the balance of the four humors, in the same way that we might describe a person today as having a "positive outlook" or a "Type A" personality. These four humors corresponded to four qualities—hot, cold, wet, and dry—and to the four basic elements in the Aristotelian universe—earth, air, fire, and water. The organs were viewed primarily as channels for the humors, rather than as having only one specific function. Disease was primarily regarded as an imbalance of bodily humors, which could be diagnosed by taking a patient's pulse or examining his or her urine. Treatment was thus an attempt to bring the humors back into balance, which might be accomplished through diet or drugs—usually mixtures of herbal or mineral substances regarded as therapeutic—or through a direct attempt to rebalance the humors through emetics, purgatives, or bloodletting. The bodily humors were somewhat gender-related—women were regarded as tending toward the cold and wet, men toward the hot and dry—so that therapies were also gender-distinctive. The exact balance of humors was different for each individual, however, with the healthy body capable of maintaining this on its own. Treatment—whether diet, drugs, or bloodletting—was thus viewed as eliminating any obstacles to this natural balancing, rather than as directly changing the balance.

Blood was viewed as in some ways the dominant humor. According to Avicenna, phlegm was "imperfectly matured blood" that could be transformed into blood if heat were applied correctly. In his opinion, blood also carried phlegm, black bile, and yellow bile throughout the body, and it was these substances that were partially responsible for the different textures of body parts—the hardness of bones and the softness of the brain, for example. Though some commentators thought the source of semen was the brain, as both were soft and whitish, most saw semen—and milk—as transformed blood, gradually "cooked" until it was whitish. The agent in all of these transformations was heat, which was also important in many issues concerning reproduction. The sex of an infant, for example, was determined largely by the amount of heat present during intercourse and gestation; males resulted when there was the proper amount of heat, which caused their sexual organs to be pushed outside the body, and females when there was too little heat, which caused their sexual organs to remain internal. Men's greater heat continued throughout their lives, causing them to burn up their hair and go bald and to develop broader shoulders and bigger brains (because heat rises and causes things to expand).

Though medical theorists agreed about a great deal, there were also areas of sharp disagreement. In the area of reproduction, the sharpest disagreement was between the ideas of Aristotle and those of Galen and his followers regarding the roles of the mother and the father in conception. Aristotle held that the mother provided the matter out of which an infant was formed, and the father provided the "active principle," the force that brought this inert matter to life (although he did not provide any material part of the embryo); women were "passive" in reproduction, and their menstrual fluid was a deficient form of semen. Galen and his followers held that both the male and female produced seed, so that both contributed both materially and actively to the generation of the child. (The word *generation* was generally used in the ancient and medieval West to describe the process that we label *reproduction.*) Each sex produced both strong and weak seed, with strong seed the source of males and weak seed the source of females; the sex of a child depended on the balance of these two and the amount of heat present during generation.

Despite disagreements, the ideas of this body of medical literature spread throughout Europe, North Africa, and the Near East, and familiarity with this literature became the mark of a professional physician. In the Islamic world medical teaching was carried out largely in hospitals; in Europe, it was carried out at the new universities, where medicine became one of the standard areas of advanced study, along with law and theology. The influence of this Galenic/Islamic tradition did not stop with those who could read learned languages, however, for beginning in the fourteenth century in Europe translations into the vernacular languages and compilations of these works became available. (Translation is less of an issue in the Islamic world; because the Qur'an was revealed to Muhammad in Arabic, study of that language was even more central to all learning than study of Latin was in Europe.) Once the printing press was developed in the mid-fifteenth century, these vernacular medical works and the Latin translations were very frequently reprinted. It is difficult to gauge how often the treatments they recommend were actually applied, but the ideas they contain were shared by most of the population, from the highly learned to the illiterate.

Like the Western Galenic/Islamic tradition, the Chinese medical tradition is also linked closely with ideas about the natural and social world, but it is more dynamic than the western view, with a basis in forces rather than in matter or elements. As laid out in the *Huangdi Neijing*, the primordial underlying undifferentiated force was *qi*—a word that originally meant "breath"—which was conceptualized as flowing in the body along with blood to maintain life. This original *qi* was differentiated into two basic principles of operation, yin and yang; yin generally represents darkness, cold, wetness, night, passivity, the moon, contraction, and the female, while yang represents light, heat, the sun, activity, expansion, day, and the male. In the body, yin corresponds to the lower half and the right side, and yang to the upper half and the left side. These two are not completely dichotomous, however, for, to be complete, each yin must contain some yang, and vice versa.

Tensions created by the yin/yang polarity generated more complex processes, based on what are usually termed the Five Agents (*wu xing*): Wood, Fire, Earth, Metal, and Water. These sound somewhat like the basic Aristotelian elements, but they are understood more as forces, always changing and always affecting one another in specific relationships and a set sequence. Fire, for example, is seen as conquering Metal, but the process can be controlled by Water. These Five Agents are correlated with Five Organ Systems (*zang*) of the body, sites from which each of the Five Agents operates to initiate key processes in the body: Wood with Liver, Fire with Heart, Earth with Spleen, Metal with Lung, and Water with Kidney. (Both the Agents and the Organ Systems are generally capitalized to differentiate them from the normal usage of these words; thus the *zang* Heart includes the heart, but also other parts of what we would now label the circulatory system as well as the small intestine and the tongue.) The main system for reproduction in both men and women is Kidney, because of the various watery substances involved; according to the *Huangdi Neijing*, "at fourteen a girl's Kidney *qi* is flourishing . . . her menses flow regularly and she can bear young . . . at sixteen a boy's Kidney *qi* is abundant, and he comes into his reproductive capacities; his seminal essence overflows and drains; he can unite yin and yang and so beget young."[1]

In the healthy person, all of these correspondences would be in balance, just as in the healthy society and the healthy state, everything would be in balance. Illness was thus conceptualized as a disharmony in the equilibrium, or a blocking of the flow of activating energy caused by external agents such as infection or climate (classified as yang factors), internal dysfunctions (classified as yin factors), or a combination of the two. The task of the doctor was thus to determine the cause or causes of the illness and to bring the person back to health by redirecting the proper flow of energy through a variety of means, including herbal and mineral remedies, diet, and breathing exercises. Several of the early texts collected in the

1. Translated and quoted in Charlotte Furth, *A Flourishing Yin: Gender in China's Medical History, 960–1665*, (Berkeley: University of California Press, 1999), p. 45.

Huangdi Neijing mention bloodletting as a means to remove bad blood, and also to balance blood or *qi* and to stimulate their flow around the body. The movement of *qi* could also be influenced by moxabustion, the burning of powdered mugwort plants on the skin at specific points. Surgery was generally not recommended because it was too localized to be of much help.

By the first century B.C.E., the use of acupuncture (needles inserted into the skin, generally without causing any external blood flow) came to be a significant therapeutic technique. The origins of acupuncture are unclear, but it came to be integrated into yin/yang theory, which identified twelve cardinal tracts through which *qi* flowed through the limbs and an extra eight tracts along the head and trunk interlacing with these. Some of these are yang tracts and some of these are yin tracts, and acupuncture needles of various lengths and thicknesses are inserted at the hundreds of points around the body where these tracts cross and converge.

These tracts are sometimes called "channels," and in addition to the twelve cardinal tracts there are two additional channels, the Highway Channel and the Conception Channel, which in women combine with Kidney to regulate reproductive and gestational functions. Both blood (*xue*) and *qi* are involved in reproduction, as is Essence (*jing*), which came to be conceptualized as the male contribution to conception. Materially Essence was identified with semen, but it was also seen as a life-giving vitality and linked to cosmological processes. The female contribution was Blood, which encompasses not simply the blood that nourishes the fetus but also breast milk and other fluids.

The system of correspondences fit very well with Confucian ideology about the importance of balance, structure, and hierarchy, and this made these medical ideas particularly powerful during the Han dynasty and then later during the Song Neo-Confucian period. They did not completely overturn earlier ideas about demonic causes of illness, however, nor did they prevent other medical traditions from developing, such as Taoist techniques designed to increase longevity or sexual potency. There were also significant differences of opinion within the tradition, just as there were in the West between Galenists and Aristotelians. Liu Wan-su (1110–1200), for example, viewed fire and heat as the cause of many illnesses, for they led to excessive amounts of yang influences in the body; he recommended treatments involving drugs and acupuncture that would cool the body and replenish yin. By contrast, Li Gao (1180–1251) thought that internal heat centered in the Stomach and the Spleen was always in danger of diminishing, so that treatments should supply the body with substances that generated heat and aided digestion. Such differences of opinion, plus the complexity of the tradition itself, meant that medical personnel in China had a wide range of diagnostic and treatment options available and could modify treatment based on the needs or desires of the individual patient.

The training of medical personnel in China, as in Islamic areas and medieval Europe, occurred by a variety of means, including informal oral instruction in practical techniques, apprenticeship to a physician, and study at a medical academy. Beginning in the Han dynasty (206 B.C.E.–220 C.E.), the highest-status level of training took place at schools sponsored by the emperor that prepared men to take state examinations in medicine and other subjects. Official physicians were appointed to fill the needs of the royal palace and also often of the army and other branches of the administration. In the Song dynasty (960–1279), the state sponsored an expansion of formal medical education based on approved medical classics, made possible by the new technology of printing. Scholars who were not themselves physicians often took great interest in medicine and wrote works of medical theory; these were often framed as demonstrations of the filial piety required by Confucianism, in which a dutiful son considered ways in which he could prolong the lives or alleviate the sufferings of his aged parents. Included in this expanded medical education was training in *fuke,* the branch of medicine devoted to women's disorders and illnesses (what we would term gynecology). *Fuke* was regarded as socially useful, as were considerations of problems associated with the male role in procreation, for both helped families secure descendants—who would then honor their ancestors. There were thus large numbers of treatises on both subjects written by physician-scholars, though the training of midwives who handled normal births continued to be carried out orally.

THE METHOD

One of the greatest dangers in exploring the history of science or medicine is viewing people who lived in earlier centuries as stupid or ignorant. How, we ask, could they have held such idiotic ideas? Couldn't they see what was in front of them? How could they claim to see what wasn't in front of them? Many of the earliest historians of science, and even more the earliest historians of medicine, who were often retired physicians, themselves gave in to this, for they viewed the story of science and medicine in a linear fashion, as constant advance from the ignorance of the past to the great knowledge of the present. Increasingly, however, historians of science point out that in every era, including our own, scientific knowledge is shaped by people's preexisting ideas; these ideas allow even the most "objective" scientists to see things only in certain ways. (This can perhaps best be seen in contemporary subatomic physics, where attempts are now being made to trace the paths of types of particles whose existence was not known about until very recently, or in the discussions among astrophysicists and astronomers about the presence of "dark matter." Now that dark matter or the neutrino is a concept, scientists begin to see it and try to trace its effects.)

Thus it is important that, as you read and look at the sources for this chapter, you do not view them solely from the vantage point of medicine in the twenty-first century, but first try to understand the view of the body and reproductive processes that they contain; this will also help you make comparisons among them. Many of the medical works from which these sources come are extremely long, and some are still available in their entirety only in Latin or Arabic or Chinese. As you read them, it might be best to make a list of the key ideas and topics that emerge. These might include such topics as basic anatomy and physiology, sexual intercourse, conception, sexual differences, fetal development, difficulties in conception and birth, and the relations between general health and reproduction. Not every topic will be covered by every author, but through this list you can begin to discern key ideas and prepare to make comparisons. At the same time, it will be useful if you also keep a list of proposed remedies for problems, for this will help you answer the second main question and also give you further clues to the general understanding of reproductive processes in this period.

Source 1 includes selections from the *Canon* of Avicenna, written in Arabic at the beginning of the eleventh century and translated into Latin by Gerard of Cremona, who translated many medical and scientific works, during the second half of the twelfth century. How does Avicenna compare the male and female reproductive organs? What happens at the moment of conception? How is the embryo formed in the uterus?

Source 2 is a short treatise about impotence, written by Constantine the African in the late eleventh century as part of his longer work *Pantechne.* It was frequently copied in later medical works, usually without naming him as the author (a very common practice). What sort of spells does Constantine view as interfering with intercourse? What remedies does he propose?

Source 3 is an excerpt from the treatise *The Diseases of Women,* attributed to Trota or Trotula of Salerno, a woman medical practitioner active in Salerno in the eleventh century. Trotula is a very mysterious figure whose work and even existence have been the source of great debate for centuries. Many treatises that she did not write, including the one excerpted here, were attributed to her, but it has now been proved conclusively that she did write some works and was a real person. Most of the medical writers and practitioners of medieval Europe, however, regarded Trotula as an important authority and cited her along with male authors when they were attempting to demonstrate the validity of a particular idea. How does Trotula characterize the differences between men and women? Does she adopt an Aristotelian or a Galenic view about the role of the two sexes in reproduction? Why do women menstruate? Is menstruation harmful or beneficial? What are some of the causes of failure to conceive? What are the remedies for these? What does the author suggest doing to encourage the birth of a boy? Why do you think there is no corresponding advice to encourage the birth of a girl? How does a fetus develop, and how can a woman tell if it is a boy or a girl?

Source 4 is an excerpt from *Ethical Conduct* by Moses Maimonides (1135–1204), a Jewish rabbi, philosopher, and physician. Maimonides was born in Cordoba, Spain, but emigrated to Egypt and became the chief physician at the court of the sultan Saladin in Cairo. He was reputed to have been invited to become the physician for Richard the Lionhearted in England, but he never left Egypt. He wrote numerous religious and philosophical works in Hebrew, including a massive commentary on the Torah, and at least ten medical works in Arabic, many of which were later translated into other languages. What does Maimonides see as important to general health? How does this relate to his views about sexual intercourse?

The works we have looked at so far, though they combine learned and popular medicine and were often eventually translated, were directed specifically to a learned—and therefore male—audience. Source 5 is somewhat different, an excerpt from one of the earliest printed midwives' manuals in Europe, the *Rosegarden for Midwives and Pregnant Women* written in German by Eucharius Rösslin, a pharmacist and physician in Frankfurt, and printed for the first time in Strasbourg in 1513; it was later translated—often with a different title—into Latin, French, Czech, Polish, Spanish, Dutch, and English. By the later sixteenth century, it was mentioned in city midwifery ordinances as recommended reading. Rösslin draws on a huge range of Greek and Arabic authorities; these, rather than any hands-on experience, form the basis of his advice, though he also includes remedies that come from popular traditions. The *Rosegarden* includes sections on diet and conduct for pregnant women, specific instructions for midwives during normal and difficult births, and instructions for care of newborns. It also includes sections dealing with rather grim topics, such as how to deliver a child that has died in the uterus. The section included here is that dealing with the period just before and during a birth. As you read this, note what advice Rösslin gives to the mother and to the midwife. How does this fit with the more general ideas about health and bodily processes that you have encountered so far? What is the midwife's role in a normal birth procedure?

The next four sources take us from the Western to the Chinese tradition. Source 6 is an extract from the chapter titled "General Survey of the Origins of the Viscera and Bowels" from the treatise *Tu shu bian,* written in the sixteenth century by the physician Zhang Huang. How does Zhang Huang describe the roles of the male and female in generation? How does the fetus develop in the uterus? How does this development relate to more general theories of the body, such as yin/yang and the five Organ Systems?

Sources 7 and 8 are from earlier works detailing the opinions and actions of scholar-doctors. Source 7 is from a treatise written around 1200 titled *How a Confucian Scholar Serves His Parents.* It was ascribed to the medical theoretician Zhang Congzheng (1156–1228), but it was actually written by one of his students and describes the activities of Zhang Congzheng (called Dairen in the text). Source 8 is from *Yishuo (A Discussion of Medicine),* written in 1224 by Zhang Gao, describing the activities of Zhu Xinzhong (1097–1167), better known as Zhu Yi, a famous official and Confucian scholar of the Song era, and his associates, the physicians Li Jidao and Pang Anchang. What are the problems in these cases? What sorts of remedies have been tried? What treatments do the physicians undertake? How does the telling of these stories reinforce the ideal of the scholar-physician developing in China during this period?

Source 9 comes from *Veracious Explanation of the Blessing of Heirs* (1591), one of the works of a later scholar-doctor, Yuan Huang, whose family had practiced medicine for four generations. Yuan Huang combines many different traditions in his book—Confucian, Buddhist, and Taoist—which was itself inspired by his own quest for a son. His describes the techniques to best assure reproduction as ones of "inner alchemy," guiding the body toward greater longevity and fertility, with attention to Essence in men, Blood in women, and *qi* in both sexes. In the early seventeenth century, Yuan Huang's work became part of the main compendium of medical knowledge regarding women, *To Benefit Yin,* which was frequently reprinted. In this selection, what advice does Yuan Huang give to men to increase their Essence? What does he say is useless? What should a husband pay attention to in his wife to assure conception? To assure the conception of a boy? What determines whether the child will be a boy or a girl?

Medical ideas were largely transmitted through words during this period, but treatises were occasionally illustrated, or issues surrounding reproduction were portrayed visually elsewhere. Sources 10 through 12 are three illustrations of births: Source 10 is a caesarean section shown in a fourteenth-century manuscript of the Arabic writer al-Biruni's *Chronology of Ancient Nations,* Source 11 is a sixteenth-century engraving of a birth scene that was frequently used to illustrate works on women's health, and Source 12 is a fourteenth-century wall painting of a birth scene, from the Baoning temple in Shaanzi province in China. In Source 10, male physicians attend directly to the patient, while in Sources 11 and 12 the mothers are surrounded by women; why do you think this might be so? The male scholar-physician in Source 12 sits calmly on the right, while the men in the background of Source 11 appear to be casting a horoscope; why do you think the artists chose to portray the men in the scene in these ways? What other similarities and differences do you see in the three birth scenes?

THE EVIDENCE

Source 1 from Avicenna, Canon, *tr. Gerard of Cremona, translated and reprinted in Danielle Jacquart and Claude Thomasset,* Sexuality and Medicine in the Middle Ages, *tr. Matthew Adamson (Cambridge, Polity Press, 1988), pp. 36, 55, 63, 77.*

1. From Avicenna, *The Canon of Medicine,* 11th century

I say that the instrument of reproduction in the woman is the womb (*matrix*) and that it was created similar to the instrument of reproduction in the man, that is to say the penis and what goes with it. However, one of these instruments is complete and stretches outwards, whereas the other is smaller and held on the inside, to some extent constituting the opposite of the male instrument. The covering of the womb is like the scrotum, the cervix [= vagina] like the penis. There are two testicles in women as in men, but in men they are larger, turned outwards and tend to be spherical in shape; in women they are small, of a rather flattened roundness, and they are located on the inside, in the vulva. . . .

The sublime God created the testicles to be, as you know, the principal members which engender sperm from the moisture that is brought to them in the veins; this moisture is like the residue of the food that has reached the fourth stage in the whole body.[2] It is a better-digested and subtler blood. . . .

As soon as the two seeds have been mixed, the ebullition[3] of which we have spoken takes place and the swollen part and the first membrane are created; then all the sperm is suspended from the horn-shaped protuberances,[4] and it there finds its nourishment as long as it is still sperm, until it starts to draw its nourishment from the menstrual blood and from the cavities [the openings of the veins] to which the membrane which has been formed is attached. According to Galen, this membrane is like a protective coating left behind by the sperm of the female when it flows towards the place where the male's sperm also flows, and if it does not join with the sperm of the male at the very moment it is shed, it nonetheless mixes with it during intercourse. . . .

After that, the blood which is voided by the woman at the time of menses is used for nourishment. Part is transformed in accordance with its similarity to the spermatic substance: it forms the parts of the body that have come from the sperm, and it increases the sperm by nourishing it. Another part does not act as nourishment but, through coagulation, is used to fill the empty spaces of the

2. Food was thought to be digested in stages within the body.

3. **ebullition:** the process of bubbling up.

4. The uterus was thought to have "horns," or growths sticking out on each side, which were shown in anatomical illustrations into the seventeenth century; these horns were thought to contain blood vessels.

principal parts of the body, and makes flesh and fat. A last part consists of superfluous matter and is no good for either of the above-mentioned purposes: it stays put until childbirth, when nature expels it as being superfluous.

Source 2 from Henry E. Sigerist, Essays in Biology *(Berkeley: University of California Press, pp. 541–546. Reprinted in Edward Grant,* A Source Book in Medieval Science *(Cambridge: Harvard University Press, 1974), pp. 768–769.*

2. Constantine the African's Treatise on Impotence, 11th century

A short treatise about the people who, impeded by spells, are unable to have intercourse with their wives.

There are people who, impeded by diabolical spells, are unable to have intercourse with their wives. We do not want to deprive our book of their applause, for the remedy, if I am not wrong, is most sacred.

Now, if this should happen to somebody, he must set his hope in the Lord and He will be merciful. Since, however, there are many kinds of spells, it is necessary that we discuss them. Some spells are made of animated substances such as the testicles of a cock. If they are put under the bed with blood of the cock, they bring it about that the people lying on the bed cannot have intercourse. Some are made of letters written with the blood of a bat. Some are made of inanimate substances, for instance if a nut or an acorn is divided in two, and one half is put on one side, the other on the other side, of the road along which the bride and bridegroom must proceed.

There are others also which are made from beans which are not softened with hot water nor cooked on the fire. This spell is very bad if four such beans are placed on the roof or on the road or over or under the door.

There are others also which are of metal, such as those that are of iron or lead, for instance, the iron ones made of the needle with which the dead men or women have been sewn. And because these spells are devilish and are particularly in women, they are sometimes cured by divine, sometimes by human measures.

If therefore bridegroom and bride are disturbed by the above-mentioned spells, it is better to talk about them than to keep silent, for if the victims are not succored they are separated and thus disgraced, and doing this evil they seem to sin not only against their relatives but also against the Holy Ghost.

If we wish to extirpate the spell properly, we must look out: if the above-mentioned spell is under the bed, it must be removed. But if the author of this spell removes it in daytime and puts it back at night, or vice versa, then bridegroom and bride must acquire another house and lie down there.

If the spell is made of letters, which is recognized by the fact that bridegroom and bride do not love each other, one must search above and under the threshold of the door, and if something is found it must be taken to the bishop or priest. If not, one must do what is indicated below.

If a nut or an acorn are the cause of this spell, the woman shall take a nut or an acorn and divide it in two. And with one half the man shall proceed on one side of the road and deposit it there; the woman, however, shall put the other half on the other side of the road. Thereupon bridegroom and bride shall take both parts of the nut without having removed the shell. And then the nut shall thus be made whole again and shall be kept for seven days. Having done this they shall have intercourse.

If, however, it happens on account of beans, it can be cured with divine rather than human means. If it is on account of the needles for the dead, the spells must be sought either in the pillow or in the mattress. If they are not found, the victims shall lie together in another house.

Bile of a male dog purifies the house and brings it about that no evil remedy be brought to the house.

Sprinkle the walls of the house with dog's blood, and it will be liberated from every spell. . . .

If, however, on account of impending sins, the above-mentioned measures did not help at all, they shall go to a priest or the bishop. And if the bishop has permitted it and no remedy is found, after having confessed to the bishop or an ordained priest they shall take Holy Communion on the day of the Holy Resurrection or Ascension in Whitsuntide. Having received the Body and Blood of the Lord, bridegroom and bride shall give each other the kiss of peace.

And after they have received the benediction of the bishop or priest, the bishop or priest shall give this verse of the prophet written on paper: The voice of the Lord is upon the waters: the great Lord is upon many waters [Psalms 28:3]. Thereafter they shall go home and shall abstain from intercourse for three days and three nights. Then they shall perform it, and thus all diabolical power is destroyed.

The little treatise on spells has come to an end. Thanks be to God. Amen.

Source 3 from Trotula of Salerno, The Diseases of Women, *translated by Elizabeth Mason-Hohl, M.D. (Los Angeles: Ward Ritchie Press, 1940), pp. 1–3, 16–25. Reprinted in Edward Grant,* A Source Book in Medieval Science *(Cambridge: Harvard University Press, 1974), pp. 761–763, 764–766.*

3. From Pseudo–Trotula of Salerno, *The Diseases of Women*, 12th century

PROLOGUE

Since God, the author of the universe, in the first establishment of the world, distinguished the individual natures of things each according to its own kind, He differentiated the human race above the other creatures by means of extraordinary dignity. To it, beyond the condition of other animals, He gave freedom of reason and of intellect. Moreover, desiring its generation to subsist perpetually, He created it male and female in different sexes that by means of their fertile propagation future offspring may never cease to come forth. Blending their embraces with a pleasing mixture, He made the nature of the male hot and dry and that of the female cold and wet so that the excess of each other's embrace might be restrained by the mutual opposition of contrary qualities. The man's constitution being hot and dry might assuage the woman's coldness and wetness and on the contrary her nature being cold and wet might soothe his hot and dry embrace. Likewise that the male having the stronger quality might pour seed into the woman as into a field and the woman endowed with a weaker quality, subject as it were to the function of the man, might naturally take unto her bosom the poured out seed. Since then women are by nature weaker than men it is reasonable that sicknesses more often abound in them especially around the organs involved in the work of nature. Since these organs happen to be in a retired location, women on account of modesty and the fragility and delicacy of the state of these parts dare not reveal the difficulties of their sicknesses to a male doctor. Wherefore I, pitying their misfortunes and at the instigation of a certain matron, began to study carefully the sicknesses which most frequently trouble the female sex. Since in women not so much heat abounds that it suffices to use up the moistures which daily collect in them, their weaknesses cannot endure so much exertion as to be able to put forth that moisture to the outside air as in the case of men. Nature herself, on account of this deficiency of heat, has assigned for them a certain specific purgation namely the menses, commonly called flowers. For just as trees do not produce fruit without flowers so women without menses are deprived of the function of conception. This purgation occurs in women just as 'pollutio'[5] occurs in

5. **pollutio:** nocturnal emissions, or "wet dreams."

men. . . . If such purgations have been of normal time and regularity, Nature sufficiently unloads women of superfluous moisture. If the menstruation has taken place too copiously various sicknesses arise from it. . . . Sometimes the periods fail because of excessive grief or anger or excitement or fear. If they have ceased for a long time there is a suspicion of serious future illness. Often the urine is changed into a red color or into a color like the washings from fresh meat; sometimes the woman's appearance is changed into a gray or leaden color, or into the color of grass. . . .

CHAPTER 11
ON THE HINDRANCES TO CONCEPTION AND OF THE THINGS WHICH MAKE FOR IMPREGNATION

Certain women are useless for conceiving either because they are too thin and lean or because they are too fat. In these latter the flesh folded around the opening of the womb binds it and does not permit the seed of the man to enter it. Some have a womb so soft and slippery that the seed having been received cannot be retained in it. Sometimes this happens through a defect of the male who has seed so thin that when it is poured into the vagina it slips out because of its own liquidness. Some men also have testicles cold and dry; these men rarely or never beget, because their seed is useless for procreation. It is evident therefore that conception is hindered as often by a defect of the man as of the woman. If it is by a defect of the woman it happens either from excessive warmth or from excessive moistures of the womb. Sometimes on account of its natural softness the womb cannot retain the seed injected into it, and often because of its excessive moisture it suffocates the seed. Often because of its excessive heat the womb burns the seed up and she cannot conceive. . . .

If conception be hindered because of a defect of the male it would be from a lack of force impelling the sperm, a defect of the organ, or a defect of heat. If it be from a defect of heat, the sign is that he is not eager for copulation. Hence he ought to anoint his loins with arrogon or take seed of colewort and euphorbia and reduce them to a fine powder. Then mix them with the oils of fleabane[6] and of weasel and with this anoint his loins. If it happens through a defect of the spirit the sign will be that he has desire but the penis is not erected. We aid him with an ointment that generates spirit. . . .

If the woman or the man be sterile you will ascertain it by this method: take two jars and into each put bran. Into one of them put the urine of the man and into the other put the urine of the woman and let the jars be left for nine or ten days. If the barrenness be from a defect of the woman you will find many worms and the bran foul in her jar. On the other hand you will have similar evidence from the other urine if the barrenness be through a defect of the man. But if you have observed such signs in neither urine neither will be the cause of the

6. **arrogon, colewort, euphorbia,** and **fleabane:** all plants.

barrenness and it is possible to help them to conceive by the use of medicines. If they wish to have a male child let the man take the womb and vulva of a hare and have it dried and pulverized; blend it with wine and let him drink it. Let the woman do the same with the testicles of the hare and let her be with her husband at the end of her menstrual period and she will conceive a male. . . .

CHAPTER 12
ON THE FORMATION OF THE SEED WHEN CONCEIVED

In the first month occurs a small clot of blood. In the second occurs the formation of the blood and of the body; in the third the nails and hair are produced. In the fourth motion and therefore women are nauseated. In the fifth the foetus receives the likeness of father or mother. In the sixth, the binding together of the sinews. In the seventh, the bones and sinews are strengthened; in the eighth nature helps and the child puts on flesh. In the ninth, it proceeds from darkness into light. . . .

CHAPTER 14
ON SIGNS OF PREGNANCY

For knowing whether a woman is carrying a male or female child take water from a spring and let the woman draw out two or three drops of blood or of milk from the right breast. Let them be poured into the water and if they seek the bottom she is bearing a male; if they float on top she is bearing a female. Hippocrates said that the woman who is bearing a male is well colored and has the right breast larger; if she is pale she is bearing a female and has the left breast larger.

Source 4 from Jacob Minkin, The Teachings of Maimonides *(Northvale, N.J.: Jason Aronson, 1987), pp. 384, 386–387.*

4. From Moses Maimonides, *Ethical Conduct,* ca. 1190s

Another great principle of hygiene, physicians say, is as follows: As long as a person takes active exercise, works hard, does not overeat and keeps his bowels open, he will be free from disease and will increase in vigor, even though the food he eats is coarse. . . .

Whosoever indulges in sexual dissipation becomes prematurely aged; his strength fails; his eyes become dim; a foul odor proceeds from his mouth and armpits; the hair of his head, eye-brows and eye-lashes drop out; the hair of his beard, armpits and legs grow abnormally; his teeth fall out; and besides these, he becomes subject to numerous other diseases. Medical authorities have stated that for each one who dies of other maladies, a thousand are the victims of sexual excess. A man should, therefore, be careful in this regard if he wishes to lead a happy life. He should only cohabit when he finds himself in good health and vigor, experiences involuntary erections which persist after he has diverted his mind to other things, is conscious of a heaviness from the loins downwards as if the spermatic cords were being drawn and his flesh is hot. Such a condition calls for cohabitation which then is conducive to health. One should not cohabit when sated with food, nor when one is hungry, but only after a meal has been digested. Before and after coition, attention should be paid to the excretory functions.

Source 5 from Caroline Gisela March-Long, "Early Modern German Obstetrical Manuals: Das Frawenbüchlein *(c. 1495) and* Der Rosengarten *(1513)," M.A. thesis, Duke University, 1993, pp. 125, 127–129.*

5. From Eucharius Rösslin, *Rosegarden for Midwives and Pregnant Women,* 1513

When the pregnant woman nears delivery, she should drink mature wine mixed with water. She should also have a regimen of food and drink, a regimen a month before birth which makes one moist but not too fat, and one should avoid what makes one dry, constipated, weighs down, presses or constricts. When the woman is even nearer to delivery, when she still has twelve or fourteen days and feels some pain and pressure, she should sit in a bath up to her navel every day, sometimes more often, but not too long (so that she doesn't get weak). She should move around with easy work and movements, walking and standing more than she did before. Such things help the fetus come into position.

Another regimen for the time of delivery which the woman should need if she feels pressure, pain and some moistness begins to show and flow out of the vagina. This regimen takes place in two ways. The first is that one brings on a quick descent and delivery. The other way to lessen complications, labour pains, and pain is for her to sit down for an hour and then stand up and climb up and down the stairs shouting loudly. The woman should force out and hold her breath (breathe heavily) so that she puts pressure on her intestines and bears down. ITEM: The woman should also drink those medicines that are written about afterwards for they force the child downward into delivery position. When she feels the uterus dilate and plenty of fluid flow to her genitals (i.e., water breaks), she should lie on her back, but not completely lying down or standing. It should be a middle position between lying and standing. She should tilt her head more towards the back than the front. In southern German and in Italian/French areas, the midwives have special chairs for delivery. They are not high, but hollowed out with an opening in the inside. The chair should be prepared so that the woman can lean on her back. One should fill and cover the back of the same chair with cloth and when it is time, the midwife should lift the cloth and turn them first to the right and then to the left side. The midwife should sit in front of her and pay careful attention to the child's movement in the womb. The midwife should guide and control her arms and legs with her hands which are coated with white-lily or almond oil or the like. And with her hands in the same way, the midwife should also gently grasp the mother, as she well knows. The midwife should also instruct, guide, and teach the mother, and strengthen her with food and drink. She should urge the woman on to work with soft, kind words so that she begins to breathe deeply. One should dry her stomach off gently above the navel and hips. The midwife should comfort the woman by predicting a successful birth of a baby boy. And if the woman is fat, she should not sit, rather lie on her body and lay her forehead on the ground and pull her knees up underneath so that the womb has pressure applied to it. Afterwards, she should anoint her internally with white-lily oil and, if necessary, the midwife should open the woman's cervix with her hands and afterwards, the woman will deliver quickly.

Source 6 from Chang Huang, T'u shu pien, *translated in Paul U. Unschuld,* Introductory Readings in Classical Chinese Medicine *(Dordrecht: Kluwer, 1988), p. 57.*

6. From Zhang Huang, *Tu shu bian,* 16th century

Man has life because he is endowed with the yin and yang (influences) of heaven and earth. When the father's semen and the mother's blood contact each other, they unite and congeal to become the fetus in the womb. If it takes the way of heaven, a male is generated; if it takes the way of the earth, a female is generated. In the beginning, (the children are) carried on the back and need a swaddling cloth; (life continues to the time when they wear) tufts of hair on their heads and when they shed their milk teeth, until they become boys and (adults) in their strongest age. How could anybody speak (of this process) lightheartedly! The (state of) pregnancy of the first month is called "white dew". The embryo of the second month is compared to peach blossoms. When, in the third month, the right kidney grows first, (the child) will be a male; if the left kidney grows first, it will be a girl. Next, the kidneys generate the spleen, the spleen generates the liver, the liver generates the lung, the lung generates the heart, because each (viscus) generates (the viscus) by which itself can be overcome. The kidneys belong to (the phase of) water. Hence the five viscera are yin. Next, the heart generates the small intestine, the small intestine generates the large intestine, the large intestine generates the gallbladder, the gallbladder generates the stomach, the stomach generates the bladder, and the bladder generates the triple burner, because each (bowel) generates (the bowel) that it can overcome. The small intestine belongs to (the phase of) fire; hence the six bowels are yang. Next, the triple burner generates the eight (single conduit) vessels, the eight (single conduit) vessels generate the twelve conduits, the twelve conduits generate the twelve network (vessels), the twelve network (vessels) generate the one hundred eighty linking network (vessels), the linking network (vessels) generate the one hundred eighty connecting network (vessels), the connecting network (vessels) generate the thirty-four thousand tertiary network (vessels), the tertiary network (vessels) generate the three hundred sixty-five bone-sections, the bone-sections generate the three hundred sixty-five large insertion points (for the needles), the large insertion points generate the eighty-four thousand pores with hair; finally, the body with all its ears, eyes, mouth, four limbs and hundreds of bones is completed. When it is (commonly) said that during the fourth month the figure (of the human body) is prepared, that during the fifth month sinews and bones are generated, and that during the sixth month the hair on the head grows, this refers exactly to this (process outlined above). During the seventh month, then, the *hun*-soul arrives and (the fetus) is able to move its left hand. During the eighth month the *p'o*-soul arrives and (the fetus) is able to move its right hand. During the ninth month the body (of the fetus) turns over three times. After ten months are full, mother and child separate. Those children who exceed this (number of) months will become rich and of noble status; those who are born short of (this number of) months will be poor and needy.

Source 7 from Chang Ts'ung-cheng, How a Confucian Scholar Serves His Parents, *translated in Paul U. Unschuld,* Medicine in China: A History of Ideas *(Berkeley: University of California Press, 1985), pp. 323–324.*

7. From Zhang Congzheng, *How a Confucian Scholar Serves His Parents,* ca. 1200

A thirty-four-year-old woman dreamt at night of having sexual intercourse with demons and spirits. She lived in fear of strange things, and the hall of the spirits and the palaces of the departed appeared to her in visions; she also saw boat paddles and bridge beams. All of this had continued for some fifteen years, and during the entire period she had never once been with a child. She sought help in the prayers of shamans and supplications of sorcerers—there was nobody to whom she had not turned already. The wounds where needles had pierced her muscles and where her flesh had been cauterized numbered in the tens of thousands. She grew increasingly yellow and emaciated, she developed hot spells, and refused to drink. Her abdomen grew full and her feet were swollen. She herself had already placed her destiny into the hands of heaven. One day she sought aid for her suffering from Tai-jen [Dairen]. Tai-jen spoke: "An excess of yang fire manifests itself in the upper [part of the body], an excess of yin fire in the lower [part of the body]. Demons and spirits are yin forces; the hall of the spirits is a yin place. Boat paddles and bridge beams are used in the water. The [movement in the] vessels at the 'inch[-openings]' of both hands is deep and subdued. All this reveals that the chest is filled with phlegm." After three repetitions of vomiting, purgation, and sweating, all of the woman's dreams disappeared in fewer than ten days. After one month she was already pregnant. Tai-jen spoke: "I have restored life to a woman and enabled her to become pregnant. This technique cannot be wrong!"

Source 8 from Chang Kao, I-shuo, *translated in Paul U. Unschuld,* Introductory Readings in Classical Chinese Medicine *(Dordrecht: Kluwer, 1988), p. 351.*

8. From Zhang Gao, *Yi Shuo* *(A Discussion of Medicine)*, 1224

Chu-Hsin-chung's [Zhu Xinchong's] grandfather lived in the city of Tung. At one time, a pregnant woman among his relatives was about to deliver. After seven days the child had still not come down. Cakes filled with drugs, amulets dissolved in water, everything was used on her. Finally she awaited only her death. Coincidentally, the renowned physician Li Chi-tao [Li Jidao] resided at Mr. Chu's [Zhu's] (home), and Chu took him to the home of that woman. Li took a look at her and said: No drug could be of use here, only needling (may bring help). My own skills have not yet reached (the level needed) in this case; I do not dare to set my hand to her. Hence he went back again, and it happened that Chi-tao's [Jidao's] teacher P'ang An-ch'ang [Pang Anchang] just passed by the gate, and (Li and P'ang) together went to see Chu. Chu informed (P'ang) of what had happened, and said (to him): "Her family would never dare to bother you, Sir! Still, human life is most important. Sir, could not you feel pity with her, and proceed to her immediately in order to save her?" An-ch'ang promised (to do so), and joined the others to proceed (to the patient). As soon as he saw the pregnant (woman) he said: She need not die! Then An-ch'ang asked one of the family to warm the (patient's) waist and abdomen with hot water, and he patted her upper and lower (waist and abdomen) with his hands. The pregnant (woman) felt a slight pain around her intestines and stomach, and amidst her moaning and groaning she gave birth to a male child. Mother and child were both well. Her family was both startled and happy. They expressed their gratitude, and revered (P'ang) as if he were a spirit. Nobody knew how he had done this. An-ch'ang said: The child had left the womb already when one of its hands inadvertently grasped the mother's intestines and stomach. Hence it could not come further down. Consequently, even though she was given drugs, this was of no use. Just now, I pushed her intestines aside and felt for the child's hand. Then I needled its tiger mouth, whereupon the child felt some pain and drew its hand in, and was born immediately. There was no other technique involved. To test (his words) he asked the child to be brought, and examined its right hand. The tiger mouth (location) had a mark resulting from a needle. (P'ang An-ch'ang's skills) were as miraculous as this.

Source 9 from Yuan Huang, Qi si zhenquan (Veracious Explanation of the Blessing of Heirs), *12–13, 18–20, quoted and translated in Charlotte Furth,* A Flourishing Yin: Gender in China's Medical History, 960–1665 *(Berkeley: University of California Press, 1999), pp. 202, 209, 212.*

9. From Yuan Huang, *Veracious Explanation of the Blessing of Heirs,* 1591

Master Yuan Liaofan [Yuan Huang] says, "The Way of gathering Essence [reabsorbing semen] is: one, reduce desire; two, avoid overexertion; three, restrain anger; four, abstain from wine; five, moderate diet. Nowadays those who talk of 'nourishing life' often speak of 'gathering yin to replenish yang,' and of prolonged [sexual] combat without emission. This is a great mistake. The Kidneys are the storehouse of Essence, and when males and females engage in the sex act they must disturb Kidney function. When Kidneys are activated, Essence and Blood follow and flow out. Even if one emits nothing externally, Essence has already left the palace. Before one has managed to curb it, even as one's member softens a few drops of true Essence may leak out. This is [a common] experience. When the fire is blazing, who can restore the firewood? . . .

. . . Living creatures all have a mating season. . . . The classics of inner alchemy [*dan jing*] teach that each month there is one hour of one day, in keeping with the rhythm of the menstrual cycle, when a woman will have a fertile period. In that hour, her *qi* will be steaming and hot. When she is swooning and longing, unable to control her desire, the moment is at hand. At this time one may reverse course and hold [semen] to make an immortal embryo, or let flow and release it to make a fetus. . . . When her desire is intense, within the womb something like a budding lotus flower . . . protrudes into the vagina. A wife will feel it when she washes herself below, but, ashamed, she is unwilling to speak. If the man can privately advise her beforehand, and have her speak of it herself, he will straightaway hit the mark. . . .

. . . To speak of the male leading is not about [his] youth or age, strength or weakness, health or sickness, or whether ejaculation is easy or difficult. If at the time of amorous arousal "the hundred pulses arrive in unison" [*bai mai qi dao*] . . . one can conceive a child. . . .

. . . When a young man 'rides' a woman, in the beginning he feels an intensity and thirst for his goal; after ejaculation his whole body is joyful and at ease. This is what is called 'one hundred pulses arrive in unison' to conceive a child. . . .

. . . The woman's Blood is able to complete and consolidate it because her "hundred pulses gather together" [*bai mai heju*]. Compared with the male's Essence [Blood] is necessarily less strong. . . .

. . . As for the sex of the child, it's not a matter of whether Essence or Blood arrives first, or of the day of the woman's cycle, or of whether intercourse is before or after midnight, nor is it a matter of a strong woman mating with a weaker man, or vice versa. Only the difference between their two climaxes can determine victory or defeat. Thus if Essence in attaining climax has the wherewithal to defeat Blood, the child will be male; if Blood in attaining climax has the wherewithal to defeat Essence, the child will be female.

Source 10: University of Edinburgh Library, Oriental MS 161.

10. Caesarean Section, 14th-century Arabic Manuscript

Source 11 from Albertus Magnus, Daraus man alle Heimlichkeit des weiblichen Geschlechts erkennen kann *(reprint Frankfurt, 1977), p. 7.*

11. Birth Scene from Pseudo–Albertus Magnus, *On the Secrets of Women,* 16th-century German Illustration

Source 12 reproduced from the Baoning si Ming dai shui lu hua *(Ming Dynasty Wall Paintings of the Baoning Temple): Photo: Cultural Relics Publishing House, Beijng.*

12. Chinese Wall Painting Portraying a Stillbirth, 14th century

QUESTIONS TO CONSIDER

If you have been making lists of the ideas and treatments presented, you now have what may appear to be a great amount of disparate material, and it is time to pull this together and make comparisons. Turn first to the issues of anatomy and physiology. How does Avicenna (Source 1) describe the differences between the male and female reproductive organs and role in intercourse? How does pseudo-Trotula (Source 3) describe these? To what do they ascribe these differences? Do they see the reproductive organs in women and men as anatomically similar or completely distinct? How do the authors relate the process of menstruation to sexual difference? How do they explain why there is no similar process in men? How do they value anatomical and physiological differences—in other words, which is superior, male or female? In the medieval West the right/left dichotomy was a very strong intellectual concept, with right being seen as good and left as bad. (This is reflected in the word *sinister,* which comes from the Latin word for "left.") How does this dichotomy relate to that of male/female in matters of reproduction? Yuan Huang (Source 9) also describes gender differences in intercourse and conception. How are his ideas different from those of Avicenna and pseudo-Trotula?

Now look at issues of impediments to conception, discussed by Constantine the African (Source 2), pseudo-Trotula (Source 3), and Zhang Congzheng (Source 7). What can make men impotent or women infertile, in their opinions? What sorts of treatments could overcome these hindrances? Maimonides (Source 4) and Yuan Huang (Source 9) both discuss the importance of moderation in sexual activity for men. How is their advice similar, and how is it different?

Now look at issues of fetal development, Pseudo-Trotula and Zhang Huang both use words taken from food processing, such as *coagulation* or *congealing,* to describe the first part of fetal development. For pseudo-Trotula, how does this fit with humoral theory and ideas about the role of heat? For Zhang Huang, how do these fit with theories about yin/yang and five phases correspondence? What do both authors see as the significant milestones in fetal development?

Rösslin (Source 5), Zhang Gao (Source 8), and the illustrations in Sources 10 through 12 all depict birth procedures. How would you compare Rösslin's advice to midwives with the birth shown in Source 11? How would you compare Zhang Gao's description of the birth with that shown in Source 12? In both of these instances, you are comparing a written and a visual illustration from within the same culture. How would you then compare these illustrations *across* cultures, that is, Sources 8 and 12 with Sources 5 and 11? How would you compare all of these scenes with the Caesarean section shown in Source 10?

Now consider issues of medical treatment and advice. How would you compare the advice given by Constantine the African to aid conception to that given by pseudo-Trotula? How do these fit with the treatments proposed by Rösslin to aid in an easy delivery? What might account for the differences between these authors? How would you compare the treatments undertaken by the physicians in Zhang Congzheng's description with those in Zhang Gao's? How would you compare the western treatments with those advocated by Chinese writers?

Putting all of this information together, what similarities and differences do you see in ideas about the relations between general health and reproduction for either men or women? How would you summarize the authors' primary advice for those who want to have a long life and many children?

You have probably recognized that not all medical ideas and treatments in the West arise from strict humoral theory, nor all those in the East from theories of systematic correspondences; ideas and treatments also arose from other sources, such as local familiarity with the therapeutic properties of various plants and mixtures, popular notions of black and white magic, general ideas about gender hierarchy, and religious or philosophical concepts about God or the universe. We may often try to draw a sharp line between science and superstition, but, as you have noticed, that line was not sharp for medical writers in this period, nor was the line between magic and religion. As you are answering the central questions for this chapter, it might be good to keep in mind how the many sources of medical ideas might have benefited medieval people. Why might both physicians and patients have preferred a range of theories and treatments?

You are now ready to answer the questions for this chapter: What were some of the basic ideas regarding reproduction in the western and Chinese traditions? How were these translated into practical advice for patients and medical practitioners? In what issues do you see similarities, and where do you find differences?

EPILOGUE

Ideas about reproduction changed very slowly in both the West and the East. During the seventeenth century, many university-trained physicians in Europe began to give up humoral theory for other systems of anatomy and physiology based largely on experiments and observation. In 1628, William Harvey discovered the circulation of the blood. (The blood's circulation through the lungs had been discovered in the thirteenth century by the Islamic physician Ibn-an-Nafis, although it was not widely recognized until the Spanish physician Michael Servetus's treatise on the subject in the sixteenth century.) The increasing use of human dissection slowly built up enough evidence to lead people to doubt Galen on a variety of anatomical and physiological issues.

Observation alone was not necessarily enough to change ideas, and it could, in fact, lead to what may appear to be even more bizarre notions. During the seventeenth and eighteenth centuries, the debate between the Galenist and Aristotelian views of conception continued in Europe, but now both sides were armed with microscopes. Those who supported a basically Aristotelian position—that the active principle came from the man—claimed to have observed tiny men in human spermatozoa, complete with arms, heads, and legs. William Harvey thought that sperm was so powerful that it could act at a distance like a magnet. He backed up this idea not by quoting ancient authorities, as medieval authors did, but by experimentation; he dissected large numbers of does just after coition and could see no sperm in their uteri, and so he determined that sperm did not need to touch the egg to fertilize it. Those who supported a more active role for the ovum also claimed that humans were preformed in it, but they were somewhat hampered by the fact that it was not definitively identified until 1827, a remarkably late date considering its size relative to that of spermatozoa, which the Dutch scientist Anton von Leeuwenhoek identified correctly in the 1670s.

Misconceptions continued in the nineteenth and twentieth centuries. Until the 1840s most authorities believed that females—both human and other mammalian—ovulated only with intercourse, despite physiological evidence to the contrary; that the female experience could be so different from the male was a notion that was very hard to accept, though by this point medical writers no longer believed, as Avicenna had, that the "womb is like the scrotum and the vagina like the penis." In the 1870s the removal of healthy ovaries became a popular treatment in the United States and Europe for women judged to be psychologically abnormal, though the physicians who performed the procedure were less certain about the exact link between the brain and reproductive organs than Trotula had been seven centuries earlier. Learned ideas such as these were part of the "scientific" medicine brought into China and other parts of Asia by western missionaries and physicians, which may explain why many people chose (and continue to choose) to stay with their own theories. [Many of the medical procedures described in this chapter, generally labeled "traditional Chinese medicine" (TCM), are still widely practiced today.] These learned misconceptions were accompanied by popular ones, many of which still exist. Many people in the United States today swear that they can tell the sex of a fetus by some aspect of the mother's body, and recently a state senator commented that he knew a woman's allegations of rape were false because she subsequently became pregnant, which was impossible if this had been "true" rape.

Except in cases such as those of the state senator, we don't yet know which of our contemporary ideas about reproduction will appear as bizarre seven hundred years from now as those in this chapter do to us. What we do know is that today's ideas are just as connected to realms beyond medicine as were those surveyed in this chapter. The kinds of issues that concerned earlier medical writers on reproduction—What should one do if one has difficulty with reproduction? What is the source of differences between men and women? When does life begin?—are still with us, and not simply in medical textbooks.

CHAPTER THIRTEEN

SACRED JOURNEYS: PILGRIMAGES IN BUDDHISM, CHRISTIANITY, AND ISLAM (629–1324)

THE PROBLEM

Early in 1964, a thirty-eight-year-old American boarded a plane for Germany, his ultimate destination the city of Mecca in Saudi Arabia. As a Muslim, his faith required that he visit the holy sites of Islam and perform the prescribed rituals of the *hajj*. As a black man coming from a society deeply divided by race, the strongest impression this pilgrimage left on him was the complete irrelevance of racial concerns amongst his hosts and fellow pilgrims. He wrote his wife:

> You may be shocked by these words coming from me. But on this pilgrimage, what I have seen, and experienced, has forced me to *re-arrange* much of my thought-patterns previously held, and to *toss aside* some of my previous conclusions. . . . During the past eleven days here in the Muslim world, I have eaten from the same plate, drunk from the same glass, and slept in the same bed (or on the same rug)—while praying to the *same* God—with fellow Muslims whose eyes were the bluest of blue, whose hair was the blondest of blond, and whose skin was the whitest of white. . . . We were *truly* all the same (brothers)—because their belief in one God had removed the "white" from their *minds*, the "white" from their *behavior*, and the "white" from their *attitude*. . . . All praise is due to Allah, the Lord of the Worlds.[1]

A year after his realization that true brotherhood was possible across racial lines, the author was felled by an assassin.

The experiences of Malxolm X in Mecca were highly personal, but they were also part of a larger fabric of history. His journey to Mecca, and the

1. *The Autobiography of Malcolm X,* as told to Alex Haley (New York: Ballantine, 1964), pp. 391–393.

rites he performed while there, repeated the experiences of generations of Muslims over a thousand years. Like so many of these pilgrims, Malcolm brought his own concerns and the issues of his own society with him, only to have his preconceptions challenged by the international, cosmopolitan experience of the hajj.

It is logical to begin this chapter on sacred journeys with an account from the world of Islam. No other religious tradition has placed more emphasis on the sacred pilgrimage, requiring a very specific set of rites of *every* believer who has the resources to make at least one journey to the heartland of its prophets. But Islam is remarkable only for the intense centralization and codification of its sacred journey. The impulse to travel to holy sites appears to be a nearly universal component of human spirituality.

For most people in most places and times, the destinations of these journeys have probably been relatively local. Sacred spaces, often associated with nature or with the presence of living or departed spiritual leaders, might be relatively easy to visit. But with the rise of major world religions, such as Buddhism, Christianity, and Islam, sacred journeys came to involve long sojourns in which pilgrims, like Malcolm X, crossed significant cultural frontiers. In the process, pilgrims performed the same role that long-distance traders often played in disseminating culture. Pilgrimage routes became broad avenues on which people and ideas, cultures and languages, moved and mixed.

In each of these traditions there is a sense of the need for a return to places associated with the founding of that religion: to the parts of India most closely associated with Siddhartha Gautama, the Buddha; to places in Palestine, most notably Jerusalem, where Jesus lived and died; and to Mecca and Medina, where Islam states that Muhammad received God's final revelation and initiated the incredible expansion of the world's fastest-growing religion. Modern transportation has made such journeys relatively easy today, although political and economic circumstances can still create dangers and uncertainties. In the period covered in this chapter, from the seventh through the fourteenth centuries, the decision to set out on a long-distance pilgrimage was not one that could be taken lightly. As we will see, such an act of spiritual devotion could take years of the pilgrims' lives and expose them to extreme hazards.

In the sources that follow, you will consider the motivations and experiences of Buddhist, Christian, and Muslim pilgrims. What role does pilgrimage seem to play in each particular religion in general terms and in the faith experiences of the individual pilgrims? Why did these pilgrims set out? What do their experiences along the way tell us about their own view of the world and that of the societies through which they pass? As outsiders, how are they viewed and how do they view others? What types of challenges did they have to overcome to reach their destination? Were they ultimately successful in their spiritual quest?

BACKGROUND

In comparing the religions to be considered in this chapter and their traditions of pilgrimage, it is important to note that Christianity and Buddhism share the common trait of having ultimately gained millions of followers outside their places of origin while becoming minority religions in the lands of their founders, Siddhartha Gautama (the Buddha) and Jesus. Islam, by contrast, has remained dominant in the areas where Muhammad lived and preached. As a result, patterns of pilgrimage in Buddhism and Christianity have been less centralized than those in Islam, less focused on a particular route or a predictable pattern.

The early success of Buddhism in India following the death of Siddhartha Gautama (ca. 483 B.C.E.) reached its height in the reign of Emperor Ashoka (ca. 264–223 B.C.E.), who made Buddhism the state religion and patronized its art and architecture (see Chapter 5). The *stupas* and pillars erected under Ashoka still attract pilgrims. Most importantly for our story, Ashoka sponsored missionary activities outside of India. By the time caste-based Hinduism reasserted itself in South Asia, Buddhist monasteries had been founded across Central and Southeast Asia, as well as in China.

The pilgrimage impulse was strong in Buddhism from the beginning. It is said that when the Buddha died, his disciples cremated his remains and scattered the ashes among the most important of their communities. Before long, the Buddha's followers began visiting the sites of his life's most important activities: "To visit the scenes of the eight great events is to experience in a direct way the life of the Buddha as both a demonstration of his perfection and the perfection of all Buddhas."[2] The further across Asia the religion spread, however, the more difficult it was for Buddhists to visit these original sites, and as Buddhism waned in India, social and political circumstances made such journeys much more problematic.

That did not stop intrepid travelers from going to India to visit the holy sites. A number of Chinese Buddhist monks made such journeys in the fourth through sixth centuries. Their numbers were never great, but they were very important in the development of East Asian Buddhism. Buddhism had arrived in China via the Silk Road during the Han dynasty. Christian, Zoroastrian, and Manichean communities were also established in China at this time, but Buddhism became far and away the most prominent of these imported faiths, even while having to contend with competition from two well-established religious and ethical traditions: Confucianism and Daoism. In spite of occasional persecution, Buddhism flourished, and by the time of the T'ang Dynasty (626–960), monasteries had been established throughout the land. From this time forward, Chinese Buddhism was relatively self-sufficient, and pilgrimages to India became more infrequent.

2. John Huntington, "Sowing the Seeds of the Lotus: A Journey to the Great Pilgrimage Sites of Buddhism," *Orientations*, November 1985, p. 48, cited in Sally Hovey Wriggins, *Xuanzang: A Buddhist Pilgrim on the Silk Road* (Boulder, Colo.: Westview, 1996), p. 82.

As well as personal spiritual fulfillment, Chinese pilgrims to India were concerned with gathering material that could be used to purify and rectify the Chinese practice of Buddhism. In returning to the source, they sought out original texts and learned to read them in their original languages, consulting with Buddhist sages in the monasteries they visited along the way. Buddhism had adapted itself to local customs as it spread from its original homeland. These monks saw the need to return to its place of origin to purify their faith. Meanwhile, missionaries from China had reached Korea and Japan by the sixth century. As Buddhism once again flourished and adapted itself to local culture, Korean and Japanese monks were fired by the same impulses that had led Chinese monks to India. Now China itself became a destination for pilgrimage.

The resources that earlier pilgrims had previously sought in India—sacred texts, relics, learned authorities, and holy sites—became widely available in China. The Mahayana school, to which the Chinese belonged, appealed to a wider population than the stricter and more ascetic Theravada school primarily because it offered an easier path to Enlightenment and emphasized the passage of the individual soul to a blessed realm rather than the complete extinction of the individual. The deification of Siddhartha Gautama under Mahayana gave an outward focus to spirituality, meaning that veneration of statues of Buddha became a focal point of worship. Particularly impressive images of Buddha could become destinations of pilgrimage wherever they might be found. Mahayana Buddhists also emphasized that common people could be helped toward Enlightenment through the aid of compassionate beings known as *bodhisattvas.* These were individuals who were further along on the path to *nirvana* but who remained in the world as benefactors of humanity. As they achieved Buddhahood themselves and passed from the earth, their places of residence could also becomes shrines to which pilgrims flocked. In other words, the multiplicity of bodhisattvas and Buddhas in China itself meant that there was no special need to go to the land of Siddhartha Gautama, who could at any rate be prayed to at local shrines.

Just as Chinese monks had once looked to India, Japanese and Korean monks now saw China as a destination for sacred journeys. By the seventh century, Buddhism was taken up by Japanese emperors. In the early days it was missionaries from China who brought doctrines, images, relics, and sacred texts to Japan. Soon, however, Japanese monks made the journey in the opposite direction, to visit the holy sites and scholars of China. In 607 the Emperor Shotoku authorized an embassy to China to establish diplomatic relations and sent hundreds of young men, Buddhist monks included, to study in China. The best known of the Japanese Buddhists who traveled to China was a monk named Ennin who kept a diary of his long and arduous trip (838–847 C.E.). You will encounter Ennin's story later in this chapter.

Like Buddhists in the same period, medieval Christian pilgrims could choose from a wide variety of possible destinations. Geoffrey Chaucer's *Canterbury Tales,* which follows a group of such voyagers from London to the cathedral town of Canterbury sixty miles distant, shows that the impulse to visit sacred places could be satisfied without sacrificing years of one's life or crossing significant cultural frontiers. As Christianity expanded in the late Roman and early medieval periods, sacred places of pilgrimage were established all across Europe. In some cases these sites were inherited from the pagan past. As Europeans grafted Christian beliefs onto their long-established traditions, places that had once been identified with pagan gods and nature spirits came to be associated with Christian saints or the Virgin Mary. Sites associated with martyrs of the early church were also popular, as were monasteries where saints had performed miracles during their lives and continued to offer spiritual aid after death. The purpose of this "cult of saints" was to seek their intercession so that prayers to God would be more successful. Even if one could not travel to the exact place where the saint's power was focused, it was still often possible to venerate him or her locally: The emphasis on such relics as sacred bones allowed the saints' blessings to be widely dispersed; even minor villages and towns were likely to have at least one such relic.

In spite of this decentralized pattern of pilgrimage, there were some particularly holy sites that required more ambitious journeys. Perhaps the most famous place of pilgrimage within Europe was the shrine of Santiago de Compostela in northwestern Spain. By the sixth century a tradition had been established that the body of St. James had been returned to Spain after his execution in Palestine. In the ninth century a church was built at the spot where he was said to have been buried. As pilgrims thronged to the shrine, hostels were built to house them. As various routes to Santiago de Compostela from different starting points in Europe were established, subsidiary sites of pilgrimage grew up around them. At the highest levels of the hierarchy of pilgrimages stood Rome (for Roman Christians), Constantinople (for Orthodox Christians), and Jerusalem. Given medieval conditions of transport, a trip to Rome or Constantinople would be a daunting adventure. A journey to Jerusalem would be almost beyond reach. Yet the Christian focus on Jerusalem, which eventually culminated in the Crusades of the late medieval period, should not be underestimated.

It did not start out that way. The earliest Christians showed little interest in Jerusalem as a sacred place. In the first three centuries of Christianity, Jerusalem was seen either as the "Guilty City" for its role in Christ's death or as a center of Roman (and therefore anti-Christian) power. Another factor that served to deemphasize the physical Jerusalem was the emphasis that early Church leaders placed on the "eternal" Jerusalem. Christian theologians such as St. Augustine of Hippo and Origen lived in a Greek-speaking world in which Hellenistic philosophy was influential. Origen was a Platonist who believed that the physical world was merely a distorted image of the ideal: Believers should "seek the heavenly city in place of the earthly."[3] The Book of Revelation predicted that a "New Jerusalem" would descend from the heavens at the end of time to replace the tarnished one on earth, further lowering the prestige of the actual city in which Jesus had lived and died. Jews, who were prevented by Roman law from living in or visiting Jerusalem after the destruction of the Second Temple in 70 C.E., were also inclined to focus on the city as a metaphysical construct rather than as a physical destination.

The conversion of the Roman Emperor Constantine in 313 was a turning point. By 335 a great basilica had been built that incorporated the Rock of Golgotha, the site of Christ's crucifixion. Churches were also built at other sites associated with Jesus Christ, and Jerusalem became the ultimate focal point of Christian pilgrimage. As Karen Armstrong points out, "Pilgrims did not visit Golgotha and the tomb as modern travelers visit a historical site: these earthly relics of Christ's life on earth introduced them to a transcendence . . . the holy places were not mere mementoes but were experienced as earthly replicas of the divine."[4] The earlier metaphysical notion of Jerusalem was being replaced by a more "tactile spirituality" in which physical contact with holy places and holy relics had great meaning. Many of the relics found throughout Europe were carried back (actually or purportedly) by the fortunate few who managed to visit Palestine in the three centuries between the conversion of Constantine and the rise of Islam.

Jerusalem was conquered by an Arab army in 638. They came to call it *al-Quds*, meaning "the holy." The land of Abraham, Moses, and Jesus had great meaning for Muslims, who traced their spiritual history back to the same sacred spaces. Muhammad was believed to have ascended to heaven in the company of the prophets from the Temple Mount in Jerusalem itself. While a small number of Jews and Muslims settled in the city, Christians remained a majority and pilgrimages continued. When Charlemagne (r. 771–814) set his sights on Jerusalem as a destination for pilgrims, the Abbasid Caliph Harun-al-Rashid exchanged gifts with him and allowed the European king to build a new church in the holy city as well as a place for the travelers to stay. The emphasis that Charlemagne placed on a stronger European connection with Jerusalem would later have violent consequences.

With the weakening of the Abbasid caliphate in the ninth and tenth centuries, political turmoil engulfed Palestine. As various Muslim forces fought for control, the Byzantine Empire launched a holy war against Islam. Ultimately this was unsuccessful, but the attacks added a note of anti-Christian feeling that had previously been absent: In 938 a procession of Christians was attacked in Jerusalem. For the next century and a half the rulers of Jerusalem were alternatively accommodating and hostile as European pilgrims flocked to the holy city. A particularly large contingent appeared in the year 1000, when some expected

3. Cited in Karen Armstrong, *Jerusalem: One City, Three Faiths* (New York: Knopf, 1996), p. 171.

4. Ibid., p. 213.

to witness the Second Coming of Christ. Over the next century, several large-scale, well-organized pilgrimages were undertaken.

This tradition of the mass pilgrimage took quite a new form in 1095, when Pope Urban II, responding to a call for help from a Byzantine Empire besieged by Muslim forces, declared what became known as the First Crusade. The military campaigns launched from Europe over the next two hundred years had the conquest and control of Jerusalem as their central motif, but they bear very little relation to the spiritual journeys with which this chapter is centrally concerned. In 1099 Jerusalem fell to the crusaders; it was retaken by Muslim forces under Salah al-Din in 1187. Jerusalem was to remain under Muslim control for over seven hundred years. Christian pilgrimages to the holy sites continued throughout that period, but later pilgrimages generally lacked the fervor of the medieval ones and were no longer undertaken on a mass scale.

Jerusalem has also been a place of pilgrimage for Muslims for nearly fifteen hundred years. Pilgrims who make the *hajj* have long been anxious to add Jerusalem to their itinerary. But a trip to Jerusalem is only a bonus: Mecca is the required destination for all believers. The world of Islam, like those of Christianity and Buddhism, also contains subsidiary pilgrimage sites. Many Muslims, especially Shi'ites and Sufis, believe that the special grace (*baraka*) that surrounds certain holy people continues after death and that visiting the tombs of saints can promote spiritual growth. But if these shrines become too popular, they are frowned upon by the most orthodox believers, who fear that popular veneration of saints' tombs might displace the God-ordained focus on Mecca.

Of the five "pillars" of Islam—the statement of faith, the five daily prayers, the requirement of charity, the need to fast during the month of Ramadan, and the Qur'anic injunction to perform the hajj—none is more difficult to achieve than the pilgrimage to Mecca. For most Muslims in today's world, it has been an unachievable goal: Two million pilgrims from 125 countries come to Mecca for the hajj each year, but that accounts for only two in a thousand adult Muslims. For those who have the means and the opportunity, however, it is the journey of a lifetime.

In the second half of the first millennium, Islam expanded beyond its original Arabian heartland with amazing speed. It was not long before most believers neither spoke Arabic as their native language nor fully connected with the Arab culture in which Islamic belief and practice was so deeply rooted. Even in the immediate geographic environs of the Arab world, cultural diversity soon became the rule rather than the exception in the world of Islam. The Persians are close neighbors, but their language is Indo-European rather than Semitic, and their cultural and religious traditions are quite different from those of the Arabs. The Turks originated in the very different environment of the Central Asian steppes, and again both their language and their culture were and are nothing like those of the Arabs among whom Islam had originated.

Needless to say, when Islam spread to West Africa and Southeast Asia, its cultural complexity increased dramatically. The possibility has always existed that interaction with local languages and cultures would dilute the purity of the faith. The hajj acts as a check on that process. Every year pilgrims arrive from across the world, representing diverse cultural backgrounds. But in the hajj all distinctions are removed: The pilgrims adopt the same dress, speak the same words, and precisely follow the same rituals. When the pilgrims circle the black building known as the *ka'ba* at the center of Mecca, they are at the physical and spiritual center of the Islamic world.

The ka'ba is a very ancient building that already stood where it does today when Muhammad was a child. At that time it was filled with images and objects sacred to many faiths, representing the religious pluralism that prevailed in seventh-century Arabia. After Muhammad received his first revelation and spread the word about the one true God, the polytheism of the ka'ba could only seem an abomination. When he returned from his exile in Medina, Muhammad ordered that the ka'ba be cleared of the objects and images it contained and be sanctified for God. The fact that religious travelers were already accustomed to visiting the ka'ba might have eased the adjustment of converts to the new religion. Muhammad himself established the precedent for all the main elements of the pilgrimage as still practiced today, and to the believer those directions came straight from God.

Only Muslims may enter Mecca, which is seen as *haram,* a sanctuary of their faith. As they enter, the pilgrims exchange their personal clothing for special white garments, which eliminate all distinctions of rank and status. Men and women wear different types of garments, but women who are in Mecca as pilgrims are not veiled, and men and women mix very freely. Ritual bathing prepares the pilgrims for the holy rites that are about to begin. No violent thoughts or actions and no sexual activity are allowed. Seven counterclockwise circuits of the ka'ba are performed at three key points during the hajj, though few pilgrims are lucky enough to achieve their goal of actually touching this edifice as thousands swirl about the ka'ba in unison. Five times each day every Muslim faces the ka'ba in order to pray; for believers to actually be there is to feel that they are at the center of human communication with God. After leaving Mecca, and after a night spent in desert tents, the pilgrims move on to Arafat to perform the ritual known as the Day of Standing Together Before God. After another night in the desert, the pilgrims participate in a ritual stoning of the devil before returning to Mecca and repeating their circuit of the ka'ba. Most will then go on to Medina to visit the Prophet's grave.

While the world has changed dramatically, the pilgrimage itself has changed little over the centuries. It therefore serves to connect Muslims not only with their contemporaries, but with past generations. Above all, it is the ultimate expression of the personal religious devotion of the pilgrim:

> Muslims are drawn to Mecca like filings to a magnet, attracted by the integrative

> power of a journey to the heartland. More than a city, Mecca is a principal part of speech in a sacred language and the direction Muslims pray in throughout their lives. Simply to set foot there may answer years of longing. . . . Over the centuries, in times of peace and war, Mecca has offered its visitors a dependable retreat, a sort of ritual greenhouse reserved for forcing the spirit into blossom no matter what may be going on beyond the Haram borders. As a reminder of how life ought to be lived, the journey has inspired peasants, princes, mystics and revolutionaries. For all these reasons, it represents a literal trip of a lifetime.[5]

Islam has clearly invested much of its spiritual energy in the hajj.

Politics and historical chronology are not irrelevant to the story of the hajj: Whoever controls the holy sites has a position of great power and responsibility in the Islamic world, an authority exercised today by the royal house of Saudi Arabia. Certainly political and military circumstances in the world outside Mecca have greatly affected the ability of pilgrims to reach the holy city over time. Having said that, there is a timeless quality to the hajj that sets it apart from its Buddhist and Christian equivalents. While the stories of the Buddhist and Christian pilgrims that follow seem to come from a far different world, the essential experiences of Muslim pilgrims in the city of Mecca have never fundamentally changed.

THE METHOD

The first thing to bear in mind when reading the pilgrimage accounts that follow is the variety of narrative styles. Some are first-person narratives, while others are impersonal chronicles. As always when reading historical documents, you should ask: Who wrote this, and why? How might these documents have affected the attitude of a reader at that time toward pilgrimages and holy sites?

Because the sources are so different in structure and intent, not every one will be relevant to each of the questions we pose. But as you read, keep separate lists for Buddhist, Christian, and Islamic sources and make note of any information you run across that is relevant to the following questions:

- What were the primary religious factors that inspired the pilgrims to set out on their journey? What were their most powerful spiritual experiences? Did their religious beliefs or attitudes change in any way as a result of the pilgrimage?
- How was the pilgrimage organized—on an individual basis or in a large or small group? What might account for each form or organization?

5. Michael Wolfe, introduction to *One Thousand Roads to Mecca: Ten Centuries of Travelers Writing About the Muslim Pilgrimage* (New York: Grove, 1999), p. xxiv.

- How were the pilgrims affected by the political systems they encountered? Did political leaders along the way do more to help or to hinder the pilgrims? What hazards did the pilgrims face, and how did they overcome them? How did the pilgrims sustain themselves economically?

- As the pilgrims observed peoples whose cultures and customs were different from their own, what did they especially notice, and how did they react? Alternatively, how did people from different backgrounds seem to view the pilgrims?

With these questions as a starting point, you will return to make systematic comparisons among the documents. Meanwhile, the following paragraphs provide some additional background for each. You will want to refer back to this section as you consider the evidence.

Source 1 consists of a series of extracts from the diary kept by the Japanese monk Ennin during his nine-year pilgrimage to China. Ennin's journey of 838 to 847 took place during the period mentioned above when the Japanese emperors, who were interested in learning from Chinese examples in government, culture, and religion, sponsored "embassies" to achieve that end. As you will see in this reading, however, official sponsorship from Japan was not sufficient to guarantee the success of a pilgrimage. Apart from the sometimes grave difficulties Ennin encountered in traveling by both sea and land, Chinese officials both great and small placed impediments in his path. Showing remarkable fortitude, however, Ennin and his companions were successful in their sacred journey, learning from Buddhist monks in various monasteries and visiting holy sites. Ennin's experience in China was an international one, for while he was there he met and interacted not only with Chinese Buddhists but also with monks from Korea, India, and other lands. His diary demonstrates that pilgrimages of this type had cultural and linguistic as well as spiritual dynamics.

A portrait of Xuanzang, the greatest of all Chinese pilgrims to India, is shown in Source 2. Xuanzang's journey of 629 to 645 resulted in a religious renaissance. The sacred texts and relics he brought back to China served as a foundation for the further development of Buddhism in the context of the powerful and centralized T'ang state. He also composed a record of his travels entitled *Record of the Western Regions* and was the subject of a well-known biography, *The Life of Xuanzang*. This work helped to establish the legend of Xuanzang as a man of great fortitude, wisdom, and compassion. The portrait reproduced here gives us some insight into how Chinese Buddhists conceptualized Xuanzang as the "ideal pilgrim" in terms of both his physical and spiritual attributes.

Source 3, which describes the great German pilgrimage to Jerusalem in 1064–1065, takes us to the world of medieval European Christianity. It is quite different from the world of Asian Buddhism, although here as well religion and politics are intertwined. This pilgrimage took place just thirty years before the beginning of the Crusades. At that time, such mass journeys were increasingly popular, although the political and military situation in Palestine was unsettled. While the pilgrimage itself was not military in nature, the fairly aggressive attitude of the Western Europeans toward the peoples they encountered (including their fellow Christians in Constantinople) is clear.

What did Christian pilgrims experience when they were in Jerusalem? Source 4, an extract from a Scandinavian pilgrim's guide from the twelfth century, translated from Icelandic, gives us some insight into the religious goals of such journeys while also reminding us of the great distances that were traveled in medieval Europe. Abbot Nicholas, who spent four years making this difficult journey, composed this guide to give future pilgrims advice on the route they could take and an idea of what they might find along the way. Earlier sections describe the route by sea and land from Iceland to Rome and Nicholas's experiences there. This passage describes Jerusalem and the Holy Land itself, then briefly indicates the way home. It is worth noting that in the 1150s, when this pilgrimage took place, European Christians were in political control of Jerusalem. In 1187 the Muslims retook Jerusalem, and the already difficult journey became even more problematic.

Whatever the political and military situation in Palestine, Jerusalem exercised the Christian imagination. It was not only a physical destination, but a spiritual and metaphysical one as well. Guillaume de Deguileville's *Pilgrimage of the Human Life* (1331) given as Source 5, describes a very different sort of "pilgrimage" from the ones in the previous sources; it takes place in a dream and gives us to a deeper understanding of the metaphysics of medieval Christianity. This document is included to remind us that the concept of the "New Jerusalem" as a perfect heavenly destination, so important to the early Church, still influenced the medieval imagination. It emphasizes how difficult it was to reach the "New Jerusalem," but also indicates what types of help the pilgrim of the spirit could find along the way. Guillaume de Deguileville, like the early Church leader Origen a thousand years earlier, might advise the faithful to "seek the heavenly city in place of the earthly."

The rest of the documents take us to the world of Islam. Source 6 is the story of Naser-e Khosraw, a Persian pilgrim who performed his hajj in the 1060s, at about the same time that the great German pilgrimage headed for Jerusalem. Khosraw was an administrator in Persia (today's Iran) who seems to have had a midlife crisis: Disenchanted with the corruption of government and concerned about his own moral failings, he had a dream that led him on a new path, and he departed for Mecca. The full text of his story has much to say not only about the hajj itself but also about the whole Islamic world through which he passed.

The final readings in this chapter, Sources 7, 8, and 9, take our view of the Islamic world even further. These documents by three Arabs—al-Maqrizi, al-Umari, and Ibn Khaldun—concern a great West African king, Mansa

Musa. This king of Mali was perhaps the best-known African of his period, and his story is still considered central to African history today. In the fourteenth century, the Islamic kingdom of Mali was the latest of the large-scale states that had appeared in the West African region known to Arab geographers as the Sahel. The wealth of Mali, and therefore of its king, had several sources. Trade in goods produced in different environmental zones within West Africa was one source of wealth and urbanization, as was trade across the desert with the Arabs and Berbers of North Africa. The most important foundation of Malian power, however, was control of gold, and it is as a man of gold that Mansa Musa is still remembered. His story is quite important to world economic history, since the supply of gold he commanded played a crucial role in the economic growth of the Mediterranean region in this period. In these sources, however, while Mansa Musa's wealth and power are not forgotten, we also see him as a Muslim who took his faith seriously enough to brave the difficult journey across the Sahara to complete the hajj. The authors collected stories of Mansa Musa and his kingdom as part of a larger effort to inform their cosmopolitan audience about the *Dar al-Islam* ("the Abode of Islam") in the world at large.

THE EVIDENCE

Source 1 from Ennin's Diary: The Record of a Pilgrimage to China in Search of the Law, *trans. Edwin O. Reischauer (New York: The Ronald Press Company, 1955), pp. 6–23 passim, 58–63 passim, 93–117 passim, 148–153 passim, 235–259 passim, 302, 305, 347–376 passim.*

1. From the Diary of Ennin, 838–847

[*In 838 Ennin boarded a "tributary" ship to China sent by the Japanese government to foster political, economic and cultural exchange between the two empires.*]

When the waves came from the east, the ship leaned over to the west, and when they came from the west, it inclined to the east. They washed over the ship [to a number] beyond count. All on board put their faith in the Buddha and in the [Shintō] deities, and there was none but did pray. The men were desperate, and all from the head of the mission down to the sailors stripped and bound their loin cloths fast about them. Since the ship was about to break in the middle, we rushed to stern and bow, and each of us looked for a place that remained intact. Because of the shock of the waves the structural joints [of the ship] were all pulling apart, so they fastened ropes to the right and left railings and pulled them together, striving to find a way to survive. Bilge water filled [the ship], which thereupon settled onto the sand bottom, and the official and private goods [in the hold] washed about in the bilge water. . . .

In the northwest we saw at a distance something floating along with the waves. The men all said that it perhaps was a boat come to meet us. While we were speculating, it came on towards us against the wind, and at last we knew that it was a boat. . . .

We straightway drew up to the boat and moved the national tribute articles to it. . . .

. . . The Ambassador and some others went ashore and lodged, but they have not yet met the government officials. . . .

. . . At 4 P.M. we alighted from our boat and lodged at the official inn on the south side of the river. We two monks stayed in separate rooms.

[*Ennin's goal is to reach the monastery of T'ai-chou, but first he must receive permission from the Chinese officials. Meanwhile, Ennin waits at the monastery of Yangchou.*]

. . . It is the festival of the winter solstice. Monks and laymen all offer congratulations. Those who are laymen pay their respects to the officials and congratulate them on the festival of the winter solstice. When they see the Minister of State, they say, "Moving by degrees, the sun has reached its southern extremity. We humbly hope for a myriad of blessings for the Minister of State's honored self." Officials of high and low rank and the common people all offer one another congratulations when they meet. Clerics offer each other congratulations when they meet, uttering phrases about the winter solstice and making obeisance to one another. Laymen on entering the monastery also show the same courtesy.

The congregation of monks said to us foreign monks, "Today is the festival of the winter solstice. May you have a myriad of blessings; may the propagation of the lamp [of the Law] be without end; and may you return soon to your own land and long be National Teachers." After we had all paid our respects to one another, they remarked that it was extremely cold. One monk came and said, "This being the winter solstice, may you have a myriad of blessings; may your scholarship illumine the 'three learnings'; may you soon return to your homeland and for long be National Teachers." There were all sorts of [such] speeches.

This festival is exactly the same as New Year's Day in Japan. Each lay and monastic establishment provides rare delicacies, and all sorts of dishes are assembled. All use congratulatory phrases on the season, conforming to the tastes of the men of former times. Clerics and laymen alike offer congratulations on the winter solstice for a period of three days. This monastery also arranges a three-day offering, and various sorts [of things] are gathered. . . .

Today was a national anniversary day. . . . Early in the morning the monastic congregations gathered in this monastery and seated themselves in rows in the flanking buildings on the east, north, and west. At 8 A.M. the Minister of State and the General entered the monastery by the great gate. The Minister of State and the General walked in slowly side by side. Soldiers in ranks guarded them on all sides, and all the officials of the prefecture and of the regional commandery followed behind. They came as far as the foot of the steps in front of the lecture hall, and then the Minister of State and the General parted, the Minister of State going to the east and entering behind a curtain on the east side [of the courtyard], and the General going to the west and entering behind a curtain on the west side. They quickly changed their slippers, washed their hands, and came out again. In front of the hall were two bridges. The Minister of State mounted the eastern bridge and the General the western bridge, and thus the two of them circled around from the east and west and met at the center door of the hall. They took their seats and worshiped the Buddha.

After that, several tens of monks lined up in rows at both the east and west doors of the hall. Each one held artificial lotus flowers and green banners. A monk struck a stone triangle and chanted, "All be worshipful and reverence the three eternal treasures." After that the Minister of State and the General arose and took censers, and the prefectural officials all followed after them, taking incense cups. They divided, going to the east and west, with the Minister of State going towards the east. The monks who were carrying flowered banners preceded him, chanting in unison a two-line hymn in Sanskrit, "The wonderful body of the *Nyorai*," etc. A venerable monk followed first [behind the Minister of State] and then the soldiers guarding him. They went along the gallery under the eaves. After all the monks had burned incense, they returned toward the hall by this route, chanting Sanskrit hymns without cease. The General went to the west and burned incense, performing the same rite as [that performed by the Minister of State] in the east, and [the two of them] came [back] simultaneously and met in their original place [before the central door of the hall].

During this time, there was beautiful responsive chanting of Sanskrit hymns by [the groups of monks] on the east and west. The leader of the chants, standing alone and motionless, struck a stone triangle, and the Sanskrit [chanting] stopped. Then they again recited, "Honor the three eternal treasures." The Minister of State and the General sat down together in their original seats. When they burned incense, the incense burners in which their incense was placed stood side by side. A venerable monk, Yüan-ch'eng Ho-shang, read a prayer after which the leader of the chants intoned hymns in behalf of the eight classes of demi-gods. The purport of the wording was to glorify the spirit of the [late] Emperor. At the end of each verse he recited, "Honor the three eternal treasures." The Minister of State and the officials rose to their feet together and did reverence to the Buddha, chanting three or four times. Then all [were free] to do as they wished. . . .

[As time passes, he grows impatient to reach T'ai-chou. Local officials tell him that he cannot proceed without an Imperial order, and the Japanese ambassador informs him that the Emperor has refused to grant permission for the monks to travel. Ennin consults a Japanese diplomat about his dilemma.]

I presented a letter to the Ambassador Consultant Counselor, [saying that] I should remain in China because I was having difficulties in accomplishing my search for the Law. . . . The Consultant Counselor notified me saying, "If you desire to remain, that is for the sake of Buddhism, and I dare not stand in the way of your determination. If you wish to stay, then do remain. The government of this land, however, is extremely severe, and, if the officials learn of this, it will [entail] the crime of disobeying an Imperial order, and you will probably have trouble. You should think it over."

[Faced with these bureaucratic obstacles, Ennin and his fellow monks make the difficult decision to stay in China illegally, sailing up the coast while posing as Korean monks.]

I, the Scholar Monk, while at Ch'u-chou, had planned with the Korean Interpreter Kim Chŏngnam that, when we reached the Mi-chou region, we would stay in a private house, and, when the tributary embassy departed, we would live in hiding in the mountains and would then go to [Mt.] T'ien-t'ai and also to Ch'ang-an. . . .

Here we monks were in this isolated valley, suddenly encountered by this situation. We did not know what to do. We gave all the baggage and even the food we had brought with us to the boatmen, not keeping back a single thing. We feared that, if we said that we had gold, they would agree among themselves to kill us. We therefore said that we would go to a village. . . .

. . . The village elder, Wang Liang, wrote, saying:

> You monks have come here and call yourselves Koreans, but I see that your language is not Korean, nor is it Chinese. I have been told that the ships of the Japanese tributary embassy stopped east of the mountains to wait for [favorable] winds, and I fear that you monks are official visitors [to China] who have fled to this village from the ships of your own country. I dare not let official visitors stay. I ask you to tell the truth and not make up falsehoods. This village has just had a communication from the prefecture, and three or four representatives of the Guard Officer are here investigating, so I fear that they will see you monks and arrest you and take you to the prefectural [capital].

In order to search for the Buddhist Law, we monks have several times made schemes, but we have not yet been able to carry out these plans. On the point of returning to Japan, we with difficulty devised a plan for staying behind, but again it did not work, and we were discovered by them. We have tried every idea, but we cannot stay. The officials are vigilant and do not permit the slightest [irregularity]. Therefore, I have decided to board the second ship and return to Japan. I left on the eighth ship all the Buddhist teachings and the materials which I had previously sought out in Yang-chou and Ch'u-chou, and I gave to others between Hu-hung Island and the prefecture all the baggage we took with us when we expected to be left behind, so we board the ship empty-handed. But my sighs are caused entirely by our failure to accomplish our search for the Law. . . .

I, the Scholar Monk, in order to return quickly to Japan to fulfill the vows made in recent years, had the diviner pray to the [Shintō] gods and offered a fire crystal to the Great God of Sumiyoshi, a rosary of rock crystals to the Dragon-King of the Sea, and a razor to the patron deity of ships, in order to pray for our safe return to Japan.

[*After this setback, Ennin and his fellow pilgrims change their minds and decide to stay in China after all. They reach the Mt. Ch'ih cloister and there hear about a new pilgrimage destination in the north, Mt. Wu-t'ai. Ennin writes to the government minister in charge of monasteries.*]

We monks, having in mind merely our longing for the Buddhist teachings, have come from afar to this benevolent land with our hearts set on sacred places and our spirits rejoicing in the pilgrimage. It is said that Mt. [Wu]-t'ai and some other places are the source of the teaching and the places where the great saints have manifested themselves. Eminent monks from India have visited them, crossing their precipitous slopes, and famous patriarchs of China have there attained enlightenment. We monks have admired these glorious places, and having chanced to meet with this happy destiny, have by good fortune come to this holy land. Now we wish to go to these places to fulfill our long-cherished hopes, but we fear that on the road [others] will not honor our reasons for traveling. We have heard that the Learned Doctor Prajñā petitioned for official credentials on behalf of some mendicant monks, and that they [were allowed] by Imperial edict to practice [their mendicancy. Thus,] this started of old and has continued until recent times.

We humbly hope that this monastery, in accordance with the laws and precedents of the land, will address the prefecture and the subprefecture, asking for official credentials. If it does so, the . . . glorious fame of the Monastery Administrators will stir foreign lands afar, their encouraging magnanimity will make gloriously manifest the sun-like Buddha, and we shall be more than indebted to you.

[*While waiting for permission to travel, Ennin and the other Japanese monks participate in the rituals of Korean Buddhist monks at Mt. Ch'ih.*]

At 8 A.M. they struck the bell for the scripture lecturing, apprising the group, after which the congregation spent quite a little time entering the hall. At the moment the bell sounded for the congregation to settle down, the lecturer entered the hall and mounted to a high seat, while the congregation in unison called on the name of the Buddha. Their intonation was wholly Korean and did not resemble the Chinese sounds. After the lecturer had mounted to his seat, the invocation of the name of the Buddha stopped. A monk seated below him chanted in Sanskrit, entirely in the Chinese manner, the one-line hymn, "How through this scripture," etc. When he reached the phrase, "We desire the Buddha to open to us the subtle mystery," the crowd chanted together, "The fragrance of the rules, the fragrance of meditation, the fragrance of deliverance," etc. After the singing of the Sanskrit hymn had ended, the lecturer changed the headings of the scripture and dividing them into the three parts, explained the headings. After that the *Ina* came forth in front of the high seat and read out the reasons for holding the meeting and the separate names of the patrons and the things they had donated, after which he passed this document to the lecturer, who, grasping his chowry, read the patrons' names one by one and made supplications for each individually. After that the debaters argued the principles, raising questions. While they were raising a question, the lecturer would hold up his chowry, and when a questioner had finished asking his question, he would lower it and then raise it again, thank [the questioner] for his question, and then answer it. They recorded both the questions and the answers. It was the same as in Japan, except that the rite of [pointing out doctrinal] difficulties was somewhat different. After lowering his hand at his side three times and before making any explanation, [a debater] would suddenly proclaim the difficulty, shouting with all his might like a man enraged, and the lecturer would accept the problem and would reply without raising problems in return.

After the debate, he took up the text and read the scripture. At the end of the lecture, the congregation chanted praises together in drawn-out syllables. Among these praises were words of blessing. The lecturer descended from his seat while a monk chanted the hymn, "Being in this world is like [living] in emptiness." It sounded very much the way it does in Japan. The lecturer mounted the worship platform [in front of the deities], while a monk chanted the three praises. Then the lecturer and the congregation, singing together, left the hall and returned to their rooms.

[*After being further delayed by bureaucracy, Ennin finally sets out for Mt. Wu-t'ai, an area known as the home of the bodhisattva Monju, also referred to in this document as Monjushiri. Monju was a great spiritual leader who delayed his own achievement of nirvana in order to help his fellow men attain Enlightenment. Ennin's long stay at Mt. Wu-t'ai was the spiritual center of his pilgrimage.*]

. . . When one enters this region of His Holiness [Monju], if one sees a very lowly man, one does not dare to feel contemptuous, and if one meets a donkey, one wonders if it might be a manifestation of Monju. Everything before one's eyes raises thoughts of the manifestations of Monju. The holy land makes one have a spontaneous feeling of respect for the region. . . .

. . . We opened the hall and worshiped an image of His Holiness the Bodhisattva Monju. Its appearance is solemn and majestic beyond compare. The figure riding on a lion fills the five-bay hall. The lion is supernatural. Its body is majestic, and it seems to be walking, and vapors come from its mouth. We looked at it for quite a while, and it looked just as if it were moving.

The venerable monk told us that, when they first made the Bodhisattva, they would make it and it would crack. Six times they cast it, and six times it cracked to pieces. The master was disappointed and said, "Being of the highest skill, I am known throughout the empire, and all admit my unique ability. My whole life I have cast Buddhist images, and never before have I had them crack. When making the image this time, I observed religious abstinence with my whole heart and used all the finesse of my craft, wishing to have the people of the empire behold and worship it and be specially moved to believe, but now I have made it six times, and six times it has completely cracked to pieces. Clearly it does not meet the desire of His Holiness [Monju]. If this be correct, I humbly pray that His Holiness the Bodhisattva Monju show his true appearance to me in person. If I gaze directly on his golden countenance, then I shall copy it to make [the image]." When he had finished making this prayer, he opened his eyes and saw the Bodhisattva Monju riding on a gold-colored lion right before him. After a little while [Monju] mounted on a cloud of five colors and flew away up into space. The master, having been able to gaze on [Monju's] true appearance, rejoiced, [but also] wept bitterly, knowing then that what he had made had been incorrect. Then, changing the original appearance [of the image], he elongated or shortened, enlarged or diminished it [as necessary], so that in appearance it exactly resembled what he had seen, and the seventh time he cast the image it did not crack and everything was easy to do, and all that he desired was fulfilled. After he had made this image, he placed it in the hall, and with tears welling up in his dewy eyes, he said, "Marvelous! What has never been seen before, I have now been able to see. I pray always to be the disciple of Monjushiri, generation after generation and rebirth after rebirth." And so saying, he died.

. . . Regardless of rank or position, here all persons make one think of Monju. Long ago, the Ta-hua-yen-ssu held a great maigre feast, and commoners, both men and women, and beggars and the destitute all came to receive food, but the patron was displeased and said, "My intention in coming here far up the mountain slopes and holding a maigre feast was merely to provide for the monks of the mountain, and it was not my intention that these worldly laymen and beggars should all come and receive my food. If such beggars are to be provided for, then maigre feasts can be arranged in their native places. Why should I come all the way to this mountain [to feed them]?" The monks persuaded him to have food given to all. Among the beggars was a pregnant woman, heavy with child, and, when at her seat she received her full portion, she demanded a portion for the child in her womb. The patron cursed her and would not give it to her. The pregnant woman said several times, "Although the child in my womb has not yet been born, he counts as a person, so why don't you give him his food?" The patron said, "You are a fool. Even though the child in your belly should count as one, he does not come out to ask for it. If he gets the food, to whom should we give it to eat?" The woman replied, "If the child in my belly does not get food, then I too should not eat," and, rising, she left the dining hall. Just as she went out of the door of the hall, she was transformed into Monjushiri, emitting light which filled the hall with dazzling brightness. With his bright jade-[like] countenance and seated on a lion with golden hair and surrounded by a myriad of Bodhisattvas, he soared up into the sky. The whole assembly of several thousand persons rushed out together and fell dumbfounded and insensible to the ground. They raised their voices in repentance and wept bitterly, raining down tears, and called out together, "His Holiness Monjushiri," until their voices gave way and their throats were dry, but he never deigned to turn around and grew indistinct and then disappeared. The whole assembly had no appetite for the food, and each one of them made vows. Thenceforth, when offerings were sent and maigre feasts arranged, all were provided for equally, regardless of whether they were clerics or laymen, men or women, great or small, noble or lowly, poor or rich. Accordingly, the custom of the mountain is to have a system of equality. There have been many other miracles of divine manifestation besides this one, of which the whole empire knows.

[*After years of study at the monastery in Mt. Wu-t'ai, Ennin's achievements in Buddhist knowledge are confirmed.*]

. . . My instruction in the Great Law of the *Kongōkai* was concluded, and I made offerings to the *Kongōkai Mandara* and received Baptism as a Transmitter of the Law. Five jars of water were poured on my head. At night I made offerings to the Twelve Heavens. Everything went auspiciously.

I finished copying the newly translated scriptures of the Hsing-shan-ssu and the *Methods of Reciting Religious Formulae* on the twenty-second day of the fourth moon. [Yüan-cheng] Ho-shang said to me, "I have told you all that I understand about the Great Law of the *Kongōkai,* and you have copies down all of these practices. If there is anything further that you lack, you should seek it elsewhere."

[*Just as Ennin achieves the main goals of his pilgrimage, the political situation becomes volatile. As Uighur armies attack from Central Asia, foreigners and foreign religions come under attack. The Emperor begins to suppress Buddhism and promote Taoism.*]

In the wards within the city of Ch'ang-an there are more than three hundred Buddha halls. Their Buddhist images, scripture towers, and so forth are as magnificent as [those described] in the Law, and all are the work of famous artisans. A single Buddha hall or cloister rivals a great monastery in the provinces. But in accordance with the edict they are being destroyed. I do not know how many Buddha halls and cloisters of the land in the various provinces are being done away with. There [also] was an Imperial edict ordering the destruction of all the revered stone pillars and the grave monuments of monks. [Another] Imperial edict called upon the University for Sons of the State, the Scholars, those who had achieved the status of Accomplished Literati of the land, and those of learning, to take up Taoism, but so far not a single person has done so.

The Taoist priests, Chao Kuei-chen and others, made a memorial to the throne, saying:

> The Buddha was born among the western barbarians and taught "non-birth." "Non-birth" is simply death. He converted men to Nirvana, but Nirvana is death. He talked much of impermanence, pain, and emptiness, which are particularly weird [doctrines]. He did not understand the principles of spontaneity and immortality.
>
> Lao-tzu, the Supreme, we hear, was born in China. In the Tsung-p'ing-t'ai-lo Heaven he roamed about and spontaneously and naturally became transformed. He concocted an elixir and, taking it, attained immortality and became one of the realm of spirits and produced great benefit without limit. We ask that a terrace of the immortals be erected in the Palace where we may purify our bodies and mount to the heavenly mists and roam about the nine heavens and, with blessings for the masses and long life for the Emperor, long preserve the pleasures of immortality.

[*Finally, the Emperor declared that all Buddhist monks and nuns were to be returned to lay life, and that foreign monks were to be sent home. As he departs from Mt. Wu-t'ai, Ennin's main concern is with the scriptures and other sacred material he has collected on his journey.*]

. . . The Commissioners of Good Works, in accordance with the Imperial edict, included us in the return to lay life. They also notified the monasteries that, if a monk or nun does not submit to being returned to lay life, he is guilty of disobedience to an Imperial edict and will be condemned to death on the spot.

On hearing this I bound up my written materials, wrapping up all the scriptures I had copied, the teachings on devotion, and my *mandara.* In all I had four hampers of writings and clothes. Then I bought three donkeys and waited for a decision [on my case]. I do not regret my return to lay life. I merely regret that I shall not be able to take with me the holy teachings I have copied. Buddhism has been proscribed on Imperial order, and I fear that, [were I to take the writings with me], on my way the various prefectures and commanderies would examine me and, discovering the truth, would accuse me of disobedience to an Imperial edict. . . .

After fifteen *li* I turned around and saw the Chief Administrator Ilsin far to the west, coming after us on a horse . . . dashed up the road. We had tea with him in a wayside store and talked for a long time. When we parted he said, "Buddhism no longer exists in this land. But Buddhism flows toward the east. So has it been said since ancient times. I hope that you will do your best to reach your homeland and propagate Buddhism there. Your disciple has been very fortunate to have seen you many times. Today we part, and in this life we are not likely to meet again. When you have attained Buddhahood, I hope that you will not abandon your disciple."

. . . We reached Yang-chou and saw the monks and nuns of the city being sent back to their places of origin with their heads wrapped up. The monasteries are to be destroyed, and their money, estates, and bells are being confiscated by the government.

[*The journey is a difficult one.*]

. . . At dawn we went with some government hirelings to the home of the Interpreter Yu. The Interpreter gave three hundred cash to the government hirelings and conferred with them privately, saying, "The monks are going on a distant trip just at the hottest time of the year, and already they are in distress. I should like to be able to keep them in my home and have them rest for two or three days. You, sirs, go home and come here early on the eighth." The government hirelings agreed to the suggestion and returned home. The Commissioner and the Interpreter did all they could to take care of us.

I have been told that the road from Ch'u-chou to Teng-chou is all mountains and wilderness, the trees and grasses are high and thick, and the mosquitoes and horseflies like rain. All day long one crosses mountains and moors, and the village stockades are far apart. Dwellings are rarely to be seen, and the people are evil at heart. One goes seventy or eighty *li* before coming across a house or two, and people are frightened [when one does meet them]. If we were to take our hampers of writings with us and call them our goods, we would be despoiled by the people, and I fear that we would fail. Moreover, since Buddhism is banned by Imperial edict and has been completely proscribed and since the people of the prefectures and subprefectures to the north are evil at heart, if we were discovered taking Buddhist images with us, they would surely make obstacles for us, and our crime would be that of disobedience to an Imperial edict. Therefore, I consulted with the Interpreter Yu and put all four of the hampers of holy teachings, pious pictures, and clerical clothing which we had brought from the capital, into the Interpreter's house and entrusted them to him, bidding him take charge of them. Earnestly I charged him, saying, "If I reach Teng-chou and can stay there, then please bring my books. If not, let your chief concern be to take care of them and not let them get lost." The Interpreter agreed and put our baggage in order in a special place.

[*As he faces these dangers, Ennin gets the news that the anti-Buddhist emperor has died. The dark cloud of repression is lifted as the new emperor immediately takes steps to restore the monasteries to official favor. Reunited with most of his sacred treasures, Ennin begins his homeward voyage.*]

. . . Tei Yuman returned, and I received a letter from my Ch'u-chou patron, Yu Sinŏn. Among the pious pictures and the writings which I had previously entrusted to him, the *Double Great Taizō and Kongō Mandara* in full colors had been burned by Yu Sinŏn because of the severity of the Imperial orders in Huainan, but [Tei Yūman] was able to bring all the other drawings, writings, and the rest.

. . . We boarded the ship and waited for a wind.

. . . We heard bad news and were extremely frightened, but since there was no wind, we could not start. The group on board cast away mirrors and the like in sacrifice to the spirits to obtain a wind. We monks burned incense and recited prayers on behalf of the spirits of the soil of this island and the spirits of the great and the lowly, praying that we might safely reach our homeland. Then at this place we read the *Diamond Sutra* in one hundred scrolls on behalf of the spirits of this soil and the spirits of the great and the lowly. In the fifth watch (4 A.M.), we started out even though there was no wind. Scarcely had we gotten out of the mouth of the inlet when a west wind suddenly blew up, so we hoisted sail and headed east. It seemed as though the spirits were aiding us.

We went among the mountainous islands, with row upon row of mountainous islands scattered about both north and south of us.

. . . At dawn, far to the east we saw the Island of Tsushima. At noon we saw ahead of us the mountains of Japan stretching out clearly from the east to the southwest. At nightfall we reached Shika Island in the northern part of Matsura District in the Province of Ilizen and tied up.

Source 2 based on a traditional Xi'an rubbing, from a scroll by Ma Jianping. From Sally Hovey Wriggins, Xuanzang: A Buddhist Pilgrim on the Silk Road, *© 1996 by Westview Press. Photo by Abe Dulberg.*

2. Modern Portrait of Xuanzang

Source 3 from Annalist of Nieder-Altaich, "The Great German Pilgrimage of 1064–65," trans. James Brundage, Internet Medieval Sourcebook, [*http://www.fordham.edu/halsall/source/1064pilgrim.html*].

3. Annalist of Nieder-Altaich: "The Great German Pilgrimage of 1064–65"

1. An almost incredible multitude set out for Jerusalem this year to worship at the sepulcher of the Lord. So many people took part in the pilgrimage and so much has been said about it that, lest its omission seem serious, we should briefly summarize here what transpired.

2. The leading personages who took part in the pilgrimage were Archbishop Siegfried of Metz, Bishop William of Utrecht, Bishop Otto of Ratisbon, and Bishop Gunther of Bamberg. Bishop Gunther, though younger than the others, was not inferior to the rest in wisdom and strength of spirit. Although now, after his death, we can scarcely record it without sorrowful groans Gunther was at that time the glory and pillar of the whole realm. Those who were acquainted with his secrets used to say that in many virtues he was perfection itself, down to the most minute details.

3. These leaders were followed by a multitude of counts and princes, rich and poor, whose numbers seemed to exceed twelve thousand. As soon as they had crossed the river known as the Morava, they fell at once into constant danger from thieves and brigands. Prudently avoiding these dangers, they cautiously made their way to the city of Constantinople. There they conducted themselves so honorably in every way that even the imperial arrogance of the Greeks was taken aback by them. The Greeks were so astounded by the noble appearance of Bishop Gunther that they took him to be, not a bishop, but the King of the Romans. [i.e. The King of Germany] They believed that he had disguised himself as a bishop, because he could not otherwise pass through these kingdoms to the sepulcher of the Lord.

4. They left Constantinople a few days later and, after passing through various difficulties and tribulations, came to Latakia. Bishop Gunther made their troubles clear when he wrote from Latakia to his people who were still at home. He said, among other things: "Brethren, we have truly passed through fire and water and at length the Lord has brought us to Latakia, which is mentioned in the Holy Scriptures as Laodicea. We have had the Hungarians serve us without faith and we have had the Bulgarians prey secretly upon us; we have fled from the open raging of the Uzes [i.e. The Byzantine name for the Oghuz Turks] and we have seen the Greek and imperial arrogance of the citizens of Constantinople; we have suffered in Asia Minor, but worse things are yet to come."

5. While they were staying for a few days in Latakia, they began to meet each day many people returning from Jerusalem. The returning parties told of the deaths of an uncounted number of their companions. They also shouted about and displayed their own recent and still bloody wounds. They bore witness publicly that no one could pass along that route because the whole land was occupied by a most ferocious tribe of Arabs who thirsted for human blood.

6. The question before the pilgrims was what to do and where to turn. First of all, they quickly agreed in council to deny their own wishes and to put all hope in the Lord. They knew that, living or dying, they belonged to the Lord and so, with all their wits about them, they set out through the pagan territory toward the holy city.

7. They soon came to a city called Tripoli. When the barbarian commander of the city saw such a multitude he ordered that all of them, without exception, be slaughtered cruelly with the sword; he hoped thereby to acquire an infinite sum of money. Immediately there arose from the sea (which beats against one side of the city) a dark cloud, from which there issued a great many lightning flashes, accompanied by terrifying claps of thunder. When this storm had lasted until noon of the next day and the waves of the sea had reached unusual heights, the pagans, united by the urgency of the situation, shouted to one another that the Christian God was fighting for his people and was going to cast the city and its people into the abyss. The commander, fearing death, changed his mind. The Christians were given leave to depart and at once the disturbance of the sea was calmed.

8. Harassed by various trials and tribulations, the pilgrims at last made their way through the whole country to the city called Caesarea. There they celebrated Holy Thursday, which fell that year on March 24. They even congratulated themselves on having escaped all danger, since it was reckoned that the journey from there to Jerusalem would take no more than two days.

9. On the following day, Good Friday [March 25, 1065] about the second hour of the day, [about 6:30–8 AM] just as they were leaving Kafar Sallam, they suddenly fell into the hands of the Arabs who leaped on them like famished wolves on long awaited prey. They slaughtered the first pilgrims pitiably, tearing them to pieces. At first our people tried to fight back, but they were quickly forced, as poor men, to take refuge in the village. After they had fled, who can explain in words how many men were killed there, how many types of death there were, or how much calamity and grief there was? Bishop William of Utrecht, badly wounded and stripped of his clothes, was left lying on the ground with many others to die a miserable death. The three remaining bishops, together with a considerable crowd of various kinds of people, occupied a certain walled building with two stone towers. Here they prepared to defend themselves, so long as God allowed it.

10. The gate of the building was extremely narrow and, since the enemy was so close, they could not unload the packs carried by their horses. They lost, therefore, their horses and mules and everything that the animals were carrying. The enemy divided these things among themselves and soon hastened to destroy the owners of the wealth. The pilgrims, on the other hand, decided to take up arms and with weapons in hand they courageously fought back. The enemy more indignant than ever, pressed the attack more vigorously, for they saw that the pilgrims, who they had thought would not attempt anything against them, were resisting manfully. For three whole days both sides fought with full force. Our men, though handicapped by hunger, thirst, and lack of sleep, were fighting for their salvation and their lives. The enemy gnashed their teeth like ravening wolves, since it seemed that they were not to be allowed to swallow the prey which they had grasped in their jaws.

11. At last, on Easter Sunday, about the ninth hour of the day, [i.e. mid afternoon] a truce was called and eight pagan leaders were allowed to climb up into the tower, where the bishops were, to find out how much money the bishops would pay for their lives and for permission to leave.

12. As soon as they had climbed up, the one who seemed to be their chief approached Bishop Gunther, whom he took to be the leader of the pilgrims. The sheik removed the linen cloth with which his head was covered, and wrapped it around the neck of the seated bishop. "Now that I have taken you," he said, "all of these men are in my power and I shall hang you and as many of the others as I wish from a tree." Gunther acted as he did because the just man was fearless as a lion. As soon as the interpreter made known what the sheik had done and said, Gunther, who was not at all terrified by the numerical strength of the surrounding enemy, immediately leaped up and knocked the pagan to the ground with a single blow of his fist. The venerable man brought his foot down on the sheik's neck; then he said to his men: "Quick now! Set to and cast all these men into chains and put them out naked to ward off the missiles which their men are throwing at us." There was no delay; as soon as he had spoken his orders were carried off. Thus the assault of the attacking pagans was quelled for that day.

13. On the following day, about the ninth hour, the governor of the King of Babylon [i.e. Al-Mustansir, the Fatamid Caliph of Cairo] who ruled the city of Ramla, came at last with a large host to liberate our men. The governor, who had heard what the Arabs, like heathen, were doing, had calculated that if these pilgrims were to perish such a miserable death, then no one would come through this territory for religious purposes and thus he and his people would suffer seriously. When the Arabs learned of his approach, they dispersed and fled. The governor took charge of those who had been captured and tied up by the pilgrims and opened the gate so that our men could leave. They made their way, after leaving, to Ramla, where, at the invitation of the governor and towns-

people, they rested for two weeks. They were finally allowed to leave and on April 12 they entered the holy city.

14. One cannot describe with words the fountain of tears which was shed there, the number and purity of the prayers and consecrated hosts which were sacrificed to God, or the joyful spirit with which, after many sighs, the pilgrims now chanted: "We shall now pay reverence at his foot stool." [Ps. 131; 1]

15. After they had spent thirteen days there, fulfilling with intimate devotion their vows to the Lord, they finally returned in exultation to Ramla. Large numbers of Arabs gathered together at many places along the route, lying in ambush at all the entrances to the road, for they still sorrowed over the prey which had been snatched from their jaws. Our men, however, were not unaware of this. They presently gave passage money to the merchants. When they saw a favorable wind they boarded the ship. After a prosperous voyage they landed on the eighth day at the port of the city of Latakia. Leaving there a few days later, they joyfully arrived at last, though not without great difficulty and travail, at the Hungarian border and the banks of the Danube river.

Source 4 from Joyce Hill: "From Rome to Jerusalem: An Icelandic Itinerary of the Mid-Twelfth Century," Harvard Theological Review, *76, no. 2 (1983), pp. 178–181 (spelling modernized).*

4. Icelandic Pilgrim's Guide, 12th century

Then it is up to Jerusalem; it is the most splendid of all the cities of the world and is celebrated in song everywhere throughout Christendom because wondrous signs of Christ's passion are still seen there. Here is the church . . . where the Lord's cross stood, where one can clearly see Christ's blood on the stones as if it were newly bled and so it will always be until Doomsday. Men receive light down from heaven there on Easter Eve. It is called the Church of the Holy Sepulcher. . . . The center of the earth is there, where the sun shines directly down from the sky on the feast of Saint John. Here is the hospice of John the Baptist, which is the most magnificent in the whole world. Here is the Tower of David. In Jerusalem also is the Dome of the Rock and Solomon's Temple.

Southwest from Jerusalem is the mountain that is called Zion where the Holy Ghost came upon the apostles and where Christ ate on the evening of Maundy Thursday, and the table at which he ate still stands there. Four miles further south is Bethlehem, a small and beautiful town, where Christ was born. From there it is a short distance to Bethany, where Christ raised Lazarus from the dead. Southeast of Jerusalem is the Dead Sea, where God destroyed two cities, Sodom on the far side and Gomorrah on this side. The Jordan flows through there and does not mix with the waters of the lake because it is very holy water.

East of the city is the Mount of Olives, where Christ ascended into heaven. Between the Mount of Olives and Jerusalem is the valley of Josaphat where there is the tomb of queen Mary. Then it is a long way to the mountain of Querencium, where God fasted and where the devil tempted him. . . . There stood Jericho and the plains of Abraham. Then it is a short distance to the Jordan, where Christ was baptized. . . . On the bank of the river stands a certain small chapel where Christ took off his clothes and so the chapel remains in after times as a witness to the spot. . . .

Homewards from the Jordan it is five days' traveling to Acre, a further fourteen days by sea to Apulia, which is 1800 miles, a further fourteen days on foot from Bari to Rome, a short six weeks' traveling from the south to the Alps, and a further three weeks north to Jutland. . . .

This guide and list of cities and all this information is written at the dictation of Abbot Nicholas, who was both wise and famous, blessed with a good memory, learned in many things, sage and truthful, and there ends this narration.

Source 5 from Guillaume de Deguileville, The Pilgrimage of Human Life (Le Pèlerinage de la vie humaine), *trans. Eugene Clasby (New York and London: Garland Publishing, 1992).*

5. From Guillaume de Deguileville, *Pilgrimage of Human Life*, 1331

BOOK I

To those of this country, who have no home here, but are all pilgrims, as St. Paul says—men and women, rich and poor, wise and foolish, kings and queens—I want to recount a vision that came to me the other night as I was sleeping.

. . . Everyone can learn from it which path to take and which to leave and abandon. This is something very necessary to those who are pilgrims in this wild world. Now listen to the vision that came to me as I was in my bed during my religious life at the Abbey of Chaalis.

As I was sleeping, I dreamed I was a pilgrim eager to go to the city of Jerusalem. I saw this city from afar in a mirror that seemed to me large beyond measure. The city was richly decorated both inside and out. The streets and lanes were paved with gold. The foundation was set up high, the masonry was made of living stones, and a high wall enclosed it on all sides. It had many houses, squares, and mansions. Inside, all was gladness and joy without sorrow. To be brief, all those within it had, in general, more of all good things than they could ever think of or ask for. But I was greatly disturbed that people could not enter as they pleased, because the entrance was very strongly guarded. Cherubim was the gate-keeper, and he held a polished sword, double-edged, well-sharpened on both sides, and easily turned this way and that. He knew how to wield it well and no one was skillful enough with a shield to pass through without being wounded or killed. Even the Prince of the city, because of his human nature, suffered death at the entrance and was pierced through his side with the blade. He left his blood as payment, although he owed no debt there. His knights, his champions, and his servants did the same. They all drank from his cup and met their death at the entrance. I saw pennants, stained red with blood, hanging on the battlements over the gate—the porter of that gate spares no one. When I had seen all this, I knew for certain that one had to enter here by force if there were no other way in. However, I did not see anyone pass through this way. They were all completely overcome when they saw the Cherubim, and from then on he could put away his fiery sword.

Just as I looked up, I saw a marvelous thing that astonished me greatly. I saw St. Augustine sitting high up on the battlements and he seemed to be a fowler or a bird-keeper. With him there were many other great masters and teachers who were helping to feed and nourish the birds. To get the food they were holding and the seeds they were scattering—their honeyed morsels and their sweet, beautiful words—many people were becoming birds and flying up on high. Indeed, I could see many Dominicans, Canons, and Augustinians, all kinds of people, lay and secular, clergy and religious, beggars and the needy, gathering feathers and making great wings for themselves. Then they began to fly, rising high up into the city. They flew over Cherubim and paid little heed to his power.

As soon as I turned and looked in the other direction, I was even more astonished at what I saw there. Up on the walls of the city I saw other persons of authority helping their companions to get inside by clever means. First, I saw St. Benedict, who had placed against the wall a great ladder made up of the twelve rungs of humility. His companions—many black monks, white monks, and grey monks—climbed quickly up these into the city without hindrance from anyone. Next I saw St. Francis, who proved to be a good friend to those of his order. As I saw in my vision, he had let down over the walls a strongly-braided rope with knots in it and all his true companions were climbing up it. None of them had hands so slippery that they could not climb right to the top if they grasped the knots firmly. I saw many others on top of the wall, but I am not sure I can tell you all their names or how they were helping their companions to climb up on all sides, because I was looking only at the side that faced me. I could not see beyond this, much to my regret. But I can tell you that in the wall facing me I saw a small narrow door [Luke 13.24] that the king of the city had placed under guard for the sake of justice. He had given the key to St. Peter, whom he trusted. That trust was surely well-placed, because he let no one pass through except the poor, for the one who does not lie has said that the rich cannot enter there any more than a camel can pass through the eye of a needle [Matt. 19.24]. Entering was very cleverly arranged, for all the people were taking off their clothes and stripping naked at the entrance [Eccles. 5.14]. Old clothes piled up there quickly. None of the people passed through there clothed, unless they wore the king's robes, but those who did so could always pass through anytime they wanted. This way of entering pleased me very much, because all the people had an advantage in common if they became truly poor. There was no difficulty at all, as long as they would take off their old clothes and leave them outside, in order to have new ones within. This arrangement should be quite agreeable, because there is not much to do. In truth, people cannot be so rich that they may not become poor, if they want. And surely it is good to be so, in order to enter into such a beautiful state. It would be good to fast a little, in order to feast at dinner-time.

Now I have told you briefly how I saw the fair city in a beautiful mirror and how I was inspired to go there as a pilgrim, if I could, by any means. Indeed, in my dream I could see no rest anywhere else. It seemed to me that I would find great peace if I could be within its walls.

Source 6 from Naser-e Khosraw (Safarnama), *trans. Wheeler Thackston (CUNY Press, 1985), the Persian Heritage Series No. 36.*

6. From Naser-e Khosraw, *Book of Travels*

I was a clerk by profession and one of those in charge of the sultan's revenue service. In my administrative position I had applied myself for a period of time and acquired no small reputation among my peers. . . .

In the month of Rabi II in the year 437 [October 1045], when the prince of Khurasan was Abu Solayman Chaghri Beg Daud son of Mika'il son of Seljuk, I set out from Marv on official business to the district of Panjdeh and Marv Rud, where I stopped off . . .

From there I went to Juzjanan, where I stayed nearly a month and was constantly drunk on wine. (The Prophet says, "Tell the truth, even if on your own selves.") One night in a dream I saw someone saying to me, "How long will you continue to drink of this wine, which destroys man's intellect? If you were to stay sober, it would be better for you."

In reply I said, "The wise have not been able to come up with anything other than this to lessen the sorrow of this world."

"To be without one's senses is no repose," he answered me. "He cannot be called wise who leads men to senselessness. Rather, one should seek out that which increases reason and wisdom."

"Where can I find such a thing?" I asked.

"Seek and ye shall find," he said, and then he pointed toward the *qibla* and said nothing more. When I awoke, I remembered everything, which had truly made a great impression on me. "You have waked from last night's sleep," I said to myself. "When are you going to wake from that of forty years?" And I reflected that until I changed all my ways I would never find happiness.

On Thursday . . . [19 December 1045] . . . , I cleansed myself from head to foot, went to the mosque, and prayed to God for help both in accomplishing what I had to do and in abstaining from what he had forbidden.

Afterwards I went to Shoburghan and spent the night in a village in Faryab. From there I went via Samangan and Talaqan to Marv Rud and thence to Marv. Taking leave from my job, I announced that I was setting out for the Pilgrimage to Mecca, I settled what debts I owed and renounced everything worldly, except for a few necessities.

. . . After Jerusalem I decided to voyage to Egypt by sea and thence again to Mecca. . . .

. . . Whoever wants to go to Mecca from Egypt must go east. From Qolzom there are two ways, one by land and one by sea. The land route can be traversed in fifteen days, but it is all desert and three hundred parasangs long. Most of the caravans from Egypt take that way. By sea it takes twenty days to reach Jar, a small town in the Hijaz on the sea. From Jar to Medina it takes three days. From Medina to Mecca is one hundred parasangs. Following the coastline from Jar, you will come to the Yemen and the coast of Aden; continuing in that direction, you will eventually wind up in India and China. Continuing southward from Aden and slightly westward, you will come to Zanzibar and Ethiopia. . . . Going south from Egypt through Nubia, you come to the province of the Masmudis, which is a land of broad pasturelands, many animals, and heavyset, strong-limbed, squat, black-skinned men; there are many soldiers of this sort in Egypt . . .

A DESCRIPTION OF THE CITY OF MECCA

The city of Mecca is situated low in the midst of mountains such that from whatever direction you approach, the city cannot be seen until you are there. The tallest mountain near Mecca is Abu Qubays, which is round like a dome, so that if you shoot an arrow from the foot of the mountain it reaches its top. Abu Qubays is to the east of the city, so that if you should be in the Haram Mosque in the month of Capricorn you see the sun rise from behind the top of the mountain. On top of the mountain is a stone stele said to have been erected by Abraham. The city lies on a plain between the mountains and measures only two arrow shots square. The Haram Mosque is in the middle of the plain, and the city lanes and bazaars are built all around it. Wherever there is an opening in the mountain a rampart wall has been made with a gate. The only trees in the city are at the western gate to the Haram Mosque, called Abraham's Gate, where there are several tall trees around a well. On the eastern side of the Haram Mosque a large bazaar extends from south to north. At the south end is Abu Qubays. At the foot of Abu Qubays is Mount Safa, which is like a staircase, as rocks have been set in such a fashion that people can go up to pray, which is what is meant by [the expression] "to do Safa and Marwa." At the other, the north end of the bazaar, is Mount Marwa, which is less tall and has many edifices built on it, as it lies in the midst of the city. In running between Safa and Marwa the people run inside this bazaar.

For people who have come from faraway places to perform the Minor Pilgrimage, there are milestones and mosques set up half a parasang away from Mecca, where they bind their *ihram.* To bind the *ihram* means to take off all sewn garments and to wrap a seamless garment about the waist and another about the body. Then, in loud voice, you say, "*Labayk Allahumma, labayk,*"[6] and approach Mecca. When anyone already inside Mecca wants to perform the Minor Pilgrimage, he goes out to one of the markets, binds his *ihram,* says the Labayk, and comes back into Mecca with an intention to perform the Minor Pilgrimage. Having come into the city, you enter the Haram Mosque, approach the Ka'ba, and circumambulate . . . always keeping the Ka'ba to your left [shoulder]. Then you go to the corner containing the Black Stone, kiss it, and pass on. When the Stone is kissed once again in the same manner, one *tawaf,* or circumambulation, has been completed. This continues for seven *tawafs,* three times quickly and four slowly. When the circumambulation is finished, you go to the Station of Abraham opposite the Ka'ba and stand behind the Station. There you perform two *rakats* called the Circumambulation Prayer. Afterwards you go [to] the Well of Zamzam, drink some water or rub some on the face, and leave the Haram Mosque by the Safa Gate. Just outside this gate are the steps up Mount Safa, and here you face the Ka'ba and say the prescribed prayer, which is well-known. When the prayer has been said, you come down from Safa and go from south to north through the bazaar to Marwa. Passing through the bazaar, you go past the gates to the Haram Mosque, where the Prophet ran and commanded others to run also. The length is about fifty paces, and on either side are two minarets. When the people coming from Safa reach the first two minarets, they break into a run until they pass the other two at the other end of the bazaar. Then they proceed slowly to Marwa. Upon reaching the end they go up Marwa and recite the prescribed prayer. Then they return through the bazaar and repeat the run until they have gone four times from Safa to Marwa and three times from Marwa to Safa, making seven runs the length of the bazaar. Coming down from Marwa the last time, you find a bazaar with about twenty barbershops facing each other. You have your head shaved and, with the Minor Pilgrimage completed, come out of the Sanctuary. The large bazaar on the east side is called Souk al-Attarin [Druggists' Market]. It has nice buildings, and all the shopkeepers are druggists. In Mecca there are two [public] baths each paved with a green stone from which flints are made.

I reckoned that there were not more than two thousand citizens of Mecca, the rest, about five hundred, being foreigners and *mojawirs.*[7] Just at this time there

6. The words of the *labayk* mean approximately "[Thy servant] has answered thy call, O God."

7. ***mojawir:*** a sojourner, one who resides for an unusually long period near a holy place on sacred shrine to receive the blessings attendant upon it.

was a famine, with sixteen maunds of wheat costing one dinar, for which reason a number of people had left.

Inside the city of Mecca are hospices for the natives of every region—Khurasan, Transoxiana, the Iraq, and so on. Most of them, however, had fallen into ruination. The Baghdad caliphs had built many beautiful structures, but when we arrived some had fallen to ruin and others had been expropriated. All the well water in Mecca is too brackish and bitter to drink, but there are many large pools and reservoirs, costing up to ten thousand dinars each, that catch the rainwater from the hills. When we were there, however, they were empty. A certain prince of Aden, known as Pesar-e Shaddel, had brought water underground to Mecca at great personal expense. This water was used to irrigate crops at Arafat and was limited to there, although conduits had been constructed and a little water reached Mecca, but not inside the city; therefore, a pool had been made to collect the water, and water carriers drew the water and brought it to the city to sell. Half a parasang out on the Borqa Road is a well called Bir al-Zahed [the Ascetic's Well]. A nice mosque is located there, and the water is good. The water carriers also bring water from that place for sale.

The climate of Mecca is extremely hot. I saw fresh cucumbers and eggplants at the end of the month of Aquarius. This was the fourth time I had been to Mecca.

From . . . [19 November 1050] until . . . [5 May 1051] I was a *mojawer* in Mecca. On the fifteenth of Aries the grapes were ripe and were brought to town from the villages to be sold in the market. On the first of Taurus melons were plentiful. All kinds of fruit are available in winter, and [the markets] are never empty.

THE HAJJ

On the ninth of Dhu al-Hijja 442 [24 April 1051], with God's help, I completed my fourth pilgrimage. After the sun had set and the pilgrims and preacher had left Arafat, everyone traveled one parasang to Mash'ar al-Haram [Sacred Shrine], which is called Muzdalifa. Here a nice structure like a *maqsura* has been built for people to pray in. The stones that are cast in Mina are gathered up here. It is customary to spend the holiday eve in this spot and then to proceed to Mina early the next morning after the dawn prayer for making the sacrifice. A large mosque called Khayif is there, although it is not customary to deliver the sermon or to perform the holiday prayer at Mina, as the Prophet did not establish a precedent.

The tenth day is spent at Mina, and stones are cast, which practice is explained as a supererogatory act connected with the Pilgrimage.

On the twelfth, everyone who intends to leave departs directly from Mina, and those who intend to remain awhile in Mecca go there. Hiring a camel from an Arab for the thirteen-day journey to Lahsa, I bade farewell to God's House.

A DESCRIPTION OF BASRA

The city has a large wall, except for the portion that faces the water, where there is no wall. The water here is all marsh, the Tigris and Euphrates coming together at the beginning of the Basra district, and when the water of the Hawiza joins the confluence, it is called Shatt-al-Arab. . . . To the southwest of Basra is open plain that supports neither settlement nor agriculture. . . .

When we arrived we were as naked and destitute as madmen, for it had been three months since we had unloosed our hair. I wanted to enter a bath in order to get warm, the weather being chilly and our clothing scant. My brother and I were clad only in old *lungis* with a piece of coarse fabric on our backs to keep out the cold. "In this state who would let us into a bath?" I asked. Therefore, I sold a small satchel in which I kept my books and wrapped the few rusty dirhems I had received in a piece of paper to give the bath attendant, thinking that he might give us a little while longer in the bath in order for us to remove the grime from our bodies. When I handed him the change, he looked at us as though we were madmen and said, "Get away from here! People are coming out of the bath." As he would not allow us in, we came away humiliated and in haste. Even the children who were playing at the bathhouse door thought we were madmen and, throwing stones and yelling, chased after us. We retired into a corner and reflected in amazement on the state of the world.

Now, as we were in debt to the camel driver for thirty dinars, we had no recourse save the Vizier of the King of Ahwaz, Abu al-Fath Ali son of Ahmad, a worthy man, learned in poetry and belles lettres, and very generous, who had come to Basra with his sons and retínue and taken up residence but who, at present, had no administrative position. Therefore, I got in touch with a Persian, also a man of learning, with whom I had some acquaintance and who had entrée to the Vizier but who was also in straightened circumstances and totally without means to be of assistance to me. He mentioned my situation to the Vizier, who, as soon as he heard, sent a man with a horse for me to come to him just as I was. Too ashamed of my destitution and nakedness, I hardly thought it fitting to appear before him, so I wrote a note of regret, saying that I would come to him later. I had two reasons for doing this: one was my poverty, and the other was, as I said to myself, that he now imagines that I have some claim to being learned, but when he sees my note he will figure out just what my worth is, so that when I go before him I need not be ashamed.

Immediately he sent me thirty dinars to have a suit of clothing made. With that amount I bought two fine suits and on the third day appeared at the Vizier's assembly. I found him to be a worthy, polite, and scholarly man of pleasant appearance, humble, religious, and well-spoken. He had four sons, the eldest of whom was an eloquent, polite, and reasonable youth called Ra'is Abu Abd Allah Ahmad son of Ali son of Ahmad. Not only a poet and administrator, he was wise and devout beyond his youthful age. We were taken in and stayed there from the first of Shaban until the middle of Ramadan. The thirty dinars due the Arab for our camel were paid by the Vizier, and I was relieved of that burden. (May God thus deliver all his servants from the torment of debt!)

When I desired to depart he sent me off by sea with gifts and bounteous good things so that I reached Fars in ease and comfort, thanks to the generosity of that noble man. (May God delight in such noble men!) . . .

After our worldly condition had taken a turn for the better and we each had on decent clothing, we went back one day to the bathhouse we had not been allowed to enter. As soon as we came through the door the attendant and everyone there stood up respectfully. We went inside, and the scrubber and servant came to attend to us. When we emerged from the bath all who were in the dressing room rose and remained standing until we had put on our clothes and departed. During that time the attendant had said to a friend of his, "These are those very young men whom we refused admission one day." They imagined that we did not know their language, but I said in Arabic, "You are perfectly correct. We are the very ones who had old sacks tied to our backs." The man was ashamed and most apologetic. Now these two events transpired within twenty days, and I have included the story so that men may know not to lament adversity brought on by fate and not to despair of the Creator's mercy, for he is merciful indeed.

Source 7 from Corpus of Early Arabic Sources for West African History, *trans. J. F. P. Hopkins, ed., N. Levtzion and J. F. P. Hopkins (Cambridge: Cambridge University Press, 1981), Bibliothèque Nationale, Paris, MS. 4657.*

7. From al-Maqrizi's Account of Mansa Musa

Mansā Mūsā arrived in Egypt in 724/1324 with magnificent gifts and much gold. The sultan al-Malik al-Nāsir Muhammad b. Qalāwūn sent the *mihmandār* to receive him and Mūsā rode to the Citadel on the day of his official reception. . . . He refused to kiss the ground and said to the interpreter: "I am a man of the Malikite school and do not prostrate myself before any but God." So the sultan excused him and drew him near to him and did him honour. The sultan asked him the reason for his coming and he replied: "I wish to make the Pilgrimage." So the sultan ordered the *wazīr* to equip him with everything he might need.

It is said that he brought with him 14,000 slave girls for his personal service. The members of his entourage proceeded to buy Turkish and Ethiopian slave girls, singing girls, and garments, so that the rate of the gold dinar fell by six dirhams. Having presented his gift he set off with the caravan. The sultan had committed him to the care of the emir Sayf al-Dīn Itmish, commander of the caravan (*amīr al-rakb*), and he [and his companions] travelled as a self-contained company in the rear of the pilgrim caravan. When he had completed his Pilgrimage he remained behind for several days at Mecca after the ceremonies. Then he turned back but many of his followers and camels perished from cold so that only about a third of them arrived with him. Consequently he needed to borrow much money from the merchants. He bought several books on Malikite jurisprudence. The sultan presented him with horses and camels and he set off for his own country, having given away much wealth as alms in the two holy cities. Whenever his companions addressed him on any subject they bared their heads while speaking to him according to a custom of theirs.

Source 8 from Corpus of Early Arabic Sources for West African History, *trans. J. F. P. Hopkins, ed. N. Levtzion and J. F. P. Hopkins (Cambridge: Cambridge University Press,* 1981*), Bibliothèque Nationale, Paris, MS. 5868.*

8. From al-Umari's Account of Mansa Musa

The king of this realm sits in his palace on a big dais . . . , on a big seat . . . made of ebony like a throne. . . . Over the dais, on all sides, are elephant tusks one beside the other. He has with him his arms, which are all of gold—sword, javelin . . . , quiver, bow, and arrows. . . . About 30 slaves, . . . stand behind him, Turks and others who are bought for him in Egypt. One of them carries in his hand a parasol . . . of silk surmounted by a dome and a bird of gold in the shape of a falcon. This is borne on the king's left. His emirs sit around and below him in two ranks to right and left. Further away are seated the chief horsemen of his army. In front of him there stands a man to attend him, who is his . . . sword-bearer . . . , and another, called *shā'ir* "poet" who is his intermediary . . . between him and the people. Around all these are people with drums in their hands, which they beat. Before the kings are people dancing and he is pleased with them and laughs at them. Behind him two flags are unfurled, and before him two horses are tied ready for him to ride whenever he wishes. . . .

They wear turbans with ends tied under the chin like the Arabs. Their cloth is white and made of cotton which they cultivate and weave in the most excellent fashion. . . . Their brave cavaliers wear golden bracelets. Those whose knightly valour is greater wear gold necklets also. If it is greater still they add gold anklets. Whenever a hero . . . adds to the list of his exploits the king gives him a pair of wide trousers, and the greater the number of a knight's exploits the bigger the size of his trousers. These trousers are characterized by narrowness in the leg and ampleness in the seat. The king is distinguished in his costume by the fact that he lets a turban-end dangle down in front of him. His trousers are of twenty pieces and nobody dares to wear the same. . . .

The king of this country imports Arab horses and pays high prices for them.

His army numbers about 100,000, of whom about 10,000 are cavalry mounted on horses and the remainder infantry without horses or other mounts. They have camels but do not know how to ride them with saddles.

The emir Abū 'l-Ḥasan 'Alī b. Amīr Ḥājib told me that he was often in the company of sultan Mūsā the king of this country when he came to Egypt on the Pilgrimage. He was staying in [the] Qarāfa [district of Cairo] and Ibn Amīr Ḥājib was governor of Old Cairo and Qarāfa at that time. A friendship grew up between them and this sultan Mūsā told him a great deal about himself and his country and the people of the Sūdān who were his neighbors. One of the things which he told him was that his country was very extensive and contiguous with the Ocean. By his sword and his armies he had conquered 24 cities each with its surrounding district with villages and estates. It is a country rich in livestock—cattle, sheep, goats, horses, mules—and different kinds of poultry—geese, doves, chickens. The inhabitants of his country are numerous, a vast concourse. . . . He has a truce with the gold-plant people, who pay him tribute.

Ibn Amīr Ḥājib said that he asked him about the gold-plant, and he said: "It is found in two forms. One is found in the spring and blossoms after the rains in open country (*ṣaḥrā'*). It has leaves like the *najīl* grass and its roots are gold (*tibr*). The other kind is found all the year round at known sites on the banks of the Nīl and is dug up. There are holes there and roots of gold are found like stones or gravel and gathered up. Both kinds are known as *tibr* but the first is of superior fineness (*afḍal fī 'l-'iyār*) and worth more." Sultan Mūsā told Ibn Amīr Ḥājib that gold was his prerogative and he collected the crop as a tribute except for what the people of that country took by theft.

. . . A custom of this sultan is that he does not eat in the presence of anybody, be he who he may, but eats always alone. And it is a custom of his people that if one of them should have reared a beautiful daughter he offers her to the king as a concubine . . . and he possesses her, without a marriage ceremony as slaves are possessed, and this in spite of the fact that Islam has triumphed among them and that they follow the Malikite school and that this sultan Mūsā was pious and assiduous in prayer, Koran reading, and mentioning God. . . .

"I said to him (said Ibn Amīr Ḥājib) that this was not permissible for a Muslim, whether in law . . . or reason . . . , and he said: 'Not even for kings?' and I replied: 'No! not even for kings! Ask the scholars!' He said: 'By God, I did not know that. I hereby leave it and abandon it utterly!'

"I saw that this sultan Mūsā loved virtue and people of virtue. He left his kingdom and appointed as his deputy there his son Muḥammad and emigrated to God and His Messenger. He accomplished the obligations of the Pilgrimage, visited [the tomb of] the Prophet [at Medina] (God's blessing and peace be upon him!) and returned to his country with the intention of handing over his sovereignty to his son and abandoning it entirely to him and returning to Mecca the Venerated to remain there as a dweller near the sanctuary . . . , but death overtook him, may God (who is great) have mercy upon him.

"This sultan Mūsā, during his stay in Egypt both before and after his journey to the Noble Ḥijāz, maintained a uniform attitude of worship and turning towards God. It was as though he were standing before Him because of His continual presence in his mind. He and all those with him behaved in the same manner and were well-dressed, grave, and dignified. He was noble and generous and performed many acts of charity and kindness. He had left his country with 100 loads of gold which he spent during his Pilgrimage on the tribes who lay along his route from his country to Egypt, while he was in Egypt, and again from Egypt to the Noble Ḥijāz and back. As a consequence he needed to borrow money in Egypt and pledged his credit with the merchants at a very high rate of gain so that they made 700 dinars profit on 300. Later he paid them back amply. . . . He sent to me 500 mithqals of gold by way of honorarium. . . .

From the beginning of my coming to stay in Egypt I heard talk of the arrival of this sultan Mūsā on his Pilgrimage and found the Cairenes eager to recount what they had seen of the Africans' prodigal spending. I asked the emir Abū 'l-'Abbās Aḥmad b. al-Ḥāk . . . and he told me of the opulence, manly virtues, and piety of this sultan. "When I went out to meet him (he said), that is, on behalf of the mighty sultan al-Malik al-Nāṣir, he did me extreme honour and treated me with the greatest courtesy. He addressed me, however, only through an interpreter despite his perfect ability to speak in the Arabic tongue. Then he forwarded to the royal treasury many loads of unworked native gold and other valuables. I tried to persuade him to go up to the Citadel to meet the sultan, but he refused persistently, saying: 'I came for the Pilgrimage and nothing else. I do not wish to mix anything else with my Pilgrimage.' He had begun to use this argument but I realized that the audience was repugnant to him because he would be obliged to kiss the ground and the sultan's hand. I continued to cajole him and he continued to make excuses but the sultan's protocol demanded that I should bring him into the royal presence, so I kept on at him till he agreed.

"When we came in the sultan's presence we said to him: 'Kiss the ground!' but he refused outright saying: 'How may this be?' Then an intelligent man who was with him whispered to him something we could not understand and he said: 'I make obeisance to God who created me!' then he prostrated himself and went forward to the sultan. The sultan half rose to greet him and sat him by his side. They conversed together for a long time, then sultan Mūsā went out. The sultan sent to him several complete suits of honour for himself, his courtiers, and all those who had come with him, and saddled and bridled horses for himself and his chief courtiers. His robe of honour consisted of an Alexandrian open-fronted cloak . . . embellished with . . . cloth containing much gold thread and miniver fur, bordered with beaver fur and embroidered with metallic thread, along with golden fastenings, a silken skull-cap with caliphal emblems, a gold-inlaid belt, a damascened sword, a kerchief [embroidered] with pure gold, standards, and two horses saddled and bridled and equipped with decorated . . . saddles. He also furnished him with accommodation and abundant supplies during his stay.

"When the time to leave for the Pilgrimage came round the sultan sent to him a large sum of money with ordinary and thoroughbred camels complete with saddles and equipment to serve as mounts for him, and purchased abundant supplies for his entourage and others who had come with him. He arranged for deposits of fodder to be placed along the road and ordered the caravan commanders to treat him with honour and respect.

"On his return I received him and supervised his accommodation. The sultan continued to supply him with provisions and lodgings and he sent gifts from the Noble Ḥijāz to the sultan as a blessing. The sultan accepted them and sent in exchange complete suits of honour for him and his courtiers together with other gifts, various kinds of Alexandrian cloth, and other precious objects. Then he returned to his country.

"This man flooded Cairo with his benefactions. He left no court emir . . . nor holder of a royal office without the gift of a load of gold. The Cairenes made incalculable profits out of him and his suite in buying and selling and giving and taking. They exchanged gold until they depressed its value in Egypt and caused its price to fall." . . .

Merchants of . . . Cairo have told me of the profits which they made from the Africans, saying that one of them might buy a shirt or cloak . . . or robe . . . or other garment for five dinars when it was not worth one. Such was their simplicity and trustfulness that it was possible to practice any deception on them. They greeted anything that was said to them with credulous acceptance. But later they formed the very poorest opinion of the Egyptians because of the obvious falseness of everything they said to them and their outrageous behaviour in fixing the prices of the provisions and other goods which were sold to them, so much so that were they to encounter today the most learned doctor of religious science and he were to say that he was Egyptian they would be rude to him and view him with disfavour because of the ill treatment which they had experienced at their hands.

Muhanna' b. 'Abd al-Bāqī al-'Ujrumī the guide informed me that he accompanied sultan Mūsā when he made the Pilgrimage and that the sultan was very open-handed towards the pilgrims and the inhabitants of the Holy Places. He and his companions maintained great pomp and dressed magnificently during the journey. He gave away much wealth in alms. "About 200 mithqals of gold fell to me" said Muhanna' "and he gave other sums to my companions." Muhanna' waxed eloquent in describing the sultan's generosity, magnanimity, and opulence.

Gold was at a high price in Egypt until they came in that year. The mithqal did not go below 25 *dirhams* and was generally above, but from that time its value fell and it cheapened in price and has remained cheap till now. The mithqal does not exceed 22 *dirhams* or less. This has been the state of affairs for about twelve years until this day by reason of the large amount of gold which they brought into Egypt and spent there. . . .

Al-Zawāwī also said: . . .

"The king of this country wages a permanently Holy War on the pagans of the Sūdān who are his neighbours. They are more numerous than could ever be counted."

Source 9 from Corpus of Early Arabic Sources for West African History, *trans. J. F. P. Hopkins, ed. N. Levtzion and J. F. P. Hopkins (Cambridge: Cambridge University Press, 1981).*

9. From Ibn Khaldun's Account of Mansa Musa

According to *al-ḥājj* Yūnus, the interpreter for this nation at Cairo, this man Mansā Mūsā came from his country with 80 loads of gold dust . . . , each load weighing three *qinṭārs.* In their own country they use only slave women and men for transport but for distant journeys such as the Pilgrimage they have mounts.

Ibn Khadīja continues: "We returned with him to the capital of his kingdom. He wished to acquire a house as the seat of his authority, solidly constructed and clothed with plaster on account of its unfamiliarity in their land, so Abū Isḥāq al-Ṭuwayjin made something novel for him by erecting a square building with a dome. He had a good knowledge of handicrafts and lavished all his skill on it. He plastered it over and covered it with coloured patterns so that it turned out to be the most elegant of buildings. It caused the sultan great astonishment because of the ignorance of the art of building in their land and he rewarded Abū Isḥāq for it with 12,000 mithqals of gold dust . . . apart from the preference, favour . . . and splendid gifts which he enjoyed."

There were diplomatic relations and exchanges of gifts between this sultan Mansā Mūsā and the contemporary Merinid king of the Maghrib, sultan Abū 'l-Ḥasan. High-ranking statesmen of the two kingdoms were exchanged as ambassadors. The ruler of the Maghrib chose with care such products and novelties of his kingdom as people spoke of for long after . . . and sent them by the hand of 'Alī b. Ghānim, the emir of the Ma'qil, and other dignitaries of his state.

QUESTIONS TO CONSIDER

The questions relating to "sacred journeys" that might be of greatest interest to us as modern readers, those having to do with the inner spiritual lives of the pilgrims, can be very difficult to answer given the nature of the sources available to us. Individual, personal narratives are often not available. Nevertheless, several documents here give us some insight. In reading the sources, how would you compare the *intentions* of the pilgrims? Did the Buddhist, Christian, and Muslim pilgrims you have read about seem to have similar goals in undertaking their journeys, or were their intentions specific to their particular religion? You will have to speculate to answer the next questions, but do you think the experience of pilgrimage had any permanent effects on these travelers after they returned home? What new perspectives might Ennin, for example, have brought back to the Buddhist monasteries of Japan? How might the experiences of the German pilgrims have affected their ideas concerning the establishment of a "New Jerusalem"? How might Mansa Musa's experiences have affected political and religious practices in Mali? What other evidence of changed attitudes or practices do you see in these sources?

Scale of organization was one factor that clearly had a major effect on the experiences of pilgrims. As a general rule, the smaller the group you travel with, the more you need to rely on the help of strangers and the more culturally accommodating you have to be, learning other people's languages and adapting yourself to their customs. Does that statement seem to hold true in these texts? How different were the experiences of pilgrims who traveled alone or with a few people (Naser-e Khosraw or Ennin) from those who traveled as part of much larger groups (Mansa Musa or the German pilgrims)? How might you relate Guillaume de Deguileville's "pilgrimage" to this question?

A related issue is the life of the pilgrims on the road and the reception they met from the people among whom they traveled. In what ways did the government and bureaucracy of China, for example, aid or hinder Ennin in achieving his goals? How would you compare his experiences with those of Christian or Muslim pilgrims moving through what we now call the Middle East? Considering other dangers the pilgrims faced on the road, were they better off traveling in an area of strong or weak government? Some pilgrims, like Mansa Musa, brought considerable wealth with them when they journeyed and were able to pay their own way. If they were not as rich as the king of Mali, how did they sustain themselves while living in foreign lands?

A central question in today's world is the dynamic of cross-cultural exchange in a rapidly globalizing human society. While the pace of such interactions has certainly quickened dramatically, world historians have stressed that we should not assume that people in earlier times lived in utter isolation within separate "civilizations."[8] Pilgrimage routes could act as pathways of cultural borrowing in areas such as language, music, architecture, technology, taste in foodstuffs, and many other areas of life. For world historians, travelers' tales such as these in this chapter can provide valuable information regarding cross-cultural exchanges in pre-modern times. So how *did* the pilgrims relate culturally to the people they encountered on their travels, and how were they viewed by their hosts? What might these pilgrims have brought back from their journeys that would have had an influence back home?

8. Jerry Bentley, *Old World Encounters* (New York: Oxford University Press, 1993).

How did the Arabs who returned to Mali with Mansa Musa, for example, leave their mark on his capital?

Finally, you may want to compare these sources in terms of their relevance or lack of it to today's world. Does Ennin's story have anything to tell us about the relationship between nationalism and religion that might be applied to our own times? Do the attitudes and actions of the Christian and Muslim pilgrims have any continuing relevance to the situation in the Middle East today? Are there other questions raised by these sources that seem to have continuing relevance?

EPILOGUE

The final questions above lead us to consider the issue of sacred journeys in today's world. In some ways, it seems that little has changed. While improvements in transportation and the creation of modern facilities have certainly had an effect, Muslims still perform the same hajj rituals as Naser-e Khosraw and Mansa Musa. Many more Christians and Jews are able to make pilgrimages to Jerusalem than ever before, but when they enter the Holy City, the sites they visit are the same as those their ancestors longed to see a thousand or more years ago. Buddhism is still an international religion with significant movement of believers across national and cultural boundaries (and the Communist government of China seems to be just as interested as its T'ang-era predecessors in the regulation of religion). On the other hand, our world sometimes seems so urbanized, commercialized, and focused on recreation and entertainment that the whole concept of "sacred spaces" seems to be on the wane. Does it seem that we are less likely than our ancestors to aspire to sacred journeys? Or do our journeys take us to places regarded as "sacred" in a nonreligious sense, such as the Lincoln Memorial or the national Baseball Hall of Fame?

Whatever the answer, there can be no doubt about the importance of religiously inspired pilgrimages over the long course of world history.

CHAPTER FOURTEEN

THE VILLAGE AND THE STATE

(1400–1650)

THE PROBLEM

Political history is often told as the story of military conquests and the careers of leaders and generals. According to these accounts, the era around 1500 was a time of significant developments in many parts of the world. In England, the years 1455 to 1471 saw bitter conflict between competing claimants to the throne—the Wars of the Roses—and then unification under a new dynasty, the Tudors. In the Andes, the people who came to be known as the Incas first slowly and then more quickly expanded their authority over other peoples, creating by the end of the fifteenth century the largest empire ever built in South America. In Japan, the period between 1467 and 1568—known as the age of the Warring States (*Sengoku*)—was one of nearly constant warfare between local military leaders, followed by a period of regional consolidation and ultimately the establishment of peace after 1590 under a series of military leaders, including Toyotomi Hideyoshi and Tokugawa Ieyasu.

All large-scale governments—nations, empires, states, kingdoms—depend on extracting revenues from their populations that enable them to carry out their aims, whether these are conquest, further centralization, or simply the maintenance of power. This may take the form of monetary taxation, as it does in most of the modern world, or of taxes paid in the form of goods and services, as it did in most of the pre-modern world. Governments may also require and demand labor services for a variety of purposes, of which military conscription has been the longest lasting. Large-scale governments can collect these taxes and obligations directly, as the United States government does today through the Internal Revenue Service, or they can depend on intermediaries. In England and Japan, these intermediary authorities were often members of the hereditary aristocracy who also had jurisdiction over certain aspects of life and collected their own taxes and payments. In the Andes, the Incas relied on both leaders of the conquered people and officials sent out from their capital at Cuzco to enforce their demands for payments. Better exploitation of surpluses from largely agricultural populations was a major part of political developments in all three of these areas in the period around 1500.

Central and regional governments and members of the nobility were not the only political authorities that had an impact on people's lives. Throughout the pre-modern world, most people lived in villages, supporting themselves and providing the required taxes and payments by growing agricultural products of various types. In many places these villages developed political structures of their own, institutions of self-governance that regulated what went on and conducted relations with national or regional authorities. These institutions changed over time depending on a variety of factors; the impositions of authorities beyond the village was one of these, but new agricultural techniques, epidemic diseases, climate change, and cultural developments such as the introduction of new belief systems also influenced village self-government and political life. As historians have studied village life more closely over the last thirty years as part of their growing interest in the lives of ordinary people, they have discovered that although villages are often portrayed as passive and timeless, they can be quite dynamic. Thus, to be comprehensive, political history must include not only the story of large-scale governments, but also that of local structures of power, which in the pre-modern world generally meant those of kin groups and villages.

Your task in this chapter is to use sources from three widely divergent areas, England, the Andes, and Japan, to explore some of the ways in which villages and states interacted and the ways different levels of political authority sought to shape people's actions in the centuries around 1500. How did the state seek to control villages and their resources? How did villages respond to these efforts and themselves seek to regulate the lives of their inhabitants? What similarities and differences can you see across these three cultures, and how might the life of peasants in them have been different or similar as a result?

BACKGROUND

Scholars of village life often spend their entire career exploring a single village in great depth, investigating family relationships, land ownership and settlement patterns, legal developments, and other issues. They point out that every village is distinct, and that there are often great differences between villages that are quite close together. Some of them might be horrified at the type of analysis and comparison we are doing in this chapter, but their intensive local research is what has allowed us to gain the knowledge we have of individual villages, and makes such comparisons possible. In order to understand village–state interactions in these three areas, we must rely first on the work of local historians to learn something about the organization of villages in each area, then on the work of political historians to learn about the larger political structures within which these villages were enmeshed.

In England, most of the villages were nucleated; that is, the houses were clumped together, with the fields stretching beyond this compact center. In many parts of England, the fields of the village were farmed in what is termed open-field agriculture, a pattern that differs sharply from modern farming practices. In open-field agriculture, the village as a whole—or actually the adult male heads of household—decided what crops would be planted in each field, rotating the crops according to tradition and need. Some fields would be planted in crops such as wheat and rye for human consumption, some would be planted in oats or other crops for both animals and humans, and some would be left unworked, or *fallow,* to allow the soil to rejuvenate. Most families were also allowed to run some animals, such as pigs, cattle, and sheep, in the woods or meadows outside the cultivated fields.

The open-field system and many other local issues were largely handled by the village itself, but much of the economic and political life of the village fell under the jurisdiction of lords, members of the nobility or gentry who might live in a large house in the village but often lived elsewhere. The territory controlled by a lord, generally termed a *manor,* might consist of one village, a number of villages, or even only part of a village. Within each manor, the lord established the duties each villager owed, which generally included labor obligations and payments of taxes in cash or goods such as wheat or animals. Lords generally appointed officials termed *bailiffs* or *reeves* from outside the village to oversee the legal and business operations of their manors, and additional officials were chosen by the village residents themselves from among the adult men to supervise the harvest, watch over the use of the mill, or perform similar tasks.

Several times a year in most English villages, the villagers, or at least some of them, gathered for court proceedings during which the legal and financial affairs of both the lord and the village were dealt with; these courts handled matters such as land transfers or inheritance disputes. The courts often went beyond what we would recognize as judicial activities and issued new ordinances—which historians now term *by-laws*—in the name of the lord and the village to regulate activities in the village or its fields and forests. In the thirteenth century, manorial courts began keeping formal records written on pieces of parchment that were stitched end to end and then rolled up; they were generally made while the court was in session, not written up afterward. Such court rolls are the most important type of documents surviving for exploring English villages during this period.

Along with laws passed by the manorial courts, England had national laws and ordinances that were issued by the king, sometimes in conjunction with Parliament. These were generally sent out as written documents to the sheriffs in every county, who would then be the main agents of enforcement. So that people could know the law, the sheriff would often order it to be read out loud at places where people gathered, such as marketplaces and churches. Once a national law became known, those who broke it could be tried at higher-level courts, or at manorial courts if the amount set as the fine for breaking the law was not too great. Protests against national and manorial laws generally took the form of evasion rather than outright disobedience, although opposition to a royal poll tax levied in 1378 to pay for war with France led to a nationwide rebellion in 1381.

In the Andes, the main staple crops were various types of potatoes in highland areas and maize in more low-lying areas. Villagers often built terraces, separated by stone retaining walls, on the steeper slopes to plant their crops, and irrigation channels and ditches to bring water to the fields. At the time of the Inca conquest, families in most Andean cultures were organized into *ayllus,* groups of related kin that cooperated in farming and ritual activities. Each ayllu was located in a specific territory and organized the agricultural work for that area, such as clearing fields, planting and harvesting crops, and building irrigation channels, but the boundaries between the areas were not always clearly delineated. The ayllus were economically independent, but most villages were actually made up of more than one ayllu. Land was owned by the ayllu, not by individuals, with parallel lines of descent; women achieved access to resources such as land, water, and herds through their mothers, and men through their fathers.

Along with the ayllus, several other forms of social organization were important in Andean culture. One of these was a division of society into two parts, termed *moieties,* which were related to other categories that were regarded as binary, such as light and dark or right and left. The moiety system divided society into an upper moiety called the *hanansaya* and a lower moiety called the *hurinsaya;* within each village, ayllus were grouped into one of these two moieties, with the larger and more prominent ayllus having a higher rank within that moiety. The two moieties together made up a whole, with both of them viewed as necessary for social stability, but the hanansaya were also regarded as superior to the hurinsaya, and the leader of the hanansaya in any village was viewed as the village's leader. After the Inca conquest, this division between upper and lower also came to be associated with the Incas and those they had conquered, with the Incas and those who had dealings with them being regarded as having more social prestige than others. Luis Capoche, a Spanish official, described this social division in 1585 in this way: "And the *hanansaya,* which means the group from above, held the first rank of nobility and they rallied as military people to the calls for war made by the

Inca; and the *hurinsaya* are understood to be the people from below and the class of the common and simple people, who carried the provisions and necessities of the warriors."[1]

The word *Inca* originally meant a single person, the Inca king, who picked his successor from among his sons. Though most Incas were monogamous, the king had many wives and children, and his ayllu could be very large; on his death, that group continued to live off his wealth, and the new king formed a new ayllu. By the 1530s, the time of European conquest, there were eleven royal ayllus, corresponding to the first eleven kings. Each of them had to extract a surplus from villagers somewhere in order to provide food and other necessary goods; this system may have been one of the reasons for the Inca wars of conquest.

The Inca system for collecting taxes was quite different from that in England. Instead of paying in a combination of goods, cash, and labor, conquered peoples within the Inca empire paid their tribute solely in labor. The food produced on conquered land was divided into three parts, with one part supporting the Inca bureaucracy, one part the religious personnel of the Inca empire, and the third the people who actually worked the land. (These parts were not always equal, and appear to have been adjusted if Inca officials decided that a family or ayllu did not have enough land to feed itself.) Along with this agricultural labor, all heads of household were also required to send a person (or themselves) to work a certain number of days per year at other tasks, including road building and military service. This labor tax, called the *m'ita,* was rotated among households throughout the year, with some labor required of each household every year.

The Incas did not develop a system of writing before the arrival of the Spanish, but Inca officials recorded statistical information, including tax data, on *quipus,* which were collections of knotted cords of various colors and lengths, all suspended from one thicker cord. The ability to read quipus has been lost; however, early Spanish officials sometimes recorded the words of people who were reading these quipus and a few native or mixed-race individuals wrote chronicles based in part on quipus, so that the information they contained has not been completely lost. These records were, of course, written in Spanish or Latin, not Quecha (the language of the Incas), and there were certainly some misunderstandings, but they are still very valuable. They were also generally written from the perspective of the conquering Incas rather than that of other Andean peoples; for other peoples' perspectives, we must rely on archaeological evidence.

In Japan, the major crop was rice, grown either on dry fields or on flooded, enclosed paddies, which produced significantly more than the dry fields. Villages were different in size and structure, but in the fourteenth and fifteenth centuries many of them,

1. Luis Capoche, "Relación general de la villa imperial de Potosi . . ." [1585], translated and quoted in Brian S. Bauer, *The Development of the Inca State* (Austin: University of Texas Press, 1992), p. 126.

especially those near the capital of Kyoto, formed themselves into semiautonomous communities (*so*) made up of one or more villages, with economic, social, religious, and political functions. The so developed means of handling disputes among villagers, issued and enforced ordinances, owned some property in common, controlled irrigation and common lands collectively, and assumed collective responsibility for tax payments. The so as a whole decided how much each family farmed and paid in taxes, and redistributed land if it seemed that certain families were not able to support themselves. So signed agreements with authorities beyond the village and often existed as permanent institutions for centuries. Disputes with higher authorities were often expressed in the form of collectively written petitions of grievances or litigation, and sometimes led to revolt.

During the Warring States period, the central government of the shogun was very weak, and the main agents of political authority were the *daimyo,* local military leaders who began to develop into territorial rulers in control of all aspects of life. Daimyo sometimes granted land to military retainers, who administered their own holdings somewhat independently, handling legal issues and collecting taxes. The daimyo and their retainers relied on shares of the rice and soybean harvest along with payments of cloth for their income, so they encouraged more intensified farming; greater yields would also make more rice or other grains available for sale at local markets, whose transactions also yielded revenue to them. By 1550 many of the more powerful daimyo sought to restrict the independent authority of their military retainers while still keeping them loyal, and to assess land values and land holdings more accurately in order to maximize both rice production and the resultant income. Thus, as in England, village–state interactions really involved three actors—the ruling daimyo, lower-level military retainers, and the villagers acting through their communal so—each of which could work with one of the others against the third. In some cases, villages also joined together in leagues (*ikki*) to defend their interests against the actions of overlords.

During the sixteenth century, a series of powerful military leaders began to create a national political structure based on a coalition of daimyo, from whom they demanded strict obedience. As part of his efforts at centralization, one of these generals, Toyotomi Hideyoshi (r. 1590–1598), created models for tax collection and encouraged surveys of all land that would classify land according to its level of productivity. These surveys were supposed to encourage peasant landownership and create uniformity in landholding, but in many areas drastic reorganization never occurred. In addition, Hideyoshi did not undermine the importance of the so in villages that were organized in this way, but instead used the so to ensure order at the local level. Hideyoshi's successor, Tokugawa Ieyasu, also allowed so to continue issuing ordinances, handling disputes, and carrying out religious observances, though his government also appointed new types of officials on lands he directly controlled to represent the village and oversee tax collection and household registration. These centralizing rulers (Tokugawa Ieyasu took on the old title of *shogun,* a title that had earlier been given to the supreme military commander over all Japan) thus became a fourth force in village–state interactions. Scholars have paid great attention to the daimyo and to centralizing rulers, and there are many sources that represent their point of view. Individual so maintained records regarding laws and administration that stretch over many centuries as well, however, and through these we can have some insight into the villagers' own view of their situation. These records are generally made from paper made of the bark of mulberry trees, stitched together into book form. Access to them is still sometimes controlled by village officials or the families of former village leaders, with the collections including thousands or even tens of thousands of documents.

THE METHOD

As with many other aspects of life in the pre-modern world, we have much more information about the way village–state interactions were *supposed* to be than about the way they were. Many of our sources are clearly prescriptive, such as laws and ordinances issued by the villages themselves or by higher governmental authorities. Others are idealizations; they may look like descriptions of reality, but they are strongly influenced by the opinions of the author about proper political relations. Historians have sometimes been misled into thinking that such sources describe the actual operations of political authority, which has led them to overemphasize the power of large-scale governments. The first two questions for this chapter have been posed carefully to avoid such misunderstandings, for they ask you to examine ways in which states *sought* to control villages and ways in which villages *sought* to respond to these measures and to control their own residents. These questions can be answered using both prescriptive and idealizing sources, and your method in interpreting the written sources for this chapter should be one of careful reading and analysis. As you read each source, note the actions and the aims of the village structures of power and those of the higher-level authorities; making a list of these would be very helpful. The first two questions require you to put together information from the sources for each culture, and the third question asks you to compare the three cultures and make some inferences based on these comparisons. You will thus need to develop your answers to the first two questions before moving on to the third.

Along with written evidence, the

chapter includes a visual source from each of the three cultures that portrays some aspect of the enforcement of political power. We may think of visual depictions as descriptive, as portraying an actual scene; this is sometimes true, but they may just as often be intended to describe an ideal or to make a point that the artist wished to stress. This does not limit our use of them in this chapter, but, as with law codes, we must be careful not to assume that they are simply representations of reality.

Sources 1 through 4 come from England. Source 1 is a series of by-laws from the village of Great Horwood in central England, which you should read carefully. What types of activities did these laws seek to prohibit? What punishments were set for those who broke these regulations? Who is described as issuing these laws? In which situations do the villagers enforce their own laws, and in which is the lord involved? Source 2 is the record of a manorial court held in the village of Teynton in central England in 1541; it is the only document in this chapter that describes the actual operations of a court and the enforcement of laws. What types of taxes and fees do the villagers pay to the king? How else does he exert his authority? What by-laws do villagers appear to have broken, and how are these infractions punished? Source 3 is a Statute of the Realm, issued by Henry VIII in 1511, which to a great degree repeats a statute issued by Edward III in 1363 during the Hundred Years' War. What does Henry order villagers to do? What does he forbid them to do? What justifications does he give for these measures? How is this law to be enforced? Source 4 is an illumination from the Smithfield Decretals, a manuscript from a slightly earlier period that depicts many scenes of English life, especially in its small marginal paintings. This one shows the king dispatching a messenger. How does the artist convey the speed of the messenger? In what form is the message he takes?

Sources 5 through 8 come from the Andes. Source 5 is from the report of a Spanish inspector dating from 1549; the area concerned, the Huallaga Valley, had put up strong resistance to Spanish rule and had been conquered only in 1542. Spanish authorities wished to know about the obligations imposed by the Incas on the Chupaychu, the main ethnic group in this area, whom the Incas deemed to have consisted of 4000 households. The record was written in Spanish by a European scribe, based on an Andean's reading of a quipu. According to this report, what types of labor had the villagers been required to do? If all of these labor obligations were actually met (which we have no way of knowing), how many villagers were engaged in labor for the Incas, and how many in basic food production or care of animals? Sources 6 and 7 are chronicles written in Spanish that also describe the taxation system of the Incas. Source 6 is from the chronicles of Pedro de Cieza de León (1520–1554), a Spanish soldier and writer who compiled a history of Peru during his seventeen years there. Source 7 is from the chronicles of Garcilosa de la Vega (1539–1616), the son of a Spanish conquistador and an Inca princess, who grew up in Peru but left there as a young man and spent the rest of his life in Spain. Both of these authors are generally favorable to the Incas, viewing them as benign conquerors, which may have influenced their reporting on Inca demands. According to these authors, what types of labor are required of the villagers? How are the laws requiring tribute enforced? Who was liable to pay labor tribute? How do these authors assess the level of labor service required? How does their assessment fit with the information recorded in Source 5?

Source 8 is from another chronicle, this one by the Andean noble author Filepe Guaman Poma de Ayala; his very long chronicle, written between 1584 and 1615 and addressed to the Spanish king, includes hundreds of illustrations that have been an important source for many aspects of Peruvian life, including gender relations and agricultural techniques. In this illustration, an Inca official labeled "governor of the royal roads" is talking with a runner, whom Guaman Poma describes as having "the speed of sparrow-hawks." Along the road are special huts, which the Incas built every mile or so; runners carried oral messages and perhaps quipus to the runner in the next hut, a system that allowed news to travel about 150 miles a day. In the written sources, you have already read about demands for labor tribute for road building, and roads were an essential part of the Inca empire. How would these runners further enhance the strength of the empire? Why might the Inca have selected "the most nimble" from their subject peoples and trained them for this task, rather than training their own young men as runners?

Sources 9 through 13 are from Japan. Source 9 is a series of regulations from several so in the region around Kyoto. What actions on the part of villagers are required? What is prohibited? Who is responsible for enforcing these regulations? Source 10 is an extract from a petition from a group of villagers to their overlord. What are they requesting? What obligations do they wish to have lessened, and what reasons do they give? Source 11 includes two decrees, the first dating from 1587 and the second from the following year, from two different sides in the battle for centralized power. The first decree comes from Hojo Ujimasa, one of the last major opponents of Hideyoshi, who was being pressed militarily, and the second from Hideyoshi himself. What does each of them order? What does each set for punishments if the order is not followed? How does Hojo Ujimasa justify the need for military conscription? How does Hideyoshi justify the need to *prevent* villagers from having weapons? What are they to do instead of fighting? (Hideyoshi's method was ultimately more successful, and the conscripted army of Hojo Ujimasa was no match for Hideyoshi's professional army, though commoners were involved in battles into the seventeenth century.)

Source 12 is a series of regulations for villagers, issued by the shogunate in 1643. What are villagers prohibited from doing? Why are certain crops and foods to be encouraged and others prohibited? Source 13 is a detail from one of the screens painted by

Kusumi Morikage (ca. 1620–1690), one of the few Japanese artists from this period who depicts rural life in a sympathetic manner. In this scene, people are engaged in agricultural activities and a tax collector is visiting the village. Which of the so's own regulations and of those imposed by the shogunate are being followed? What else do you notice about rural life in this painting?

You have now developed three lists of some of the ways in which higher-level authorities impinged on villagers' lives and, for England and Japan, some of the ways in which villagers responded and regulated themselves. (No records comparable to English by-laws or Japanese so regulations exist for the Andes, though scholars are now using archaeological evidence to discover many details about village life. Large-scale agriculture and irrigation projects indicate that villages and ayllus certainly imposed some type of regulations, passed down through oral tradition and perhaps recorded on quipus.) These lists will provide you with numerous examples with which to answer the first two questions in the chapter. Before starting your comparisons in answer to the third question, we recommend turning to the Questions to Consider section, which offers some suggestions for lines of comparison.

THE EVIDENCE

Source 1 from Warren O. Ault, Open-Field Farming in Medieval England: A Study of Village By-Laws *(London: George Allen and Unwin, 1972), pp. 125, 132, 134, 136, 138, 141.*

1. Village By-laws from Great Horwood

1433

Plebiscite. It is ordered by all the tenants that no one shall have his beasts on the green of the town by night until the end of autumn next to come under pain each one of 4d.[2] And there were chosen as wardens John Hayes and Robert Baynard.

Plebiscite. And that every tenant be at Nether forde next Monday about Vespers with tools to clean the watercourse under pain of 1d. for default and John Baynard of Nether Ende is chosen warden.

2. **d.** = denarius, or penny; 12 pennies made a shilling, abbreviated s.

1465

It is ordered by the consent of all the tenants there that no one henceforth shall wilfully allow his foals openly to go into the fields of grain after they are three weeks old unless tethered to their mothers under pain of each one doing the contrary paying 12d. namely for each foal every time.

1480

The township of Great Horwood is ordered to make anew part of the butts[3] this side the Feast of the Nativity of St John the Baptist[4] under pain for each one in default of 8d., 4d. of which to the parish church there pay 4d.

And if any one shoots with arrows at the metes[5] and does not close the bars after him he shall forfeit to the lord as often as he does it 4d.

1503

It is ordered by common consent and assent that all tenants having hedges on the eastern part of the town aforesaid shall cause them well and sufficiently to be repaired, namely from Colles Lane to the eastern end of the aforesaid town leading toward Little Horwood, under pain for each of them failing in default of 12d.

And under the aforesaid pain that each of them who puts his cattle on their land adjacent to their closes next to sown land shall keep them safely and securely under guard.

And that henceforth each of them who has land next to his close shall plough it and bring it into cultivation under the aforesaid pain.

1516

It is ordained that all the tenants and inhabitants shall tether their foals and mares in the sown fields and not allow them to go at large in the grain of the tenants under pain for each delinquent of 40d.

And that none of the inhabitants shall cut or carry furze[6] from the common called the Priourswode except by order of the bailiff under pain each delinquent of 20d.

And that no one shall take fish in the common fishing stream called 'le brok' flowing within the aforesaid town unless it be on his own ground under pain for each delinquent of 40d.

3. **butt:** a mound of earth on which a target is set.
4. **Feast of St. John the Baptist:** June 24.
5. **mete:** boundary.
6. **furze:** a spiny evergreen shrub.

1531

It is ordered that they shall not allow their beasts to go at large before the end of autumn under pain of 40d.

It is ordered that no tenant by copy of court [roll] shall have several . . . sub-tenants in one house without the lord's leave, under pain of 40s.

It is ordained that no one shall pasture any beast except oxen in the wheat field before the Feast of Pentecost[7] under pain of 40d.

1534

It is ordered that no one shall harbour or entertain any woman or women of ill fame more than one night under pain for each delinquent, of 6s. 8d.

Source 2 from Nathaniel J. Hone, The Manor and Manorial Records *(Port Washington, N.Y.: Kennikat Press, 1971), pp. 177–178.*

2. Court Roll of Teynton, 1541

Court of the manor of the lord King held there 13th Dec. 32 Hen. viij.

Essoins[8]—none.

The homage[9] there to wit Robert Frebury, William Burchall, Robert Baker, William Bedell, Thomas Mychell, Ralph Tayllor, Robert Stokes, John Agas, Thomas Frebury, Robert Shelffocke, William Ansley, Clement Michell, Thomas Hill, and John Hychene, being sworn and charged by the Steward present, upon their oath that the lands and tenements[10] [of the] late George Lord Cobham's remain in the hands of the lord King by reason of an exchange for other lands.

And that Robert Lambard, John Edwards, Robert Payne, John Ward, and Robert Stokes are free tenants and owe suit of Court and have appeared.

And that Laurence Pemerton, who held of the lord King according to the custom of the manor, three messuages[11] whereof one is called Hornes Barne another Stayarhows and a third late in the tenure of William Welles, and before him of Richard Michell, and three virgates[12] of land by a rent for the whole per ann. is dead since the last court; whereupon there falls to the lord of heriot[13] for

7. **Feast of Pentecost:** The seventh Sunday after Easter; in 1531, this was May 28.
8. **essoins:** people's excuses for not appearing in court, brought in by others.
9. **homage:** free male residents of the town required to swear an oath to their lord.
10. **tenement:** building.
11. **messuage:** land surrounding a house.
12. **virgate:** roughly 25 to 30 acres of land.
13. **heriot:** fee due to the lord on the death of a tenant, usually the best animal owned by the family.

the two messuages one young ox and a cow valued both at 18^d delivered to Ralph Norwood esq. the King's farmer there, and for the third messuage no heriot as yet. And let there be an inquiry thereof before the next court, because the homage present the said messuage is not heriotable. And the first proclamation is made. And no one comes.

To this court comes Robert Lamberd, son and heir of Thomas Lamberd, deceased, and does fealty to the lord for a messuage and virgate of land with appurtenance late of Thomas his father, and gives for relief 6^s 8^d.

And Robert Tayllor, since the last court, has cut down an elm, to wit a timber tree worth 6^d, without licence of any of the lord King's officers; but the said Robert used the same tree for repair of his tenement; therefore let him have a talk thereupon with the King's officer before next court.

And the aforesaid Laurence Pemerton, in his life time, substituted Walter Milleward as his subtenant in the said messuage called the Stayarhows, contrary to the custom of the manor, without licence; therefore let him have a talk thereon with the King's officer before the next court.

And that William Bedell, Robert Baker, John Agas, Thomas Frebury, Robert Stokes, and Clement Michell have forfeited to the lord King each of them 40^d because they have not repaired the defects of their tenements before the feast of All Saints last past as they had in precept at the last Court. But they are bound till the next court, because no one was assigned to deliver them timber for the said repairs.

And Robert Huchyns, the miller there, has not restored his encroachment of the land by the mill, as he had in precept at the last Court, under pain of forfeiture to the lord King 40^d but said pain in respite till next Court, upon view thereof to be had.

It is ordained that no keeper shall place his penning sheep on the wheat field after the feast of St Martin in future, under pain for each offence of forfeiture to the King 6^s 8^d.

Sum of Court 24^s 8^d.

Source 3 from Statutes of the Realm, 3rd. Henry VIII, c. 3, p. 25. *Spelling and orthography modernized.*

3. Statute of Henry VIII Regarding the Shooting of Longbows, 1511

The King our sovereign lord, calling to his most noble and gracious remembrance, that by the feat and exercise of the subjects of this his realm in shooting of longbows there hath continually grown and been within the same great number and multitude of good archers which hath not only defended this realm and the subjects thereof against the cruel malice and danger of their outward enemies in time heretofore passed . . . and albeit that diverse good and profitable statutes in the time of his noble progenitors and predecessors kings of this land for the maintenance of archery and longbows heretofore have been made, amongst which the right famous king of noble memory Henry VII, father to our said sovereign lord by authority of diverse parliaments caused good and noble acts and statutes to be established and made . . . yet nevertheless archery and shooting in longbows is right little used but daily diminishes, decays, and abates more and more. . . . And also by means and occasion of customable usage of tennis-play, bowles [lawn-bowling], classhe [skittles], and other unlawful games, prohibited by many good and beneficial estates by authority of parliament in that behalf provided and made, great impoverishment hath ensued. And many heinous murders, robberies, and felonies be committed and done. And also the divine [service] by such misdoers on holy and festival days not heard or solemnized to the high displeasure of the Almighty God.

Wherefor the King . . . hath ordained, enacted, and established that the Statute of Winchester for archers be put in due execution. And moreover that every man being the King's subject not lame, decrepit, or maimed, nor having any other lawful or reasonable cause or impediment, being within 60 years, (except those men, spiritual men, justices of one bench or of the other, justices of the assize and barons of the exchequer) do use and exercise shooting in longbows, and also to have a bow and arrows ready continually in his house to use himself, and do use himself in shooting. And also that the father, governors, and rulers of such as be of tender age do teach and bring upon them the knowledge of the same shooting. And that every man having a man child or men children in his house shall provide, ordain, and have in his house for every man child being of the age of seven years and above till he shall come to the age of seventeen years, a bow and two shafts to induce and learn them and bring them up in shooting and shall deliver all the same bow and arrows to the same young men to use and occupy. And if the same young men be servants that then their masters shall abate the money that they shall pay for the same bows and arrows of their wages. And after all such young men shall come to the age of seventeen years every of them shall provide and have a bow and four arrows continually for himself at his proper costs and charges, or else of the gift and provision of his friends, and use and occupy the same in shooting as is afore rehearsed. . . . And every person that shall be found by inquiry or examination in default or not providing and having bows, arrows, and shafts ready by the space of one month shall forfeit and pay for every such default 12d. . . .

And that all statutes heretofore made against them that use unlawful games be duly put in execution, and punishment had according to the penalties of the same, as well against the offenders and occupiers of such unlawful games as against them that be owners or keepers of houses or other places where any such unlawful games be used. . . . And furthermore that all justices of the peace, bailiffs, sheriffs, constables, and all other head officers, and every of them finding or knowing any mans person or persons using or exercising any unlawful games contrary to the said estate, shall have full power and authority to commit every such offender to ward [jail], there to remain without bail to such time he or they so offending be bound by obligation to the king's use in such sum of money as by the discretion of the said justices, mayors, bailiffs, or other head officers shall be thought reasonable that they nor any of them shall not from thence forth use any unlawful games. And that every bower [bow-maker] within this realm always make for every bow of ewe that he maketh to sell at least two bows of elm or other wood of mean [moderate] price.

Source 4: British Library, Royal MS 10. E. IV, fo. 302V.

4. King and Messenger, from the Smithfield Decretals, ca. 1340

Source 5 from John V. Murra, "The Mit'a Obligations of Ethnic Groups to the Inka State," in The Inca and Aztec States 1400–1800: Anthropology and History, *ed. George A. Collier, Renato Rosaldo, and John D. Wirth (New York: Academic Press, 1982), pp. 240–243.*

5. Report from the General Inspection of the Chupaychu, 1549

[Cord 1] They were asked what services did [the Chupaychu] give to the Inca in Cuzco *a la continua*[14]
and they said that 400 Indian men and women remained in Cuzco *a la continua* to build walls and if one died they gave another.

[Cord 2] They also gave 400 Indians to plant the fields in Cuzco so people could eat

[Cord 3] They also gave 150 Indians *a la continua* as *yana*[15] of Guayna Capac.[16]

[Cord 4] 150 more to guard the body of Topa Ynga Yupanqui[17] after he died, *a la continua*

[Cord 5] 10 *yana* more to guard his weapons

[Cord 6] 200 Indians more to guard the Chachapoya[18]

[Cord 7] 200 Indians more to guard Quito[19]

[Cord 8] 20 Indians more for the guard of the body of Guana Cava[20] after his death

[Cord 9] 120 Indians more to make feathers

[Cord 10] 60 more to extract honey

[Cord 11] 400 Indians to weave fine cloth

[Cord 12] 40 Indians to make more dyes and colors

[Cord 13] 240 Indians to guard the sheep [camelids]

[Cord 14] 40 Indians to guard the fields which they had throughout this valley; the maize grown was mostly taken to Cuzco and the rest to the warehouses [at Huanuco Pampa].

[Cord 15] 40 additional Indians to plant hot peppers which were taken to Cuzco

[Cord 16] and they also gave 60 Indians and sometimes 45 to make salt

14. ***a la continua:*** full time.
15. ***yana:*** personal attendant to the nobility.
16. **Guayna (or Huayna) Capac:** the Inca king who ruled from 1493 to 1527.
17. **Topa Ynga Yupanqui:** the Inca king who ruled from 1471 to 1493.
18. **Chachapoya:** a region of the Inca empire on the edge of the jungle, now northeastern Peru.
19. **Quito:** a city in the Andes, now in Ecuador.
20. **Guana Cava:** Guayna Capac.

[Cord 17] 60 Indians to make [raise] the coca leaf which they took to Cuzco and to the warehouses of Huanuco [Pampa] and sometimes they hauled 200 sacks and at others 40

[Cord 18] 40 Indians to accompany the Inca in person to hunt deer

[Cord 19] and 40 Indians more to make soles and they took them to Cuzco and to the storehouses

[Cord 20] 40 more carpenters [woodworkers] to make plates and bowls and other things for the Inca and they took them to Cuzco

[Cord 21] 40 more potters to make pots and they took them to Huanuco [Pampa]

[Cord 22] and 68 more Indians to guard the *tampu*[21] at Huanuco

[Cord 23] 80 more to carry loads from the *tampu* to Pumpu [some five to six days' march] and from Sutun Cancha to Tambo [one day's, coming back]

[Cord 24] 40 more Indians to guard the women of the Inca

[Cord 25] 500 to go with the person of the Inca to war, to carry him to hammocks, and they went to Quito and to other places

[Cord 26] 500 more Indians, to plant and [do] other things without leaving their territory

Source 6 from Pedro de Ciez de León, The Incas, *trans. Harriet de Onis (Norman: University of Oklahoma Press, 1959), pp. 161, 163–165.*

6. Pedro de Cieza de León, *Crónicas*, 1553

As in the previous chapter I described the way in which the Incas carried out their conquests, in this it would be well to tell how the different nations were taxed, and how the returns of this taxation were handled in Cuzco. For as is well known to all, not a single village of the highlands or the plains failed to pay the tribute levied on it by those who were in charge of these matters. There were even provinces where, when the natives alleged that they were unable to pay their tribute, the Inca ordered that each inhabitant should be obliged to turn in every four months a large quill full of live lice, which was the Inca's way of teaching and accustoming them to pay tribute. We know that for a time they paid their tax in lice until, after they had been given flocks and had raised them, and made clothing, they were able to pay tribute henceforth.

On these visits of the envoys of the Incas to the provinces, as soon as they arrived they could tell from the quipus the number of people, men and women, old folks and children, and gold or silver miners, and they ordered that so many

21. ***tampu:*** a small way station along the Inca highways; this one is located two days' walk west of the Huallaga Valley where the Chupaychu live.

thousand Indians be put to work in the mines, to dig the amount of those metals that had been set to be turned over to the inspectors assigned for that purpose. And as during the time the Indians appointed to work the mines were doing this they could not cultivate their fields, the Incas ordered those from other provinces to come and plant the crops at the proper season in lieu of tribute, so that they [the fields] would not lie fallow. If the province was a large one, it furnished Indians both to mine the metals and to sow and work the land. If one of the Indians working in the mines got sick, he was allowed to return home at once, and another came to take his place; but none was assigned to the mines unless he was married so that his wives could look after his food and drink, and, aside from this, it was seen to it that they were supplied with food in abundance. With this way of doing things, none of them considered it hard work even if they spent their whole life in the mines, and none of them died from overwork. Besides, they were permitted to stop work several days in the month for their feasts and recreation; and the same Indians were not continuously in the mines, but every so often they were sent away and others came in their place.

So well had the Incas organized this that the amount of gold and silver mined throughout the kingdom was so great that there must have been years when they took out over fifty thousand arrobas[22] of silver, and over fifteen thousand of gold, and all this metal was for their use. These metals were brought to the capital of each province, and the same system of mining and delivering them prevailed throughout the kingdom. If in certain regions there were no metals to be mined, so that all should contribute their share, they set tribute of small things, and of women and children who left their villages without any sorrow, for if a man had only one son or daughter, they did not take the child, but if he had three or four, they took one in payment of his service.

Other regions paid as many thousand loads of corn as there were houses in it, which was done at every harvest, and was credited to the province. In other areas they similarly supplied as many loads of *chuño*[23] as the others of corn, and others *quinoa*,[24] and others tubers. Some places gave as many blankets as there were married Indians in it, and others as many shirts as there were people. Others were obliged to supply so many thousand loads of lances, and others, slings and *ayllos*;[25] and the other arms they use. Certain provinces were ordered to contribute so many thousand Indians to go to Cuzco to work on the public buildings of the city and those of the Incas, supplying them with the necessary food. Others contributed cables to haul stones; others, coca. In this way all the provinces and regions of Peru, from the smallest to the most important, paid

22. **arroba:** a measure of weight, about 25 pounds.

23. ***chuño:*** freeze-dried potatoes.

24. ***quinoa:*** a grain grown at mid-altitude.

25. ***ayllo:*** a sling with stones attached used to entangle the feet of warriors or animals. Now called a *bola*, it is still used in Argentina.

tribute to the Incas, and all this was accomplished in such orderly fashion that neither did the natives fail to pay what they owed and were assessed, nor did those who collected these tributes venture to take one grain of corn in excess. And all the food and articles necessary for making war which were contributed were expended on the soldiers or the regular garrisons that were established in different parts of the kingdom for its defense. When there was no war, most of this was eaten and consumed by the poor, for when the Incas were in Cuzco they had their *hatun-conas,* which is the name for a bondsman, and in such number that they sufficed to work their lands and care for their houses and sow the necessary food supplies, aside from that which was always brought for their table from the different regions, many lambs and fowls and fish, and corn, coca, tubers, and all the fruits they raise. And there was such order in these tributes which the natives paid and the Incas were so powerful that they never had a war break out again.

To know how and in what way the tributes were paid and the other taxes collected, each *huata,* which is the word for year, they sent out certain *Orejones* as supervisory magistrates, for they had no authority beyond visiting the provinces and notifying the inhabitants that if any of them had a complaint, he should state it, so that the one who had done him a wrong could be punished. And when the complaints were heard, if there were any, or it was learned that somewhere a debt was pending, they returned to Cuzco, from which another set out with authority to punish the culprits. In addition to this, there was another important provision, which was that from time to time the headmen of the provinces appeared on the day appointed for each nation to speak to bring to the knowledge of the Inca the state of the province and the shortage or abundance that existed in it, and whether the tribute was too large or too small, and whether they could pay it or not. After which they were sent away satisfied, for the Inca rulers were certain they were not lying but telling the truth. For if there was any attempt at deceit, stern punishment followed and the tribute was increased. Of the women given by the provinces, some of them were brought to Cuzco to become the possession of the Lord-Incas, and some of them were sent to the temple of the sun.[26]

26. Girls were selected from conquered peoples to be Chosen Women (*acllyas*), and were dedicated to the Sun or other gods, or married to the Inca king or other prominent men.

Source 7 from Garcilosa de la Vega, Royal Commentaries of the Incas and General History of Peru, *trans. Harold V. Livermore, vol. 1 (Austin, University of Texas Press, 1966), pp. 272–274.*

7. Extract from Garcilosa de la Vega

Coming to the subject of the tribute levied and collected by the Inca kings of Peru from their vassals, this was so moderate that when one realizes what it consisted of and how much it was, it can truthfully be affirmed that none of the kings of the ancients, nor the great Caesars who were called Augustus and Pius can be compared with the Inca kings in this respect. For properly speaking it seems that they did not receive taxes and tributes from their subjects, but rather that they paid their subjects or merely imposed taxes for their benefit, such was their liberality toward their vassals. Considered in relation to the general circumstances of those times, the daily pay of laborers, and the value of commodities, and the expenses of the Incas, the tribute was so small in quantity that many Indians barely paid the value of four reals of the current time. Although there could not fail to be some inconvenience attached to the payment of the tribute or the service of the king or the *curacas,*[27] it was borne cheerfully and contentedly owing to the smallness of the tribute, the perquisites the Indians received, and the numerous advantages that arose from the performance of the tasks. The rights of the tribute payer and the laws in his favor were inviolably preserved so that neither the judges nor the governors, nor the captain generals, nor the Inca himself could pervert them to the disadvantage of the vassals. They were as follows: the first and most important was that no one who was exempt from tribute could be obliged to pay it at any time or for any reason. All those of royal blood were exempt, as were all captain generals and other captains, even the centurions and their children and grandchildren, and all the *curacas* and their kinsmen. Royal officials who were commoners and held minor posts were exempted from paying tribute during their term of office, as were soldiers on active service and youths of under twenty-five since they were required to serve their parents until that age. Old men of fifty and upwards were exempt from tribute, and so were all women, whether married or maidens, spinsters or widows. The sick were exempt until they were completely recovered, and all the disabled, such as the blind, lame, limbless, and others who were deprived of the use of their limbs, though the deaf and dumb were allotted tasks for which they did not need to hear or speak.

The second law was that all the rest apart from these were obliged to pay tribute unless they were priests or officials in the temples of the Sun or of the chosen virgins. The third law was that no Indian was ever obliged for any reason to pay anything instead of tribute, but only to pay in labor, with his skill or with

27. **curaca:** an official with jurisdiction over a certain number of households.

the time he devoted to the service of the king and the state. To this extent rich and poor were equal, for none paid more or less than others. The word rich was applied to anyone who had children or family to help him in his work and so to finish his share of the tributary labor sooner: anyone who had no children or family, though he might be well off in other respects, was accounted poor. The fourth law was that no one could compel anyone to perform or undertake any craft but his own, unless it was the tilling of the soil or military service, two duties to which all were liable in general. The fifth law was that each should pay his tribute in whatever goods were found in his own province, without being forced to go abroad in search of things that did not occur where he lived: it seemed to the Inca a great injustice to ask his subjects to deliver fruits their own earth did not produce. The sixth law required that each of the craftsmen who worked in the service of the Inca or his chiefs should be supplied with everything necessary for his work: thus the smith was given gold, silver, or copper, the weaver wool or cotton, the painter colors, and all the other requirements of their respective callings. Each craftsman was therefore only obliged to supply his labor and the time needed for the work, which was two months, or at most three. This done, he was not obliged to work any more. However, if there was any work left unfinished, and he wished to go on working of his own free will and see it through, what he did was discounted from the tribute he owed for the following year, and the amount was so recorded by means of their knots and beads. The seventh law required that all craftsmen of whatever occupation should be supplied if they fell ill with all they required for food, clothes, comforts, and medicine, instead of having to pay tribute: if the Indian concerned was working alone, he alone was helped, but if he had brought his wife and children so as to finish the work sooner, they too were fed.

In the allocation of such tasks, the question of time was not taken into consideration, but only the completion of the job. Thus if a man could take advantage of the help of his family and friends to complete two months' work in a week, he was regarded as having fully satisfied his obligation for the year, and no other tribute could be pressed upon him. This alone is sufficient to refute the contention of those who say that formerly tribute was paid by sons, daughters, and mothers, whoever they were. This is false, for although these all worked, it was not because the obligation to pay tribute was imposed upon them, but because they helped their fathers, husbands, or masters: if the man did not wish his dependents to share in his work, but preferred to work alone, his wife and children remained free to busy themselves about the house, and the judges and decurions were unable to bring any compulsion to bear on them, as long as they were not idle. It was for this reason that in the days of the Incas those who had many children and large families were accounted rich: those who had not were often taken ill owing to the length of time they had to devote to their work until their tribute was settled. In order to remedy this there was a law that those who were rich by reason of their families and the rest who had finished their tasks should help them for a day or two. This was agreeable to all the Indians.

Source 8 from Guaman Poma de Ayala, El Primer Nueva Corónica y Buen Gobierno *(Caracas: Ayacucho, 1980). Photo: Det Kongelige Bibliotek.*

8. Illustration from Guaman Poma de Ayala, *El Primer Nueva Corónica y Buen Gobierno*

Source 9 from Hitomi Tonomura, Community and Commerce in Late Medieval Japan: The Corporate Villages of Tokuchin-ho *(Stanford: Stanford University Press), pp. 199, 203, and 206; and David John Lu,* Sources of Japanese History, Vol. I *(New York: McGraw-Hill, 1973), p. 157.*

9. *So* Regulations

1448

1. Those who do not come to the meeting after two beats of the drum shall be fined 50 *mon.*[28]
2. A penalty of 500 *mon* shall be imposed for cutting down forest trees and seedlings.
3. A penalty of 100 *mon* shall be imposed for taking firewood [or leaves] and mulberry leaves.

1489

Regulations commonly agreed to by the people of the village of Imahori, dated first year of Entoku . . . , eleventh month, 4th day.

1. Anyone who receives his right to residence from the *sō* (village self-governing association) will not be permitted to board anyone from outside of this village.
2. No one from other villages will be permitted to reside in this village, unless someone from this village serves as his guarantor.
3. If there is any boundary dispute between privately-owned land and land owned by the *sō,* the matter must be settled with the payment of money.
4. No one will be permitted to keep dogs.
5. From the common fund of the *sō,* an amount of one *kan* will be paid each year for the performance of *sarugaku*[29] to be held on the sixth day of the second month.
6. Anyone who sells his house must pay to the *sō* three *mon* out of one hundred *mon,* and thirty *mon* out of one *kan* realized from the sale. Anyone who disobeys this rule shall be expelled from the *za* (in this instance, *za* signifies a worshipper's group of the village shrine).
7. Anyone who conceals the amount of the sale price of his house shall be punished.
8. No house shall be built to the east of the moat.

28. ***mon:*** a unit of money; 1000 *mon* equaled one *kan.*
29. ***sarugaku:*** a form of popular theatrical entertainment.

1583

1. Those listed on the register shall have the right to discuss [matters concerning the survey].

2. Do not cover other people's land. Once the owner is agreed upon, do not make different claims.

3. Should there be troublesome people among the landholding peasants [*hyakushō*], dissociate from them as the regulations stipulate.

[Signed] Imabori *sōchū*

1626

Items stipulated:

1. For harvesting grass in someone else's paddy, 1 *koku*[30] of rice shall be charged as a penalty.

2. Breaking off branches and leaves by hand shall also invoke a penalty of 1 *koku.*

3. Breaking off branches and leaves in the *sō* forest will invoke the same penalty. Anyone violating these rules shall be driven out [of the village] by the *sō.*

Thus commanded.

[Signed] *sōchū*

Source 10 from David J. Lu, Japan: A Documentary History *(Armonk, N.Y.: M. E. Sharpe, 1997), pp. 162–163.*

10. From Joint Petition by Villagers, 1407

We beg your indulgence in the following matters:

1. We request that the rice offered to the temple which is earmarked for festivals be distributed to the farmers. . . .

3. We wish to report that the flood damage has resulted in a reduction of eight *koku* and four *to*[31] in rice production, and there is an additional damage of three *koku* and one *to* of rice.

4. On account of poor crops or abandonment of land, you previously ordered us to pay one half of the rent due from Nishidai (part of Oyama *shō*),[32] which amounts to twenty-four *koku,* eight *to* and three *shō.* However, cultivators of

30. ***koku:*** a unit of dry measure for grain, about five bushels.

31. ***to* and *sho:*** units of dry measure for grain; 100 *sho* = 1 *to,* 100 *to* = 1 *koku.*

32. **Oyama *shō:*** the estate (*shō*) on which these villagers lived.

these fields come from other distant *shō,* and we cannot force them to work. Therefore, this year please count this as a complete loss. . . .

8. After having paid our annual rent, we wish to report that those farmers who absconded have now returned.

9. The illegal acts of the deputy (*daikan*) were the root cause of the absconding of the farmers in the way they did, after exhausting all available means [to fight against such illegal acts]. Relying on the help you are granting us, they have returned. However, if the deputy continues to occupy his position, then their return will be in vain. We venture to speak out in this manner, because the sinful and illegal deeds of the deputy are many. If [a new] deputy can be dispatched from the temple, it will benefit the farmers greatly. We have heard that the *ryōshu*[33] of Ōyama *shō* is consulting with the *shugo*[34] to summon the farmers [for additional duties]. We are very much surprised. This makes us to have no other recourse but to think of [moving to] other provinces.

May we submit our humble thoughts?

With trepidation, respectfully
Farmers from Kazuidani

To the Chief of the Administrative Department (*bugyōshu*) [of Tōji].

Source 11 from David J. Lu, Japan: A Documentary History *(Armonk, N.Y.: M. E. Sharpe, 1997), p. 186.*

11. Decrees Regarding Military Service of Villagers

DECREE OF HŌJŌ UJIMASA, 1587

1. All men, without distinction as to being of the samurai class or of common people, in this county (*gō*) are ordered to come and register for the service of this province in an emergency. Of these, eight [are to be drafted].

2. They are to bring with them any of the following three weapons: an arrow, spear, or gun. However, a spear, whether its shaft is made of bamboo or wood, is useless if it is shorter than two *ken* [about twelve feet]. Even if one claims to be an official of the higher authorities, and does not follow the above injunctions, he must still be treated the same as merchants or petty artisans. The registration applies to all men from fifteen to seventy years of age.

3. Those who respond to the call must prepare their daggers and military emblems in such a way as to make them look like worthy warriors.

33. ***ryoshu:*** lord of the estate.

34. ***shugo:*** military governor of a province or several provinces.

4. If an able-bodied man is deliberately left behind, he and the one who has ordered him to remain will be beheaded immediately by the Minor Deputy (*shō-daikan*) of the county upon hearing of it.

5. Anyone who abides by the provisions of this circular diligently, whether he be of the samurai class or of common men, can expect to receive rewards.

The above provisions describe the need in time of emergency. Everyone is directed to complete preparation of their implements of war by the end of the eighth month. The names of those who register must be submitted by a responsible party by the twentieth day of the next month. The above provisions must be widely circulated within the county.

Fifteenth year of Tenshō [1587], last day of the seventh month.
To the Minor Deputy and People of the Iwase Village.

DECREE OF TOYOTOMI HIDEYOSHI, 1588

(a) The Edict:

1. The farmers of all provinces are strictly forbidden to have in their possession any swords, short swords, bows, spears, firearms or other types of weapons. If unnecessary implements of war are kept, the collection of annual rent (*nengu*) may become more difficult, and without provocation uprisings can be fomented. Therefore those who perpetrate improper acts against samurai who receive a grant of land (*kyūnin*) must be brought to trial and punished. However, in that event, their wet and dry fields will remain unattended, and the samurai will lose their rights (*chigyō*) to the yields from the fields. Therefore, the heads of provinces, samurai who receive a grant of land, and deputies must collect all the weapons described above and submit them to Hideyoshi's government.

2. The swords and short swords collected in the above manner will not be wasted. They will be used as nails and bolts in the construction of the Great Image of Buddha. In this way, the farmers will benefit not only in this life but also in the lives to come.

3. If farmers possess only agricultural implements and devote themselves exclusively to cultivating the fields, they and their descendants will prosper. This compassionate concern for the well-being of the farmers is the reason for the issuance of this edict, and such a concern is the foundation for the peace and security of the country and the joy and happiness of all the people. In China, in olden days, the sage ruler Yao pacified the country and converted precious swords and sharp knives into agricultural implements. But there is no precedent for such an act in this country. Thus, all the people must abide by the provisions of this edict and understand its intent, and farmers must work diligently in agriculture and sericulture.[35]

35. **sericulture:** the raising of mulberry trees as food for silkworms.

All the implements cited above shall be collected and submitted forthwith.

Vermilion seal of Hideyoshi
Sixteenth year of Tenshō [1588], seventh month, 8th day.

Source 12 from David J. Lu, Japan: A Documentary History *(Armonk, N.Y.: M. E. Sharpe, 1997), pp. 213–215.*

12. Regulations for Villagers Issued by the Tokugawa Shogunate, 1643

1. Hereafter, both the village headman (*shōya*) and higher village officials (*sōbyakushō*) may not build houses which are not consistent with their stations in life. However, town houses (*machiya*) may be built under the direction of the fief holder (*jitō*) or magistrate (*daikan*).

2. Concerning farmer's clothing, in accordance with the previous *bakufu*[36] edict, the village headman and his family may wear silk, pongee, linen, and cotton; lower village officials (*wakibyakushō*) may wear only linen or cotton. Other materials may not be used to make the neckband (*eri*) or waist sash (*obi*).

3. Neither the village headman nor the higher village officials may dye their clothing purple or crimson. Other colors may be used to dye clothing for wear but no design is permitted.

4. Farmers must be told that their normal meals must consist of grains other than rice and wheat. Rice especially must not be consumed indiscriminately.

5. In villages, hot noodles, thin noodles, buckwheat noodles, bean-jam buns, bean curds and the like may not be traded. This is to prevent wasteful use of the five grains.

6. *Sake* (rice wine) must not be brewed in villages. Nor can it be bought from elsewhere to be sold locally.

7. Do not go to market towns to drink freely.

8. Farmers must be told that they must take good care of their wet and dry fields, and weed them attentively and conscientiously. If there are insolent farmers who are negligent, the matter will be investigated and the offenders duly punished.

9. If a single farmer is unmistakably overburdened, and cannot carry on his share of farm work, not only his five-man group (*goningumi*)[37] but also the entire village must [in the spirit of] mutual help, assist in his rice planting, and otherwise enable him to pay his annual taxes (*nengu*).

36. ***bakufu:*** shogunate.

37. ***goningumi* or five-man group:** neighborhood groups that higher authorities sought to establish, responsible for mutual surveillance of each other and paying taxes.

10. From this year on, planting of tobacco on either old fields or new fields is strictly forbidden, because its cultivation wastes the lands that can be used to grow the five grains.

11. The village elders (*nanushi*) and higher village officials, both men and women are forbidden to use any kind of conveyance.[38]

12. Farmers must be told that no shelter can be given in the district to anyone who comes from another village and does not cultivate the fields, and is not reliable. If any farmer gives shelter to such a person, the gravity of his offense is to be investigated, and he becomes subject to arrest and imprisonment.

13. Wet and dry fields may not be sold in perpetuity.

14. Farmers may not, on account of disputes involving annual taxes and other matters, desert their places and take refuge with those who have absconded. Anyone who violates this, after an investigation may be considered as committing a culpable offense.

15. If the *jitō*[39] or *daikan*[40] administers the area so poorly that the farmers find it impossible to endure it any longer, they may first pay up all the annual taxes, and leave the village. They may even establish their residence in a neighboring county. If there is no tax overdue, the *jitō* or *daikan* cannot punish them with banishment (*kamae*).

16. Even in the matters of Buddhist ceremonies and religious festivals, overindulgence beyond one's own status must be avoided.

17. Within the city limits of Edo, no one is to ride on top of a horse loaded with wood, hay, goods in straw sacks and the like.

The above articles must be made known to all the villages, to secure immediate observance of their intent. Care must be taken continuously to conform to these injunctions.

Twentieth year of Kanei [1643], third month, 11th day.

38. **conveyance:** here, a sedan chair or other item carried or pulled by people.

39. ***jito:*** vassal of the shogun or a *daimyo* who had the right to collect his own taxes.

40. ***daikan:*** an official in charge of collecting taxes for a *daimyo* or the shogun.

Source 13: Rice Cultivation in the Four Seasons *(detail). Photo: Kyoto National Museum.*

13. Screen with Village Scene by Kusumi Morikage

QUESTIONS TO CONSIDER

As you look over your lists, some points of comparison among all three cultures or at least two of them will be immediately obvious. One of these is military conscription, training, and supplies. Who provides the weapons in Henry VIII's and Hojo Ujimasa's decrees (Sources 3 and 11)? What is the age range of the men who are expected to be prepared to fight? Is anyone exempt from these provisions? According to Cieza de León (Source 6), who makes the weapons for the Incas? According to the general inspection of the Chupaychu (Source 5), how much of the labor demanded of conquered villages is for military purposes? Why do you think Cieza de León and de la Vega make so little reference to military service in their discussions of labor tribute?

The village by-laws and court roll from England (Sources 1 and 2) and the *so* and Tokugawa regulations from Japan (Sources 9 and 12) offer many points of comparison. Why do you think the villagers and their overlords in both places were concerned about the cutting down of trees and the harvesting of grass and shrubs? Why might they have been concerned that strangers not be allowed to board or to become subtenants? The English by-laws frequently mention animals roaming around at large and getting into sown land, while this is not mentioned in the Japanese regulations. What might account for this difference? Does Morikage's painting (Source 13) support your speculations about this? The Japanese regulations refer often to religious ceremonies and obligations, whereas these are mentioned only once in the English by-laws or court roll. Given that most English villages had a church in them, and that everyone in England during this period was baptized as a Christian, why do you think religious matters are not mentioned more often in these sources? What other concerns are particular to one of these areas but not the other?

Sources 2 and 10 both provide examples of villagers disobeying laws or carrying out prohibited activities. In Source 2, what are Robert Tayllor, Laurence Pemerton, Robert Huchyns, and the group of people beginning with William Bedell accused of doing? How do they justify their actions? What are the consequences of their actions? In Source 10, how is the absconding of farmers explained by the petitioners? What have they heard that the consequences of this will be, and how do they respond to this? How do the consequences of illegal actions in both of these cases fit with the general tone regarding penalties in many of the sources in this chapter? Would you expect that the death penalty set for not enlisting in the military in Hojo Ulimasa's decree (Source 11) or the requirement that taxes be paid in live lice described in Cieza de León's chronicle (Source 6) was actually enforced? If not, why would the rulers have prescribed such penalties?

Both Cieza de León's chronicle (Source 6) and the petition by the Japanese villagers (Source 10) refer to requirements of labor or produce that have been set too high. How do the villagers in each case seek to have these lessened? De la Vega's chronicle (Source 7) and the Tokugawa regulations (Source 12) both discuss some form of communal responsibility if obligations are not met. In each case, who is to assist those who cannot carry out the required work?

Look at the two pictures of messengers (Sources 4 and 8). How do the artists indicate that the king in Source 4 and the governor of the roads in Source 8 are figures of authority? What differences between the two pictures do you see? Why might Guaman Poma have chosen to place his figures in a background showing the system of roads and huts?

A point of comparison that may not emerge immediately is the way in which historical examples are used to justify the actions of contemporary rulers. Read the opening section of Garcilosa de la Vega (Source 7). To whom does he compare the Inca rulers? Now read the decree of Toyotomi Hideyoshi carefully (Source 11). Who is set up as an example of a former ruler who beat swords into plowshares (to use the phrase in the Book of Isaiah in Hebrew Scripture), an image found in many cultures? Why might these authors include references such as these? To whom does Henry VIII refer when he orders the shooting of longbows? Why might he use this type of example, rather than one from the distant past?

You are now ready to use your information about the specific cultures and your comparative analyses to answer the questions for this chapter. Though these states are widely separated geographically, are there some concerns that appear to be common to all rulers and authorities as they seek to extract surpluses from their populations? How do these concerns differ from those of the villages themselves?

EPILOGUE

This chapter is both the final one in the first volume of this book and the opening one in the second volume for a reason. The interactions you have traced here—between states and villages, between higher-level officials and individuals, between individuals and village authorities—actually began much earlier than 1400 and continued much later than 1650, making this chapter both a culmination and a beginning.

Since the agricultural revolution, people have lived in villages planting crops and raising animals, and devising ways to best do this given the climate and terrain in their area. Almost everywhere this has involved communal activities, which means that some method of local decision-making had to be devised and some means of punishing those who did not abide by these decisions developed. Since the first growth of large-scale states in Mesopotamia, China, and elsewhere, leaders and officials have extracted revenues from those villages, and the villages and their residents have responded to these demands in various ways. In the millennia before about 1400, very few records of those responses and other aspects of village life were left, so that what we can learn about local political structures or other issues is often quite limited. This chapter begins at the point where those sources start to emerge for a few parts of the world, allowing us for the first time to get a glimpse of the structures that have shaped people's lives throughout much of the time covered in the first volume of this book.

The development of different forms of government after 1650, including monarchical, democratic, and Communist nation-states, did not immediately alter the relationships you have seen here. Most people throughout most of the world continued to live in agricultural villages for centuries, and in many parts of the world continue to do so today. Those villages made communal decisions in various ways, and punished wrong-doers or requested that higher-level authorities do this. Those of you who are reading this chapter as part of a course that begins around 1500 might be tempted to view what you have evaluated here as part of a "traditional" or "pre-modern" world, very foreign to the industrial and postindustrial world that came later. Certainly the concerns of villages and states about cutting down trees, tethering animals, or providing bows and arrows for boys seem quite archaic, unrelated to the development of industrialism, imperialism, and international war that you will trace later in this book.

Viewing the issues we have discussed here as part of a "world we have lost" (the title of a well-known book on English village life) might be misleading, however. Not only could you easily find local regulations about cutting trees (or grass), tethering animals (at least dogs and cats), or providing weapons to children in the most highly developed American cities and suburbs today, but those local regulations continue to have repercussions on the larger political realm. As the American presidential election of 2000 made eminently clear, telling political history as if it were only the story of large-scale governments can miss the point. Speaker of the U.S. House of Representatives Tip O'Neill famously said that "all politics is local"; the fact that the choice of the leader of the world's most powerful country may have ultimately been determined by the shape of the ballots in one county only reinforces O'Neill's point.

TEXT CREDITS

Chapter 1 **Page 12:** From Joseph Needham, *Science and Civilization in China,* Vol. 4, Part 3. Reprinted with the permission of Cambridge University Press. **Pages 14, 16:** From Cho-yun Hsu, *Han Agriculture: The Formation of Early Chinese Agrarian Economy.* Copyright © 1980. Used with permission of the University of Washington Press.

Chapter 2 **Page 27:** Reprinted by permission from W. G. Lambert and A. R. Millard, *Atra-hasi: The Babylonian Story of the Flood* (Winona Lake, Ind.: Eisenbrauns, 1999), pp. 57, 59, 61. **Page 29:** From *The Beginnings of Indian Philosophy,* trans. Franklin Edgerton (Cambridge, Mass.: Harvard University Press, 1965), pp. 60–61, 67–68, 73, 74. **Page 33:** From *The Torah: A Modern Commentary.* Copyright © 1981. Reprinted by permission of The Union of America Hebrew Congregations. **Page 37:** From R. Wilhelm and Cary F. Baynes (trans.), *The I Ching [Yijing] or Book of Changes,* 3d ed. Copyright © 1967 by Princeton University Press. Reprinted by permission of Princeton University Press.

Chapter 4 **Page 87:** Copyright © 1994 by Raymond Dawson. Reprinted from *Sima Qian: Historical Records,* translated with an introduction and notes by Raymond Dawson (World's Classics, 1994) by permission of Oxford University Press. **Page 93:** From *Sources of Chinese Tradition* by William Theodore de Bary. Copyright © 1960 by Columbia University Press. Reprinted with permission of the publisher. **Pages 95, 98:** From *Roman Civilization* by Naphtali Lewis and Meyer Reinhold. Copyright © 1955 by Columbia University Press. Reprinted with permission of the publisher.

Chapter 5 **Page 120:** From *The Edicts of Asoka,* edited and translated by N. A. Kikam and Richard McKeon, 1959, pp. 27–29, 30, 34, 51–52, 58, 66, 67–68. Reprinted by permission of publisher, The University of Chicago Press. **Page 124:** From John S. Strong, *The Legend of King Asoka: A Study and Translation of the Asokavadana.* Copyright © 1983 by Princeton University Press. Reprinted by permission of Princeton University Press. **Page 132:** From A. J. Arberry, *The Koran Interpreted.* Copyright © 1964. Reprinted by permission of HarperCollins Publishers Limited. **Pages 132, 136:** From Al-Khatib al-Tibrizi, "Niches of Lamps," in John Alden Williams (ed.), *Themes of Islamic Civilization.* Copyright © 1971. Reprinted by permission of John Alden Williams. **Page 134:** From Ibn Ishaq, *The Life of Muhammad, Apostle of Allah,* edited and translated by Michael Edwards. Copyright © 1964. Reprinted by permission of The Folio Society.

Chapter 6 **Page 155:** From Adam of Bremen, *History of the Archbishoprics of Hamburg-Bremen,* translated by Francis J. Tschan (New York: Columbia University Press, 1959), pp. 75–76, 190–191. **Page 160:** Inscription from R. I. Paige, *Runes,* University of California Press, 1987, pp. 46–51. Reprinted by permission of the Regents of the University of California. **Page 162:** From Gwyn Jones, *The Norse Atlantic Saga* (London: Oxford University Press, 1964), pp. 142–152. Copyright © Oxford University Press 1964. Reprinted by permission of Oxford University Press. **Page 171:** Excerpts from David Malo's Early-19th-Century Hawaiian Antiquities. Translated by Nathaniel Emerson (Honolulu: Bishop Museum, 1951), pp. 4–7. Reproduced with the permission of Bishop Museum Press. **Page 172:** From Samuel H. Elbert and Torben Monberg, *From the Two Canoes.* Oral Traditions of Rennell and Bellona (Honolulu and Copenhagen: University of Hawaii Press, 1965), pp. 82, 174–176, 188, 257, 301. Reprinted by permission of the University of Hawaii Press. **Page 176:** Based on charts in Patrick V. Kirch, *The Evolution of the Polynesian Chiefdoms* (Cambridge and London: Cambridge University Press, 1984), pp. 43, 27. Reprinted with the permission of Cambridge University Press.

Chapter 7 **Page 191:** From ibn-Munqidh, *An Arab-Syrian Gentleman and Warrior in the Period of the Crusades,* translated by Philip K. hitti. Copyright © 1987 by Princeton University Press. Reprinted by permsision. **Pages 193, 195:** From Francesco Gabrieli, *Arab Historians of the Crusades: Selected and*

Translated from the Arabic Sources, translated/edited by E. J. Costello. Copyright © 1969 Routledge & Kegan Paul Ltd. Reprinted by permission of the University of California Press. **Page 198:** From Peter Tudebode, *Historia de Hierosolymitano Itinere (History of the Jerusalem Journey)*, translated by John Hugh Hill and Laurita L. Hill, 1974, pp. 54–55, 58–59, 115, in *Memoirs of the American Philosophical Society*. Reprinted by permission. **Page 200:** From *A History of Deeds Done Beyond the Sea*, translated by Emily Atwater Babcock and A. C. Krey. Copyright © 1943 by Columbia University press. Reprinted with permission of the publisher.

Chapter 8 **Page 215:** From *The Tale of Genji* by Murasaki Shikibu, trans. Edward Seidensticker. Copyright © 1975 by Edward G. Seidensticker. Reprinted by permission of Alfred A. Knopf Inc. **Page 224:** From Giovanni Boccaccio, *The Elegy of Lady Fiammetta*, edited and translated by Mariangela Causa-Steindler and Thomas Mauch, 1990, pp. 1, 3–4, 7–8, 25–26, 113–155, 116, 118, 119, 124–125, 127, 156–157, 159. Reprinted by permission of the publisher, The University of Chicago Press.

Chapter 9 **Page 244:** From *The Decameron* by Giovanni Boccaccio, translated by Mark Musa and Peter Bondanella. Copyright © 1982 by Mark Musa and Peter Bondanella. Used by permission of W. W. Norton & Company, Inc. **Page 248:** Translated and selected by H. A. R. Gibbs (New York: August M. Kelley, Publishers, 1969), pp. 305, 68, 69. Reprinted by permission of the publisher. **Page 249:** From Christos S. Bartsocas, *Two Fourteenth Century Descriptions of the "Black Death,"* Journal of the History of Medicine, October 1966, pp. 395–397. Reproduced by permission of Oxford University Press. **Pages 250, 253, 258, 259, 263:** From *The Black Death*, translated and edited by Rosemary Horrox, 1994. Manchester University Press, Manchester, UK. Reprinted by permission of Manchester University Press. **Page 253:** From Manfred Ullman, *Islamic Medicine* (Edinburgh: Edinburgh University Press, 1978), p. 94. Reprinted by permission of Edinburgh University Press, Edinburgh, Scotland. **Page 255:** From Michael Dols, *The Black Death in the Middle East*. Copyright © 1977 by Princeton University Press. Reprinted by permission of Princeton University Press. **Page 255:** Reprinted by permission of American University in Beirut.

Chapter 10 **Page 285:** From *The Travels of an Alchemist*, translated by Arthur Waley. Copyright © 1923. Reprinted by permission of Routlege & Kegan Paul. **Page 290:** From *The Travels of Marco Polo* by Manuel Komroff. Copyright 1926 by Boni & Liveright, Inc., renewed 1953 by Manuel Komroff. Copyright 1930 by Horace Liveright, Inc., renewed © 1958 by Manuel Komroff. Used by permission of Liveright Publishing Corporation. **Page 294:** Reprinted with the permission of Scribner, a Division of Simon & Schuster, Inc., from *The Civilization of China* by Dun J. Li. Copyright © 1975 by Dun J. Li.

Chapter 11 **Page 312:** From *Contemporaries of Marco Polo*, edited by Manuel Komroff. Copyright 1928 by Boni & Liveright, Inc., renewed © 1955 by Manuel Komroff. Used by permission of Liveright Publishing Corporation. **Page 314:** From *The Conquest of Constantinople* by Robert of Clari, translated by Edgar Holmes McNeal. Copyright © 1936 by Columbia University Press. Reprinted with permission of the publisher. **Page 318:** From Deno John Geanakoplos (trans.), *Byzantium: Church, Society and Civilization Seen Through Contemporary Eyes*. Reprinted by permission of the publisher, The University of Chicago Press. **Page 327:** Reprinted by permission from *The Florentine Codex: General History of the Things of New Spain* by Fray Bernardino de Sahagún. Book 8: Kings and Lords, pp. 58 and 29. Translated by Arthur J. O. Anderson and Charles E. Dibble. Copyright 1954 by the School of American Research, Santa Fe.

Chapter 12 **Page 345:** From Avicenna, *Canon*, translated by Gerard of Cremona, translated and reprinted in Danielle Jacquart and Claude Thomasset, *Sexuality and Medicine in the Middle Ages*, translated by Matthew Adamson. Copyright © 1988. Reprinted by permission of Blackwell Publishers. **Page 350:** From Jacob S. Minkin, *The Teachings of Maimonides*. Reprinted by permission of the publisher, Jason Aronson Inc., Northvale, N.J., © 1987. **Page 351:** From Caroline Gisela March-Long, *Early Modern German Obstetrical Manuals: Das Frawenbüchlein (ca. 1495) and Der Rosengarten (1513),* M.A. Thesis, Duke University, pp. 125, 127–129.

Chapter 13 **Page 374:** From *Ennin's Diary: The Record of a Pilgrimage to China in Search of the Law,* trans. Edwin O. Reischauer (New York: The Ronald Press Company, 1955). Reprinted by permission of John Wiley & Sons, Inc. **Page 386:** From *Internet Medieval Sourcebook,* James A. Brundage, trans. Reprinted by permission of James A. Brundage. **Page 389:** From "From Rome to Jerusalem: An Icelandic Itinerary of the Mid-Twelfth Century," *Harvard Theological Review,* 76:2 (1923), pp. 175–203 (spelling modernized). Reprinted by permission. **Page 390:** Guillaume de Deguileville, *The Pilgrimage of Human Life (Le Pèlerinage de la vie humaine),* translated by Eugene Clasby (New York and London: Garland Publishing, 1992). Reprinted by permission of the translator. **Page 392:** Reprinted by permission of the Persian Heritage Foundation, New York, New York. **Pages 397, 398, 402:** From *Corpus of Early Arabic Sources for West African History,* trans. J. F. P. Hopkins, ed. N. Levtzion and J. F. P. Hopkins. Copyright © 1981 by University of Ghana, International Academic Union, Cambridge University Press, 1981. Reprinted with the permission of Cambridge University Press.

Chapter 14 **Page 421:** Excerpt from "The Mit'a Obligations of Ethnic Groups to the Inka State," by John V. Murra, in *The Inca and Aztec States 1400–1800: Anthropology and History*, edited by George A. Collier et al, copyright © 1982 by Academic Press, reprinted by permission of the publisher. **Page 422:** Excerpts from *Incas of Pedro de Cieza de Léon*, translated by Harriet de Onis. Edited with an introduction by Victor Wolfgang von Hagen, pp. 161, 163–165. Reprinted by permission of the University of Oklahoma Press. **Page 425:** From *Royal Commentaries of the Incas and General History of Peru* by Garcilosa de la Vega, translated by Harold V. Livermore. Copyright © 1966 by permission of the University of Texas Press. **Page 428:** From Tonomura, *Community and Commerce in Late Medieval Japan.* Copyright © 1992 by the Board of Trustees of the Leland Stanford Junior University. With the permission of Stanford University Press, www.sup.org. **Pages 429, 430, 432:** From David J. Lu, *Japan: A Documentary History* (Armonk, N.Y.: M. E. Sharpe, 1997), pp. 162–163, 186, 213–215. Reprinted by permission of the author.